ISBN 978-0-282-79039-4
PIBN 10268706

1 MONTH OF
FREE
READING

at

www.ForgottenBooks.com

By purchasing this book you are eligible for one month membership to ForgottenBooks.com, giving you unlimited access to our entire collection of over 1,000,000 titles via our web site and mobile apps.

To claim your free month visit:

www.forgottenbooks.com/free268706

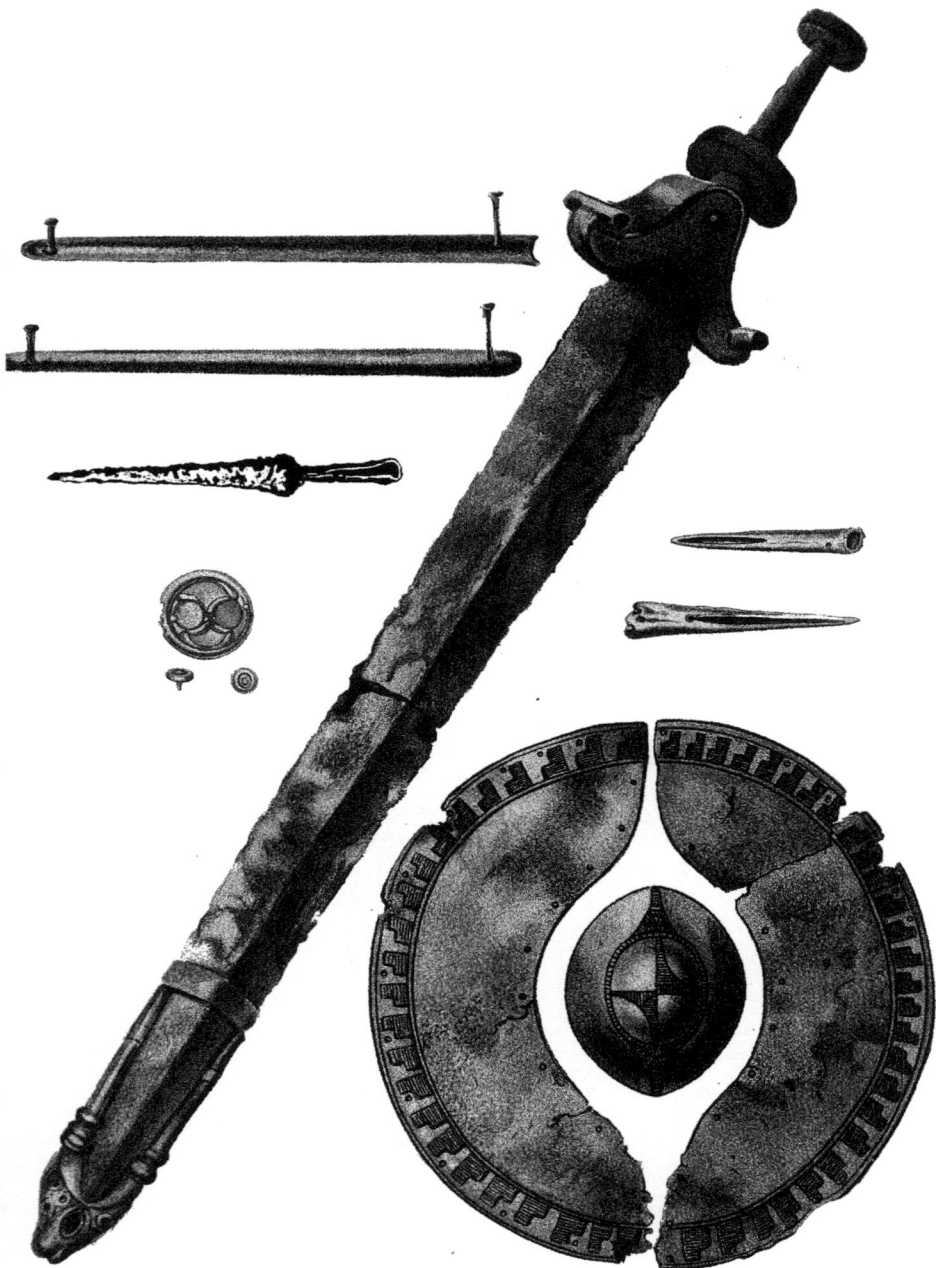

Objects found with a Skeleton on Grimthorpe Wold, near Pocklington. (Page 150).

OWN & SONS, LTD., LONDON, HULL & YORK.

INCLUDING ROMANO-BRITISH DISCOVERIES, AND A DE

ANCIENT ENTRENCHMENTS A SECTION

YORKSHIRE

J. R. M

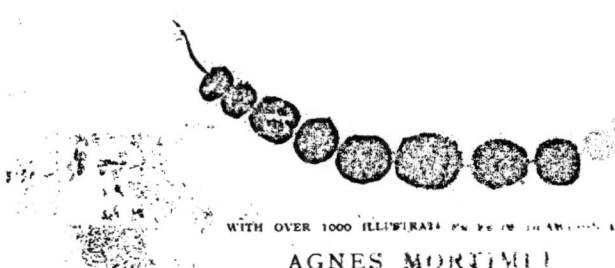

WITH OVER 1000 ILLUSTRATIONS

AGNES MORTIMER

FORTY YEARS' RESEARCHES

IN

BRITISH AND SAXON BURIAL MOUNDS

OF

EAST YORKSHIRE.

INCLUDING ROMANO-BRITISH DISCOVERIES, AND A DESCRIPTION OF THE
ANCIENT ENTRENCHMENTS ON A SECTION OF THE
YORKSHIRE WOLDS.

BY

J. R. MORTIMER.

WITH OVER 1000 ILLUSTRATIONS FROM DRAWINGS BY

AGNES MORTIMER.

LONDON:

A. BROWN & SONS, Limited, 5, FARRINGDON AVENUE, E.C.
AND AT HULL AND YORK.
1905.

PRINTED AT BROWNS' SAVILE PRESS,
DOCK STREET, HULL.

To

THE MEMORY OF THE LATE

Christopher Sykes, M.P.,

AND THE LATE

Mary E. Sykes, of Sledmere,

WHO KINDLY OBTAINED THE

NECESSARY PERMISSION TO EXCAVATE, AND GAVE

ENCOURAGEMENT AT THE COMMENCEMENT

OF THESE RESEARCHES,

This Volume

IS GRATEFULLY AND RESPECTFULLY

DEDICATED BY

THE AUTHOR.

EDITORIAL.

WHEN preparing the Catalogue of Mr. Mortimer's Museum at Driffield a few years ago, I was forcibly impressed with the great scientific value of the collections there housed. It was also obvious that their worth would be enormously increased were the voluminous notes upon them—prepared by Mr. Mortimer at the time his various discoveries were made—given to the world in the form of a volume. This had naturally been Mr. Mortimer's wish, but from the desire for completeness and accuracy, which has characterised him in his long and successful career as an antiquary, he wished to still further peruse and revise his volumes of MS. The publishers of this work were eventually approached, and after frequent interviews with author and publishers, an arrangement was entered into which has resulted in the present publication.

From the excellent manner in which both have done their work, I feel that no apology is needed from me for any efforts of mine to bring "Forty Years' Researches" into existence. As an ample reward for my interference, I have had the pleasure of seeing the work through the press, which has occupied, to my great profit, what little spare time I have had during the past two years.

In a careful examination of these written descriptions of the opening of the barrows, &c., such as has necessarily been my lot, it is clear that every possible care has been exercised in preparing them, and the amount of labour that has been bestowed upon them is simply astonishing. It must also be remembered that the various vases, crania, and other relics from the barrows were generally found in a damaged and fragmentary condition, the repairing and restoring of which he might possibly never have accomplished had it not been a labour of love.

It is so unusual for anyone beginning life as Mr. Mortimer did to take such an interest in antiquarian matters, and still more unusual for that interest to result in such a glorious collection as is in the Museum at Driffield, that one may be pardoned for briefly referring to one or two facts in connection with his career.

He is the survivor of three children, and was born on June 15th, 1825, at Fimber.* His parents, in common with other old time inhabitants of the Wolds, also lived to a ripe old age. The collecting instinct showed itself at an early age, when the walls of the cottage were ornamented by strings of birds' eggs.

* A walnut tree stands in front of this cottage, grown from a nut planted on Mr. Mortimer's birth by his father.

Subsequently, fossils and flint implements picked from the fields occupied his attention. It was the great Exhibition of 1851, however, that first gave Mr. Mortimer a desire to follow up scientific research. Fortunately, he was situated in what eventually has proved to be one of the most productive districts for British relics in the country.

Wisely restricting his work to his own area, he has gathered together by his individual labours a collection, not only of antiquities but of geological specimens, of which any well endowed institution might be proud.

After having amassed a collection of flint implements and fossils, he commenced his systematic excavations of the burial mounds of the southern section of the Wolds, of which during the past forty years he has opened some three hundred. These explorations were the means of adding many most valuable objects to his collection. In 1878 his collections far outgrew the accommodation to be found in a private dwelling-house, and the Museum in Lockwood Street, Driffield, was built for their reception. Since then they have been visited and consulted by the leading antiquaries and geologists in the country, and many of his specimens have been described in standard works.

It is only natural that "Mortimer" should be a household word in East Yorkshire. The flint implements found on the Wolds are called "Mortimers" wherever one goes; and "tak it ti' Mortimer" is heard whenever any curious stone or unusual object is found in the district.

Under the title of "Some Recollections of my Boyhood," Mr. Mortimer has gathered together a most valuable collection of facts relating to the manners and customs of the inhabitants of the Wolds sixty or seventy years ago, and it is hoped that they will shortly be issued in the transactions of one of the local societies.

With regard to the future of the Mortimer collection, the writer is much more hopeful than is Mr. Mortimer himself. There is little fear of it being split up and squandered. It is only natural that Mr. Mortimer should like the collection to remain at Driffield if possible. If this cannot be, arrangements have already been made whereby his wish that they shall remain in the Riding can be carried out, as he has agreed to the collection being offered to Hull upon certain conditions, and the writer has every reason to believe that those conditions will be met by the inhabitants of the city. The Museum at Hull is the only really permanent Museum in the Riding, and unquestionably the collections would there be made much more use of than if they remained at Driffield.

T. SHEPPARD.

PREFACE.

THIS work, and the discoveries it makes known, have been the occupation of my leisure hours during the period of a busy commercial life, ranging from 1860 * to the present time, and carried on under many difficulties and obstacles. As I possess no claim to any literary attainments, having had in my youth no higher training than that obtainable from a village school, while I was often in delicate health, thus interfering with the benefit I might have otherwise received from the crude and scanty instruction afforded by those primitive seats of learning, I must ask the kind indulgence of my readers in perusing the records now placed before them. My intention being rather to supply information to the antiquary than to gratify the taste of the "general" reader, much descriptive repetition has been rendered unavoidable.

However, I trust that whatever this narrative may lack in literary merit will be somewhat counterbalanced by the attention and care that has been bestowed upon the researches it describes. These were all conducted under my personal supervision, with a few exceptions, which were superintended with equal care by my late brother, R. Mortimer, the loss of whose help I deeply lament. It should here be mentioned that with the view of preventing error, the facts collected during this long period were accurately recorded at the time the various inspections took place.

Ancient burial mounds, like many ancient manuscripts, can reveal the secrets of the past. It is therefore highly desirable that the whole of their contents should be, as far as possible, carefully interpreted before they are entirely swept away from the land, and their precious relics permitted to crumble into dust, and thus become for ever lost. The objects they contain can only be preserved in cabinets, and the history they possess must be recorded in type. At the commencement of these excavations we estimated that over twenty-five per cent. of the original number of the barrows had been removed by the occupiers of the land; and since then the rate of destruction by agricultural and other operations has been even greater. It is therefore obvious that the time is not far distant when all but a few

---

* The first notes, relating to Barrow No. 4 (see p. 113), were taken in 1860, though previous to that time, even soon after the great Exhibition of 1851, which fired me with a love for scientific knowledge, I collected fossils and, later, flint weapons and tools.

of the larger mounds will have disappeared from view, leaving no trace of their former existence.

The title of the Rev. Canon Greenwell's book, viz., "British Barrows," enabled him to enrich it by figuring a few of the interesting vases, &c., not discovered by his own researches, which did not belong to the neighbourhood of his excavations. This privilege I must not take. I have therefore only figured and described the relics which belong to my own district, and an occasional article that has been found in close connection with it. The labours, of which the details contained in the following pages are the result, include the opening of nearly three hundred British burial mounds of the Stone and Bronze periods, and over sixty mounds of the early Iron Age;* a few Romano-British interments; several Anglo-Saxon grave-yards, together with an examination and careful mapping of a considerable part of an extensive system of earthworks, evidently of great antiquity, which are spread out like a vast net-work over this same region. These researches are confined within an area of about seventy-five square miles, which is included in the map of a portion of the mid-wolds of Yorkshire.

It has been my chief desire, from the commencement, to limit my investigations to this special area, so that there might be brought together in one collection all the treasures I could obtain. This collection is now a large and representative one for the neighbourhood, and I venture to think that it is of much archæological value. Probably never again in this country will it be possible to form such a museum of locally obtained specimens.

Several of the mounds had been previously opened by various explorers at different periods. The first of which I have any knowledge was conducted by the late Sir Christopher Sykes,† of Sledmere, towards the end of the eighteenth century. This was followed by excavations made by the Yorkshire Antiquarian Club from 1849 to 1853, by some made by the late Jas. Silburn, of Pocklington, during 1851-2, and a few at about the same time by the late Lord Londesborough. So recently as the autumn of 1881 Mr. Thomas, Town Clerk of Boston, opened four barrows on the Huggate Wold. Besides these, it is believed that a few have been plundered at various times by operators who left behind no record of their discoveries.

Traces of many of these early openings were not infrequently noticed at the time of my re-opening the mounds. Moreover, several burial mounds have been carted away and spread over the surrounding land; while many more have been considerably lowered by the plough, and a large number have been entirely obliterated by these and other agencies. That such has taken place is strikingly

* These are only partially alluded to in this volume.
† Grandfather to Christopher Sykes mentioned in the dedication.

shewn along the Garton Slack, between Driffield and Wetwang, where the mounds have been so far lowered by tilling the land, that at the time of the Ordnance Survey, about 1843, only four were sufficiently prominent to be observed and mapped, whereas since then I have, by a careful examination of this small area, discovered and successfully excavated the sites of thirty-two more, bringing the total number to thirty-six, thus shewing that even with the additional barrows I have marked on the map, we have probably but a portion of a still larger number which once dotted this landscape, forming, perhaps, its most noticeable feature.

I cannot here omit to mention the many obligations I owe to the great kindness afforded by the late Miss M. E. Sykes, of Sledmere, whose enlightened encouragement was a great stimulus, and to the late Christopher Sykes, M.P., then of Sledmere, through whose influence we were able to obtain the permission to excavate upon the estates of the adjoining proprietors. Amongst these I may mention the names of Lord Middleton, Lord Halifax, Lord Londesborough, Sir Tatton Sykes, Bart., Mr. Jessop, and, indeed, I may add all the land-owners in the neighbourhood who have allowed us to pursue our enquiries without any hindrance, and in many instances manifested a personal interest in our proceedings.

The farmers and occupiers were by no means reluctant in giving their assent, though in a few instances the cautious stipulation was made that if any *gold* was found they should be allowed to have a share. I may perhaps mention one amusing exception, when a dissentient, after having somewhat reluctantly given us permission, designedly placed a manure heap on the top of a low mound we were about to open, and thus effectually checked our proceedings for the time being.

For literary assistance I am indebted to the Rev. Canon Greenwell, F.R.S., F.S.A., who has kindly permitted me to make use of such paragraphs from the very able introduction to his work on "British Barrows" as I cared to select. I tender my best thanks to the Rev. E. M. Cole, M.A., F.G.S., and to Mr. T. Sheppard, F.G.S., Curator of the Municipal Museum, Hull, for reading the proofs, also to the latter gentleman for preparing the index, and for seeing the book through the Press. My thanks are also due to Dr. R. Wood, J.P., to Mr. G. W. Lamplugh, F.R.S., F.G.S., for revising certain portions of my manuscript, and to Sir John Evans, K.C.B., F.R.S., &c., for perusing my manuscript introduction. For the sketches of the specimens figured in this book, and for numerous illustrations used elsewhere, I am solely indebted to my daughter Agnes, who from the time she was thirteen years of age until she was nineteen, devoted many of her leisure hours to the completion of this, which at her age, must have been a tedious and irksome task.

Lastly, I cannot refrain from referring to the noble munificence of Sir Tatton Sykes. Bart., who generously supplied the necessary funds to enable me, during the latter period of my diggings, to open and examine several very large mounds which I had previously passed over, and should not have undertaken alone.

The enormous amount of labour necessary in obtaining the requisite material for the compilation of this volume, together with the fact that my leisure hours have been somewhat few, has resulted in some delay in the publication of the result of my work.   I hope, however, that the length of time occupied in its preparation has had a beneficial effect upon it.

Few pursuits can be more fascinating than enquiring into the history of past ages, tracing out the manners and customs of mankind in early times, investigating their origin and antiquity, and following the rise and progress of bygone races. But when these explorations are conducted on our native soil, more especially near the cherished spot which gave us birth, and in which our present joys and future hopes—as to this life—are chiefly centred, they then acquire the deepest interest and become invested with a special charm and value.   Remembering this, it has been for many years my desire to see the collection which I have got together permanently established in the neighbourhood.

Unfortunately so far my endeavours to dispose of it to the County and Local Authorities have been unsuccessful.   Circumstances do not permit me to offer it as a free gift, although I am willing to sell it at a price half that at which it may be valued.

In conclusion, I may state that I have often found the pursuit of archæology, and the diversion it affords, a delightful relaxation as well as a soothing anodyne for many of the cares and troubles which so frequently beset the paths of a business life ; while I feel that so long as my normal health and faculties remain, these researches will continue to be a source of pleasurable remembrance.

J. R. MORTIMER.

CONTENTS.

PART II.—ANGLO-SAXON REMAINS, BRITISH EARTHWORKS, &c.

INDEX TO BARROWS.

ERRATA.

———

Page xliv., line 23—*For* "scapula" *read* "spatula."

,, xlvii., line 35—*For* "Hordes" *read* "Hoards."

,, 59—*For* "Fig. No. 119" *read* "Fig. 115."

,, 86, line 5—*For* "size" *read* "side."

,, 109, line 12—*Insert* "it" *after* "others."

,, 183, lines 4, 15, and 16—*For* "No. 31" *read* "No. 23."

,, 208, line 4—*For* "thirty-five" *read* "thirty-six."

,, 208, line 6—*For* "thirty-one" *read* "thirty-two."

INTRODUCTION.

" The proper study of mankind is man."—POPE.

" The more I think of it," writes Ruskin, " I find this conclusion more impressed upon me—that the greatest thing a human soul ever does is to see something, and to tell what it saw in a plain way."

During the past forty odd years * I have exposed, or assisted in exposing, every interment in the district, described in this volume. I observed every-thing *in situ*, and with my own hands removed the relics. I have, therefore, seen something of the ancient Britons, and I have attempted to tell in a plain way what I have seen. In this portion of the book I have freely availed myself of Canon Greenwell's kind permission to make extracts from his very able intro-duction to " British Barrows," which in a great measure refers to a part of the Wolds adjoining my field of work. The extracts I have made from tables and text are such as equally apply to my own explorations.

He begins as follows :—" The almost universal custom of raising a mound— the so-called barrow—over the buried dead, to mark the place where they lay in the grave, has been variously discussed and by many different writers. This form of memorial (*monumentum ære perennius*) as ancient as it has been lasting, is found in almost all parts of the globe, from the extreme West of Europe to the Eastern limit of the Continent of the New World. Barrows under diverse names line the coasts of the Mediterranean, the seats of ancient empires and civilisa-tions, before whose rise they were in existence, and whose decay they have witnessed and outlived. So numerous are they that they spread like a covering over the wide plains, the steppes of Northern Asia, from the Euxine almost to the Icy Sea, where a few wandering nomads represent a population which was once large, wealthy, and powerful. The Continent of India possesses them in abundance, and their buried contents present an identity in many particulars so close with those of Britain, that some have considered it as affording a proof of a near connection between the two peoples who erected them. Egypt knows them as the sepulchres of her early kings, and the Pyramids have remained an unchanging legacy from the dead. The red man of America still places his dead beneath them ; and the huge mounds, so common in some parts of that Continent, are the evidence of an early occupation."

They abound in Great Britain and Ireland, and in few districts are they more numerous than in some parts of Yorkshire. Over the area covered by the map they are somewhat thickly spread, mainly in groups † often with one or more isolated mounds between the groups.

The practice of barrow building was probably evolved from the mere heaps which, even before the advent of the most primitive burial ceremony, were

---

* Since 1860.
† See p. 298, and the " Transactions of the East Riding Antiquarian Society," vol. 3, 1895, page 53, and the " Proceedings of the Yorkshire Geological Society " for 1897, p. 201.

instinctively raised to cover the small artifical underground dwellings in which the occupants were sometimes interred * and also from the small heaps which at first would be almost instinctively cast over the dead body to hide it. Those heaps in the earliest ages of mankind would simply be the protective coverings for the habitations of the living and the dead alike ; but as civilisation slowly advanced, it was evidently desired to more effectually protect and respect the great and good, by raising over their graves a lasting memorial. † In many cases the mounds are of great size, and able by their simplicity of construction and imperishable nature to endure as long as the natural hills themselves, unless removed by man. These mounds are amongst the oldest existing monuments of man's labour, and at one time their numbers were far greater than now, and must have greatly encumbered the ground. Solon observed this and forbade the raising of tumuli on account of the space they occupied.

The Form of Barrows.—"The barrows differ in shape and size, and are made of various materials. They are known as barrows (mounds of earth) and cairns (mounds of stone), ‡ and popularly in some parts of England as Lows, Howes, and Tumps. § They vary in size, from a few feet in diameter to a miniature mountain—like Silbury Hill in Wiltshire, which covers about five acres of ground, and measures 130 feet in perpendicular height." ‖

They differ considerably in outline, and the slope of the side is sometimes very gradual, at other times quite sharp. In most cases (on the Wolds) they have become greatly altered during the course of years of cultivation of the surface, and in many cases have been entirely removed ; but judging from some which still remain untouched by the plough, and from the present appearance of the whole of them, they may be described as being bowl-shaped and conical—those of the former shape being, perhaps, the most numerous.

LONG BARROWS.

As a rule they are circular, though at times approaching an oval form, but a long mound is somewhat common in some parts of England,¶ and has been regarded

---

* See barrows Nos. 110 and 23 and others. Such a practice survived to a much later and more civilised period. Diodorus informs us that Semiramis, wife of Ninus, the founder of the Assyrian Empire, buried her husband in the palace and raised over him a great mound of earth, which remained after the destruction of the City. This would not be a solitary case.

† Ulysses, in Hecuba, cared not how meanly he lived, so he might find a noble tomb after death.—— *Sir Thomas Brown on Urn Burial*, p. 137.

‡ " Barrows and cairns often occur in close proximity, there being nothing in the mode of interment or in the remains found in them to imply that there was any difference in point of time between the two kinds of mounds."

§ And on the Yorkshire Wolds by the double appellation of Howe Hills.—J.R.M.

‖ This mound has been twice opened. First by the Duke of Northumberland and Colonel Drax, in 1777, by sinking a shaft 5 feet in diameter from the summit to the base ; and again by the Dean of Hereford in 1849. A tunnel sufficiently wide to admit two men was then driven from the circumference to the centre. No interment was found, but the observation of an inner core of sods of turf piled together and covered with the large mass of loose chalk which formed the mound above, proved it to be entirely artificial. However, it could hardly be expected that these two small openings would be more likely to find the primary grave under Silbury Hill, than two rat holes would be likely to come upon the ashes of a mouse placed under a mound ten feet in diameter. Such has been the ineffectual opening of many of the large tumuli in other countries.

¶ Dr. Thurnam says that long barrows are rare throughout England, but are more numerous in Wiltshire than in any other part of England, there being about 1 to 35 round ones. But even here they are isolated, two being seldom less than a mile apart, while the round ones are nearly always in clusters.— *Archæologia*, vol. xlii. p. 9.

by some as the earliest form of barrow, and belonging to a period before the introduction of the use of metal into the country. Dr. Thurnam was of this opinion. Only a very few of these long barrows occur on the Wolds of Yorkshire, and but two have come under my examination. One (No. 110) is within the area of my map, and the other is on Helperthorpe Wold, and is described on page 333. Each long barrow possesses the distinguishing feature of having a wide and deep trough-shaped trench running close to each margin the whole length of the barrow, but not round the ends. The material from the trenches has in the main been used in the construction of the mound.*

On the Wolds, as well as in other parts of England, these barrows are strikingly similar in form and orientation, occurring mainly east and west, after the manner of churches, between which probably there may have been, in the orientation, some kindred sentiment. The broad end is almost invariably to the east. To the writer's knowledge, these trenches have never been observed to pass round the ends of a long barrow. The form and mode of construction of the long barrows differ greatly from the circular ones, and may have originated by an interment having been made, a ditch on each side being dug to obtain the material for the mound. After a time a second and adjoining interment was made, the two parallel ditches being lengthened to obtain material to cover the second grave. In this way the mound would grow to the long narrow form described.

In "Rude Stone Monuments," page 358, Mr. Fergusson gives a section of a long barrow situated at Carnac, in Brittany, which appears to exhibit evidence of this repeated lengthening of the barrow, and shows clearly that the west end of the barrow was *also* used for interment.

A long barrow in the parish of Kilham—described in "British Barrows," page 553, by Canon Greenwell—and at page 333 in this volume, also supports this view. Cremation (though, Canon Greenwell thinks, after a singular and imperfect fashion) seems to have been the rule in the long barrows on the Wolds; and this mode of burial seems also to have prevailed in the unchambered long barrows opened in the south of England. The contents of the two explored by me do not show any features of interest differing from those found in round barrows.† I cannot agree with Dr. Thurnam's theory, that the unchambered long barrows in Britain were built by men with long heads, anterior to the building of the round barrows, which latter he thinks have been built in the main by men with round heads. The chambered long barrows, as far as I can gather, differ from the unchambered ones no more in form than does the round barrow, containing a cist, differ in form from the round barrow without a cist. Dr. Thurnam also remarks, "The evidence before us appears to favour the conclusion that while in Britain the chambered long barrows were erected by a dolichocephalous (long headed) race, in Gaul such tombs were raised by a brachycephalous one.‡ In Scandinavia they seem to be monuments of an old round-headed and probably Turanian race."§

---

* The Rev. W. C. Lukis, F.S.A., was of opinion that most, if not all, of the elongated tumuli of Brittany were originally circular and enlarged by subsequent additions.—*Archæologia*, vol. xlii. p. 74.

† Neither do the long barrows opened by Canon Greenwell. See "British Barrows," Nos. ccxxii., ccxxiv., ccxxvi., and ccxxxiv.

‡ Thurnam's "Round Barrows."—*Archæologia*, vol. xlii.

§ "Prehistoric Man and Beast," p. 210, by the Rev. H. N. Hutchinson.

Though the long barrows are designedly of a type so very different from that of the circular barrow, I am inclined to believe there is but little evidence of their greater age. They might just as probably be later, as absence of relics with most of the interments in long barrows does not alone prove their age.* Be this as it may, their form and manner of construction differ so widely from those of the round barrows, that it seems difficult to attribute the two forms to the same race of people.

ROUND BARROWS.

The Round Barrows are, as their name implies, circular in form, and by early writers have been divided into several kinds.

" What Sir Richard Colt Hoare calls Druid barrows, consisting of one or more very small mounds having a circular bank surrounding them at some distance, do not occur upon the Wolds, though it is possible that such may at one time have existed and been entirely destroyed by cultivation. At the same time, as they have not been met with on the Moors to the North of the Derwent, it is more probable that they were always absent on the Wolds. Nor do the twin barrows of Sir R. Colt Hoare, or a group of three mounds surrounded by a ditch, which are found, though rarely, in Wiltshire, find any representative on the Wolds."

An exception to this occurs on Acklam Wold, where barrows Nos. 204 and 205 were found to be surrounded by one trench, which, from the tilling of the land, was not visible on the surface.

CIRCLES ENCLOSING BARROWS.

Many of the Wold barrows had originally an encircling mound or ditch— and in most instances both—at their base, which from cultivation have long since disappeared.

Most of the Wold barrows I have opened were found to have a filled-in trench encircling their margin, not visible on the surface, the filling in being the result of tilling the land and atmospheric influences. These trenches are, except in very rare instances, of a circular form.

The Yorkshire Antiquarian Club noticed a mound on Arras, near Market Weighton, that was enclosed in a square foss ; also one on Skipton Common, with a square foss set out by the cardinal points. I also remember seeing a small barrow close to Cawthorne Camps, which was within a four-sided trench.†

The barrows on the Wolds differ considerably in size, and at the present time range from 15 to 125 feet in diameter, and from a few inches to 22 feet in height ; though at the bottom of Garrowby Hill there is a flat-topped mound (mainly artificial) 250 feet in diameter and 50 feet in height, which has not been opened.

MATERIAL USED IN THE CONSTRUCTION OF BARROWS.

The barrows " have been made with the materials which came the readiest to hand, and these appear to have been collected for some distance round each mound, for no indication of any hollow marks the place from whence the earth or chalk was taken. As might be expected, they are more commonly made of earth than of chalk,

---

* The Rev. W. C. Lukis believed the long barrows of Brittany were later than the round barrows.

† It is just possible these particular mounds were long after their erection used as Moot-Hills, and might then have been enclosed in square earthen embankments to serve as protections and shelters for the attendants at the Folk-Moots.

but it is rare to find one without some admixture of that stone, or of flint, the former, no doubt, obtained from the grave,"* which is almost always found at the centre. They occur but very rarely made entirely of chalk.

"With the imperfect tools and other appliances possessed by the people who erected them, the task of collecting the earth, and much more of quarrying the chalk, must have been by no means an easy one. Chalk, however, from its tendency to become broken up, especially in the upper beds, by cracks, is easier to work, even by means of so humble an implement as a pick of deer's horn or a pointed stake, than might at first be supposed. I have frequently noticed indications of turfs or sods of earth having been used; in a few instances the remains of grass and other plants being distinctly visible. In some of the barrows the appearances were such † as to suggest that the material was collected in small quantities, probably in baskets, and that the mound was constructed piecemeal, here a basket full of earth, there a few turfs, then two or three blocks of flint, and so on." Sometimes a central core of chalk-stones exists at the base of the barrow.

"In some cases the material has been placed with greater regularity, and the way in which a barrow had gradually increased from the centre was most clearly shown by the parallel layers of different coloured matter, which were distinguishable in the section of it."

Canon Greenwell adds, "I have never seen anything to lead to the conclusion that a material, foreign to the spot on which the barrow was erected, had been used in its construction, with the exception of slabs of stone used in making cists, and that has occurred, within my experience, in only one case upon the Wolds. Nor have I ever found that the body had been placed among any peculiar soil, or brought in contact with any other substance than that which might have been obtained in close proximity to the barrow."

The perusal of the following pages will, however, show that in the case of the barrows I have opened, it was more the rule than the exception for clay, foreign to the spot, to be used in the erection of these barrows. It occasionally occurred in large quantities, and had sometimes been fetched from a considerable distance. I have also noticed, not infrequently, that clay, peaty matter, and sometimes fine loamy earth, brought from a distance, had been specially placed near the interment and the cinerary urn. Occasionally the interment rested on a few inches of clay, and not infrequently a thin layer of the same material covered it. In Barrow No. 12 the grave in the chalk rock had a flooring of Oolitic flagstones; while there were ten interments on a flooring of Liassic stones in Barrow No. 275; and in Nos. 61, C 38, and 281, were cists of the same foreign rock; while under the centre of Nos. 55 and 83 was concealed a broken or incomplete circle of large Oolitic sandstone blocks (Calcareous Grit) enclosing interments.

The use of material from a distance in building these barrows seems to have been practised over wide areas. Canon Atkinson, when opening barrows on the Cleveland moors, observed layers of white sand used in making the mound, which he considered was not obtainable within seven miles of the site of the barrows,

---

* I may add also at times from an encircling trench either within or round the circumference.

† See barrow 90, page 97 (and others) ; also for an account of the ferns, grass, roots, and remains of small beetles found in a barrow in good preservation, see an account of " Castle Hill," near Newton-in-Makerfield, by Rev. Ed. Gibson, opened in July, 1843.

and the greater part of another barrow was whinstone from a dyke three miles distant.*

The Rev. R. Kirwan, Rector of Gittisham, opened three tumuli at Honiton in 1868, in which he observed peat and blue clay, which the workmen said did not belong to the locality.†

Furthermore, earth, foreign to the locality, has been observed to cover the bodies in the American burial mounds ("Pre-historic America," p. 95, by the Marquis de Nadaillac).

CIRCLES WITHIN BARROWS.

"In some rare instances they certainly had enclosing circles within the barrow. I have met with this feature in the form of a circle of flint stones, and of a circular trench. In both cases the circle was an incomplete one. In the ring of flint stones there was a space left vacant; in the trench, which was hollowed out of the chalk rock, there was one portion, or more, which was necessary to complete the circle, not excavated. The same peculiarity is found to exist in the barrows and cairns of other parts of England and in Scotland ; and, indeed, this incompleteness appears to be almost invariable in connection with sepulchral circles."

The incompleteness of these circles is so frequent a feature in their construction that it cannot be accidental.

"They have, moreover, been left incomplete in some cases in a way which must show a design in the operation. It has been suggested by some that the enclosing circles were merely made to support the mound at the base. It is only necessary to remark, in refutation of this surmise, that the circle is often within the mound, is sometimes a trench, and is, as before mentioned, nearly always incomplete. Others have, and with some reason, supposed them to be marks of taboo, a fence to preserve the habitation of the dead from desecration. The fact that so many are within, and must always have been concealed by the barrow, appears to be inconsistent with this explanation."

Several examples of concealed circles are described in this volume. All, except one of stone, were trenches in the ground. I incline to the belief that they are marks of taboo, or enclosures which were made at the beginning of the ceremony to mark off and protect the sacred spot in which the ceremony and interment were afterwards to be conducted, and that the break in the circle had no other significance than to serve as a place of ingress and egress during the performance of the obsequies or funeral rites. The frequent addition of a circle which more often enclosed the whole barrow also supports this view.

SITE OF THE BARROWS.

"It is usual to find the Wold barrows associated in groups, of greater or less number, though a single one is not very uncommon. As a rule they crown the heights, and, though frequently placed on the slope of the hills, it is rare to find them in the bottom of the valley." ‡

* "Forty Years in a Moorland Parish," pp. 147 and 152.
† "Memoirs of the Excavation of Three Barrows at Broad Down," *Transactions of the Devonshire Association for the Advancement of Science, &c.*, 1868.
‡ "British Barrows," p. 8.

The writer has found this to hold good in the main; and Dr. Thurnam, in alluding to the barrows in the south of England, says "Mounds occupy the escarpments like watch towers." This I have found to be the case along the northern and western escarpments of the Yorkshire Wolds, where they are most numerous, and mainly grouped in clusters, arranged in lines along the elevated ground on the brow of these escarpments. They also run from these ridges into the interior of the Wolds, along elevated ground, as do Groups I. and II. from Aldro to near Sledmere; and in other places, possibly along the lines of ancient track-ways, which they would the more distinctly mark.

Besides the barrows in the interior of the Wolds which are placed along the ridges of elevated ground, there is Group No. XI., most of the barrows of which are placed along the bottom of a broad valley, which, in early times, had frequently been flooded (see footnote, p. 233).

Probably the commune to which the dead belonged fixed the site of the burial mounds near their settlement, whether on high or low ground.

HOLES IN BARROWS.

"There are certain features in connection with many of the barrows which, as they do not appear to have reference to any particular burial, but rather to the sepulchral mounds themselves—though perhaps the two can scarcely be separated—it will be better to explain, before giving a description of the manner in which the mounds have been made. Though, as has been stated, these features do not connect themselves immediately with the burials, they are nevertheless so commonly found in the barrows that they must have reference to and originate in customs pertaining to the rites of sepulchre. It is a frequent occurrence to find holes sunk below the natural ground within the area of a barrow, and not usually in close proximity to any interments, though in some instances such has been found to be the case.

"Sometimes as many as four or five have been met with in a single barrow.[*] They are of various sizes, and differ in shape, but they are generally circular, about $1\frac{1}{2}$ feet in diameter, and the same in depth. In the greater number of cases they are filled with the ordinary materials of which the mound itself is composed, [†] and contain nothing besides. But at other times, pieces of animal and —much more rarely—of human bones, charcoal, potsherds, and burnt earth and stone are found in them." [‡]

Those holes which show no traces of fire very probably contained posthumous tributes of food to the dead, while those in which traces of fire are visible—as well as a few long trenches of considerable size—(see Barrow No. 254, p. 320) may very probably have been used in sacrificing and in depositing food.[§] The Laplanders interred a quantity of provisions along with the dead body, and during the first three years after the death of a relative, were accustomed from time to

* Nos. C 61, p. 211, and others in this volume.
† This may be due to their having contained something perishable, which on decaying admitted the material into the place as it became empty; or to their having been empty at the time of raising the barrow.
‡ Similar dish-shaped holes are found under barrows in America. "Primitive Man in Ohio," by Moorehead, p. 177.
§ See Potter's "Antiquity of Greece," vol. i. pp. 228 and 252.

time to deposit, in holes dug beside the grave, small quantities of tobacco, or of whatever was most agreeable to their departed friend during his lifetime.* When these holes contain burnt matter only, they may have served for cooking the funeral feasts. The New Zealander's oven is a hole, about one foot deep, in which a great quantity of dry wood is placed, and covered over with a number of stones.† The Australian aborigines adopt a similar method.

ANIMAL BONES IN BARROWS.

"The occurrence of animal bones is another frequent incident. It is rare, indeed, to meet with a barrow (where the material is such as to favour the preservation of bone) without a considerable number of animal bones being found scattered indiscriminately throughout the mound ; and where they have not been so found, their absence is no doubt in many cases to be attributed to decay of the bones. In some barrows they are very abundant.

"They are nearly always, when of a nature that admits of such a process, broken, so as apparently to extract the marrow. There can, I think, be little doubt that these bones are the remains of feasts held at the time of the funeral, or at some subsequent one, such as the anniversary.

"Practices of a like kind have been common to many different peoples, and so prevalent was the custom in some parts of Europe in the early times of Christianity, that frequent orders directed against holding feasts or sacrificing at the graves of the dead are to be found in the Frankish capitularies."

HUMAN BONES.

The fact that broken and dismembered human bones—often associated with animal bones—mixed in the grave and in the mound, have been found in so many of the barrows I have opened, would seem to indicate that they had often served the same purpose as did the animal bones. These scattered human bones, like the associated animal bones, are generally in far better preservation than those of the interment below. They have also a different appearance, as if they had been somewhat changed, probably by some process of cooking. Repulsive as cannibalism is, the evidence of its existence in the barrows of this neighbourhood seems to me so strong as to place its former practice beyond doubt. All races of men, in their march towards civilisation, appear to have passed through the stages of cannibalism. ‡ Every carnivorous animal would feed on its own species rather than hunger to death. Man is not an exception to this feeling, and in all parts of the world, during early uncivilised ages, from sheer necessity alone he must have been frequently driven to this practice. As regards the Britons, let us hope that they may have been partially civilised and seldom resorted to cannibalism except in their revered funeral customs, which would be the last to disappear.

These broken bones found scattered in the mound on the old surface line, and in the grave beneath it, are largely—whether animal or human—unquestionably

* "The Last Act," by William Tegg, p. 190.
† "Flint Chips," by Stephens, p. 59.
‡ The Agheri Fakirs of India eat human flesh, and they believe some of this sect have the power to eat human flesh and then make it alive again. They make drinking cups of human skulls. See "Journal of the Anthropological Institute," vol. xxvi. p. 345.

the remains of feasting during the funeral obsequies and the making of the mound, and they give valuable and indisputable evidence of the domestic and wild animals then killed for food ; also, from the pieces of charred and decayed wood, we are able to ascertain many of the kinds of trees that then clad the adjoining hills and valleys.

POTSHERDS AND FLINTS.

" There are two other series of objects which are found still more constantly, and even more abundantly, than the bones, and for the presence of which it is much more difficult to account—namely, flints and potsherds. They occur at times in very large quantities ; the flints generally in the shape of mere chippings and waste pieces, but often as manufactured articles, such as arrow-points, knives, saws, drills, and scrapers, &c. The potsherds are sometimes fragments of the ordinary sepulchral pottery, but more frequently of vessels, which, on account of their better firing and the absence of ornament, appear to be those of domestic utensils. Both flints and potsherds are found distributed throughout the whole of the mounds, and in some instances in such quantities as to suggest the idea that the persons who were engaged in throwing up the barrow scattered them from time to time during the process. They are certainly not there accidentally.

" It is difficult to account for the occurrence of the flints and potsherds in question, except on the supposition that they symbolised some religious idea, though what that idea was we may not be able to conjecture."

PROTECTION OF THE BODY.

The manner in which the dead have been disposed within the barrow differs very considerably. Sometimes the body, whether burnt or unburnt, seems to have been placed in the mound without anything to protect it from the surrounding earth or stones.

Sometimes it has been placed in a small box of stone—a cist; and at other times in the hollow trunk of a tree; but most frequently of all in a grave sunk below the surface of the ground. Not infrequently the body was protected in a wooden structure within the grave, and, when cremated, often in an urn. In some instances the mound encloses the remains of a large structure (Barrows Nos. 23, 41, 110, C 34, and others), suggesting an abode originally built for the living and afterwards appropriated as a resting-place for the dead.

The interments—both burnt and unburnt—are found in various parts of the barrows. The central, which in the case of no subsequent disturbance is the primary burial, was usually made in a grave sunk into the chalk rock. This grave is either oval or circular; generally the former. It varies considerably in size, from less than 3 feet to 15 feet† in diameter, and from 1 foot to 19 feet in depth below the original surface of the ground. In some few instances the primary burial has been made upon the surface level. The graves containing inhumed bodies are mainly oval, whilst the graves or holes containing cremated bones only are almost invariably circular and more or less dish-shaped. This persistent distinction between the graves of the two modes of burial cannot be attributed to the makers following

---

* In some cases the flints would be found mixed with the surface soil used to raise the mound.

† See Barrow 54 in this volume, p. 64.

the most yielding lines in the rock as has been suggested. I have never found sufficient proof of a primary burial having ever been placed above the base line of the barrow. Where Canon Greenwell has thought he had found it so situated, the true primary burial below must have either completely decayed or have been passed over.

"The number of burials in a barrow is very uncertain; nor is the size of the mound any criterion in that respect. A large mound may contain a single interment, or a small one several. When more bodies than one are found in the mound they are mostly placed at greater or lesser distances from the centre, upon or beneath the natural surface, or above it, at different levels. Some of these appear to have been buried when the primary interment took place, while others are evidently the bodies of persons interred at a time subsequent to that of the first erection of the barrow. These secondary interments have been made either by placing the body in the mound as the building proceeded; on the surface of an existing barrow; or on the surface ground just beyond its limits, and then covering them by adding more material to the mound; or by making an excavation into it. Secondary burials occur in all parts of the barrows, and the several levels at which they have been met with seem to show that a mound has sometimes been increased in size.* They have been made on all sides of the barrow, but much more frequently on the south and east than on the north and west. It is probable that the desire to face the sun guided them in this, as it has other peoples."

"In most cases there is nothing remaining to protect the body against the pressure of the overlying soil; but now and then a few large blocks of flint or thin slabs of chalk have been placed round it, thus forming a kind of rude covering. The interring in cists—that is, in coffins made of four or more stones set on edge, with a cover—so common ·in other parts (not only in this country, but in almost all parts of the world where suitable stone was to be had) is, as might indeed be expected, almost entirely wanting upon the Wolds." In a chalk district like this it was impossible to procure the requisite slabs, except by bringing them from a distance. I only know of three instances on the Wolds,† two of which I have examined, viz., in barrows Nos. C 38 and 61. In the former mound the stones forming the cist have been recognised as belonging to the Oolitic beds at Filey Brig, a distance of nearly twenty miles; while those forming the cist in the latter mound had been obtained from the outcropping Oolitic beds at the foot of the Wolds, about half a mile westwards from the barrow. The third example was a double cist, which Canon Greenwell found placed in a deep grave sunk in the chalk rock under a barrow near Rudston,‡ only a few miles to the east of my field of operations, and where the Oolitic stones of which it was composed must have been brought from a place at least twelve miles distant— probably from Filey Bay. In some rare cases the inhumed body was protected in a coffin made out of a split and hollowed tree trunk, of which the well-known Gristhorpe burial, now in the Scarborough Museum, is an example. A similar discovery was made at Sunderlandwick (Barrow No. 279a, Group XII. p. 296), but

---

* As Barrows Nos. 17 and 229, Groups IX. and XIII., also Nos. 122, C 59, and 116, in this volume.
† At Eddlethorpe, a short distance from the northern edge of the Wolds, I opened a barrow in which were five cists, arranged in the form of a cross. See fig. 1010, p. 347.
‡ "British Barrows," p. 238.

I know of no others from a barrow in East Yorkshire. An oaken tree coffin seems to have been the rarest of all forms of protection to a dead body, and it was probably the most difficult to supply with the tools then in existence,* even when, as is probable, a trunk was chosen which had been somewhat hollowed by decay.

"The bottom of a grave has sometimes been laid with slabs of wood ; and in one instance a wooden flooring had been placed upon the short posts, driven in at the head and foot of the grave, the sides of which also showed, by the impressions on the clay, that it had been lined with wood. The body seems not infrequently to have been placed upon wood, not extending much beyond the bones, and in one case protected on each side by a thin slab of willow, there being no appearance of wood either above or beneath it ; but in other cases wood —apparently planks—had been laid over the body." †

My own work fully confirms the above observations. In the barrows described in these pages, it will be observed that traces of wooden protection for the body in the grave are numerous, taking the place of stone cists where no stone was readily obtainable. On the beach at Easington, in Holderness, under a tide-demolished barrow, Dr. Hewetson and the writer on April 21st, 1894, discovered a double cist made of broad slabs split from the outer shell of the decayed trunk of a willow tree. This barrow had been swept away by the waves, and its site was at about half-tide-line, and a considerable way from the the very low cliffs. Lining the grave with wood (the branches of trees) would not be difficult to accomplish, and would be practised as a protection to the body.

INTERMENTS IN ABANDONED DWELLINGS.

Four varieties of dwellings have been discovered, some of which had afterwards been given up to the dead.

One kind—of which I have met with two examples (pages 155 and 182)—had been built entirely above ground, with circular side walls consisting of vertical stakes interlaced with wattled work plastered with clay, and the roof thatched. In the centre of one of these was a grave containing an inhumed body.

Another kind (pages 221 and 258) had been sunk into the ground in the shape of a shallow well, having had a leaning roof meeting at the top, and most probably also thatched. The other two forms were sunk in the ground sufficiently deep to admit the erection of a horizontal roof. Of this latter I have met with five examples ; three with a sloping passage each leading into the pit (Barrows 241 and 260, Group XV., and Kemp Howe, Cowlam, p. 336) ; and two others, each with two inclining passages twenty-five feet long, slanting from opposite sides into the

---

* Professor Williamson, in his account of the Gristhorpe tumulus, says (referring to the oak tree coffin), " Of this mode of burial only two similar examples have been recorded, one of which was in a tumulus opened by Sir R. C. Hoare, I think in the neighbourhood of Stonehenge, where the body was deposited in the trunk of an elm. The other is recorded in the Chronicle of the " Annual Register," of March 12th, 1767. It was in a barrow opened at Storbough, near Wareham, in Dorsetshire. The coffin was formed of a very large and rudely-excavated trunk of an oak, ten feet long and four feet in diameter. It contained the bones of a human body, wrapped up in a large covering of several deerskins, neatly sewn together, a part of which was ornamented with a piece of gold lace four inches long. Under the covering was found a small vessel of oak, of a dark colour, something in the shape of an urn. The top of the coffin was even with the natural surface of the ground, the barrow raised over it."
† "British Barrows," p. 14.

centre of the pit (Barrows 110, p. 103, and C34, p. 258). Two at least of these dwellings had also been appropriated as receptacles for the dead.*

The two last-named underground dwellings and passages were covered with a horizontal roof, upon which was heaped soil and stones, more or less in the form of a barrow.† Except when they are occasionally protected by a barrow, no trace of the first kind could possibly have remained to the present time. The last-named variety, with its long inclined passage, is very primitive, and little superior to the burrowings of wild animals, which probably may have been copied by early man. Probably this somewhat frail latticed dwelling was mainly occupied during the summer months, the underground structure being a winter habitation and a hiding-place during periods of alarm.‡ They would also serve as sleeping dens and give protection to occupants against the cold and attacks of wild animals. The earliest home of primitive man was most probably a natural shelter or cave in the rock; and the rude dwellings found under the barrows, in the form of a cave, seem to give further proof of the great age of some of the barrows.

BURNT BODIES.

Burning the body was undoubtedly long posterior to inhumation, yet it was practised during the Trojan and Theban Wars, and is of remote antiquity. Its origin is lost in the mists of time, and must for ever remain uncertain. Nevertheless, its introduction indicates a considerable advance in civilisation.

"Eustachius assigns two reasons why burning came to be of general use in Greece. The first is because the bodies were thought to be unclean after the soul's departure, and, therefore, were purified by fire. The second reason is that the soul being separated from the gross and inactive matter, might be at liberty to take its flight to the heavenly mansions." §

Perhaps the fable of the phœnix rising again from its own ashes originated from the practice of burning the human body and the belief of its liberating the spirit.

I have found cremated bones placed in all positions, sometimes in urns, but more frequently alone, both in the barrow and in the ground beneath it. They occur as primary burials in the centres of large graves, as in Barrows Nos. C34, C68, C90, 69, and 275, and a few others, but far more frequently in dish-shaped and bowl-shaped excavations in the ground under the barrow, wood ashes and

---

* The primitive Greeks were buried in places in their own houses.—Potter's "Grecian Antiquities," vol. ii. p. 217.

† The remembrance of these mound-covered cave dwellings seems to linger in old stories. In "Gaelic Mythology" one story tells how an old woman went to a knoll for shelter, and began to fix in it the tether peg of the tether of two calves, when the knoll opened and a woman put out her head and all above the middle, and rebuked her for what she was doing. The owner of the calves apologised, and pleaded weakness and poverty as an excuse. The inhabitant of the knoll directed her where to feed her calves, and told her that if she acted as she was bidden she would not be a day without a cow as long as she lived.—"Journal Anthropological Institute," Nov. 1879, p. 169.

‡ Tacitus, in describing the dwellings of the ancient Germans, says, "Besides their ordinary habitations, they have a number of subterranean caves, dug by their own labour and carefully covered over with soil, in winter their retreat from cold and the repository for their corn. In these recesses they not only find a shelter from the rigour of the seasons, but in times of foreign invasion their effects are safely concealed. The enemy lays waste the open country, but the hidden treasure escapes the general ravage, safe in its obscurity, or because the search would be attended with too much trouble."

§ Potter's "Grecian Antiquities," vol. ii. p. 209.

burnt soil accompanying the bones and filling the upper portion of the excavated receptacle, the sides of which are generally more or less burnt. It would seem from this that in many instances the ashes were not cool before being interred, but were gathered hot from the funeral pyre and deposited in that condition. In this way the sides of the cavities containing them were burnt, and bones of an inhumed body, with which the cremated bones were in contact, were sometimes partly charred, as in Barrows 51, 73, C 43, and several others.

Cremated interments are still more frequently found in small pockets or heaps, either circular or elongated. These two forms were probably mostly determined by the bones having been collected from the wood-ashes, and either tied in a ball or rolled in a skin of cloth, which in many instances had left, by its decay, a vacant place round the bones, as in Barrow No. 52, Group III., &c. These deposits seldom contain wood-ashes and burnt soil, so generally found with cremated bones in the dish-shaped excavations. Cremated bones are also found in this district, mostly in urns, generally upright, but sometimes inverted. Most probably, as Canon Greenwell suggests, the mouth of the urn was covered with cloth or hide, while instances occur where the urn itself had been protected, as in Barrow No. 241, Group XV. Canon Greenwell did not find on the Wolds burnt bones in connection with any protection of wood. I have been more fortunate, however, and have observed cremated bones which had been placed in a hollowed log or other wooden receptacle (Barrows Nos. 90, C 34, C 73, C 74, and others). Similar interments have been found in other parts of England.* From these it would seem probable that, as with the inhumed bodies, so with the burnt bodies, more or less protection had been generally given, and that where no trace remains of a protection to the interment, it had probably completely decayed, or the mouldered remains had been overlooked at the time of research. In all the preceding instances the cremated bones are in small pieces, seldom more than two inches in length. Probably, after collecting the fire-splintered human bones from the ashes of the pyre, it was a custom to break them into smaller pieces at the side of the grave.

Most rarely of all, the bones of burnt bodies, greatly shattered and warped by heat, but not in small pieces, have been found remaining, apparently on the site of the place of cremation, mixed with the embers of the funeral pyre. (See account of Barrows Nos. 80, 81, C 34, C 56, and 224, Group XI.).

Canon Greenwell has noticed this, and writes: "In some rare cases the bones were not collected after the burning, but were left in the position they occupied before the fire was applied." From a perusal of the detailed account of the two barrows referred to, it is evident that they are not of the same nature of those I found. The Canon says the body was in each case placed in or over a circular hollow, in one case but 2½ feet, and in the other case 3½ feet in diameter, with an average depth of 9½ inches only ; and in each case the hollow contained a great quantity of charcoal under the body. In a footnote he gives an instance of a similar discovery of two bodies by Mr. Bateman. But, as the bodies described in all these cases were in the usual flexed position of an

---

* Four instances are given of Sir R. Colt Hoare having found the deposits of burnt bones placed in a wooden box, and of the Rev. W. C. Lukis having met with burnt bones enclosed in a hollow tree trunk in a barrow at Collingbourne, Dorset, Wiltshire.—"British Barrows," p. 14, footnote.

unburnt body, with all the bones still in their proper position, and preserved in their natural order, and hardly affected by heat—which could not have been the case had they been subjected to the ordinary action of the pyre—I am inclined to believe that the partial calcination of each of these bodies is due to their having been placed on the top of one of the dish-shaped cavities immediately after it had been filled with cremated bones, and the glowing embers of the fire that had probably reduced a previous body to ashes. These having been quickly covered up, sufficient heat would be retained to partly calcine the portion of the body placed immediately above them, without much warping or splintering of the bones. The fact of two of the bodies named by Canon Greenwell being accompanied by a food-vase, and one by a food-vase and a bronze pricker, placed as we find them with ordinary unburnt interments, strongly supports the view here expressed. Besides, the hollows themselves would have been unsuitable and quite too small for the effectual cremation of full-grown individuals.*

I agree with Canon Greenwell that "A deposit of burnt bones is sometimes found to comprise the remains of more than one body. In some instances they are those af a woman and child, probably a mother and her offspring; but in other cases they are the bones of adults.

"It is not an uncommon occurrence to find pins, generally made of bone, but sometimes of wood, with a deposit of burnt bones. In most cases they are calcined, and no doubt represented the fastening of the dress or covering in which the body was enclosed before the burning took place. But in others the pin is found to be untouched by fire, and it is probable, where this is the case, that it had served to fasten a cloth or hide in which the bones had been deposited after they were collected from the funeral pile."

The remains of such cloth or portion of a dress I obtained in the form of tinder from barrow No. 15, and I have not infrequently noticed with burnt bones what seemed to be flakes of burnt skin or leather. Further instances of the remains of burnt clothing and the fastenings for such have been found with cremated bones. Sir R. C. Hoare found traces of linen cloth in at least six instances with burnt bones. The same has been noticed in urns in other parts of England (Thurnam's "Round Barrows," page 42).

---

* Similar appearances of partial cremation, almost certainly from a similar cause, were observed in the Royal tombs at Mycenae, and I think there is no doubt that Dr. Schliemann (see "Mycenae," by Dr. Schliemann) was mistaken in his frequently repeated assertions, that cremation of the bodies had actually taken place at the bottom of the tombs. At page 337 he says, "The funeral pyres were not yet extinguished when they (the bodies in the bottom of the tombs) were covered with a layer of clay and then with a layer of pebbles, on which the earth was thrown at once;" and then adds, "To this circumstance chiefly are we indebted for the preservation of so large a quantity of wood, and the comparatively good preservation of the bodies; for in no instance were the bones consumed by the fire, and on several bodies, which were covered with gold masks and thick breastplates, even much of the flesh had remained." This might have been due to the body having been embalmed. Had an attempt been made to cremate the bodies in the graves, their destruction, as well as that of the quantity of accompanying objects, would have been much more complele, as but a little heat so confined would have had a much greater effect on the bodies, and would have quite melted most of the thin gold leaves. That fire had entered largely into the Mycenaean funeral ceremonies is quite certain, and at that early period it seems to have been universally applied in performing the funeral rites. This custom still lingers, as the Australian aborigines are said to kindle a fire in the grave, probably to purify it. The traces of burning observed in the Mycenaean tombs were no more than those which would have been caused by a few of the glowing ashes of the pyre, and probably also those of a sacrificed slave or attendant, having been cast on the floor of the grave, or on and around the bodies, and the whole immediately covered with the layer of clay noticed by Dr. Schliemann.

Of the belief that clothing and other articles so burnt would be of service to the spirit of the dead we have historical proof. Hector's store of raiment, rich and rare, his wife promises to burn for his use.* Herodotus also relates that Periander stripped all the women of Corinth and burnt their clothing as an offering to his dead queen, the shade of whom appeared to him, and said she was cold and had literally nothing to put on, for the robes buried with her were of no use since they had not been burnt. This indicates a former belief that burning articles did not destroy them, but made them of service to the dead. In the funeral customs of the Gauls (which were similar to those of the Britons) letters were even thrown on the pile, which it was thought would be received by the dead to whom they were addressed. † In the Lithuanian and old Prussian district, even as late as the Middle Ages, the belief was that things burnt would rise again with their owners, and serve them as before.‡ Strange as such a custom is, it still seems to be believed in, and has recently been practised in this neighbourhood.§

A deposit of human bones is sometimes found to contain a small number of animal bones mixed up with it. From the fact that they are not present in all cases, and when they do occur are only in small numbers, it is probable that in most cases they were there accidentally, having been gathered when the bones of the burnt body were collected from the funeral pile. It is quite possible, however, that these bones may represent animals killed at the funeral and burnt with the body.‖ In Barrow No. 71 I took from a deposit of cremated bones nearly the whole of one antler of a roebuck, which was calcined and would not have got there unobserved.

In a few areas cremation had been almost entirely practised. One such area occurs between Huggate and Haywold (part of Group XIV.); and Canon Greenwell found similar groups at Cherry Burton, Etton, and Goodmanham—about five miles south-east of Huggate. Further, the Rev. Canon Atkinson, of Danby, in Cleveland, opened a large number of barrows in Danby, Westerdale, Skelton, and Guisborough, and in part of two adjoining parishes—roughly estimated as an area of 70,000

* Homer's "Iliad," V. 11, book xxii. lines 597 and 598.   † "Crania Britannica," p. 116.
‡ Taylor's "Primitive Culture," vol. i. p. 444.
§ " A singular scene was witnessed at Withernsea, near Hull, on Saturday afternoon. On the previous Tuesday a party of gipsies encamped on a piece of ground near the promenade, and included amongst their number was John Young, better known as ' Fiddler Jack,' who was exceedingly ill, and who died on Thursday. There was much lamentation in the camp, and on Saturday the strange ceremony of burning his effects took place in connection with his funeral. The deceased was interred in the parish graveyard, and owing to rumours afloat as to the after-proceedings many persons gathered to witness the event, and there was much excitement. It is stated that some of the personal effects of the dead were burnt on the night before the funeral, but the principal destruction of his property took place on Saturday afternoon near the camp, a short time after the return from the burial. The waggon that had belonged to Young, and which was said to have cost £40, was set on fire, and the clothes, bedding, and other effects of the deceased, including a set of china and a fiddle, were thrown into the flames and consumed. It was rumoured that the horse that had been owned by the deceased would be shot and cremated, but this was not done. This strange custom, which is of great antiquity, and is said to have originated in order to prevent quarrelling among the relatives, and also that the widow might not be wooed for the property she might possess. It is also stated that the widow will for a period of three months have to depend entirely upon herself for her sustenance, and in no way participate in any of the earnings of her relatives. The woman is said to be well known to the inhabitants of Withernsea."—Yorkshire Post, Sept. 18th, 1894.
‖ A very valuable account, illustrative in many respects of what has been met with by Canon Greenwell and myself, is contained in the "Iliad," xxiii. 166-7. Homer there, writing of what Achilles did at the burning ot the body of Patroclus, says that, after placing the fat of many sheep and oxen (whose carcases were heaped round the pyre) about the body of Patroclus, from head to foot, he set vessels— (food vessels ?)—with honey and oil, slanting towards the bier. He then threw horses, pet dogs, and captured Trojans, after slaying them, on the pile, to be burnt with the body of his friend.

to 80,000 acres—all of which contained cremated interments only. The following note appears in his "Forty Years in a Moorland Parish," page 149:—"I hardly think that on these wide and wild moors in this division of the district of Cleveland the custom as to actual placing of what remained of the body after cremation (for no one actual instance of inhumation simple has so far been met with) varies at all, except in the rarest instances. The incinerated remains were simply laid on the natural surface, whether with the protection or accompaniment of an urn or without, and then covered with earth, or a protection of some sort of rough or rude stonework."

In the British Isles, cremation has been repeatedly practised at various times; firstly, by the Britons; secondly, by the Romans; and thirdly, by the Anglo-Saxons. Probably it was adopted for a considerable time by each of these, though apparently never to the exclusion of inhumation, as we have no proof that the latter was not always practised to some extent.[*] We have also evidence that in some instances it was a custom to inhume the adult bodies and to cremate the children (as in Barrows Nos. C 76, 264, &c.); while at other times the children were inhumed and the adults cremated (Barrow No. 88, &c.).   There are also instances where the chief interment in the barrow was inhumed and the sacrificed attendants were cremated (as in Barrows Nos. 273, C 76, 242, 250, 265, and others).   In several instances, where the body of the chief burial was reduced to ashes, the attendants were inhumed (as in Barrows Nos. 33, 276, and others).   From these examples it would seem that at times interment by inhumation was considered more honourable than by cremation.   At other times cremation was most in esteem, and was reserved for the principal interment, while the attendant was inhumed.[†]   The Jews also burnt the body as a mark of honour;[‡] whilst Buddha's remains were cremated amidst great pomp, and quarrels arose for the possession of the remains.   They were at last divided into eight portions, over each of which a tope was built ("Childhood of Religion," by E. Clodd, p. 183).

SECONDARY INTERMENTS.

It has already been mentioned that interments occur at various levels in the barrows, and Canon Greenwell thinks "There can be no doubt that a few of the burial mounds were used over a considerable period for later interments.   When this has been done by making excavations in an existing barrow, disturbance of the bodies already there has occasionally taken place.   But some of these cases are probably only apparent, and suggest the idea that a practice, which has been the custom amongst many peoples, may have prevailed in Britain.   Amongst the Patagonians the habit prevailed of keeping the bones of the body from which the flesh had been removed, and afterwards, on certain occasions, taking them to the burial-place of the tribe, where they were laid in the grave in order, together with the arms, &c., of the deceased.

"Many of the secondary interments must have taken place either at no great interval after the erection of the mound, or at all events before any change had

---

[*] Cremation societies are now being established, and the time may soon come when inhumation will again be the exception.

[†] Such practices account for the frequent occurrence of the two modes of interment in one grave.

[‡] Wellbeloved's "Eboracum."

taken place in burial customs or in the manufacture of pottery, implements, and ornaments; for such as are associated with the introduced bodies differ in no respect from those which are found to accompany the primary occupant of the barrow."

DISMEMBERED BODIES.

In the descriptions of the barrows given in this volume are detailed accounts of deposits of dismembered bones, containing remains of two and sometimes several bodies, packed so closely together as to leave no doubt that the bodies had been cut to pieces, and in some rare cases probably by some means divested of the flesh, or most of it, previous to burial (see Group III., Barrows Nos. 50, 52, 53, and 54; and Group I., Barrow No. 72, and a few others). But in no case have I found what may strictly be called a true ossuary.

BURIAL BY INHUMATION.

"The dead were buried in the barrows both by inhumation, when the body was interred in the condition in which it was when life departed, and after cremation, when it had undergone the process of burning." *

Probably soon after death, the body was often put in the flexed posture with the hands placed in the positions frequently adopted in sleep and during rest, and thus made ready for the grave.

I can also support Canon Greenwell's views that inhumation and crema- tion were practised in Britain at the same time. "This applies both to primary and secondary interments. Nor does the evidence afforded by the barrows show that the one process was earlier then the other. It has been held by many archæologists that burning the body was more frequent, if not the universal practice during the bronze period; and indeed this seems to be true as regards Denmaık; but the facts supplied by the Wold barrows by no means corroborate that view. It is perhaps natural, and what might be expected, that in the rudest states of society the body, if interred at all, should be simply buried without having been subjected to the action of fire. And this is confirmed by the knowledge we possess of the burial rites of modern savages. But the whole series of the Wold barrows belongs to a time when civilisation had made some considerable progress, and when there was nothing to prevent the use of so artificial a process of disposing of the body as cremation implies."

BURIAL AFTER CREMATION.

Though inhumation has been by far the most frequently practised within my field ot operatıons, ın some ot my small groups, or divisions ot barrows, cremation was the rule, and there is nothing connected with the barrows themselves to show that they are earlier or later than the neighbouring ones. For instance, a little east of Huggate (part of Group XV.) there were eight adjoining barrows, containing ten burials, nine being of burnt and one of unburnt bodies. Canon Greenwell gives† particulars of a similar discovery made at Goodmanham, eight

---

* "Among the Greeks both practises prevailed at the same time. The Romans at first buried the dead without burning them; afterwards they practised cremation, and finally reverted to the first mode; but at no time was the observance in either way universal." † " British Barrows," p. 19.

miles to the south of Huggate, where there were six burials, five being of burnt bodies and one unburnt. The proportion of burnt to unburnt bodies in the barrows I have opened are 328 by cremation, and 565 by inhumation, making a total of 893 burials in the 288 barrows I have tabulated, which gives 37 per cent. for burnt bodies, and 63 per cent. for unburnt bodies. Canon Greenwell, in referring to the barrows he has opened on the adjoining Wolds, adds—" It may suffice to mention that out of 379 burials only 78 were after cremation, whilst 301 were by inhumation, which gives only 21 per cent. for burials of burnt bodies. And to show that in the Wold barrows bronze is by no means more commonly found with burnt bodies than with unburnt, out of fourteen instances where I have discovered bronze articles associated with an interment, it was only in two that that the body had been burnt."

Out of thirty-five instances where the writer found bronze articles with interments, ten were associated with burnt bones. It is shown, both by Canon Greenwell and myself, that burial after cremation is nothing like so common as burial by inhumation. Occasionally within or adjoining large groups of barrows, where inhumation was mainly practised, a small group of barrows existed which was almost entirely confined to interment after cremation.

On the moors to the north of the Wolds, the late J. Ruddock and Thomas Kendall, of Pickering, opened a large series of barrows, chiefly in the neighbourhood of Pickering. The researches * of the former gentleman are recorded in "Ten Years' Diggings," by Thomas Bateman; and from the thirty-seven barrows there described, Mr. Ruddock exhumed twenty-six cremated bodies and only twenty-one inhumated ones, which reverses the proportions noted by Canon Greenwell and myself, and approaches more closely to Canon Atkinson's discoveries. It is to be regretted that Mr. Kendall has left no written record of his work, and therefore we have no means of ascertaining the proportion of burnt to unburnt bodies found by him. Too much reliance, however, must not be placed on the results obtained by the three last-named workers, as I believe that in many cases the primary interments (probably in graves under the barrows) were not discovered. If so, these undiscovered primary interments might somewhat alter the proportions of burnt and unburnt bodies.

CONTRACTED POSITION.

The ordinary inhumed interment is nearly always found to have been laid in a doubled position, with the knees drawn up towards the head, generally on the right or left side, not infrequently on the back, but rarely on the chest, and when in this position the knees are always, and the head generally, pressed over to one side.

"This remarkable doubled-up position of the body—which has, nevertheless, prevailed in many countries and at very different times—was certainly not caused by the desire to compress the body within the limits of a grave of small dimensions. In those barrows where a grave of nine feet or ten feet in diameter has occurred, the single body, which is all that in many instances has been buried there, is found to be contracted and placed at one side of the grave, thus occupying but a very

* These were conducted during 1849 to 1854.

small portion of its area. Where the body has been simply laid upon the ground, and when it might have been extended at full length without any difficulty, the same curved form is preserved. Even in the process of burning the body, the contracted position seems to have been retained." Canon Greenwell gives instances of these latter, but, as already expressed, I question those being more than ordinary interments by inhumation, which has been placed over a cavity containing the glowing embers of the funeral pile. While it is very probable that the body would be placed on the funeral pile at the time of cremation, in a flexed posture, as was the inhumed body when prepared for the grave, I must admit that I know of no proof of this.

"The position, therefore, was not due to the requirements of space, but originated in some settled principle, the meaning and purpose of which it may be said we have not the means of fully understanding, though I think a satisfactory explanation can be given. Nor does the question receive elucidation from any knowledge we possess of the cause of its adoption by modern savages; for though it is a common practice amongst many of them, no reason, except custom, is given for its use. This manner of disposing of the body has been so common and so widely diffused that it cannot be accidental. Some writers have thought that, in placing the body in the ground after this fashion, reference was made to the way in which man lay in the womb before he came into the world, and that as his entrance was, so his departure from this, or rather perhaps his entrance into another world, should be. This explanation, I think, can only claim a doubtful acceptance, for it is one which supposes a mental process beyond the power of the persons who originated the custom, and also would show a knowledge of the human frame such as these people, though they might be considered beyond the savage state, were not likely to possess. A more simple and, at the same time, a more probable explanation of this custom has, however, been offered, and one which cannot be considered an unnatural or unlikely one.*

"Where the sleeping-place was not well protected against cold, and when covering for the body at night was scanty and limited, the contracted position was that which was best adapted to afford warmth and comfort. In fact, it has been observed that most savages sleep after that fashion. What was more natural then, than that the body should be interred in the same posture in which the person was accustomed to rest in sleep, and in which, in many cases, he probably may have died."

"Bodies are said to be found in Britain buried in a sitting position.† This is probably a mistaken view of the contracted body, taken by persons who, seeing the head lying close to the knees, have come to the conclusion that it had fallen down upon the knees when the ligaments decayed. There seems, however, reason to suppose that they were sometimes placed in a sitting position in the chambered barrows of Scandinavia, where, in some cases, they appear to have been arranged in stone cells or stalls running round the chamber."‡

"A very remarkable discovery by Mr. Lukis shows that in the Channel Islands bodies were, in some cases, interred in a kneeling posture. He found in a cist, within a dolmen called 'Du Tus,' in Guernsey, two skeletons amongst

---

* Evans's "Ancient Stone Implements," p. 125.   † Bateman, "Ten Years' Diggings," p. 23.
‡ Nilsson, "Stone Age," Lubbock, p. 128.

sand, with the bones so arranged that the correctness of the description cannot be disputed." *

In "The Pictorial History of Scotland," p. 21, the purpose of interring the body in a flexed position is explained as follows :—"In all probability the earliest mode of interment was to place the body in a cist in a contracted posture, with the knees drawn up to the breast, that the warrior with his weapons by his side might be ready to spring up, fully equipped for the conflict."†

The custom of interring the dead in a doubled-up position seems to have been at one time maintained throughout the habitable world. As suggested by Sir John Evans, this posture probably originated from a wish to follow an attitude taken during sleep and rest. Occasionally the body seems to have been placed on its haunches, as in Barrows Nos. 52, C 59, Group III.; 264, Group XIV., and probably 261, Group XV.

Canon Greenwell records no burial in a sitting position.

EXTENDED POSITION.

In only two reliable instances out of 565, have I found the body extended at full length, as in Barrows Nos. C 39 and 100, and Canon Greenwell alludes to four instances of extended bodies out of 301 burials of inhumed bodies. While Mr. Bateman, referring to the Derbyshire barrows, says—"Nor have we seen any skeletons accompanied by relics of the early ages [British] fully extended." But in the same volume, in his descriptions of the barrows opened by Mr. Ruddock in the neighbourhood of Pickering, he mentions four extended bodies in twenty-five inhumed burials, two of which are described as extended side by side at the bottom of a grave eleven feet deep.‡ This is high percentage, and there may have been a mistake in the positions of some of these bodies.

DISMEMBERED BODIES.

I have noticed, as described in Barrows Nos. 50, 52, 53, 54, and a few others, one other method of dealing with the dead, viz., of cutting the bodies to pieces, and placing the parts in a heap. In some cases, they were apparently with the flesh on, and in rare cases certainly with the flesh removed, as in Barrows 54 and one or two others.§

---

* See a paper by Mr. Lukis in the Journal of the "British Archæological Association," vol. i., where, on page 27, is an engraving of the skeletons in the positions in which they were discovered.

† The very unusual and, as far as I know, exceedingly rare position named by Mr. Lukis might favour the above explanation, and show that in his particular case the bodies had been placed in such a position. I have not seen Mr. Lukis' engraving, but it might be detected that the bodies had been merely buried on their chests, face downwards, with the legs drawn up. I have found both British and Anglo-Saxon bodies in this position, but I doubt very much whether placing them absolutely on their knees was ever practised. At all times the wish seems to have been to place the body in a position of ease. This most unusual position of the body named by Mr. Lukis might also have resulted from its having been placed in a sitting position and the back secured to the sides of the cist, so that on the decay of the flesh, &c., the head and chest fell forward, thus giving it the appearance of being in a kneeling posture. I have occasionally found bones which seem to have fallen into positions giving a somewhat similar appearance.

‡ "Ten Years' Diggings," p. 206.

§ Diodorus says that the Carthaginians have a strange custom of burying the dead. They cut the body up in pieces and put all the parts in an urn, and then rear a heap of stones over it ("The Celtic Tumuli of Dorsetshire," p. 16). In the mounds on the Western River, South Carolina, many urns have been found containing human remains, in some cases calcined, but in others packed within the vessels in their natural state, after the flesh had been removed ("Ten Years' Diggings," by Thomas Bateman, p. 9).

POSITION OF THE HANDS.

"The position in which the hands have been placed varies considerably. They are found up to and in front of the face—and this is perhaps the most frequent position—at the neck, under the head, crossed over the chest or stomach, at the knees and hips, and extended down the side, or (occasionally) out from the body, in fact, arranged in almost every way in which it is possible to place the arms of a body laid upon its side, and just as they would naturally be adjusted during sleep." Canon Greenwell does not name the hand having been placed over the pelvic region, several cases of which I have noticed. In two instances an adjoining body had its hand on the pelvis of its companion. There is no rule as regards the direction of the body, the head being laid with the face opposite to any point of the compass. Three hundred and eighty-three interments, examined by myself, were in a sufficient state of preservation to admit of the position of the head and face being ascertained, together with the side on which the body had been laid. Without having regard to the minute division of the compass points, they may be thus classed :—

Direction of Head.	On the Right Side.	On the Left Side.	On the Back.	On the Chest.	Position not known.	Total.
Head pointing to N.	14	16	8	0	4	42
,,　　　,,　　N.N.W. .	4	3	0	0	0	7
,,　　　,,　　N.W. . .	6	2	3	0	3	14
,,　　　,,　　W.N.W. .	1	0	1	0	0	2
,,　　　,,　　W. . .	45	17	13	0	7	82
,,　　　,,　　W.S.W. .	2	0	1	0	1	4
,,　　　,,　　S.W. . .	13	2	3	0	2	20
,,　　　,,　　S.S.W. . .	4	1	2	1	1	9
,,　　　,,　　S. . . .	20	8	12	0	3	43
,,　　　,,　　S.S.E. .	4	0	0	0	0	4
,,　　　,,　　S.E. .	5	9	6	0	1	21
,,　　　,,　　E.S.E. . .	3	1	1	0	0	5
,,　　　,,　　E. . . .	41	25	9	1	8	84
,,　　　,,　　E.N.E. .	0	3	0	1	0	4
,,　　　,,　　N.E. . .	12	12	6	0	1	31
,,　　　,,　　N.N.E. . .	4	4	3	0	0	11
Total	178	103	68	3	31	383

To compare with this table I give on next page Canon Greenwell's list of the 234 bodies he obtained from the adjoining Wold barrows.

Entire adult bodies were found placed in large jars interred in a tumulus at Hanai Tepeh, in the Troad—date about 400 B.C. ("Archæological Journal," vol. xvi. p. 2), and a recent discovery made by Mr. F. Petrie, in Egypt, and figured in the *Illustrated London News*, of the 17th July, 1897, showed that a skeleton of the 5th Dynasty, about 3500 B.C. was found, the bones of which had been cut up and put in a box, with an effigy of the deceased by the side of it ("General Pitt Rivers," vol. iv. p. 21).

Direction of Head.			On the Right Side.	On the Left Side.	Total.
Head pointing to N. . . .			8	11	19
,,	,,	N.N.W. . .	3	3	6
,,	,,	N.W. . .	12	6	18
,,	,,	W.N.W. . .	6	1	7
,,	,,	W. . . .	20	5	25
,,	,,	W.S.W. . .	7	1	8
,,	,,	S.W. . . .	16	3	19
,,	,,	S.S.W. . .	4	5	9
,,	,,	S. . . .	11	8	19
,,	,,	S.S.E. . .	1	5	6
,,	,,	S.E. . . .	3	18	21
,,	,,	E.S.E. . .	1	9	10
,,	,,	E. . . .	13	24	37
,,	,,	E.N.E. . .	1	4	5
,,	,,	N.E. . .	6	15	21
,,	,,	N.N.E. . .	0	4	4
			112	122	234

DIRECTION OF THE HEAD.

It will be observed from the above tables that the most prevalent position of the head is to the west and the east. Though it is most commonly found that a grave contains but a single body, it is by no means an infrequent occurrence to find two or more bodies which have evidently been all interred together and at the same time, or at least before the grave was filled in.

In Barrow No. 273 and others, there were the remains of two to five inhumed and cremated interments in each grave. And often in these instances each had its head towards a different point of the compass. That this was accidental is very improbable.

Why the body was placed sometimes on its right side and at other times on the left side, not infrequently on its back, and still more rarely on its chest or on its hips, I cannot say.

CENOTAPHS.

" Barrows are sometimes met with in which, upon examination, no burial appears to have been placed, since no remains of the body are to be discovered. In the greater numbers of these instances there can be little doubt that, in consequence of the imperfect exploration of the mound, the place of burial has been missed, and in other cases that a small deposit of burnt bones or the almost entirely decayed bones of an unburnt body have been overlooked. Large numbers of barrows have been opened by various diggers by merely cutting a narrow trench through the centre. It will be readily understood how, in a process like this, the central burial might not be discovered ; for in throwing up a mound of considerable size, that part which was at one time the centre might eventually be at some distance from the central point of the complete barrow. Graves, also, have very frequently been overlooked,"* the explorers not being aware that it was the habit to bury beneath the natural surface. To this fault the writer pleads guilty during his early researches, as shown by the detailed account of his openings ; and Canon Greenwell, at the commencement of his explorations was, for some years, unaware of the existence of graves beneath the base of the barrows he explored. "There are other cases when the most careful excavation has failed to discover any trace of an interment. These empty barrows have been spoken of as cenotaphs—monuments raised to commemorate but not to contain the dead. In the greater number of instances, however, as has already been stated, the barrows are found empty, not because they are so in reality, but because they have not been searched exhaustively. The absence of any signs of burial, where a barrow has been fully and minutely examined, is due, in my opinion, to the entire decay of the skeleton, in cases where no weapon, implement, ornament, or vase accompanied the body. . . . I have myself opened several cists where there was not the slightest trace of bone to be seen, but where the occurrence of flint and jet and food vessels showed plainly that a body had once been placed therein. In other cases there was absolutely nothing within the cist."

With this I quite agree. In the burial mounds I have examined, only two cists have been constructed, and where the body had been placed in the ground without anything of a durable nature, the admission of air and damp might easily lead to the total disappearance of the bones; and if nothing of a more lasting character had been associated with the body (as in Barrows Nos. 44, 86, 213, and others), we should have an empty barrow—the so-called cenotaph. So far Canon Greenwell and I agree in this matter.†

DECAY OF THE BODY.

When the bodies have been interred where they could be reached by a free access of rain water, carrying a little air and probably also a small quantity of the acids obtained by water in passing through the superincumbent soil, they were slowly dissolved, and in time finally disappeared. It is, therefore, not strange—considering the very long time many of the bodies have been interred—that we should sometimes find a grave where no visible trace of a body remains. We might have rather expected to meet with but few instances where any trace did remain; and probably such would have been the case had not the Britons generally chosen a dry soil for their graves and taken much precaution to prevent percolating

---

* " British Barrows," p. 28.

† Some thirteen years later he thus writes:—"On the other hand, the examination of the mounds just described convinced me that the opinion I had hitherto entertained, that where no remains of an interment were found in a grave or otherwise in a sepulchral mound, such absence was due to the decay of the bones, was an erroneous one. In some of these barrows, notably Nos. ccxl., ccxlvi., ccxlix., and cclii., there was an entire absence of human bones under circumstances where it is certain that, had a body been interred, its remains must have been found. In the case of No. cclii. (Willie Howe), small fragments of animal bone, in a quite sound condition, were met with in the grave, showing that the surrounding material was a sufficiently preservative one. I have, therefore, felt obliged to come to the conclusion that on rare occasions a mound was raised, not to cover an interment, but presumably to be a memorial to a person whose body for one reason or other—and many may be suggested—it was found impossible to bury in the usual way, or perhaps at all ; that in fact, these early inhabitants of Britain erected cenotaphs."—" Recent Researches in Barrows : " " Archæologia," vol. lii. 1893. As already stated, my observations do not enable me to agree with this.

water from reaching the interment by covering the grave with clay, or, not infrequently, by partly using clay in building the mound over the grave. This almost impervious material, frequently brought from a distance, must have been intended to serve some such important purpose.*

CHARCOAL IN THE GRAVES.

Nearly every barrow-digger must have observed an incident intimately connected with burials by inhumation—which is rarely, if ever, wanting—the occurrence of charcoal, in greater or less quantities, in contact with the body.†

BURIAL IN DRESS.

Owing to the perishable nature of the material, it is difficult to come to any certain conclusion as to whether the corpse was interred in the ordinary dress of the deceased person, in something like a shroud, or without any covering. Upon the whole, it seems most probable that the body was laid in the grave clothed. Several facts bearing upon this question have been discovered. The impressions of various fabrics upon the oxidised surface of associated implements of bronze has afforded some information as to the nature of the clothing.‡ But the occurrence of bronze is so rare, and when found is so often in the shape of drills, awls, and other articles too small to afford a surface sufficient to exhibit any impression, that we possess but scanty evidence in this respect from its presence in the graves. The finding of articles used in fastening and ornamenting the dress affords, however, more satisfactory proof. Such articles are rings and links of jet (figs. 216 and 320), buttons of amber (fig. 213), of jet (figs. 290 and 525), and of bone (figs. 293, 531, and 739), and even of baked clay (fig. 587). Buttons of jet, stone, and bone were also found by Canon Greenwell. From these instances it would seem fair to infer that it was the custom to bury the body in its everyday clothing.

Hair Pins.—Bone pins, of the type shown by fig. 167, have been found by the writer, mostly at the back of the skull of a female, as in Barrows Nos. 113, 81, and others. These pins were undoubtedly used for securing the back hair, as shown in the photograph (fig. 602), and further support the highly probable inference that the body was placed in the grave in its everyday attire. Canon Greenwell alludes to the finding of bone pins, which he justly remarks is uncommon. He found twelve unburnt bodies each accompanied by a pin, and amongst burnt bones they occur in four cases. I have found seventeen inhumed bodies accompanied by one pin each, and one body by six pins;§ and seventeen cremated bodies were each accompanied by a pin, and with one deposit were two pins. Only one-third of the whole number are of the skewer-like type (fig. 518), while

---

* The aborigines of Australia raised a mound over the body, and coated it over with a layer of wet clay.—" The Aborigines of Australia," p. 60, by J. Worsnop.

† See " British Barrows," p. 29, for further particulars.

‡ Mr. Bateman mentions the finding of a body of a man . . . who had been interred enveloped in a skin of dark red colour, the hairy surface of which had left many traces both upon the surrounding earth and upon the patina coating a bronze axe-shaped celt and dagger, deposited with the skeleton.—" Ten Years' Diggings," p. 34.

§ Dr. Thurnam mentions six pins having been found with one body, in a long barrow.—"Archæologia," vol. xlii. p. 148.

the rest are mostly formed of the longitudinal half of the scoop-bone of a goat or sheep, frequently pierced at the broad end (fig. 167).

Bone Pins.—I have in my description of the barrows designated this shape as "hair-pins." * They have not only accompanied the inhumed body to the grave, but have also accompanied their owners to the funeral pile, though as far as I am aware only in the case of the females. This indicates that they frequently wore their black hair in a bundle behind the head, while the men probably wore their hair short, | or allowed it to hang loosely, as nothing for securing it, to my knowledge, has ever been found with the body of a male. ‡ The skewer-shaped pins (figs. 518, 619.) previously referred to appear to have served some other purpose. They are found with burnt as well as unburnt bodies, but most frequently with the former. When found with the latter, they are generally away from the back of the head, and have most probably secured some garment or a portion of the dress. In the former cases they had merely secured the wrapper containing the collected calcined bones. So far as I am aware no trace of a comb made of any substance whatever has been found with a British interment in East Yorkshire.

Traces of clothing seem to be indicated by the remains of cloth found in Barrow No. C 38, Group XII., and portions of woven material from No. 82, Group XI. ; in both cases connected with an inhumed body. In the York Museum is a thick piece of woven cloth measuring about 6 inches by 3 inches, made of very fine, short, soft hair or wool, from a barrow on Skipwith Common in 1819.§

I have frequently also noticed decayed matter, sometimes in considerable quantities, at the head or feet of bodies, and sometimes both. Such in grave "B" Barrow No. C 63, Group XI., and two others much resembled decayed leather. For further accounts of burials in dress see "British Barrows," p. 32.

DRESS FASTENINGS.

Fastenings for the dress have already been alluded to. They include buttons of wood, amber, jet, stone, bone, and baked clay (figs. 468, 213, 290, 525, 293, 531, and 587) in some cases highly decorated ; a peculiar ring (fig. 216), the application of which as a mode of fastening the dress—in this case, at least, apparently that of a male—is difficult to understand ; a jet article (fig. 320), probably to brace the belt generally found about the loins ; a link or fastening of bone (fig. 293), pins of bones (fig 619), and articles of boars' tusks (Barrows Nos. 273 and 294).

IMPLEMENTS.

"The nature of the materials of which weapons and implements were made has enabled us to obtain a considerable amount of information with respect to them.

---

* The hair-pins found in the Egyptian tombs are usually made of wood, bone, ivory, metal, or alabaster. The Roman hair-pins found with bodies are of jet and bone.

† Cæsar says the Britons wore their hair long—Book v. ch. xiv.

‡ In Australia the *male* aborigines wear their hair in the form of a chignon through which they thrust a hair-pin 6 inches to 12 inches in length.—"The Aborigines of Australia," by T. Worsnop, p. 160.

§ The Rev. Allen Borman Hutchins found in a barrow seven miles east of Sarum near Winters Low Hut Inn, a cinerary urn measuring 18 inches by 18 inches, and says, "With the assistance of my two men, the urn was removed, and immediately some linen, beautiful to the eye and perfect for a time, of a mahogany colour, presented itself to our view, and resembled a veil of the finest lace. I made an accurate drawing of the linen, which originally contained the burnt bones, of a yellow hue."—"Archaeological Journal," vol. i. 1845, p. 156.

These various articles are met with, associated with the bodies, both burnt and unburnt, as well as placed, without reference to any particular interment, within and at different parts of the mound. They are numerous, and it is difficult to say of some of them whether they should be classed in the catalogue of weapons or implements."

They may be divided into articles of stone (including flint), of bone [*] and deer's horn, and of bronze. The list of those made of stone other than flint found in the barrows I have opened are, a wrist-guard (fig. 741),[†] perforated hammers (fig. 233), and perforated axe-hammers (figs. 9, 513); also hand weapons (fig. 609) from Barrows Nos. 37 and 13, grain-rubbers (fig. 22, Barrow No. 18), hammer-stones from Barrow 37 (fig. 519), whetstones (fig. 201a) picked from the surface;

FIG. 150a. ‡
Found with a Flint Knife ground on the edges,
and a crushed Cinerary Urn, about 1 foot
from the surface, on the Rookdale Farm,
Sledmere, 1869.

FIG. 201a. ‡
Whetstone of the Neolithic Period.

portion of the only large whetstone (fig. 150a) I know of from a British interment, which is finely and well hollowed on the broad flat side, suitable for sharpening and polishing flint and stone axes, a use to which it had evidently been put. The narrow edges of this stone are rubbed flat, and may have been used to sharpen flint and bronze knives, possibly the flint knife which accompanied it. It has been much after the shape of fig. 181 (which, however, was not found with an interment) in Sir John Evan's "Ancient Stone Implements of Great Britain," but

---

[*] The four large articles, one made of a tine of a red deer (fig. 523), one of the antler of a roebuck (fig. 500), one of the leg bone of an ox (fig. 408), and one of a human femur (fig. 533), all seem to be tools for some similar purpose.

[†] Wrist-guards have occurred in connection with an interment of an unburnt body in several instances; in Wiltshire, on Roundway Down, near Devizes ("Crania Brit.," pl. 42), and near Sutton (Hoare, "Ancient Wilts.," vol. i., pl. 103); in Hertfordshire, near Tring ("Archæologia," vol. viii., p. 429, pl. 30); in Suffolk, near Brandon; this guard is now in the Christy collection. In Scotland they have been met with in the Isle of Skye (Whilson, "Prehistoric Annals of Scotland," vol. i., p. 223), near Cruden, Aberdeenshire ("L.C.," vol. i., p. 76), and near Evantown, Rossshire ("Proc. Soc. Ant. of Scotland," vol. vi., p. 233). They have also been found casually in other places in Great Britain and Ireland. They have been discovered in Denmark, associated with burials. See also Sir John Evans, "Stone Implements," p. 380.

was apparently much larger. The large whetstone (fig. 150a) just referred to is an exceedingly rare article. It was found in 1869 while working in a marl pit on Rook Dale, near Sledmere. I procured it and a fine flint knife—2¾ inches long, ground at the edges—from the man soon after he found them. They were found with burnt bones in a crushed cinerary urn. The knife shows traces of fire, while the whetstone shows none; but the latter had been broken into not less than four pieces, of which, unfortunately, two are all that had been preserved. Its uniform breadth has been 2 inches, and its thickness from 1 inch to 1¼ inches, and its length not less than 12 inches, but more probably 16 inches. Dr. Thurnam, in his "Round Barrows," page 139,* says—"No stones with hollowed surfaces, suitable for grinding celts or other large implements, seem to have been met with in our

FIG. 301a. ⅓
Found at Keld Slack,
Newton, near
Pickering, 1889.

FIG. 209a. ⅓
Flint and Pyrites.

barrows"—meaning the barrows in the south. Neither does Canon Greenwell seem to have found connected with interments this particular kind of hollowed whetstone. They are not, however, says Sir John Evans,† of uncommon occurrence in Denmark, Sweden, Scandinavia, France, and in the Swiss lake dwellings.

IMPLEMENTS AND WEAPONS OF FLINT.

The implements of flint include hatchets (fig. 475), scrapers, round and elongated (figs. 7, 252, and 452), knife-daggers (fig. 209), oblong knives (fig. 160), oval (fig. 336), chisel-ended (fig. 180), circular (figs. 181a to 181b), triangular (fig. 208), elongated (figs. 284 and 361), and lanceolated (figs. 197 and 95½). Of sickles (figs. 254 and 253a), saws (fig. 285 and fig. "A"), drills, fabricating tools (figs. 451 and

* "Archæologia," vol. lxiii.   † "Ancient Stone Implements of Great Britain," p. 235.

909), sling-stones (fig. 459), hand weapons (figs. 462 and 946), grinders (fig. 22a), rubbers (564), polishers picked from the surface (fig. 200a). arrow points, leaf-shaped* (fig. 17), triangular (fig. 413), and barbed (fig. 129). Some of these are figured on the adjoining plate E.

Heads of darts or javelins (figs. 301a, 302, 918, and 16), some of which may have been used as goads by herdsmen and charioteers ; small button-shaped articles (figs. 30a and 80). numerous worked globular stones; the smaller, most probably, have been used as sling-stones, and the larger balls as hand weapons used in close combat † (figs. 435, 459, and 462) ; flint for striking lights (fig. 209a), Barrow 124, Group IV.), and numerous other shapes, the use of which it is not easy to make out. Some of the finely-chipped discs of flint (fig. 80, and figs. 30 to 32c, Pl. IV., from Barrow No. 43, and many others picked from the surface of the land), may just possibly have served as British currency.‡ They are very numerous, and the smaller ones would hardly have served as tools or instruments for any purpose.

Probably many of the flint and other stone axes and axe-hammers were blocked into rough form and then bartered, the purchaser sharpening and polishing them at his convenience.

IMPLEMENTS OF BONE.

Implements of bone, owing to their less durable nature, are only rarely found. The writer possesses two large poignard-like instruments, one made from a human femur (fig. 533), the other (fig. 408) from the leg-bone of an ox ; a knife (fig. 917) or scraping instrument, a stiletto (fig. 344) ; three scapula-shaped articles, which may have been used in the manufacture of pottery (figs. 260, 268, 937) ; a small gouge-like tool, and two curved instruments (54 Pl. VII.), made of boars' tusks.

In addition to these, I have a bone article (fig. 126), probably a whistle or some other instrument for producing sound, § which may have been used at the burial ceremonies.

Implements made from the antlers of red deer and roebuck are not numerous. I have discovered two hammers (fig. 152), one from Howe Hill, Duggleby (fig. 63, Pl. VIII.) ; two piercing tools (?) (figs. 500 and 523), one made from the tine of an antler of a red deer, the other formed of an antler

---

* In the four Royal tombs at Mycenæ, there were, as well as the great number of gold articles, thirty-five arrow-heads of obsidian, of two distinct types, fifteen of which are figured in Dr. Schliemann s "Mycenæ," p. 272. One is leaf shaped, the other fourteen are wing shaped, with varying outlines. This latter is a somewhat rare form in Yorkshire. The common barbed Yorkshire type is not represented in the Mycenæan find.

† Such weapons were used freely by the ancient Greeks and other nations at the time of the Trojan War, and are frequently mentioned in the " Iliad " as being used by the Gods as well as mortals.

‡ The Baganda of Central Africa now use Cowrie shells as money ; but prior to their introduction *round* stones were used as money.--The Rev. J. Roscoe, " Journal of the Anthropological Institute," vol. xxxii, pp. 70 and 71—(1902). Formerly in England there was no regular copper coinage. Merchants and traders supplied their own small change in the form of tokens of lead and other material. During the reign of Elizabeth there was an extensive issue of tokens of lead, tin, and even leather. It was only in 1672 that an authorised issue of halfpennies and farthings was undertaken.

§ A somewhat similar instrument was taken from a barrow in Wiltshire (Thurnam's " Round Barrows," "Archæologia," vol. xliii.). Another was taken from a barrow in Staffordshire (T. Bateman's " Ten Years' Diggings," p. 155). Similar instruments (called whistles) have been found in America, and a bone flute of similar shape, but ornamented with encircling grooves, is figured in " Troy and its Remains," p. 25, by J. H. Schliemann.

FIG. 181 b.   ¼
In the York Museum.   Found near Thwing.

FIG. 253a.   ¼
Found at Kilnwick, near Driffield.

FIG 22a.—Mealing Stone.   ⅔

FIG. 200a.   ¼
Burnisher of portion of a Flint Nodule.

FIG. A.   ¼
Flint Saw.
In the Scarbro' Museum.
Found near Scarbro'.

FIG. 181a.   ¹

of roebuck by removing the side branches; an instrument with eight points (fig. 727),* probably used for netting or weaving, and five articles in the form of picks (figs. 457, 59, and 337), which probably were used for digging the graves in which they were found.

Ox horn implements have never been found by the writer, and are rarely, if ever, found on account of their liability to decay. However, traces of the fibre of horn are preserved on the oxydised blades of the bronze daggers, where it had unquestionably formed the handles.†

BRONZE.

The bronze implements found in barrows by the writer include six knife-daggers (see. figs. 590, 8, 12, and 391), four knives (fig. 428), ‡ thirteen drills, and awls or prickers (figs. 350 and 363), two ear-rings (560), in all twenty-five articles. Canon Greenwell found sixteen awls or prickers, four dagger-knives, one plain axe, two knives and two ear-rings, making in all twenty-five bronze articles from barrows of the bronze period. He also found two armlets and one fibula of bronze, but these certainly belong to the late iron age. Canon Atkinson, of Danby, examined no fewer than eighty to one hundred barrows in Cleveland alone, and only in one instance found any trace of bronze, and that was with a cremated body.

POSITION OF IMPLEMENTS.

"In the barrows of the Wolds, though implements of any kind have been but rarely found in connection with an interment, those of stone are much more abundant than those of bronze." § This is also my experience of the adjoining area.

These implements of stone, bone, or bronze have been discovered in various positions, in front of the face and chest, behind the head, shoulder, and back, at the hips and under the knees. I have observed but few instances where the position was such as to lead one to infer that it was a custom to place any kind of weapon in the hand.

Among the several articles of flint, stone, bone, and bronze which can fairly lay claim to be considered as weapons, are arrow points, javelin points, daggers of flint, flint axes, perforated axe-hammers of stone, and of stag's horn, to which may be added undoubtedly the dagger and knife-dagger of bronze.

BRONZE KNIFE DAGGERS.

This instrument has its prototype in the fine flint dagger, and perhaps is more a weapon than an instrument, though its edges are often found much worn by

---

* A somewhat similar tool, having eight to ten teeth, and also made from the horn of a stag, was found in a Scotch Broch.—"The Orkneys in Early Celtic Times," by J. Macbeath, p. 55.

† An article called a horn spoon has been found in a vase in Scotland.

‡ In the British Museum there is a similar bronze knife, about 4½ inches long, with a broad chisel point.

§ He adds, "The converse of this appears to be the case in Wiltshire, where Sir R. Colt Hoare met with bronze implements in the proportion of two of that metal to one of stone; and though it is possible he may have overlooked some of the small flint articles, still it is evident that in Wiltshire stone was less frequently deposited with the dead than was bronze."

repeated sharpening (fig. 391), showing it to have been used as a knife.* "The knife-dagger, which is usually called a dagger and believed to have been a weapon, can scarcely be regarded as being such. It is so thin in the blade, and at times the point is so much rounded, that it would ill serve the purpose to which a dagger had to be applied. It partakes much both of the shape and character of a knife, and seems to have been intended rather for cutting than for stabbing. At the same time, it probably served more than one purpose."

This would almost certainly be the case, yet one found at High Towthorpe (fig. 12), approaches very closely the form of the true dagger. It possesses a mid-rib † and shows no sign of wear on the edges through having been sharpened to serve as a knife.

The Wold barrows did not yield to Canon Greenwell one of this description, but strong blades similar in character to the dagger from High Towthorpe have occurred in several of the Wiltshire barrows opened by Sir R. Colt Hoare, as well as in other parts of England. It has been observed that these knife-daggers, wherever found nearly always occur with bodies unaccompanied by any vessel of pottery. I have discovered, in all, six daggers or knife-daggers of bronze, and in each instance there was a total absence of pottery. This is not quite the case with respect to the flint daggers, as in the case of these one was accompanied by a drinking cup (Barrow 37, Group XI.). The occurrence of a flint knife with a bronze dagger (Barrow C 39, page 3), and at other times accompanying a flint dagger (as in Barrow C 52, described at page 217), is significantly interesting, as such a fact favours the supposition that the dagger—whether of flint or bronze— did not always serve the purpose of a knife, but was, as well as the axe-hammer, mainly a weapon of war.

AXE-HAMMER.

"The perforated axe-hammer could scarcely have been used for any other purpose than that of offence, for the edge, instead of being sharp as in the case of the ordinary stone hatchet, is always rounded and squared.‡ This would be sufficiently efficacious for assaulting an enemy, but would never have been applied to such a use as that of cutting wood. The care bestowed upon some of these axe-hammers, and the ornament which is found upon some of them, are also greatly in favour of their having been used as weapons, upon which so many peoples have been in the habit of lavishing decorations."

HORDES OF BRONZE IMPLEMENTS.

My researches enable me to confirm Canon Greenwell's remark that "The barrows are found to contain examples of almost all the stone implements which occur elsewhere. I do not remember, indeed, to have seen any article of stone which has not, in one form or another, been met with in a barrow. The contrary, however, is the case with regard to bronze. The number as well as variety of weapons and implements belonging to the bronze period, which have been discovered under

* Dr. Thurnam thinks the leaf-shaped daggers were imported.—"Archaeologia," vol. xlii.
† Canon Greenwell found a portion of a bronze dagger with a mid-rib accompanied by a flint knife 4½ inches long and 2 inches wide, lying side by side, but without any sign of an interment, in a barrow on Wykeham Moor.—"Archaeological Journal," vol. xxii. p. 243.
‡ See Sir John Evans' "Stone Implements," p. 175.

many different circumstances, and in great abundance, is very large.* Not to particularise each one, it may be sufficient to mention swords, daggers, spear-heads, axes (plain, flanged, and socketed, the so-called pallstabs and celts), gouges, chisels, knives, drills, and awls.   Now, out of this long list but a very small proportion has ever been found in barrows in association with interments, or indeed in any part of a sepulchral mound."

SCARCITY OF BRONZE IMPLEMENTS.

Those that have occurred may be comprised under the head of the plain axe, dagger, knife-dagger,† knife, drill, and awl.

" It appears strange that out of all these implements and weapons belonging to the bronze period in Britain, only the six above mentioned should have been found in the barrows, and the fact is not easily to be accounted for."

I have not even in one instance found a plain or any other form of bronze axe in any barrow I have opened.‡

I know of no instances of either a sword or a spear-head ever having been discovered in connection with a British interment in the barrows, and Canon Greenwell remarks, " The fact that so few of the ordinary bronze implements and weapons have been met with in barrows is a very important one as regards the age of these sepulchral mounds, for if the barrows belong to the same period as that which was so prolific in the various articles of bronze mentioned above (namely, those found in hoards and unassociated with burials in tumuli), it is difficult to understand how so small a number of them should have been met with accompanying interments in mounds.   It must not, however, be supposed that because in some barrows no other implement than those of stone have been

---

* In vol. ii., " York and the East Riding," p. 168, is found recorded the finding at Brough, on the Humber, in 1719, of a bushel of celts; and in a bank at Skirlaugh a large quantity of celts, spear-heads, sword-blades, &c., were discovered in 1809.   A hoard of these was found at Sproatley about 1857, at Middleton in 1858 ; one at Westow in 1840 (" Journal of the British Archæological Association," vol. i. page 51), and another at Acklam in about 1860, and a sixth at Hanging Grimston in 1882—all East Yorkshire, also at Lowthorpe in 1843, when two portions of a large sword and twelve large battle-axes of bronze were found while making a drain, in a hole, lying side by side.   None of them had any shaft, but the oval hole for its insertion still remained, and some of them had a chain attached.   An account of this find, written by John Brown, late of Driffield, was published in the *York Herald*, June 16th, 1843, and other local papers.   Three of these axes were offered to Mr. W. Hargrove, the proprietor and editor of the *York Herald*, for 20s., but in a letter of his which I have seen he declined the offer, adding that 4s. or 5s. was enough for them.   Several more of these axes were found by another individual.   In a barrow on Willoughby Wold Canon Greenwell, in 1888, found a hoard of four flat bronze axes *un*associated with an interment; and a hoard of celts was found in 1843 at Everthorpe, near North Cave ; and in 1840 a collection of bronze weapons was found at Bilton, in Yorkshire.   In addition, Canon Greenwell has a bronze mould for casting bronze axes, found at Hotham in 1867.   For figures and description of this mould, as well as of some other objects referred to above, see " Pre-historic Man in Holderness," &c., by T. Sheppard.—*Trans. Hull Sci. and Field Nat. Club*, vol. i. pp. 52, 71, and 120.   In the Sheffield Museum there is a bronze mould for casting socketed axes, from Roseberry Topping.

† The knife-dagger and knife found in the barrows are quite different implements from the knives which frequently form part of the hoards of bronze articles, such as swords, spear-heads, &c.

‡ Canon Greenwell, in " British Barrows" p. 186, describes the finding of a plain axe, and in fig. 38 he gives an illustration of the same.   So far as I know, this is the only authenticated instance of a bronze axe having been found with an interment on the Wolds of Yorkshire (Sir R. C. Hoare found in the Wiltshire barrows five of these axes—one with a burnt body and four with unburnt bodies (Thurnam's " Round Barrows," " Archæologia," vol. xliii.), and three of these bronze celts were found by Mr. Bateman in the tumuli of Derbyshire (" Ten Years' Diggings," p. 34).   It would have been more satisfactory had the Canon himself been present at the opening of this rich and very interesting barrow.   The opening was conducted entirely by an amateur assistant in Canon Greenwell's absence.

found, such barrows belonged to a time before the introduction of bronze, for its absence by no means proves that it was unknown. In many cases there may have been small articles, such as awls or prickers, buried with the dead which have entirely decayed. Indeed, in a barrow at Rudston, but for the stain upon the cheek bone of a woman, there would not have been the slightest evidence that anything of bronze had been buried with her, and that evidence would have been wanting unless the metal had been in contact with the bone.[*]

I have observed instances where a slight stain of bronze on the bone with which the instrument happened to have been in contact was all that remained. It is also an interesting and suggestive fact that few, if any, of the knife-daggers of the barrows are ever found with any of the hoards of bronze weapons ; and it is difficult to account for it except on the supposition that the knife-dagger and the plain axe were of the earliest introduction, and the only ones in use during the period of the erection of the barrows, all or most of the weapons so frequently found in hoards being of later introduction.[†]

"It may be asked, if the ordinary barrows are none of them the burial-places of the people who occupied the country during the highest development of the bronze period, where do their burial-places exist?[‡] The question certainly is one which it is not possible to answer ; but the inability to offer any explanation is not sufficient to make us, in the face of what appears to be greater difficulties, accept the view that the barrows belong to that time. There are other periods during which the people must have buried in large numbers, and yet there is scarcely any trace left of their sepulchral remains. For instance, the time which elapsed between the introduction of iron, and the full occupation of Britain by the Romans, was by no means a short one, and yet the burials which can be attributed to that period are but few."

Probably, however, to that period belongs the discovery made at Grimthorpe, and described in this volume at page 151, and the find in the two barrows at Cowlam ;[§] also the one on Beverley Westwood,[||] and that made by Thomas Kendall, in a barrow on Caythorne Moor, near the Camps, about 1849, containing the remains of a British chariot. The discovery made in the group (said in Oliver's "History of Beverley" to number about 200) of small mounds on Arras and Hessleskew by the Rev. W. Stillingfleet, in 1816-7, most probably also belongs to this period,[¶] as well as the two recently explored groups of barrows at Seorborough and Danes Graves.

WEAPONS AND IMPLEMENTS.

"It has been stated already that various implements of flint are found in the barrows, both associated with interments and disposed casually amongst the materials of which the mounds are composed. There is a fact connected with these implements, of interest in itself, which becomes of some importance from

---

[*] " British Barrows," p. 45.
[†] For further evidence see " British Barrows," p. 49.
[‡] Possibly, then, the custom of depositing relics with the dead and burying in barrows was in the main abandoned, at least for a time. Several instances have come under my notice where graves, with and without bodies, have occurred where no trace of a mound existed, and such graves may be of that period.
[§] " British Barrows," page 208. [||] *Ibid*, page 436. [¶] *Ibid*, page 50.

the evidence it affords in relation to the cause of such articles being deposited with the dead. Those implements of flint which are found placed in imme-diate connection with the body appear in most instances to be perfectly new, and as if made for the burial,* while those found in the barrows and not associated with an interment have, as a rule, been evidently in use ; some of them, indeed, show abundant signs of having answered their purpose for a lengthened time. Bronze implements, on the contrary, when discovered · in a barrow and there deposited with the dead appear to be such as had been the property of the living and had been in ordinary use" (see fig. 391). Occasionally, however, as is shown by fig. 12, there is no visible trace of the weapon having been used.

Weapons and implements, either of bronze or stone, are, however, rarely found accompanying a burial (see summary of the tables of relics, page 443).

THE BREAKING OF WEAPONS AND TOOLS.

It is difficult to explain the origin of the practice of burning and breaking tools and weapons, evidences of which are found with interments. The burnt instruments found accompanying cremated bones would seem to be the least difficult to explain. They probably were placed on the pyre along with the body as part of its equipment for the next world.†

The discovery of tools which must have been purposely broken at the time they were placed in the grave, is most difficult to account for. Possibly this custom originated with some wily individual, who, at the interment of a relation or a friend, wishing to minimise the temptation there 'might be to deprive the dead body of its accompanying articles, made them useless, in this world, by breaking. On the call of its owner to spirit-land they would come forth, like himself, restored to their former shape.‡

Such a belief would account for the apparently purposely broken arrow-points taken from Barrows No. 275, 88, 276, and 100, and also the tool with eight points found in Barrow C 37. This practice is not confined to Yorkshire.§

* See the beautiful specimens, figs. 413 and 414, which seem quite new and far too delicate for any use upon earth.

† "Primitive Culture," vol. i. p. 449.

‡ The American Indians believe in killing (breaking) the tools before interring them. Mr. E. W. Nelson observed scattered on an Eskimo grave a musket and numerous spears with other implements ; all broken so as to render them useless to the living.—*The 18th Annual Report of the Bureau American Ethnology*, p 322.

§ Dr. Thurnam figures three leaf-shaped arrow-heads of flint from a chambered long barrow in the outh of England which are similarly broken at their points, and he adds, "It is curious that in every's instance the points of these arrow-heads were broken off when found" ("Archæologia," vol. xlii. p. 71). He also mentions the finding of thirty polished stone axes in the chambered long barrow of Mount St. Michel, at Carnac in Brittany, in 1862, and remarks—"Many of these implements appear to have been purposely broken before being deposited" (*Ibid*, page 73). He also gives other instances. The same treatment of arrow-heads has been observed in America ("Primitive Man in Ohio," Moreland, p. 160). That such a strange custom and belief is not confined to the rude culture of the Stone Age, but was practised even by a race that had reached a very high state of culture, is most interesting. During the palmy days of the Eighteenth and Nineteenth dynasties, the ancient Egyptians seem to have made use of such a practice. In the tomb of Seti I. it is thought that many of the articles of furniture, pieces of armour, weapons, &c., were broken intentionally when they were placed there ("The Mummy," by E. A. Wallis Budge, Litt. D., F.S.A., 1893, p. 347). In the cemetery of Haward, jars of Roman coins, buried as funeral offerings, had been cut in pieces to prevent their being used again ("Haward, Biahmn, and Arsinoe," by W. M. Flinders Petrie, 1889, p. 13). The belief that the breaking of weapons did not make them useless to the dead seems to have survived in this country even down to Anglo-Saxon times (see p. 277 of this work).

ORNAMENTS.

Objects of personal decoration, also, are sometimes found placed with the burials in the barrows, but these are much less frequently discovered than weapons or implements, and seem to occur principally with the remains of women. They accompany both modes of burial. When met with in association with a burnt interment, in many cases they have not been burnt with it, but have been placed with the calcined bones after they were collected from the funeral pile ; and the same is observed in certain implements of flint and bone—and probably ivory —as in Barrows No. 47 and others. Out of the 893 burials discovered by the writer, only 57 possessed anything of the kind. Ornaments seem to have been equally rare in the barrows of the adjoining neighbourhood opened by Canon Greenwell, as out of 379 burials only 8, that did not belong to the iron (Anglo-Saxon) age, possessed any. These personal ornaments are, however, very similar to those discovered by myself. They consisted of beads and earrings (figs. 48 and 49 in " British Barrows "), * and were almost identically the same shape as those shown (fig. 560). I have found only four British necklaces,† one with cremated bones on Garrowby Street (Barrow No. 114, fig. 426); three with inhumed bodies, viz., one at Garton Slack (Barrow No. 75), and two on Garrowby Street (Barrows Nos. 13 and 64, Groups VII. and VIII., figs. 362 and 418a). Jet‡ studs or buttons (fig. 118) have been found in thirteen instances.

Amber.—Buttons of this substance have occurred in two instances. One of these was found by myself with an inhumed body on Acklam Wold (fig. 213, Barrow 124), and three—also with an inhumed body—were found at Kelleythorpe by the late Lord Londesborough in Barrow No. C 38 (fig. 743 of this work, also figured in "Archæologia," vol. xxxiv. p. 255, pl. xx.), and a small lump of amber was found in a barrow at Huggate, in 1852, by Jas. Silburn ("Crania Britannica," p. 82). A ring of red amber, 1⅜ of an inch in diameter, occurred near the neck of a skeleton in the Queen's Barrow on Arras, near Market Weighton ("Proceedings of the Archæological Institute at York, 1846 ").§ There are also jet beads (fig. 275) and rings (fig. 216). All these may have been used as ornaments as well as for dress fasteners, though they appear to have been associated with males also. In one instance (Barrow No. 114, Group VIII.) were associated some double beads of a glass-like substance or vitreous paste, of small size and peculiar shape (fig. 426).‖ With a cremated body in Barrow No. 13, Group VIII., were two convex discs of opaque glass, three-eighths of an inch in diameter. Beads of bone (fig. 39) are also met with. Of all the substances then used for ornamentation, gold seems to have been the most rare in connection with barrows. The only occurrence of gold with a British interment in this neighbourhood—except a find belonging to the early

---

* T. Bateman apparently also found a pair.—"Ten Years' Digging," p. 80.

† In addition to these, I possess portions of a fine jet necklace, accidently found with a British interment in the village of Middleton, in 1901.

‡ By the ancients, jet and amber were not only sought after for ornaments, but found a place amongst drugs and amulets. They were believed to exert a wonderful power over the brain, nerves, and uterine system, and were believed to afford a test of female chastity (Thurnam's " Round Barrows ").—"Archæologia," vol. xliii. p. 211.

§ This barrow, however, belongs to the early iron age.

‖ Similar notched beads have been discovered in Wiltshire, associated with burnt bodies (Thurnam's " Round Barrows ").—"Archæologia," vol. xliii. p. 211.

iron age *—is that forming the heads of four bronze rivets which had been used to fasten the stone-plate of a wrist-guard to some flexible material, to enable it to be secured to the arm of the wearer. This was found in a cist at Kelleythorpe, near Driffield (Barrow No. C 38, fig. 741), and was described by the late Lord Londesborough. Sir R. Colt Hoare records only six or seven instances in Wiltshire, where it has occurred more abundantly.

Of silver, I know of no instance occurring with a British burial. " In the barrows on the Wolds " (remarks Canon Greenwell) " neither gold, glass, ivory, nor amber has been found as far as I know."

As my objects of glass, amber, and ivory, and bronze daggers of elaborate form, have been added to the list which Canon Greenwell gives from the northern part of the Wolds of Yorkshire, the people formerly inhabiting this neighbourhood would seem to compare more favourably with those of the south of England than he has shown.

CONDITION OF THE WOLD-DWELLERS.

Canon Greenwell states—" There is nothing in the implements and ornaments to show that there was any traffic going on between the Wold-dwellers and other people at a distance, except to a very trifling extent." The finds I have made hardly enable me to coincide with this view. Some of the implements and ornaments indicate that these Wold-dwellers either possessed a much greater amount of skill in the manufacture of their implements and ornaments than has been assigned to them, or their traffic with people at a distance cannot have been quite so limited. The gold, glass, and probably some of the fine leaf-shaped dagger-knives of bronze, were most probably obtained from a distance by barter, and the amber and the ivory to some extent also procured in exchange in the same way. The amount of skill and finish bestowed upon the wristguard with the gold headed rivets attached to it (fig. 741), and the beautiful bronze daggers (figs. 12 and 590) seem to show that these articles were probably manufactured and exported by some nation more advanced in the art of metallurgy. Besides, the skilfully executed boring of some of the spindle-shaped and large flat beads of jet as well as the very delicate manner in which some of the discs of jet are cut (see figs. 362 and 418a), seems to me to indicate their foreign manufacture rather than that they are of British make from native jet. Not so, however, with the stone tools and weapons; their native production can hardly be doubted, as, though the flint from which all the most beautiful specimen are made is not the characteristic flint of the Yorkshire chalk, it would be in places readily obtained from boulders in the drift, found on the surface of the land or along the sea beach. From the latter place some of the jet, amber, and ivory might have been obtained. The jet would also be found *in situ* in the cliffs near Whitby, whilst the ivory might be obtained from portions of mammoths' tusks washed from the cliffs along the coast, and at times sufficiently sound to be made into pins and other small articles †, though I believe only a small portion of the articles were derived from this source.

---

* The Rev. W. Stillingfleet, in describing the finds in the Queen's Barrow on Arras, says, " At this barrow I received from the hands of my labourer a ring very nearly standard gold, in weight 3 dwt. 21 grs."—"Archæological Institute at York," 1846.

† Instances are recorded of the tusks of the mammoth—some portions of which I possess—having been obtained at Hessle and Sewerby, and at several other places on the coast between Flamborough and Spurn Head.

The Britons kept and domesticated animals, they cultivated cereals,* and were considerably advanced in culture, and far removed from the time when primitive man

> " Perished in winter winds, till one smote fire
> From flint stones coldly hiding what they held,
> The red spark treasured from the kindly sun ;
> They gorged on flesh like wolves, till one sowed corn,
> Which grew a weed, yet makes the life of man ;
> They mowed and babbled till some tongue struck speech
> And patient fingers framed the lettered sound.
> What good gifts have my brothers, but it came
> From search and strife and loving sacrifice."
> —EDWIN ARNOLD.

MOTIVE FOR PLACING ARTICLES IN GRAVES.

Weapons, implements, ornaments, and the remains of animal food, it has been seen, are often found deposited in the barrows with the dead. Many other things certainly would be deposited, all trace of which are gone. "The custom has usually been accounted for by the most natural explanation, that it was the result of a belief of an after state of existence of the same nature as that which had just terminated, and where food and other things would again be required† that when the dead man passed to the happy hunting fields where the ox and the red deer roamed in herds unnumbered, and which no slaughter makes less, he might have his faithful dog to bear his company ; that when he joined the departed brave in the halls of Odin, there to quaff without satiety the ever-replenished mead from the skull‡ of his enemy, he might bear with him the trusty dagger, the unerring arrow or javelin, wherewith to subdue the foes that never failed and yet were ever vanquished. The practice has been all but universal ; every ancient burial-place testifies to it ; almost every modern savage gives the like evidence of the custom.§ To archaeological science it has been of inestimable service. What should we know of Ancient Egypt, or her cultivation, her art, her manufactures, except as far as the imperishable monument of stone bear witness, had not the tombs preserved an endless storehouse of pictures as well as the very things themselves, those pictures represent? Denmark's stone, bronze, and iron ages might have remained a subject of dispute amongst the learned, but for the barrows and their buried contents, which have handed down to us a book in whose record of flint and metal we may again read something of the history of the past."

* Mr. Grant Allen in an ingenious paper published in the "Fortnightly Review" of May, 1894, argues that cultivation began by the accidental sowing of grain upon the tumuli of the dead.

† Such a belief is not confined to a low culture ; it obtained in Ancient Egypt. During the earlier dynasties, the stelae found in the Egyptian tombs are inscribed with prayers to Osiris for cakes, bread, meat, wine, oil, milk, wax, bandages, ducks, oxen, &c. Such prayers to the gods for sepulchral meals are common in the tombs.—"The Mummy," p. 219.

‡ The calvarium possibly found lying on the chest of body marked M. in barrow 118 might have served such a purpose. Amongst the Australians, when a mother dies, her skull is made into a drinking cup, to be used by her daughter.—"The Aborigines of Australia," by T. Worsnop, p. 88.

§ The Samoyads of the Great Tundra inter with their dead a lasso, cup, spoon, axe, knife, and even a gun, or at any rate a bow and arrows. If a woman ; needle, scraper, &c. But every deposit is somewhat damaged, even the sledge and harrow which are placed beside the grave—probably to prevent the unscrupulous from stealing them.—"Journal of the Anthropological Institute," for May, 1895, p. 406.

POTTERY.

A more frequent accompaniment of the body, whether burnt or unburnt, than either weapon, implement, or ornament, is a vessel of earthenware. This is found, in the greater number of cases of unburnt bodies, in front or at the back of the head, but occasionally behind the back, in front of the chest or knees, and sometimes, though rarely, at the feet. In a few instances a sepulchral vase has occurred in a barrow not in close proximity with an interment (as in barrows Nos. 17, 116, 9, 247, 250, C 90, 131 and 132). It is usually placed on its bottom, upright, occasionally inverted, but is found not infrequently on the side, a position which appears to have been caused by its having been overthrown by the pressure of the surrounding earth.

"Vessels of pottery are associated with the burnt bodies in two ways. They occur containing the bones, and are also met with accompanying them (as food vases) much after the fashion in which they are found with unburnt bodies. They are in this case on the top or at the side of the deposit of burnt bones, and occasionally amongst them, even, in rare cases, where the bones themselves are enclosed in an urn."

They are also found in the form of "incense-cups," with burnt bones, most frequently associated with those contained in cinerary urns.

"The vessels vary almost indefinitely in size, shape, and ornamentation, as they do in the composition of the clay and the rudeness or skill of their manufacture."

They may be classified as *food-vessels*, in which the remains of animal food have occasionally been found (see Barrows 37, 40, and 74, fig. 516); *drinking-cups*, the form of which is the most suitable for that purpose (fig. 542); *cinerary urns* (fig. 412), in which cremated bones are nearly always found; and the so-called *incense-cups* (fig. 421), which are nearly always connected with burnt bones, and often show traces of intense heat.

"The cinerary urn and the incense-cup have hitherto been found to accompany burnt bodies, though on Langton Wold, and in a few other cases, a vessel which is in every respect of form and ornament a cinerary urn was placed close to an unburnt body. The food-vessel and drinking-cup are met with in association with burnt and unburnt bodies, though it is very rare to find a drinking-cup accompanying burnt bones. I have only found it so deposited in one barrow at Rudstone, where three bodies, one unburnt and two burnt, were placed in a deep grave, each having a drinking-cup of very similar shape and ornamentation buried with it."

Though these earthenware vessels are easily divided by their shapes and sizes into the four above-named groups, yet not infrequently a food-vase* is of the cinerary urn type, though its size is that of an ordinary food-vase. And in rare instances a real cinerary urn, both in size and type, seems to have been used as a food-vessel, and placed near a heap of burnt bones, and not containing them, as in Barrows Nos. 202, C 90, and 100. In one instance (Barrow No. C 41, Group XI.) a vessel, quite of the incense-cup type (fig. 724), and but a little larger than the average size of this class of vessel, was found accompanying an ordinary shaped food-vase with an unburnt body. This, if it has served the same purpose

* As in barrows No 118 (fig. 513), No. 96 (fig. 423), No. C 29 (fig. 148), and others.

as the incense-cup found with cremated bodies, is an exceedingly rare occurrence; and it might be urged that the use this kind of vessel served when placed with burnt bones may probably not have been exactly the same as when placed with an unburnt body. It is still more rare to find the true drinking-cup (fig. 527) with a burnt body. No such instance has occurred in my experience, and the one given by Canon Greenwell from Rudstone (fig. 120 in "British Barrows") does not appear to me to be a drinking-cup at all, but probably one of those domestic vessels which had been placed in the grave to serve as a food-vase. *

The more or less over-hanging lip of these vessels (fig. 20 in "British Barrows") makes them unsuitable for drinking from. Dr. Thurnam rightly remarks that the true type of the drinking-cup is *not* recurved at the top. I believe the real drinking-cup had generally a straight vertical lip (like fig. 527), a form which would be found far the best adapted for its every-day use; and that any vessel bearing another form of lip had not been specially made for this purpose. Probably the finer class of vase with recurved lip (figs. 131 and 134) and the drinking-cup were two special kinds of domestic pottery. They are made of a superior paste to that of most of the food-vases and of all the cinerary urns.

Though these vessels are found with burials much more frequently than are weapons, implements, or ornaments, they are by no means associated with the majority of interments. Thus, out of 893 burnt and unburnt bodies met with in the barrows I have opened, only 258 had any vessels of pottery buried with them, and of these 43 were cinerary urns holding the ashes of the dead.

In the series of adjoining Wold barrows opened by Canon Greenwell, out of 379 interments only 108 had any vessel of pottery buried with them, and of these nine were cinerary urns.

As a rule, the drinking-cups are more or less ornamented.

During my excavations I have met with 38 drinking-cups (fig. 93), 162 food-vases (fig. 183), and 46 cinerary urns (fig. 143), and 12 incense-cups (fig. 114). Some of each kind are quite plain.

"The clay of which they are made differs much, both in quality and preparation, by means of tempering, which it has undergone. As the vessels were probably not infrequently manufactured on the spot, or in the immediate neighbourhood, the clay necessarily varied with the several localities; and as greater or less skill was at times employed, and they were more or less hastily made, these differences are only such as might be expected.

"In the greater number of all the vessels, and in the whole of the larger ones, broken stone in various proportions is found to have been mixed with the clay. In some very few cases there is almost as much broken stone as clay in the composition. The stone usually consists of such as was at hand; on the Wolds, chalk and flint, quartz, sandstone," and in one case (fig. 527) bits of finely-pounded iron pyrites had been used, which sparkle and shine like particles of gold in the

* This view is supported by Canon Greenwell's following remarks, speaking of the vessels found in the two adjoining cists at Rudstone:—"In the south-east corner of the cist was placed a drinking-cup, standing upright (adjoining burnt bones), which, like that in the first cist, contained some dark-coloured matter, the remains, it is to be presumed, of whatever had been originally deposited in them;" and he adds, "This drab-coloured matter has been shown by analysis to contain a large quantity of nitrogen, and is, therefore, probably of animal origin." This trace of organic matter indicates the residue of food rather than that of drink ("British Barrows," p. 240).

texture of the vase.* This pyrites would occur in the Kimeridge clay of which the vessel was probably made.

Some of the vessels appear to have been made from one mass of clay, and at once ; but others show that they were formed of separate pieces (rings) laid one upon the other (fig. 376), being gradually built up. This is apparent from the smooth and rounded edges of the pieces into which a vessel has sometimes separated from long exposure to damp in the ground and from pressure of the earth upon it. In many of the cinerary urns the clay appears to have been made use of in the rough, but in other cases the finer vessels have had the clay carefully prepared.

With regard to Canon Greenwell's observation that "Some of the pottery seems to have been made by overlapping a coarse and ill-worked clay with a coating of finer paste ; and it is not improbable that in many cases the vessel was shaped at the first out of inferior clay and partly dried, and that afterwards an additional layer of better-tempered clay was laid over the surface, upon which the ornamental patterns were executed, the whole being then fired ; " I must say I have never observed any well-marked trace of a coating of finer paste having been laid over a framework of inferior clay, though I have frequently noticed an apparent difference between the inner and outer sides of the walls of an urn. But this seems to me to be at least partially due to some peculiarity in firing the vessel. Similar evidences of the unequal baking of the walls of Roman and Anglo-Saxon pottery are also observable.

"There is no instance where any process of artificial colouring appears to have been employed, nor has there been ever seen any appearance of true glazing. Upon most of the drinking-cups, and also upon some of the other vessels, there is, however, found a polished surface which almost amounts to glazing. This may have been produced by rubbing the hand over the partially-dried vase, but more probably by the use of a smooth stone or an implement of bone," as, for example, fig. 937 ; or still more probably by the inside of a pad of a raw hide, which would have produced the somewhat greasy-looking glazing, which occurs more or less on most of the finely-polished vessels. Possibly this slight polish was occasionally given to the domestic vessels by cleaning them after use.

The ornamentation of the pottery—which will, however, be considered more in detail under the description of each class of vessel—has never been found to exhibit any representation of animal or vegetable form.† It consists principally of combinations of straight lines in an almost inconceivable variety.

The patterns have been made by a sharp-pointed instrument drawn over the moist clay ; by stamping with a narrow piece of bone or hard wood, cut into alternate raised and sunk squares, or simply notched ; by rows of dotted markings, round, oval, and triangular, of greater or lesser size ; by the impressions of the finger nails (or occasionally the end of the thumb and thumb and forefinger

* I have fragments of North American Indian pottery which seem to be mixed with a similar substance.
† Dr. Thurnam figures a rim of a cinerary urn on which is an almost unique ornamentation, and in a foot-note remarks, "At first I thought it might have been produced by the impressions of the spikes of some grass or cereal ; " and he adds, "It is not certain whether they could have been produced by any plaiting of cord or thong." Believing that such a process would give this form of ornamentation, I plaited together three pieces of a leather bootlace, from which I obtained an almost identical impression to that figured by Dr. Thurnam ("Archæologia," vol. xliii. p. 65). It much resembles the impression taken from a head of barley. It is the only instance of the impression of a plaited thong on a vase that I know of, all others having been given by a twisted thong or rope.

together) ; and most commonly by the impression of a twisted thong, generally made of a strip of hide, but certainly in many cases of string manufactured out of vegetable fibre and consisting sometimes of two, if not three, twisted strands. Curved lines and circular markings, though they occur now and then, are uncommon, the pattern being generally made up of straight lines arranged in cross, zigzag, chevron, reticulated, and herring-bone fashion.*

It has been suggested that the ornamentation originated in an imitation of basket-work.

So far as I know, no vase has been found possessing an ornamentation strikingly imitative of any kind of basket-work. Had the one been an imitation of the other, we ought to find in the ornamentation a much closer resemblance to basket-work.

The sepulchral pottery, as has already been stated, may be divided into cinerary urns, incense-cups, food-vessels, and drinking-cups.

These different vessels have been found in the barrows I have opened in the following numbers :—Food-vessels are by far the most frequent. In this class I include all those vessels (except drinking-cups), which are associated with unburnt bodies, and all those which accompany burnt bodies (except cinerary urns and incense-cups), whatever the form may be. Of these food-vessels discovered with 893 interments, 119 have occurred with unburnt bodies, and 43 with burnt bodies. Cinerary urns are the next most numerous, 46 containing deposits of burnt bones have been found. Drinking-cups come next in number ; 38 have been met with by me associated with unburnt bones. The rarest class is the incense-cup, of which I discovered only 12, 8 with burnt bodies, and 4 with apparently unburnt bodies.† In the neighbouring Wold barrows, Canon Greenwell met with 73 food-vases— 57 with unburnt and 16 with burnt bodies. Of drinking-cups he names 24, of which 22 were associated with unburnt bodies and two with burnt ones. An analysis of the 135 vessels of pottery obtained by the late Thos. Kendall, of Pickering, from the barrows on the neighbouring moors (now in Mr. Thomas Mitchelson's museum at Pickering) gives 27 cinerary urns, 29 incense-cups, 77 food-vases, and only 2 drinking-cups. As Kendall has left no notes of his excavations, it is impossible to make out what proportion of the vessels were found with inhumed bodies and what with cremated deposits. However, the large number of food-vases compared with the small number of drinking-cups is very remarkable, and differs widely from the experience of Canon Greenwell and myself.

The incense-cups, Canon Greenwell also says, are the rarest class. He only found six in the barrows he examined on the Wolds, and he remarks, "The exact converse of this appears, from Sir R. Colt Hoare's account of the barrows, to have been the case in Wiltshire, where the order is reversed, incense-cups being the most common vessels, and food-vessels the rarest. The Dorsetshire barrows also seem to contain very few food-vessels, and drinking-cups and incense-cups are also very uncommon."

These classes differ very much from each other, as also do the vessels of each class amongst themselves. It is, therefore, desirable to give a more minute description of them than has hitherto been attempted.

---

* Similar bands of rope-like markings and slanting lines placed in herring-bone fashion encircle the ancient gold vessels found in the Royal tombs at Mycenæ. (See Schliemann's " Mycenæ," figs. 319 and 453).

† See detailed account of Barrows Nos. C 62, C 41, and 250.

g

CINERARY URNS.

"The cinerary urns, [*] those vessels which contain a deposit of burnt bones, are of different size, and vary to some extent in shape.   They range in height, from 5 or 6 inches to about 3 feet, the breadth at the widest part being usually about the same as the height."

In this estimate I think the Canon must have included some of the food-vases occasionally found with burnt bones, which may have in rare instances been mistaken for cinerary urns from the occasional similarity of type, and from their having been crushed into fragments and so become partially mixed with the bones they accompanied.

I have occasionally found a food-vase of 5 to 6 inches in height lying crushed among a heap of burnt bones, and in such an instance it might easily be taken for a cinerary urn, though it probably would not have held more than a quarter of the bones it accompanied.   The smallest vessel I have ever discovered which could without doubt be shown to be a cinerary urn is 8 inches high (fig. 368, Barrow C 69).

"A common shape is that of two truncated cones placed the one upon the other, the broadest parts in opposition, the upper rather overlapping the lower and being about half its depth (figs. 401 and 424).   The mouth is, therefore, more or less contracted, and the upper cone constitutes the rim, which is over-hanging.   The ornamentation is very often confined to the rim, but is also frequently continued below it, and in some rare cases extends over the whole surface of the urn.   The inner part · of the lip has also, in many cases, a pattern upon it.   The bottom of the urn is small in comparison with the mouth, and is usually not above one-third of its diameter.   This ·form is found distributed over nearly the whole of Britain.

"A second form (fig. 923) differs somewhat from the first described.   It has an overhanging rim, but does not present that feature in so marked a degree as in the first type ; and the sides of the urn below the rim, instead of sloping gradually to the bottom, have at that part a concave belt of greater or lesser depth, from the lower part of which they contract to the bottom of the urn. The overhanging rim may be said to be the principal · characteristic of the cinerary urn."

The one shown in fig. 143 is unusually tall in proportion to its width, being more cylindrical in form, and resembling those from Dorsetshire and the neighbouring districts.   There are numerous minor varieties (figs. 406, 412, 419, 185, 937, 940, 957, 904, 446, 234, 99, 730, and others).   For still further types found in other parts of Britain, reference should be made to "British Barrows."

The vases in the British Museum from Ashford, Middlesex, are all remarkable for being about the same width from top to bottom, and generally shallow.   Except a well-marked one of this type in T. Kendall's collection at Pickering, I know of no others of this shape of cinerary urn having been found in Yorkshire.

[*] It is thought that Leland in his Itinerary is the first to mention cinerary urns in "British Barrows"— "Archæological Journal," vol. xxviii.

"The urns are rarely found to be quite destitute of ornament. The most common forms of ornament are alternate series of parallel, horizontal, and vertical lines, now and then in a double series; triangles set in rows, the triangular spaces formed being filled with parallel diagonal lines, which have a different direction in each alternate space; lines forming a reticulate pattern; lines placed herring-bone fashion, or in a zigzag. The lines are often made by the impression of a twisted thong or cord, but sometimes are drawn on the clay with a sharp-pointed instrument."

Occasionally the ornamentation consists of circular punctures, star-shaped impressions, or short wedge-shaped gashes; also of rows of impressions given by the thumb and forefinger, and sometimes by the finger-nail alone.

The large cinerary urns in some instances contain a second vessel besides the burnt bones. These I have found in four cases, each being the so-called incense-cup. In one case (Barrow C 94, Group XV.) there was a food-vessel also; whilst in Barrow C 79, Group III., an incense-cup and a food-vase accompanied a heap of burnt bones, no cinerary urn being present.

It is far from being the rule to find the remains of a burnt body interred in an urn. Out of a series of 328 burnt bodies that I have discovered of the *British period* (pre-iron age), 45 or 13.7 per cent. were placed in urns, while out of 78 burnt bodies which occurred in the neighbouring Wold barrows opened by Canon Greenwell, only 9 per cent. were deposited in urns.

INCENSE-CUPS.

The second class of vessels—that to which the name of "incense-cup" has been given—has been found throughout the whole of Britain. They also occur in Ireland, and are found in Scandinavia, Germany, and France. Out of 328 burnt bodies discovered in the barrows I have opened, only 8 were accompanied by an incense-cup; while out of the 565 unburnt bodies, 3 (Barrows Nos. 40, C 41 and C 62) have occurred with vessels which in form and size would almost, without hesitation, have been classed as an incense-cup* had it been found with a cremated body; therefore I have classed them as such in my written description of the barrows. A somewhat similar vessel was found alone in barrow No. 250.

Canon Greenwell, in referring to the northern section of the Wolds, says:— "Incense-cups are not numerous, and were associated with but 6 out of 78 burials after cremation," being 7.7 per cent.

This proportion is much greater than that from the burials I have exhumed. It, however, would seem to be far below that indicated by the discoveries of the late Thomas Kendall, in the barrows on the moors in the neighbourhood of Pickering, as the incense-cups in his collection amounted to 21.5 per cent. of the whole of his British pottery. This great disparity between the percentage of incense-cups found by Kendall and those discovered by Canon Greenwell and myself might be partly accounted for by the probability that Kendall did not always collect and restore the crushed fragments of many of the larger vessels he discovered, while the smaller and less crushed incense-cups were generally

* Mr. C. S. Greaves adverted to the discovery of somewhat similar incense-cups in the Troad in burials without cremation.—"Journal of the Royal Archæological Institute," vol. xxviii. p. 68.

intact. This explanation does not, however, account for the still larger percentage of the somewhat larger food-vases, which would often be found crushed into numerous pieces.

This class of vessel is mainly circular. There are, however, exceptions, such as fig. 421, which is oval in shape. A similar one was found by Kendall, and is now at Pickering. These vessels also differ considerably in size, and are found to measure from a little more than an inch to about 4 inches in diameter, and from 1 inch to about 3 inches in height. The circular ones vary in shape, but perhaps the most common form is one with the expanded middle (fig. 161, Barrow C 74, Group III.).

The ornamentation consists of almost all the patterns noticed in the account of the cinerary urns. Many of them have the pattern extended on the bottom—a very rare feature in the other vessels. This pattern on the bottom assumes peculiar forms, of which the cross is by no means the most uncommon.

Occasionally quite plain ones are found. Some have occurred in other parts of the country, having open work all round the sides, the piercings taking the place of ornamentation (see "British Barrows," fig. 67), whilst one much resembling a model of Stonehenge is figured in Hoare's "Ancient Wilts," vol. i. plate xxx.

"There is one feature very common in the incense-cups, but which very rarely occurs in any other classes of fictile vessels. They are often perforated with holes. These, which are usually two in number, are found at different places on the side. They are most commonly near the top, but often midway down one side, and sometimes near the bottom of the vessel. A second pair of these perforations occur now and then opposite to the first pair, and at other times three sets of two holes are placed at intervals in the sides."

One example (fig. 588, Barrow 40, Group XI.), though not found with a burnt body, seems to come under the class of incense-cups. Its opposite sides are pierced with two holes each, near the top, and also punctured externally to about half their thickness. These punctures cover—probably as an ornament—the greater portion of the exterior of the cup. A somewhat similar vessel, so far as the perforations are concerned, having four rows of small holes encircling it, was found in a barrow at Hutton Cranswick, near Driffield, but in this case with a deposit of burnt bone.[*] A cup as wide or wider at the bottom than at the top is rarely found in this neighbourhood. This remark applies to all other kinds of British pottery, though such a feature is common in Middlesex. Many other forms have been found.[†]

"Incense-cups," writes Canon Greenwell,[‡] "when discovered invariably accompany deposits of burnt bones, placed both amongst and upon them, but scarcely ever, except accidentally, containing them." He, however, in a footnote, refers, though somewhat doubtfully, to one having been found by Mr. Ruddock[§] in the North Riding of Yorkshire, with an unburnt body. The writer's discovery of this class of vessel with three unburnt bodies fully supports the probable accuracy of Mr. Ruddock's discovery.

---

[*] "Proceedings of Yorkshire Antiquarian Club." It is engraved in "Reliquiæ Ant. Eboracences," p. 38, by W. Bowman.

[†] See "British Barrows," pages 75 to 78; also Dr. Thurnam on "Round Barrows" ("Archæologia," vol. xliii.).

[‡] "British Barrows," p. 80.   [§] Bateman's "Ten Years' Digging," p. 227.

"They have been found not infrequently with burnt bones inside a cinerary urn. They have sometimes been met with in pairs. In the cases where this has occurred, it is probable that the deposit of burnt bones contained the remains of two bodies. I am acquainted with one instance "where an incense-cup had apparently been burnt with the body, amongst the bones of which, themselves enclosed in a cinerary urn, it was found; but, except in that single case, so far as I know, these vessels have been placed with burnt bones after the latter had been collected from the funeral pile."* (Canon Greenwell here refers to fig. 421 found by the writer).

In addition to the one mentioned above, I possess two others (figs. 179 and 161), which show traces of intense heat; being, in fact, almost vitrified. They were probably burnt with the body, or buried with the glowing ashes. Incense-cups sometimes occurred in association with bronze articles, at other times with implements of flint and ornaments of jet and bone. Various opinions have been given as to their use, some of which are based upon the belief that the vessels which accompanied burials were once used for domestic purposes. This supposition is somewhat supported by the position in which one specimen was found, in Barrow No. 40, partly pushed into the mouth of the occcupant of the grave (fig. 585), as if it were in the act of taking food. Near this vase were some of the bones of a small animal, determined by Mr. E. T. Newton to be those of a sucking-pig.

"The incense-cups, as indeed the name given to them implies, have been regarded as vessels in which to burn incense, aromatic oils, or perfume."

"The Hon. W. Owen Stanley and Mr. Albert Way, in a valuable essay upon ancient interments and sepulchral urns found in Anglesea and North Wales, printed in the "Archaeologica Cambrensis," † seem to lean to the belief that they may have been chafers, for conveying fire, whether a small quantity of glowing embers, or some inflammable substance, in which the latent spark might for a while be retained, such for instance as touchwood, fungus, or the like, with which to kindle the funeral fire."

"The occurrence of ornament upon the bottom, which is found at that part much more frequently upon them than upon any other of the sepulchral vessels, affords a presumption that they were meant to be seen from below, and may seem to favour the theory that they were lamps; but it can only be regarded as corroborative evidence at the most."

"The fact that incense-cups are [nearly] always associated with burials after cremation, brings them into intimate connection with the burning of the body, and perhaps may be considered to favour the view which regards them as the means of conveying the fire to kindle the funeral pile. Neither the form nor the peculiarity of the holes and piercings is inconsistent with this explanation of their use. Their size is what we might expect to find in vessels made for the purpose of carrying a piece of ignited touchwood or other suitable material, and the holes and piercings are not ill adapted for keeping it, by means of a draught, in a state of ignition."

* Mr. Bateman records the finding of a small vase which had passed through the fire, in company with a deposit of burnt bones. This may possibly have been an incense-cup ("Ten Years' Digging," p. 161). He also mentions the fact that portions of earthen vessels were sometimes burnt along with the human bodies (p. 190). Sir R. Colt Hoare ("Ancient Wilts," pl. xviii.) figures an incense-cup, which he says (vol. i. p. 174) has been burnt and cracked by the heat of the funeral fire.   † Third Series, vol. xiv.

This supposition, however, does not, as already stated, so well account for their being found occasionally with unburnt bodies.

FOOD VESSELS.

The vases to which this name has been applied are found accompanying both burnt and unburnt bodies, though most commonly the latter. They occur more frequently than any of the sepulchral vessels met with in the barrows within the area of my researches. Of the 162 cases where they have occurred in this series of barrows, 119 were associated with unburnt bodies. To compare with the above, I give below the results of Canon Greenwell's researches, and also some results obtained by other explorers in various parts of Britain. Of the 73 food-vases found by Canon Greenwell, he says, "They were all, with the exception of 16, associated with unburnt bodies, 9 of which were *not* of purely food-vase type. The proportion has not been so great, though still very large, being 12 with unburnt to 5 with burnt bodies, in the barrows I have opened in other parts of England ; and the same appears to have been the case in the Derbyshire and Staffordshire barrows, in which Mr. Bateman and Mr. Carrington discovered 25, and of these 19 were placed with unburnt bodies. In the large series of Cleveland barrows, however, in which, as has already been mentioned, Mr. Atkinson met with no burials by inhumation though the number of burnt bodies he found was very great, there was not one which had a distinctive food-vessel accompanying it."

In the barrows opened on the Moors north of Pickering by Kendall, they appear to have been more numerous than any of the other classes, as out of the 135 British vessels now at Pickering, 77 are food-vases, being more than all the other three classes added together. This is a very large percentage. In the south of England they seem to have been very rarely met with. Two or three vessels, which probably answer the same purpose as this class is supposed to have done, were all that were discovered by Sir. R. Colt Hoare in Wiltshire ; nor do they appear to have more frequently been found in Dorsetshire and the other south-western counties. They are, however, common in the northern part of England, as they are in Scotland. In Ireland they are also numerous, many of them being artistically made and very beautifully ornamented.

"When they are deposited with burials after cremation, they do not contain any of the bones, but are placed sometimes amongst them, but more frequently upon or at the side of them. * There is no difference in the form or style of ornament between those found with burnt and those found with unburnt bodies. They vary in size from about 3 inches to 8 inches in height, and are more diversified in shape than those of any other class."

The prevailing type is one which is in form like figs. 37, 358, 360, 371, 377, 380, 515, 517, 483, 547, 576a, and 951, sometimes, but not always, contracted towards the mouth. "One type of this series frequently has projecting knobs or ears placed round the shoulder of the vase, which are sometimes perforated and at other times without any piercing. A few of this type [fig. 456] have two

---

* Bateman, speaking of one, says it is that class of vessel indifferently deposited with human remains, burnt or unburnt, and which may probably have contained food or drink, but never the remains, as is the case with cinerary urns.—"Ten years' Diggings," p. 19.

rows of projections, pierced or unpierced, the object of the piercing being most probably to allow a thong or cord to be passed through the holes, by which to suspend the vases. When they ceased to be suspended the ears were still retained, in accordance with the common principle of survival, but were not pierced, becoming mere ornamental appendages, and indeed, as such, they are very effective."

This supposition probably also accounts for the holes being so very small in some of the projections that it would be very difficult to pass a string through them sufficiently strong to bear the weight of the vase.

These projections or ears have generally been formed by fixing pieces of clay into a previously-formed groove encircling the vase, and then piercing them, always horizontally. During the whole of my researches, I have not found one unmistakable food-vase possessing ears which are *pierced vertically;* neither I believe have Greenwell, Bateman, or Thurnam figured any.* The only British examples of vertically pierced ears I know of are on incense-cups.

" Many of this type of food-vase are very well and symmetrically made, and the ornament also is applied with much taste ; and they may be said to excel in fineness of paste, care in manufacture, and beauty of ornament, any food vessel of the other types which are found on the Wolds and in other parts of Yorkshire [see figs. 369, 380, and 483]. Another common type in the Wold barrows, and more frequently found there than in other parts of England, is one which approaches somewhat to the globular shape [fig. 93]. It is made of coarse clay, and is less skilfully manufactured than the last-mentioned class ; the ornamentation also is not so carefully designed, and shows less taste in its application. There are many also which cannot be classed with any type, as they differ too much amongst themselves, and more or less from any of the before-mentioned forms [as figs. 15 and 248]. Others are of very peculiar shape and of rare occurrence."

The writer has a semi-globular vase with four pierced feet, as if for suspension (fig. 205), and a much-decayed, but apparently very similar one was found close to a body in Grave C., Barrow No. 101. Its feet were the only parts that had not returned to the condition of the original clay. The vessel in question is of a quite different type from the one found by Canon Greenwell, at Weaverthorpe, on the Wolds, and also from the one discovered in Lincolnshire, and from another from Northumberland. The two former are figured in "British Barrows," pp. 88-9. The four so-called feet of fig. 76 in "British Barrows" are, like the feet of my vase, perforated, as if it were intended to either hang this vase with the mouth upwards or downwards, as desired. Similar perforations, as far as I can remember, passed through the feet of the one found in Barrow No. 101. The somewhat square and peculiarly-shaped bottom of the vase (fig. 990) looks as if the maker might have intended to give feet to it, but did not carry out the intention. Others having the equally rare addition of a cover or lid (figs. 105 and 448) I have met with in two cases (Barrows Nos. 116 and 117) ; and Canon Greenwell mentions his discovery of three similar ones with covers; and in "British Barrows,"

* Vertically-pierced ears are frequently figured by Dr. Schliemann in his "Ilios, the City and Country of the Trojans," from the 1st, 2nd, and 3rd burnt cities.

p. 90, he figures one of two found on Potter Brompton Wold.* I have discovered four of the class of food-vessel having an ear or small handle each (figs. 353, 944, 990, and 725†), and one with an unpierced knob or rudimentary handle fig. 26).

There is another form (figs. 423 and 932), the exact type of the first-named class of cinerary urn with the deep overhanging rim. Still more distinct are two semi-globular types, one of medium size (fig. 15, Barrow 18, Group I.), and the other and a larger one (fig. 248), 12 inches in diameter. Both varieties have an out-turned lip. Of the former of this kind I have three examples; and at Pickering are three similar ones. They have been placed in the grave as food-vases. The larger kind is nearly always found broken, and the whole of the fragments are hardly ever found together. This type of vessel was possibly used also as a cooking pot which served at the funeral feast and was afterwards broken and its fragments left near the grave. Probably both these, like some of the other types, were originally domestic utensils. Fig. 335 gives an exceedingly rare form of vase. Canon Greenwell, in "British Barrows" (fig. 84), shows a similar form, which he classes as a drinking-cup.

There is another type, of elegant shape (figs. 134, 246, 597, 608, and 745), carefully made, with out-turned lip, which Canon Greenwell classes as a drinking-cup.

I also possess portions of two vessels (figs. 142 and 219), with turned-in lips. This very rare type, Canon Greenwell writes, is unknown to him; and the only other example known to me is figured by Lieutenant General Pitt Rivers in his work (vol. iv. plate 241, fig. 14). It was found in the body of the rampart of South Lodge Camp, Rushmore Park, and is described as British.

The food-vases are the most varied class of British fictile ware. There are scarcely two of them exactly alike. Each differs from the other in some slight form of outline or ornamentation, being almost as much diversified as the human countenance.

"It is quite impossible to give anything like a complete account of the ornamental designs found upon them, for they are endless."

"The ornamentation is sometimes confined to the upper part of the vase, but more frequently covers the whole, and is found on the inside of the lips of the rim, and in rare instances on the bottom of the vessel. The pattern has been made by thong, or cord impressions, by lines drawn with a pointed instrument, by dotted markings, by the cut end of a reed, and by wedge-shaped gashes. In colour the vessels vary as much as those of the other classes of sepulchral pottery. They are ashen-grey, yellowish-brown, straw-coloured, dark brown, and almost as red as pale brick."

Position.—"The position they occupy relative to the body differs considerably. They are met with before and behind the head; in front of the chest; behind the

---

* By the way, the illustration shows that the cover of Canon Greenwell's vase does not match the body of the vessel, and scarcely could have belonged to it, the ornamentation being so very different. Two of these vases being found together, possibly the covers have been crossed. Dr. Thurnam, in his "Ancient Round Barrows" ("Archæologia," vol. xliii.), names a food-vase with a cover from Acklam Wold in 1849. This vase is figured by Professor Phillips in "Rivers, Mountains, &c., of Yorkshire," plate 33, but without the cover.

† This might have served also as a drinking-cup.

shoulders and back ; in front of the knees ; at the feet ; " and sometimes at the top of the head, while in rare instances they are found some little way from the remains as if they had been deposited after the body had been partially covered up ; and occasionally they are apparently posthumous insertions. They generally occur, however, near the skull.

"Though it is not possible to say with absolute certainty what was the purpose for which they were placed in the grave, a more probable reason for their occurrence there can be assigned than any that has been suggested with regard to the incense-cup. The name given to them, there can be little doubt, answers to their use—namely, that of containing food for the dead. In several instances a dark-coloured substance has been found in them, and in others a black deposit is to be observed on the inside near to the bottom, which may easily be the remains of animal or vegetable matter. Unfortunately, analysis does no more than show that such is the nature of the deposit. The fact, however, that remains of such a nature are found in them goes far to prove that they were receptacles of food ; for in what other shape is it likely that any animal or vegetable substance would be placed in connection with the dead?"* Besides, the writer in three instances found small pieces of bone (Barrows 37, 40, and 74), in food-vessels, in one case accompanying cremated bones. There are other instances where food—or what could scarcely be anything else—was sometimes deposited with the body, with or without the food-vase—as shown by the not infrequent occurrence of the remains of portions of the bones of animals. As well as the bones of such animals as the ox, deer, fox, pig, and others; there are not infrequently dismembered and broken human bones accompanying those of the buried person, in a manner showing beyond doubt that cannibalism existed among the Britons, in their funeral ceremonies, at least.

Canon Greenwell says, " It appears to me that in these broken skulls and disjointed bones we have the results of feasts at the interments, where the slaves, captives, or others were slain and eaten. In what other way are we to account for circumstances connected with these deposits?" †

DRINKING-CUPS.

Whatever may have been the purpose for which the food-vessel was deposited in the grave, the same, there can be little doubt, was answered by the next class of sepulchral vessels, the drinking-cup. Though not so commonly met with as the food-vessel, it is, nevertheless, sufficiently abundant. I have found it associated with inhumed burials in 38 cases.

Canon Greenwell found, in the adjoining Wold Barrows he opened, 24 examples, of which 2 (if these be really drinking-cups) were with cremated remains. While out of 135 vessels in the collection made by the late Mr. Thomas Kendall, of Pickering, only 2 are of this class. The drinking-cup occcurs over the whole of Britain, and with few exceptions varies less in each different locality than those of any other kind of sepulchral pottery.

* Dr. Thurnam, in "Ancient British Round Barrows" (" Archæologia," vol. xliii.), says the majority of the food vessels from the barrows seem to have been employed for some pultaceous food or pottage, which almost everywhere formed the staple diet of man before—and often for ages after—he adopted the use of bread.   † " Archæological Journal," vol. xxiv. p. 99.

h

"There is a considerable difference in their size, and they vary in height from 5 inches to 10 inches. In shape they arrange themselves into two principal forms, though there is a great similarity between the two. The one (fig. 543) is more flowing and easy in outline, narrowing from the mouth to about the middle, then gradually swelling, and then again narrowing towards the bottom; the other form (figs. 527 and 540) is somewhat rounder than the last near to the bottom, and from the upper part of this globular portion of the vessel the sides widen towards the mouth without any curvature."

The latter type is the true and natural form of the drinking-cup, its upper part and mouth being of the most convenient shape for drinking from; though there are several slightly varied forms, such as figs. 93, 44, 597, 109, and 106. Occasionally they occur with a handle, but this is of exceedingly rare occurrence. The writer possesses one (figs. 101 and 103)* with this appendage, and it is also of the rare drum-shape, of equal width from top to bottom. Canon Greenwell only found one† with a handle, in a barrow on Goodmanham Wold, and he names only three more reliable instances in Yorkshire. One of these is my own specimen; another from near Pickering, in the North Riding; and a third in the Mayer collection at Liverpool, said to have been found near Whitby, also in the North Riding. This makes altogether only four with handles from Yorkshire.

"The ornamentation upon them is very varied, though not more so, perhaps, than it is found to be on the food-vessels."

The drawings, however, will give a better idea of the designs upon these earthenware vessels than can any description. The vessels are usually ornamented all over the outside, sometimes to a considerable depth within the rim, and occasionally on the bottom.

Canon Greenwell figures one from Goodmanham ("British Barrows," p. 101). Another was found at Kellythorpe in a cist (Barrow No. C 38, fig. 745). In all three cases the ornament on the bottom is a cross pattern. Dr. Thurnam, in his paper on the "Round Barrows," figures several of these variously ornamented bottoms.

The true drinking-cup is never to my knowledge associated with burials after cremation. Why burnt bodies are frequently found accompanied by a food-vessel, but never by a drinking-cup, is very difficult to account for.

Canon Greenwell, however, says that in a barrow at Rudstone "a burnt and unburnt body were discovered in adjoining cists. With each was a drinking-cup [?], of similar shape and character, and outside the cist was a second deposit of burnt bones, having with it another similar cup." ‡

The class to which these two vessels belong resembles the true drinking-cup more in the fineness of the paste of which they were made, and by the ornamentation upon them, than they do in shape, the two types being more or less distinct.

If food was essential, so would liquid be, to the requirements of the spirit of the tomb; and I do not know of an instance of the remains of animal matter having ever been found in any vase of the true drinking-cup type. That they

---

* Two of the vessels with handles I have classed as food-vases are not ill-adapted for drinking-cups.
† "British Barrows," p. 99, fig. 86.   ‡ *Ibid.*, p. 99.

served the purpose of holding liquid, there can be little doubt. It is reasonable to suppose that they were not placed in the grave empty any more than were the food-vessels ; and the remains found in the latter show at times that something of a more or less solid nature had been originally deposited there.

The conclusion to which all the evidence we are able to put together appears to lead is, Canon Greenwell thinks, that cinerary urns, incense-cups, food-vessels, and drinking-cups were especially made for the burial, yet he admits that the occasion must sometimes have arisen when no vase, properly sepulchral, could be obtained, and therefore a domestic one was made to serve in its stead ; and he remarks that the slightest acquaintance with Roman burials will show how common it is to find ordinary household vessels answering to a sepulchral use.

This common custom among the Romans of taking domestic vessels for sepulchral use is hardly likely to have been a new introduction of theirs, but rather a continuance of an old and probably, at one time, universal custom ; and affords some evidence that in much earlier times the Britons would also frequently deposit domestic pottery with their dead. It is fair to presume that the first vessel or tool placed with the dead would be one which had been in use previous to the death of its owner, and that an article specially made for the grave was a later introduction.

VASES ALSO DOMESTIC.

Canon Greenwell [*] thinks that even the strongest of the food-vessels and the drinking-cups are but ill-adapted for most household work, and would certainly not bear the knocking about to which such vessels must necessarily be submitted. I do not quite agree with this, however. The form of the typical drinking-cup is well chosen for the purpose its name implies, and most of the food-vessels are the prototypes of our ordinary culinary porringers, jars, and pancheons.[†]

SEMI-GLOBULAR VESSELS.

This class of vessel—which Canon Greenwell thinks is the only one which can have been for domestic use—is not only distinct in form, but also in colour, and in the texture of the clay of which it is made, from any of the preceding types. It is nearly always semi-globular, with a more or less overhanging lip externally, and, so far as I know, possesses no ornamentation, except the few indentations given by the thumbnail[‡] (Tumulus 18, Group I., fig. 14), which probably in this instance were not intended for ornamentation at all, being merely casually impressed. These vessels vary considerably in size. The smaller have apparently served as food-vessels accompanying inhumed bodies, as in Barrows Nos. 18 and 94, Groups I. and III. The larger ones measure from 10 to 14 inches in diameter, and are all rounded at the bottom. They have all accompanied

* "British Barrows," p. 104, discusses this question.
† Dr. Schliemann figures several vessels of silver from the "treasures of Priam," which he found in his excavations at Troy. They are very similar in shape and size to at least two types of our British drinking-cups, and show that this shape of vessel was then considered the most suitable for domestic use. —"Troy and its Remains," p. 329.
‡ Dr. Thurnam thinks, judging from those ornaments made by the finger and finger nail on some of the vases, that the female sex made the pottery ("Archæologia," vol. xliii.).

cremated bodies. I possess portions of four, from Barrow No. 110—a long barrow. They accompanied burnt bodies, but from the incomplete fragments of each vase it was not certain whether they had contained the bones or served as food-vessels. Fig. 248 is a restoration. I have also frequently found fragments of both the large and the small size of this kind of pottery scattered in the material forming the round barrows, but more frequently on the old surface line under them. Many fragments of one or more of the larger kind of this type were found in the pit-dwelling under "Kemp Howe," and this vessel has been made of a somewhat lighter-coloured clay than usual, and contains a much greater number of small white chalk-like particles.

The larger vessels may have served for boiling and cooking food, and probably, like the drinking-cup, were often used at the funeral feasts, and afterwards broken and left on the site of the obsequies. These broken fragments are mostly found either on the ground near the grave, or in the trench, as in Barrow No. 254, Group XIV., where they are nearly always associated with traces of fire. Canon Greenwell discovered a vessel of this class on Heslerton Wold, which also was found in fragments in a trench containing much burnt matter, but no interment.

He describes this vessel in "British Barrows," p. 143, as "hand-made, with a rounded bottom, 5 inches high, and 10 wide at the mouth. The lip or rim turns over. It is of palish brown colour, and the paste is remarkably fine, and without any admixture of broken stone; and in point of density it is so light as to rival in that respect the best Greek pottery."

As previously mentioned, Canon Greenwell believes this kind of pottery to be the only one having been put to domestic use. judging, however, from the many fragments I possess of several of this type, the paste of which I find is mostly mixed with a considerable quantity of broken stone—mainly flint and calcite— I certainly do not think that it is likely to have been more durable for domestic purposes than the drinking-cup and the better kind of food-vessel. The substance and colour of this kind of pottery seems to me to be in most instances mainly due to its having been made of the dark-coloured Neocomian and Kimeridge clays underlying the chalk which come to the surface along the outer edge of the Wolds and in many of the valley-bottoms in this neighbourhood. It seems strange that these dark clays have not been more frequently used for the construction of other types of pottery. The only drinking-cup I know of made of one of these clays is shown in fig. 84.* It is of very rude workmanship, without any ornamentation upon it, and had most probably been hurriedly made from the neighbouring Kimeridge clay. I only possess five vessels made of this clay which can be classed as food-vases. They are figs. 14, 15, 317, 442, and 441 from Barrows Nos. 18, 33, and 118, and are all quite plain. Whenever this dark clay was used, for whatever type of vessel, no ornamentation was given to it. Having regard to this, and the fact that the clay was easily obtainable from the vicinity of the barrows, it seems probable that this plain, dark-coloured pottery was of local make.

---

* The clay of which some of the vases were made must have come from a distance, and been well tempered and worked into a very fine, soft, plastic condition to have received such clear ornamentation.

CONSTRUCTION OF VASES.

The diversity of type and ornamentation of the vessels used as food-vases is much greater than that of any other class of pottery, and no two are exactly alike. The plan of building up the vessel seems also to have been more varied. Besides moulding the vessels out of one mass of solid clay, we find that they have also been made by adding bevel-edged rings of clay one above the other, until the vessel was finished (fig. 375).[*]

I possess no examples of cinerary urns or incense-cups which had been built up in this way, and I do not remember an instance of the drinking-cup having been so made.

ANIMAL BONES IN THE BARROWS.

The bones which have been found in the barrows are those of the ox (*Bos longifrons*); of another species of ox, the pig, the goat, and probably the sheep, the horse, and the dog, all of them being domestic animals. The most frequent bones are those of the ox, followed by those of the pig, and then the goat, the horse and dog being uncommon.

Antlers of the roebuck (*Cervus capreolus*) I have met with in three barrows, in two of which the antler has a small part of the skull attached, which suggests that the animals were slaughtered. Canon Greenwell has met with them in two barrows. Most of the antlers of the red deer found in the barrows appear to have been shed ones, however. I possess a large left antler from Barrow 284, with portion of the skull attached; probably the animal was killed and its flesh eaten at the time of the raising of the barrow.

The wild boar is represented by tusks (fig. 479, Barrow C 33). They also occur in other barrows. Bones of the fox occur rather frequently in some of the barrows, notably in Nos. 275 and 28. The teeth of the beaver were found in two instances. Possibly both these animals were then used as food. Some bones and a large tooth of the Urus[†] were found in Barrow No. 284. I possess several other teeth of the Urus from other barrows; and I took the lower end of the humerus of the same animal from a pit-dwelling in Garton Slack, close to a group of barrows which are probably of the same age. I also possess the greater portion of a large skull of this animal found in a bed of peat at Brigham, near Driffield. This skull shows rough cuts and other marks left by some very crude instrument, and the animal had evidently been slaughtered and its head smashed, probably for the purpose of procuring the brains for food. It would seem that almost every animal—at times including man[‡]—that fell by the sling and the arrow, or was captured by the net or the pitfall, was then eaten.

VEGETABLE FOOD.

Of vegetable food, only the merest trace can be expected to remain; and when this is found, it must have been preserved under very favourable conditions. The partial carbonisation of fruit or grain, by over cooking, may have in some

---

[*] The Kaffirs build their pottery very much in this manner.—"Natural History of Man," by J. G. Wood, p. 233.

[†] Determined by E. T. Newton, of Jermyn Street.

[‡] Professor Huxley said, "In the early ages of the world, the first impulse of man was not to love his neighbour but to eat him." J. M. Wheeler, in "Footsteps of the Past," p. 138, says cannibalism was a religious ceremony; and at p. 157, that eating the body was a religious rite.

few cases preserved it to the present time. That such deposits of food were frequently made there can be no doubt.

The observance of a little dark-coloured matter at the bottom of many of the food-vases (even where there was no trace of bone) seems to indicate that the vase had held provisions. Canon Greenwell[*] names three instances where this dark-coloured matter remaining at the bottom of a food-vase was proved by analysis to be of vegetable origin. While he also says,[†] "In front of the knees of a child was placed a large quantity of round dark objects, apparently the seeds of some plant, bearing, indeed, a strong resemblance to the fruit of the juniper."[‡]

My discovery of carbonised grains of wheat in Barrow No. 27 (p. 111) proves that wheat, and probably other kinds of grain, were then, even so far north, cultivated and used for food. Dr. Thurnam says[§] the remains of charred wheat were found with a burnt body, in a barrow at Upton Pyne, Devon.[||]

COOKING THE FOOD.

Cooking food, firstly by roasting and secondly by boiling, would be practised by primitive man at a very early period ; but the barrows have produced only one class of vessel (fig. 248)[¶] at all likely to have been of much service in holding water for boiling food, either by placing it over a fire or even by heating the water in it with stones made hot by fire. judging from the frequency in which partly-charred animal bones have been found in connection with the interments and in the mound, roasting seems to have been the more general process.

Many of the small dish-shaped cavities containing burnt matter that are found scooped into the old turf-line under the barrows were probably made to serve as cooking ovens for roasting the funeral feasts.[**]

SOCIAL CONDITION.

I quite agree with Canon Greenwell's views that a critical examination of the bones found in the barrows "shows very clearly that a different state of existence prevailed on the Wolds from what *was* generally believed to be the case. It was commonly thought that these people subsisted principally by the chase ; and, though it was not doubted that they possessed domesticated animals, it was scarcely believed that the flesh of such was the main support of these early Wold-dwellers. Such, however, appears undoubtedly to have been the case, for we cannot imagine that the bones found in the barrows represent other than their ordinary and daily food. The chase must, however, have been followed very

---

[*] " British Barrows," pp. 311, 312, and 313.

[†] *Ibid.*, p. 141.

[‡] Similar deposits have occurred elsewhere. In a cist at Terrchie, near Stonehaven, with a contracted body, were not fewer than 150 small black balls, which on examination proved to be vegetable, and were most probably acorns.—" Proc. Soc. of Ant. of Scotland," vol. i. p. 140.

[§] " Archaeologia," vol. xliii.

[||] This depositing food with the dead in the grave is not confined to low grades of civilisation. The highly-cultivated Egyptians were most profuse in administering to the supposed requirements of the tenants of the grave. In the tombs of about the first century B.C., in the cemetery of Hawara, Egypt, have been found pomegranates, stones of fruit, heads of wheat, wheat bread, lentils, several varieties of seeds, and numerous other vegetable products.

[¶] This shape is retained in some of the thin bronze vessels of the Roman period, and even in later times.

[**] The Australian Aborigines cooked their food in similar holes in the ground.

extensively by the Wold ʻinhabitants, as is shown by finding in the barrows the osseous remains of so many wild animals, and by the abundance of arrow points which are found scattered about in every part of the district."

The writer possesses thousands of arrow-heads picked from the surface of the land in a small area. These were no doubt used equally in war and in the chase, but it is impossible to suppose that the enormous numbers met with can have been intended solely for war-like purposes. Many were probably expended, not only in the pursuit of the larger animals, but of birds, amongst them probably being the bustard, which until quite lately was an occupant of the Wolds, and has given the name of "Bustard Nest" to a farm-house a few miles from Driffield.

Remarks have been made incidentally concerning the social condition of the people who erected these burial mounds, their food, clothing, arms, implements, ornaments, and other accessories of daily life. The barrows, indeed, only give a very imperfect, and, at times, but a doubtful outline with respect to some of these subjects. Sufficient evidence, however, has been brought together to admit of certain conclusions being arrived at. A brief account, then, of what we appear to have learned concerning the people and their progress in civilisation, their art and manufactures, and their social habits, as evidenced by the contents of the barrows, may not be out of place.

" That they lived in an organised condition of society may be considered as quite certain ; and, as a necessity of such a state, they must have been under the government of a head, most probably the chief of a sect or clan. They had unquestionably long passed beyond the stage when family is the only community, and they were ruled by an order and constraint embracing wider bounds than those comprised within the authority of relationship in its more limited sense. The magnitude of the burial mounds would in itself imply this, as, from the amount of continued labour bestowed upon them, they could never have been erected except by a community which included several families."

The barrows being chiefly found in groups favours the view that the Britons lived in small settled communities for a considerable time. I agree with Canon Greenwell that " To the heads of these smaller communities, if such existed, the greater number of the barrows must probably be attributed, if the supposition is correct which regards them as the burial-places, not of the mass of the people, but of those who occupied a position of authority, of whatever nature that might be, amongst them. This view appears to be most consistent with facts, for it cannot be supposed for a moment that the whole population was buried in the sepulchral mounds. Had that been the case, the barrows would have been far more abundant than they are, even though the time during which the practice was in use was short. But as it is evident that the period when burials in the barrows took place was a lengthened one, it becomes still more certain that only a very small part of the population received such a distinction. These mounds must be regarded as the places of sepulchre of chiefs of tribes, clans, and families, or of the people in authority claiming and being allowed a position of respect, and of those who were nearly connected with them, as wives, children, and personal dependents. Some of the barrows, indeed, appear to have been in use over a lengthened period, and assume somewhat of the character of a family burying-place. * The mass of the

* In most cases the interments seem to have all taken place at the time of raising the mound.

community were probably buried at no great depth beneath the surface, and with no mound over them, or at all events a very trifling one, to mark the spot.[*]

Possibly the great numbers of small cairns which even yet exist on the un-cultivated moors of Yorkshire, and which, as well as the small mounds of earth, were at one time very much greater, belong to this class of the community, all traces of their interments having long since been removed by the free percolation of air and water through the small superstructure.

As already stated, carbonised grains of wheat have been found in the Wold Barrows (No. 27), and as this discovery was due to the merest accident, probably other varieties of grain, were also used, and grown on the Wolds—the adjoining low land at that time being all morass and forest. The numerous stone-pounders found, which seem to have been used for bruising or grinding grain, also indicate that corn and seeds of various kinds were not of uncommon use. These stone pounders might also have been used for bruising roots and breaking bones and the stones and seeds of wild fruits, which would then most probably abound in the adjoining vales of York and Pickering and the low ground of Holderness. These pounders (fig. 22) are found in considerable numbers on the surface of the ground, and I have met with them in three instances in barrows. I am not aware that any fragment of a quern or hand millstone has ever been discovered in a barrow upon the Wolds, except where there is unmistakable evidence of Romano-British or Anglo-Saxon disturbance. Neither have I found in the barrows any hand mealing-stone, with a broad flat grinding surface, like fig 22a. I possess three of this kind, all of which were found on the surface of the land.

Mr. T. Boynton, of Bridlington, has one of this type, which he took from a lake dwelling at Ulrome, where the only metal object found was a socketed spear-head of bronze. Its flat grinding surface is also half an oval, and somewhat larger (11½ inches by 7 inches) than the one I have figured.

To use the words of Dr. J. Barnard Davis—"The Ancient Britons had dwelt long in the islands, following the free lives of hunters, and to a limited extent cultivated the soil. They lived in small settlements, were warlike and quite able to defend their homes. They had ingeniously accepted the resources Nature offered to their hands, wrought them with unlimited diligence, and risen from the use of stone to that of metal implements ; and they were ready to avail themselves by imitation of the improvements in arts and arms resulting from a contact with superior races who surrounded them."[†]

PROGRESS IN MANUFACTURES AND ART.

Progress in Art.—Their dress, the use of metal, their weapons, implements, ornaments, and pottery have already been treated of at some length, so that it is only necessary here to give a slight account of them. That woollen and probably linen fabrics were manufactured is evident from the remains of such which have been discovered. The evidence is naturally but scanty, on account of the perishable

---

[*] At the time of the Pyramids the common people were of no account, and were buried in pits huddled together anyhow. Probably during the barrow period in Britain, a somewhat simliar practice was in operation.

[†] " Crania Britannica," p. 237.

nature of the material. Portions, however, of woollen stuffs have been found by Canon Greenwell, "either the remains of the dress of the person interred or of some wrapping in which the bones had been collected from the funeral pile.*

Strands of apparently a coarse linen fabric (fig. 595) I possess, from a body in Barrow No. 82, in Garton Slack, and also fragments converted into tinder from Barrow 15, and traces of a quantity of linen cloths were found under a body in Barrow C 38, Group XII.

The Wold dwelllers were undoubtedly clothed in garments, fastenings to which are frequently found in the form of jet, amber, bone, and wood buttons (figs. 239, 213, 293, 468, &c.) ; but as to the form of these garments, and whether loose or tight fitting, we have no evidence to show.

However, in one instance (Barrow No. 123) I found two of these jet buttons so placed near the ankles of each leg as to suggest the probability that they might have been to secure a pair of skin leggings, or leggings and boots combined.

These buttons are also found placed a little distance from the body, as in Barrow No. 200, where they could scarcely bave belonged to any garment the body was interred in. Buttons and pins have occurred in many instances ; and a jet ring with perforations on the circumference (fig. 216), has sometimes been met with— usually in connection with buttons. I have only found two of these rings, and in one instance it accompanied a kidney-shaped button of amber (fig. 213, Barrow No. 124). Canon Greenwell also found two similar jet rings, which in both cases were associated with jet buttons. I have found three oblong narrow link-shaped articles of jet or lignite, having a large slit which widens towards the middle and occupies about two-thirds of the whole length, accompanying inhumed interments (fig. 445). Canon Greenwell found one with a body on the adjoining Wolds, and they have been discovered in other places in Britain.† They were probably used in fastening the dress, perhaps by a belt having been passed through the slit. No bronze fastenings have been discovered in barrows of the bronze age, except the small bronze buckle‡ said to have been found with the wristguard on the arm of a male in a cist in Barrow No. C 38, at Kelleythorpe. The dress was probably fastened more commonly by loops or laces, of which no trace remains.

"The pottery is quite equal to what has been discovered in other parts of Britain, though perhaps the designs upon some of the vessels do not show so much artistic skill as is seen upon those from the south-west of Scotland. It manifests, however, a long-continued experience in the manufacture of fictile ware. The ornamentation upon the vases and urns is not wanting in certain tasteful arrangements ; but in ignorance of the use of the wheel, in the imperfect firing, in the absence of glazing, and of any other form of design in the patterns than simple combination of lines or circular markings, it cannot be said that they had attained to any great perfection in the art of the potter."

Though undoubtedly the plain and more rudely manufactured pottery was often made specially for the grave, and occasionally at the time of interment, when the clay could be procured from the neighbourhood of the barrow, yet we

---

* "British Barrows," p. 375.

† One from the Isle of Skye is figured in Wilson's "Prehistoric Annals of Scotland," vol. i. p. 441. Another is figured by Lieut.-General Pitt Rivers (vol. iv. plate 294, fig. 1).

‡ This buckle may have belonged to one of the several Anglo-Saxon bodies buried round the cist, and by accident been thought to belong to the body in the cist.

do not possess sufficient evidence to show whether or not some of the finer kinds of pottery (which vie with that of any other parts of England) and the thin-bladed bronze daggers (the moulds for which I have not met with) were importations or manufactured in Britain.

The personal ornaments, which have, however, occurred in a very few instances, give indications of some artistic skill. They consist of necklaces, generally made of jet or lignite ; of buttons and rings of jet (and occasionally amber). In some cases these are tastefully decorated, and therefore have a claim to be classed under the head of ornaments. There are also ear-rings of bronze ; beads and pendants of bone, jet, and glass, or vitreous paste and other substances, not found in sufficient numbers to constitute a necklace ; and some humbler articles, such as perforated teeth.

Canon Greenwell seems to think that, "the whole evidence of the barrows appears to show that the people living on the Wolds were to some extent isolated from the rest of the country, with which they seem to have held but little intercourse, this state of things originating partly in the natural features of the district in which they dwelt, surrounded as it was on all sides by low-lying ground, swampy, and largely covered by wood. They were apparently not possessed of much in the shape of gold, bronze, amber, or glass. Their condition may perhaps be described as that of people who were living in the pastoral state, but at the same time cultivated grain, though probably not extensively."

"Their clothing, no doubt, consisted largely of skins, though they certainly used textile fabrics ; and such ornaments as they possessed were of a simple, though by no means of an inartistic, description. The presence of a lump of ochre, which has been found in more than one instance * associated with the body, may perhaps be considered as affording some evidence of the use of colour as a means of personal adornment, probably for colouring their hair ;† nor is it easy to account for its occurrence on any other supposition. When these people are compared with the inhabitants of some other districts of Britain—as, for instance, of Wiltshire and even Derbyshire, who, to judge by the pottery, implements, and ornaments, must have been occupying the country at the same time—they cannot be regarded as having been in possession of the same amount of wealth of various kinds, as of bronze and other materials, or to have arrived at quite the same height of cultivation."‡

My experience does not enable me to quite agree with the views just expressed. Though in barrows of the bronze age gold has only been found in one case (Kellythorpe), I have found both pottery and bronze daggers which compare very favourably with those from most other districts ; and as regards the skill in working flint into the many beautiful daggers, knives, spear-heads, arrow-heads, &c., they are unsurpassed, if not unequalled, by any other community of men in any part of Britain. And, perhaps, of later date, more British chariots (see p. 358), with their accompanying productions of advanced art, have been found in East Yorkshire, on the Wolds, than in a similar area in any other part of England.

---

* Three cases by myself, and one or more by Canon Greenwell. Similar finds occur in America. "Near the right thigh of a body lay a disc of yellowish ochre, one side of which had been rubbed off, probably for use as paint."—Moorhead's "Primitive Man in Ohio,' p. 160.
† Pliny tells us the Ancient Gauls coloured their hair,   ‡ "British Barrows," p. 118,

The chariot, of course, is of much later introduction than the erection of most of the barrows. Most striking is the advance in the arts discovered in the small barrows which contain the chariot, when compared with the contents of larger barrows in which only articles of stone, bone, or bronze are found. I believe the chariot has been but rarely found in France, though it was extensively used by the Ancient Gauls. The presence of the chariot with its artistic accompaniments would seem to point to a somewhat sudden introduction of a higher state of civilisation, as we do not find in any of the barrows indications of a gradual development of the arts reaching anything near to that attained by the chariot-builders.

The suggestion that this higher state of culture was introduced by the Phœnician or some other traders and settlers seems highly probable, and it must have been at a somewhat early period to have enabled the chariots to become so numerous and so widely dispersed at the time of Cæsar's invasion, which his description of them and the discovery of their remains from time to time go to show (see page 358).

To briefly summarise, the Britons, in addition to all kinds of small game, hunted and killed the large animals, such as the urus, the deer, and the wild boar; they chipped their flint weapons into forms with consummate skill; they moulded their pottery, frequently into elegant shapes, often embellishing it with variously-arranged cuts and impressions, produced by simple appliances. They also cultivated cereals; domesticated animals; had pressed the horse into their service; had learnt the use of the chariot; and were well advanced into the iron age, probably long before the landing of Julius Cæsar in Britain.

GOVERNMENT.

It cannot be expected that the contents of the burial mounds should give much information upon the social relations of these people, the position the wife occupied in the family, and questions akin to this. Some few inferences may, however, be drawn from the facts the barrows have disclosed. For instance, the central and, indeed, the primary burials in Barrows No. 17, 42, 51, 70, C 76, and C 97 had been those of a very young child, placed in a grave sunk into the chalk rock, in some cases the barrows being of large size. Similar occurrences are also recorded in "British Barrows," and Canon Greenwell thinks that "From these and similar instances we may gather that the family tie had much influence with these people, and that the child of the chief or other person of distinction held an important position in the estimation of the tribe. The affection of the father might prompt him to honour with full ceremonial of the burial rites the child whose early death be mourned, but unless the social importance of the infant had been likewise recognised in the eyes of the people, it is scarcely likely that so high a mark of consideration as a separate barrow implies would have been accorded to so young a member of the community. Perhaps it may not be considered to be an unfair inference to regard a circumstance like this as indicating that something like hereditary headship prevailed amongst them."

"The great labour and pains bestowed upon the burial of the dead, the large mound, the deep grave, the various attendant ceremonies of the funeral, may not necessarily show any high advance in civilisation, for in very rude conditions of society the disposal of the body after death has generally been attended with somewhat of care, and regarded as requiring the presence of some rites of burial. But, making allowance for this, we cannot look upon the barrows and their varied contents without being impressed with the belief that the semi-savage had been well-nigh passed, and that the dawn of an advanced civilisation was approaching. The pottery, with the simple yet effective ornamentation, the bronze knife, dagger, and awl, the necklace of jet, the button tastefully decorated, the ear-rings of metal may all be regarded as heralds of advancing civilisation and refinement."

There are, on the other hand, some features pointing to a condition of things which ill accords with much advance beyond savagery.

It can scarcely be questioned that it was the habit to slay at the funeral and to bury with the chief, wives, children, and others, probably slaves.*

Colonel Meadows Taylor found in a large number of the sepulchral places he examined in Dekham, the remains of bodies, with bones disturbed and lying confusedly about. In many cases the skulls were separate from the bodies. The conclusion at which he arrives is that these fragmentary skeletons are the remains of people slain at the burial of a chief person.†

This custom is not yet extinct. " Father Dorgere, a Roman Catholic missionary, who has just arrived at Paris from Dahomey, says the funeral ceremonies for the late king will last twelve months, during which 4000 slaves will be sacrificed on his tomb. He says that the slave trade between Dahomey and Portugal is still carried on to a large extent, an order for 10,000 slaves having been given just before he left Dahomey."—*Yorkshire Post*, July 31st, 1981.

The frequent occurrence of several bodies, all certainly interred at the same time, the finding of a man and woman in adjoining graves (Barrows Nos. 56 and others) which must have been made together, or of two persons of different sexes in the same grave (Barrows Nos. 75, C 32, C 62, C 63, C 71, 273 and others) with the remains of children, or with deposits of burnt bones, are incidents difficult to interpret in any other way than that described. The custom of " suttee " (which still, in spite of the most stringent enactments, lingers in India), shows that under an elaborate religious system and in highly-organised communities a habit so repugnant to our ideas may nevertheless prevail.‡

That women, however, were not in the condition of slaves, but held a position of trust as the equals in some degree of the husband, may perhaps be considered as not improbable, when the manner in which they seem to have received burial in the barrows is remembered. They have been found interred apart from any male, and occupying important positions in the burial mounds, in some cases a woman

* Alexander commanded the battlements of houses to be pulled down, mules and horses to have their manes shorn off, and many common soldiers to be slain to accompany his dear Hephestion's death.— " Burton's Anatomy of Melancholy," p. 235.

† Cairns, Cromlechs, &c., in the Dekham.—" Transactions of the Royal Irish Academy," vol. xxiv. p. 339.

‡ That it was in use amongst the ancient Scythians, the account of the burial of the kings given by Herodotus (and amply confirmed by the examinations of the burial mounds of the countries occupied by that people) abundantly proves.—(" Herodotus," iv. c. 71).

being the sole tenant of a barrow—a circumstance which is quite inconsistent with their place in the house being merely a servile one.*

BELIEF IN A FUTURE STATE.

For an account of the religious beliefs of the Ancient Britons, see "British Barrows, p. 121, by Canon Greenwell, and a paper by the present writer in the "Transactions of the East Riding Antiquarian Society," vol. xii.

PHYSICAL CHARACTERISTICS.

"One of the most important and interesting subjects of inquiry which a knowledge of the contents of the barrows has enabled us to discuss is that of the people themselves, with reference to their physical characteristics. There are two classes of barrows upon the Wolds, so different in their appearance and construction as to suggest at once without any further investigation of their contents, that they belong to different periods of time, and the probability that they are the burial-places of different peoples. The one is eminently a long mound, the other is circular in its outline." †

The long mound is exceedingly rare on the Wolds. I have only met with two, and only five are on record from the adjoining parts of the Wolds described by Canon Greenwell.

In the two long barrows I have explored, no entire inhumed body was found. All the remains had been subjected more or less to burning. Canon Greenwell, speaking of his researches on the adjoining Wolds, says: "In every case, except one, the bodies have been in a greater or less degree submitted to the action of fire."

Though the long barrows are so markedly distinct from the round barrows, and though the difference in form may indicate a difference in race, yet I possess no conclusive evidence to show that the long barrows on the Wolds are of an earlier or of a later date than the round barrows, by which they are so frequently surrounded. However, I think it probable that the long barrows may, in this neighbourhood at least, belong to a rather recent period in barrow building.‡

The true long barrow is invariably accompanied by a deep and wide trench running along both sides, but not round the ends, the material from the trenches having gone to form the mound. Probably the trenches were principally made to obtain material for the mound. If so, this is a method which would be adopted by men possessed of suitable tools, which enabled the material for building the mound to be obtained more easily than by scraping it up from the surface of the surrounding land, and carrying it to the mound from a distance, as was the general practice in building the round barrows.

* It may not be out of place to give an account of the burial of a Fiji chief. "The dead chief lay in state, with his dead wife by his side, on a raised platform ; the corpse of his mother (who had been strangled) on a bier at his feet, and a murdered servant on a mat in the middle of the house. A large grave was dug in the foundation of a house near by, in which the servant was laid first, and upon her the other three corpses, wrapped and wound up together."
† "British Barrows," p. 121.
‡ Mr. Lukis says long barrows in Brittany are much rarer and more recent than round barrows ; whilst Dr. Thurnam strongly advocates their priority in time to all other mounds. On the other hand, Mr. Cunningham at one time was inclined to think the long barrows to be of more recent origin than the round form.—"Archæologia," vol xlii. In Wilson's "Annals of Scotland," p. 54, it is noted, "Long barrows have been stated to belong, apparently, to the rude primeval period ; but the numbers of examples which have been carefully examined are still too few to admit of any positive conclusion being assumed."

"The round barrows contain two very distinct forms of skull, a long and a round one, together with other less characteristic forms which may be supposed to have belonged to people who were descended from inter-marriage between persons whose heads were of the two different types in question. The dolicho-cephalic head of the round barrows does not differ from the dolichocephalic head of the long barrows."

Judging from the evidence I possess from the round barrows, their builders were of a mixed race, with heads varying in type almost as much as do the heads of the people occupying the same neighbourhood now vary.* There is no evidence in favour of the supposition that there was a period when men, possessing either form of cranium, were the sole denizens of the Wold arca.†

Considering the physical characteristics of the two peoples of the round barrows on the Wolds, there was a wide difference in their appearance, and also in stature. In a comparison of five dolichocephalic with five brachycephalic skulls from seven barrows, reaching from near Driffield to Aldro, the average length of five femoral bones found with the former crania is 18.7 inches, while the average length of five similar bones found with the latter is 17.6 inches only.‡

This shows the stature of the owners of the long heads to exceed that of the round heads, in proportion to the difference of one inch in the length of the femoral bone.

Probably a larger number of comparisons would give a somewhat less marked difference.

The dolichocephalic people were also ·of a somewhat softer outline, in all the features of the head and face, than the more rugged brachycephalic people. The cheekbones are by no means prominent, nor, as a rule, are the supraciliary ridges so much or so early developed as in the round-headed skull, both of which would make the face soft in its expression. The forehead is of an average height and breadth, rather higher than broad, however, in its general proportions. The head is long, as indeed the term given to it implies, and has the parietal bosses quite rounded off. The occipital region of the skull is prolonged in a marked degree, and adds much to the lengthened appearance of the head. Taken as a whole, it may be said that regularity and smoothness of outline is the main characteristic; and that those prominences are wanting which must have given such harshness of features to the brachycephalic head. This form of head differs in almost every particular from that just described. The lower jaw is massive, and in a certain degree square at the chin. The malar bones are prominent, and the supraciliary ridges strongly and early marked; thus affording, in the rugged and fierce expression which the face must have presented, a strong contrast to the pleasing

* Both these types of crania were obtained from the tumuli in the valley of Ohio. See Morehead's "Primitive Man in Ohio," p. 197. This gives further proof that the blending of races was widespread, and probably long preceded the period of raising tumuli.

† Huxley, in referring to the two forms of crania, states: "Furthermore, brachycephaly, even in ancient times, seems, so far as the imperfect data allow us to judge, to have been more abundant in Switzerland and France than in Scandinavia and England; in the East than in Scotland; and more abundant in Scotland than among the Anglo-Saxons, or the South Germans of the grave-rows. In all these countries a long-headed people has existed, side by side with a broader-headed one, for a longer or shorter period. In Scandinavia, Scotland, Ireland, and England, the long-headed type has overcome the other, and predominates at the present day. In Germany and Switzerland, on the other hand, it is the broad head which has vanquished.— "Pre-historic Remains of Caithness," p. 177.

‡ See paper by the writer in the "Journal of the Anthropological Institute," vol. vi. pp. 328-334.

appearance of the other people. The forehead is broad, though not low. The head is remarkably short and square. The occiput is so much flattened as to have suggested to some that it is due to an artificial process, such as the habit of placing the infant with its head resting at the back against a board or other contrivance; or to the child having been carried for long during the period of infancy.

"The skull of both types is capacious, and the different parts are well balanced; nor is there anything in it to lead to the belief that either people was wanting in mental power."

In comparing the brachycephalic adult male skull with that of the female, there is generally a striking difference. The facial outline of the male is in the main exceedingly rugged, the supraciliary ridges being very prominent On the contrary, the supraciliary ridges of the adult female are much less developed, and the facial outlines are much finer than those of the male skull. This same comparatively soft appearance of the features is always observed in the crania of male children, and in youths from thirteen to eighteen years of age.

Time and civilisation have done much to erase some of the coarse and prominent facial features of the Britons; yet such occasionally exist, even to a marked degree, in the brachycephalic male skull of the present time.

Dr. W. Wright, M.B., F.R.C.S., of the Birmingham University, has been so kind as to give me the following report upon the skulls I have obtained from these barrows: *—

"I examined in all sixty-two skulls from the Round Barrows of East Yorkshire. I found the cephalic index of breadth range from sixty-nine to ninety-two. Twenty of the skulls were dolichocephalic, twenty-four were mesaticephalic and eighteen brachycephalic. There were more of the mean type than of the extreme types. The cranial capacity, as taken by millet seed, ranged from one thousand three hundred and forty-five to one thousand six hundred and twenty cubic centimetres. The skulls were either orthognathous or mesognathous, and lepthorine or mesorhine. Classifying the skulls according to the method advocated by Sergi, I found that forty-two belonged to the ellipsoid class, ten to the sphenoid, seven to the ovoid and beloid, and three to the cuboid. From the indices, and, perhaps, still more clearly from the classification according to shape, it will be seen that we have skulls of the most divergent types.

"A study of the norma facialis leads to the same conclusion : some of the male skulls have massive jaws, projecting cheek-bones, and overhanging supraciliary eminences; others of the same sex are smooth and delicately rounded.

"My results agree with those of Professor Rolleston (Greenwell's "British Barrows"), in that we both found the two most common types to be the long ellipsoid and the short sphenoid. I cannot, however, agree with him in thinking the intermediate types rare. We have, in fact, a very mixed series of skulls from these barrows. Further, since the same form of burial seems to have been in vogue for long-skulled individuals as for round-skulled ones; since the burials seem to differ in no essential or fundamental way, we have some reason for assigning them to the same date—to the Bronze Age, since bronze articles have

* For further particulars see " Journal of the Anthropological Institute," for 1903; also the " Journal of Anatomy," vol. xxxviii.

been found in some of them. The interesting question now presents itself—with which type of skull were the bronze articles found? On referring to the tables, prepared by Mr. Mortimer, of the relics buried with the bodies, I find that of the six skulls with which bronze articles were found two were dolichocephalic, two mesaticephalic, and two brachycephalic, or, according to the other classification, two were ellipsoid, one sphenoid, two ovoid, and one intermediate in shape between the ovoid and the pentagonoid. If, then, we admit that the East Riding was inhabited during some part of the Bronze Age by a mixed race, we are next led on to enquire if the race became mixed after arriving in England, as is usually supposed, or before its advent. While unable to give a categorical answer to this question, an examination of these skulls incline one to the latter view. It seems also incredible that a round-headed race could have swept across Europe without intermixture with the long-headed race which is known to have inhabited Western Europe in Neolithic time.

"The conclusions at which I arrived were that these skulls belonged to a very mixed race closely related to Continental types, particularly to the Reihengraber race, and if Retzuis and Ecker are right to the Swedes of the present day, and that in all probability intermixture began before their arrival in Yorkshire."

COLOUR OF THE SKIN AND HAIR.

As regards the colour of the skin of those ancient dwellers on the Wolds and neighbouring moorland hills, there cannot possibly be any evidence remaining. Most likely it differed but little (except that it was covered with a larger amount of hair) from that of the present inhabitants. Of the colour of the hair[*] of the head some little is known, though, as must be expected, the instances where the remains of it have been found in barrows are very few. The following description, by Dr. J. B. Davis, is an instance from a barrow on the moors a little west of Scarborough. "In a British barrow of the extensive series of the eastern moors of Yorkshire, which present such proofs of a Brigantian population, opened by Mr. Kendall a few years ago, human hair was discovered which had been formed into a personal ornament. The excavation first exposed a British urn in an inverted position. When this was lifted up it was found to cover a small vase placed upright, round the foot of which lay, upon the bottom of the cist, a beautiful chaplet of light auburn hair. This pledge of affection was quite perfect when first exposed, and had been carefully braided in four plaits, fragments of which are still preserved."[†]

In July, 1896, I visited Mr. Thomas Mitchelson's museum at Pickering, which now contains the late Thomas Kendall's collection of British relics, but no portion of this chaplet remains. However, I got a very vivid confirmation of this find from old Mr. Dowson, who accompanied me to the museum, and who assisted the late Thomas Kendall in all his barrow excavations, and was present when the chaplet was found. Mr. Dowson pointed out to me the two vases which accompanied the chaplet, and told me that a bone pin and a bone hook were also found with the plaited hair.

[*] It is said Boadicea had flowing yellow hair, and that the Gauls added to the prevalent red colour of their hair by the use of an alkaline ley or soap.—"Crania Britannica," pp. 75 and 77.
[†] "Crania Britannica," p. 170.

Dr. J. B. Davis gives another instance. " In 1843, the remains of an Ancient Briton were discovered at a depth of about 14 feet in Scalby Moss, Cumberland. The hair, which had been worn short, is perfectly preserved, the colour being a dark brown, nearly black." *

The Rev. Allan Borman Hutchins found in a barrow 7 miles East of Sarum, near Winterslow Hut Inn, some human hair among burnt bones in a cinerary urn. This hair was short, brittle, and of bronze colour. †

At York, a Roman sarcophagus was found in 1875, containing the remains of a female with beautiful black hair, plaited at the back of the head and secured with three jet pins. It is now in the York Museum. Such relics are of rare occurrence, and in the future their discovery will be even less frequent.

RELATIVE AGE OF THE ROUND AND LONG BARROWS.

From the limited information I have gathered from my researches and those of Canon Greenwell respecting the relative ages of the two forms of barrows, I am slightly inclined to consider that the long barrows of this district are more recent than the greater number of the round ones. This view of their relative age seems to be somewhat supported by the following passage from "British Barrows," p. 129. "It must not be overlooked that in the early iron age—so far at least as the limited number of interments which have been discovered ‡ and noticed enable us to judge—the skull form seems to have been dolichocephalic." §

This form of skull was also found with a chariot on Arras, in the East Riding of Yorkshire, and is figured in "Crania Britannica."

With regard to the age of the round barrow, there is much uncertainty ; and I should assign a more remote age to many of them ‖ than Canon Greenwell does in "British Barrows." Whether or not they continued to be raised as late as the Roman invasion, I know of no conclusive evidence.

THE EARLY IRON PERIOD.

In this district I know of no object of iron having been found with any undoubted British burial, with the exception of those at Grimthorpe (page 150), Danes' Graves, ¶ Arras, Hessleskew, and Beverley, where iron implements and the remains of British chariots have been found. In all these instances the mounds were very small compared with the barrows of the stone and bronze periods. Each group consists of a greater number, and they are much nearer each other than are the barrows of the stone and . bronze periods. No part of Britain of the same area has yielded so many remains of this iron age than has East Yorkshire.

---

* " Crania Britannica," p. 170.   † " Archæological Journal," vol. i, p. 156.

‡ Since the Canon wrote this, a considerable number of small barrows of this age (known as Danes' Graves) have been opened by the writer, the skulls from which are strikingly dolichocephalic.

§ " British Barrows," p. 129.

‖ Except, of course, the groups containing a considerable number of small barrows of the early iron age on Arras, at Danesdale, and Scorborough, near Beverley, nearly all the skulls from which are somewhat extremely dolichocephalic.

¶ At Scorborough, near Beverley, there is a group of about 170 similar small mounds, closely placed together, but in which no iron has yet been found, though they clearly belong to this period (See " Transactions of the East Riding Antiquarian Society," vol. iii., page 21). For some account of Danes' Graves see the " Annual Report of the Yorkshire Philosophical Society " for 1897).

By whom, or at what period iron was first introduced into Britain, may ever remain unknown.*

Dr. Thurnam, in speaking of the Arras finds, says, "There can be little doubt that the culture represented by them is Gaulish, and that it was brought by emigrants from the Continent." † Probably the introduction of iron was mainly brought by an influx of settlers, Gaulish or Phœnician, who in pre-Roman times succeeded the people of the bronze age. Possibly some of the settlers of this period may have excavated the extensive class of British entrenchments, as this particular kind of earthworks is certainly later than the bronze-bearing barrows.‡

ROMANO-BRITISH PERIOD.

Of the period during which Britain was governed by Imperial Rome, I have much less to say than I had hoped. Nevertheless, we find that the field of our researches was crossed at right-angles by two main roads—one leading eastwards from York to Flamborough, the other running nearly southwards from Malton, crossing the former road near Fimber, where we have evidence of a small Roman station (see p. 194). There is also a road from Malton southwards to Brough, which cuts the one from York to Flamborough at a point near the top of Garrowby Hill. This seems to be traceable for some distance southwards, nearly in the direction of Millington. It passes near several barrows in Group No. VIII., and cuts through British entrenchments.

CEMETERIES.—ROMANO-BRITISH PERIOD.

The cemeteries of this period which I have met with are neither numerous nor important. § The most westerly cemetery is near Millington; a description of which is given on p. 171. The other is at Blealands Nook, at the junction of the two Roman roads near Fimber, ‖ see p. 194.

Probably another is indicated by a fine glass cinerary urn, now in fragments, in the York Museum, and labelled "found in a mound near Wharram le Street in 1820, and presented by the Rev. J. W. Stillingfleet." The inhumed interments at Driffield (p. 297), and the remains found in a mound in the Green-lane, near Craike Hill (p. 227), also seem to belong to this Romano-British period.

The writer obtained a considerable quantity of broken Roman pottery which was found while making a pond in the valley about a quarter of a mile south-east of the village of Thixendale, but no trace of an interment was observed by the workmen. The excavation, however, was too shallow to reach the bottom of a Roman grave, did any exist. In January 1895, a small plain Roman vase was found at the depth of about five feet in Mr. Marshall's brickyard at the north end of Driffield. No trace of anything was found with it. About half a mile north-east from Millington, in the year 1845, the foundations of a circular building, and of two

---

* It is said that the chariot was in use in Palestine in 1480 B.C.—"The Antiquary," for June, 1893, p. 276.
† "Archæologia," vol. xlii.   ‡ (See chapter on Entrenchments, p. 365).
§ No stone coffin of this epoch has, to my knowledge, been found.
‖ Between the two meres there is the site of an old filled-in well, called "Well-hole" and "Spring-hole," which if excavated might yield objects giving important historical evidence bearing on the history of this village in Roman times.

oblong buildings were found, as well as Roman pavements, tiles, various other relics, and a hoard of Roman coins.* In 1902, an interesting interment, accompanied with two swords, was accidentally found on North Grimston Brow. These seem to be Roman. During the summer of 1904, a Roman tesselated pavement was accidentally discovered on the high ground between Harpham and Kilham. It measured 18 feet by 17 feet, and consisted of small cubes, mainly of chalk and sandstone, varying from half an inch to one inch square, which were arranged after the pattern of a maze. Two other pavements have also been found, and all have been given to the Hull Museum by Mr. St. Quintin, the owner of the estate on which they were found.

HOARDS OF ROMAN COINS.

At Cowlam, in 1858, a large black vase was ploughed up in the first field to the south of the church. It contained fourteen hundred Roman bronze coins, many of which I possess, through the kindness of the late Christopher Sykes.

Many Roman coins have been picked from the surface of the land near the small cemetery at Blealand's Nook, between Fimber and Wetwang. In May, 1887, one silver and sixteen bronze Roman coins were found on a farm called " Copper Hall," a little to the east of the village of Skerne, near Driffield.

ANGLO-SAXON PERIOD.

Of this epoch, the discoveries recorded in these pages are almost entirely relating to the pagan Saxons, who are found to have been interred in graveyards and grave-rows, generally occupying the sites of British barrows or entrenchments. Barrows Nos. 127, C 33, C 34, 112, C 38, and 4, as well as the adjoining barrow marked X opened by Greenwell (see p. 135 in " British Barrows "), had been converted into graveyards, while several others have been similarly made use of. But it has very rarely been observed by the writer that an Anglo-Saxon interment had disturbed the original British one.

In numerous instances Anglo-Saxon remains have been casually found in the entrenchments, and in one instance (described on page 265) the entrenchment near the monument at Sledmere had become an extensive grave-row. In three cases (Fimber, Acklam Wold, and Garton Slack, described on pp. 237 and 249) no mound was visible ; † but the interments in the latter place were adjoining, and some of them in the foss of an obliterated British entrenchment. ‡

No truly Anglo-Saxon barrow is known in this neighbourhood. If such ever existed they were probably of small size. §

* J. J. Sheahan and T. Whellan, "York and the East Riding," vol. ii. p. 562.
† At Londesborough is a graveyard which has from time to time yielded Anglo-Saxon remains; and a somewhat similar extensive—and I believe unrecorded—cemetery was many years ago (1850 to 1855) discovered in a brickyard at Nafferton. Many urns and other relics were found and disposed of, and no trace of them remains. Another was discovered in 1824 at Kilham, several relics from which were presented by the late Rev. E. W. Stillingfleet to the York Museum.
‡ In the "Antiquary" for November, 1891, p. 189, is a short account of an Anglo-Saxon cemetery at Southover, Lewes. Here the interments were also in a line, two and three abreast, and apparently under a bank or rampart of an entrenchment, much resembling the arrangement and position of the interments near Garton Station and Sir Tatton Sykes' memorial (pp. 249 and 265).
§ Very probably many of the so-called Anglo-Saxon mounds which have been explored in other parts of England were also originally British barrows. Mr. Akerman, in his "Archæological Index," p. 18, mentions a British barrow surrounded by a number of Anglo-Saxon barrows. Probably, after fully occupying the area of the British barrow they constructed small mounds round it.

Both inhumation and cremation were practised by the Anglo-Saxons, and in this district the former was apparently the most frequent practice.

Which custom was most generally adopted by them on their first arrival is uncertain ; but that both modes of interment had then been some time in practice is almost certain.* They probably abandoned cremation soon after they embraced the Christian faith.

Though we cannot fix the time when the pagan Saxon mode of interment ceased in this neighbourhood, yet there was a very considerable period during which it must have prevailed. This would extend from the first settlement of the Saxons in East Yorkshire down to their final conversion to Christianity, namely, from about the middle of the fifth to about the middle of the seventh century, when the heathen mode of burial was probably discontinued in this neighbourhood except with occasional reversions to the old practice.†

Charlemagne, a century later, forbids the old Saxons to bury *more paganorum*, and directs that interments should take place on consecrated ground.‡

The form of the Anglo-Saxon grave, as shown at p. 249, Group XI., is a comparatively small, oblong one, and very different from that of the British oval grave. The body is found mostly on its side, occasionally with the legs doubled up, but most frequently at full length, and occasionally with legs crossing below the knees after the manner of a Knight Templar. The head is found pointing in every direction, but most generally to the west. By the side of the body is frequently a knife (fig. 624), sometimes accompanied by a sharpening-iron (fig. 680), and in one instance what seemed to be a rude fork (fig. 683),§ accompanied the knife. These tools are chiefly found as if they had been carried in a belt worn round the loins. Occasionally, with the male skeletons, a long, straight two-edged sword is found (fig. 224), but much more frequently a spear (figs. 759 and 746)—the cusp of which generally lies near the skeleton—and near the feet a spike (fig. 759), belonging to the butt-end of the spear is sometimes found, showing that the ordinary length of this weapon was about six feet. An iron umbo of a shield (fig. 765) sometimes occurs, generally on the upper part of the body. In one case two iron bridle bits (figs. 659 and 660) occurred on the chest of a young man, and in another instance a large cooking ladle (fig. 225) accompanied a body. Fibulæ (figs. 784 and 828) of various forms occur frequently. Those found on the shoulders are chiefly circular. Buckles (fig. 755) and clasps (fig. 890) at the waist—indicating that the dead had been interred in their ordinary clothing—are often accompanied by such articles as the steel for procuring a light (fig. 804) and numerous other requisites.

With the women a knife also is often found, as well as shears (fig. 798), and such articles as satchels (fig. 281), bronze boxes with thread and needles (fig. 643), combs (figs. 799 and 671), spindle whorls (fig. 650), jewelled ornaments (figs. 672

---

* Woden had enacted a law that the dead should be burned with all their removables, especially their money, deeming that they would be more welcome to the gods.—"Britannia Antiqua," illustrated by Atlett Sammes, p. 440.

† We have the testimony of Beda that after the planting of Christianity many of the converted or half-converted Anglo-Saxons lapsed into idolatry.—"Hist. Ecclesiasta," lib, iii. c. 30.

‡ Archbishop Cuthbert obtained, in A.D. 741, a dispensation from the Pope for the making of *caemitories* or churchyards within the towns or cities, whereas here in England, until this time, within the walls thereof none were buried.—"Inventorum Sepulchrale," by C. Roach Smith, p. 38.

§ Akerman's "Pagan Saxons," p. 72, gives an account of a somewhat similar object found near Salisbury, accompanied by a knife and flint and steel.

and 222), armilla (fig. 815), and beads of glass and amber (figs. 811, 851, and 888).

It is also interesting to note that, as in the case of the Britons, food had in many instances been deposited with the dead. This custom is clearly indicated by the frequent occurrence of small heaps of animal bones found near the interment ; also by the presence of small earthenware vessels (fig. 654) and the iron hoops, &c., belonging to wooden buckets * (fig. 636). I have rarely met with instances of the placing of ashes in an urn.

The presence of sherds of pottery, teeth, and bones of animals in the earth above, and round the interments has frequently been noticed, and possibly indicates some funeral ceremony.

In the future, other cemeteries will probably be discovered in the district. Undoubtedly a few have been carelessly destroyed in excavations for surface alterations ; whilst others have been encroached upon to their complete destruction by those of a later period. That churches were not infrequently built in the immediate vicinity, or on the actual site of pagan cemeteries, is probable. Of such an occurrence we have evidence at Fimber, Garton, and Kirby Grindalythe † (see page 191).

Garton and Fridaythorpe may be expected to yield further Anglo-Saxon remains in the future.

CROSS EXCAVATIONS IN BARROWS.

In perusing the descriptions of the barrows, it will be observed that their exploration has revealed the interesting fact that the Anglo-Saxons not only frequently used the British barrows as grave-yards, but that they also made Folk-Moots of several of them. A British barrow, conveniently situated near an Anglo-Saxon settlement, was chosen or appropriated as a Moot-hill. ‡

They also seem to have often excavated in their Moot-hills § a large figure of the cross. ‖ The four arms of each cross are approximately directed towards the four cardinal points of the compass. A full account of each cruciform structure, with a plan, is given at pages 188–206, 339, and others, in the description of the barrows in which it occurs. Besides the four crosses I have exhumed, Canon Greenwell, during his researches in the barrows on the Yorkshire Wolds in 1866, found one in a mound at Helperthorpe, very similar to the one I discovered in Barrow No. 5 at Fimber. And about the same time another was discovered at Swinton, near Malton, by the Rev. James Robertson. This one also was very similar to that at Fimber.

---

* Possibly many of these food-vessels were entirely of wood, horn, or other perishable substances, and, therefore, no trace of them remains.

† The writer has been told of many instances where bodies have been found when digging the foundations of buildings, and in making other excavations near the above-named churches ; and in 1892 he was present when several bodies were exposed in digging the foundations of some new cottages that Sir Tatton Sykes, Bart., was about to erect at Kirby Grindalythe. Nothing was found with these bodies, but they clearly belonged to an old burial-ground some little distance from the present churchyard.

‡ A Witena Gemot was held at York in 627, at which it was decided to profane the temple of Goodmanham, —Kemble's "Saxons in England," vol. ii., p. 241.

§ "They dug a grave in the centre of the Folk-Moot, when the ground was first consecrated, and threw in ashes, a coal, and a tile."—"Primitive Folk-Moots," Gomme, p. 36.

‖ A cross was used in summoning a Heepp meeting at the Thing.—Du Chaillu in "The Viking Age," vol. i. pp. 520-521.

These buried crosses date back far before the Conquest, and probably also before the erection of any Anglo-Saxon church.   Many of these old Folk-Moots, under the various names of Moot-hill,* Mill-hill, Mall-hill, Miln, Gallows-hill, and various other names, still exist near many old settlements throughout Yorkshire and other parts of England.   Moot-hills occur also in various parts of Scotland.   In Denmark they are known as Thing-mounds.   Though the purpose they once served is well known, probably but few persons are aware that a deep cross-shaped trench was often cut into these Moot-hills, generally through the mound and to some depth into the firm rock below.   These cruciform excavations in the Moot-hills seem to mark the dawn of Anglo-Saxon Christianity in England.†   They are possibly also the progenitors of the preaching, market, and other upright crosses of stone which were so numerous throughout the country during the Middle Ages.

In reply to an inquiry of mine respecting embankment crosses, &c., the late Canon Atkinson, wrote, November 19th, 1894, "I had a series of old Boundaries" (referring to the Easingwold district of a period of three centuries since), "under hand, two or three weeks ago, and in one of them in particular I was struck by the occurrence of the phrase 'a cross in the ground.' . . . It did not seem to me from the context that a mere stone with a cross on it was stuck into the ground at the places indicated."

Possibly in later times upright stone crosses were occasionally placed on the summit of the Moot-hill.   Evidence that such had sometimes been the case and afterwards destroyed is in the form of a large flat piece of grit-stone with curved lines engraved upon it (a portion of a cross taken from the Mill-hill at Wetwang, in which is excavated a large deep cross), see p. 206. ‡

EMBANKMENT CROSSES.

Besides the buried crosses I have named, there still remain exposed a few large horizontal embankment crosses formed by two ridges of earth crossing each other at right angles, and also, like the excavated crosses, directed to the cardinal points of the compass.   They vary in size, the arms measuring from 21 to 250 feet in length (see p. 388).   They are mostly found near the sites of old settlements, and where no Moot-hills existed they possibly served a similar purpose to that for which the cross trench was cut into the Moot-hill.

* These Folk-Moots (and Parish Councils) are really again in existence, but revised and re-shaped to meet modern requirements by the Parliaments of 1888 and 1894.

† The excavation of a cross in the Moot-hills (barrows?) and the erection of a church on or near to them, show the great reverence in which these mounds were held in pre-Christian times.

‡ Many barrows throughout the island bear the names "Cross-hill, "How-hill-cross," "Stump-cross," &c., and have doubtless derived these appellations from either the buried cross or the upright stone cross erected at a later period on their summits.   On a tumulus at the top of Knightlow-hill, five and a half miles north-west of Coventry, stands the remains of an old wayside cross.—Gomme's "Primitive Folk-Moots."

PART I.

DESCRIPTION OF THE BARROWS.

The Edge of the Wolds.

The Western Edge of the Wolds

FORTY YEARS' RESEARCHES IN BRITISH & SAXON BURIAL MOUNDS OF EAST YORKSHIRE.

· No. 1.—THE TOWTHORPE GROUP.

This series of barrows may appropriately be termed the Towthorpe Group. It consists of twenty-one barrows, all of which, except the one marked "A" on the Plan, have been opened; only fourteen barrows are marked on the Ordnance Map. The group stretches for four and a half miles, and is part of a chain of barrows which extends for a considerable distance parallel with the existing green lane from Aldro nearly to Sledmere. This lane probably follows, more or less closely, the route of an ancient British track-way. Adjoining this group are the detached barrows which we have also opened.

BARROW No. 1.*

This mound is situated near the centre of the group, close to High Towthorpe. Here the green lane already mentioned is crossed by the high road from Malton, through Wharram-le-Street, to Beverley and Hull. Part of this road, for some distance south and north of the barrow, is called "High Street" by the old inhabitants of the neighbourhood. Unfortunately this name is not retained on the Ordnance Map. No. 1, and the five barrows next described, are on the estate of the late Rev. Yarburgh Lloyd Greame, of Sewerby, whose kindness in so readily granting the requisite permission to explore is most gratefully acknowledged.

On the 4th of May, 1863, the writer, with the assistance of R. Mortimer and

FIG. 1.

two workmen, commenced to open this mound. It was the first British barrow he had the pleasure of examining. A trench 10 feet wide was cut across its centre from the northern to the southern margin. The section thus exposed is shown in fig. 1.

The upper portion (E), to a depth of 16 inches, consisted chiefly of the surface soil of the neighbourhood, the bottom part of which was reddened as if by the action of fire. Close below this was a stratum of wood and ashes and other dark matter, 2 to 3 inches in thickness; and then a lenticular bed of tough drab-coloured clay, 29 feet in diameter, and 12 to 14 inches thick in the

---

* The barrows are numbered in the order in which they were opened, and the relative positions of the groups can be seen in the general map of the district.

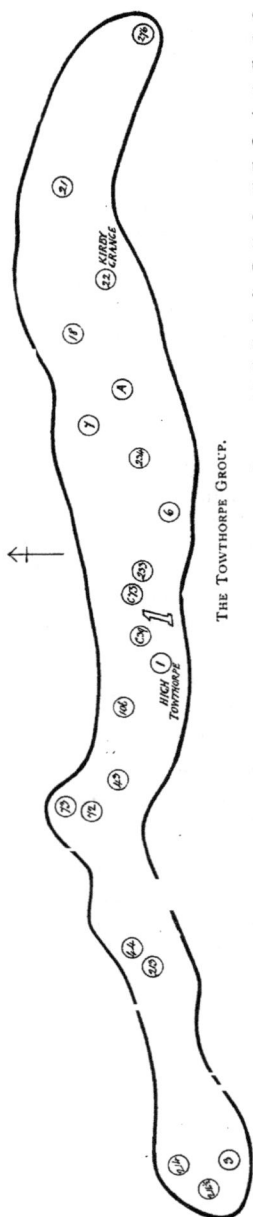

THE TOWTHORPE GROUP.

centre, gradually thinning towards the circumference. The upper part of this bed of clay, which was in contact with the stratum of wood ashes, was reddened by fire; its under surface had a similar appearance, and rested upon what seemed to be a second stratum of burnt and decayed matter, 2 to 3 inches in thickness, similar to that already described. The clay forming this lenticular bed contained numerous small fragments of grey flint, characteristic of the chalk of the neighbourhood. It must have been obtained from one of the valley bottoms (either Burdale, Wharram-le-Street, or Duggleby), in which are exposures of the Kimeridge clay. In these places angular pieces of flint and chalk crumble from the hill-side, and mix with the clay, imparting a greyish colour to it. This is especially the case at Burdale, where there is a fine spring at the base of the chalk, and a small pond resting on the Kimeridge; and it is probably from this place that most of the clay for the construction of this barrow was obtained. It is not easy to explain the method by which the clay was transported, but several tons had certainly been used in this case. Many other instances in which material from a distance has been used in the erection of the barrows of this neighbourhood are recorded in the following pages. In the centre of the mound, at the base of the lenticular bed of clay, and below the ashes (which probably represent the residue of a funeral pyre) stood two food vases, close together (figs. 2 and 3), and near to these, decayed bones (the remains of a body) and a chipped flint. The smaller and more ornamented vase (fig. 2) was situated to the south of its fellow. It measures 4½ inches in height, 5½ inches in diameter at the top, and about the same across the shoulders. The ornamentation had been impressed on the plastic clay by a thin square-ended tool, about half-an-inch in length, which showed in the impression a fine notched structure, and was equally divided into ten ridges about the size of the indentations on the milled edge of a shilling, and almost as truly cut. In the lower groove which runs round the vase are four pierced projections.

Vase (fig. 3) is about 5 inches high, and about 6 inches in diameter at the top and across the shoulders. Three encircling lines of short vertical cuts, rudely and apparently hastily made, previous to baking the vase, represent its entire ornamentation.*

* Mr. Bateman in "Ten Years' Diggings," page 283, describes two very similar vases, which had been found under similar conditions. Unfortunately, through an accident to one of my cases, the two vases just described have been much injured.

During the excavation we collected from the material of the mound a dozen hand-struck flint flakes of various sizes, and a small splinter from the cutting-edge of a green-stone celt.

Re-Opening, December 24th and 25th, 1865.

Believing that a grave might exist under the mound which had been missed at the time of our first examination, we made further search on the above dates. On this occasion we re-opened a large portion of its centre, our cutting extending sideways considerably beyond the limits of the former excavation, and the ground was probed everywhere beneath, but no interment could be found. All we obtained was a finely-chipped knife of black flint (fig. 4), 2¼ inches long, and eight hand-struck splinters of a similar kind of flint, taken near the base of the mound. We also found a small thin piece of bronze, but its original position in the barrow was uncertain.

BARROW "C 39." *

Stands in the western end of the Towthorpe plantation. It is about 300 yards to the north of Barrow No. 1.

November 7th, 1870.—This barrow had just been cleared of the large trees which grew on its sides and summit, thus offering a favourable opportunity for excavation previous to its being re-planted in the following autumn. It measured 132 feet in diameter, and 12½ feet in elevation. These dimensions will show that to open the barrow properly was no light undertaking, and must necessarily have occupied a considerable time. The operations were superintended by my brother and myself alternately, and the result is given in the form of a diary, this being, in the present instance, the simplest and clearest method of description.

We first marked out in the centre of the mound a rectangular portion measuring 92 feet east and west, and 30 feet north and south. We then, with the aid of nine diggers, commenced simultaneously at opposite ends of this area, and turned the material over towards the centre, carefully trenching the ground beneath as we proceeded. Owing to the numerous large roots of the recently-felled trees, we had

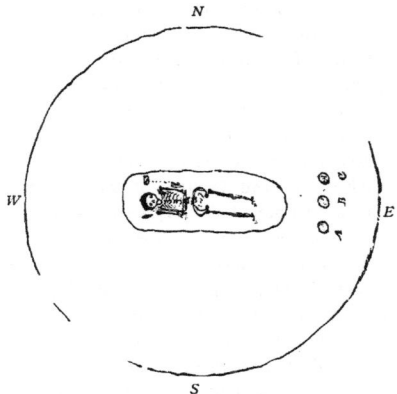

Fig. 5.

Fig. 6.

considerable difficulty in sinking the two openings down to the base of the mound. Close under the opening, at the eastern end of our excavation, shown at *A, B, C,* on the plan and section (figs. 5 and 6), were three cup-shaped excavations in the

* The letter "C" in connection with the number of these barrows, stands in all cases for "100," when placed in this position. "C 39" therefore = "139."

rock. These, commencing with the most northern, measured respectively 2½ feet, 2 feet, and 1½ feet in depth, and each had a diameter of about 4½ feet at the top, and about 3 feet at the bottom. The average distance between them was about 18 inches. They principally contained a mixture of the original local soil, with a bluish clay. This latter, which must have been carried from a distance, contained numerous small angular and sub-angular flints and a few fragments of chalk. Pieces of burnt wood were found in all the holes, and in the central one was a small sherd of British pottery, but no trace of burnt or unburnt bone was observed. These holes must have been made previous to the raising of the barrow, as the layers of earth in the mound above were unbroken.

November 8th and 9th.—The same number of workmen employed, and nothing found but a few splinters of flint.

On the 10th and four following days our labours were interrupted by frost and snow.

November 16th.—Diggers ten in number, and nothing found.

November 17th.—Our staff consisted of twelve labourers, but nothing was obtained except splinters of flint.

November 18th.—Workmen the same as yesterday. A few splinters of flint, and a rudely-formed, leaf-shaped, arrow-head of the same material, were taken from the substance of the mound.

November 19th.—Nine diggers. At 22 feet E.S.E. of the centre, 3 feet from the base of the mound, and 6 feet from its surface, were a few calcined bones of a child in the midst of decayed wood. As there was no trace of an urn, probably these remains had been buried in a receptacle of wood or some other perishable substance; a small splinter of dark-coloured flint accompanied them. It was clear that this interment was not intrusive, but had been made during the erection of the barrow, as the numerous strata of ochry-coloured soil, alternating with clay and laminæ of dark matter, which formed the mound throughout, from base to apex, had not been cut through.

November 21st.—Ten diggers. Only a few worked flints were picked up. We were, however, stimulated by observing at the base of the mound, on the east of the centre, a quantity of gritty chalk, which we believed indicated a grave in the centre of the mound.

November 22nd.—We had twelve workmen. Only chips of flint found.

November 23rd.—Number of diggers and result same as yesterday, except that we picked up, near the base of the mound, a knife of black flint 2½ inches long, $\frac{7}{10}$ inch wide, much resembling fig. 4, and nicely chipped at the points and edge.

November 24th.—Rainy day. No digging.

November 25th.—Seven diggers in the forenoon, and nine in the afternoon. At the close of this day's labours, the workmen on the eastern side reached the edge of a grave in the rock, beneath the centre of the mound.

November 26th.—Ten workmen. The excavation was driven from the east 7 feet over the grave, without finding anything but a few flint splinters and a decayed piece of a human leg-bone, at the southern brink of the grave.

November 28th.—Twelve diggers. By noon the grave was passed over completely, and we observed that a small mound had been first raised over the grave,

FIG. 2.   ⅓

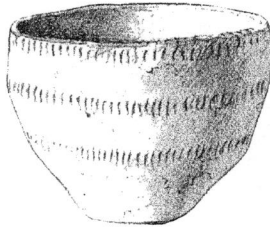

FIG. 3.   ¼

FIG. 4.

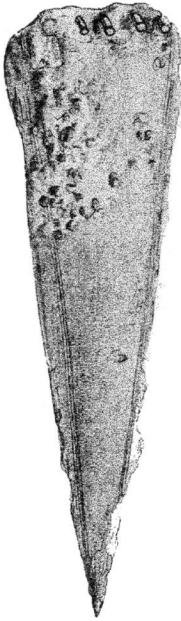

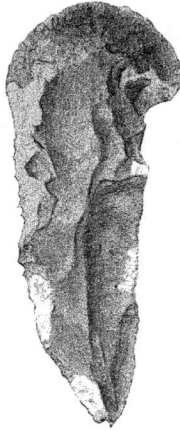

FIG. 11.   ⅓

FIG. 7.   ½

FIG. 8.   ⅔

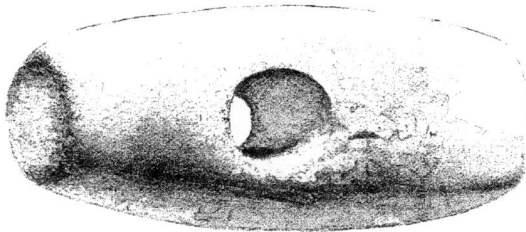

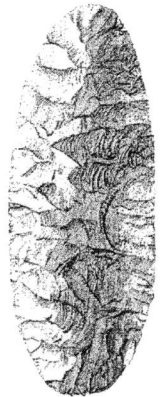

FIG. 9.   ½

FIG. 10.   ½

and that afterwards, probably leisurely, the monument had been raised to its final limits.   In the material over the grave were some splinters of flint, two saws, a rough spear-head, and a fine spoon-shaped scraper of black flint, $3\frac{1}{8}$ inches long (fig. 7).   More chalk and chalk rubble, which had been cast from the grave and not replaced, was noticed.   This, as we afterwards observed, was owing to the grave being partly filled with a boat-shaped block of clay.   It is also worthy of note that under this chalk and rubble, which had not been put back into the grave, there was a quantity of clay, 3 to 4 inches in thickness, lying on the ancient surface.   This indicated that the procuring of non-local clay for the building of the mound, and the digging of the grave, were carried on simultaneously. During the afternoon we dug down into the east end of the grave, and at the distance of $3\frac{1}{2}$ feet touched the decayed bones of the feet of the body forming the primary interment.

November 29th.—Diggers same as yesterday.   As the writer could not be present, nothing was done in the grave ; however, besides operating on the western side of the centre, trenches were made on the southern and northern margins of the mound, and cut towards the centre, but without discovering any encircling fosse, or finding anything but flakes of flint, two thin pieces of an urn, and a few much decayed splinters of a human leg bone, at a point about 3 feet from the base and 8 feet from the centre of the barrow.

November 30th.—Again 12 workmen.   On this date the remaining portion of the grave was very carefully emptied by the writer and an experienced workman. It was charged in a manner observed several times previously in our excavations.   A boat-shaped block of clay and soil, identical with the substance of the mound, occupied the centre of the grave, reaching to within one foot of the sides all round the top, and narrowing considerably at the bottom. Between this block of clay and the sides of the grave, rough chalk was piled all round.   At a depth of $3\frac{1}{2}$ feet we reached the floor of the grave, and found in the centre the remains of an interment of a male, on his back, at full length, with the head to the north-west (see fig. 5).   A careful measurement showed the length to be 5 feet 11 inches from head to feet.   Owing to the floor of the grave not allowing proper drainage, and to the body being in contact with the moist clay above, most of the small bones had quite disappeared, while the crushed skull and limb bones were very soft, and crumbled to pieces on being touched.   The left arm was bent over the body, and the right arm was doubled, with the hand at the shoulder.   There was a quantity of fine carbonaceous matter under the skeleton, especially about the feet, and close below its sides all round was a row of rather large pieces of chalk, forming a trough or bed in which the corpse had been placed.   Touching the outside of the left humerus was a dagger-blade of whitish-coloured bronze (fig. 8), $7\frac{3}{4}$ inches long, 2 inches wide at the butt end, with an exceptionally sharp apex pointing to the feet.   Its good state of preservation is doubtless due to the fact of it having been interred in the sheath, which was apparently made of bronze.   This was found for the most part in green powder, which had coloured the lower end of the left humerus.   Of the handle, which had been secured to the blade by four rivets, nothing remained.   Under and over this weapon was a large quantity of dark matter, resembling decayed and compressed leaves.   On the left side of the head was a fine hammer-head (fig. 9) of hard white stone — probably crystalline limestone—measuring 3½ inches long and 4½ inches in circumference. The position in which it was found shewed that its handle extended to the side of the dagger, and, from the few decayed pieces picked up, appeared to have been about 18 inches long, and probably of ash. Close to the right facial bones was a fine knife of black flint (fig. 10), with two very sharp cutting edges. One side is flat and the other raised in the centre by means of very beautiful chipping. From the appearance of these relics, they seem to have been quite new at the time of interment. The two following days, seven, and six workmen, respectively, were employed in restoring the form of the mound.

About two-thirds of this barrow consisted of clay, probably from Burdale, which is about 1 mile to the west; and from the neighbourhood of Duggleby, about 1½ miles to the north of the barrow. The clay from the latter place is much darker in colour than that obtained from Burdale, and each kind of clay predominated at the side of the mound nearest the place whence it had been brought. Layers of these clays, alternating with layers of reddish surface soil, formed the whole of the mound, and filled the centre of the grave beneath.*

BARROW "C 73"

Stands a little to the east of the last, and is also in the Towthorpe Plantation, the trees of which, in the neighbourhood of the mound, had been cut down a short time previous to the examination. Its diameter was 60 feet, and elevation 7½ feet. During the first week in December, 1874, an area 20 feet wide, extending from the eastern to the western margin, was turned over. Approaching the centre, in an excavation a few inches below the base of the mound, were the greatly decayed portions of a small coffin, made from the trunk of an oak, and measuring 3½ feet S.E. by N.W., and 17 inches across. Impressions of the squarely-cut ends and rounded sides of the coffin were sharply defined on the soil and subsoil of the old land surface. At its north-west end was a large heap of cremated bones of an adult, upon which was some decayed oak, probably the remains of a lid or cover. The other end of this receptacle contained nothing except the ordinary compact soil from the barrow which had settled into it, but at the time of the interment this portion may have held food.

The material of this mound was similar to that of the last mentioned, except that it had a less proportion of foreign clay. Thirty-five flint chips and flakes, ten scrapers, two globular lumps, or small sling stones, three knives, and two portions of knives, were obtained from the mound during the excavation.

BARROWS Nos. 233 and 234

Were opened during the fortnight between July 3rd and July 15th, 1882. The old trees of the plantation covering the mounds had been cut down unknown to us, and the area replanted. Permission to remove the young trees, however, was kindly granted.

No. 233 had an elevation of 7 feet 8 inches and a diameter of 68 feet. A

---

* The total cost of opening this barrow cannot be put down at less than £30, as we paid £25 13s. for the manual labour alone.

portion was cut from the centre, 28 feet S.S.E. by N.N.W., and 24 feet across. Near the east corner, at a depth of 1 foot from the apex, were the crushed fragments of a food-vase (fig. 11), without any accompanying interment. At the base of the mound, near the north corner of the excavation, the pointed end of a stake of oak, 2 inches in diameter, was found. Adhering to it was a small piece of bone, which had greatly decayed. This possibly indicated an interment on or near the original surface line. The stake penetrated the old surface soil about 12 inches, and, though no actual connection was observed, probably had formerly been connected with a piece of wood about 4 feet long and 6 to 8 inches thick, of which the impression and decayed remains were observed lying horizontally a foot or so above. These may have been the remains of a cist of wood. Near the western side of the excavation, some 8 or 9 feet from where we had supposed the centre of the mound to be, an oval grave measuring at the top 7½ feet S.S.E. by N.N.W., and 6 feet 4 inches across, and 6½ feet by 4 feet 8 inches at the bottom, was reached. Its depth was 4 feet 7 inches. Close to the east brink of the grave, on the undisturbed ground at the base of the barrow, were pieces of human bones, indicating an interment (No. 1), in the last stage of decay. No other relics were observed. At the bottom of the grave were the decayed remains of the body of a male (No. 2) of middle age, on its right side, with knees drawn up at right angles with the body, and its head to the east. The right arm was doubled back, with the hand to the face, and the left arm bent to a right angle, with the hand over the body. A femur measured 19 inches in length. Touching the right side of the hip was the blade of a very fine bronze dagger-knife (fig. 12), with its point towards the feet. It had been secured to the handle by three rivets, in addition to which were the rudiments of a "tang," a feature which is probably almost unique. The longitudinal mid-rib and two lateral ribs are also rare features, and seldom met with in such weapons from the barrows. The handle, probably of wood, had decayed, and, as was the case of the dagger in Barrow "C 39," no trace of a pommel remained. Probably the handle of this type of dagger-knife rarely possessed one. No other relic was observed. Around the head, shoulders, and hips was much decayed matter, in some places very like lamp-black. A section of the barrow showed that a small mound about 2¾ feet high and about 15 feet in diameter, containing only a little clay that had been brought from a distance, had first been heaped over the grave. Part of this had apparently settled into the grave after some perishable substance covering it had decayed. Some time after the building of the inner core or mound, a considerable quantity of foreign clayey matter, intermixed with soil from the surface of the surrounding land, had been heaped upon it (as was also the case in some of the adjoining barrows), until the mound was finally completed.

The dagger is in fine preservation, and exhibits beautiful workmanship. It was probably new when placed in the grave, as there does not seem to be any trace of its ever having been re-sharpened or used.

A few hand-struck splinters of flint were picked from the centre of the mound.

BARROW No. 234

Had an elevation of 5 feet and a diameter of 65 feet. Commencing a little way from the northern margin of the barrow, we turned over the greater portion of the mound, and trenched the original surface ground beneath, at distances of about a foot apart, without, strange to say, finding any traces of an interment, or even the least piece of pottery, and only two or three hand-struck splinters of flint. There was a little foreign clay mixed with the ordinary soil of the mound, chiefly on the south side.*

BARROW No. 6.

On the 18th of November, 1863, work was commenced on this mound, which is situated a little to the east of the last. It had been reduced to an elevation of 18 inches by tilling the land, whilst its diameter was 60 feet. We began by making a cutting from north to south 24 feet long and 10 feet wide, which on nearing the centre was increased to 14 feet in width. At the centre, and only a few inches from the surface, a skull † was obtained, which had been protected by a piece of chalk breccia. The facial bones and lower jaw had been carried away by the plough, and the long bones of the skeleton—of which there were traces—were so much broken that the original position of the interment could not be ascertained. A little below these remains was found a second body (No. 2), and about 6 inches lower a third (No. 3), which was on the floor of the grave. Both were flexed, with their heads to the west.

To the south of the bodies just mentioned, near the base of the mound, were four small skulls, with other bones, of children of various ages, while to the west, a little below the base of the mound, were three adult bodies, two of which had pieces of chalk breccia placed near their heads. All, except one, lay with their heads to the north-west. The exception had its head in the opposite direction. It is rather remarkable that not a fragment of an urn, nor the rudest flint tool, nor even a worked splinter of flint, was found. This barrow consisted entirely of soil and small chalk gravel from the neighbouring subsoil. No trace of foreign clay was observed.

Re-opening.—This interesting barrow having been explored in the early days of our researches, on the 3rd of September, 1867, it was decided to make a second examination, with the hope of finding interments under the bodies we had previously exhumed, but in this we were disappointed. A search was then made on the west side of the first opening, and about 10 feet N.E. of the centre of the barrow there was a body doubled up and much decayed, on its right side, with its head to the south. No relic was found. About the same distance S.W. of the centre was a food vase (fig. 13), 4¾ inches high, and 5¼ inches wide at the mouth. It had been carefully placed with the mouth downwards, a rare position for these vessels. It accompanied the remains of a child, which had almost disappeared. With the exception of a few pieces of charcoal, nothing more was found.

BARROW No. 7.

In the first week in April, 1864, a square was cut from the centre of this small barrow, which was only a little over a foot in elevation. In the centre was a small grave filled with dark soil matter, from which a few splinters of

---

* The total cost of opening and filling in these two mounds was £10.
† Marked *D* in my Collection.

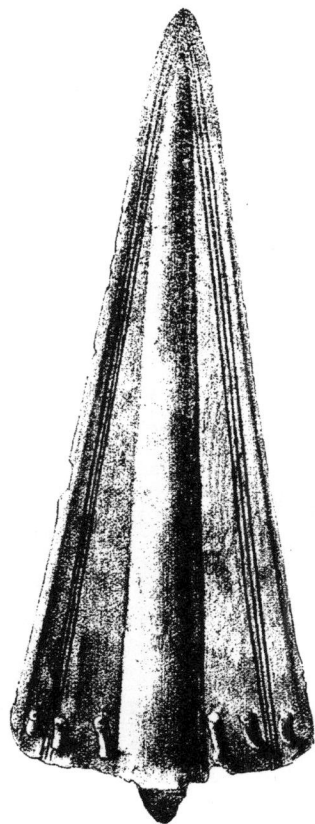

FIG. 12.   ¾

FIG. 14.   ¼

FIG. 15.   ¼

FIG. 17.

FIG. 18.

FIG. 13.

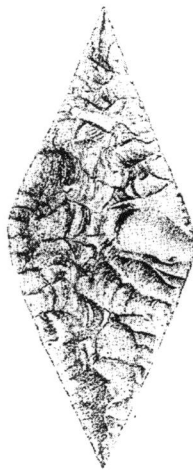

FIG. 16.   ¼

FIG 19.   ¼

animal bone and two fragments of an urn were picked up. A small quantity of a substance resembling calcined ·bones was also noticed, but nothing more.

The barrow marked "A" on the plan of the group on page 2 is a little to the south-east of No. 7. It is covered with fir trees, and has not been opened.

BARROW No. 18

Is about half-a-mile east of the last, and a little N.N.W. of "Canada Cottages." It is on the estate of Sir Tatton Sykes, Bart., from whom, through the kindness of the late Christopher Sykes, we received the necessary permission to explore. From August 19th to the 23rd, 1864, researches in this very interesting barrow were carried out. Its elevation was ascertained to be only 3 feet, while its circumference measured nearly 75 yards. This indicated that the apex had been much lowered and spread about by the frequent passage of the plough over its surface. Work was begun by making a cut 14 feet square in the centre of the mound, which was carried downwards to the undisturbed ground beneath. Close to the centre, only a few inches under the summit of the barrow, was a small heap of calcined human bones, mixed with a little burnt wood. Lower down, and in various places in the mound, detached teeth and bones of the ox and pig were found. Probably some of these bones had been cast there by the barrow builders after they had eaten the flesh. A little to the south and east of the centre, and about 2 feet from the apex were the skulls and part of the bones of three small dogs or foxes, possibly placed there as food. The heads of these animals were of small size, though the canine teeth appeared to be larger and more pointed than is usual with dogs of small size. From the positions of some of the bones in the three deposits, it seemed probable that the bodies of these animals had been cut to pieces before being placed in the barrow, as in one case two leg bones, crossing each other at right angles, were on the top of a skull. About 12 inches lower down, and south-west of the centre, were six bodies about the level of the old surface, and in the small space of about 5½ feet square. The crowding together of these remains was such that we were unable to make out their positions further than that they had been placed in flexed postures with their heads pointing in different directions, and generally with their faces looking upwards, indicating that most of them had been placed on their backs. On the west side of the bodies stood a semi-globular vase (fig. 14), mouth upwards, completely filled with dark soil, free from bones or ashes. It measures 4½ inches over the mouth and 3 inches in height. It is destitute of ornamentation, except a vertical row of 14 impressions made by the thumb-nail when the vase was in a plastic condition. On the N.E. side of the interments stood another vase (fig. 15), similar in size and form to the previous one, containing dark soil.*

A few inches south-west of the first-named vase was a beautiful spear-head of black flint (fig. 16) which, by pressure, was affixed to a femoral bone. Also about 12 inches north of the same vase were four large leaf-shaped arrow-heads of fine workmanship (figs. 17, 18, 19, 20). Close under the thigh-bone of another

---

* The form of these vases, as well as the texture and the dark colour of the paste, are of comparatively rare occurrence among British remains. The clay forming one had been freely mixed with small fragments of material, probably broken chalk, which have been since dissolved, and have left the surface, both inside and out, full of small irregular cavities or pits.

B

body, a second spear-head (fig. 21) was found, about one foot to the south of the first (fig. 16). There were also three deposits of flint-flakes—one on the west, the second on the south-west, and the third on the south-east side of the interments. Some of these flakes were very finely serrated. Lastly were three pear-shaped "pounders" of gritstone. The largest (fig. 22), which is 3½ inches in length, was obtained at the south-east side of the interments. The two smaller ones (figs. 23 and 24) were taken from different places. The late Christopher Sykes, of Sledmere, and the late Robert Topham, of Low Mowthorpe (at that time tenant of the land), were present when most of these fine instruments were found.

From the midst of the bodies the rib of an ox was taken. On the north-east margin nests of rats' bones were found, consisting of the remains of not less than 20 individuals, and a few others occurred on the west side of the interments. This was the first barrow in which the remains of these rodents had been observed by us, though from Mr. Bateman's "Ten Years' Diggings" it appears that such deposits were frequent in the mounds he opened.

This barrow consisted almost entirely of Kimmeridge clay brought from the nearest locality, "Low Mowthorpe," a distance of one mile. This was mixed with a little soil from the surface of the land in the neighbourhood of the barrow. Possibly soil was spread over each layer of clay as the building of the mound proceeded. The clay appears to have been trodden into an impervious mass, thus keeping out the wet and protecting and preserving the bodies from decay. Two smaller excavations were made, one to the south-east and the other to the north-west of the central one, without finding anything more.

Re-opening.—Soon after the first opening, it occurred to the writer that the ground at the base of the barrow had not been sufficiently probed; therefore, on the 19th of September, 1864, a cut 7 feet square was made from the mound so as to fall upon a place previously noticed, slightly north of the centre, which was originally thought to be a sand-pipe.* Even on the re-opening we were not certain that it was of the nature of a grave until we had dug one foot below the base of the barrow. At this depth there was a mass of dark clay, similar to that forming the body of the mound, in which, at a depth of about 2 feet, the upper portion of the antler of the red deer bearing two tines occurred. This oval, trough-shaped mass of clay measured 7 feet long by 4½ feet wide, and was 31 inches deep, but it contained no visible trace of an interment.

Second Re-opening.—Still under the impression that this mound had not been sufficiently examined, we again began work on it on June the 10th, 1868, continuing until June the 16th, turning over the whole of it. At a point 20 feet north of the centre, a funnel-shaped hole cut 4½ feet into the chalk rock, 3½ feet wide at the top, and 1 foot wide at the bottom, was discovered. Nothing but small pieces of burnt wood and two small bits of greatly decayed bone were found in it. It seemed as if this hole had been cut through the body of the mound; consequently, if any interment had taken place, it would be a secondary one. About 11 feet north-north-east of the centre was a small oval dish-shaped grave, 12 inches deep, on the bottom of which lay the body of a strong middle-aged person, on the right side, doubled up, with its head to the north-north-west, and both hands bent

* These sand and clay-pipes, or pockets in the chalk, are very deceptive and misleading, even to the most practiced workman, if not examined with the greatest care.

PLATE III.

FIG. 20.   ½

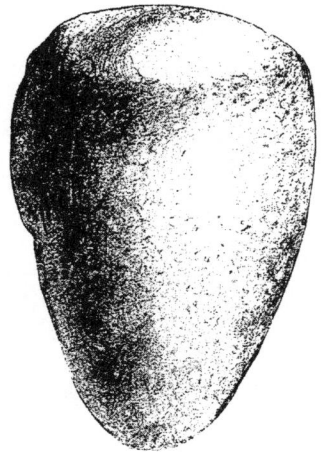

FIG. 21.   ½

FIG. 22.   ¼

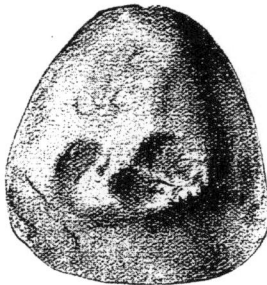

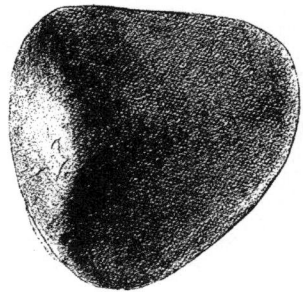

FIG. 23.   ½

FIG. 24.   ½

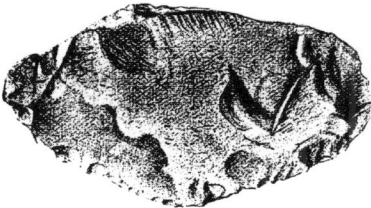

FIG. 25.   ½

FIG 26.   ⅓

under the chin. No relic accompanied it. There was no sign of the mound having been cut through to insert this burial. A partly-destroyed body (near to which had stood a food-vase, pieces of the bottom of which alone remained) was found 15 feet west of the centre, and within reach of the plough ; while 12 feet south-west of the centre, also in contact with the tilled surface, was another disturbed body, on its left side, and head to the east. Behind the shoulders in this case were portions of the bottom of another small vase. A few splinters of flint, and several bones of animals, were taken from various places in the barrow.

It was noticed that a shallow ditch had once encircled the mound, the material from which formed a ring of gritty chalk lying on its outskirts.

During the winter of 1887, this mound was altogether removed by Mr. William Byass, the tenant of the farm, and spread over the surface of the adjoining land, leaving not the slightest trace of its former existence. Had it not been explored, it would have been one more addition to the large number of barrows thus removed before having yielded its well-kept secrets of the past.

BARROW No. 22.

Nearly south of the last, and close to the west side of the Kirby Grange Farm buildings, there once stood a large mound. Its removal was carried out about the year 1850, by Mr. D. Leadly, at that time tenant of the farm. The motives which induced him to remove this barrow were that he might obtain material to make a level road over the narrow end of a valley between the Malton high road and part of his farm, and also that he might level the ground close to the west side of some new buildings, to which a farmhouse, &c., were soon to be added. Mr. Leadly told the writer that he distinctly remembered finding a whole human skeleton, a little beneath the apex of the barrow, and that in numerous other places in the mound detached bones were found ; and at its base, not far from the centre, a cavity had been scooped into the soil and rock below, which, to give his own description, was "of the form and dimensions of a medium-sized, round-sided kitchen copper with rounded bottom," such as the farmers in the neighbourhood used. A few burnt bones and wood ashes at the base were all he remembered finding. Above these was nothing but a little gritty chalk filling the grave. It is worthy of note that he also observed that the mound was streaked throughout with layers of dark matter, alternating with layers of reddish soil.

BARROW No. 21

Was opened March 1st, 1865. It stands in the fourth field east-north-east of the last barrow. Though its elevation was 2 feet above the adjoining ground, and 1½ feet above the old surface line beneath it, and had a diameter of 45 feet, the Government Ordnance Survey had omitted to map it. A piece 13 feet square was cut from its centre, shewing that the material of which it was composed was soil mixed with a dark and rather clayey substance. About the centre, and on the old ground surface, were a few calcined bones and wood ashes thinly scattered over a space measuring nearly 3 feet by 2 feet. Close to the north side of these was a line of six rough pieces of flint, extending for about 3 feet. On the south-western edge of the burnt bones and ashes were the remains of a small and very thin cup-shaped vase, without ornament, and too fragmentary to repair, which had measured about 3½ inches in its greatest diameter, and 3¼ inches in depth.   Lastly, a few feet to the west of the centre was what appeared to be a small oval grave.   It measured 2 feet by 16 inches, its greatest diameter pointing north and south.   Nothing was found in this trough-like hollow but dark-coloured earth and pieces of burnt wood. Only one portion of a hand-struck flint splinter was found in the material forming the barrow, and the burnt wood seemed to have been derived from oak and ash.

Re-opening.—On June 27th and 28th, 1881, we carried out, as in the case of all our early openings, what the writer had for a long time considered necessary—a re-examination.   On reaching the base, appearances clearly indicating a large grave were visible.   A little west of the centre was the shallow hole we had emptied at our first opening, containing clayey soil only.   Under this, at a depth of 18 inches below the base of the mound, lay a doubled-up and much decayed body, on its right side, with the head to the south-west. Close to the knees was a rudely chipped flint (fig. 25), and near to the head was a crushed food vase (fig. 26), possessing a rudimentary handle in the somewhat uncommon form of a button-shaped knob.   This kind of knob-handle is exceedingly rare on British pottery.   Under the left arm were fragments of the skull of an infant, on a mass of dark matter 12 inches by 5 inches in area. At the bottom of the grave was a second adult body, greatly decayed, probably a female, in a flexed position, and also on its right side.   At its back were the remains of an infant, and near to it a fine but much-crushed drinking cup, which has since been partly restored (fig. 27).   It shows the broken condition in which many of these vases are found.   It is 7¾ inches high, 5¾ inches wide at the mouth, 5 inches at the middle, and 3½ inches over the bottom. This oval grave measured 7 feet 3 inches east and west, and 5 feet 9 inches north and south, with a depth of 4 feet 10 inches.   The sides were vertical. We picked from the material filling the grave, a little above the upper interment, two rather large pieces of the upper portion or rim of a drinking cup, part of the remainder of which was found dispersed between this body and that at the bottom of the grave, while one large piece of a rim, matching those found above the upper interment, was taken from the floor of the grave. These fragments are covered externally with a very delicate pattern and ornamentation, most skilfully incised, and have belonged to a very fine vessel which, after having served at the funeral obsequies, was probably broken and cast into the grave.   Also, scattered at all depths between the two bodies, were many detached and splintered bones of a large individual, and along with these a tine from the antler of a red deer.

The writer is compelled to believe that, in this case, as in many others which have come under his notice, the detached and broken human bones found in the grave are not those of bodies disturbed by the introduction of later or secondary interments, but are the remains of victims who have been sacrificed in obedience to some cruel superstition.

BARROW No. 106.

This barrow is near No. 1, and a little to the west-north-west of the centre of this group of barrows. It was reduced to a central height of about 10 inches, and its circumference was hardly traceable. On September 25th and 26th, 1867, we worked from the southern and towards the northern margin, and at about the centre found and emptied an oval grave, measuring at the top 5 feet north-west to south-east, 3½ feet across, and 16 inches deep. At the bottom of the grave "A," on the undisturbed rock, with the head to the south-east, and partially on its back, as shown on the accompanying plan (fig. 28), were the remains of a rather strong-boned female. The femur measured 17⅞ inches, tibia 14½ inches, humerus 12 inches, ulna 10 inches, and radius 9½ inches. No relics were found, but 6 inches behind the pelvis were the bones of an infant, apparently only a few days old, doubled up and on its left side. Close above the adult body, as well as in many other places in the grave, were detached bones of a child from 12 to 18 months old—judging from the size of the bones. It seems probable that this body had been barbarously severed and buried piecemeal, as portions of the skull and other bones were found in places widely separated. About one foot north-west from the grave described above, was a second one (*B* on the plan) with nearly vertical sides, measuring at the top 8 feet by 4½ feet, and 3 feet deep, on the floor of which were the crouched remains of a female (?) in the position shown. Length of femur 18 inches and tibia 14⅜ inches. At the time of interment small stones had been packed closely all round the body. A few pieces of burnt wood were

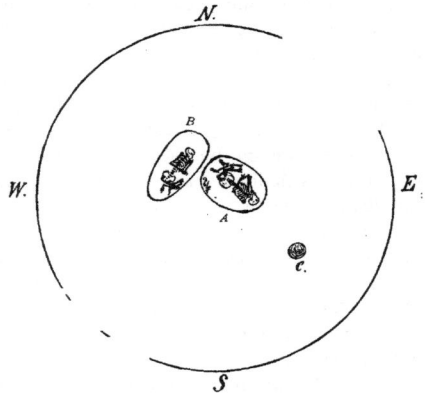

FIG. 28.

found here and there, but no dark matter was observed above or beneath the body, neither was the smallest piece of pot, bone, or worked flint found in any part of the grave. A compact boat-shaped piece of non-local clay, containing a few large unworked flints, stretched lengthwise over the body at the bottom of the grave. Fully 12 feet south-east from the centre grave, a shallow dish-shaped hole (marked *C*) 2 feet in diameter, with sides much reddened by fire, had been scooped into the original surface previous to the raising of the mound. It contained nothing but dark earth resembling peat.

BARROW No. 43

Is situated about a quarter of a mile to the west of the last. It is the first one opened on Lord Middleton's estate, and the ready permission of his lordship was obtained in this case also through the kindness of the late C. Sykes. This was an oval barrow, with a diameter of 92 feet, extending nearly east and west, and a transverse diameter of 76 feet. As it only measured 18 inches in height, probably its elliptical form was mainly or in part due to the action of the plough, as the old high-ridged lands run over it in the direction of its longer axis.

On February 14th, 1866, we commenced to open it by cutting a rectangular piece from the centre measuring 16 feet by 12 feet. Near the middle of this excavation, at about the base of the mound, was the greater portion of a human calvarium in a far-advanced state of decay, but no teeth were present, which shows that probably the whole skull had not been interred. Throughout this excavation, at about the same depth as the calvarium, were many hand-struck splinters of flint, ornamented fragments of a food-vase, and a drinking-cup, also detached human and animal bones. The human as well as the animal bones were frequently in separated splinters. At about 4½ feet north of the centre of the excavation, the appearance of the ground at the base of the barrow changed, indicating the presence of a grave, and the ends of two human thigh-bones protruded from this place. In following these downwards, some leg bones and a few other human remains were found, not at all connected, but in separate places, surrounded with unctuous earth and gritty chalk. Some pieces of animal bone were also observed here. A little lower, at a depth of 18 inches, measured from the base of the barrow, were the remains of a young person of medium size, with the head to the east, on its right side and the legs doubled up ; the right arm reaching downwards with the bones of the fingers passing partly under the left femur ; the left arm was doubled back to allow the hand to be brought to the right side of the skull, which is a very fine one. A small food-vase had been placed just in front of the face, but when found was crushed into many pieces. It has since been put together (fig. 29), and measures 5½ inches in height, 6 inches across the mouth, 2½ inches across the bottom, and is of the ordinary shape and quite plain. This is one of the few vases procured which is not ornamented in some form or other. No other article of man's device was found in connection with this body.

On February 19th, work was resumed by following downwards and sideways the filled-in material of the grave from which we had previously taken the above-mentioned skeleton, and on reaching the depth of 2 feet 8 inches, measured from the ancient surface line, and rather to the west of the above-mentioned remains, we bared a second skeleton, that of a person of about 40 years of age, which had been placed on the bottom of the grave, on its right side, with its head to the south, and the hands brought up to the head, and knees almost touching the chin. Close behind its head was a collection of worked implements, consisting of six nearly circular discs of flint (figs. 30, 31, 32, 32 A, 32 B, and 32 C), measuring from ¾ inch to 1½ inches in diameter, chipped nearly all round the edges ; one small lump, nearly an inch in diameter, flaked on all sides ; six small splinters, and two shapeless pieces ; all except three are of black flint (see figs. 32 E, 32 F, 32 G, 32 H, and 32 I). These had evidently been designedly placed where we found them, possibly in compliance with some belief. No urn or other article was found with this body, which was in such an advanced state of decay that the vertebræ and the upper side of the skull had quite disappeared. A femur and a tibia measured respectively 18 inches and 15 inches. Seven feet west of the

FIG. 29.   ⅓

FIG. 27.   ⅓

FIG. 30.

FIG. 31.

FIG. 32.

FIG. 32 A.

FIG. 32 B.

FIG. 32 C.

FIG. 32 E.

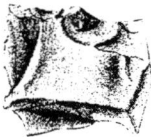

FIG. 32 F.

FIG. 32 G.

FIG 32 H.

FIG. 32 I.

grave we found a dish-shaped hollow, measuring 2½ feet in diameter, and 8 inches in depth, which contained only soil burnt red, mixed with wood ashes. Though nothing more was found in this strange receptacle, it apparently served some purpose or other at the performance of the funeral obsequies. Lastly, we drove the excavation eastwards, westwards, and northwards into the mound without finding anything but splinters of bone and flakes of flint. The whole barrow was composed of soil, mixed in some places with chalk, which probably was partly obtained ·when digging the grave. Here and there, at its base, were slight traces of a tenacious earth foreign to the immediate neighbourhood.

We also collected twenty-nine flakes and splinters, five nearly circular discs, in every way resembling the six found behind the head of the body No. 2; four pieces rather over an inch in diameter, which may have been cores or sling-stones; the point-end of a spearhead, an inch long; and a small rudely-fashioned leaf-shaped arrow-head, all of black flint, as well as one rough spearhead, 2¼ inches long, and 1½ inches broad; three large splinters, and one unshapely fragment roughly flaked over the greater part of the surface, the latter measuring 2¼ inches long, 2 inches wide, and 1 inch thick. All these last mentioned are of native grey flint, and, together with those already enumerated, make up the sum total of what was picked from the material of this barrow and from the. old surface beneath it.

BARROW No. 72.

This barrow is the southernmost of two shown on "Bella Sheepwalk," and is about a quarter of a mile north-west of the last. We worked upon it on August the 2nd, 3rd, and 13th, 1866. At that time its height was 2 feet and its diameter about 70 feet, having been considerably reduced in size by the frequent passage of the plough. The first discovery was about 5 feet north-west from the centre, and is shown at *A* and *C* on the plan (fig. 33). Here, at depths varying from one foot above to one foot below the base of the barrow, were the greater portions of three full-sized skulls, one of which seemed to have been interred whole, but without the under jaw, while the other two had been broken. Within the calvarium * of one of these were tightly jammed a large portion of

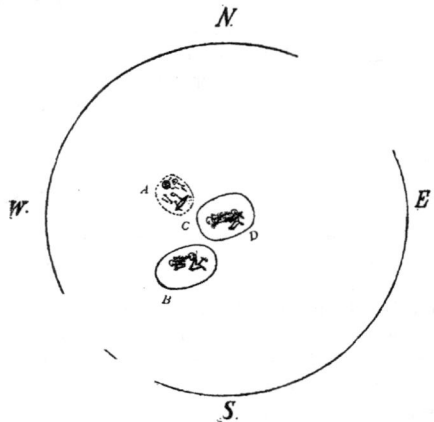

FIG. 33.

a pelvis, and a large dorsal vertebra. Within the hollow of another broken calvarium was the head of a large femoral bone. .The long bones and others

* Similar to what was found at Aldro', Barrow 54.

found in this deposit were in the greatest confusion and much broken. With these adult remains were found some leg bones and the ilium of a child; also a large brow tine from the antler of a red deer, and the greater portion of the scapula of probably the same animal; also several fragments of a food-vase and eleven flint splinters, two irregular lumps, and two small oval discs chipped round their broad ends. Close under these broken-up bodies was a circular heap of burnt adult bones (shown at *A*, on the plan), and associated with it, a bone pin (fig. 34), which measured nearly 2¾ inches long, and showed traces of fire. Also, about 14 inches eastwards and 6 inches deeper was a second mass of calcined bones (shown at *C*), 22 inches long and 6 inches wide. These had probably been rolled up in a skin or some other perishable covering, which had decayed. Close under was a knife (fig. 36) of flint, 1¾ inches long, and 1⅛ inches broad, with two cutting edges. This shewed no trace of fire. All these burnt and unburnt bones were within an oval space which measured only 3 feet in its greatest diameter, and was consequently too small for an ordinary grave. Its contents, however, were very suggestive. Next, 5 feet south of the interments just described, and only from 8 to 10 inches below the base of the mound, were the contracted and badly-preserved remains of an old person, in the position shown at *B*, on the plan. A femur measured 16½ inches. Four pieces of an urn, and seven splinters of dark-coloured flint, were taken from the mound over and around this body. Finally, about 4 feet eastwards of the cigar-shaped deposit of burnt bones, "C," was a small oval grave dug 18 inches below the base of the barrow, in which lay a contracted body as shown at *D* on the plan. Except that the right arm was stretched at full length with the hand on the pelvis, the position of the body was in every way similar to that of the body *B*. No relic was found with the remains of this skeleton. I possess many fragments of the skulls, but was not able to obtain the measurement of the long bones. Though I hesitate to say positively that all the burials in this mound were contemporaneous, it appeared almost certain that the deposition of the two incinerated deposits (*A* and *C*), under the remains of the fractured bodies shown within the dotted line above them, was effected at one and the same time.

BARROW No. 73.

Opened August 14th, 1866. A slight rise in the hedge adjoining the north side of the last barrow having attracted attention, the ground was examined, and found to be a small and almost demolished barrow, which is not mapped on the Ordnance sheet. About the centre was a small hole excavated about 6 inches into the original surface soil, containing a few burnt bones, at the north side of which stood an elegantly-fashioned food vase of somewhat unusual outline and ornamentation (fig. 37). Close to the north side of this deposit was a knife of black flint, unburnt, 2½ inches long, 1 inch broad, with two neatly-chipped cutting edges (fig. 38). It is double-pointed. About 3 feet to the east was a triangular excavation, also sunk 6 to 8 inches below the base of the mound, completely filled with red burnt earth, and mixed with wood ashes, in which were fragments of an urn. The bottom and sides of this excavation were also reddened by fire. Nearly 5 feet south-westwards, and about

6 inches lower than the incinerated remains, was a body doubled up on the bare floor of a small oval grave, with its head to the north-west and the arms across the chest. Although no relic was found with this interment, we noticed the presence of a quantity of wood ashes and red soil, which had evidently been cast hot into the grave upon the feet and legs of the body, so that the limbs were burnt and blackened. This fact is of some archæological value, as it affords an almost certain indication that the inhumed interment and the incinerated burial were contemporaneous. A femur measured 16½ inches, tibia 13½ inches, and humerus 11¾ inches. They probably belonged to a female of about 30 years of age.

BARROW No. 44.

This mound is half-a-mile west of the two last barrows, and close to the north side of Raisthorpe Plantation. It was opened on February 21st, 1866, when it had a diameter of 75 feet and an elevation of 20 inches. We commenced by removing entirely from the heart of the barrow a portion measuring 23 feet north and south, and 15 feet east and west. During this operation nothing was found beyond one small circular disc, and five small splinters of dark flint, and one lump of burnt wood about the size of a small bean.

The mound consisted of earth throughout the extent of our excavation with the exception of a thin bed of bluish clay, in some places broken, which covered the turf line at the base of the barrow. We removed this old surface soil and bared the gritty chalk below, and then everywhere probed the rock, but, strange to say, could find no trace of an interment anywhere. The Ordnance Surveyors had sunk the base of a signal staff in the centre of this mound, and may therefore, in inserting it, have destroyed the interment, if one ever existed in this part of the barrow.

BARROW No. 213

Is companion to the last-mentioned, and is partly covered by the south side of the Raisthorpe Plantation. On August 23rd, 24th, and 25th, 1880, we turned over the whole of this mound, except a small portion covered with trees, without finding any trace of a burial, or even the smallest bit of bone, flint, or pot. It was built of the local surface soil, mixed freely with a considerable amount of foreign clayey matter, arranged in layers. There was no indication of the layers having been cut through by any previous opening, and it is difficult to account for the absence of any interment in these two neighbouring barrows, except on the supposition that the interments had entirely decayed.

BARROW No. 214

Is one of three adjoining barrows still further to the west. Some entrenchments pass its southern margin.

On November 22nd, 1881, when we excavated it, it was so far reduced by the tilling of the land as to measure only 6 to 8 inches in height and about 20 feet in diameter. We turned over the greater portion of the barrow, and tested the ground beneath it, without finding anything whatever beyond an almost entirely destroyed body which had been broken up by the plough.

BARROW No. 3

Is about 200 yards to the south of the last, and is close to the south side of one of a chain of six curious natural hollows in the ground. On the 19th and 21st of August, 1863, we found it to measure 56 feet east and west, and 41 feet north and south, with an elevation of about 3 feet. We commenced near the western edge, and dug a trench from 7 to 8 feet wide towards the centre. The barrow was found to be mostly composed of rough pieces of chalk, of all sizes, which may have been procured from the brow of the adjacent natural hollow. This chalk was slightly mixed in places with soil from the surface, especially on its south side, which was the distant side from the place from which the chalk is supposed to have been taken. At the end of the first day we had reached the centre, and had found only the shoulder blades of an ox or deer, and a few bones of a smaller animal, mixed with wood ashes, lying on the old surface line. On the second day the excavation was continued eastwards from the centre for 6 or 8 feet further, and we came upon a brecciated material composed chiefly of chalk, mixed with wood ashes, sandy soil, and, in places, with what was thought might be traces of bones. After clearing- away part of the loose material surrounding this mass, it measured 10 feet in length from west to east, and 5 feet in width at the west end, and the same to about half its length, but it then narrowed to a point at the east end. It was about $2\frac{1}{2}$ feet in thickness. The top of this mass was nearly destitute of soil, and must have arrested the passage of the plough. It was quite apparent that fire had been an active agent in its formation, as the soil all round it was reddened by intense heat and blackened with burnt matter. The material of which it consisted may have been heaped over the glowing embers of a funeral pile, the confined heat of which may have caused the mass to adhere together, as the rest of the mound had a very loose appearance. We carefully broke this breccia to pieces, and at the east end found a cylindrical bead or ornament, slightly burnt (fig. 39), which had been made from a leg bone of a small animal. Near the same place were calcined bones and much charcoal, from which was picked a partly-burnt human lower jaw, apparently belonging to a young female. After the whole of the brecciated mass had been removed, we observed under it the residue of a large fire, from which at the west end we took the lower jaw-bones of three adults, and a thigh-bone measuring 17 inches. These had been less injured by the action of the flames than other portions of the bodies, very little trace of which remained.* No urn or worked flint was observed.

During our research in this barrow we were visited by the late Christopher Sykes, and Miss Mary E. Sykes, of Sledmere, who, as in many other instances, watched the proceedings with much interest.

Re-opening.—On July 20th and 21st, 1891, with Capt. Burstall's kind permission, we made our unavoidably-delayed re-examination. We had long believed that at the previous opening of this barrow we had passed over a grave near the centre of the mound. In this, however, we were mistaken, as, after two days' careful search, we failed to discover anything more.

---

* The question suggests itself, were these the remains of a sacrificial feast?

FIG. 34.

FIG. 36.

FIG. 37. $\frac{1}{2}$

FIG 38. $\frac{1}{1}$

FIG. 39. $\frac{1}{1}$

FIG. 41. $\frac{1}{3}$

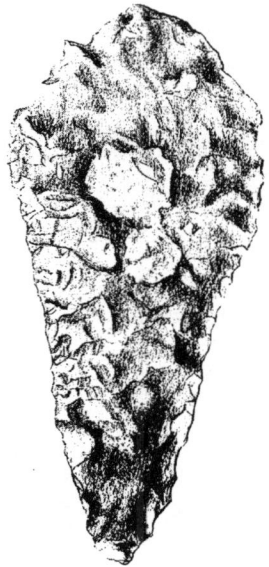

FIG. 40. $\frac{1}{1}$

FIG. 41 B. $\frac{1}{1}$

BARROW No. 214½.

A little west of Barrows Nos. 3 and 214, and close to the west side of the road from Raisthorpe to the Wold Barn, is a chalk-pit. Bodies had here been found in quarrying the chalk. On June 20th, 1883, a workman discovered a much-decayed skeleton, and on the following day my brother examined the place and obtained part of the skull and a rude article of bone (fig. 40). No urn or portion thereof was observed. One of the quarrymen remembered a body having been found in this quarry about two years before. The ground on the west side of the pit is slightly raised, indicating the former existence of a small barrow, of which only the outskirts now remain.

No. 211½.

On October 7th, 8th, and 9th, 1879, the writer, for geological reasons, cut three sections across the western end of the westernmost of a line of naturally-formed mounds which skirt the foot of the southern hillside of Back Dale, a little north of Thixendale, and near the last-described barrow. These mounds extend about a quarter of a mile, and seem to have been caused by the slipping of masses of chalk from the adjoining hillside. To the writer's surprise, the first section exposed a large British grave of the usual oval form, cut 4 feet into the summit of the slipped mass—a barrow raised by Nature. At about half the depth of the grave, on a ledge of the rock at the east end were the remains of an infant (No. 1). On the floor of the grave were two bodies (Nos. 2 and 3). No. 2 was the remains of a young female of small stature, with head to west, on its right side, and minus legs, and No. 3 that of a youth from twelve to fifteen years of age, which had been placed on its left side, with the legs pulled up at right angles with the trunk, and with head to the east. Close behind the head of No. 3 was a crushed drinking-cup, which has since been rebuilt (fig. 41), and a slightly-worked flint. From the material filling the grave we picked pieces of burnt wood, a few fragments of human bone, and some leg bones of a pig. At the time it was thought highly probable that further search along the summits of these natural hillocks would discover other interments of a similar nature, and on July 22nd and 23rd, 1891, we probed with a crowbar the remaining portion of the ridge of this mound and the summits of the other four mounds, but failed to find any further trace of a grave.

BARROW No. 276.

This barrow, covered, until recently, with the trees of "Greenland Plantation," is on "Maramotte"* Farm, near Sledmere. It is known by the name of "Dog Hill," from the fact of its having been used during the 18th Century as a cemetery for several favourite dogs belonging to the Sykes' family. This barrow

---

* Also spelt "Marramatte," and tradition says that the name of the farmhouse was given after two favourite dogs—"Marra" and "Matte." Our discovery in the mound goes to substantiate this.

is not shown on the 6-inch Ordnance Maps, but was pointed out to the writer by the present Sir Tatton Sykes, who had frequently observed it when shooting in the woods.

August 23rd, 1892.—We found its shape much defaced by agricultural operations. It measured about 2½ feet in elevation; five days were devoted to its examination.

In the body of the mound, at various depths, but not reaching quite to the base, were the bones of about 10 dogs, much decayed, most of which had been interred in wooden coffins, a copper coin having been placed with four of them. The wood of the coffins had almost entirely decayed, and was mainly in the condition of a dark-coloured powder, except some small pieces upon which the coins had rested. These pieces owed their preservation to their having been impregnated with the oxide of copper from the coins. This is not an isolated case of the intrusive interment of animals. I have met with four instances where animals that died during the cattle plague in 1877 and 1878 had been buried in mounds.* A little N.W. of the centre, at about the base of the mound, we found all the bones of an adult human foot (No. 1), lying in their true positions.

On the same plane, but 2½ feet north-eastwards were the contracted remains of two children, No. 2 with the head to N.E., and No. 3 with the head in the opposite direction, their ages being about 2 and 8 years respectively. A metatarsal bone of an adult foot was on the pelvis of No. 2, and two flakes of flint were placed near the hips of the other body. About 2 feet to the east of these bodies we reached the edge of an oval grave, which, after much labour, was emptied and found to measure 5½ feet east and west, and 5 feet across, retaining the same dimensions to the bottom. Its depth below the base of the barrow was 5½ feet, and the excavation was entirely filled with chalk that had been obtained in making it. Mixed with this material, from top to bottom, were the following :—Within the east side of the grave, at a depth of 1 foot, most of the cranial bones of a small pig, part of the under jaw of another pig, and various pieces of animal bone, also three small portions of an urn; in the south side of the grave, at a depth of 2 feet 9 inches, a detached human leg bone (tibia), two fragments of ribs, and a portion of some other bone; at a depth of 3 feet 10 inches, an ulna, and at the depth of. 4 feet a humerus. All these belonged to an adult.

Besides the above bones, the positions of which have been defined, there were scattered at various depths in the grave the following detached human bones :— 2 scapulae, 6 lumbar and 6 neck vertebrae, 1 patella, 1 heel bone, several bones of the foot, portions of two ulnae, parts of 3 radii, portions of a humerus, 2 collar bones, and a portion of a sternum. There were also 11 pieces of an ornamented drinking cup, and portions of an antler of a red deer, similarly dispersed, while a few bits of cremated human bones were distributed here and there in the lower half of the grave. Among the numerous pieces of bone belonging to at least two adults, not a single fragment of a skull was found. In the centre, on the smooth chalk rock forming the bottom of the grave, was a heap of the cremated bones of an adult, surrounded and partly covered with selected flat

* Unfortunately these intrusions had, in three instances, destroyed the original contents of the barrows.

pieces of chalk rock, placed apparently as a means of protection. On the east end of this deposit, was an axe-hammer (fig. 41A) of basalt, with its narrow end downwards, probably originally held in that position by the handle which had decayed. Close to the hammer was a large portion of a human left pelvic bone, unburnt, with one half of the head of the thigh bone in its socket. It appeared to have been cut from the other portion with a saw or some keen-edged metal instrument. It is difficult to account for this portion of the unburnt human pelvis accompanying the hammer, unless it was a remnant of food intended for the occupant of the grave on his resurrection. The other unburnt human and animal bones dispersed in the grave seem to have been placed there for a similar purpose, while others may have been cast in by the relatives and friends of the deceased, as relics of the funeral feast after or before they had eaten the flesh. Strange as such a repulsive custom appears to us, living in the 20th Century, it is difficult in any other way to account satisfactorily for the human bones being freely mixed with those of animals, and dispersed throughout the grave, as in this and many other instances that have come under my observation. Probably at the time of building these barrows this barbarous proceeding was not usually practised, except at funeral solemnities, and may be regarded as a survival of a custom which, in still earlier times, was more generally adopted.

Connected with the south-west side of the last-named grave by an opening 2 feet wide, was a second one, similar in outline, measuring 6 feet east and west and 4½ feet across, the depth being 3 feet. About 10 inches inside this was body No. 4 on its right side, with its knees pulled up, its hands to its face, and the head to the south-west. A femoral bone measured 12½ inches, and had probably belonged to a person from 10 to 12 years of age. At a depth of 2 feet within the grave were the much crushed bones of a very young child (No. 5) which had been doubled up, on its right side, with its head to north-east. The child lay immediately on the flexed legs of an adult (No. 6), whose head was pointing to the south-west. It was laid on its right side, with its hands to its face, and appeared to be the remains of a person of middle age—perhaps the mother of the child lying above. A humerus of this body measured 12¼ inches, and was of slender make. Below, on the floor of the grave, at a depth of 3 feet, was an adult body (No. 7) on its left side, with head to the east, knees drawn up, and hands to its face.

A flint flake and a rather poor flint scraper occurred together behind the head. A femur was ascertained to measure 17½ inches, a tibia 15¼ inches, and a humerus 13 inches, and belonged most probably to a person about fifty years of age.

From the inside of the mound, which consisted of soil-like matter, was picked one spear head, 2 inches long, a fine circular disc, and ten flakes, all of foreign black flint.

This barrow presents another point of interest, as it furnishes an example of the fact that an advanced state of decay in bones does not always constitute a reliable test as to the age of the burials. As already mentioned, the bones of the dogs, which had been protected in coffins, and had not been buried more than 150 years, were very much decayed, while the human and animal bones found 3 feet to 5 feet below them, and which had been interred for twenty to thirty centuries—perhaps more—were in good preservation. It is due to this slow decomposition of the bones under favourable conditions that we owe much of the knowledge we possess of the physical features of the ancient inhabitants of this island, while to the exploration of the barrows we are indebted for the greater part of what is known concerning the social, moral, and religious tendencies of the people of those early times.

DETACHED BARROWS,

All outlying barrows, which are near to any group of barrows, but too far distant to be included in the group, will, from time to time, be described under the head of "detached barrows."

BARROW No. 7a

Stands on the elevated ground a little to the north of, and overlooking, the small village of Thixendale. Its diameter was 53 feet, and elevation 3 feet. On the 18th of April, 1864, an area of about 9 feet square was cut from the centre of this barrow. On reaching the base the remains of a medium-sized body were observed just about the centre, lying on the right side, with the legs and hands drawn towards the face, and the head pointing to east-south-east. It measured from the crown of the head to the bottom of the pelvis 3 feet 4 inches, and a femur and a tibia, though of very strong make, only measured 17¼ inches and 13¾ inches respectively. No relic accompanied the body, but we took the skull, a femur, and a tibia. We then continued the excavation eastwards and westwards until it measured 30 feet by 9 feet, and in doing so picked out fragments of an urn, the tooth of an ox, and two splinters from a leg bone of the same animal, all lying apparently on the old turf line under the barrow, and at various distances from where the body had been interred.

On April 19th, the excavation was continued by making a cut 21 feet long by 3½ feet, parallel with and about 2 feet to the north of the former one. Here, more fragments of an urn were found on the same horizon. We also dug a square hole on the south side of the centre pit. Having failed to find any interment in the two former excavations, the surface soil in all the openings was removed to the rubbly chalk rock below, but we found nothing except three splinters of black flint. It seemed clear that the mound had been raised by heaping gritty chalk and soil over and around the corpse indiscriminately, and that part of these materials had been obtained from an encircling trench at a little distance from the margin of the barrow. At the time of our search the trench was filled in by frequent ploughing of the land, and quite invisible. We proved its existence by an excavation made on opposite sides of the barrow, which showed it to be 98 feet in diameter and 3 to 4 feet deep.

It may not be unworthy of note that in this, as in other cases which have been observed, the old turf line under the barrow was from 10 to 12 inches higher than the present land surface in the neighbourhood of the barrow.

In the field adjoining, to the east-south-east of the last mound, we were tempted to try a low elevation resembling a barrow, which is not shown on the Ordnance Survey Map, but after trenching over its centre for about 18 yards square we were unable to discover any trace of an interment, though about 12 to 14 inches from the surface we discovered here and there traces of a black substance much resembling burnt wood, and a few splinters of hand-struck flints in the soil turned over.

Re-opening.

On November 4th, 5th, and 6th, 1867, in the hope of finding further inter-ments, this barrow was re-opened by turning over the greater part of it and testing the ground beneath. About 6 feet south-south-east of the centre was a circular hole 15 inches in diameter and about the same in depth, containing at the bottom a few pieces of burnt wood and a whitish substance, the residue of some object which had decayed. About 5 feet south of the centre was an oval excavation in the rock, measuring 4 feet by 2 feet, and about 2 feet deep. It contained loose chalk rubble mixed with a little soil, and at the bottom some dark matter, but no trace of a body. During the progress of the work, several pieces of a large urn, four fragments of foreign flint, and several splinters of bone belonging to an animal about the size of a small ox or deer were picked up, chiefly at the base of the mound.

BARROW No. 273, "HOWE HILL, DUGGLEBY."*

This large flat-topped circular barrow (fig. 45) was opened by the writer for Sir Tatton Sykes, Bart., of Sledmere, during July and August, 1890. It stands on the sloping hillside, about 13 chains S.S.E. of the village of Duggleby, in and near which rise the springs which form the Gypsy Stream. It resembles in size and form two other large barrows on the neighbouring chalk wolds; one, Mickle Head, about nine miles S.W. of Duggleby, at the foot of Garrowby Hill;† and the other near Wold Newton, named "Willy Howe," eleven miles distant, in an easterly direction. The latter has been similar in size (about 125 feet in diameter) to the Duggleby Barrow, and it also stands on the foot of the southern side of the same mid-wold valley, and about the same distance south of the Gypsey Stream. In short, the two barrows are in every respect so much alike that their resemblance would seem to be more than accidental. They may have been erected in memory of two neighbouring and kindred chiefs held in equal honour, over whose remains similar monuments were raised. Of the three barrows the Garrowby one is by far the largest, having a diameter of 250 feet at the base, and an elevation of about 50 feet. This mound does not appear to have been opened, but "Willie Howe" has been twice examined; once by the late Lord Londesborough in 1857,‡ and again by Canon Greenwell in 1887. The latter search was made

* Barrows Nos. 273, 291, 292, and 293, are detached barrows, situated some distance from the north side of group No. 1.
† This mound is not marked as a tumulus on the ordnance maps; the writer, however, believes it to be artificially shaped.
‡ This opening, which was made east and west through the centre, was not more than 18 feet wide at the bottom, and probably not more than 16 feet. Therefore the experience gained in opening "Howe Hill," Duggleby, renders it possible that the primary burial in "Willy Howe" yet remains undiscovered, probably near to the north side of the opening made by the late Lord Londesborough. Had the excavation in "Howe Hill," Duggleby, been no wider than that made in "Willy Howe," the two graves containing the primary interments would not have been found.

within the limits of the former opening, with a view to discovering the primary interments which might have been passed over by the previous explorers.   No indication of a body was observed on either occasion.

   Owing to the sloping nature of the ground on which Duggleby Howe had been raised, its elevation appeared much greater viewed from the north side than it did from the south.   Its diameter at the base was about 125 feet, and its flat top was 47 feet in diameter.   By drawing a line east and west across the centre of the barrow its elevation was found to be 22 feet on the east side, and 19 feet

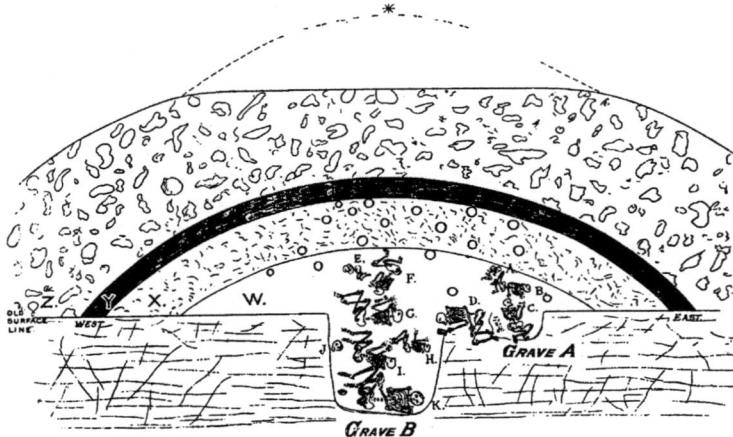

FIG. 45.

w. The inner mound of a clayey or earthy matter, 5½ feet in thickness.
x. A bed of small chalk grit, 4½ feet thick, in which were most of the cremated bodies.
y. Blue Kimeridge clay, 12 inches in thickness, sealing up all the inhumed bodies, as well as the
      cremated interments, which were found at various elevations, as shown by the small circles ;
      but only a few were vertically over the grave.
z. Roughly quarried chalk, 9½ feet in thickness, in the centre of the mound.
* Marks the assumed original height of the barrow, which was probably 8 or 10 feet higher
      than the present flat top.
o. Indicates cremated interments.

on the west.   In all probability this mound was originally 8 to 10 feet higher, measured along the same line.   It is said that the Duggleby Barrow was opened by the late Rev. Christopher Sykes,* brother to the late Sir Tatton Sykes, of Sledmere, not more recently than the year 1798 or 1799, as he left Sledmere in 1800.   I am afraid there is no written account of this opening, and there is no record of anything having been found.

   * Mr. Sykes explored other barrows in the neighbourhood ; and it is recorded, in the preface to the eighth edition of the hand-book of the Antiquities in the York Museum, that the Rev. Christopher Sykes was the first donor to the Museum.   The gift was a small number of Anglo-Saxon cinerary urns from a cemetery on the Wolds.
   A short paper, by Mr. Sykes, on the finding of a bracelet on the wrist of a skeleton found by the road side in Wetwang field, was read May 15th, 1794, at a meeting of the Society of Antiquaries of London. It is therefore to be hoped that some account of Mr. Sykes' explorations of the Duggleby and other barrows may yet exist.

PLATE VI.

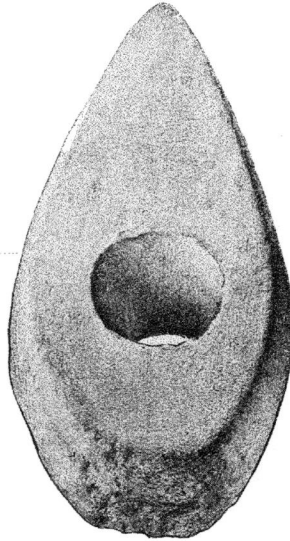

FIG. 51. ½

FIG. 41 A. ½

FIG. 41 A. ½

FIG. 52. ½

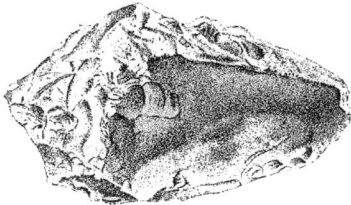

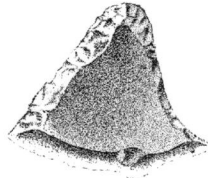

FIG. 46. ½

FIG. 47. ½

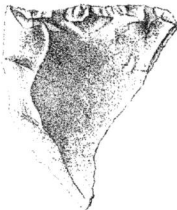

FIG. 48. ½

FIG 49.

FIG. 50.

On July 21st, 1890, a commencement was made by the writer and a number of experienced workmen. An area of 40 feet square over the centre of the barrow, and a portion of the east side, were removed. From the central area and mainly from the filled-in excavation (which was small for so large a mound, and did not reach within 12 feet of the base), made by the previous explorers, the following articles of iron were found:—a few nails and flat bits of iron much corroded, and one side of a pair of small shears, probably Anglo-Saxon; there was also the pointed end of a bone pin, and a piece of bone apparently from the side of an Anglo-Saxon comb.

Twenty-five flint flakes were found, some of which were variously shaped by secondary chipping; including a punch-shaped tool 2½ inches long; a portion of a toothed double-edged flake saw; and a sharply pointed triangular knife 2 inches in length, and 1 inch broad at the base, made of a very thin flake of light-coloured native flint; (one side of this knife shows a portion of the rough drab-coloured skin of the block from which it has been struck); four large flakes most skilfully removed from the side of the knife leave, without the usual finer chipping, an edge almost as sharp as a razor; while its back has been formed by removing numerous small chips, mainly from the same side of the knife, leaving it only about one-eighth of an inch in thickness. The other side has been left flat as struck from the core, with the exception of a short distance along the back where it is slightly chipped. There was also a large rejected core (fig. 46) of black flint, probably used as a hammer, from which four large flakes had been struck from opposite sides. About 250 pot-sherds were found, among which was one small piece of British ware; a few fragments of Roman and Anglo-Saxon vessels; and many portions of vessels of a more recent period, some glazed and some un-glazed. There were also several pieces of gritstone, a few inches in diameter, all more or less reddened by the action of fire. In addition, the remains of the following animals were collected, viz.:—bones and fifteen teeth of a horse;* bones and five teeth of an ox; part of the under-jaw with teeth of a goat or sheep; two under-jaws with teeth of a small dog or fox; teeth and portions of the antler of a red deer. There are also three-quarters of a human lower-jaw, probably of a female; several other pieces of human bone, notably a portion of very large femur, and another portion of a rather small femur, both of which had been deeply cut with a sharp instrument, probably by some of the workmen engaged in the previous opening. These human bones indicate the removal of at least two adult bodies, which were probably secondary Anglo-Saxon interments, and had been buried in the upper part of the mound. The great quantity of various kinds of pottery found in the upper and disturbed portion of the barrow is interest-ing and very unusual. It corresponds, in quantity and variety, with the pottery which the writer has obtained from three other mounds, one at Fimber, one at Wetwang, and one at Cowlam. But in each of these cases it was found either in, or connected with, large cross-shaped trenches which had been cut north and south, east and west, through the centre of the mounds, and into the rock below, to a depth of from 8 to 9 feet. Possibly these sherds are the remains of pottery used and broken at the opening of, or other ceremonies connected with these

* The teeth of this animal were found only at the summit of the mound, in ground disturbed by secondary interments, and by the digging of the cross-formed trench, probably in Anglo-Saxon times.

D

excavated crosses. From the finding of so large an amount of pottery in this instance, we were led to believe that an excavated cross, similar to the three named above, and serving a similar purpose (probably a sacred Moot-hill symbol), had once existed on the summit of the Duggleby Howe, and that, when the present Sir Tatton Sykes, in 1870, placed a wooden cross on the summit of this mound he was unconsciously replacing an old sign, of similar import, which had been removed by the excavations made by the Rev. C. Sykes nearly a century before. The symbol of an excavated cross dates back, probably, from the 5th to the 7th century, when the top of the mound was made flat, and in other ways fitted for a Folk Moot, for which purpose it possibly served for many centuries. Whether or not "Willy Howe" had a flat top at the time it was first opened seems somewhat uncertain; but the mound "Mickle Head," at the foot of Garrowby Hill, has a flat top 60 feet in diameter, and several other large mounds in other parts of Yorkshire possess this feature.

As the excavation proceeded, and the central opening had reached a depth of 9 feet, it was observed that portions of the old cutting made by the Rev. C. Sykes, as well as the bottoms of the southern and eastern arms of an excavated cross, extended nearly to this depth. The undisturbed portions of the two arms of the cross contained about 18 inches of pure clay at the bottom, as well as a block of grey limestone, worked into the form and about the size of an ordinary building brick; and a piece of grit-stone which seems to have had a circular hollow cut into the middle of it, which may be a portion of the bottom stone of a primitive bandmill. In addition to the remains found in the upper portion of the mound we took from the material filling the old opening, and in the disturbed portion of the arms of the cross, a few more pieces of the two previously mentioned human bodies; portions of the heads and other bones of two large dogs; the right side of a hoof, and other bones of an ox; four teeth of a horse and two pieces of burnt animal bone. One portion of the broken leg bone of an ox has had a round hole about half an inch in diameter bored through it, probably in order that it might be used as a tool. There was also a portion of another iron knife, seemingly Anglo-Saxon, nine rusty nails and other bits of iron; fifty-nine pieces of pottery of the same kinds (except British) as previously found, and twelve chips of flint. Seven cremated interments were taken from a small area on the north side of the central excavation. They were all laid on the same plane, fourteen feet from the level of the flat top of the barrow, under an arched bed of Kimeridge clay, as shown on the plan (fig. 44). A portion of a bone pin (fig. 61) was found with No. 4, and one of the workmen picked up an instrument of flint (fig. 52) chipped to a very sharp point. It was about three feet north of the deposit No. 3, and on the same level. It was found that there was an inner mound, the centre of which did not, as shown in the plan, quite correspond with the centre of the completed barrow. This may have occurred through the chalk material that formed the upper portion of the mound having been quarried from the rising ground to the south, and consequently piled more on this side than on the north and distant side of the mound.

A section (fig. 45) which was obtained from measurements of the southern and eastern radii, shows this inner mound to have a diameter of 75 feet, and to measure 11 feet in height, the upper 10 to 14 inches being almost pure Kimeridge Clay,

containing no remains, under which was 4½ feet of small chalk grit, in which most of
the cremated interments were found ; and below this was a core of clayey soil of a
hazel colour, mixed with a little chalk grit, which was 5½ feet high in the centre, and
had been obtained from the adjoining ground. This core was afterwards found to rest
on the old turf line, and to contain or cover all the inhumed primary interments, and a
few of the cremated ones. A large heap of chalk lying on the south side of the central
grave (from which it had been cast) still remained on the old surface line. Fifteen
additional deposits of burnt bones were found in the same central area in which the
seven previously named deposits were taken, but at depths varying from two to
six feet below, and reaching downwards from the lower portion of the chalk layer
to near the base of the core of clayey soil. Except a few burnt portions of a bone
pin found with No. 20 on the plan, and a piece of the lip of a food-vase with
No. 12, no relic accompanied any of the deposits. Near the deposit No. 19, and
about two feet from the base of the mound, was found the greater half of the lower

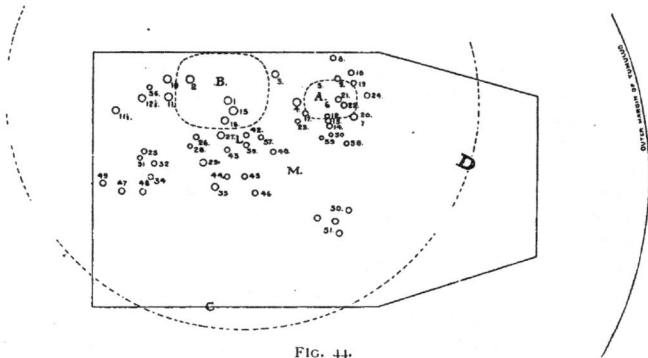

FIG. 44.

Plan of Duggleby Howe, showing positions of interments, size of excavations, &c.

jaw of a young person, the back molar just rising from its socket. Two more
cremated deposits (Nos. 21 and 22) were found. Just to the east of No. 21 were
the much decayed unburnt remains, marked *A*, of a very young child, and 10
inches lower was the inhumed body, marked *B*, of a youth from 6 to 10 years of
age, on the right side, with its knees up and head to the east. A femur and tibia
measured 13 and 10½ inches respectively. This body was 19½ feet from the apex
of the mound, and one foot from its base. No relic accompanied it, but about
2 feet to the south and 2 feet higher in the mound was a stag's-horn pick (fig. 60),
with the point broken off ; and about 1 foot above this and a little further south
was another pick (fig. 59), also of stag's horn, with the point much worn. Only
one deposit of burnt bones (No. 23 on the plan) was found, at a depth of 17 feet
from the apex of the mound ; but in a very shallow grave, 9 to 10 inches below
the ancient turf line, and at the depth of 22½ feet from the flat top of the mound,
vertically under the body marked "B," was a body, marked "C," on its left side,
head to N.N.E., both hands near the face, and the knees brought up to a right
angle with the trunk. A femur measured 16¾ inches, a tibia 13½ inches, and the

humerus 13 inches respectively. These are of medium strength. The skull is
dolicocephalic, the bones of great thickness, and belonged to a person about 50
years of age, with fine features. A large bone pin (fig. 62) 9¼ inches long, was
found about 3 inches behind the back of the body, with the point to the hips.
Close to the shoulders were several flint flakes, also worked flints, as well as
several tusks of the boar. There was a similar deposit a few inches behind the hips.
In all there were thirteen flakes and six worked flints (figs. 47 to 52) all of dark-
coloured foreign flint. There were also two incisor teeth of the beaver (fig. 55) ;
and twelve boars' tusks, fig. 53 being one, and fig 54 another which has been made
into an instrument of uncertain use. Just above the body were found the neck
vertebræ of an ox and other pieces of animal bone. On the western edge of this
shallow grave, marked " A " on the plan, were the inhumed remains of an adult,
marked " D," about 70 years of age, of large stature, with head to the west, and
lying over the eastern edge of the centre grave, marked " B," into which it had
settled some 10 inches. It was on its right side in the position shown on the plan.
The femur and tibia measured 20 inches and 17½ inches respectively. In front of
the face was a beautiful knife (fig. 58), of almost transparent glass-like flint. It is
of a rare type* and very thin, having been ground down on both sides to not more
than $\frac{1}{16}$ of an inch in thickness. Its length is 2⅜ inches, and breadth 1$\frac{3}{16}$ of an inch.
Its smoothly rounded ends are so formed that it might be used equally well as a knife
or a spoon. A deposit of burnt bones was found in the position numbered 24 on the
plan, and about the same depth in the mound as Nos. 1 to 7. Nothing was found
with it. Over the centre grave, marked " B " on the plan, and about 3 feet above
the base of the barrow, was the much decayed body of a child, marked " E," and
about 2 feet under it the body of a youth 8 to 12 years of age, marked " F," on
the left side, head to S.W., knees pulled up, and hands in front of face: Femur and
tibia measured 14 inches and 11½ inches respectively. No relics were found with this
burial. About 2 feet lower than the last body and about 1 foot into the grave " B "
was an adult male, marked " G," who probably had reached the age of 60, laid on
its right side in a flexed position, and head to N.E. Femur and tibia measured
18 and 14 inches respectively. This body was distorted by the unequal settling
of the grave below. In front of its chest was a hammer head (fig. 63) made of
the base of a shed antler of a red deer, and near it was a diamond-shaped
arrow-head (fig. 64) of dark-coloured flint, which unfortunately had lost its point.
There was also a most beautiful axe (figs. 56 and 57) made of drab-coloured flint,
9½ inches long. The flint might have been obtained with careful selection from the
neighbouring beds of chalk. The broad cutting edge was towards the knees of the
body. The hammer-head was laid on its edge, showing that it had at the time
of interment been held in that position by a shaft, most probably of wood, which
had since decayed. The bottom of the central grave, " B," was next reached, and
other parts of the excavation lowered. In proceeding downwards, at a depth of 3
feet, the doubled body of a child, marked " H," was found on its right side, and the
head to the east. It appeared to have been about 2 to 3 years old. No relic was
found with it. This body lay at the bottom of a boat-shaped mass of clayey matter,
in the centre of the grave ; all round the outsides at this horizon being gritty
chalk. About 2 feet below the last body was an adult, marked " I," probably a

* The writer only knows of one similar knife, which was found by him in a barrow on the " Aldro Farm."

PLATE VII.

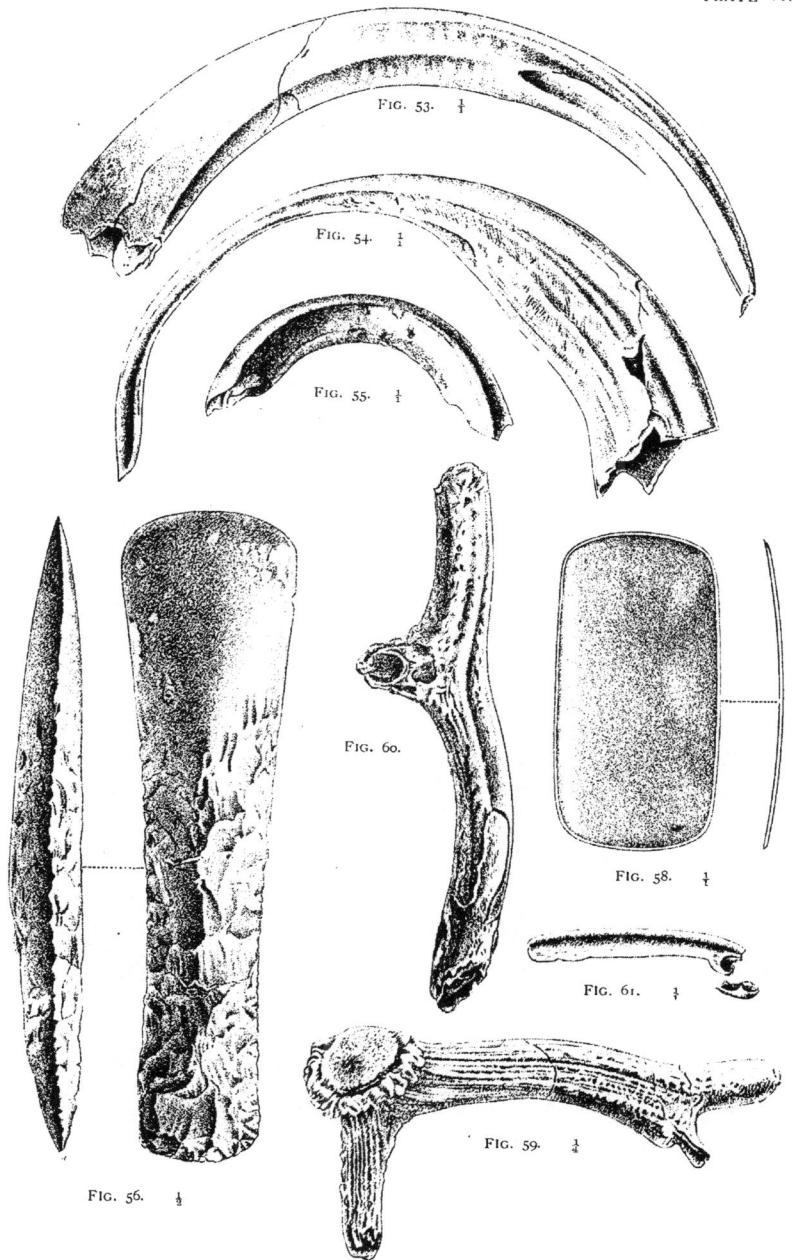

FIG. 53.   ¼

FIG. 54.   ¼

FIG. 55.   ¼

FIG. 60.

FIG. 58.   ¼

FIG. 61.   ¼

FIG. 59.   ¼

FIG. 56.   ½

male about 60 years of age, in the same bent position, but considerably contorted by the unequal settling in the grave. Its head was placed to the east. The femur and tibia measured 17¾ and 14½ inches respectively. Nothing accompanied this body; but near its feet was the skull, marked "J," of a person about 20 years of age, with the back upper left molar fully grown, minus its under jaw; and there is a large suspicious-looking circular hole in the left parietal bone. At a depth of 9 feet from the base of the barrow the firm undisturbed floor of this grave was reached. At about half its depth, the grave measured 11 feet east and west, and 10 feet north and south; and at the bottom 7 feet east and west, and 5½ feet north and south. In the grave was an adult body, marked "K," on its back, head to east, knees drawn up, right arm bent over the chest, and hand on the left shoulder; the left arm was bent at a right angle over the abdomen, with the hand near the right elbow. Femur, tibia, and humerus measured 19, 15, and 13 inches respectively, and were of strong make. Mr. Mark Sykes, of Sledmere, much interested, assisted the writer to uncover this body. At the knees were the irreparably crushed remains of a semi-globular food-vase, of which a restored drawing is given (fig. 65). It was made of dark-coloured Kimeridge Clay, obtained in the neighbourhood. Near the vase nine small flint flakes were found, some of which were slightly notched on one edge as if intended for saws; there were also two cores from which a few flakes had been struck; all of dark-coloured flint. These were very poor specimens, none of them seeming suitable even for the most inferior tool. Possibly they were placed there during some burial ceremony. A quantity of decayed wood and several thin patches of ferruginous matter (not the residue of any oxidized iron implements) were in contact with the body, over and under it. At various depths in the centre of the mound, a little to the south of the grave, were 13 more deposits of burnt bones, shown on the plan by the Nos. 25 to 37 inclusive, and with No. 30 there was a bone pin (fig. 66).

About 3 feet above and near the outside of the southern edge of the large grave, "B" on the plan, were the remains, distorted from unequal settling, of a young person, marked "L," having only two molar teeth on the sides of the jaws, and there was no appearance that there ever had been or would have been, a third molar. This interment originally had been placed with its head to the north, knees pulled up, right arm crossed over the body, and the left arm doubled, with hand brought to the shoulder. Femur and tibia measured 16¼ and 13½ inches respectively. This body seemed to have been interred with its head and shoulders considerably raised, and probably was protected by a cist-like receptacle of wood, this being sufficiently durable to allow the flesh to decay, thus permitting the under-jaw to fall some distance from the head, the head to roll over, and other bones to fall into the unnatural position in which they were found. There was a small deposit of cremated bones close to the hips of this body, but no relic accompanied it. About 16 feet south-east of the centre of the large grave, and one foot above the base of the barrow, was a body, on its back, head to south-west, with knees pulled up and head pressed over to the north-west. Femur and tibia measured 18 and 14 inches respectively; the right humerus 13 inches, whilst the left measured 12½ inches only. Over this body were the greatly decayed remains of two very small infants, the positions of which could not be made out. About 20 feet west of these and about 3 feet above the base of the mound and in the bottom bed or core of hazel-coloured clayey soil were most of the bones of one leg of a fox,[*] the flesh of which had probably been consumed by the mound builders, and the bones dropped where they were found. The total number of cremated interments, which were found in circular heaps 6 to 18 inches in diameter, and 1 to 6 inches in thickness, was 53,[†] of which 9 or 10 were found in the core of hazel-coloured clay, and the remainder in the layer of gritty chalk close above. Excepting portions of burnt bone pins with Nos. 4, 10, and 30, previously alluded to, nothing accompanied any of them. It is remarkable that not one of this very large number of burnt bodies had been placed in a cinerary urn. The barrow is also remarkable for the almost entire absence of British pottery and potsherds. Excepting the crushed vase with the body at the bottom of the grave, 4 very small sherds from the substance of the mound, and a very small fragment of a food-vase with the cremated deposit No. 12, no other pottery was found.

The following Report on the Duggleby Crania, &c., has been kindly prepared by Dr. J. G. Garson :—

ON THE CRANIA AND OTHER HUMAN REMAINS FOUND IN THE BARROW AT HOWE HILL (No. 273), DUGGLEBY.

"The specimens from Howe Hill Barrow which have been placed in my hands for examination by Mr. Mortimer, consist of the skulls belonging to the skeletons he has designated in his paper on the exploration of the barrow, by the letters C, D, F, G, H, I, J, K, L, and M, and some of the long bones of the extremities of D, I, and K (p. 24, fig. 45, and p. 27, fig. 44). He has also been good enough to furnish me with the measurements of some of the long bones, which have unfortunately not been preserved, belonging to C, D, G, I, L, and M, together with his notes and diagrams relating to the exploration of the barrow, which have been of the greatest assistance to me. The skulls and bones are in a very fragile condition, and many of them are very incomplete, notwithstanding that Mr. Mortimer has bestowed much time and patience in restoring them as far as was possible.

"Eight of the specimens belonged to adult males, and two to children of about six and ten years of age respectively. No female's bones appear to have been found in the barrow. According to the usual rule, the description of the specimens I am about to give will only include the adults of the series.

"*Stature.*—As is generally the case with human remains from ancient barrows, the stature of the persons whom the skeletons represent can only be determined by calculation from the long bones of the extremities. Of these I have personally only measured the right femur of D, the right and left femora and tibiæ of I, and the two femora, the right humerus, and left tibia of K. The measurements of the other bones which I have given in the 'Table of Measurements of the Long Bones,' were made by Mr. Mortimer, on whose accuracy in measuring I must entirely rely. It is necessary to state that his measurements were not made with

---

[*] Determined by E. T. Newton, F.R.S., F.G.S.

[†] It will be observed from the plan (fig. 44) that most of the cremated deposits are at the south side of the grave, and that they are sparingly distributed vertically over the grave. Had our excavation reached as far beyond the north as it did on the south side, very probably many cremated deposits would have been found on that side of the grave also. Therefore, the number of burnt bodies remaining in the unexplored portion of the mound might possibly be nearly as great as the number discovered.

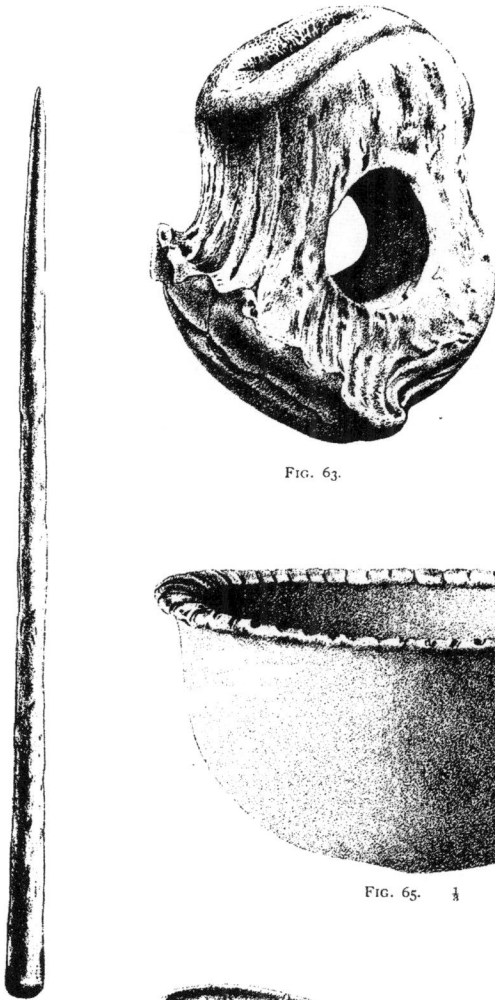

FIG. 64. $\frac{1}{1}$

FIG. 63.

FIG. 65. $\frac{1}{3}$

FIG. 62.
$\frac{2}{3}$

FIG. 66

instruments of such precision as were at my disposal for measuring those of the bones submitted to me, and although I have found some differences between his measurements and my own in the bones of D, I, and K, which we have both measured independently, I have little doubt that his measurements of the bones of the other skeletons which I have not measured are sufficiently correct for comparison with measurements taken before such rigid accuracy as is now required was practised in anthropological research. The measurements made by Mr. Mortimer were supplied to me in inches and parts of inches, but for convenience I have carefully converted them into their equivalent in millimetres. By taking my own and Mr. Mortimer's measurement together, I have been able to calculate the probable stature of seven of the adults, no long bones being found with the eighth adult skull (marked ʝ). In doing this I have used the following formulæ given by Topinard in his *Eléments d' Anthropologie :—*

$$\frac{\text{Femur} + \text{Tibia} \times 100}{49.4} \qquad \frac{\text{Femur} \times 100}{27.1} \qquad \frac{\text{Tibia} \times 100}{23.3} \qquad \frac{\text{Humerus} \times 100}{20.7}$$

"As in my opinion the best and most reliable estimate of stature is obtained from the lengths of the femur and tibia added together, I attach most importance to the results yielded by the first of these formulæ. Having the measurements of both these bones in each of the seven skeletons, I have been able to estimate the stature in this way in each instance, and find that the average of the series is 1 m. 661, or 65.4 inches. Estimated from the length of the femur alone, the average is 11 mm. more, namely 1 m. 672, or about 66 inches, while from the length of the tibia it is 1 m. 575, or about 62 inches.

"The tallest individual was that to whom the skeleton D belonged. His stature estimated from the femur and tibia is 1 m. 927, from the femur alone 1 m. 874, and from the tibia 1 m. 905, or 75.9, 73.8, and 75 inches respectively. It is fortunate that the right femur of this skeleton is preserved, and that its length can be demonstrated to be 508 mm., otherwise it might be thought that there was some mistake regarding its measurement, on account of its being so unusually long. The two shortest skeletons are those marked C and L, each of which have an estimated stature from the femur and tibia of 1 m. 555, or 61.2 inches. From these figures it will be seen that there is a considerable degree of variation in this small series. The occurrence of D measuring 9 inches more than the tallest of the other six, without there being any skeleton correspondingly short, gives an erroneous idea of the average stature of the series. I have, therefore, had resource to Mr. Galton's method of arranging the different specimens according to their centesimal grades, by which means we get rid of the disturbing effects of the extremes at each end of the series, and so obtain the mean of the group. When treated in this way the actual mean stature of the series is 1 m. 628 (64.1 inches). For the information of those who are unacquainted with this method of dealing with statistics, I may state that at the 25th centesimal grade the stature is 1 m. 564 (61.6 inches), the 50th, 1 m. 616, and at the 75th, 1 m. 692 (66.6 inches) ; the value of Q, therefore, is 64 mm., giving a corrected mean for the series of 1 m. 628. This height indicates as nearly as possible, I consider, the mean stature of the persons represented by the skeletons we have to deal with. It is considerably lower than the mean stature of the male population of this country at the present time, which, at prime of life between the ages of 23 and 51, . is 1 m. 715 (67.5 inches), according to the extensive observations of the Anthropo-

metric Committee of the British Association* (See Report for 1882). The
tibiofemoral index, which shows the relative length of the tibia to that of the femur,
varies from 77.7 in G and M to 87.4 in D, and averages in the whole series 81.1, but
excluding D, in which the index is very high, it averages 80 in the 6 other skeletons,
which is almost the same as that given by Broca, Topinard, and Rollet for Europeans.
Although in persons of tall stature Topinard found that the index is somewhat higher
than in short persons (averaging 81.1 in males with statures between 1 m. 70 and 2
m. 06, and 79.7 in those with statures varying from 1 m. 43 to 1 m. 60) the index is so
high in D as to lead us to suspect that some error has occurred in recording the
length of the tibia in that skeleton.

"The index of Platycnemism, or the relation between the transverse breadth of
the tibia to its antero-posterior diameter was ascertained only in the two specimens K
and I which were measured by me ; in the former it is 64.9, and in the latter 67.6,
giving an average of 66.3 for the two specimens. The measurements for this index
were taken by Busk's method about 4 cm. below the nutrient foramen of the bone.
The average index in English people is 73, so that the specimens from Howe Hill
Barrow, are markedly platycnemic as compared with the existing inhabitants.

"To trace the relations of. the people represented by these skeletons, it is
necessary to study, as far as materials will permit, the characters and dimensions
of those of the earlier races who have successively inhabited various parts of England.
For this purpose, I have calculated the stature of all the Barrow specimens of adult
males described in the 'Crania Britannica' by Dr. Barnard Davis. As, however,
he only gives the dimensions of the femur, I have only been able to do so from it, and
not from the femur and tibia, as I would have preferred to do. The results are as
follows :—The average stature of 8 Long Barrow skeletons is 1 m. 698 (66.8 inches),
the average length of the femur being 460 mm., while that of twelve Round Barrow
skeletons is 1 m. 793 (70.6 inches).

" Between the average stature, estimated from the femur, of the Howe Hill series,
which I have previously stated, is 1 m. 672, and that of the Long Barrow specimens,
the difference is only 26 mm. ; while between the former and Round Barrow series it
is 118 mm. It is therefore clear that the skeletons from Howe Hill correspond very
closely to Dr. Barnard Davis's Long Barrow series, which, I may mention, includes
specimens from Yorkshire, Staffordshire, Gloucestershire, and Wiltshire, from which
counties also the Round Barrow specimens were likewise obtained. The tallest Long
Barrow skeleton in the 'Crania Britannica' series has an estimated stature of 1 m.
874, his femur being 508 mm. long, which is exactly the same length as the longest
femur from Howe Hill ; the shortest man has an estimated stature of 1 m. 546, which
is also exactly the same as that of the shortest skeleton from Howe Hill. The range
of variation in stature of both series is practically the same ; in both there is a
disturbing element owing to the presence of an unusually tall individual, which raises
the average stature of each group to a figure higher than it should be. To get at the
true mean stature of the groups, I have again employed Mr. Galton's graphic method,
which shows that the stature at the 25th and 75th centesimal grades is respectively
1 m. 585, and 1 m. 715 in the Howe Hill specimens, and 1 m. 652, and 1 m. 730 in the
Long Barrow series, the respective values of Q (*i.e.*, half the difference between the

---

* When these observations, as tabulated, are treated by Mr. Galton's method of centesimal grades, the
corrected mean stature is 1 m. 703 (67 inches).

statures at each of these two grades), are 65 and 39 mm., giving to the former series a corrected mean stature at the 50th grade of 1 m. 650, and the latter of 1 m. 691, the observed mean of the former being 1 m. 653, and of the latter 1 m. 702.

"On the other hand, the tallest Round Barrow skeleton in the 'Crania Britannica' has an estimated stature of 1 m. 920 (75.6 inches), and the shortest of 1 m. 686 (66.3 inches), while the rest of the series range themselves regularly between these extremes.

"In the 'Memoirs of the Anthropological Society of London,' Vol. III, p. 41, Dr. Thurnam gives the average length of the femur of 25 males from Long Barrows as 457 mm., which gives an estimated stature of 1 m. 686, while the femur in 27 males from Round Barrows averaged 477.5, which gives an average stature in them of 1 m. 761.

"The Howe Hill specimens may also be compared with skeletons obtained by General Pitt Rivers, from Rotherley, Woodcuts, and Winklebury. The medium stature of 11 skeletons found at Rotherley was 1 m. 562 (61.5 inches), and of 7 from Woodcuts which were rather more mixed in type, 1 m. 644 (64.7 inches).

"The general conformation of the skulls obtained from these two places agrees with that of the Howe Hill series in being, as we shall afterwards see, markedly dolichocephalic. On the other hand, the medium stature of 12 Anglo-Saxon skeletons from Winklebury was 1 m. 700. Thus, we see that the stature of the Howe Hill Barrow series agrees very closely with that of the dolichocephalic race in the Pitt Rivers series, and is considerably less than that of the Anglo-Saxons in the same collection. The tibiæ of the Rotherley specimens are somewhat platycnemic, the average index in these being 70.2.

"SKULL—*Characters of the Calvarial portion.*—The ridges for muscular attachments on the cranial vault are of very moderate size, but in one or two instances are fairly well developed in the stephanic region. The under surface, however, presents a marked contrast to the upper in this respect, the superior curved line of the occiput being in some cases very strongly developed; a well-marked torus is present in three specimens, and a smaller one on a fourth; the other muscular attachments on the base are well-marked except the mastoid processes, which are only moderately large. The bones forming the calvarial vault, are thick and heavy, and in one instance might be called massive. The sutures are moderately closed in some specimens and obliterated in others; stenosis of the sagittal suture is present in a greater or less degree in the majority of cases. Where the sutures can be traced their character is simple. In only one instance are worm-eaten bones present, these are of small size and situated in the lambdoidal suture. The antero-posterior outline or curve of the calvaria is regular; in one case the forehead is vertical, in several it is low, and in others its curve is medium. Occipital elongation occurs only once, and in that instance it is probably more apparent than real, owing to post-mortem distortion. I may mention here that post-mortem distortion of some kind is noticeable in almost all the specimens, but varies in character; sometimes affecting the right and sometimes the left side. When viewed from above, the outline of the calvaria is seen to vary considerably; in four cases it may be described as extremely long and narrow, the forehead rounded, narrow, and with the orbital processes little marked; the sides straight, and the occiput elongated; in three specimens it is somewhat shorter and broader, and more or less pear-shaped in form, or, as it has been termed by some

E

writers, 'coffin-shaped.' In one of these latter (L) the forehead is very rounded, the frontal bosses are well-marked, and the occipital region terminates very abruptly, so as to give a truncated appearance to the back of the head. The fourth specimen (G) presents characters intermediate between these two kinds; it agrees with the first four in being long and narrow, but in the details of its outline it agrees with the second three. When the skulls are placed in a row and viewed from the front, the form of the arch of the cranial vault is observed to be very characteristic, being pointed in the first four specimens, while it is flat in the other four. These varieties in the form of the cranial arch are equally observable when the skulls are looked at from behind. As the differences mentioned seem to me to be no mere accidental variations, but probably racial, I have divided the series into two groups, the first of which is composed of the specimens C, D, I, and K, while the second includes G, L, J, and M. It will be noted that the skull of the primary interment belongs to the first group. The immature specimens F and H belong to this group.

"On each parietal bone of J, just above the parietal boss, a rounded opening occurs, that on the left side being 33 mm., and that on the right 20 mm. in diameter, the edges are bevelled inwards, and from them stellated fracture rays extend. There is little doubt that these holes are the result of sharp and quick blows delivered with considerable force, and would have been sufficient to have caused the death of the person. The skull was found by itself without the rest of the skeleton, in the middle of the grave below the centre of the barrow.

"*Characters of the facial portion.*—The broken condition of the facial portion of the skull renders it impossible to give anything like a satisfactory description of the characters of the face, but it appears to be longer in proportion to its breadth in the first group than in the second. As a rule the facial bones harmonise with those of the calvaria, except in L, in which the weakness of the former presents a marked contrast to the massiveness of the latter.

"The glabella and superciliary regions vary from being almost quite flat in some specimens to being moderately or even markedly developed in others. In the case where it is most developed (I), the superciliary bosses and the glabella form a continuous ridge across the forehead. The orbits appear to be set at about the same angle with the horizontal in each case, and their upper margins are thin; in form they are broadened rectangular to nearly square in the specimens complete enough to admit of their shapes being determined.

"The nasal spine is small, the lower margins of the nasal openings are sharp and well-defined, the outline in profile of the nasal bones appears to vary within the outlines of Nos. 1, 2, and 3 of Broca's nasal curve. The profile of the upper jaw is straight, or nearly so, there is therefore no tendency to prognatism. The direction of the incisor teeth is vertical. In the majority of cases, the teeth are moderately worn, but in one case (I) they are much worn, and in two (K and J), they are little worn. The last molar is sometimes absent through not being developed. The form of the palate, or rather the outline of the alveolar arch, is somewhat parabolic. The chin is narrow and pointed in the majority of cases, but it is more rounded and less pointed in M.

"*Measurements.*—Turning to the measurements of the skull and comparing them, as far as possible, with the characters observed by inspection, we find that while some of these do not vary much in the two groups, others are markedly different. The measurements of G show that in some respects it agrees with those of the first group, but in the majority it resembles those of the second, among which it has been placed from its general characters.

"The cephalic index of the series ranges from 65.5 to 79.6; five of the crania are hyperdolichocephalic, and one is dolichocephalic, and two are mesaticephalic. All the specimens belonging to the first group, and G, belonging to the second group, are hyperdolichocephalic. The higher cephalic index in the other specimens is due not only to their breadth being greater, but also to their length being less than those of the first group. The cephalic index of L being considerably higher than the others (79.6) is probably due to irregular or premature closure of some of the sutures, which has caused abnormal bulging of the parietal regions, its biauricular or base breadth being only 100 mm., or no less than 20 mm. less than any of the other specimens, so that it cannot be considered quite normal.

"The height measurement and the height to length index are slightly less in the first group than in the second. The appearance of greater height imparted to the eye in the former is therefore due to the want of filling out of their lateral walls, and the acuteness of the arch formed by the upper and curved parts of the parietal bones, as it will be seen that there is little variation in the biauricular diameter in the whole series, except in L, which is unusually narrow in this region. Only in K does the height exceed the maximum breadth. Owing to the imperfect condition of the specimens it was not possible to measure the cranial capacity, but as estimated from the cephalic module of Schmidt it is a little larger in the second group than in the first, though the antero-posterior or sagittal, the horizontal, and the traverse circumferences of the cranium are practically similar in both groups.

"The narrowness of the cranium in the first group is not confined to the maximum breadth only, but extends to the minimum, and the maximum (bistephanic) diameters of the frontal bone, and also to the external biorbital and bizygomatic diameters, all of which are less than in the second group. This shows that the upper part of the face is quite in harmony with the width of the calvaria in each group. The minimum traverse diameter of the maxillary bones, that is, the maximum alveolar breadth, is if anything less in the second group than in the first, while the bigonial diameter of the mandible averages 6 mm. less in the former, showing that the lower part of the face is narrower in them than in the latter, thus reversing the conditions present in the upper part of the cranium. This narrowing of the lower part of the face in the second group appears more accentuated on account of the greater breadth of the upper part, and gives a somewhat wedge-shaped appearance to the face. Details of the characters of the nose, orbits, &c., from the measurements is unfortunately impossible.

"The skulls are in all respects similar to those of Long Barrow specimens which have passed through my hands from different parts of the kingdom, but I have never examined a series of skulls in which there were such a large pro-portion of hyperdolichocephalic specimens. The two types found in this series I have long been familiar with among Long Barrow skulls. That which I have dis-tinguished as Group 2 may be thought from the description to be somewhat like the skulls of the Round Barrow period, but this is not the case, as although somewhat coffin-shaped they are quite distinct from them. It is very unfortunate that in the exploration of this barrow the importance of preserving most carefully every bone of each skeleton found was not understood, as the anatomy of the two types which existed in that remote period has not been worked out yet. As far as I am able to see, there does not seem to be any difference in stature between the two groups, nor was there preference, apparently, as to the places of interment given to the one type more than the other, which were thoroughly mixed together, some of each group were in the grave with the primary interment, and some of both kinds were found outside it.

"Let us now turn to the skulls from Long Barrows described in the 'Crania Britannica' and by Dr. Thurnam in the 'Memoirs of the Anthropological Society of London,' Vol. III., and to the specimens figured by General Pitt Rivers from Rotherley and Woodcuts. The cephalic index of 17 Long Barrow skulls, including the 9 specimens whose height has been estimated from the femur, previously discussed from the 'Crania Britannica,' varies from 67 to 75; 3 are hyperdolichocephalic, 13 dolichocephalic, and 1 mesaticephalic. The measurement of length from which Dr. Davis calculated the index was that from the ophryon to the occiput, which generally is a little shorter than the maximum length measured from the glabella, as now universally done, consequently the cephalic index calculated from the former is somewhat higher, and it is probable that several of the 13 dolichocephalic specimens would have fallen within the limits of the first group had Dr. Davis measured their length from the glabella, many of them having indices, according to him, of 70, 71, and 72. In a more recent paper Dr. Thurnam [*] gives the cephalic index of 48 Long Barrow skulls as varying from 65 to 75. Of these 16 are hyperdolichocephalic, 29 dolichocephalic, and 3 mesaticephalic; their length averaged 195, the breadth 139 mm., the height 143, the face length (probably from the ophryon to the chin) 111 mm., face breadth 128 mm.; the cephalic index of the series averages 71, and the altitudinal index 73. Coming to the same race in post-Roman times we find that the cephalic index in the specimens from Rotherley varied from 68.9 to 82.6, and that 3 were hyperdolichocephalic, 6 dolichocephalic, 3 mesaticephalic, and 1 brachycephalic. The Woodcuts specimens are not so markedly dolichocephalic, and not so pure in character.

"Arranged in tabular form, the cephalic index in these series are as follows :—

	Hyperdolicho-cephalic.	Dolicho-cephalic.	Mesaticephalic.	Brachycephalic.
Howe Hill Barrow...	5	1	2	0
Long Barrows, 'Crania Britannica' ...	3	13	1	0
,, ,, Dr. Thurnam ...	16	29	3	0
Rotherley, General Pitt Rivers ...	3	6	3	1
Woodcuts ...	0	5	7	1

"From this it is evident that the general form of the Howe Hill Round Barrow skulls agrees entirely with the Long Barrow skulls of Davis and Thurnam. In neither group of the Howe Hill skulls, if we except L, which, as I have already said, is an abnormal specimen, have we any approach towards the brachycephalic type, as the only other mesaticeptic specimen is at the lowest end of the group, four above the dolichocephalic group. As it is very imperfect in the posterior part of the base, as it

[*] 'Memoirs Anthrop. Soc., Lond.,' vol. iii., p. 41.

is shorter than any of the others, it is not unlikely that in drying, the unsupported part of the occipital may have curved inwards somewhat and so reduced the length, in which case it would also fall into the dolichocephalic group.

" I have not been able to compare these specimens from Howe Hill with any of the actual specimens described by Drs. Davis and Thurnam, but I have done so with drawings of them. On plate 33 of the ' Crania Britannica ' is an engraving and on the opposite page of the letterpress are some woodcuts of a skull from West Kennet Barrow in Wiltshire, of which the cephalic index is 67.0 ; both of these specimens resemble the skull C from Howe Hill. Again on plate 59 we have an engraving of a skull from the Long Barrow of Rodmarton, Gloucestershire, with a cephalic of 72 which agrees in its characters with M of our series. The skull depicted on plate 5 from the Long Barrow of Ulley, Gloucestershire, fairly represents D, I, and K of our series. In the ' Crania Britannica,' therefore, we have specimens from the Long Barrows which represent very accurately both groups of our series from Howe Hill Barrow. I need scarcely occupy space in comparing them with the Round Barrow skulls described by Drs. Davis and Thurnam, as these are all brachycephalic and of very different type, except in cases where crossing has occurred.

" Having established the fact, sufficiently clear I hope, of the identity as regards the physical characteristics of the Howe Hill specimens with the Long Barrow race, there remains to be considered the question of the archæological evidence of their affinities. For this we have to refer to the abstract of Mr. Mortimer's notes which I made previously to examining the skeletons, so as to do away with the chance of any bias being produced on my mind by the specimens. In the outer layer of the barrow we find flint, bone, and *iron* implements ; British, Roman, and Anglo-Saxon pottery, and some of more recent date ; of animal remains those of dog, red deer, ox, and horse. There were well marked traces of this outer layer having been used for secondary interments, but neither these nor the various explorations which had been previously made had extended beyond this layer. Next there is a layer of Kimeridge Clay 1 foot in thickness, in which no relics were found, which, as it were, cemented in the interior mound containing the interments, which may be considered as the *raison d'être* of the barrow. The inner mound consisted of two layers, in which there were 7 deposits of burnt bones, with flint and bone implements and pieces of food vase. In the inner or core of the barrow were numerous cremated deposits extending to half its thickness, but fewer in number below that. Towards the base line of the barrow and in the central grave we have the skeletons placed in different directions, chiefly lying on one or the other side, with the limbs drawn up towards the body. With them were found in this deeper part of the core, flint implements carefully manufactured, worked flints and flakes, bone pins, some of which were burnt. With K, the primary interment at the bottom of the grave, was a semi-globular vase of Kimeridge Clay, but no cinerary urns were anywhere found ; the animal remains found in connection with the skeletons were those of fox (identified as such by E. T. Newton, Esq., F.R.S.), ox, deer, boar, and beaver. It is a matter of regret that the pieces of bones from the cremated deposits so numerous in the barrow, were not preserved, as it might have been possible to determine from them whether they were human or belonged to domestic or other animals. From these data I think we have undoubtedly to deal with the remains of a Neolithic people interred in an age before metal had been introduced among them. The bronze age, which succeeded the stone period, is totally unrepresented in the barrow, from which I think we may conclude that a considerable interval of time elapsed between the primary interments in the inner mound and the secondary ones in the outer layer.   Although the various flints and other articles found have not, as far as I am aware, been submitted to the examination of a well-known acknowledged expert, the full description which Mr. Mortimer has given us of them leads me to the conclusion that the archæological evidence corroborates the conclusion I have arrived at from the examination of the skeletons, and shows that the people interred in this barrow are identical with the Long Barrow people.

"NOTE.—Since the above was written I have calculated the stature of the skeletons by Rollet's formulæ for the *femur* and *tibia*, which are almost identical with Topinard's latest for these two bones.   The stature from the *humerus* is calculated from Topinard's latest revised formula.

	Humerus x L.	Femur x L.	Tibia x L.	Fem. & Tib.	H. F. & T.
	20.0	27.3	22.0	49.3	...
C ...	1,650	1,556	1,559	1,558	1,588
D ...	...	1,861	2,018	1,931	...
I ...	...	1,608	1,577	1,594	...
K ...	1,710	1,707	1,700	1,703	1,706
G ...	...	1,677	1,618	1,651	...
L ...	...	1,535	1,586	1,558	...
M ...	1,625	1,677	1,618	1,651	1,640
	4,985	11,621	11,676	11,646	4,934
	1,662	1,660	1,668	1,664	1,645
Average excluding D.					
	1,662	1,627	1,610	1,619	

"As the length of the tibia in D is quite out of proportion to that of the femur, I am inclined to think that some error has occurred in recording its measurement. The above formulæ appear to give better results than the earlier ones of Topinard used in the paper, as the estimates from the femur and tibia more closely correspond to one another.   The earlier formulæ are those used by General Pitt Rivers in his works on 'Excavations in Cranborne Chase'; the formulæ used in the paper for the estimate of stature from the lengths of the femur and tibia added together is almost the same as that just given, and the difference between using the one or other is only 3 mm. on the indicated stature ; that is to say, when the divisor 49.4 is used the stature indicated by the answer is 3 mm. less than when 49.3 is used as the divisor.

"The length of the humerus in these specimens being longer than usual, possibly from the longest bone having been measured instead of the mean of the two, Topinard's last formulæ has been given in this additional note in preference to that of Rollet's which would have given a still higher estimate, and therefore differed more from the results given by the other bones."

SKULLS FROM HOWE HILL BARROW, YORKSHIRE.

	(1) Maximum length	(2) Maximum breadth	(3) Basio-bregmatic height	(4) Minimum frontal breadth	(5) Stephanic breadth	(13) Horizontal circumference	(6) Frontal curve length	(7) Parietal curve length	(8) Occipital curve length	(9) Antero-post. curve length (nasion to opisthion)	(10) Length of foramen magnum	(11) Basio-nasal length	(12) Total longitudinal circumference	(14) Auriculo-bregmatic curve length	(15) Bi-auricular breadth	(16) Nasio-mental length	(17) Nasio-alveolar length	(18) Basio-alveolar length	(19) External bi-orbital breadth	(20) Bizygomatic breadth	(21) Maximum breadth of maxillae	(22) Minimum breadth of maxillae	(23) Bigonial breadth	(24) Interorbital breadth	Orbital breadth	Orbital height	Nasal length	Nasal breadth	Palato-maxillary length
C	200	133	—	100	118	536	145	140	113	398	—	—	—	815	c110	120	70	—	104	124	88	60	104	(34)	—	33	c50	c23	53
D	198·5	139	133	87	c116	540	139	147	130	409	—	—	—	814	118	—	—	—	—	—	—	—	—	—	38	33	c54	c25	—
I	205	132	135	94	c111	c500	133	137	123	—	—	—	—	c290	c116	130	73	—	101	c198	102	60	c100	26	38	33	54	48	54
K	198	131	—	—	—	531	suture obliterated	—	—	371	41	114	595	312	121	96	143	—	205	136	190	180	307	26	38	66	104	24	107
Total	794	535	367	281	345	2,107	409	414	248	1,178	41	114	596	1,231	465	346	143	—	205	252	190	235	307	26	—	66	104	48	107
Average	198·5	133·7	133·5	93·7	115	527	136·3	138	121·5	388	41	114	596	810·4	116·2	115·3	71·5	—	102·5	126	95	60	102·3	26	—	33	—	—	53·5
G	205	142	140	106	122	555	133	145	123	401	—	—	—	811	190	124	75	—	114	192	61	57	88	—	—	33	53	c22	—
J	196	140	—	100	c120	c513	200	146	—	—	—	—	—	—	—	—	—	—	c116	—	—	—	—	—	—	—	108	—	—
L	191	152	140	108	125	549	143	146	114	394	43	103	523	341	100	—	64	97	c102	134	!	54	98	c23	40	33	54	c22	54
M	194	145	133	100	129	540	136	139	114	379	43	108	528	309	121	114	139	97	109	138	100	63	106	23	40	33	108	23	54
Total	776	579	413	409	496	2,157	402	430	351	1,174	43	103	523	961	341	238	139	97	441	266	235	235	291	23	40	33	63	69	54
Average	194	144·7	137·7	102·2	124	539	134	143	117	391	43	108	528	810	113·7	119	69·6	97	110·2	133	100	59	97	23	40	33	54	23	54

INDICES.

	Cephalic	Height	Sup. facial	Total facial	Nasal	Stephano-zygomatic	Gnathic	Orbital
C	65·5	—	56·4	103·3 / 96·8	46·9	95·2	—	—
D	68·8	c65·3	—	—	—	—	—	—
I	68·0	—	—	—	46·8	85·9	—	86·8
K	66·2	68·2	56·4	96·8	93·2 / 46·6	181·1	—	86·8
Average	67·1	133·5	56·4	96·8	—	90·5	—	86·8
G	69·3	68·3	56·8	106·4 / 98·9	39·3	92·4	—	—
J	75·3	—	—	—	—	—	—	—
L	79·6	c73·8	—	—	—	96·8	—	—
M	74·7	68·6	47·8 / 117·5 / 85·1	117·5 / 85·1	46·2	96·8	94·2	82·5
Total	298·9	210·2	104·6	179·0	85·5	188·7	94·2	82·5
Average	74·7	70·0	52·3	69·5	42·7	94·8	94·2	82·5

Measurements of the Long Bones, and Stature Estimated from them by Formulæ stated in Paper.

	Humerus.	Femur.	Tibia.	F. and T.	From humerus.	From femur.	From tibia.	From F. T. and H.	From F. T. and T.	Tibio-femoral index.
C	†330	495	343	768	—	—	—	—	—	80·7
D	—	*508r	444	852	1,394	1,569	1,472	1,546	1,555	87·4
I	—	*439	*347‡	*786	—	1,574	1,565	—	1,527	79·0
K	*342r	*465	356	840	1,652	1,690	1,489	1,659	1,591	80·2
G	—	458	314	814	—	1,719	1,605	—	1,700	77·7
L	—	419	349	768	—	1,690	1,538	—	1,648	84·9
M	325	408	356	814	1,570	1,690	1,528	1,596	1,555	77·7
Total	997	3,173	2,569	5,742	4,816	11,707	11,025	4,890	11,624	5,070
Average	332	453	367	820	1,605	1,672	1,575	1,600	1,661	81·1

* Means measured by myself; when only one bone has been measured it is marked r or l as it was right or left:—Femur, r 488, l 440; Tibia, r 348, l 346; Femur, r 407, l 463 worn

All measurements unmarked have been supplied to me by Mr. Mortimer.

† The relation which the length of the tibia bears to that of the femur shows that probably some error has occurred in measuring, as the record of the measurement of the tibia in D.

‡ The average tibio-femoral index of the six specimens, omitting D, is 800.

Four parcels of disjointed and splintered bones scattered in the body of the mound, and found under the dome-shaped bed of blue clay, have been submitted to Mr. E. T. Newton, F.R.S., who has supplied me with the following list of animals, which he has been able to identify.

Parcel No. 1, containing the bones found immediately over the grave B, comprised :—

> Bos taurus, probably var. longifrons.
> Capreolus caprea (Roebuck).

Parcel No. 2, taken from the soily material at the base of the barrow, contained :—
> Homo sapiens (human).
> Cervus elaphus (red deer).
> Bos taurus (calf)? var. longifrons.
> Canis vulpes (fox).
> Sheep or goat.
> Gnawed bones,

Parcel No. 3. The bones were removed from the body of the mound at depths varying from 13 to 18 feet, and consisted of :—
> Homo sapiens.
> Bos taurus? var. longifrons.
> Sus scrofa (pig).
> Canis vulpes (fox).
> Sheep or goat.

Parcel No. 4, taken 3 feet below the bed of blue clay, included the bones of :—
> Canis vulpes (fox).
> Capreolus caprea (Roebuck).

Referring to Dr. Garson's descriptions of the skeletons it will be observed, probably with some surprise, that he had met with no female bones, the 8 adult specimens all belonging to males. The height of the tallest he calculated to have been about 6 feet 3 inches, and the shortest about 5 feet 1¼ inches. It will also be noticed that their average height and cranial measurements correspond very closely with those usually found in Long Barrow interments, and are very different in type from other Round Barrow specimens with which Dr. Garson has compared them. But according to the prevalent theory the Round Barrows were raised by a round skulled race, and the Long Barrows by men with long skulls—a theory which is decidedly negatived by the evidence obtained from this Round Barrow, and also from numerous other examples which have come under my observation. It is to be regretted that Dr. Garson has omitted giving the approximate ages of the 8 adults. From my own examination of the teeth at the time when I was engaged in repairing the crania, I was led to believe the ages of the adults varied from 18 to 70, or even more, whilst those of the children extended down to the period of infancy. From this it would seem that in the grave and immediately above it there must have been the representatives of three generations who had, from some cause or another, been buried at the same time. As there was no break in the layers of soil covering the grave, this must be taken as affording a proof that no intrusive interment had taken place at any subsequent period.

As a specialist Dr. Garson naturally attaches the greater importance to the collecting of the osseous remains. But an ordinary archæologist probably considers the collecting of other relics more important than securing the bones, for these are, except in the hands of a specialist, comparatively useless. I possess nearly two cart loads of crania and other portions of human skeletons (properly labelled and stored away) which have been collected at various periods from British barrows.

From a more recent examination made of no less than forty of the cremated deposits obtained from Howe Hill, now in my possession, I found them to consist of about twenty-five per cent. of infants and young children, and about sixty-five per cent. whose ages appeared to range from boyhood to manhood ; while there did not seem to be more than ten to fifteen per cent. assignable to very old persons judging from the closed sutures observed in the fragments of the skulls.

It is difficult to avoid speculating as to the meaning of such a large number being met with in the mound. Why were they burnt and dispersed in the manner and in such abundance as that in which we found them? Were they the remains of slaves or servants, who, with their families (as they were evidently of all ages), had been sacrificed and interred during the raising of the mound?

The absence of any cinerary urn, food vase, or flint instruments with these cremated deposits is significant, and would seem to imply that very little respect or care was bestowed on their disposal. They appear to have been placed merely in small heaps, occasionally comprising more than one body, as the mound was being raised. If these deposits were not the remains of cremated attendants they may have been those of prisoners taken during a war with some hostile clan.

The disjointed and fractured bones found during the excavations most probably represented the animals that were slaughtered and eaten by the builders of the mound. Their presence in this instance can scarcely be otherwise accounted for. The bones of the fox having been taken from each division of the mound under the blue clay show that these animals were then numerous and used as food. As regards the human bones, two of which are the lower ends of humeri belonging to adult persons, they show the sharply jagged fractures * similar to those observed on the splintered animal bones, with which they were associated. The larger portion of the humerus is blackened in consequence of having been scorched, probably in cooking the flesh.

The human bones which had been broken, whilst in a similar fresh condition, might also have been the remains of feasts. Cannibalism has undoubtedly existed at one time or another all over the world, and probably this repulsive practice would long survive, especially at great funeral gatherings or other religious ceremonies. As before stated, very few bones were found in the large mass of rough chalk forming that portion of the mound above the bed of blue clay, with the exception of those met with in the disturbed portion at the apex of the barrow. These, as already mentioned, were detached and broken bones of the ox, the dog, and the horse, also a few human bones. The remains of the horse were not found below this disturbed portion of the mound. All these were evidently of a secondary character, belonging to an unknown but comparatively

---

* Bones which have been buried for a long time lose their gelatine, and consequently break short like the rotten decayed branch of a tree without showing any splintering.

recent period ; probably they were Anglo-Saxon interments. These bones were
not included in the collection submitted to Mr. Newton for determination.

In conclusion it can only be observed that in spite of the efforts of this ancient
race to perpetuate the memory of their dead, how scanty is the record which
reaches us, and how great are the blanks which still remain in our knowledge of
their lives and their customs even after we have, by careful search, exhausted every
evidence from their burial mounds. But the little we have been able to gather,
and now place upon record, will, we trust, remain in some degree as a memorial,
even though vague, of the savage customs and low culture under which this
early people lived.

BARROWS Nos. 291, 292, and 293

Are three mounds in Howe Hill Field, on Duggleby North Wold, near the
northern escarpment of the chalk hills. They are arranged in a line north and
south, and are about 315 feet apart.

No. 291 was partly opened by Canon Greenwell in 1866, and the following
extract in reference thereto is quoted from his "British Barrows," page 140:—
"Upon Duggleby Wold there was at one time a group of three barrows lying
very close together. Of these, one was removed several years since, and of the
two remaining I opened the larger. This was 74 feet in diameter and 6 feet high.
The upper part consisted of layers of loamy earth, below which the material
employed was very stiff clay, with chalk and flints intermixed. Twenty-five feet
south of the centre was an oblong hollow with rounded ends, excavated in the
chalk, 6 feet by 4¾ feet, and 2½ feet deep, and having a direction south-west by
north-east. Like nearly all of these enigmatical holes, it contained nothing besides
the filling-in of earth and clay. Twelve feet south of the centre there was another
hole, 2 feet in diameter and 1½ feet deep, containing, like the larger one, nothing
more than the filling-in. At the centre was a flat-topped conical mound, composed
of chalk rubble, 1½ feet high and 4 feet in diameter at the top. Upon the flat
summit was a layer of charcoal, and upon it was deposited the body, apparently,
of a man, laid on the right side, with the head to west, but in such a decayed
state that the position of the hands could not be ascertained. At the hips were
two flint flakes, and close to the body were four flint chippings and three water-
worn quartz pebbles. Beyond the head were four holes, made apparently by the
ends of stakes, similar to some found in a grave under a barrow on Ganton Wold,
and which are fully described in the sequel.* These now under notice were
10 inches deep, and varied from 1½ inches to 2 inches in diameter. Three of them
were angular and one round, and the remains of the decayed wood in the holes
were quite distinct. On both the east and west sides of the central mound was
a similar one, but without any layer of charcoal, and showing no signs of a body
having ever been placed upon either of them. Within the barrow were a few
potsherds, some chippings of flint, a well-formed flint flake 2¾ inches long, much
worn by use along both edges, and a thin piece of sandstone, 4 inches long,
1⅜ inches wide at the narrow end and 1¾ at the broader, the latter being rounded.
The surface is quite smooth, apparently from use, and the stone seems as though
it might have served for rubbing down hides or some similar purpose."

* "British Barrows," page 170.

August 12th to 18th, 1895, under the patronage of Sir Tatton Sykes, Bart.,
I opened the three mounds of this group, commencing first with the one partly
opened by Canon Greenwell, thinking that something more might be discovered.
This mound (No. 291 of our series) is the centre one of the group, and the
largest of the three. Its present diameter is 78 feet and height 4 feet, having
lost 2 feet of its elevation since 1866, partly from the cultivation of the
land, and had become much flattened at the top. We turned over an area in the
centre measuring 14 yards north and south by 7 yards east and west, and trenched
the ground beneath to the bed rock, at distances of a foot apart, but no grave
could be found. About 3 yards north of the centre, at the base of the mound,
we picked up a flint spear-head 4½ inches long (fig. 41*b*), and a grit-stone
pounder. There were indications that an interment had entirely decayed, though
no remains of a body were found. From the substance of the barrow we took
a flint knife, three good scrapers, many flakes and rudely chipped flints, but no
potsherds or fragments of bone were observed.

No. 292 is the most southerly barrow. Its diameter measured 65 feet and
elevation 4½ feet. It had evidently never been previously opened. Under the apex
was a core of blue clay brought from a distance, 18 inches in thickness. As in
the previous barrow, we turned over a portion 36 feet by 18 feet, and probed the
ground below. Near the centre, about 18 inches from the tilled surface, we found
about three parts of a flat-bottomed dish-shaped vessel of apparently late mediæval
date. This dish had been inverted over something which had decayed, and
appeared to have been broken and a portion of it carried away by the plough.
A few feet north of the centre, at a depth of 15 inches, were two arrow-heads, one
barbed, the other wing-shaped.

Eight feet south of the centre, on the original surface, were traces of a
decayed body, and a portion (about 8 inches long) of some article of hard wood
which had been well shaped into four sides about 1 inch in width.

Eight feet north of the centre was a small grave about 18 inches deep, filled
with clayey matter resembling that of the mound above, and on the bottom was
a thin covering of burnt wood, but no trace of human remains.

From the mound were taken 10 flint flake saws, several of which show distinct
appearances of having been used, one punch-shaped tool, many flakes and several
worked pieces of flint of doubtful use.

No. 293 is the mere site of the northern barrow of this group which, as
mentioned by Canon Greenwell, was removed many years ago by Mr. Heseltine,
the then tenant of the land. We trenched the ground under all the central
area of this barrow, but could not find any trace of a grave.

No. II.—THE WHARRAM PERCY GROUP.

THE ten barrows comprising this small series are situated a little to the west of the last group, and the central ones are somewhat crowded together. Only eight of these barrows are shown on the Ordnance Map. They form a link in the chain of groups which cling to the elevated western edge of the wolds.

BARROW No. 45,

Which had not been observed by the Ordnance Surveyors, is the most easterly of this series, and is situated towards the north-west of Wharram Percy House.

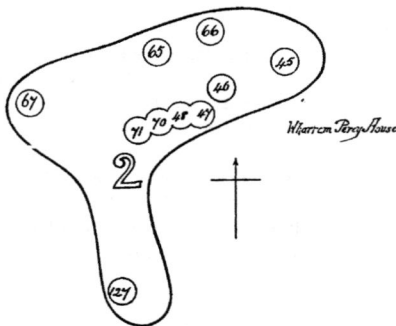

FIG. 67.
The Wharram Percy Group.

From February 26th to the second week in March, 1866, we explored No. 45 barrow, and three others to be next described. First we turned over the greater portion of this small mound, and near the centre came upon a dish-shaped hole scooped into the old turf-line to a depth of 12 inches, and having a diameter of 18 inches at the top. The upper half of this receptacle was filled with unctuous earth, freely mixed with wood ashes, and the lower half contained burnt human bones, from which we took a portion of a bronze instrument much burnt. The diameter of this mound was 35 feet, while, in consequence of tilling the land, its height was only 8 to 9 inches, the passage of the plough having destroyed the upper portion of the dish-like hollow. Three splinters of flint and a spear head of the same material were found in the mound.

April 10th, 1883.—We re-opened this mound, but nothing more was found.

BARROW No. 46

Is a little to the south-west of the last, and the most easterly of a line of five contiguous barrows standing on the high ground called Greenlands. Its diameter was 66 feet, with an elevation of 2 feet above the adjoining surface, and 18 inches above the natural ground beneath it. We removed from the heart of this barrow a square mass measuring 17 feet each way. This operation, however, only resulted in our finding five small hand-struck flakes of black flint and a fragment of British pottery.

We next cut trenches outside the central excavation, but in these also failed to find any interment.* Pieces of burnt wood and twelve more flint flakes were picked up from the base of the mound.

---

* One of the workmen remarked that the mound was a "deaf 'un" (meaning an empty one).

PLATE IX.

FIG. 69.   ¼

FIG. 68.   ½

FIG. 70.   ¼

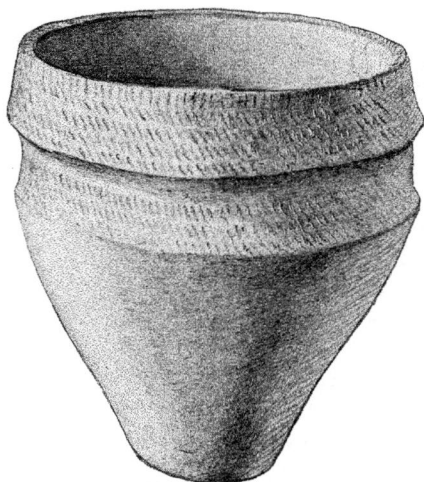

FIG. 73.   ⅓

FIG. 71.   ¼

FIG. 74.   ¼

FIG. 72.   ⅓

FIG. 75.   ¼

Re-opening.—On April 13th and 14th, 1883, we were permitted to satisfy ourselves as to the possibility of having missed the principal interment at the time of our first opening, by again turning over the greater portion of the mound and trenching the ground beneath. It was then observed that at our first opening we had followed to some extent a disturbed piece of ground under the barrow. This particular spot was now found to be a grave measuring 7 feet east and west, 5 feet north and south, and 2 feet deep. No inhumed body was found, but as the grave had been dug in a ferruginous subsoil such an interment may have entirely disappeared. In close contact with the west end of the grave, at the bottom, was a small heap of burnt bones belonging to a child, near to which stood a small food vase (fig. 68). This relic seemed, from its position, to belong to the cremated remains, and not to an inhumed body which might have entirely disappeared.

BARROW No. 47

Had a diameter of 70 feet and an elevation of 2 feet 3 inches when measured from the old ground surface beneath it. Our plan in this instance, as well as in that of several other barrows of this group, was first to cut away from the centre of the mound an 18 ft. square, and afterwards, if necessary, to make small excavations in other places. Under the mound, near the centre, a slight rise was observed, and the old surface-line was covered with a thin layer of soil reddened by fire. Immediately above this was a bed of blue clay, 12 inches thick in the centre, but thinning towards the edge. This bed extended all over the surface of the excavation, and seemed to be of circular form. Three splinters of black flint were all that was found in the mound.

In removing the slight rise in the centre already named (which was found to be the upper part of a boat-shaped mass of clayey matter, filling the upper portion of an oval grave and pointing east and west), only two pieces of black flint, apparently shaped for slinging, were picked up. At a depth of about 18 inches in the grave, and within three inches of the bottom of the boat-shaped mass, was a much-decayed body, doubled up. This rested on a layer of unctuous clay 3 inches in thickness, and above it, to a height of 18 inches, the clayey earth was of a dark colour, and contained several irregularly-formed cavities, measuring from 2 to 8 inches in length and having greasy-looking sides, indicating decayed matter. As we got deeper the grave became circular, and at a depth of 2 feet 7 inches the bottom was reached, which measured $2\frac{1}{2}$ feet in diameter. Upon this was a heap of burnt human bones, occupying a space of 20 inches east and west, and 9 inches in the opposite direction. At the west end of this deposit was an unburnt bone pricker, $1\frac{3}{4}$ inches long, with a circular hole through the head (fig. 69), probably an instrument used for piercing skins; also a knife of black flint (fig. 70), $2\frac{3}{4}$ inches long and $1\frac{1}{4}$ inches broad, together with a punch-like article or chipping tool (fig. 71) of flint, nearly $3\frac{1}{2}$ inches long, about the thickness of a man's little finger and triangular in section nearly the whole of its length. The ends, which are obtusely pointed, are somewhat polished and show signs of use. Oddly enough, this tool has a white vitreous appearance from having been subjected to the action of fire, although the knife and bodkin show no sign of this. About 7 inches above the elongated heap of calcined bones, and 12 inches north-eastwards, stood a food-vase (fig. 72) in an erect position, which contained nothing but a small quantity of greasy-looking earth at the bottom. It measures 5½ inches in height, 7¼ inches across the mouth, 8½ inches in the thickest part, and 3½ inches across the bottom. The upper edge of the mouth has a chevron pattern formed of rude cuts about ½ inch in length ; two similar lines run round the outside just beneath the lip, and below these are four rows of vertical gashes, followed by a band of three rows of punctures made by means of a blunt and slightly-notched tool. Three more rows of vertical gashes extend to the bottom of the vase. A quantity of clay was observed throughout the mound.

BARROW No. 48

Has a radius of 25 feet and an altitude of 1 foot, and lies about 70 yards to the west of the last barrow. While digging near the centre, one of the workmen struck his pick into a cinerary urn, which had been inverted over burnt bones, placed on the old surface-line. The bottom of the urn being so near the upper part of the mound, a portion of it had been previously carried away by the plough. After having been restored from the recovered fragments (see fig. 73), it measured 10 inches high, 9 inches in diameter at the mouth, and 10 inches at the widest part. About 5 feet northwards from the urn a circular dish-shaped hollow, 3½ feet in diameter, had been scooped through the ancient surface-soil into the subsoil below, to the depth of 16 inches, and was charged with burnt soil mixed with a large proportion of wood ashes, a few burnt human bones adhering to the sides. Around the edge were traces of great heat, indicating that most probably the ashes and burnt soil had been thrown into it and covered up while intensely hot. A thin layer of blue clay shrouded this receptacle and its contents. Two very rough sling-stones of native flint taken from the body of the barrow were all the relics found.

April 11th, 1883.—A re-opening was made, but nothing more was discovered.

BARROW No. 70

Was opened July 23rd, 24th, and 25th, 1866. This measured 70 feet in diameter, and 5 feet 4 inches from base to apex, and had been lowered but little by the plough. A circular mass 20 feet in diameter was cut away from the centre without finding any interment ; but at the base there were two heaps of chalk rubble, resting on the old turf-line, indicating a grave. In the centre of the mound a small circular hole was observed, probably the bed of an upright stake* two inches in diameter, and rising perpendicularly from the base to a height of 2½ feet into the body of the mound. The mound consisted mainly of clay brought from a distance, and soil from the neighbourhood, arranged in separate layers and patches, streaked with wood ashes and soil burnt red. From these materials we took two pieces of the neck of a food vessel, 1 slingstone, 2 small discs worked round the edges, and a flake two inches long chipped to a cutting edge, also 27 splinters, all of which, with one exception, being of foreign flint.

* This may have been thus placed so as to mark the grave and keep the centre of the barrow.

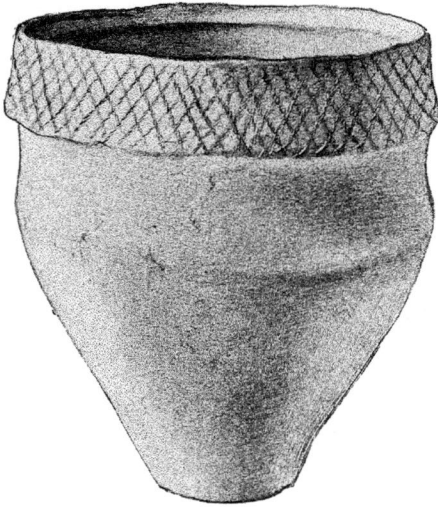

FIG. 79.   ¼   FIG. 78.

FIG. 76.   ⅓

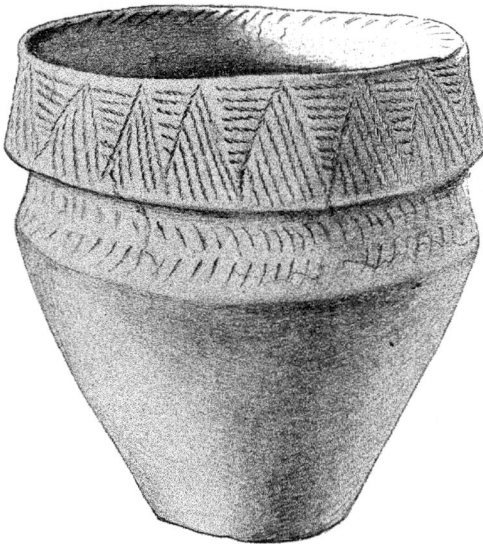

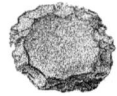

FIG. 80.   ¼

FIG. 77.   ⅓   FIG. 83.   ¼

Not being able to find any disturbance of the ground under the barrow, within the limits of our excavation, excepting in the centre, between the heaps of rubble and vertically below the stake hole, we followed this indication by working carefully downwards, and presently emptied a dish-shaped grave 2 feet deep, 6 feet 9 inches long, south-east and north-west, and 4 feet 9 inches from side to side. At the bottom, on the bare chalk rock, reposed the remains of a young person about 14 years old, on its back, head to the south-east, hands brought to the face, and the knees pulled up and pressed over to the left side. A femur measured $14\frac{1}{4}$ inches, tibia $11\frac{1}{4}$ inches, and humerus $10\frac{1}{4}$ inches. No food-vase accompanied the body, but close to the right side of the head was a small hole in the floor of the grave, which may have served the purpose of a vase, as it contained what appeared to be decayed or partly-burnt bone mixed with dark matter. Two articles of jet resembling studs, (figs. 74 and 75),[*] which probably had been used for securing some garment, or worn as ornaments in the ears, were found close to the neck and partially under the much-crushed skull. The body was covered and the grave everywhere occupied with a lenticular mass, consisting of very impervious blue clay, in many places stained black, closely resembling the filling-in of numerous other graves described in these pages. It also contained, as did barrow 47, many small greasy-sided cavities, apparently caused by something that had decayed. From the material filling the grave 13 splinters of foreign and 3 of native flint, 3 chipped sling-stones, and 4 pieces worked round the ends or around the sides were taken. All or nearly all of these must have been cast over and into the grave at the time of covering the body.

This barrow has not been re-opened, but might possibly yield something more, as it may be we did not quite reach the bottom of the grave.

BARROW No. 71

Is the most south-westerly of a line of five barrows. On July 25th, 1866, its altitude was 18 inches, and diameter 44 feet. In the centre of the barrow stood a cinerary urn (fig. 76) measuring 9 inches high, 8 inches across the rim, and 9 inches across the shoulders, with its mouth only 7 inches from the surface of the mound. It is adorned with impressions made by a rope or twisted thong, and was about half full of burnt bones unaccompanied by any relic. Directly under this one, in a hole a little below the base of the mound, was a second cinerary urn (fig. 77) inverted, $10\frac{1}{2}$ inches high, $9\frac{1}{2}$ inches in diameter at the mouth, and $10\frac{1}{2}$ inches at the widest part. It was completely filled with the finely-calcined bones of an adult, with which was the greater portion of the horn of a roebuck, showing traces of fire, and some pieces of leg bones, probably from the same animal; also a bone hair-pin (fig. 78) made from the longitudinal half of a leg bone of some small animal. This pin is $3\frac{1}{2}$ inches long, with a hole through its head, and is much distorted by the action of fire.[†] A third urn seemed to have

---

[*] Mr. Thos. Boynton, of Bridlington, has an exceedingly fine pair of large studs of jet, of a similar pattern. He bought them at a sale at Peak Hall, near Robin Hood's Bay, in August, 1895. It is almost certain that they had been found in opening a barrow some 35 years previously, on the Peak near Robin Hood's Bay.

[†] The finding of two cinerary urns placed one over the other in this way is of rare occurrence.

been destroyed by the plough, as we picked several pieces of its base from the surface of the barrow. From the mound near the interments we took seven splinters and one pointed instrument of flint.

Re-opened April 9th, 1883.—A further search was made without finding anything more.

BARROW No. 65

Lies to the northward of the five barrows situated in the centre of this group, and, although not mapped by the Ordnance surveyors, stands prominently on the brink of Birdsall Brow, at an altitude of 600 feet above the sea level. On June 4th, 1866, when we opened it, its height was 5 feet and its diameter north-east and south-west 42 feet, and it had been originally nearly conical in form. Nearly all along this elevated edge of the chalk escarpment, old landslips are visible, and about one-third of this mound, at its northern extremity, had at some time subsequent to its erection participated in one of those movements. It had slipped down the slope, but fortunately the displacement had not reached the grave in the centre of the barrow. At the commencement of our operations the crushed skull and other bones of a child were found near the summit, and above the grave. From this point downwards to the bottom of the grave, detached and broken human bones were profusely mixed with the chalk, which alone formed the mound and filled up the grave. It was surprising to find that no clay was present, although any quantity could have been obtained at the foot of the escarpment about 100 yards away. The bones belonged to nearly every part of the human frame. The leg bones had been broken crosswise or splintered longitudinally previous to interment, and the pelvis and skull had shared the same fate. The bones of mice and the shells of snails (*Helix arbustorum and H. nemoralis*) were also found scattered about from the apex of the mound to the interment lying on the floor of the grave. At the top we picked up the upper end of a bone pin (fig. 79), and down in the bottom we found the leg bone of a small goat or pig. The grave measured 9 feet west-south-west and east-north-east, 5 feet across, and $3\frac{1}{2}$ feet deep. On the floor of the grave, towards the east-north-east, was the body of an adult (No. 1) on its back, with the knees crushed over to the right side and pulled up almost to the chin; head to the west-south-west, and arms crossing the chest. Between the knees and the left shoulder was a circular piece of flint (fig. 80) flat on both sides, $\frac{1}{8}$ of an inch thick, $\frac{4}{8}$ of an inch in diameter, and chipped all round its edge. A femur measured $18\frac{1}{4}$ inches, tibia $15\frac{1}{4}$ inches, and humerus $12\frac{3}{4}$ inches in length. Near the head of burial No. 1 were the remains of another body (No. 2), on its right side, head pointing in the same direction as No. 1, with the hands near the face. The hips and legs of this body were missing, and a hole large enough to admit the end of one's finger had been punched through the frontal bone of the skull, seemingly the cause of death. One of the humeri measured $12\frac{3}{4}$ inches. Close above the head was part of a tool (fig. 81), made of the rib of an ox, 6 inches long, 1 inch broad, and rounded at the broad end. Similar instruments, which have been described as tools for modelling pottery, have been found. Not the least fragment of an urn was seen in any part of this barrow.

BARROW No. 66

Is also in close proximity to the edge of the chalk escarpment, and a few hundred yards east-north-east of the barrow last described. Opened July 6th, 1866. This small mound then measured 30 feet in diameter and 3 feet high. In the centre, and only a few inches under the sod, were (as in Barrow No. 65), portions of the skull and other bones of a child (Burial No. 1). At an equally shallow depth; but nearly 5 feet to the east-north-east of the centre were the remains of an adult (Interment No. 2), minus the legs and pelvis, which most probably had been removed in recent years while digging for rabbits. The head was to the west-south-west and the hands were brought to the face. Under the head was a small knife (fig. 82) of black flint 1¾ inches long, whilst the crushed remains of a young child (Interment No. 3), lay close to the south-south-east side of the head. After having cut a large section from the centre of this small barrow, we emptied a grave situated exactly under the remains last described; this was 2 feet deep, 6 feet north and south, and 3 feet wide. From the top of this grave the butt-end of a spear head of black flint (fig. 83), 2 inches long, was taken. At the bottom was the body of a youth (Interment No. 4), on the right side, head to the north-north-west, legs pulled up parallel with the trunk, and the arms stretched downwards. The femoral bone was 11½ inches long. Behind the head was part of a crushed food-vase of common form and medium size. Over and round the body were piled large pieces of chalk and flint, which, together with grit and a little soil, filled the grave and formed the mound. No clay had been used, though it occurs in abundance close by. A few fragments of human bone were found at different depths in the grave.

BARROW No. 67

Is also near the verge of the steep escarpment, a little to the west-south-west of the last two, and a short distance to the north-east of "Toisland Barn." On July 9th, 1866, it was found to have a diameter of 52 feet and an elevation of 4½ feet, and to be principally made up of soil obtained from the adjoining land surface, mixed with a small proportion of clay, which increased in quantity towards the centre. This material had been obtained from the foot of the adjoining slope. By excavating, it was found that a filled-in trench, 68 feet in diameter, 3 feet deep, 7½ feet wide at the top, and 1½ feet at the bottom encircled the barrow. This, however, was quite invisible on the surface. An opening was made by cutting a square block from the centre 15 feet wide, in which were found 14 splinters of flint, 2 pieces chipped at the edges (one of which is 1⅞ inches long and may have been used as a knife), 1 small slingstone, and a piece of flint of indefinite shape. All were of foreign flint. A tooth and portion of the leg bone of an ox, 3 pieces of bone, one of which had two notches and some scratches upon the surface made apparently with a flint knife or saw, were also obtained. At the base of the mound, near its centre, and at a depth of 16 inches, was a very crude drinking cup (fig. 84), without any trace of ornamentation upon it. This vessel measured 6½ inches in height, and 5¼ inches across the mouth. It is of a dark texture, and has every appearance of having been hurriedly made from the Kimeridge clay which occurs at the foot of the escarpment close by, and baked

G

probably on the spot when required. It stood close to the south side of the crushed skull of an infant, which was placed with its head near the east end of the grave, and in a position nearly similar to that of an adult body found below, shortly to be described.

Slightly lower, about 4 feet westwards and near the centre, was a heap of burnt bones of an adult, unaccompanied by any relic. At the bottom of the grave, in the centre, was a small oval enclosure formed of rough pieces of chalk and flint, placed close to each other, each being almost the size of a man's head. Within this rude cist—if it may be so termed—was the skeleton of a young man of large stature, laid on its back, and doubled up into the smallest possible compass ; head to the east, knees almost touching the chin, and the hands brought up to the side of the head. A femur and humerus measured respectively 20 inches and 14 inches. The skull and other bones were much fractured by the settling of the rough chalk everywhere present. No clay was found in this grave. Part of the leg bone of an ox was noticed on the floor a little east of the skull, and was probably the remains of food placed there at the time of burial. Behind the pelvis were two black flints, one being a short javelin head (fig. 85), 2¾ inches long, 1¼ inches broad, and ⅜ of an inch thick. The other (fig. 86), was a thin outer flake from a flint nodule, chipped to a cutting edge on one side, 1⅞ inches long, 1 inch broad, and may have served indifferently as a knife or scraper. Under the finger bones of each hand was a worked flint. That from the right hand (fig. 87), consists of black flint 1½ inches long and 1 inch wide, and has both ends obtusely pointed by chipping. The other (fig. 88), which has evidently been struck from a piece of native grey flint, is 1⅜ inch long, 1 inch broad, and has one end rounded by chipping. A patella (knee-cap) was found half-way down by the side of the femur, and a top front tooth was found close to the middle of the shaft of the right humerus.* The depth of the grave was 4 feet 10 inches below the base of the barrow, or 9 feet 4 inches measured from its apex, with a length of 8 feet east and west and a width of 5 feet, the ends being slightly rounded.

BARROW No. 127

Stands half a mile south-south-east of the last. It is cut asunder and partly invaded by an old entrenchment which at the east end of "Vessey Pasture Dale" branches from similar earthworks and runs up the west side of "Back Dale" plantation, close by barrow No. 70. This earthwork then joins the line of entrenchments running eastward along the escarpment from Birdsall Brow to Birdsall Wold, and then on to Wharram Percy. The accompanying plan and section (figs. 89 and 90) show the relationship of this barrow with the entrenchments, and the curious mutilation of the former by the latter. This section seems to indicate that the entrenchments have been erected by a later people than the barrow builders.

* At first it was difficult to account for these displacements, but finding that the tooth filled an empty socket in the jaw, as accurately as did any of those remaining, it became evident that these displacements had been accomplished by mice ; these little animals at some time having made their way through the substance of the mound, down through the open material filling the grave, until they reached the body. The remains of mice, as well as the shells of snails (*Helix nemoralis* and *H. arbustorum*) were found at all depths round the three interments. I have never found with any British interment a single specimen of the common garden snail—*Helix aspersa*.

FIG. 81. $\frac{1}{2}$

FIG. 82. $\frac{1}{1}$

FIG. 84. $\frac{1}{3}$

FIG. 85. $\frac{3}{4}$

FIG. 86. $\frac{1}{1}$

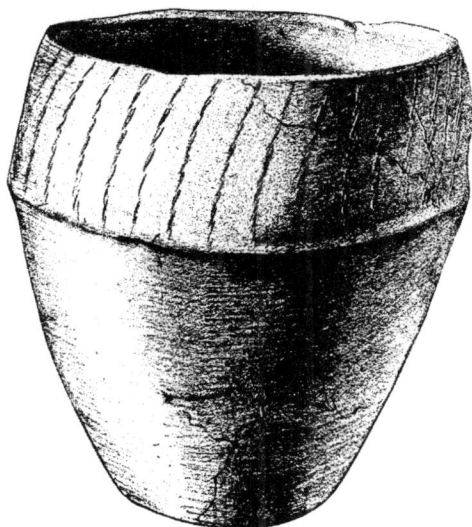

FIG. 91. $\frac{1}{4}$

FIG. 87. $\frac{1}{1}$

FIG. 88. $\frac{1}{1}$

On November 2nd and 3rd, 1868, an excavation 15 feet wide was made from the western to the eastern margin of the barrow. It was found that originally the mound had measured about 45 feet in diameter, and had mainly consisted of loamy clay. The builders of the entrenchments had cut the barrow in two, as shewn on the plan, and most probably destroyed the central interment. A

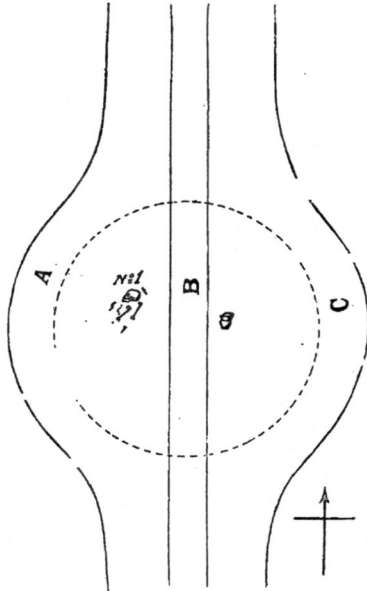

FIG. 89.—PLAN OF BARROW NO. 127.

A.—The Northern Rampart of the Entrenchments.
B.– The Ditch.
C.--The Southern Rampart.

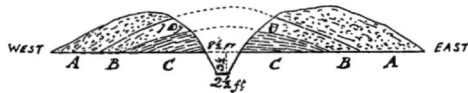

FIG. 90.—SECTION OF BARROW NO. 127.

A.—Banks of Entrenchments.
B.—Upper Portion of Barrow.
C.—Core of Barrow (Clay).

skull and other bones of a middle-aged person, and some teeth of a young ox, were found near the top of the western half of the barrow. These were probably from an interment disturbed at the time the entrenchments were made. The excavators had made no attempt to avoid the barrow and spare its contents, but judging from a slight bend in the ditch, they had apparently purposely cut right through the centre. Eastwards, 6½ feet from the centre of the ditch connected with the entrenchment, at an elevation of 1 foot 10 inches from the base of the barrow, was a crushed cinerary urn standing on the internal core of the mound and containing the calcined bones of an adult.   This urn, now reconstructed (fig. 91), is 13 inches high, 11 inches across the mouth, 12½ inches broad at the shoulders, and 6 inches wide at the bottom.   Its decoration consists of short gashes, confined to the rim of the urn (which is 5 inches deep) and arranged in nearly vertical rows.   Seven feet from the urn, in an easterly direction, and only 12 inches from the surface of the material which had been cast from the ditch in cutting through the centre of the barrow, was the greater portion of the skeleton (No. 2) of a tall man lying on his back, nearly at full length, head to south-south-west.   No relic accompanied it, but as a post-hole had at some time cut away the lumbar region and the lower part of the chest, it is just possible that an iron knife which is frequently found with these late Anglo-Saxon interments, might have been removed.   The femur measured 19½ inches, and the tibia 15⅝ inches.   Still further to the east, and at about the same depth as the last, were the leg and hip bones of skeleton No. 3.*   The upper part of this body was missing, and had probably been removed in digging for rabbits, or in planting the fence which runs over this portion of the mound.

From the above particulars it appears that at some time subsequent to the erection of the barrow, it had been destroyed in a most ruthless manner, probably by a people having no regard for the monuments so carefully and so laboriously raised, by cutting a trench right through it and squandering the once treasured contents.   Later still—but how long after we do not know—Anglian interments were made on the eastern side, in the mixed material which had been cast from the ditch.   Thus, in later times, and by people of a very different stage of culture, the same spot was once more dedicated to the burial of the dead.†

---

* Particulars of these later Anglo-Saxon burials are not included in the table of interments.

† In another part of this work more will be said about the relative ages of the barrows and the entrenchments of the neighbourhood.

No. III.—THE ALDRO GROUP.

THIS consists of no fewer than 36 barrows, 34 of which have been opened. They are arranged in five distinct clusters, which for the sake of distinction have been marked A, B, C, D, and E. Like the group previously described, it is on the northern edge of the chalk escarpment, which here projects considerably, commanding extensive views, on the right and left, over the Vales of York and Pickering, and in front, of the more distant moorland hills. Several of the barrows in this group

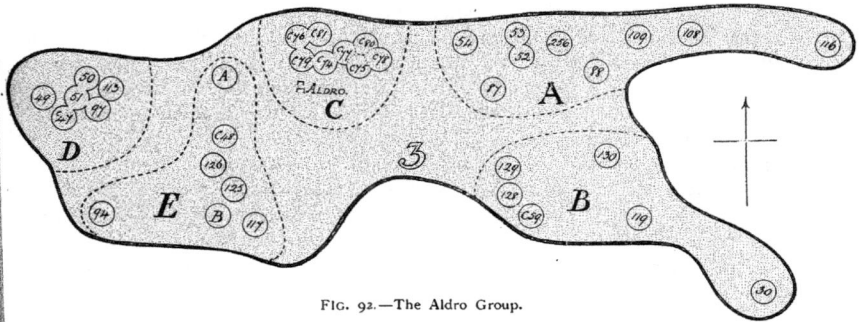

FIG. 92.—The Aldro Group.

were opened by the Yorkshire Antiquarian Club, and particulars are recorded by William Procter, M.R.C.S., in his report of the Club's proceedings. It is desirable therefore that the result of these researches should be given before describing my own excavations. His report states:—

"The examination of the large series of Wold tumuli, extending from Acklam to Huggate, was rendered complete [?] by the excavations of the Club on the mounds at Aldro, in August, 1853. On this occasion three of the British tumuli near the northern edge of the wold were examined. The first, a low one, yielded no results beyond a few burnt human bones and charcoal. The other two were close together. In the most northern, and about two feet below the surface, a food-vase* [fig. 93], of the usual sun-dried clay, ornamented with the impressed puncta in circular belts, rewarded the labour of the Club. On further investigation, layers of carboniferous matter mixed with an unctuous matter and clay, containing human bones, with a few of the mouse and bird, were found. The third, like the others, was composed of chalk rubble, mixed with small flints and layers of clay. After digging between 4 and 5 feet, a peculiar efflorescent matter covering the clay mixed with charcoal was arrived at, and below this numerous large and flat pieces of the natural rock, laid in some order and with some resemblance to a cairn. These layers of stone were followed to some distance, but yielded no results. The arrangement of the tumuli and the discovery of the vase could leave no doubt that they were of British origin."

From this description nothing more appears to have been discovered in the three barrows named above.

* Now in the York Museum.

BARROW No. 116

Is the most easterly, and is situated in the second field to the east of " Vessey Pasture " Farm-house. It is the nearest barrow to Group II.

In 1868 (from June 19th to 26th inclusive), a filled-in trench was found to encircle this barrow ; it was 90 feet in diameter, 4 feet deep, 12 feet wide at the top and 2 feet at the bottom. The diameter and elevation of the barrow could not be ascertained, owing to the centre and a large part of the east side having been removed twelve or fifteen years previously, for the purpose of obtaining flints for road repairing. It is reported that two skeletons were then found in the mound, but no relic was discovered. It is worthy of note that at about the same time a barrow a little to the west, and near to Vessey Pasture Farm-house, was removed altogether for the sake of the large flints of which it is reported the barrow was entirely composed.

Judging by the part remaining, Barrow No. 116 had a core of loamy clay and local soil, on which was a bed of large flints, about 2 feet thick in the centre, and gradually thinning towards the circumference. Above this was a capping of a similar material to that at the base. This arrangement was well shown as digging proceeded in the northern and southern parts of the mound, where less quarrying had occurred. About 26 feet southeast of the centre was an oval grave, marked A on the plan (fig. 94), measuring 5½ feet by 3 feet 11 inches, and 4 feet deep, on the floor of which were the remains of a youth from ten to fourteen years of age, in the position indicated (fig. 94' No. 1). Behind the shoulders was a crushed drinking cup (fig. 95), which, after being restored, measured 7½ inches in height and 5 inches

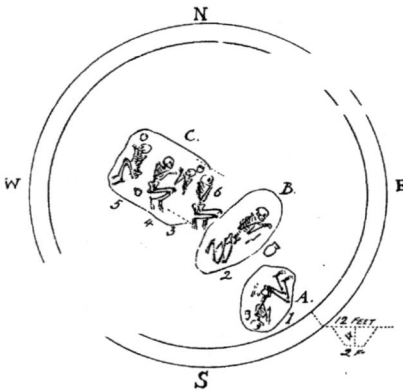

FIG. 94.

over the mouth. Its exterior is well ornamented with the impressions of a serrated tool. Behind the pelvis were the radius, ulna, and carpal bones of a small animal, probably a dog or fox; and close to these was a flake of black flint (fig. 96), upon which was the oxidised point of a bronze pricker (fig. 97). Some traces of the decayed wooden handle of this were also visible. Close above the feet was an antler of a roebuck, and the core of the horn of an ox. Near the centre of the barrow, an oblong grave, marked B on the plan, was emptied. It measured 11 feet by 7 feet, was 3 feet 4 inches deep, and was charged with earth stained with ferruginous matter, mixed with flints of various sizes. On the bottom of this grave was a decayed body, with the head to north-east, in the position shown in No. 2 on the plan. In front of this, close to the bones

PLATE XII.

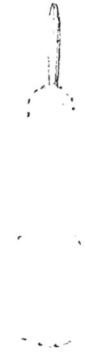

FIG. 97. ¼

FIG. 93. ¼

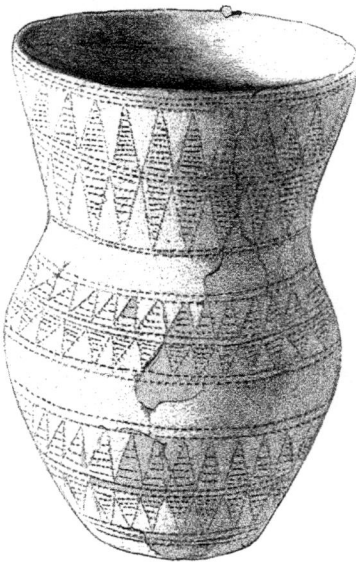

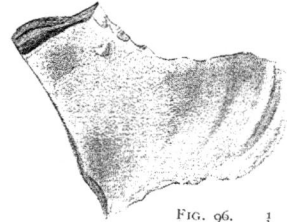

FIG. 96. ¼

FIG. 95. ½

FIG. 98.

of the fore-arm, was the greatly corroded blade of a bronze dagger (fig. 98), and a quantity of dark matter, probably the remains of the handle and sheath. After it had been restored as well as possible, it measured 4½ inches long and 2 inches wide. Three stout rivets had been used for securing it to the handle, which was of horn, judging from the impressions visible on the rivets. No other relic accompanied this body, but at the south-east edge of the grave, on a level with the base of the mound, stood a drinking-cup (fig. 99), measuring 5 inches high and 4½ inches over the mouth, beautifully ornamented externally with incised lines in various patterns. Probably this vessel contained food and was placed where found, after the filling in of the grave. About 18 inches from the north-west side of the grave *B* was a shallow and somewhat rectangular grave, *C*, measuring about 9 feet in diameter. In this, at a depth of 6 inches below the base of the mound, were the bodies Nos. 3, 4, and 5, arranged as shown on the plan. A small cup (fig. 100), ornamented with horizontal lines of cord-like impressions all over the exterior, was placed east of the head of the mutilated remains of a small middle-aged individual (No. 3). It measured 3¼ inches in height, and was the same in width across the top. There were appearances suggesting an amputation above the pelvis having taken place previous to the interment. No. 4 represents the remains of a youth, from ten to twelve years of age; the femur measuring 13½ inches. It was about 10 inches from No. 3, and near the hips was a drum-shaped drinking cup, with a handle—a rare occurrence in British vessels. After being restored, this vessel measured 4½ inches in height, and 5½ inches in diameter at the top and bottom. The sides externally are beautifully ornamented, as shown in the illustrations (figs. 101-103). At the top and bottom are rows of small rings—a type of ornament rarely met with on pottery of this period. They were probably stamped with the end of a reed. The ornamentation on the bottom, in the form of a cross, is almost as rare. No. 5 also represents the remains of a youth of not more than ten to twelve years of age, the femoral bones of which measured only 12½ inches each. In front of the face was a crushed drinking-cup (fig. 104), which after being repaired measured 4⅝ inches in height, and 4½ inches across the top. This is ornamented with bands of horizontal lines and rows of triangles, consisting of coarse impressions made with a pointed instrument, alternating with marks left by a notched tool. Almost vertically beneath No. 3, at a distance of 6 inches, was No. 6, which, for the sake of clearness, is shown in the plan, to the south of No. 3. The remains are of a person of middle age, and were not accompanied by any relic. The femur measured 17½ inches. Various detached human bones were found in the soil above bodies 3, 4, 5, and 6. A "pipe" of ferruginous earth in the chalk on the site of this barrow probably accounts for the contents being unusually decayed. A vase (fig. 105), 4 inches in height, 4½ inches across the top, with a neatly ornamented lid or cover, stood alone* 12 inches above the base of the mound, about 20 feet west of the centre. From the drawing of this very uncommon form of vase it will be observed that the lid fits around the outside of the mouth, and not in the inside, as is generally the case with the covers of modern jars. It also rises in the middle into a pro-

* We have in several instances found vases which had every appearance of having been deposited with food in them, where no trace of an interment could be discovered.

jecting boss, the top of which is oblong with rounded ends, and the sides are pierced, probably for the introduction of a thong.*

From the undisturbed portion of this barrow was taken an unusually large quantity of bones of the ox, consisting of three heads with horn cores, three pelves, six scapulae, fourteen leg bones, three vertebrae, and ribs and other bones all fragmentary, as well as a portion of the head of a goat with horn core attached; fragments of two drinking-cups, pieces of three vases of different types, 105 flint chippings, 6 cores or slingstones, 2 leaf-shaped arrow points, 1 spearhead, 1 circular disc, and 1 greenstone flake knife (fig. 106) 3½ inches long, 1¾ inches broad, chipped to a cutting edge on one side. No trace of a sharp instrument has been observed on any of the animal bones; nearly all have been smashed with a blunt tool. Most of these bones were taken from the bed of flints, which had escaped removal; and many more must have been found when the barrow was first disturbed. The quantity of bones would seem to indicate that the early inhabitants of this neighbourhood reared cattle on a large scale, the flesh of which was eaten. The fact that there were three distinct strata in this mound, and a dark streak close upon the middle one, showing traces of burning, possibly indicates that this mound may have been reared at three different periods.

BARROW No. 108.

March 10th and 11th.—This Barrow measured 27 feet in diameter, and 8 or 10 inches in elevation, and was encircled by a filled-in trench, measuring 48 feet in diameter, 3 feet deep, 8 feet wide at the top, and 3 feet at the bottom. In the centre of the barrow was a circular hollow 2 feet deep and 2½ feet across the top, containing at the bottom a heap of clean and well-calcined bones of a strongly built person. With this deposit, close to the north side, were numerous pieces of bronze weapons, burnt and fused, and probably other articles. So far as can be made out, these consist of portions of 2 or 3 swords or daggers, which had been cast in a mould, and part of a bronze handle of one of these weapons. In addition to these were many other pieces, doubled and twisted beyond recognition by the action of fire. One circular fragment of bronze, about half-an-inch in diameter, which has been larger all round, holds a circular piece of polished crystal, or glass (fig. 107), in the form of a double-convex lens; and a larger piece of bronze contains a similar glass object (fig. 108), partly hidden. They are both well formed, with one side a little more convex than the other.

---

* Small vases with covers have been met with on the Yorkshire Wolds in four other cases, to our own knowledge. We possess one (fig. 448), from Barrow No. 17, Group 9. It was taken from the base of the, mound, near the south-east margin, and, like the one just described, no trace of an interment could be found with it. Another was found on Acklam wold by the Yorkshire Antiquarian Society, and is figured in Phillips's "Rivers, Mountains, and Sea Coast of Yorkshire," plate 33, but without the cover, as only a portion of it was obtained. Two were found by Canon Greenwell, between two bodies on Ganton Wold. One of these is figured in "British Barrows," page 90. From the entirely different tooling and ornamentation of the vase and the lid, they do not seem to belong to each other. Probably this lid belonged to the adjoining vase mentioned by Canon Greenwell, which was too much injured to be restored. In "British Barrows," foot-note, pages 164-5, instances are given of similar vases having been found in several other parts of the world.

FIG. 99.   ½

FIG. 101.   ½

FIG. 100.   ½

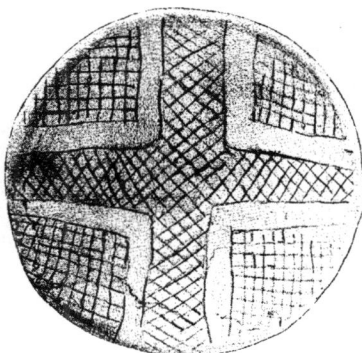

FIG. 102.   ½

FIG. 103.   ½

FIG. 104.   ½

FIG. 105.   ½

Some of the above articles were sent to Sir John Evans, who was good enough to send the following remarks on the specimens :—

"I have received your parcel of bronze relics, but I am so much puzzled by them, and they are in such fragmentary condition, that I cannot well write any detailed account of them. There appears originally to have been several distinct articles, which were more or less destroyed in the funeral pyre. That which had remained the least injured appears to be a flanged ferrule of much the same character as that from Fulbourn, my fig. 426.* The tube is ornamented by 3 groups of 4 parallel grooves. Another object seems to be the bronze covering of a dagger or sword sheath, which has been ornamented with tranverse slightly raised ribs, with a kind of ferrule of pattern in relief at what was probably the upper end. Of this sheath there were several fragments, and from their condition it seems that at the time of cremation, the blade had been withdrawn from the sheath. I do not, however, find any fragments that can be safely regarded as those either of a sword or a dagger, though there is a curved blade with two small rivet holes and provided with a curved central rib, with a smaller rib on each side of it. This may have been the blade of a halberd, but it differs materially from any others that I have seen. Another fragment with a central rib, on either side of which is a circular hole, looks more like a portion of a dagger, as from the ribs which run along the only edge that has been preserved it would seem to be part of a tapering blade, the circular holes having, however, been cast with a raised bead around them, such as I have never seen in daggers, and it is impossible to say how much may have originally existed beyond the fractured end near these holes. Another fragment of the blade, with a similar eyelet-hole, exhibits no central rib; but the most remarkable objects of all are some fragments in which similar but somewhat larger holes are filled with lenticular pieces of transparent colourless glass. Of these, two have been preserved, one of them detached from any blade. This has the appearance of the glass having been set in a circular collar or ring of bronze, which was subsequently rivetted into its place. I should infer that these lenses served to adorn some personal ornament rather than to decorate a weapon, but the unfortunate imperfect condition of these relics prevents me from arriving at any definite conclusion.

"The quantity of shapeless pieces of fused metal shows how much of bronze must have accompanied the body when submitted to cremation, and how intense must have been the heat of the fire. The fragments of the sheath are not inconsistent with the blade it was destined to contain having been of iron; and the presence of the glass ornaments (for such they seem to be, and not crystal), suggest the possibility of the interment belonging to the late Celtic period."

Above the incinerated bones, the receptacle was filled with clay, in which numerous small pieces of burnt and melted bronze were mixed. At the top were several fragments of British pottery, consisting of a portion of a very thin drinking-cup, and a thin piece of an urn well marked with the thumb-end and nail.

* "Bronze Weapons," by J. Evans.

H

BARROW No. 109.

Opened March 12th, 13th, and 14th, 1868.   This barrow, which was 2 feet
2 inches high, and about 50 feet in diameter, consisted of ferruginous surface
soil from the immediate neighbourhood, slightly mixed with foreign clay.   Four
to five inches of clay surrounded the central grave and the ground beneath the
mound for several feet.   About the centre of the barrow, at an elevation of
15 inches from the base, was an oval heap of burnt human bones, 2 feet wide
east and west, and 13 inches north and south.   It consisted of bones of a young
individual, and a few of a child.   The end of a bone needle or pin (fig. 109)
was the only relic found.   Vertically beneath this incinerated deposit was a
circular grave 6 feet deep, 4 feet in diameter at the top, and 2 feet 2 inches at
the bottom, cut into the hard chalk rock.   In the material filling the top part
of this was a basin-shaped hole 2 feet deep and fully 3 feet across the top.
The sides of the cavity were burnt, and inside was burnt soil, chalk grit, and
wood ashes.   Mixed with the soil in the lower portion were the calcined bones
of a strong adult, accompanied by a small plain vase (fig. 110), inverted.   This
stands 3 inches high, and measures 3 inches across at the mouth and shoulders.
Under the lip on each side of the vase is a small perforation, probably for the
insertion of a thong for suspension.   It occurred amongst unctuous earth and
chalk grit, mixed with small bits of burnt wood and a few pieces of burnt bones,
both human and animal.   About 11 feet southwards from the central grave a
circular hole, 3 feet deep and 3½ feet in diameter at the top, was emptied.   This
contained hardly anything but clay ; and there was no trace of any interment.

One portion of an urn, 1 barbed arrow-head (fig. 111), 2 oval scrapers chipped
on the edges, and 14 hand-struck splinters of flint were picked from the mound.

A circular trench, filled up by cultivation, encircled the barrow.   This measured
56 feet in diameter, 3½ feet in depth, 5 feet in width at the top, and 2 feet at
the bottom.

BARROW No. 88

Stands in the easternmost rampart of a series of triple dykes which defines and
traverses the eastern end of the field in which the barrow is situated.   At the time of
opening (April 15th, 17th, 22nd, and 24th, 1867) it measured 48 feet across, and 49
inches from base to summit.   It was formed almost entirely of chalk and chalk grit to
the height of 16 inches,* above which were beds of clay and soil, similarly arranged to
those in Barrow 87, to be described presently.   About 10 feet south-south-west of the
centre of the mound, at its base, was a plain food-vase, in a leaning position, which
was beyond repair.   This occurred near the head of body marked C, on fig. 115.
Close by was a human leg-bone, 3 small flakes of dark coloured flint (figs. 112-114),
and a neck vertebra of some animal.   Judging from the existence of a cavity in the
clay, 10 inches long by 5 inches wide, something perishable had also been interred.
The percolation of water through the mound had partly filled this hollow with a very
fine argillaceous sediment.   A little east of these, on the old undisturbed surface line,
were the decayed remains of four bodies, occupying a rectangular space 6 feet by 3 feet.

* Resembling the cairn in the centre of Barrow 52.

PLATE XIV.

FIG. 106.   ½

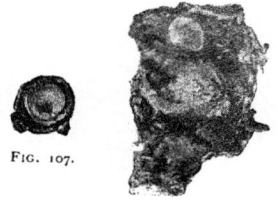

FIG. 107.

FIG. 108.

FIG. 109.   ¾

FIG. 110.   ½

FIG. 112.

FIG. 111.   ¹

FIG. 113.

FIG. 114.

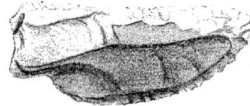

FIG. 122.

FIG. 116.   ¹

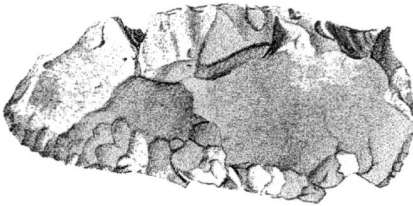

FIG. 123.   ½

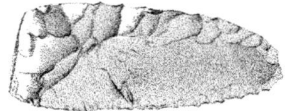

FIG. 124.

Their attitudes and relative positions are shown in fig. 115. The skeleton marked A on the plan was partly on its back, and partly on its left side. With it was a large tusk of a pig (fig. 116), close behind the pelvis. The right femur measured 15 inches, and the two back molars in the under jaw were formed within the alveoli, while the upper back molars had slightly protruded. The age of this person at death would therefore probably be from 18 to 25 years. The bones of body B on the plan were too far decayed to be measured with accuracy, but it was evident that they were larger than those of A. On examin-ing the under jaw—which was rather a slender one—it was observed that most of the molar teeth were gone, and the alveoli were closed (an unusual feature in British crania), whilst the few remaining teeth were ground down to their fangs. This indicates that the owner was of great age when buried. On referring to the plan, it will be observed that the skeleton marked C has its head to the west, a precisely opposite direction to the two last. The left back bicuspid of the lower jaw just appeared above the bone, and the corresponding one on the upper jaw had grown to the height of the first set of molars, while the next tooth was just protruding through the

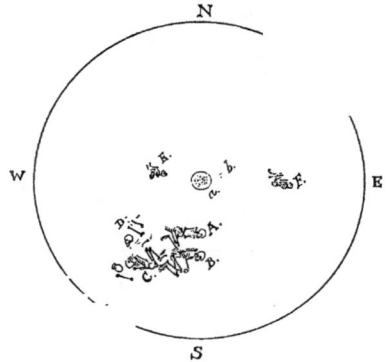

FIG. 115.

socket. The skeleton would therefore appear to be of an individual from 10 to 14 years of age. At D on the plan was a dismembered body, the bones of which are shown nearly in the position in which they were found, except a tibia and part of a humerus, which were on the breast of body C. Judging from the fact that the back molars of the under jaw had not appeared from their sockets, and that the length of the detached femur was a little short of 15 inches, this person at death would probably be a little younger than the one marked A.

From under the middle of the thigh bone of D, a nearly complete thin and finely chipped diamond-shaped arrowhead of foreign flint was taken, the part remaining measured 1⅜ inches long and ¾ of an inch broad. About ½ an inch had been broken off one end* pre-viously to being placed in position, as close under it were the remains of the decayed wooden shaft,

FIG. 117.

showing clearly that the arrow-head had been secured in a slit in the end of the shaft, as shown in fig. 117.

All the four skeletons were laid upon a thin bed of clay, and were also encased in clay mixed with a little soil, causing a break in the internal gritty core of the barrow. Many cavities with greasy looking sides were observed. Five or six feet to the north, at about the centre of the barrow, we reached a circular hollow in the substance of the mound (see fig. 119). Its depth was 3 feet, and the diameter at the top 3½ feet, without measuring the lip or flange, which turned outwards some 6 inches all round.

* Several other examples, similarly broken, have since been found, and appear to indicate that the implements were broken intentionally, at the time of burial.

Its sides were burnt red from top to bottom, to the depth of fully an inch.   At the bottom were the calcined bones of an adult (marked " *a* " on the plan, fig. 115), but no relics.   Above this was some dark coloured earth, in which were small cavities, and at the top unusually large pieces of carbonized wood.   Slightly to the east, and near the top of the gritty chalk core, were detached and broken leg and arm bones, pieces of a skull, and in one place nearly a whole skull, all seemingly belonging to a man of strong build.   A few inches south-east from the centre of the hollow was a circular heap of calcined bones of an adult (marked B on the plan) ; and about 16 inches from the west side were the contracted remains of a child (marked E) of about the age of 4 years, at the base of the mound ; and a still younger child (marked F) was buried at a distance of 2 feet on the opposite side of the hollow.

These central bodies were probably the primary interments.   Do they represent

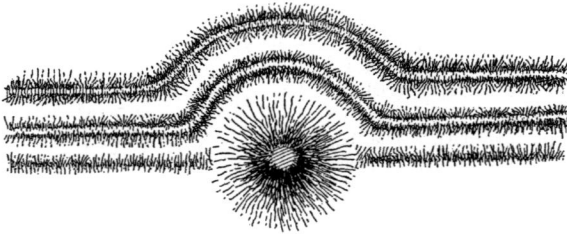

FIG. 118.
Plan of Barrow No. 88 and Adjoining Entrenchments.

FIG. 119.
A, B—Section of Barrow and Entrenchments, N.E. to S.W.
C—Section of Basin-Shaped Hollow.
D—Basin-Shaped Hollow, containing burnt bones (marked
"*a*" on the plan, fig. 115).

the burial of a family at the death of its head, the elder members being cremated, while the children were inhumed ?

From the core of the barrow was obtained the tine from an antler of a deer, a portion of the rib of an ox (?), and many small shells (*Helix virgata, Helix nemoralis, Helix arbustorum*), and a few specimens (4 at least) of the long spiral shell (*Succinea putris*).   Only 5 splinters and 1 slingstone of flint were picked from the mound during the whole of the excavations.   Originally a trench measuring 60 feet in diameter had encircled this barrow.   At the time of throwing up the obviously late entrenchments, advantage was taken of the hollow encircling the barrow, and this was followed fully halfway round the mound by the entrenchment, as shown in the accompanying plan and section (fig. 118 and 119).   That part not traversed by the entrenchment was filled in by agricultural operations ; but by excavation a section of the old fosse (c) was obtained, measuring 3 feet deep, 8 feet wide at the top, and 2½ feet at the bottom.

BARROW No. 256

Is also in the line of entrenchments, about 100 yards north of the last barrow. When it was examined on April 11th and 12th, 1883, it had a diameter of 50 feet, and was 4 feet above the original surface. It was found to resemble barrow No. C. 76, and, as shown by the plan (fig. 120), was completely within the ramparts of a line of earthworks locally called "Old Dykings." The western fosse of the entrenchments skirts the margin of the barrow, while on the north side the eastern fosse cuts considerably into the mound; so much so that the entrenchment builders had destroyed a large cinerary urn containing cremated bones, fragments of which (and portions of its contents) were found in the material removed in cutting the entrenchments. This urn may have contained the only interment, as nothing more could be found. The northern rampart of

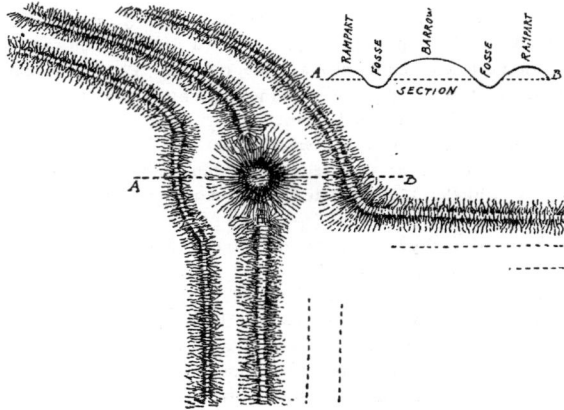

FIG. 120.—Ground Plan of Barrow No. 256 and Surrounding Entrenchments, with Section along the line, *A*, *B*.

the earthwork was much increased in height and width by the material cut from the barrow. Two scapulæ and a few other bones, belonging probably to a goat or sheep, were found, together with pieces of a food-vase and three splinters of black flint.

BARROW No. 52

Is situated a little to the west of the last, and is the southernmost of two barrows situated in the second field east of Aldro. In the Ordnance Map for the district they are shown near the elbow of Swinham Plantation.

On March 28th, 1866, the barrow had a diameter of 60 feet and an elevation of 2 feet 5 inches, measured from the undisturbed ground below. It seemed to have lost much of its original height through the action of the plough. A square piece, measuring 15½ feet on all sides, was cut from the centre; and on removing the soil a little more than a spit deep, the apex of an inner mound or cairn, formed of chalk and numerous pieces of flint, was reached. This rested on the natural surface ground, and measured nearly 18 feet in diameter, and was 18 inches in elevation. In the centre was a nearly circular hole, measuring 6½ feet east and west and 6 feet north and south, which was filled from top to bottom with unctuous earth, alternating with thin layers of clay. A few inches below the base of the cairn, and about the middle of the central hole, was

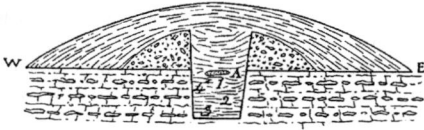

a heap of burnt bones ("a" on fig. 128), measuring 17 inches east and west and 6 to 7 inches across the middle, and tapering almost to a point at the ends. Among these bones were many splintered pieces of flint, having a porcelain-like appearance from the action of fire. These have been put together and form a knife (fig. 123) 3 inches long and about 1½ inches broad; and a spear-head (fig. 124) 2 inches long and ¾ of an inch broad. The deposit also contained a bone pin (fig. 125) 2⅞ inches long, and a hollow instrument of bone (fig. 126) 4¾ inches long, made from the leg bone of some small animal. The original shape of the bone has been somewhat altered by scraping with some instrument which has left faint scratches on the sides, while the natural aperture at each end has been widened. Possibly it is some form of flute or whistle. These articles are more or less twisted and splintered by the action of fire.

Judging from the appearance of the cremated bones, they appear to have been wrapped in something, or else some perishable substance had been deposited with them, as a cavity existed above them. Just under them, and about 12 inches below the old surface line, was a body (fig. 128, No. 1), on its back, head to the west, knees up, with the right arm crossed over the lower part of the chest, the bones of the left hand being found near the head. The femur and tibia measured 17¾ and 14½ inches respectively. This body had its head twisted sideways, and the knees, which pointed to the north, had shrunk considerably below the rest of the body by the unequal settling of the contents of the grave. No instrument accompanied this interment, but a tibia of another body was found across its head.

April 4th, 1866.—We completed our search in the grave, though the weather was very cold, with snow falling heavily for upwards of two hours. At a depth of ten inches vertically below the first body, a second interment (fig. 128, No. 2) was laid bare. This was also on its back, with its head to the west, legs drawn up, the left arm bent to a right angle, with the hand on the lower part of the chest, and the right arm doubled by the side of the body, with the hand near the head. The thigh and leg bones were almost exactly the same length as those of body No. 1. On the right side, and near the shoulder-blade, was a small food-vase (fig. 127) of common type and ornamentation, measuring 5 inches in height and 5¼ inches in diameter at the top. It contained a little dark mould. The upper band of ornamentation only goes partially round the vase. Near this vase were the bones of an entire human arm, and part of the shoulder-blade, with the exception of the finger bones and a piece of the scapula, which may have decayed. The humerus of this detached arm measured 12 inches, the radius 9¾ inches, and ulna 10¼ inches. The bones were smaller and of a much darker colour than those of the body just below them, and were similarly doubled. The close connection of this arm with the food-vase, clearly indicated that it had been placed in the grave contemporaneously with the interment below. About 16 inches from the heads of bodies 1 and 2, and a little above No. 2, was a dismembered body (No. 4), consisting of a skull with many other bones piled against it. The under-jaw was fully 12 inches from the head, and on the opposite side of the deposit. The femur and tibia measured 17¾ inches and 14½ inches respectively. We dug still deeper, and at a depth of 4½ feet from the old sur-face line reached the rocky bottom of a nearly circular grave, 5½ feet in diameter, on which rested a body (No. 3), on its back, but in this instance the head pointed west-north-west. The knees were pressed over to the west, and almost pulled up to the chin. The right arm was bent by the side, thus permitting the hand to be brought to the front of the face. The left arm had the elbow on the chest and the hand in front of the face. The femur and tibia measured 18 inches and 14 inches respectively. A small knife of grey flint, measuring 1½ inches long, and ¾ of an inch broad, was found just behind the head. The bodies Nos. 1, 2, and 3 (on fig. 128) rested on a thin layer of dark matter, which apparently represented some decayed substance.

BARROW No. 53

Is fellow to the last, and just skirts its northern margin. It was opened on April 5th, 1866. Some years previously the whole of this barrow was carted away, except some 6 to 8 inches at its base—just sufficient to indicate its circular outline, and show its diameter to be 70 feet. The remaining portion was turned over, the ground below was probed, and after considerable search, a shallow grave, sunk a little way into the gritty subsoil, was found near the centre, and was completely filled with disjointed and fractured human remains. These consisted of leg, arm, head, and other bones, compactly piled together, in a similar manner to the two heaps within the grave in barrow No. 50. Several portions of a drinking-cup accompanied this deposit, but no flint instrument was found.

Re-opening, April 9th, 1883. On this date the ground beneath this barrow was carefully searched without anything more being found.

BARROW No. 54

Is a much larger barrow than either of the two last, and stands in the same field about an eighth of a mile to the west of them. It measured 84 feet in diameter, and 5 feet in height. On April 3rd, 4th, and 9th, 1866, a square with 21 feet sides, and reaching from apex to base, was removed from its centre. This showed the mound to have been made of foreign clay and local soil in about equal quantities, and arranged in wavy layers, alternating and broken, except at the core of the mound, where chalk existed and formed an inner cairn, similar to the one in barrow 52. This was not more than 12 to 14 inches high in the middle, and had a diameter of about 25 feet. A boat-formed mass of clay and · unctuous earth occupied the centre of the cairn, as in barrow 52. It measured, at the top, 10 feet east and west, and 5 feet north and south, and extended down-wards nearly 3 feet into the middle of a vast grave. Near the centre of the barrow, at about half its height, was a very fine barbed arrow-head (fig. 129), of dark flint. From the mound were also taken twenty handstruck splinters (three only of which are of native flint); bones of animals, an ox tooth, burnt wood, a piece of a food-vase, and several portions of a drinking-cup, ornamented with impressions arranged in lines forming a diamond pattern. These fragments are remarkable for the absence of pounded quartz or other gritty matter so generally found in British pottery. A portion was put into water for a short time, and it fell to powder in the same way as dried clay does, showing how imperfectly the clay of this vessel had been baked.

On April 11th we commenced to empty the circular grave, which was situated slightly north-west of the centre. Near the south-west side, only a few inches below the old surface-line, was the crushed body of a child (No. 1 in the section, fig. 130), about six years old, in the midst of rough chalk stones, which, for the most part, filled the grave. It was crumpled up, with the head to the south and the hands near the head. Many snail shells were taken from the midst of the fragments of the crushed skull, but no relic was found. On the south-east side, at a depth of 2 feet, a second juvenile skeleton (No. 2) was found, on its left side, with the head to the east-south-east, the legs pulled up and hands near the face. A vase (drinking-cup?) had been placed at the knees, but had been crushed, and was in many pieces.

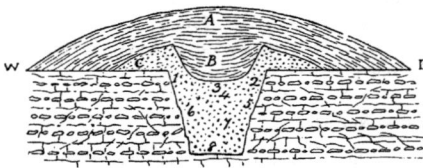

FIG. 130.—Section of Barrow No. 54.
Figs. 1-8.--Interments.
A—Upper part of mound—clay and soil.
B—Boat-shaped mass of clay and soil.
C--Chalk forming the inner mound and filling the grave.

Unfortunately the whole of the vase is not preserved, but, from the restoration shewn in fig. 131, it measured 5½ inches in height and 4½ inches across the top.

On April 16th, 1866, the mass of clay and unctuous earth which occupied the previously-named hollow in the centre of the chalk cairn was removed. On the level of the old surface, this argillaceous matter measured 8 feet east and west, and 4 feet north and south. It extended over 2 feet into the grave, and slanted inwards in all directions to the bottom, resembling the keel of a vessel. Close under this, on the rough chalk, was body No. 3, with its head due west, partly on the back and right side, and with legs pulled up, but not sufficiently to form a right angle with the spine. The remains were those of a person about forty years of age, with strong bones, and, from measurement of the skeleton made *in situ*, must have stood fully 6 feet in height. Both the humeri were parallel with the trunk, and the bones of the forearm crossed the body. The small bones had decayed, while most of the larger ones were in a state of pulp. The right side of the head and face had disappeared, leaving only the left side of the calvarium. This portion shows that the skull is of a very low type (fig. 132) if we may judge from its unusually high and strong superciliary ridges and low receding forehead.* It is a *very* small skull for a large person. No vase or implement accompanied this interment, but

* Fig. 132 gives a comparison of its outline with that of an ordinary British long skull.

PLATE XV.

FIG. 125.

FIG. 129. ¼

FIG. 127. ⅓

FIG. 137. ⅓

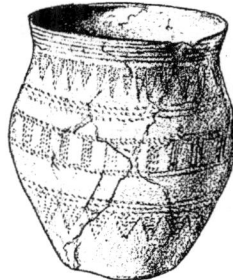

FIG. 126.

FIG. 131. ⅓

FIG. 134. ⅓

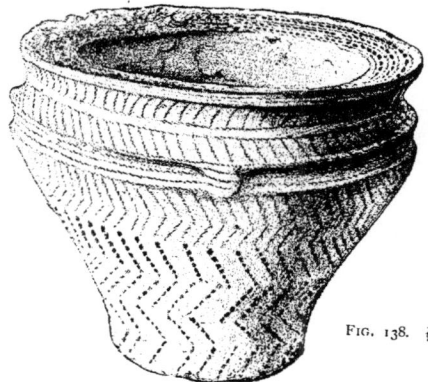

FIG. 138. ½

just below the right humerus was a long bone of a child, and about 14 inches to the
west of the skull, and at the same depth in the grave, was the base of the antler
of a red deer (fig. 133) with the two first tines attached, but worn and splintered
at the ends from having been used as a pick.   There was also the end of a flat
horn-core of a goat(?), and a fragment of a small human ilium.   Round the feet
of this interment was another piece of deer antler, the end of another horn-core
of a goat(?), three molar teeth of an ox, and portions of bones, probably belonging
to the same animal, some of which were broken and splintered longitudinally.

Among some rough chalk, to the north of the adult body, and some 12 inches
below it, were the decayed and crushed remains of a child (No. 4), the first milk
molars and canine teeth of which had grown to the level of the jaws.   The attitude
of this body was similar to that of the adult interment above, except that its knees
pointed to the north, while those of the adult pointed to the south.*

The next burial, a dismembered body (No. 5), accompanied by a little dark

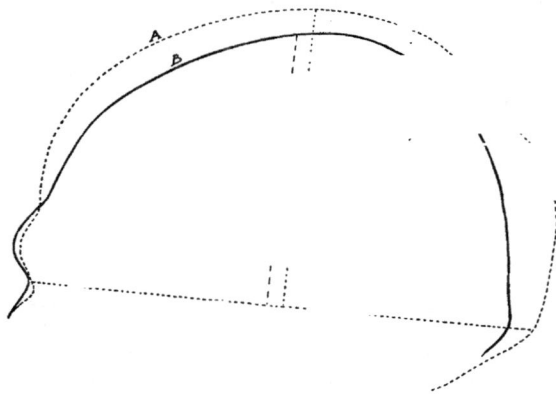

FIG. 132.
A—Typical British long skull (from Barrow C 40).
B—Skull from Burial No. 3 in Barrow No. 54.

mould, was reached on April 18th, and was on a ledge of rock protruding from the
north-east side of the grave, 5½ feet from the bottom.   The interment consisted of
portions of the skull and ribs of a child, accompanied by the tooth of a pig and part of
the under-jaw and a few other bones of a nearly full-grown but young person.   The
jaw had been split longitudinally and the teeth removed previous to interment.   Fully
a foot below, and at the north-west side, was body No. 6, that of a child, about 7 to 8
years of age.   Though this body was much broken up and its bones displaced by the
settling of the rough chalk which was in close contact, it was observed that it had
been doubled up with head to north-east.

Interment No. 7 consisted of a large heap of human bones piled up in the grave,
without any order, at a distance of 2½ feet directly below No. 5.   With it was a
drinking-cup in 48 pieces, which, after rebuilding, measured 7 inches in height and 5

* The late Miss Sykes, the Rev. E. M. Cole and Mrs. Cole (now Lady Philadelphia Cole), the Rev. T. J.
Monson and the Hon. Mrs. Monson, attended during the afternoon.

inches in diameter at the top (fig. 134). The calvarium of an adult was the receptacle of a collection of tarsal and metatarsal bones, vertebræ, the joint end of a large leg-bone, and portions of a skull. Of children's bones there were vertebræ, ends of leg-bones, small portions of a skull, and an ilium. The calvarium must have been carefully packed with these bones previous to interment, and then placed with the crown upwards. From this deposit of bones (No. 7), fragments of six separate human lower jaws were taken. Judging from the teeth, two of them represented individuals from 7 to 8 years of age, two probably 8 or 9 years each, and two adults, apparently male and female, each about 35 to 40 years of age. The adult femora measured 17 and 17½ inches respectively, and are much bent. Previous to interment a few of the arm and leg bones seem to have been broken across, and the skulls, for the most part, had apparently been smashed to pieces, so much so, that no portion, saving the calvarium containing the miscellaneous collection, was more than 2 or 3 inches across.

On April 20th work was continued, and at an additional depth of about three feet the floor of the grave was reached, upon which was interment No. 8, in two adjoining heaps of bones, forming a line east and west across the middle of the grave. We found the bones to consist of portions of two bodies; viz., those of an individual about 45 years of age, with very strong bones* and those of a youth about eight to ten years of age.† All the large bones in this deposit had been much broken, and some of the adult leg bones seemed to have been split lengthways, in the manner in which animal bones are frequently found to have been broken.‡

This unusual form of grave calls for a few remarks. Its form was that of a funnel, extending to a depth of 12 feet below the base of the mound. It was 15 feet in diameter at the top, and 5 feet at the bottom. During its construction several thick beds and large blocks of flint had been cut vertically through, showing that tools of no mean kind had been used. These broken flints (which, along with the excavated chalk, had been put back into the grave), were found to be splintered in a manner which seemed to indicate the use of metal tools. More than twenty of these pieces of flint have been preserved, and clearly show the conchoidal fracture. This kind of fracture is the result of a sharp blow given with a hard and somewhat pointed tool. It might have been produced by a stone axe, but it scarcely seems possible that so deep a grave could have been formed by stone tools alone. Had only the latter been used, some would surely have broken and splintered in excavating the hard chalk and flint, and some of the splinters would have been found in the grave. Not one was discovered, however, while three picks of stags' horn and several fragments of others were taken from the rough chalk filling. These had apparently been used in digging, but they hardly seem sufficiently strong to have made the entire excavation.

* Femur about 18 inches long.

† A very similar discovery seems to have been made by Mr. Wilhelm Boye, of Copenhagen, in a chambered tumulus in the Island of Zealand, Denmark. The bones were there heaped together promiscuously.—See " Proceedings of Society of Antiquaries," May 3rd, 1866.

‡ We placed the following inscription on the bottom of the grave before filling it in:—"April 16th, 1866. From this grave beneath a tumulus, J. R. Mortimer, of Fimber, in the presence of Miss Sykes, of Sledmere, exhumed two vases and the remains of 14 human skeletons, comprising various ages."

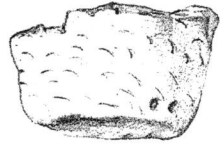

Fig. 141.   ½

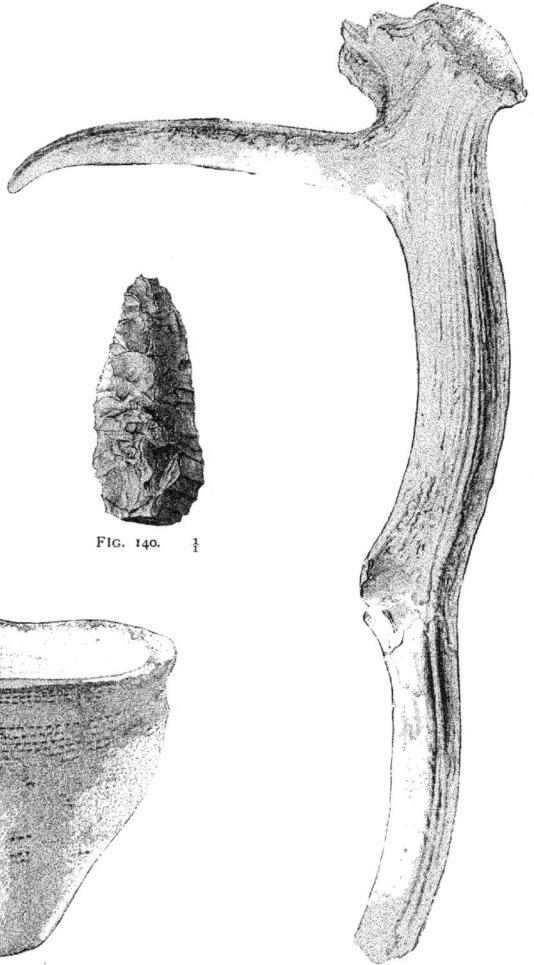

Fig. 133.   ⅓

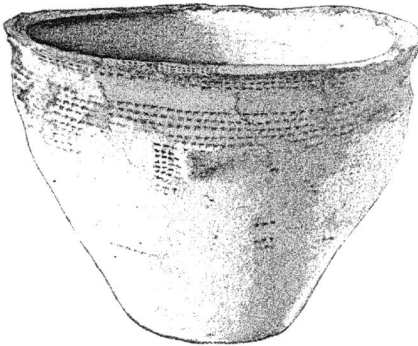

Fig. 140.   ⅟₁

Fig. 139.   ½

Fig. 135.   ⅓

BARROW No. 87

Stands about 200 yards south of the last, in the adjoining field.

On April 8th, 9th, and 10th, 1866, it had a diameter of 64 feet, with an altitude of 3 feet 7 inches. It was composed of about equal quantities of foreign clay and local surface soil, arranged in small beds. In the mound and at its base were found 23 flint chips, 1 flake knife 2 inches long, 2 flat pieces of flint of doubtful purpose, $1\frac{5}{8}$ and $2\frac{1}{4}$ inches long respectively, flaked on their sides ; and 13 oblong scrapers a little over an inch and a quarter in length, chipped all round the edge except at the butt end, where the bulb of percussion is situated. With the exception of one of the discs, these are all of foreign flint. Pieces of a drinking-cup and burnt wood were also found during the excavation.

About the centre of the mound, and not more than eight to ten inches from the apex, were some burnt human bones in the bottom of a crushed urn, the top of which had been totally destroyed by the plough. Nothing was found with it. Vertically below this urn, and in an oval grave nine or ten inches below the base of the barrow, was an adult skeleton in the usual crouched position, on its right side, head to the south-south-east. In front of the knees was a well-preserved food-vase (fig. 138). Its whole exterior is tastefully ornamented, the upper portion with very small rope impressions, while below, reaching to the bottom, are four encircling rows of short broken lines, leaning alternately to the right and to the left, producing a herring-bone pattern. These have been stamped with an instrument, probably of bone, having six evenly cut notches along its edge. At the feet was another food-vase (fig. 139) of a somewhat similar type, greatly decayed. The occurrence of two food-vases with a body is very unusual. Close to the south side of vase fig. 139, was a dish-shaped hollow in the ground, measuring about 16 inches across, containing dark unctuous earth resembling that found in the vases. A spear-point of black flint (fig. 140) nearly two inches long, was found near the skull. The whole of the bones of this interment were in the last stages of decay, and surrounding them was a thick film of dark matter, the residue of some substance decomposed. The bones, urns, and receptacle were encased in clay, and rested on a thin bed of the same substance, which seemed to have been spread on the floor of the grave. A section of the barrow showed that layers of clay and layers of soil had alternately been placed over the grave in the form of a small mound three feet high, and that afterwards the barrow had been completed. Similar cores over a grave, not conformable with the arrangement of the rest of the layers forming the completed barrow, have frequently been observed.

DIVISION "B"

Is to the south of Division "A," and consists of six barrows arranged in a manner resembling the familiar constellation "Charles' Wain," or the "Great Bear."

BARROW No. 30

Is the most easterly of this division, and about one-third of a mile east of " Dimple Hole " Plantation.

On May 29th, 1865, it had an elevation of 20 inches and a radius of 30 feet. A rectangular piece, measuring 17 feet north and south, and 13 feet east and west, was cut from the middle. In the southern part of the excavation was a. circular hollow, measuring 14 inches in diameter and 12 inches in depth, in the ground under the barrow. This was filled with unctuous earth and burnt wood, in which was a portion of the bottom of a vase (fig. 141), ornamented with indentations made by the thumb-nail; and a piece of the rim of a vase with a turned-in lip (fig. 142). This form of lip is exceedingly rare, the only other example we have met with being shewn in fig. 219, Barrow No. 211, Group IV. Possibly these are sherds of domestic pottery. Many hazel-nut shells, one of which had a carbonized kernel in it, were found in the deposit of burnt wood; also half a disc of grey flint, chipped round its circumference, the diameter and radius measuring 2 inches and $1\frac{1}{4}$ inches respectively. There was also the burnt longitudinal half of a cylindrical jet bead with rounded ends, which had been bored lengthwise from opposite ends. Its length was $\frac{3}{8}$ of an inch, and breadth $\frac{3}{4}$ of an inch. No trace of burnt bone was found. Near the middle of the barrow was a soil-pipe in the chalk, which was at first thought to be a grave, but excavation to a depth of 4 feet proved the contrary. The material forming the mound was similar to the sub-soil on the neighbouring land, and in it only one hand-struck splinter of black flint was found.

BARROW No. 119

Adjoins the last.

On July 27th, 1868, this barrow was only just visible, having been nearly levelled by cultivation. Its diameter was 15 yards. In the centre was a small deposit of burnt bones, enclosed in dark-coloured matter and wood ashes; but the upper part of this had been removed by the plough, the undisturbed portion being only 1 foot in diameter.

The only relic found was the middle portion of a slender bone pin.

BARROW No. "C 30"

Is a little to the north of barrow 119. On April 23rd, 1869, it had a diameter of 45 feet and an elevation of about 15 inches, fully one-half of which was due to the natural prominence selected by the barrow builders, or to the denudation of the surrounding ground since the erection of the artificial portion of the barrow. In the centre, on the natural surface, were many traces of burning, and a few cremated bones; and about one yard south-east of these stood a tall cinerary urn, with its mouth almost in reach of the plough, containing burnt bones of an adult. It fell to pieces on being removed, but has since been rebuilt (fig. 143), and measures 13 inches in height, 8 inches across the mouth, 9 inches across the shoulders, and $4\frac{1}{2}$ inches wide at the bottom. It is quite plain, not a single incised line being visible. This is the most cylindrical cinerary urn we have found, and much resembles the type of vessel found in Dorsetshire, some of which are figured in " The Celtic Tumuli of Dorset," by Charles Warne, F.S.A.

PLATE XVII.

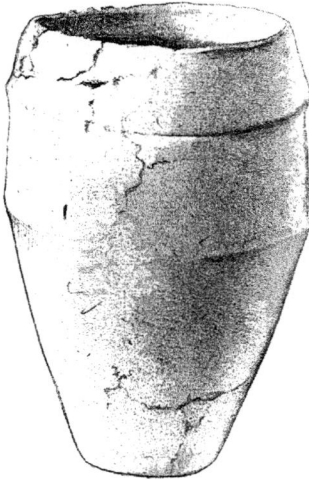

FIG. 145. ⅓

FIG. 143. ¼

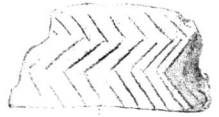

Top of Vase. ½

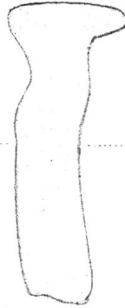

FIG. 142.

Outside of Vase. ½

Section.

Inside of Vase. ½

FIG. 146 ⅓

FIG 147. ½

BARROW No. C 59,

With the two last barrows, forms a triangle. It is the largest in the Aldro Group, which, from an elevation of 775 feet (the highest point of the north-western side of the Wolds), overlooks the vales of York and Pickering, and is visible from the distant moorland hills.

On July 24th, 1873, the diameter of this barrow proved to be 90 feet, and the elevation 7 feet. We commenced with three workmen, and cut a section 30 feet wide towards the centre, and probed the ground beneath by making trenches a foot apart down to the undisturbed rock.*

By July 28th the base of the mound was reached, and about 20 feet north-north-west of the centre a little rubbly chalk grit, which was eventually found to cover almost the whole area of the barrow, and thickened towards the centre. It rested on a thin bed of blue clay which covered the old land surface. A single chipped flint was the only relic so far found.

On July 29th the layer of chalk grit was found to extend into the body of the mound, and had a greater thickness of clay beneath it. No relic was found.

July 30th.—About 13 feet north of the centre, and 6 feet 4 inches from the upper surface of the barrow, were the flexed remains of a child about twelve months old (No. 1 on the plan, fig. 144). These were placed in an oval hollow, 4 inches deep, in the old turf-line. Near its head was a flake of black flint; in front of its face stood a food-vase (fig. 145). On the western

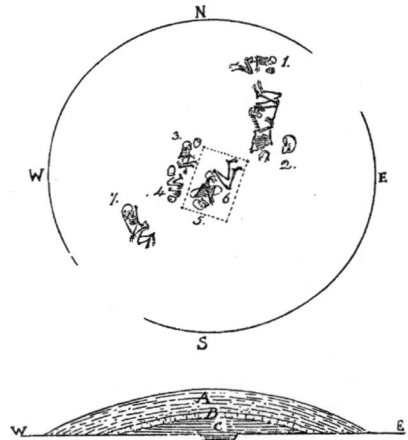

FIG. 144.
Plan and Section of Barrow No. C 59.
A—Upper part of mound.
B—Layer of chalk grit.
C—Core of blue clay.

side of the vase was a cavity in the clay, 15 inches long north and south, and 2 inches across, apparently the hollow left by some decayed object. Pieces of charcoal were found near the chest and other parts of the body. A small piece of a polished greenstone axe, one slingstone, two flakes of black flint, and a few fragments of an urn were picked from the mound.

* Workmen were employed as follows :—

July 24—3 diggers.	August 1—8 diggers.
,, 25—3 ,,	,, 2—8 ,,
,, 26— 2 ,,	,, 4—4 ,, (wet day).
,, 28—4 diggers in the morning, and 5 in the afternoon.	,, 5—7 ,,
	,, 6—8 ,,
,, 29—6 diggers.	7—3
,, 30—6 ,,	8—3
,, 31—7 diggers in the morning, and 8 in the afternoon.	

Only a few flint chippings were found on the following day.

August 1st.—On a bed of blue clay, nearly 5 feet north of the centre, and about 6 inches above the base of the mound, were the remains of a strongly-built young man, in a sitting posture, as shown in No. 2 on the plan. The wisdom teeth were not fully grown. The femur measured 19 inches, tibia 15 inches, and humerus 13 inches. The skull had fallen from its original position, leaving the lower jaw behind. This indicates that the body had been enclosed in something, probably of wood, which had kept out the earth until the ligaments had sufficiently decayed to allow the head to roll over into the position it occupied when found. No relic accompanied the interment.

From various parts of the mound were taken a few rudely worked flints and a splinter of greenstone, apparently from the same celt as the portion picked up the previous day.

August 2nd.—About the centre, and 4 feet from the apex of the barrow, were the decayed remains of an infant (No. 3) not more than 6 months old, lying in a doubled-up posture, with head to the north. A small food-vase (fig. 146), of a common type, stood near its head. Close to the south side of this body, and a little higher, were traces of another child (No. 4), apparently about the same age as its companion, and occupying a similar position, but with its head to the south. This also was accompanied by a small food-vase (fig. 147), behind the hips, but inverted, an unusual position for this class of vessel. Though on the plan bodies 3 and 4 are shown on the western edge of the grave, they really were vertically above Nos. 5 and 6. Nearly 4 inches lower were the remains of an individual of small stature (No. 5), on its right side, body flexed, head much crushed and pointing to south-south-west. The bones were of slate colour, probably from the absorption of matter from the wood used in the grave. They seemed to be those of a female from 20 to 22 years of age, but were too far gone to admit of correct measurement.*

August 5th.—A foot below Nos. 3, 4, and 5 was a quantity of calcined human bones (No. 6), which must be considered the primary or first interment. This heap was surrounded by dark matter, possibly the remains of some covering, and measured 24 inches by 8 inches, the greatest diameter pointing south-west and north-east. Round these interments were traces of timber which had apparently formed the sides and ends of a rectangular space measuring 3½ feet by 2 feet, and at each corner was a stake-hole over 2 inches in diameter. No relic was found on this date.

Fully 11 feet south-west of the centre, 1 foot above the base of the mound, and 7 inches under the stratum of chalk grit (through which no opening had ever been made), were traces of the bones of a child (No. 7), showing its flexed position, with the head to the north-west. Judging from the teeth it was probably 12 to 16 months old. No relic was found with the interment.

August 6th.—Below the layer of chalk grit, to the north of the centre, the material was pure clay (non-local), whilst to the south the clay was irregularly mixed with the ferruginous soil and subsoil adjoining the barrow. All the interments had been made previous to the spreading of the chalk grit, and the upper portion of the barrow consisted of soil and blue clay irregularly stratified to its summit. A few chips of flint, a large portion of the cutting end of a stone axe (from which the smaller

* During the last two days, Dr. Wood and Mr. R. Davison, of Driffield, accompanied us in these excavations.

splinters previously found seem to have been struck), part of the lower jaw of a dog, and a portion of the leg bone probably of a pig, were found scattered in the barrow.

This large mound appears to have been raised at two or three different times.

On August 7th and 8th, workmen were employed in filling in the excavation.

BARROW No. C. 28

Is near the last. On April 22nd, 1869, it measured 15 yards in diameter, and about 15 inches in elevation. After turning it over, we noticed that the undisturbed ground beneath it was 8 to 10 inches higher than the ground immediately surrounding it. On this old surface were considerable traces of burning, and a few calcined bones, the remains of a cremated interment, which would shortly have been completely removed by the plough. Not the smallest piece of an urn or other relic was found, excepting several hand-split pieces of black flint. A little loamy clay, brought from a distance, was noticed here and there.

BARROW No. C. 29

Is 40 yards from Barrow C. 28, and is not shown on the Ordnance map. On April 23rd, 1869, its only appearance was a slight rise on the surface, in the centre of which was a dish-shaped cavity, 8 inches deep and 15 inches in diameter. It contained dark-coloured unctuous earth, and in the centre was a food-vase (fig. 148), on its side. A portion of the upper part of its rim had been removed in tilling the land. It has been restored, and measures 6 inches high, 5 inches in diameter at the shoulders, and 3½ inches at the base. It has an unusually deep border for a food vase, which measures no less than 2½ inches, and is ornamented with horizontal "herring-bone" impressions. In form and ornamentation it has much the appearance of some of the cinerary urns. No other relic or trace of bone was observed.

DIVISION "C."

During a fortnight in November, 1874, we explored these eight burial mounds, which, though more crowded than those of the last series described, are arranged in a similarly striking manner.*

BARROW No. C. 76

Is the westernmost barrow, and being surrounded by a large fosse and ridge, and closely locked within the rampart of a double entrenchment of great extent, makes a very striking and interesting relic of prehistoric times.—See figs. 149, 150 and 151. This conspicuous mound is designated a "rath" † by Professor J.

---

* The first few days were unusually fine, but afterwards there was a heavy fall of snow, and the weather during the remainder of the time was mostly of a very wintry character, causing our work to be conducted under adverse conditions. The workmen remained in the neighbourhood, but the writer, when not relieved by his brother, rode from Driffield in the morning and returned at night, being occasionally accompanied by his Driffield friends, Dr. Wood, the late Mr. R. Davison, and the late Mr. J. Stericker, whose lively interest in the proceedings made up in a great part for the depressing effect of the inclemency of the weather.

† "Rivers, Mountains, and Sea Coast of Yorkshire," page 212.

Phillips. It measured 52 feet in diameter and 5 feet in elevation. A block eighteen feet square was removed from the centre. It had apparently been slightly excavated at some previous period. Near the centre, about 12 inches above the base of the mound, was a heap of burnt bones, but no relic. On the old land surface, a little south of the centre, under a quantity of dark greasy soil, was a hammer-head (fig. 152), 5½ inches long, made of the antler of a red deer. The perforation for the handle is circular, with a square countersink at the outside, which would enable the handle to be more securely fixed. Under the bones was an oval grave cut in the rock, measuring 5 feet east and west, 3½ feet across, and 3 feet deep. At the bottom were the crushed and decayed remains of a youth about twelve years of age, on the right side, head to the west, with knees pulled up and both arms doubled to the body

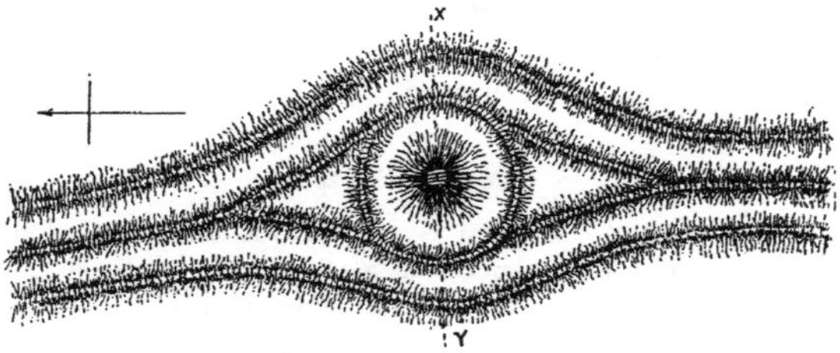

FIG. 149.
Plan of Barrow C 76 and Adjoining Entrenchments.

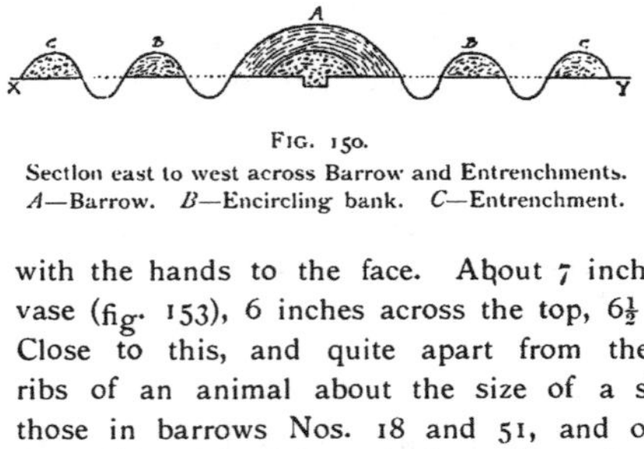

FIG. 150.
Section east to west across Barrow and Entrenchments.
A—Barrow. B—Encircling bank. C—Entrenchment.

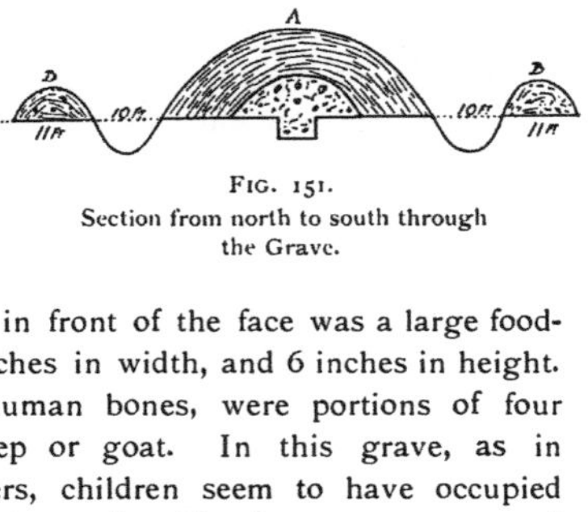

FIG. 151.
Section from north to south through
the Grave.

with the hands to the face. About 7 inches in front of the face was a large food-vase (fig. 153), 6 inches across the top, 6½ inches in width, and 6 inches in height. Close to this, and quite apart from the human bones, were portions of four ribs of an animal about the size of a sheep or goat. In this grave, as in those in barrows Nos. 18 and 51, and others, children seem to have occupied the primary burial, and these have been interred with the same care and ceremony as was bestowed upon those whom we have good reason to believe were the chiefs of tribes or distinguished heads of families. The grave was filled with broken chalk rock, and the same material formed an inner cairn above it, whilst the upper and greater portion of the mound was of earth, as shown in figs. 149, 150, and 151. Traces of burning were observed about the centre of the barrow; and in several places were obtained pieces of stag's horn, and some large pieces of human femur, tibia, and fibula, which were slightly burnt. After cutting a section where the encircling rampart of the mound unites with the rampart of the entrenchment, and otherwise carefully

PLATE XVIII.

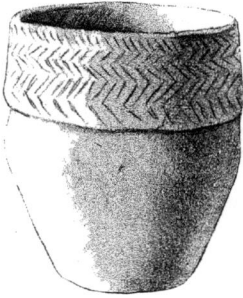

FIG. 148. $\frac{1}{2}$

FIG. 155. $\frac{1}{1}$

FIG. 153. $\frac{1}{3}$

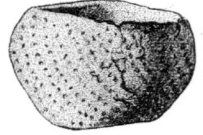

FIG. 161. $\frac{1}{2}$

FIG. 154. $\frac{1}{1}$

FIG. 163. $\frac{1}{2}$

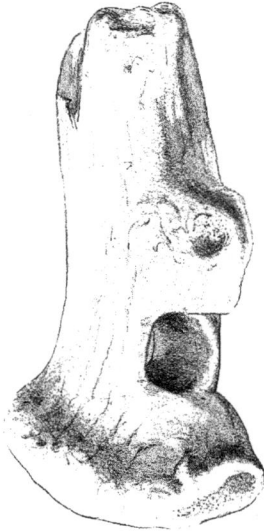

FIG. 152. $\frac{2}{3}$

FIG 159 a.

FIG. 159 b.

examining the connection of the two works, the writer is of the opinion that the formation of the barrow and the small encircling ditch (the material from which had in the main gone to form the centre core or cairn of the barrow) was earlier than that of the entrenchment; but that at some time after the entrenchment was excavated the fosse of the barrow was enlarged, and the material in places cast partly upon the adjoining ridge of the entrenchment.

BARROW No. C 81

Is not mapped by the Ordnance Surveyors, and, except to the trained eye, is hardly observable on the surface.

Its diameter was about 20 feet, and elevation 8 to 10 inches. In the ground beneath it there was a shallow depression 14 inches deep and 28 inches in diameter at the top, with the sides burnt red, containing the cremated bones of a large individual and some pieces of burnt animal bone, mixed with wood ashes and soil. No relic was found with this interment.

BARROW No. C 77

Measures 60 feet in diameter and 3 feet in height. At the base, near the centre of the mound, portions of the remains of two bodies were found, which had been broken up by the former explorers (the members of the Yorkshire Antiquarian Club), some years previously.

No grave was found. A link of jet (fig. 154) was obtained in a quantity of dark soil, about 12 inches below the surface, and a little north of the centre of the barrow. Close by was a barbed arrow-head, and a small flint knife (fig. 155). The mound consisted entirely of soil, and no mixture of clay was observed.

BARROW No. "C 80"

Was similar in size to Barrow C 77. It was formed of fine dark soil, with hardly any admixture of gritty matter. The previous explorers had turned over the greater portion of this mound, and had emptied an oval grave about 2 feet deep, from which they had extracted the interment mentioned in the Proceedings of the Yorkshire Antiquarian Club, for 1853.

Portions of a human skull and other bones were found strewed round the grave.

BARROW No. C 78

Resembled in size the two preceding barrows, and consisted entirely of gritty chalk. About the centre, a little below the base of the barrow, were the scattered bones of a youth (presumably disturbed by the Yorkshire Antiquarian Club in 1853). Behind these was a large grave which the previous excavators had slightly entered on the north side. In emptying this, a large quantity of soot-like matter was observed adhering to the sides of the grave, probably representing a wooden chest or covering which had decayed. The grave was circular, 6 feet in diameter at the top and 5 feet at the bottom, and 4½ feet deep. The lower half was charged with rough chalk, and the upper portion with chalk grit. This, like a few others we explored, contained no interment.

BARROW No. C 75

Had a diameter of 75 feet, an elevation of 12 inches, and was apparently only the lower part of the original mound.   Near the centre, at the base of the barrow, were two adult skeletons.   No. 1 (fig. 156) was on the left side, the knees bent to a right angle with the trunk, the left arm doubled with hand to chin, and right arm over the body with hand on left elbow.   Its head was to the west.   The femur measured 18 inches, and tibia 15 inches.   Touching the crown of the head were 46 flint flakes, many 3 inches in length, and one is ground on one edge (fig. 157), and another delicately serrated (fig. 158) throughout the whole of its length.   Close behind the shoulders were two flint flake knives, one of which is 4 inches long (fig. 159).   This knife has been struck from the side of a kidney-shaped nodule.   Its inner side is quite flat, without any chipping on it; but there is a large bulb of percussion at the narrow end.   Its outer side retains the weathered surface and the original curve of the

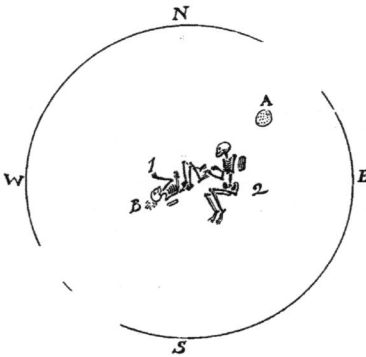

FIG. 156.

A—Burnt bones.
B— Forty-six flint flakes near the skull.

nodule, and only the slightest chipping was required, for a short distance on one side, to give it a very sharp cutting edge.

Body No. 2 was on its right side, head to the north, hands in front of chest, and the legs similarly bent and in contact with those of its companion.   The femur and tibia measured $16\frac{3}{4}$ inches and $14\frac{1}{4}$ inches respectively.   Close behind the shoulders was a very beautiful and almost unique flint knife* (fig. 160), which, by an unfortunate blow of the pick, was fractured into five pieces.   After having been carefully united, this very delicate blade measures $4\frac{3}{8}$ inches long, $1\frac{3}{16}$ of an inch wide, and is only $\frac{1}{12}$ of an inch in thickness; both sides having been so far ground down as to give it the greatest possible tenuity, and the edge all round is slightly sharpened.   This specimen may have alternately served as a knife and as a spoon.   Its unbroken condition at the time of interment indicates that great care was taken in its preservation, and that it had never been allowed to fall on anything hard—an accident which must have broken it to pieces.

About 8 feet north-east of the two skeletons, and also on the old surface-line, was a small heap of burnt bones of a small person (marked A on the plan), but no relic accompanied them.   The two skulls from the bodies were irreparably crushed.   A few chippings of flint and pieces of animal bone were picked from the mound.

---

* A similarly-shaped one, but a little smaller, has since been found in Howe Hill (Barrow No. 273) Duggleby, and is figured in the description of that barrow.

BARROW No. C 74

Is one of the four mounds of this group opened by the Yorkshire Antiquarian Club in August, 1853. Its diameter was about 50 feet, and elevation about 16 inches. Under the mound, a little south of the centre, a circular hollow, 2 feet in diameter and 14 inches deep, was found. The previous excavation had been close to its eastern side. At the bottom were some cremated human bones, mixed with burnt wood and soil, which must have been introduced while hot, as the sides of the receptacle were burnt red. Amongst these stood an incense-cup (fig. 161); and above was a crumbling trough-formed receptacle, which had been cut out of a log of oak, about two feet long and 14 inches wide, much of which remained in position. Probably it had served the purpose of a food-vase. Its sides and bottom had been converted into charcoal, probably by having been placed immediately on the top of the glowing embers, and quickly covered up. There were also the remains of a carbonised lid of oak, on the top of which were two bone pins and three small chips of flint, all of which were burnt and splintered.

BARROW No. C 79

Had a diameter of 50 feet, an elevation of 16 inches, and had not been previously opened. In the centre, about the base of the mound, was a shallow circular cavity, in which was a quantity of burnt bones mixed with dark soil and charcoal. In the midst of this, a food-vase (fig. 162) and an incense-cup (fig. 163) in fragments, were obtained.

Almost directly below these was a hole in the rock, the size and shape of a medium-sized cinerary urn, containing burnt bones of a child at the bottom, and a quantity of clean oak charcoal, in large lumps, at the top. The sides of both receptacles were burnt, probably by the introduction of the contents in a glowing condition.

The mounds of this division, like several in group No. 2, were remarkable for the absence of clay in their construction, though it could have been readily obtained close by.

DIVISION D.

Contained six barrows, arranged, as far as number is concerned, similarly to those in the last division.

BARROW No. 113

Is the most easterly of this set of barrows. On April 14th, 15th, 16th, and 17th, 1868, when they were excavated, it measured 45 feet in diameter, and 16 inches in elevation. On its western side a double entrenchment makes a slight detour, in order to avoid the mound, thus proving that it was constructed since the barrow. About eight feet east from the centre, and on a level with its base, were two heaps of burnt bones of young persons, close together; and with the most northerly one was a small but beautifully formed knife (fig. 164) of black flint. Under these was a grave, in which, at the depth of two feet, was another heap of cremated bones of a young individual. On the top of this was a fine bronze pricker (fig. 165), and on the south side a very small incense-cup (fig. 166), quite perfect. It is without ornamentation, with the exception of a few impressions given by the finger-nail, and measures $1\frac{3}{4}$ inches in height, and $2\frac{1}{4}$ inches across the top. Close by, but rather lower down, was another heap of burnt human bones, but nothing accompanied them except a piece of a bone hairpin. The grave measured 3 feet deep, $4\frac{1}{2}$ feet north and south, and 3 feet east and west, and at the bottom was a middle-aged body, on its back, head to south, both arms at full length by the sides, and legs pulled up to a right angle with the trunk. A femur measured 18 inches, and a tibia $15\frac{1}{4}$ inches, and they are of strong make. A few bits of human bone were mixed in the material filling the grave, but no other relic was found.

About the centre of the barrow was a second oval grave, 16 inches from the former, and measuring 3 feet 8 inches deep, 4 feet east-north-east by west-south-west, and 3 feet across. At the bottom were the remains of an aged female, on the right side, with head to the east, knees pulled up, and both hands brought up in front of the face. Just above the left shoulder was a bone hairpin (fig. 167A) four inches long, in a position clearly indicating that it had secured the back hair at the time of interment.* Close under the right side of the head were five more similar bone hairpins (fig. 167, b, c, d, e, f), close together, which had probably been placed there as a reserve supply.† Near the head were three black flints, one being oval (fig. 168) $2\frac{1}{4}$ inches by $1\frac{3}{4}$ inches, and $\frac{1}{4}$ of an inch thick, chipped round the edge. The others were a saw (fig. 169), and (fig. 170) probably a knife. Traces of a round piece of wood about 18 inches long and $1\frac{1}{4}$ inches thick occurred close upon this body. One end touched the chin, and the other end crossed the middle of the femur. A humerus measured $13\frac{1}{2}$ inches, tibia $15\frac{1}{4}$ inches, and femur 19 inches, and the bones were rather slender. Portions of the bones of a strong individual, and the femur and other bones of a child, were distributed throughout the upper part of the grave. Eleven chippings, 1 spear-point, and one knife of flint, shaped like a half-moon, were found in the mound. No ditch had encircled the barrow.

BARROW No. 97.

This Barrow occupied a rather smaller area than the last, and was levelled more by the plough. The contained body had been burned and the main part of the ashes placed on a thin bed of clay, which had been spread on the original surface. A spear-head, or knife of black flint, 2 inches long (fig. 171), accompanied the bones, and over them was inverted a medium-sized cinerary urn, similar to that from barrow 24 (fig. 401), and ornamented on the outside of the border and below it with deep cuneiform gashes. It was irreparably crushed by the plough-teams passing over the

---

* Dr. Thurnam, in his description of long barrows, (Archæologia Vol. xlii.) mentions 6 pins having been found with a skeleton.

† This is a rare instance in British burials, but similar finds have occurred with Roman interments. In the "Hand Book" of the Antiquities in the York Museum, 8th edition, p. 126, is recorded the finding of the extraordinary number of 14 jet pins in a stone coffin in 1840. Three jet hairpins were found in 1874 in a stone coffin under the head of another body.

FIG. 157. ¼

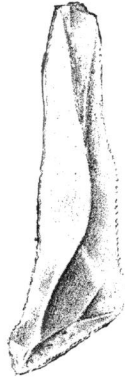

FIG. 158. ¾

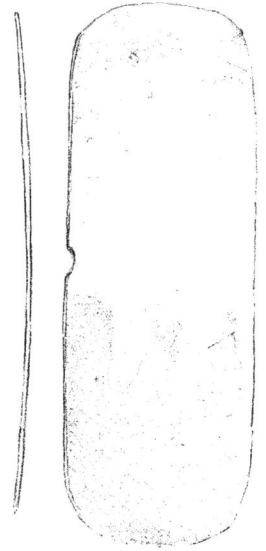

FIG. 160. ¹

FIG. 166. ½

FIG. 164. ¾

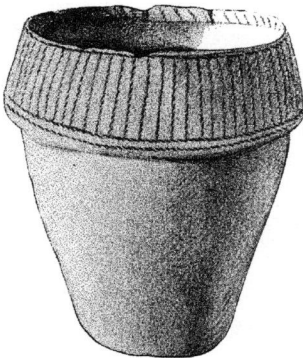

FIG. 162. ½

FIG. 165. ¹

FIG. 169. ¼

mound. Close to the south-south-west side of the urn was a circular hole in the rock, 2½ feet deep, 3 feet wide at the top and narrowing to a point at the bottom. It was filled with burnt wood and unctuous brown-coloured mould, containing a few human bones dispersed throughout the mass. Probably after placing the main portion of the bones under the urn, the remainder, with the embers, were pushed into the hole whilst hot, as its sides are burnt red. The bones may have been those of a young mother and child, as the ulna of a juvenile was recognised; and the adult bones, judging from the very open sutures observed on burnt portions of the skull, were those of a young person. A nearly complete carbonised nut or plumstone was picked from the burnt wood in the hole, and four chippings of black flint were obtained from other places during the excavation.

BARROW No. 50.

This barrow is near the western margin of some double entrenchments situated west of Aldro, and just opposite to barrow No. 113, which touches the east side of the same entrenchments. On March 19th, 1866, it measured 70 feet across, but was so far reduced as to give an elevation of 9 to 10 inches only. We turned over most of this barrow, but only found 5 handstruck pieces, and a circular disc of dark flint, several splinters of human and animal bone, and three small portions of a food-vase. In the rock below the centre was an oblong grave, 2 feet 9 inches deep, and measuring 6½ feet east and west, and 4 feet in the opposite direction. In the north corner, at the west end of the grave, was a pile of *un*burnt human bones, accompanied by the tooth of an ox. At the east end was a similar heap, consisting of the bones of two or more persons, on the top of which was a splinter of dark flint and a keen-edged and peculiarly-formed flint knife (fig. 172) of the same colour and measuring 1⅞ inches long and 1¼ inches broad. It is worthy of note that from this deposit two burnt splinters from a human leg-bone were taken. The bones of each of these deposits must have been freed, in a great measure, from the flesh, thoroughly disjointed, and some of them broken to pieces, previous to interment, otherwise they could not have been heaped together in the close manner in which they were found. Some of the bones of the legs and arms were entire, but all the lower-jaws had been broken, in two or more pieces, and the skulls into numerous fragments, and were mixed up in the heaps. Similarly puzzling deposits were also found in the neighbouring barrows Nos. 52, 53, and 54,* and they seem to have been peculiar to the barrows of this neighbourhood. The only other deposits of the kind which have come under our observation were in barrows Nos. 99, C.63, and 72.

The bottom of the grave contained unctuous earth, which 8 to 10 inches above, was replaced by rubbly chalk, which in turn was followed by another stratum of unctuous earth, reaching to the top and joining the base of the barrow. Scattered throughout the grave were numerous splinters of human bone (portions of skulls, and fragments of leg and arm bones), and bits of burnt wood, a few pieces of animal bone, two small portions of a food-vase, and one small piece of black flint.

---

* Of such a strange mode of burial we have historical proof, for Diodorus Siculus, writing of the Carthaginians, says, "They have a strange custom about burying the dead. They cut the body up in pieces and put all the parts in an urn, and rear a great heap of stones over it."

BARROW No. 51

Is about 100 yards east-south-east of the preceding barrow. During the years 1843 to 1848 Mr. Isaac Staveley, who then farmed the land, removed this and six other barrows in the neighbourhood, and spread the material over such land as was deficient in soil. He kept an account of the number of cartloads removed from one large barrow, which amounted to over 700. The writer was also told by one of the labourers employed by Mr. Staveley that the bones of a very tall man were found, the thigh-bone of which was said to have measured 24 inches.*

On March 21st, 1866, nothing remained of this barrow but a little of the east side, just sufficient to enable its position and extent to be ascertained. The sites of the other five could not be identified. We commenced at a point which we thought to be the centre, and turned over the soil to the rock below. After proceeding several feet northwards from the centre a place containing foreign earth was reached, and proved to be the north side of a circular trench 47 feet in diameter. We thoroughly emptied a segment of this circular trench, on the north side, extending 30 feet. It had been dug below the surface 2½ feet, with a width of 3½ feet at the top and 15 inches at the bottom. It contained clay, and at the bottom, on the north side, were the bases of three antlers of the red deer, apparently picks, measuring about 12 inches long, and each having the first and second brow-tines attached (figs. 173, 174, and 175). The interior of the trench was filled with stiff greasy earth to the level of the surface-line, from which a large and very roughly-chipped hand weapon of native flint (a ball or sling-stone), some small pieces of bone, and a few chips of dark-coloured flint were taken. A similar material to that in the trench had been heaped above to a height of 16 to 18 inches, as shown in a small portion of the barrow which remained. Besides emptying the trench on the north side, we made sections by sinking holes all the way round it at a distance of about ten feet, and in every place found the hollow filled with a similar material, and nearly the same in form.

A little to the south of the centre of this enclosure was a small grave. It measured 4 feet east and west, and nearly 2 feet across, and had a depth of 17 inches. At the bottom two young children had been interred, doubled up, one at each end of the grave, with their heads pointing west, as shown by a few portions of the teeth, skull, and leg bones, which had not entirely decayed. These very fragile remains rested on a thin layer of dark decayed matter. No relic accompanied them, and the grave above was filled with dark clay, almost precisely similar to that in the encircling trench. Judging from what remained of the barrow on the east side of the trench, its diameter had not been less than 75 feet, thus extending beyond the trench at least 15 feet in all directions. Probably this ditch, in common with several others which have been observed under barrows, had marked off the place of interment previous to the raising of the mound. The grave and trench alike were filled and covered by the mound.

* This may be a slight exaggeration.

FIG. 167 a. ¼

FIG. 167 b. ¼

FIG. 167 c. ¼

FIG 167 d. ¾

FIG. 167 e. ¾

FIG. 167 f. ½

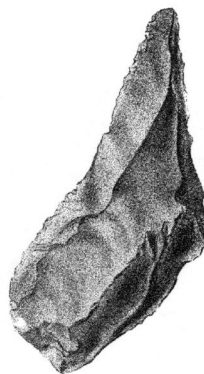

FIG 171. ¾

FIG 168.   ½

FIG. 170.

BARROW No. C 47.

On July 8th, 9th, and 10th, 1872, four workmen were employed in excavating this barrow. It measured 60 feet in diameter, 3 feet 3 inches in elevation, and consisted of soil from the neighbouring land interspersed with layers of clay brought from a distance. These were from 2 to 6 inches thick. About 12 feet east of the centre, and a foot below the surface, was a heap of calcined human bones. On the same horizon, 18 feet south of the centre, was an inhumed body, apparently a male about forty-five years of age, on its right side, with head to south, knees pulled up, left hand on the knee, and right hand on the chest. A femur measured 18½ inches. The bed underneath it was stained black. At the centre a shallow circular excavation extended 15 inches below the base of the mound, and measured 2 feet 2 inches in diameter at the top, and 18 inches at the bottom. In this were the cremated bones of an adult, probably, judging from the slenderness of some of the bones, those of a female. A little to the west of the centre, not more than 5 inches from the surface, were portions of a small food-vase. The remainder had been destroyed by the plough. Bits of burnt wood were noticed near all the interments.

No relic accompanied any of the bodies, but from the mound were taken five pieces of an urn, and the following objects of flint:—one fine slingstone, chipped into nearly the form and size of a bantam's egg ; the point of a beautifully-formed arrow-head ; one double convex disc, 1⅜ of an inch in diameter, only half-an-inch in thickness in the centre, and chipped on both sides ; one flake knife ; and the greater part of a double-edged flake-saw, the serrated edge on one side showing marks of wear.

BARROW No. 49

Is the most westerly barrow of this division, and is near to the Leavening Brow chalk-pit. On March 16th, 1866, it had a diameter of 30 feet, and was almost a foot in elevation.* A portion 18 feet long by 11 feet wide was first removed. Near the centre, between the original surface soil and some rubbly chalk, was a doubled-up body, on its back, with legs pressed to the right and the head twisted in the same direction, and pointing nearly north-west. A femoral bone measured 19 inches, and belonged to a young person, as a wisdom tooth was found only partly protruding from the lower jaw, though the grinding surface of some of the molars was somewhat worn. The skull was in numerous fragments. Some potsherds and three worked flints (figs. 176, 177, and 178) were placed near the skull. One of these, 2¼ inches long and 1 inch broad, was probably used as a spear. Another is an oval knife 2⅜ inches in length. Close to the body, in a south-easterly direction, a few bits of charcoal were observed, and the soil was reddened by fire. No grave occurred underneath this body. The southern margin of the barrow was next explored, and here a trench cut 2½ feet into the chalk rock was found, which on further examination proved to encircle the barrow.

* The ancient surface line beneath most of the barrows which we have opened is higher than the surface of the adjoining land. This may be attributed in many cases to the great length of time during which the barrows have protected the old surface soil beneath them, whereas the ground not covered by them has been subjected to denudation, the lowering action of agricultural operations, the removal of inorganic matter by repeated cropping of the land, and the constant percolation of rainwater carrying surface soil into the fissures of the rock below

DIVISION E

Completes the Aldro group. The seven mounds of which it consists differ in arrangement from the previously described divisions of this group. Two of the mounds (marked A and B on the plan) have not been opened.

BARROW No. 117

Is not shown on the Ordnance maps, but is situated a little to the north-west of "Brown Moor" Farm-house, and forms the eastern angle of this division.

On June 30th and July 1st, 1868, it measured 45 feet in diameter, and $1\frac{1}{2}$ feet above the surrounding land, but only a foot above the original surface beneath it. The west-south-west portion of the barrow is crossed by a filled-in trench,* which extends southwards to a spring of water in Brown Moor Dale, and is traceable in the opposite direction as far as the southern side of the double entrenchments which enclose Aldro. An old labourer on the farm informed the writer that when the field on the north side of the entrenchment was in tillage, this hollow-way could be seen in the crops, extending still further northwards.

Traces of loamy clay, pieces of British pot, 1 flake knife, a circular instrument, and 7 splinters of flint, were the only indications of the nature of the mound.

BARROW No. 125

Is a little north-north-west from No. 117. The excavations in this barrow and No. 126 were conducted during October, 1868. The former measured 66 feet in diameter and 3 feet in elevation. Work was commenced at its northern border, and the greater portion was turned over to its base. The ground below was also probed. The mound proved to be partly built up, like many others, with a considerable quantity of clayey earth brought from a distance. Near the centre was an oval grave, which measured $5\frac{1}{2}$ feet east and west, by $3\frac{1}{2}$ feet, and extended 3 feet below the base of the mound. This grave was sunk into ground of the nature of a sandpipe, and nothing but a film of dark-coloured matter occurred at the bottom. The earthy matter filling the grave was similar to that which formed the mound, and peeled readily from the sides, showing a good section of the sandpipe into which the grave had been cut. The excavation was then extended towards the southern edge of the barrow, and exhibited an ancient trench which had been cut across it, clearly without any regard for the contents of the mound. This hollow measured $6\frac{1}{2}$ feet in width at the top and $1\frac{1}{2}$ feet only at the bottom, and reached 4 feet below the base of the barrow. Its existence had been indicated in previous years by a green line in the corn crops, extending east and west from this barrow, and entering at a right angle the trench which passes in a northerly direction through the last described barrow.

---

* This trench appears to be one of a series, which radiates from a point near the Aldro Farmhouse, similar to those hollow-ways which radiate from the village of Fimber and described in the chapter on entrenchments. These, though now quite filled in, are at times distinctly traceable by a green streak in the corn crops before harvest.

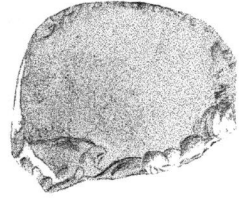

FIG. 172. ¼

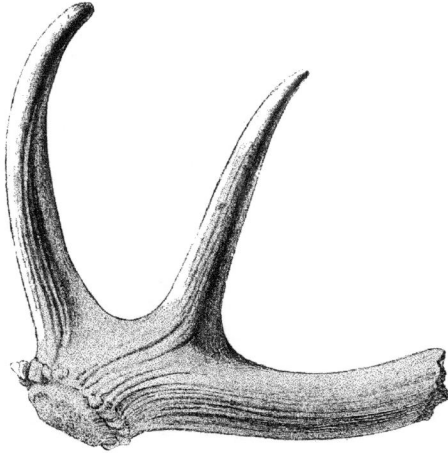

FIG. 173. ¼

FIG. 176.

FIG. 177.

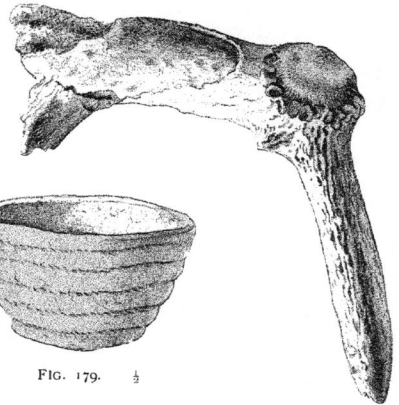

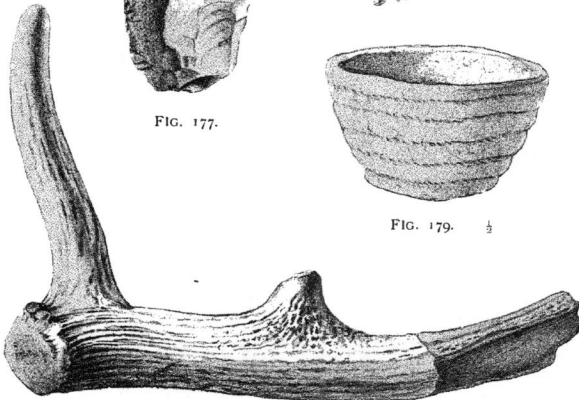

FIG. 179. ½

FIG. 174. ⅓

FIG. 175. ¼

BARROW No. 126

Is a little to the north of the last one. It measured 42 feet in diameter and 1 foot 4 inches above the adjoining ground, having been much lowered by agricultural work. It was excavated on similar lines to the last one, and near the centre were portions of the rim of a cinerary urn, which had been inverted over cremated bones placed on the old surface line. The base of the urn and part of the bones had been removed by the plough. About 2½ feet north-north-west of the urn another deposit of calcined human bones was discovered. No instrument was found with either interment.

The adjoining barrow, marked B, is in a plantation, and covered with trees. It has not yet been opened so far as we are aware.

BARROW No. C 48

Forms the northern corner of this division of barrows, and is enclosed between the ramparts of the southern side of the entrenchments which form an irregular oblong enclosure, in the eastern corner of which stands the large farm-house known by the name of Aldro. At some distant period a large portion of the northern side of this barrow has been cut away to straighten a cart-road which passes close by it, and runs for some distance along the north side of the vallum of the entrenchments.

On July 12th, 13th, and 15th, 1872, the undisturbed portion of the mound, which was 7 feet high, was excavated, and the remains of an encircling ditch were discovered. The diameter of the mound when entire had been about 20 yards. At its base foreign clay predominated, but soil obtained from the immediate neighbourhood was the most abundant in the upper part. At a point 11 feet east of the centre, and about a foot from the surface of the mound, were a few burnt bones in the bottom of a cinerary urn. The other portions of the urn and deposit had been destroyed at the time of planting a quickwood fence, which runs from east to west over the mound. Under the centre of the mound was an oval hole, extending 16 inches into the rock, and measuring 2 feet 10 inches north and south, and 2 feet 3 inches east and west at the top. At the bottom was a heap of cremated bones of an adult, on the top of which rested an inverted cup-shaped "incense-cup" (fig. 179), measuring 2 inches in height, and 3¼ inches in diameter at the top. It is partly vitrified by heat, and five horizontal rows of cord-like impressions encircle the upper portion of its exterior. Nothing else was found.

The sides and bottom of this grave were burnt red, probably by a quantity of wood ashes having been deposited therein in a glowing condition, the heat from which may also have given the vitreous appearance to the incense-cup. The grave was completely sealed up by a covering of hard black-coloured unctuous material, probably the residue of decayed organic matter. Above this was a mixture of clay and soil similar to that in the mound above. From the mound, one small disc of flint, shaped like a horse-shoe, and a finger-shaped flint 3 inches long, were taken, but no potsherds were found.

BARROW No. 94,

Though somewhat detached, properly belongs to this group.

On May 20th and 22nd,* 1867, it measured 60 feet in diameter 18 inches above the surrounding ground, and consisted for the most part of loamy earth brought from some distance. A grave, situated about 8 feet east of the centre and pointing north and south, was found in the rock. It measured 7 feet by 2½ feet at the top, 1½ feet at the bottom, and was 2 feet deep. Its contents were soil, rubbly chalk, and foreign clay, mixed with layers of wood ashes; and in the middle, near the floor, was the scapula of a small mammal. About the same distance to the west of the centre of the barrow was a second hole in the rock, about the same length and breadth as the other, but in this case only about a foot deep. It also pointed north and south, and was filled with soil, clay, and chalk rubble, but no trace of bone was observed. In the centre, on the base line of the barrow, were remains of two bodies, lying one behind the other, upon a thin bed of clay. They were both on their right sides, legs bent up, and their heads to the south. Above them was a thin layer of clay, and, underneath, the clay was covered with dark matter. All that remained of the bodies were portions of their leg-bones and part of the right side of the skull of the one which was accompanied by the knife mentioned below. Close behind the shoulders of the most easterly body was a very beautiful and probably unique knife made of a flake of black flint, on its flat side, over 3½ inches long and ⅞ of an inch broad throughout its entire length (fig. 180). Each extremity is beautifully chipped on both sides to a keen broad chisel edge, and from end to end the flat side of the blade is ground smooth by rubbing, and the two obtuse edges have been made by whetting, while the upper side has three facets partly polished. Between the shoulders of one body and the breast of the other had stood a semi-globular food-vase with a deep projecting lip, resembling those from barrow 18 (fig. 15). Part of this vase had been removed and destroyed, probably by rabbits burrowing in the mound. One lump and five splinters of black flint, two of which were finely serrated on one edge, were all that we found in the barrow.

---

* This day was bitterly cold for the end of May, and from morning to night repeated showers of snow whitened the hills.

No. IV.—THE ACKLAM WOLD GROUP.

THIS occupies the extreme west end of the chalk promontory that overlooks the picturesque villages of Acklam and Leavening, which stand on ridges of out-cropping oolitic rocks below. It contains seventeen barrows, somewhat crowded together. Several of these were opened by the Yorkshire Antiquarian Club, and

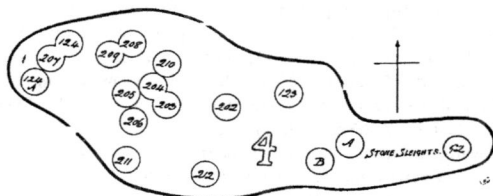

THE ACKLAM WOLD GROUP.

the result of the examination is recorded by Mr. William Procter in an account of the Society's proceedings for 1854. An abstract of that account is given below :—

> "On Acklam Wold and the surrounding hills are a large number of tumuli. To them the attention of the Club was first directed. The excavation of three were made in August, 1849. In the first [probably No. 206 on the accompanying plan], about a foot from the surface, was discovered quantities of calcined bones, and among them was a beautiful bone pin [fig. 181], 9 inches in length. Near the top a perforation passes completely through the bone. The excavation was continued to the depth of 4 feet, when a skeleton presented itself to the excavators. It was that of a male, laid on the right side, with head to the north and feet to the south, the arms brought forward and bent at the elbows, one of them touching the drawn-up knees. At this point was discovered a small urn [food-vase, fig. No. 182], unbaked, presenting no marks of the wheel, and having the other char-acters in figure and ornament of British workmanship. It was 21 inches in circumference at the upper edge, and 6 inches high.*

> "The second tumulus examined was much less elevated, and gave different results to the preceding one. About a foot from the surface was discovered a broken urn of very large dimensions, probably 60 inches in circumference, full of human calcined bones, and surrounded by blue and variously-coloured clays. This urn, though different in detail, had the same general character as that taken from the first barrow. No skeleton by further digging was discovered.

> "The third mound inspected on this occasion was the smaller of two surrounded by a fosse, commonly called a twin-barrow [probably barrow No. 205 of my series]. In the interior a curious arrangement of flint and chalk rubble occurred, frequently found in these works on the wolds, and in it some loose bones with slight marks of fire, but no urn or skeleton.

---

* The pin and urn are figured in " Crania Britannica," and are here reproduced (figs. 181 and 182).

" In the following October a second examination of the group of barrows was undertaken by the Club, and the operations were commenced on the twin barrow [No. 204] to the one last described. About 3 feet from the surface the original deposit was found, consisting of a small skeleton, the head directed slightly to the north of east, and the feet east of south, placed on the right side, with the face to the north. The arms were bent on the chest, with the legs doubled up under the thighs, which were bent at right angles to the body. About a foot from the skull, to the north, was a small vase * [fig. 183] of baked clay, measuring 5½ inches in diameter at the mouth and 3½ inches high, and capable of holding about a pint. It contained a dark unctuous-looking earth abounding in organic matter and a thin fragment of pottery which had, judging from certain characters, originally formed the cover of the vessel in which it was found. [These fragments are now lost.] Extending from the waist to the knees of the skeleton, which were curiously discoloured as if scorched,† was a large deposit of burnt human bones, among which were a few fœtal bones and a large pin.

" The largest tumulus [No. 208] of the group was now made the object of our search. It was found to be composed of chalk rubble and clay, and afforded no evidence of interment. The examinations of the larger mounds in this district render it extremely probable that they were not for the purpose of burial, but raised for the sake of observation or the performance of religious rites.‡ The seventh tumulus is placed near the brow of the wold, overhanging the village of Acklam. It had been opened before,§ but in it we found part of a broken urn, a disturbed human skeleton with evidence of cremation, and the horn core of an ox. Five other tumuli were opened, but in none was any mark of interment presented."

These constitute all the known facts connected with the early opening of any of the barrows of this group.

BARROW No. 92

Is the most easterly barrow of the group, and is situated a little to the east of Stone Sleights farmhouse. It was opened on the 15th of May, 1867, and then had a diameter of 60 feet, a height of 18 inches, and consisted mainly of loamy earth. Near the centre, and within 10 inches of the original surface, was the lower portion of a large cinerary urn, which had contained the burnt bones of a medium-sized individual. The upper part of the urn, which was within reach of the plough, was much broken and crushed. The fragments have been put together and the vessel rebuilt (fig. 185). No relic accompanied the interment. Beneath the old land surface, under the centre of the mound, a space of 20 feet square was excavated down to the rock without discovering anything further. Scattered in the mound were a large slingstone, two small implements (each having one end chipped into a semi-circular form), three flakes, each about two inches long. Two of these are slightly

---

* Now in the York Museum.

† Several similar instances are recorded in the sequel.

‡ The re-opening of these mounds shows this surmise to be erroneous.

§ This probably was the mound opened about 1838 by Messrs. P. Colby and W. Wetherell of Leavening, whom the writer remembers digging into a mound when he was a schoolboy and lived on Leavening Brow, close to this mound ; or it may be the one which was opened a little later by two of the Ordnance Survey staff, who encamped in the midst of this group.

FIG. 178.

FIG. 181.

FIG. 182. ½

FIG. 186. ½

FIG. 187. ¼

FIG. 183. ½

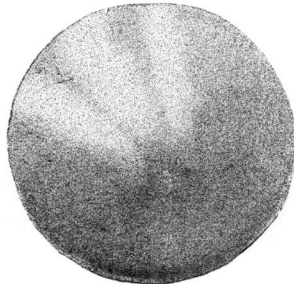

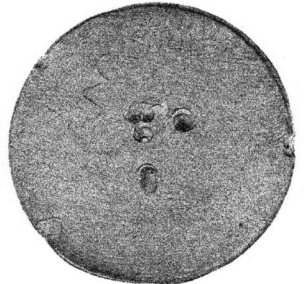

FIG. 180. ¼

FIG. 188. ¼

FIG. 188. ¼

and evenly notched on the edges, and the third has one end worked to a semi-circular form by chipping. Most of these implements are made of foreign flint. Many fragments of a food vase were also found dispersed in the mound. The two adjoining barrows (marked A and B on the map), are near together, and have not been opened. The one near to the north side of the road is very small, while the other, on the opposite side of the road, is a large one, and is planted with trees. Barrow No. 123 is about 300 yards north-west of the two last named, and close to the north side of the road, a little to the north-west of Claypit Plantation.

It was opened on October 8th and 9th, 1868, and measured about 20 yards in diameter, having a very slight elevation. It is not shown in the Ordnance Survey sheet. The greater portion of this barrow was examined down to the rock, and about the assumed centre, an oval grave was met with. It measured 7 feet by 5 feet north-north-east and south-south-west, and was 3½ feet deep. At a depth of 10 inches a plain food vase was discovered (fig. 186), which measured 3 inches in height, 4 inches across the top, and 2¼ inches at the bottom. Close to this was a barbed arrow-head of flint (fig. 187), 1½ inches long.* Small pieces of burnt wood were found throughout the whole of the grave. In a shallow trough-shaped hollow scooped out of the hard chalk floor of the grave were the greatly decayed remains of a middle-aged male, on its left side, with the knees drawn up and the head pointing to north-north-east, and having both hands up to the face. A thigh bone measured 19 inches. Upon the ankle-bones of the right foot was a beautiful jet stud or button, crown upwards (fig. 188), which measured 2⅛ inches in diameter. About 6 inches away, and on the leg bone, was a second stud, in a similar position (fig. 189), 1 inch in diameter, while under the left leg and foot were two buttons (figs. 190 and 191), respectively 1⅛ and 1⅜ inches in diameter, occupying positions exactly similar to those found on the right leg and foot, but with the crowns downwards. This appears to indicate that a pair had been worn on the outside of each leg, and had probably been used as ornaments or fastenings to secure the tops of a pair of sandals or leggings.† Nothing more, beyond a few pieces of charcoal near to the knees, was observed in the hollow. The grave for the most part contained foreign loamy earth. A stone axe (fig. 192) was picked up on the surface about 400 yards from the mound. It has a circular hollow ¼ of an inch deep in the middle on each side, probably intended for the insertion of the finger and thumb when using it. Such indentations, though of rare occurrence, are also occasionally found on hammer-stones.

BARROW No. 202.

During the last week in October and the first week in November, 1877, this and the six neighbouring barrows were opened. It had a diameter of about 55 feet, and an elevation of 4½ feet, and consisted partly of foreign clay, alternating with layers of the local surface soil. An excavation about 20 feet square was made at the centre,- but nearly the whole of the space had been previously

* This, or any other form of arrow-head, is but rarely found accompanying an interment in the Yorkshire Wold barrows, and few instances have occurred in other parts of England.
† Two straps of woollen cloth, believed to be the remains of leggings, were found with a body in an oak-tree coffin from the Threenhoi, near Rube in Jutland, but there is no mention of any kind of fastenings having been found with them.

excavated for the purpose of interring a number of beasts which had died of the cattle plague during 1866. Fortunately an interment near the centre and at about half the depth of the mound had escaped disturbance. It consisted of a basin-shaped hole, 3 feet in diameter at the top, and about 20 inches in depth. Its size and contents showed obvious traces of fire. Spread over the bottom were the calcined bones of an adult and a considerable quantity of wood ashes. These were covered with a little burnt soil, upon which was inverted a large cinerary urn (fig. 193). The inside of the lip and the outside of the rim of this are neatly ornamented with impressed cord marks, and the lines of rude star-shaped impressions, which occupy the deeply-formed neck, appear to have been made by a knot tied at the end of a piece of cord or thong. Close to this urn, and also inverted, was a small "incense cup" (fig. 194), covered externally with impressions of the thumb nail, and at the top with a cord impression. The urn did not contain any of the burnt bones, but stood inverted a little above them. It was about half filled with fine plastic clay, deposited by water which had percolated through small cracks in the sides and bottom.*

BARROW No. 203.

The diameter of this mound was a little less than that of the last, and its elevation was only 18 inches. In the centre was a large disturbed area, which also contained the remains of beasts which had been interred during the cattle plague in 1865 and 1866. This had destroyed all trace of the original burial deposit, and nothing was found.

BARROW No. 204

Had a diameter of 56 feet and an elevation of 3 feet. It consisted of a central core of chalk rubble, 18 inches in thickness, which was covered with a layer of foreign clay, mixed with the adjoining surface soil. In the rubble were observed many large pieces of freestone (Upper Calcareous Grit), from the foot of the chalk escarpment near the village of Acklam, about a mile to the west. At the base of the barrow, on the

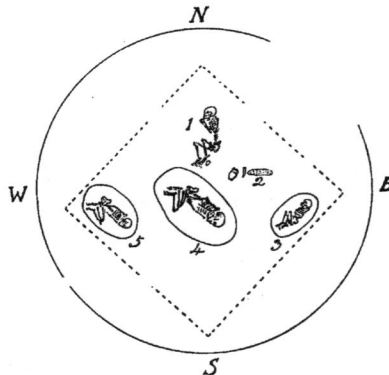

FIG. 195.

original surface of the ground, 10 feet north of the centre, were the remains of a child (fig. 195, interment No. 1) from 5 to 7 years of age. A crushed drinking cup (fig. 196) was found near its feet, and under the skull were some small pieces of another vase.

---

* This deposit of clay was a feature of much interest, as it showed many shrinkage cracks, very similar to the spar-filled cracks in "septarian" nodules from the Kimeridge Clay. Such deposits have been noticed before, not only in urns, but in the interiors of human skulls, the deposit in the latter case being at times so complete as to form a perfect cast of the interior of the skull.

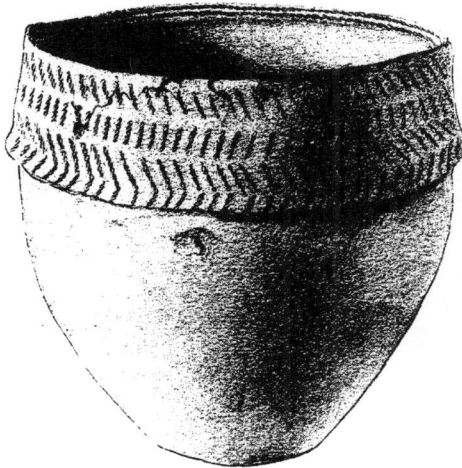

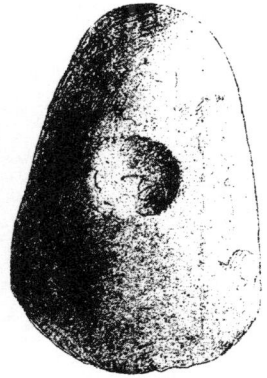

FIG. 192.   ⅟₁

FIG. 185.   ¼

FIG. 215.

FIG. 190.   ¼

FIG. 191.   ¼

FIG. 194   ½

FIG. 189.   ¼

FIG. 197.   ¼

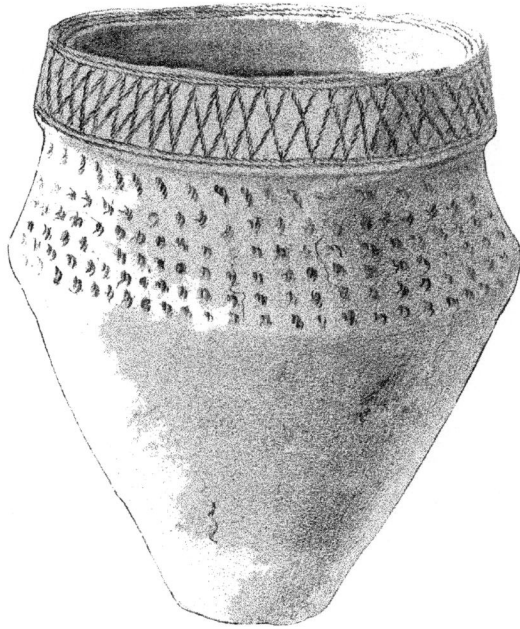

Fig. 193.   ¼

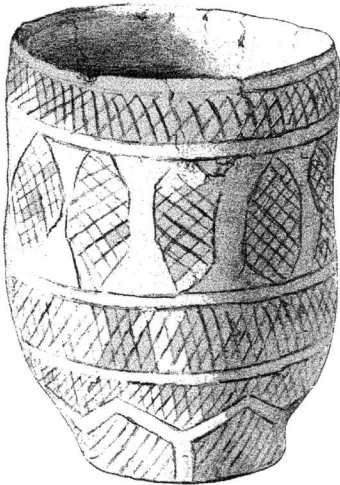

Fig. 196.   ½

Fig. 198.   ½

A second interment (No. 2 on the plan) occurred 8 feet north-east of centre, on the same plane as No. 1. This consisted of an oblong heap of burnt adult bones, measuring 24 inches east-south-east, and 10 inches across. At the west-north-west of this was a finely-flaked knife of black flint (fig. 197) 3¼ inches long, and close by it stood a beautiful little food-vase (fig. 198). In a shallow groove running round the body of the vase are eleven perforated ears or loops, a very unusual number. Eleven feet east of the centre was a small grave, sunk about 1 foot below the original level of the ground, which contained the remains of an infant (No. 3 on the plan), but no relic.

In the centre of the mound were traces of an old excavation, in which fragments of the unburnt bones of an adult were discovered. This burial had probably been disturbed by the Yorkshire Antiquarian Club in 1849. It may be the barrow described in its report as that which contained a body accompanied by a food-vase (fig. 183). A small grave about 2 feet in depth was met with at the centre, from which the skull (No. 4), though broken into numerous pieces, has been preserved. The long bones were too much decayed to enable them to be measured, but their positions are indicated in fig. 195. About 7 feet west of the centre occurred body No. 5, on the bottom of a small grave about 2 feet below the base of the mound. The remains were those of a child, probably about 6 or 7 years of age, and were so much decayed that no measurements could be taken.

BARROW No. 205

Is situated close to the north-west side of the last, and closely resembles it in size and construction. Like it, also, it contained blocks of freestone. This barrow is probably the third of the Acklam Wold mounds opened by the Yorkshire Antiquarian Club, and the one in which they found nothing. The fosse then described as surrounding the two mounds is now almost obliterated. The form of the grave—or rather series of graves—is unusual, as will be seen by a reference to the plan and section (figs. 199 and 200), and this peculiar triangular outline of the grave obtained to a depth of 18 inches. Interment No. 1 was that of an old man of large stature, and occurred 18 inches below the old surface level, upon, and extending over each side of a piece of undisturbed rock about 16 inches in width, which formed a division between bodies Nos. 3 and 5. The femur, tibia, and humerus measured 21, 16½, and 14¼ inches respectively, and the length of the spinal column measured, from the base of the skull to the apex of the sacrum, 3 feet 2 inches. These remains were crushed and injured by having been in contact with large pieces of chalk. The second body (No. 2) was placed at the same depth, but, unlike any of the other interments, was covered with a mass of clay, which filled the grave and extended to the surface of the barrow. The femur measured 18½ inches and the tibia 14¾ inches. Owing mainly to its being in contact with wet clay, which had been brought from a distance, the bones were much decomposed and the skull had almost disappeared. Near the knees was a small food-vase (fig. 201) of elegant form, and just above the left hip was a small knife of black flint (fig. 202). It was quite evident that this interment was posterior to the formation of the core of chalk rubble, the eastern side of which had been cut through. The grave was filled in with clayey earth similar to the substance of the mound itself. Burial No. 3 occurred on the floor of the grave at a depth of 4 feet from the base of the mound, and was probably that of a young female. The femur, tibia, and humerus measured respectively 17½, 14, and 12¾ inches. A small knife of black flint (fig. 202A) was found at the right side of the pelvis.

Interment No. 4 was that of a male. It also rested on the bottom of the grave, a little to the north of No. 3, in the posture shown in the plan. A femur measured 18 inches, a tibia 15 inches, and both were very strong. Between the knees and left shoulder was the blade of a bronze dagger (fig. 203) 6 inches long, pointing to the knees. No remains of the handle were found. Near it was a quantity of decayed wood and stains of green oxide, probably from the decay of the scabbard.

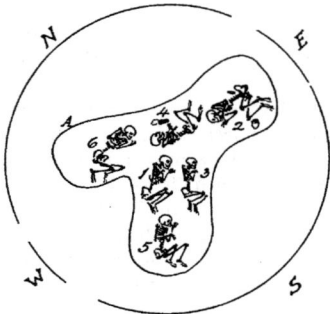

FIG. 199.—BARROW NO. 205.

The line *A* is an enlarged outline of the grave, or graves, at a depth of 18 inches below the base of the mound.

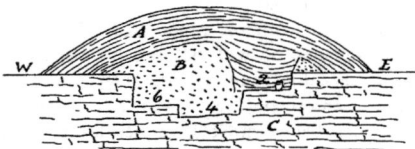

FIG. 200.—SECTION OF BARROW NO. 205.

A—Clay.
B—Chalk rubble, cut through for Burial No. 2.

Body No. 5, though placed on the floor of the grave (or probably two adjoining graves), was a foot higher than No. 4, and was separated from it by a narrow strip of undisturbed rock which stood 18 inches above the floor of the grave. On this rock, as already mentioned, interment No. 1 was partly laid. A femur measured 18¼ inches, tibia 15 inches, and humerus 13¼ inches. No relic was found. Interment No. 6 was at the same depth as No. 5, and there was no partition between them. The bones were too much broken and injured by contact with angular pieces of chalk to be measured accurately, but they were those of an adult of about the same size as the bodies No. 3 and 4. A small wedge-shaped instrument of black flint (fig. 203½) —a form seldom found with interments — occurred in front of the chest, and a few inches above the body was a sandstone pebble (fig. 204). It is battered round the edges, having been used as a hammer. With the exception of interment No. 2, all appeared to have been buried previous to the construction of the cairn of chalk rubble, with its covering of tough blue clay. This, as is shown in section (fig. 200), had not been broken through, except for burial No. 2.

PLATE XXV.

Fig. 202. ¾

Fig. 202a. ½

Fig. 201. ½

Fig. 205. ½

Fig. 203. ½

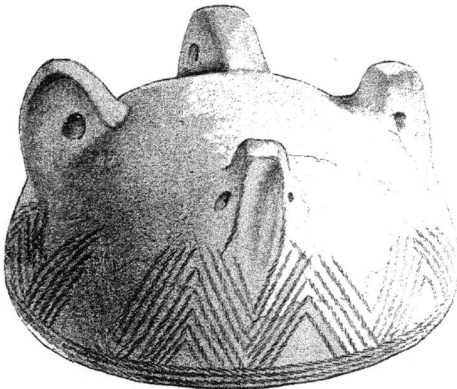

Fig. 205a. ½

Fig. 203½.

BARROW No. 206

Had a diameter of 50 feet, and was 2½ feet high. A little to the west of the centre was an oval grave of medium size, but only 18 inches deep. The mound had been previously opened, and all that was left in the grave by the explorers were the legs and pelvic bones, still in their original position. These belonged to a large-sized individual, who had been placed on the right side, with head to north-north-east and with the knees drawn up. This barrow is probably the one first opened by the members of the Yorkshire Antiquarian Club, and from which the bone pin and food-vase (figs. 181 and 182) were taken.

BARROW No. 207

Was not more than 30 feet in diameter, and 15 inches high. It had been opened at the centre, where a small oval grave was situated. Some fragments of an adult skeleton remained. As previously stated, this is most likely one of the mounds opened by a party of the Ordnance Surveyors, who were stationed on Acklam Wold from the 24th November, 1841, to the 26th March, 1842.

The writer, with other boys, frequently visited this small camp of Surveyors, and remembers being much surprised by the sight of a skull which one of the staff had taken from a small mound situated on the very brow of the escarpment.

Barrows Nos. 208, 209, and 210 were opened during the first twelve days of July, 1878, by making a square excavation 25 feet by 23 feet at the centre of each barrow.

BARROW No. 208

Is the largest of this group. It had been examined by the members of the Yorkshire Antiquarian Club in 1849, who, however, did not discover any interment. It had a diameter of 25 yards, and an elevation of over 7 feet above the ground surrounding its base. It had been erected on a natural prominence on the ground, the height of the artificial mound being 5 feet from base to apex. The natural protuberance here, as in many other cases, is due mainly to the presence of a "pipe" in the chalk containing sand and clayey matter, and which, previous to the erection of the barrow, had not been affected to the same extent by atmospheric denudation as the chalk immediately surrounding.*

About 8 feet from the centre, in an easterly direction, and about 2 feet above the surface level of the ground, were a few burnt bones placed in a dish-shaped hollow, the sides and bottom of which showed the impressions of decayed wood. A little north of the centre was an oval grave, 8 feet east and west, by 4 feet, and 3 feet 9 inches deep, containing the decayed remains of an adult which had been placed in a contracted position, on the right side, with the head to the west. This was the central or primary interment. Behind the skull, the bones of which had almost disappeared, stood a very fine semi-globular food-vase (fig. 205) of rare form. It has four feet, much resembling those of an old-fashioned cast-metal

---

* From this barrow, which is about 760 feet above the sea, there is a most extensive panoramic view of the country to the north-west and south-west.

kale-pot, of which it might well have been the prototype ; each foot having a perforation sufficiently large to admit a thong.* In front of the chest was a beautiful knife or saw of black flint (fig. 206), 2½ inches long, and serrated on both edges. Near the pelvis was a calculus about the size of a small walnut.

A few worked flints were found in the mound during the excavation.

BARROW No. 209

Stands about 100 yards to the west of the one just described. It measured 60 feet in diameter and 4 feet in height. A little north of the centre was a grave cut into the rock, 10 feet by 5½ feet, and 2½ feet deep, at the bottom of which was a skeleton, on its back, the right hand up to the face, the left arm across the abdomen, with the hand to the right elbow. The knees were drawn up at nearly a right angle to the body, and the head pointed a little east of south. Near the right elbow was a small neatly-made food-vase (fig. 207), ornamented externally from top to bottom. The left femur measured 18½ inches.

Nine feet south of the centre was a basin-shaped grave in the rock, 4 feet in diameter, and 2 feet in depth, containing at the bottom the burnt bones of an adult. A few pieces of unburnt animal bone occurred near the deposit, probably the remains of food which had been placed with the interment. Some fragments of animal bone, the tooth of the urus,† and a considerable quantity of charcoal were found in the material which filled in the grave. To all appearances both interments had been made prior to the construction of this mound.

Both barrows 208 and 209 were formed of the same materials, viz., the surface soil of the immediate neighbourhood, mixed with blue clay brought from a distance.

BARROW No. 210

Is only a surface protuberance of about 12 inches, due to the same natural cause as the partial elevation in barrow No. 208. In the centre were traces of a disturbed cremated burial. Probably an artificial capping had been added at the time of the interment, which ploughing had since removed.

BARROW No. 124

Was opened October 14th and 15th, 1868. It consisted principally of chalk and chalk grit, and was encircled by a filled-in trench, from which most of the material in the mound had been obtained. The trench proved to be 2 feet deep, 5 feet

---

* A food-vase with feet is an exceedingly rare occurrence. In only one other instance (Barrow 101) have I made such a discovery, which was in too fragmentary a state to be rebuilt. Canon Greenwell, in " British Barrows," p. 88, figures one with feet which he found in a barrow at Weaverthorpe, and mentions having seen another from a barrow at Amotherby, near Malton. (This was accidentally destroyed by Mr. G. Pycock, of Malton, who possessed it.) He also refers to two others, one from Lincolnshire and the other from Northumberland. There is a small vase measuring 3⅜ inches in height, 4⅞ inches in diameter at the top, and narrowing but a little at the bottom, which has four feet in addition to a rude handle, from the neighbourhood of Woodyates, figured in plate 2 of Charles Warne's " Celtic Tumuli of Dorset." Mr. Bateman, in " Ten Years' Diggings," p. 238, figures a small incense cup with four feet as altogether unique. But not one of these vases is semi-globular in form. They all have flat bottoms, and otherwise much resemble types of the common food-vase, and their feet are less developed and very differently formed from those on the specimen, fig. 205.

† This is not the only instance of the occurrence of remains of this animal in barrows I have opened (see barrow No. 284), and the account of Pit Dwelling following barrow C56, Group XI.

FIG. 204.   ½

FIG. 206.   ½

FIG. 209.

FIG. 207.   ½

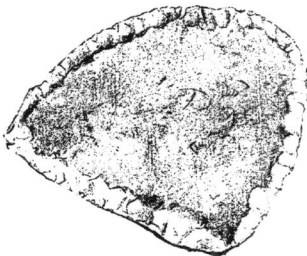

FIG. 208.   ½

wide at the bottom, and about 10 feet at the top, with a diameter of 50 feet from centre to centre of the fosse. About a year before (1867) most of this barrow had been carted away for the purpose or marling the adjoining land. It was rumoured that human remains and the whole or portion of a sword had been found. Inquiry, however, did not verify the latter portion of this rumour, though an examination of the remaining part of the mound fully substantiated the former, as the skull and upper portion of burial No. 1, probably an adult male, together with a piece of red deer's antler, were found. The body had been placed on the top of a deep grave, with the head pointing to south-south-west. This grave was an irregular- oval, measuring 6 feet. south-south-west by north-north-east, 5 feet across, and 6 feet in depth.

At a depth of 18 inches from the top were the crushed remains of a child about four years old (No. 2), but its precise position could not be made out. At a depth of 3 feet, and close to the west side of the grave, was the body of a female about twenty-five years of age (No. 3), laid partly on the back and partly on the right side, with the head and knees pointing to the south-east. A femur measured 19 inches, tibia 15½ inches, and humerus 12½ inches; all being slender bones. Close to the right side of the pelvis was a bone article, 4½ inches long, resembling a hair-pin. A triangular knife of flint (fig. 208) was cast out of the grave before being observed, and therefore its position in relation to the body could not be made out. At a depth of 6 feet, and within 2 inches of the bottom of the grave, the primary interment (No. 4) was discovered—that of a man of powerful build, not less than six feet in height, and probably about fifty years of age. The femoral bones were massive, and measured 19 inches in length. A thin layer of small grit rested on the floor of the grave * beneath the body. It was on its back, with the head to north-north-east, the knees drawn up and pressed over to the east, the left arm over the chest, the hand being in contact with the chin and right shoulder. The other arm was bent at a right angle, and had the hand near the left elbow. Below the hand was a beautiful flint dagger (fig. 209). This weapon is 7¼ inches long, 2¼ inches broad, and is of porcelain whiteness, not the result of burning, but due to having been long in contact with the chalk in the grave, and to having been subjected to the action of percolating water charged with carbonate of lime. Under the dagger were some of the finger bones, indicating that the weapon had been placed in the hand when buried. Underneath the dagger were a flint knife (fig. 210), 2⅛ inches long, chipped on both edges, a rough flake of flint, and a round-ended instrument (fig. 211) of uncertain use, chipped on one side and flat on the other, measuring 2¼ inches long, 1⅛ inches broad, and ¼ of an inch thick. Close to the point of the dagger was a small conical jet stud (fig. 212) placed crown upwards. It measured $\frac{9}{16}$ of an inch high, $\frac{4}{5}$ of an inch in diameter at the base, and is pierced on the flat side as shown in the figure. Touching the west side of the dagger was a lump of ferruginous matter † (pyrites)

---

* This we have frequently observed before, and its meaning is difficult to explain. Probably the body was buried in a hollow trunk or wicker-coffin and placed on two or more pieces of wood, leaving a space between the coffin and the floor of the grave, which, in time, became filled up by the crumbling and filling in of the grave, assisted by the percolation of water.

† The dagger (fig. 511) from barrow 37, Group XI.. is also stained on its edge by having been in contact with a similar mass of the same material, which unfortunately was broken into pieces at the time of discovery.

2 inches in diameter, much like an apple in shape, which had imparted a ferruginous stain to the two flints under it.   About 6 inches west of this was an oval stud or button (fig. 213) of red-coloured amber, pierced on its flat side with two oblique holes meeting each other in the centre without penetrating the upper surface of the stud.   Close by was a layer of decayed wood, reaching from 3 inches above the right knee to the bottom of the right side pelvis, say 13 to 14 inches, and was 4 to 5 inches broad at the middle, with the ends rounded (fig. 214), and a little above this was a bone pin (fig. 215).   Near to the lower end of the left femur occurred a fine jet ring* (fig. 216), measuring 1¼ inches in diameter, ¼ inch thick, and ¼ inch wide, having the circumference perforated with four holes placed in a groove.   Close to the right side of the skull, and near the shoulder, were the fragments of a crushed drinking-cup, a piece of which (fig. 217) shows the upper part to have been ornamented, just below the lip, with a belt of impressions made with a notched tool, and below these with belts of thickly-set impressions produced by a small thumb nail.   This cup has also been ornamented at the bottom in the form of a cross, produced by three rows of faint impressions by a notched tool.   The clay of which the vase was made had been freely mixed with pounded flint and quartz.   We have not so far attempted to build up the friable fragments.

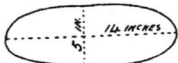

FIG. 214.

BARROW No. 124a

Is the most westerly on the point of the promontory called "Wooing Nab," and is the smallest of the group.   It was cut through on June 20th, 1871, from north to south, and near the centre were several fragments of human bones, the remains of a body which had been disturbed some years previously by Mr. Calam, the tenant of the land, in removing the barrow for agricultural improvements.   No grave or anything further was found.   It was encircled by a filled-in trench.

BARROWS Nos. 211 and 212

Were opened during the week ending October 19th, 1878.   The first is a little to the south of No. 206, which it resembles in size.   A previous excavation, about 7 feet square, had been made at the centre,† to the depth of about 12 inches below the surface level of the ground, and partly over the grave.   Near

---

° A similar jet ring from near Woodyates is figured in plate 3a in "The Celtic Tumuli of Dorset," by Charles Warne, which was also found near the thigh-bone of a large skeleton, and accompanied by a most beautiful brazen dagger, also a large and a small ornament (buttons) of jet perforated with two holes, four very perfect arrow-heads of flint, as well as some pieces of flint chipped for similar weapons, a small brass (bronze) pin, and a fine urn, broken (probably a drinking-cup) at the feet.   Canon Greenwell describes in "British Barrows" three similar jet rings, one from a barrow (LX.) at Thwing.   It was found, with a jet button, upon the middle of the right arm of a body of uncertain sex.   Another is from a barrow (XLI.) in the parish of Rudston, and was found, with a jet button, under the right tibia of a young male body.   The third was from Barrow LXVIII., also in the parish of Rudstone.   This ring, with two jet buttons and probably a whetstone, was about midway between the knees and the skull of a man.   In "Crania Britannica" is figured a rude but similar-shaped ring of Kimeridge shale, from a barrow at Affington. There is also figured an elaborately-finished jet ring from cist No. 4 at Monkton, North Wilts., also accompanied with three jet buttons.   In 1892 the writer found with a body in Collingwood, Sledmere (barrow 277), a very fine jet ring of the same type.

† Probably by the Yorkshire Antiquarian Club, in 1849.

PLATE XXVII.

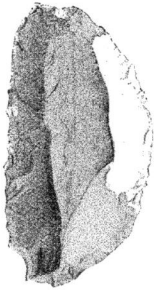

FIG. 212. ¼

FIG. 213.

FIG. 210.

FIG. 211. ⅓

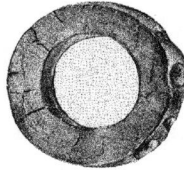

FIG. 216. ¼

FIG. 216. ⅓

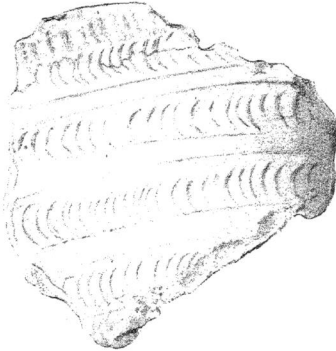

FIG. 220. ⅓

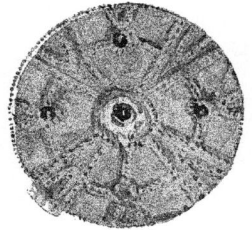

FIG. 222. ¼

FIG. 217.

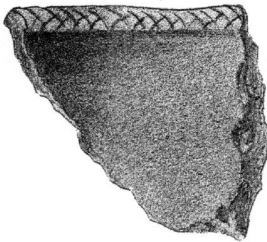

Inside.

FIG. 219. ⁴⁄₇

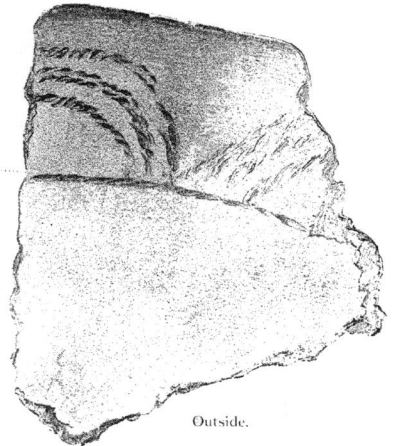

Outside.

the centre was a grave measuring $7\frac{1}{2}$ feet east and west by $3\frac{1}{2}$ feet in width and $2\frac{1}{2}$ feet in depth. At the bottom were the crushed remains of a young individual (fig. 218) of large size, lying on the left side, with the head to the east, knees drawn up and at right angle with the body. Both hands were in front of the face. The right humerus was 14 inches long, and the bones of the legs could not be measured. Near the hands was a small food-vase (fig. 219), almost entirely decayed. At the crown of the head was a piece of the bottom of a large urn. At the back of the skull were two flakes and a well-made knife or spearhead of black flint (fig. 220), and the spoon-like end of a bone article made of the rib of a large animal. Under these, partly on the floor of the grave, but mainly extending beyond its northern side, was a circular dish-shaped hole, $2\frac{1}{2}$ feet in diameter and 10 inches deep. It contained dark earthy matter, from which some teeth and pieces of the bones of pig and red deer were taken, as well as several splinters from the horn-cores, ribs, and other bones of an ox ; numerous sherds of a dish-shaped vase of dark texture (fig. 219), with

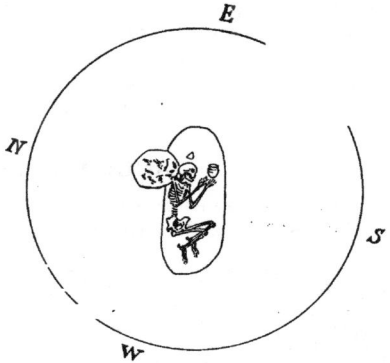

FIG. 218.

the lip turned inwards (a rare feature) ; three splinters of black flint and numerous pieces of charcoal ; and the four-tined "palm" of the right antler of a red deer, the points of which were much worn in an oblique manner, possibly indicating that they had been fixed to a shaft and used as a rake on the land.* A few splinters of animal bone and sherds of a large urn were found in the upper part of the grave and in the mound.

The dish-shaped cavity in the floor of the grave and in close proximity to the body is an unusual feature.† Possibly it had been made to contain food, &c., for the occupant of the mound, in addition to that contained in the small vase. The potsherds may be portions of a vessel used at the funeral feast and afterwards broken, some of its fragments, with probably remains of the feast, being deposited with the dead.

BARROW No. 212.

This small barrow consisted of fine clay, flints, and earth. The flints, which varied in size from a few pounds to that of two to three stones in weight, possibly had been placed over the bodies, the more effectually to prevent the predatory animals of those times from gaining access to the interments placed in the two shallow graves beneath.

---

* A similar portion of an antler was taken from barrow No. C83, the points of which were also much worn, apparently from having been put to a similar use.
† A similar one was observed in barrow 87, Group III.

The first grave, a small hole dug 6 inches below the base of the barrow, contained a body (No. 1) laid on its right side, with the legs drawn up and the hands in front of the face. The skull had a full set of teeth, much worn, indicating the advanced age of their owner. The second grave (No. 2), 5 feet east of the first, was dug 14 inches below the base of the mound, and contained the skeleton of an old person in the same position as body No. 1. Close to the feet of interment No. 2 were the legs and lower part of a third adult skeleton, the upper portion of the trunk and the skull being absent. These most probably had been severed and removed during the researches of some previous explorers. A tine from the antler of a red deer and pieces of burnt wood were found near the legs of interment No. 2.

Adjoining the west side of this group is an Anglo-Saxon cemetery.

ANGLO-SAXON CEMETERY.

The accompanying plan (fig. 221) shows the position of eight interments situated near two old chalk pits at the south side of Greet's Hill road, about

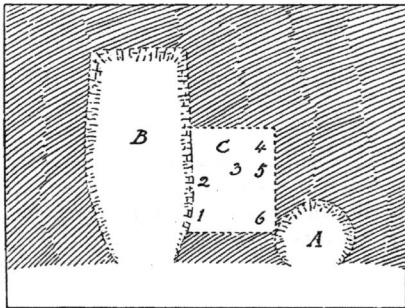

FIG. 221.

PLAN OF CHALK PITS, &C., ON ACKLAM WOLD.

A—Old Chalk Quarry.
B—Large Chalk Quarry in which interments were found.
C—Area excavated on 10th July, 1878.

500 yards south-west of Greet's Chalk Pit, Acklam Wold, 6 inch Ordnance Map (No. 159).* The area within the broken lines was excavated on July 10th, 1878, and bodies Nos. 1 and 6 were then disinterred. Previous to this, skeletons had been found at various times in both pits by the workmen quarrying for chalk. The first discovery brought to my notice was in the year 1866,† when a labourer was digging in the new pit (B), and found one or more bodies, from which he obtained a few amber and glass beads and a beautiful gold bulla (fig. 222), about 1½ inches in diameter, set with four garnets. The latter article came into the hands of an Acklam carrier, a young man, who, not knowing its value, was in the act of fixing it as an ornament to the headgear of his horse when my brother purchased it of him for half-a-crown. It is now in the British Museum. A few years after this the same labourer found another body, with which were some pieces of iron, a knife (fig. 223), and a very fine sword (fig. 224), 2½ inches in width near the hilt, and 39½ inches in length, 5 inches of which form the handle, an iron ferrule (fig. 226), part of a sharpening iron (fig. 227), and other pieces of iron (fig. 228, a, b, c, d).

july 10th, 1878, I found the six following skeletons in very shallow graves, all lying with their heads to the north-west. No. 1 was on its left side, with

---

* By the old inhabitants this place is known by the curious name of Penny-piece-field.
† I had previously heard that bodies had been found when the old pit was being worked.

FIG. 224.   ½

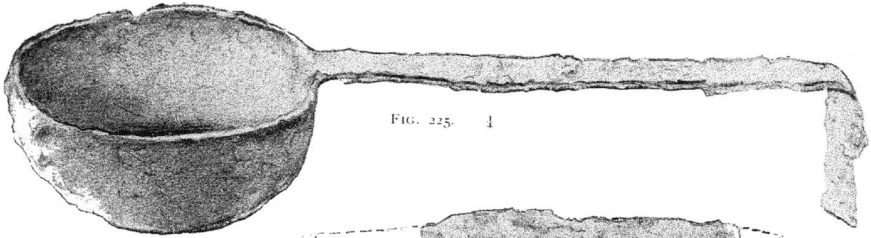

FIG. 225.   ½

FIG. 223.   ½

FIG. 226.   ½

FIG. 228a.   ½

FIG. 228b.   ½

FIG. 228c.   ½

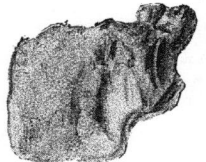

FIG. 228d.   ½

FIG. 229.   ½

FIG. 227.   ½

FIG. 230   ½

FIG. 231.   ½

FIG. 232a.

FIG. 232b.

FIG. 232c.

knees drawn up to a right angle with the body, the right arm bent over the chest, and the left arm stretched by the side. In front of the hips was an iron knife (fig. 229) of the usual type, and near the right elbow were two pieces of iron.

No. 2 was on the right side, the knees slightly drawn up, and the arms placed across the body. Close in front was a large iron ladle* (fig. 225) inverted, with its handle in front of the face. The bowl is 4½ inches deep and 8 inches in diameter; the handle is 14½ inches long, with an addition of 4 inches bent at a right angle and serving as a rest or support, which enables the ladle, when filled, to stand without losing its contents.

Interment No. 3 was placed in the same position as No. 1, and was probably a female. No. 4 was at full length on its back, the arms being stretched by the sides. No. 5 was in the same position as the last, except that it had the right arm slightly bent, and the hand upon the centre of the pelvis. Near the left side of the hips was an iron knife (fig. 230), and on the lumbar vertebræ were pieces of decayed iron. No. 6 was on its right side, the knees slightly drawn up, and, as far as could be made out, the arms were bent over the body. A knife, a buckle, and flat pieces of iron (fig. 232) occurred near the pelvis. These interments were all adults.

* In the east rampart of Fendale Camp were discovered three iron pots: the largest was broken, but the two others measured 10 inches in diameter by 4½ inches in depth; the larger one had a handle 21 inches in length. These seem to be of the type of the one from Acklam Wold, fig. 225 (Wilson's " Prehistoric Scotland," p. 436). A similar vessel, with the handle missing, is now in the Hull Museum, together with a large stone bead. It was found in a sand pit at Pontefract, together with human remains.

No. V. — THE HANGING GRIMSTON GROUP.

THIS consists of nineteen barrows, in a direction south-south-east from Group IV., mainly situated along the western brow of the chalk escarpment.

BARROW No. 61

Is the most westerly. On May 28th and 30th, 1866, it measured 70 feet in diameter and 2½ feet in height, and was formed entirely of gritty soil and chalk rubble from the surface of the surrounding land. In the centre was a partly destroyed cist composed of oolitic limestone slabs, situated a little below the old surface line. Some 12 or 15 years previous to our exploration, Mr. S. Arnell, who was then the tenant of the land, removed the obstructing covering and west side slabs, in order to facilitate the passing of the plough over the barrow. He found a body at the bottom of the cist, the bones of which were removed and re-interred elsewhere. But whether he unknowingly destroyed or removed any relic we cannot say, as we failed to find anything except small pieces of human bones. About 13 feet north-east from the cist, a little below the base of the barrow, was a body on its right side, doubled up, the left arm crossing the chest, and the other doubled back with the hand near the head. The femur and humerus measured 16 and 14 inches respectively. Over this body—but so near the surface as to have been partly destroyed by the plough— were the remains of a child. In the mound, a little way from the cist, were the detached bones of an adult, and further to the north we found a small heap of human bones, but no relic.

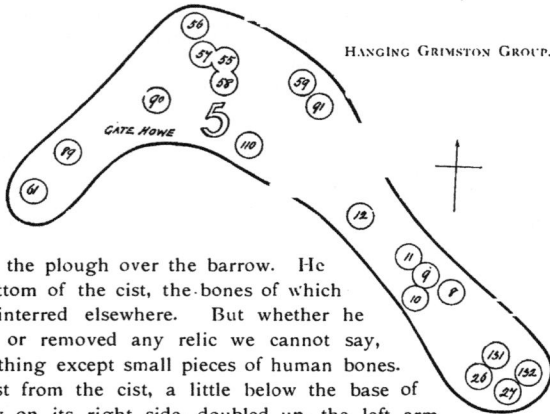

HANGING GRIMSTON GROUP.

BARROW No. 89.

On April 28th and 29th, 1867, this nearly-demolished barrow was opened. It stands on a slight natural rise of the surface, caused by a pipe in the chalk containing sandy matter, which seems to have resisted sub-aerial denudation more than the surrounding chalk.

A little north of the centre was an oval grave 2 feet deep, 5½ feet from north to south, and 4 feet across. At about half its depth, near the north end, were a few burnt human bones, and at the bottom was a film of dark matter, but no trace of a body. This grave bears a striking resemblance to the one in barrow No. 57, and very probably the absence of any trace of a body at the bottom of either was due to the free admission of air and water through the open ferruginous sandy earth contained in the graves. From the mound, which consisted of surface soil, with here and there a little foreign clay, we picked pieces of burnt wood, small portions of an urn, bits of animal bone, the tooth of an ox, and worked flints consisting of one fine circular piece nearly 2 inches in diameter, resembling fig. 252, flat on one side and chipped with a convex face on the other, and two similar but smaller discs; also three lumps—probably slingstones—from 1 to 1½ inches in diameter, 10 flakes, and 3 pieces of doubtful form, all of flint foreign to the Yorkshire chalk.

BARROW No. 90

Stands about 50 yards north of the last. At the time of opening, May 1st to 9th, 1867, it had a diameter of 82 feet, with an elevation of 6 feet, and its upper portion consisted of soil and gritty matter, with here and there a slight mixture of clay. Underneath the barrow was a core or nucleus, of similar shape to the mound, with a diameter of 26 feet and an elevation of 3½ feet. This inner mound was composed almost entirely of blue clay, a portion of which had been procured in large pieces from the dale bottoms, where the Kimeridge clay comes to the surface, the nearest place being about one mile distant and at the foot of a steep slope. In places the grassed sides of two sods had been put together. Some of these sods were 2 feet long, and here and there were shewn very distinctly, in the face of the excavation, by the lines of decayed grass, rushes, and moss, which had grown on the land at the time of their removal. We were much surprised to find part of the moss on some of the sods almost as fresh and as green as it would be at the time of its removal.[*] Though we cut a square hole measuring 20 feet across from the centre of the mound, trenched the ground beneath to the undisturbed rock, and removed the north and east sides 2 yards towards the margin of the mound, testing the ground below as we proceeded, only a single cremated interment was met with. This was situated about 6 feet south-south-east from the centre of the barrow, and only about 4 to 6 feet within the southern margin of the clay nucleus. It was also observed that this inner mound was not in the centre of the superstructure, but occupied a position considerably towards its northern side.[†] From the impression in the clay and the small pieces of decayed wood of a dark red colour, it was obvious that this incinerated interment had been placed at the southern extremity of a wooden receptacle formed apparently from the trunk of a tree, which measured about 3 feet long and 16 inches wide. The north end had been cut obliquely, thus causing one of the sides to be longer than the other. It had been placed at the base of the mound, pointing north and south, with about 1½ inches of blue clay under it, while above it ran the undisturbed beds of the inner clay mound. Among the burnt bones, and with one end protruding slightly through the top of the deposit, was a finely-made hammer-head of gritstone (fig. 233), nearly 4 inches long, and slightly burnt. No other article was found.

---

[*] A similarly fine example of early vegetation, consisting of a species of lichen, was observed upon the bark of the oak-tree coffin taken some years ago from the tumulus at Gristhorpe, and now in the Scarborough Museum. Of this, Professor Williamson, in his account of this tumulus, says—"This growth when first found was beautifully distinct." Similar features have occasionally been observed by other barrow explorers.

[†] This might be due to the greater part of the last additions to the mound having been obtained from the land on the south.

At the north end of the impression left in the clay, was a quantity of dark matter, in all probability the remains of food ; and in the clay mound immediately above were many small holes, of various shapes and sizes, with greasy looking sides, which also appeared to have resulted from the decay of some material. During the excavation a small portion of an urn, the molar tooth of an ox, a small flint arrowhead, a portion of a sandstone axe, two badly-formed discs chipped partly round the edges, and five rough splinters of black flint were taken from the mound. A thin layer of iron-stained matter marked the base of the barrow.

BARROW No. 56.

We commenced opening this barrow on May 4th, 1866, by removing a large square block from its centre, then cutting a trench 4 feet wide round the outside of this down to the base of the mound, thus leaving the central portion, where we hoped to find the primary interment, till the last. This method shewed good sections in various directions, and also exhibited the internal structure and enabled us to remove the middle portion with greater care.

It was observed that the barrow consisted of an inner cairn of gritty chalk, 30 feet in diameter and 1½ feet in elevation, resting on the old surface soil. Over this was an

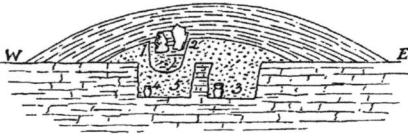

FIG. 235.

outer shell, mainly of light blue clay, 70 feet in diameter, and about 18 inches in thickness. Above this was 8 to 10 inches of tilled soil.

On May 6th, while removing the central portion, we found a heap of calcined human bones, placed slightly within the eastern edge of a basin-shaped hollow containing loamy earth. This was situated 4 feet west from the centre of the inner mound which shewed no trace of having been broken through. Immediately to the south of these calcined bones, and near the centre of the hollow just referred to, was an inverted cinerary urn (fig. 234) 17½ inches high, 14¾ inches over the mouth, and 15½ inches across the shoulders. Under this was a quantity of burnt human bones, and close to its eastern side was a slab of sandstone (Calcareous Grit) 10 to 12 stones in weight. It was placed a little higher than the urn, and apparently to protect it. After removing the urn—which was in several pieces—and the calcined bones which it contained, a third heap of dirty-looking calcined human bones was observed. These occurred slightly beneath, but distinctly separated from the bones in the urn, about 2 inches of loamy soil intervening. On the west side of these bones was a very fine knife of black flint 2¾ inches long (fig. 236). The lower jaw and some fragmentary bones of a child, and some bones of a larger individual, were noticed here and there in the loamy earth surrounding the urn. None of these detached bones showed *any trace* of fire. A slight subsidence occurred in the clayey shell over the basin-like hollow. This seemed to indicate that the clay covering had not been cut through, but had been added to the mound some time after the deposition of the urn, &c.

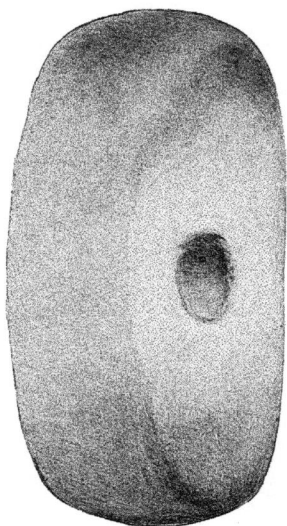

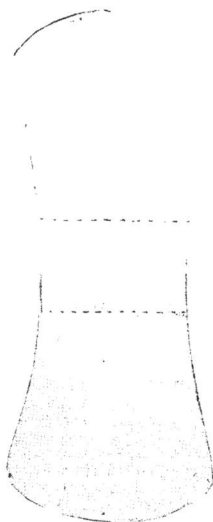

FIG. 236.

FIG. 233.   FIG. 233a.

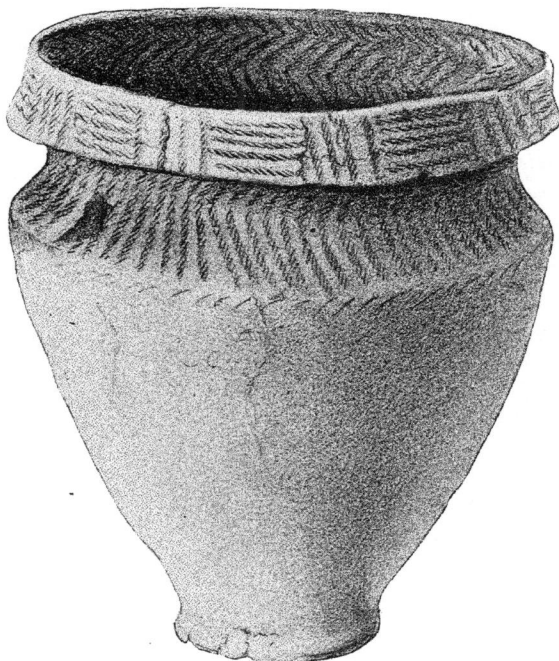

FIG. 234.   ¼

May 7th.—Having completely removed the earth within the trenches to the base of the barrow, and uncovered two interments (Nos. 1 and 2) near the centre, indications of a grave below were observed, as the old surface line was broken and rubbly chalk took the place of the original soil. Bodies Nos. 1 and 2 were on their right sides, one at the feet of the other, their heads to the west and knees pulled up. Close to the knees of No. 1 was an inferior flint tool (fig. 237), and decayed wood was observed upon the legs and pelvis. The femur and tibia measured 17 and 14 inches respectively, and evidently belonged to a young person. Body No. 2 was that of a small middle-aged individual. The femur, tibia, and humerus measured 16, 13½, and 12 inches respectively, and the teeth were much worn down. It was noticed that these two bodies had been placed at the northern edge of the western of two adjoining graves. The grave to the east measured 7 feet in length and 3 feet in depth, and was the one first examined. At the bottom, body No. 3 occurred, on its right side, with the knees doubled up, the head to the south-west. Behind the skull were the fragments of an irreparably crushed drinking-cup. The femur, tibia, and humerus measured respectively 17¼, 14, and 11¾ inches, and the teeth indicated a person of middle age, probably a female. To the west, and separated from it by a wall of natural chalk rock only 18 inches in thickness, was a second grave, of about the same size and depth. On the bottom rested bodies Nos. 4 and 5 (fig. 235), on their left sides, the knees drawn up, and their heads to the east. One was situated near the back of the other. Both skulls were crushed, probably by the workmen whilst removing the overlying material,* which consisted of earth and rough chalk rubble. The femur, tibia, and humerus of body No. 4 measured respectively 18, 14, and 12½ inches. The teeth were very much worn ; and belonged to a person about 50 years of age. The femur and tibia of No. 5 measured 18 and 14½ inches respectively, and the teeth showed only very slight indications of wear.

Near the feet of these two bodies stood a fine drinking-cup, somewhat crushed, but which has since been rebuilt (fig. 238). It is elegant in form, 7½ inches high, measures 4¾ inches over the mouth and at the middle, and 2¾ inches in diameter at the bottom.

On May 12th, the north-east corner of the excavation was extended, revealing a trench filled with loose chalk rubble. Probably this trench encircled—or nearly encircled—the inner chalk mound before the capping of blue clay was added to it. Between the clay and the chalk rubble at this place were found two longitudinal splinters of a human bone, a small portion of burnt human bone, two discs of flint slightly chipped, 1 flint flake, and three angular slingstones.

BARROW No. 57

Is about 50 yards south of the preceding one.

Opened May 11th, 1866.—From long cultivation its elevation was reduced to 12 inches, and its diameter increased to 60 feet. A square, each side of which measured 22 feet, was taken from the centre to the natural surface beneath, but only a few flint flakes were found. In probing the old surface ground, a deposit

---

* To prevent as much as possible any such injury in the future, we obtained some pieces of sheet-iron, upon which we usually stood when removing the contents of a grave. These protected everything beneath from the trampling of the workmen, and otherwise much facilitated our work.

of calcined bones in a small hole 12 inches deep was discovered, without any accompanying relic. A grave existed beneath these, measuring 7 feet east and west, 5 feet across, and 2 feet 5 inches in depth, and the heap of bone ash occurred at the eastern end, and was about 1 foot from the top of the grave. No inhumed remains were found in the grave, but at the bottom was a film of dark matter, from which was taken a jet button (fig. 239) lying on its perforated side. No other relic was found. As this grave had been made in a sandy pipe in the chalk, it is highly probable that the interment placed on the floor of this grave had disappeared, as in the case of barrow No. 89 and several others.

<h3 align="center">BARROW No. 55</h3>

Is a small mound a short distance south of the last.

March 23rd to 25th, 1866, were occupied in excavating it, and eight interments were discovered near the base, within a broken circle of stones 21½ feet in diameter.

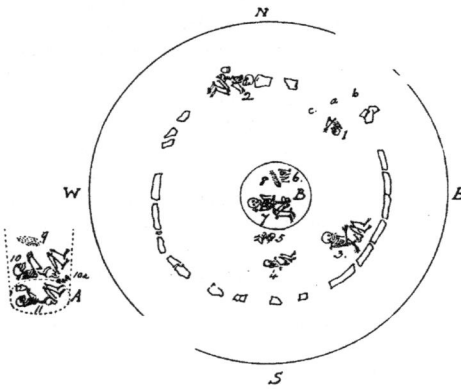

FIG. 240.

_A_—Vertical section under central grave, _B_.

The east side of this ring was formed of six slabs of Calcareous Grit and Oolitic limestone, placed on their edges, and averaging 2½ feet by 2 feet, and 15 inches in thickness. On the inside of one slab were traces of a few faintly incised vertical lines, from 2 to 3 inches in length, which apparently had been scratched by a sharp-edged tool—such as a flint flake. The remainder of this circle was marked by smaller and somewhat fragmentary blocks of similar stones placed apart at irregular distances, so that originally the ring may have been nearly complete. The nearest place from whence these blocks could have been brought is at the foot of the western edge of the chalk wolds, fully a mile distant, and a considerable amount of labour would be required to place them in the positions found. Possibly this stone circle formed a sacred enclosure, as well as a protection to the bodies, after the manner of the inner circular ditch so frequently met with. The position of the interments and the circle is shewn in fig. 240.

No. 1 on this plan is a portion of a skeleton of an individual about 27 years of age. The humerus measured 13½ inches. At _a_, _b_, and _c_, were detached human bones indicating that the interment had been disturbed, probably by rabbit digging ;[*] and during this period the circle of stones may also have been broken.

Burial No. 2 occurred just within the stone circle. The femur and tibia measured respectively 17 and 13¾ inches, and evidently belonged to a young person. Close

* This locality was at one time a rabbit warren.

FIG. 237.

FIG. 238.   ⅓

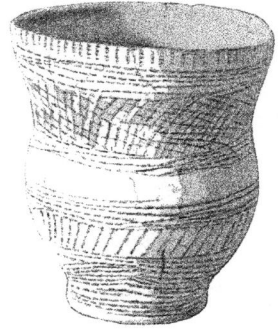

FIG. 241.   ⅓

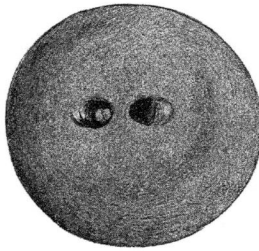

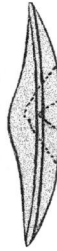

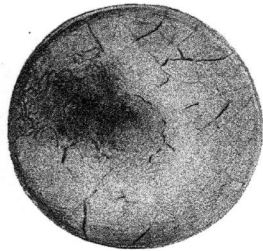

FIG. 239.   ½

FIG. 242.

FIG. 245.

FIG. 243.   ½

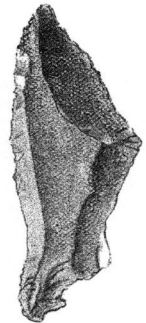

FIG. 244.

behind the pelvis were the fragments of a greater portion of an ornamented drinking-cup (fig. 241), and an angular shaped flake knife of black flint, about 1½ inches in diameter (fig. 242) chipped on one side to a cutting edge.

No. 3 is that of a small individual, probably a female, of middle age, placed in the position shown in the plan. The humerus measured 10½ inches, and the leg bones were much crushed.

The decayed remains of a child, from 10 to 12 years of age (burial No. 4), were placed in a similar position to burial No. 3.

No. 5, also the remains of a child from four to six years of age, rested on the southern edge of the grave, with the head to the east.

No. 6 was merely a heap of unburnt bones, consisting of leg bones, a vertebra, collar-bone, the half of a lower jaw broken longitudinally, and a fragment of an arm bone.

No. 7 contained the remains of an individual in the prime of life, disarranged by the settling of the grave. The humerus measured 12¾ inches.

No 8 was a long and narrow deposit of calcined adult bones lying just to the west of No. 6, and at a little lower level. Though the three last interments were over the grave, as shown in the plan, yet they were nearly on a level with the other bodies at the base of the mound, and over them was a covering of 18 inches of unctuous earth, similar to that filling the upper part of the grave.

At the base of the mound, close to the outside of the circle, was a piece of the leg bone of an ox ; and within the circle, chiefly near the centre, were found pieces of burnt wood, five worked flints, three teeth of an ox, and a portion of a drinking-cup.

On May 9th, after an interruption owing to bad weather, we were able to resume work. The grave was opened, and a few more human bones were seen at the north-east edge. These had probably belonged to No. 6, and had been separated from it by unequal settling of the contents below. This would also account for the distorted condition of body No. 7.*

Burial No. 9 occurred at a depth of 2 feet 3 inches, 16 inches from the north side of the grave, and also consisted of an elongated heap of cremated adult bones. From this portions of a flint knife, burnt and splintered by the action of fire, were taken.

No. 10, the skeleton of an individual in the prime of life, was 20 inches below the calcined bones. The femur measured 18 inches, tibia 13½ inches, and humerus 12½ inches. Just behind the pelvis were the remains of an infant (No. 10 A), near which were the fragments of a drinking cup (fig. 243). A worked flint (fig. 244) 2½ inches long, had been placed at the side of the body, and 16 inches in front of its face, close to the side of the grave, were four large pieces of human leg bones, placed together. A jet stud (fig. 245) 1⅛ inches in diameter was found on the breast bone.

No. 11 was the skeleton of a youth, resting on the floor of the grave, 6 inches below the interment No. 10. The femur and tibia measured 15 and 11 inches respectively. In front of the face had stood a gracefully-formed drinking-cup, but unfortunately it was so crushed that it had to be removed in no fewer than 91 pieces. As it had been made of well-tempered clay, however, its restoration after rebaking the fragments, was not such a very difficult operation (fig. 246). It is 8½ inches high, and 5½ inches wide at the mouth. Behind the head and shoulders were 25 hand-struck

" This distortion is not shown in the sketch.

splinters of flint, obtained from the neighbouring chalk, arranged in a heap 9 inches long. Six of these are shown at *a*, *b*, *c*, *d*, *e*, *f*, fig. 247. Not one of them showed any trace of secondary chipping, but many retained the bulb of concussion. The grave was nearly circular, 4 feet 8 inches deep, 7 feet in diameter at the top, and 5 feet at the bottom ; and the contained earth was full of numerous small pieces of broken human bones. Fragments of oolitic limestone, probably chips from the blocks forming the circle, were observed in the grave, thus indicating that the building of the circle and the deposition of the bodies had probably taken place at the same time.

BARROW No. 58.

Opened May 16th, 1866.—This barrow had a diameter of 46 feet, but from the frequent passage of the plough its altitude was only 10 inches. A portion, in form and size similar to that cut from barrow 57, was removed from the centre, and the only interment discovered was a deposit of burnt bones, without any relic. This occupied a dish-shaped cavity, scooped to a depth of 6 or 7 inches into the natural surface of the land, and measured 2 feet across the top. From the mound seven splinters of dark-coloured flint and one piece of a British urn were taken.

BARROW No. 59.

The site of this barrow is in a field to the east of and adjoining the preceding one, and on the opposite or east side of the Malton high road. On May 17th, 1866, it was a mere hillock, under which was a grave 3 feet deep, measuring at the bottom 7 feet north and south and 3 feet across. A fragment of an urn was found at the top, and at the bottom were the contracted remains of a strongly-built man, on his right side, the head pointing to south-south-east. A femur measured $19\frac{1}{2}$ inches, was of great strength, and evidently belonged to a person in the prime of life. No urn or any other relic was found.

BARROW No. 91

Is not shown on the Ordnance Sheets. On May 13th, 1867, it presented a very slight elevation indeed. It is in contact with the corner of the enclosed angular piece of ground called Queendykes Corner, and touches the south-east side of these entrenchments, which, like the barrow, are here nearly obliterated. Near the centre of this tumulus was a dish-shaped hole, 2 feet in diameter and 12 inches deep. It contained the cremated bones of an adult, and a considerable quantity of burnt wood, apparently hazel. The charred sides of this receptacle indicated that its contents had been deposited while in a heated condition.

BARROW No. 110.

This is a true long barrow, and consisted of gritty chalk mixed with the neighbouring surface soil. It measured 78 feet east and west, and 50 feet north and south, with a central height of about 3 feet. The opening of the mound occupied the whole of the time between the 16th and the 28th of March, 1868. Commencing at the eastern end, we discovered the top of what we at first thought

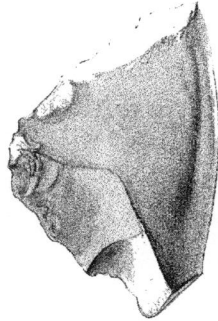

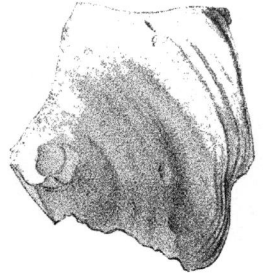

FIG. 247 a.

FIG. 247 b.

FIG. 246.

FIG. 247 d.

FIG. 247 c.

FIG. 247 f.

FIG. 247e.

FIG. 248.

FIG. 248

FIG. 250.

to be a large grave, but which afterwards proved to be a pit dwelling, charged with soil and gritty chalk mixed in a very irregular manner. On the western side, at a depth of 3 feet, was the greater portion of a much-crushed, plain earthen vessel of dark ware, and uncommon type (fig. 248), being unusually shallow. No relic accompanied it, but there were bits of burnt wood and many traces of decayed matter; while on the south side, at about the same level, was the femur of a medium-sized person, and immediately below it a lumbar vertebra of an ox or deer. At the north end, on the east side, at a depth of 2 to 2½ feet, were three somewhat scattered heaps of bones, consisting of the upper and lower jaws of pigs, chiefly young animals. At the southern end, and on the same level as the others, was a fourth heap. In all there were jaws of at least twenty pigs, and it was curious to notice that small portions of the points of most of the tusks had been broken off before interment.

At the depth of 4 feet, and near the centre of the pit dwelling, was the antler of a roebuck, about a foot below was a tine from the antler of a red deer, while at depths varying from 3 to 5 feet were portions of the leg-bones and scapulæ of the latter animal, together with fragments of bone and teeth of pigs. Shells of the common snail (*Helix nemoralis*) were found all through the deposit, and many streaks of burnt and decayed matter ran obliquely—and in some places almost vertically—into the pit dwelling, reaching in places nearly to the bottom. At a depth of 6½ feet the undisturbed chalk floor was reached, on which was a dark stratum containing small pieces of burnt wood, and near the west side was a considerable

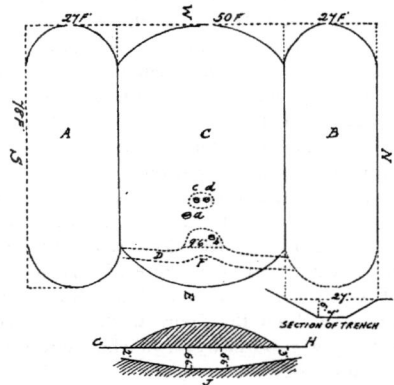

FIG. 249.

A, B—Trenches on each side of barrow. C.
D—Passage under barrow.
F—Cave floor.
G, H—Section of barrow showing underground Passage.
J—Floor of passage.

quantity of decayed substance, from which we obtained a well-preserved rib of an animal about the size of a rabbit, and also bits of bone in the last stages of decay. From the bottom of the floor, on the south side, was a sloping and slightly curved passage, which at a distance of 24 feet to the south came within 2 feet of the surface. It was charged with soil and gritty chalk, in which we observed oblique lines of black matter and carbonised wood, similar to those noticed in the interior of the pit. These appeared to nearly reach the bottom; and at a depth of 3 feet midway in the passage, were more teeth and jaws of pigs, the scapula of a deer, and the greater portion of an earthen vessel, also of the plain dish-shaped type, crushed into innumerable pieces.

A similar inclined and slightly bent passage, 27 feet in length, was also traced from the north side of this underground habitation. It was filled with soil and gritty chalk, in which were also oblique lines of black matter and burnt wood, together with animal bones and a few pieces of an urn. The measurements of the bottom are given in the ground plan and section (fig. 249). The sides everywhere leaned a little outwards.*

Altogether the appearance of this structure was strongly suggestive of a dwelling that had been covered by a horizontal roof, upon which had been heaped soil and gritty chalk, and may have been thatched with heather, rushes, or some other suitable covering. There is likewise much evidence that it had been destroyed by fire. Such a supposition would account for the position in which fragments of bone and pottery were found, and for the different lines of black matter already mentioned. The burning roof giving way and falling in would bring with it the fragments of pottery and the numerous animal bones. It is possible that these bones—including even the human thigh-bone—had been thrown from time to time by the occupants, after meals, on to the low roof of this dwelling.† In the barrow, about 5 feet from the south-west corner of the cave (at the point *A* on the plan, fig. 249), were the crushed remains of a third shallow earthen vessel, a few inches above the base of the mound. Ten feet west of the edge of the pit dwelling were many fragments of a fourth dish-shaped vessel (marked *C*), reaching from the surface to a depth of about 16 inches into the mound, and 3 feet north-west of the last was a portion of another of the same type (marked *D*). This was laid on its side, and being within reach of the plough had been much damaged. Close under this vessel was part of the jaw, with teeth, of a pig, and near by a piece of the leg-bone of the same animal. Under the two last-named vessels was an oblong grave, 2½ feet deep, and measuring at the bottom 4½ feet north and south by 2 feet. Near the centre of this, and at about half its depth, was the scapula of a pig, stood on end. There was a considerable quantity of burnt wood in the grave, and on the floor, at the south end, was a small dish-shaped hole, filled entirely with burnt wood, in which one small piece of bone was found, but no relic. All the vessels are almost exactly alike, and of a shallow, round-bottomed, dish-shaped type. Not one, however, is complete, but that shown in fig. 248 is a good restoration. They measured from 12¼ inches to 13 inches in diameter, and from 3¾ to 6 inches in depth. This form of pottery is rarely found entire in the barrows of this neighbourhood, and it seems probable that they were domestic vessels and not funeral urns, though a few of those discovered in this mound may have fulfilled the double purpose of serving the dead after having been used by the living.‡

Most of the remaining portion of this barrow was turned over without anything more being found beyond a few animal bones and some tines from the antlers of red deer, 1 scraper, 2 small discs much chipped round the edges, and

---

* The ground plan of this dwelling is very ingenious. The curved passages and their entrance into the centre portion of the dwelling afforded the greatest possible shelter and protection to the occupants, both against the ingress of cold air and the attacks of an enemy. An arrow discharged at the entrance would never reach the interior; and these curved passages had, undoubtedly, much to do with the safety of the occupants.

† Similar accumulations of the trophies of the chase and remains of feasts have been observed ornamenting the roofs of the dwellings of the Andamese, and of the inhabitants of New Guinea. (*Anthropological Journal*, vol. viii. p. 448.)

‡ An example of this uncommon type of pottery was obtained from West Heslerton Wold. It is nearly the same in form, dimensions, and colour, and is figured by Canon Greenwell in "British Barrows," page 107. On page 143 also he describes some "domestic pottery" as having been found in fragments along the bottom of a 16-ft. trench sunk into the chalk rock. This is exceedingly interesting, as these fragments seem to have been found under very similar conditions to those now described.

3 flakes. If interments had accompanied the broken vases, they had completely decayed and left no trace behind. In searching around the circumference of the barrow, a large trough-formed trench, which had become quite filled with soil, was found the whole length of each side of the mound—as shown on the plan. Each trench was 6 feet deep, 27 feet wide at the top, and about 7 feet wide at the bottom. The east extremity of the northern trench cut the end of one entrance to the pit dwelling, clearly proving the dwelling to be older than the trenches, the material from which had largely been used in building the mound. Possibly this barrow was not made all at once, but was added to at the time each interment took place, in a westerly direction from the dwelling, and possibly the erection was for a time occupied by the living and the dead conjointly. We had not time to explore the extreme west end of this barrow, on account of the farmer wishing to sow the land. It might therefore be advisable to re-examine it.

BARROW No. 12

Is situated about the middle of this group, and has no other mound close to it.

On May 11th, 1864, its diameter was ascertained to be about 50 feet, and its height 2 feet above the surrounding land. Six inches of this elevation, however, was due to a natural rise under the mound. The centre of this barrow was excavated to its base, where on a small floor of Oolitic limestone slabs, were the crouched remains of an adult, on the right side, head to N.W. To our surprise, the calvarium, crown upwards, but without the lower jaw, was placed at the pelvis.* Neither could any of the teeth belonging to it be found. Their absence could not be attributed to decay, as the skull was in good preservation. Possibly the head had been severed at the time of interment.

Re-opening.—Being under the impression that this barrow had not been sufficiently explored, on September 7th, 8th, and 9th, 1868, the ground beneath the mound was thoroughly searched, and at a point slightly east of the centre an oval grave 17 inches deep, 5 feet north and south, and 3 feet across was found, in which was a doubled-up adult skeleton, with the head to the south, on its right side, the hands to the face. Close behind the skull was a poor specimen of a flint flake-knife roughly chipped on its edge. In front of this body were the flexed remains of a child about six to eight years of age. This also was placed with its head nearly to the south, but was on its left side; consequently the two bodies were face to face. There was a small heap of burnt bones a short distance from the two skulls, but no other relic.

About 18 inches south-west of this grave, and about the centre of the mound, was a second grave, measuring 5 feet long south-west and north-east, and 3 feet wide. At a depth of about 18 inches were the decayed bones of a child from six to seven years of age, lying on the right side, with the head to the south-west; 10 inches lower the floor of the grave was reached, on which reposed the body of an adult of medium size, on its left side, head to the north-east, hands down to the pelvis, and knees pulled up. The skull and other bones were in a bad state of preservation. A dark-coloured flint

---

* Some light may be thrown on the strange position of this skull by the following :—" The best means of protection against ghosts was to burn the body and throw the ashes into the sea, or to cut off the head and put it at or between the feet, as the body had then to walk on its own head."—" The Viking Age," by Paul B. Du Chaillu, vol. I., page 447.

knife, and bone pin 1¾ inches long, made from the longitudinal half of the shank bone of some animal, occurred together on the third vertebra from the pelvis, suggesting the probability that these two articles were held in a small wallet or pocket at the right side of some garment in which the body had been interred. just in front of the face, and about 6 inches above the floor of the grave, a food-vase (fig. 250) of a somewhat uncommon form, had been placed on its bottom, but when found it was pressed to one side and fractured. At the feet of the skeleton a rectangular hole was noticed, penetrating 8 inches into the compact chalk floor of the grave, and measuring 10 inches by 6 inches.

During the excavation one leaf shaped arrow-head, one semi-circular disc chipped to an edge on its convex side, six cores, and fifty-two flakes of various sizes, all of dark-coloured flint foreign to the neighbouring chalk, were found in the mound.

BARROW No. 8

Is the most southern and the largest but one of four adjoining barrows. On April 25th, 1864, it measured 22 yards in diameter and 3 feet in elevation. A trench was cut from the western to the near eastern side, where about a cartload of light coloured blue clay was found in a heap on the natural surface under the barrow. A similar clay, containing small angular chalk flints, was observed to be mixed irregularly throughout the mound. A little within the south-west margin of the barrow a shallow dish-shaped hole scooped into the old surface line was found. It contained a quantity of burnt wood and a few calcined bones, from which was taken a small disc of flint (fig. 251), splintered and whitened by the action of fire, and a large and nearly circular disc (fig. 252) of black flint, 2¼ inches in diameter, and chipped on the convex side. This fine specimen—of uncertain use—though found with burnt bones, shows no marks of fire. The excavation was widened in the centre of the barrow, but no trace of an interment was found. From the mound was taken a fine thin flake knife, 2½ inches long, one slingstone about the size and shape of a large walnut, one small disc much burnt, and about twenty flakes and splinters, all of black flint.

Re-opening.—From May 8th to 14th, 1868, we turned over all the previously unexplored portion of this barrow, tested the ground below, and obtained sections of a filled-in ditch, 91 feet in diameter, which encircled its circumference. This ditch was 4½ feet deep, 10 feet wide at the top, and 1 foot 8 inches wide at the bottom. The barrow was found to stand on a natural elevation of 12 to 14 inches, caused by a large sand pipe in the chalk rock, and on the old surface line was some partly burnt wood. A few worked flints were picked from the mound, but no trace of an urn or an interment was observed.

BARROW No. 9

Was far the largest of this group, and had a diameter of 82 feet and an elevation of 6 feet.

On April 26th and 27th, 1864, we cut a circular portion from the centre, 14 feet in diameter, to the undisturbed ground below, which was found to be of a yellow sandy character, here and there streaked with lines of dark matter. At first, mistaking this for a disturbed place in the chalk rock, we proceeded some feet below the base of the barrow, expecting to find a grave, but eventually found that in this case, as in the last,

PLATE XXXII.

FIG. 252. ⅓

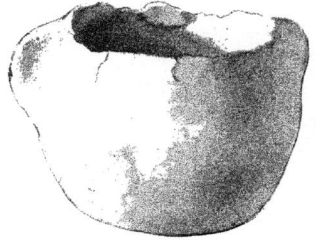

FIG. 253. ½

FIG. 121.

FIG. 254. ¼

FIG. 256. ¾

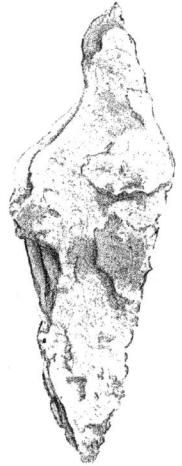

FIG. 257.

FIG. 255. ¼

FIG. 260. ¼

the barrow had been raised over a sand-pipe. The choice so often made by the Britons of a site over one of these sand-pipes was undoubtedly due to the preference given to a slight elevation on the surface, and possibly also from having discovered that it was easier to penetrate the ground on such a situation than on the level, where the hard rock was soon reached. The material of which the barrow was composed, from base to apex, consisted of blue clay brought from a distance, the natural subsoil of the surrounding land, and a yellow substance resembling that in the sand-pipe below, all mixed together, and here and there were bits of burnt wood. A small sling-stone resembling the one from the last barrow, and a few chippings of black flint, were all we obtained from this mound.

Re-opening.—April 22nd to May 7th, 1868, was occupied in turning this barrow completely over, and exploring a filled-up ring fosse, which, as in the last barrow, fringed the skirts of the mound. The diameter of this trench measured 121 feet. Its depth was 6 feet, width at top 15 feet, and at the bottom 2½ feet. That portion of the barrow which we had not previously disturbed consisted of about three parts of foreign clay to one of soil obtained on the spot, arranged in layers and patches. After the mound had been raised, the trench had been dug, and the material excavated was thrown upon the sides of the barrow round its entire circumference.

About 28 feet south-south-east of the centre, 21 inches from the tilled surface of the mound, and 10 inches from its base, were the remains of a child, on the right side, head to the west, each arm stretched at full length by the side of the body, and the knees pulled up. Near the front of the skull was a vase ($fig.$ 253), with two partly developed handles, or "ears," but without any ornamentation. It measured 3 inches high, 3¼ inches over the mouth, and 4 inches across the shoulders. Close to the north side of the excavation made at our first opening, and at the base of the mound, was a curved knife ($fig.$ 254) of black flint, 4¾ inches long, and remarkable for the bold chipping over the whole of its surface, which gives two cutting edges without the usual delicate workmanship.[*] Though no trace of any bone was observed, very probably this knife once accompanied a skeleton, but owing to the ferruginous nature of the soil the latter had entirely disappeared. On the same level, 24 feet east of the centre, was the body of an adult, partly on its back, and partly inclined towards its right side, with the left hand in front of the face, the right hand under the head, and the knees drawn up to a right angle with the body. Under the skull was a fine barbed arrow-head of flint ($fig.$ 255)—a very unusual occurrence. We also noticed some very small hand-struck splinters of foreign flint near its head and shoulders. About 6 feet from the skull, but not more than 12 inches below the surface of the mound, stood a perfect and elegantly formed food-vase ($fig.$ 256), the inside of the mouth and the whole exterior of which was elaborately ornamented with fine vertical zigzag lines, very skilfully applied. No trace of a body was near the vase, and it may have been interred later. The tusk of a boar, several animal bones, and about twenty splinters of flint were found in the barrow.

During May 9th, 10th, and 11th, 1864, we explored the two low barrows adjoining No. 9. Both these were within two chains' length from No. 9.

---

[*] I possess a yet finer sickle shaped knife (fig. 253 A). It was found at Cilnwick, near Driffield, in 1867, by a labourer when cutting a drain. It had probably accompanied a cremated interment, as the finder said he took it from a hole filled with a substance having a dark and burnt appearance.

No. 10,

The first opened, was oval in form, 2 feet high, with a diameter of 68 feet north-east by south-west, and 50 feet north-west by south-east.   Being anxious that nothing should be missed, we worked in two parties, commencing near the extremities farthest apart, and from each point excavated a breadth of 16 feet towards the centre, reaching to the undisturbed ground beneath.   This excavation was 48 feet in length.   Nearly 8 feet south of the centre, a fine barbed arrow-head of black flint was found, together with a few wood ashes, in the mound, and about 14 inches from the surface ; also about the same distance west of the centre, a delicately-formed leaf-shaped arrow-head, of horn-coloured flint, was taken from the subsoil.   During the excavation many chips of flint, some fragments of an urn, and one splinter from a polished greenstone celt, were picked up.   Just about the centre of the barrow, on a level with the undisturbed ground, was a quantity of wood ashes, in which were calcined bones, two portions of a plain urn, obviously British, and the greater portion of the blade of a bronze dagger or knife (fig. 257), measuring over 3½ inches in length, partly split at the edge, and much corroded.   These occupied a hollow, made in the original land surface previous to raising the mound, which measured 3 feet by 2½ feet, and 14 inches in depth.   The soil all round its sides was burnt to the depth of 3 inches, and the chalk at the bottom was converted into lime to about the same extent.   The barrow was composed of soil similar to that now found on the surrounding land, mixed here and there with bits of burnt wood.   At its base, in certain places, was a bed of drab-coloured clay, covering a thin layer of wood ashes, which rested on the floor of the barrow.

Re-opening, May 4th to 6th, 1868.—A further search was made without finding anything more.

BARROW No. 11.

This small barrow appeared to have been circular in form, with a diameter of 48 feet, and its slight elevation was partially due to repeated ploughing, rendering it scarcely visible above the surrounding ground.   Its position is clearly shown, however, on the Ordnance Map.   The low and unpretentious appearance of this barrow damped our enthusiasm not a little, and, had we not observed that carbonised wood, quite fresh in appearance, had been recently brought to the surface by the plough, we might have regarded it as merely a natural rise on the surface, unworthy of exploration, and have passed to a more promising mound.   Near the centre, a small deposit of calcined bones and wood ashes was found, lying in a very small dish-shaped cavity, which seemed to have been simply scratched into the turf of the ancient surface line.   No urn or weapon was found.   A few hand-struck splinters of black flint were picked up during the digging.

BARROW No. 26.

It will be observed by a reference to the map that this barrow is one of a group of four on the site of " Black Plantation."

On April 26th, 1865, owing to the trees in the plantation having been uprooted and removed from the ground during the preceding autumn, we were enabled to excavate the mounds. The ground plan of barrow No. 26 was oval, with a diameter of 58 feet north and south, and 47 feet east and west; the greatest elevation being 3½ feet.   An excavation 11 feet wide was made at a point midway between the southern margin and the centre, and driven northwards.   For a time the whole of the barrow seemed to consist of local surface soil, but as the centre was reached rubbly chalk free from soil occurred, which spread and increased in thickness towards the centre, where it was 12 feet across from east to west and 20 inches in depth. At this point was the centre of a chalk cairn, in which a basin-shaped cavity had been formed, 4 feet in diameter and 20 inches in depth. This reached from the bottom to the top of the chalk cairn, and principally contained a dark-coloured, greasy-looking substance.   In some places in it were many small cavities, and in others was mixed with wood ashes, and its contents seemed to have largely undergone some change, probably owing to the decay of some organic matter that had been placed in it.   This supposition is strengthened by the fact that the thick extremity of the shoulder-blade of an ox, together with another piece of animal bone, was found.   Still more remarkable were the three urn-shaped cavities (*f*), each containing cremated human bones, which had been formed in the dark-coloured material, and arranged in the order shown in the accompanying section (fig. 258).   The sides and bottoms of these receptacles were smooth, and ¾ of an inch in thick-

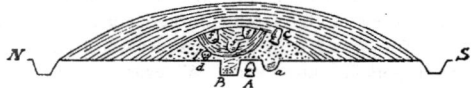

· Fig. 258.
SECTION OF BARROW 26, SHOWING ENCIRCLING TRENCHES.
A—Inverted urn of calcined bones.
B—Grave containing cremated bones.
a—Calcined bones in hollow.
c—Inverted urn.
d—Skull and detached bones.
f—Urn-shaped cavities containing cremated bones.

ness, hard and compact so as to be nearly water-tight, and when broken had a bituminous appearance.   It seems probable that these cavities had served a similar purpose to cinerary urns, being about the same size.   In the most westerly one a piece of thin bronze was found, much distorted by the action of fire.   It appeared to be a portion of a knife, as one side shows a cutting edge.   Close to the outside of the south-east edge of the basin-shaped hollow, and almost in a line with the three heaps of burnt bones, was a small cinerary urn (*C*), inverted over a few cremated bones.   It was much crushed, and only the bottom portion (fig. 259) could be built up.   This was clearly the last interment made, but whether during or immediately after the erection of the chalk cairn, and before the upper covering was added, or afterwards as a secondary interment pushed through the soily capping of the finished barrow, could not be ascertained.

On May 1st operations were again commenced, and one of the workmen struck his pick into the detached skull of a very young person (*d* on fig. 258) on the ancient turf-line, slightly to the west of and just below the side of the basin-like receptacle containing the three deposits of burnt bones.   Although this accident caused us to proceed with every care, the only other parts we could find were the arm bones.   Not the least portion of either the legs, ribs, or vertebræ was to be seen, and as the bones we found were in good preservation, it seems probable that the other parts of this body had not been deposited with the head.   A portion of a bone tool (fig. 260), made from the rib of an ox and nicely rounded at one end, was found in the chalk cairn close above where the skull occurred; while on the top of the cairn, just under the clay covering, a large hand-struck splinter of flint from the local chalk was picked up.   This may have been struck off in forming a celt or a large slingstone, and thus become accidentally buried in the barrow. The excavation was carried northwards until it measured 18 feet in length, but nothing beyond fragments of burnt wood was found.   The floor of the excavation was probed, and after careful inspection we found a disturbed place slightly to the south of where the skull had been, and at a depth of 2½ feet found the calcined bones of a full-grown person (marked *B*) placed in a grave 2 feet in diameter at the bottom.

Re-opening.—Being desirous of thoroughly testing our early explorations, from April 26th to 29th, 1869, was occupied in turning over the greater portion of this barrow, and probing the ground beneath.   At a point about 4 feet south-east from the grave (as shown in the section), was found an urn (marked *A* in the plan), inverted over the burnt bones of a child, placed in a shallow hole below the base of the mound. No other relic accompanied the interment, and the urn was irreparably crushed.   A little further to the south-east, about 2 feet from the urn, another small hole in the ground (marked *a* in the section) was discovered, containing the burnt bones of a young person, but no urn.   We examined the outskirts of the mound, and found an encircling trench, which, as usually happens in this neighbourhood, was filled up and quite invisible on the surface.   This measured 23 yards in diameter from centre to centre of the trench, was 4½ feet deep, 11 feet wide at the top, and 2½ feet at the bottom. The section (fig. 258) has been drawn so as to show all the deposits.

Reviewing the discoveries made in this barrow, it would seem that first a funeral pyre was kindled on the turf, and that three bodies—an adult and two youths—were reduced to ashes; after which the remains were collected and placed in the three little graves discovered below the chalk cairn.   Next, these cavities were filled in, and on the old surface line over them the head and arm bones of a youth were deposited. Afterwards the chalk cairn, measuring 12 feet in diameter and 20 inches high, was raised, in the centre of which, either then, or at some subsequent period, was hollowed out the basin-formed cavity, in which were arranged the three urn-shaped holes, containing cremated bones.   Then the whole was covered with a tenacious blue clay, 4 inches in thickness; and immediately above this was a quantity of wood ashes and blackened soil—possibly the remains of a second pyre.   At a later period, an urn containing cremated bones had been placed, partly in the chalk cairn, just outside the south-east side of the basin-shaped hollow; and finally, a covering of soil gathered from the adjoining land completed the barrow.

BARROW No. 27.

On May 1st, 1865, we excavated an area of 14 feet square in the centre of this barrow, without finding anything but a few hand-struck splinters of black flint.   On May 15th the excavation was continued, and in the centre were indications of a large grave cut into the chalk, measuring 9 feet east and west, 6 feet in width, and 3½ feet in depth.   In the centre of the floor of this grave was the body of a middle-aged male, on the left side, in the usual flexed position, with the head to the north, and facing east. Close above the knees was a large and much crushed food-vase, which after re-building (fig. 261) measured 6 inches in height, 7¾ inches over the mouth, 8¼ inches over the shoulders, and 3¼ inches across the base.   Two grooves encircle the neck and shoulders of this large vase, the lower one containing four unpierced stops, which divide the groove into four equal parts.   It is freely stamped with deep gashes, but no rope markings.   It contained earthy matter stained with streaks and patches of a dark greasy appearance.   The skull is brachy-cephalic, and in good preservation.   The left femur measured 18 inches, and the right femur showed a very remarkable dis-location, which Dr. Wood, of Driffield, has kindly examined for me, and described as under.—

> "This specimen represents a portion of the right side of the pelvis, along with the head of the thigh bone and a fragment of the shaft.   It illustrates in a very striking manner the changes that have been produced by an old dislocation of the femur into that part of the pelvis called by anatomists the *obturator foramen*—that is, in a direction downwards and backwards; the result being to elongate the limb and probably to evert the foot.   It is also curious to observe how far Nature has been able to compensate for such an important injury by the formation of the new socket; and this process has been so effectually carried out as to retain the bone permanently in that position, although the movements of flexion and extension may have been freely per-formed.   The original glenoid cavity is nearly obliterated, having been reduced in shape to an irregular elongated opening, barely large enough to allow the insertion of the forefinger.   The lower and inner part of the pelvis is considerably altered in form by the bulging inwards of the secondary socket, and sundry long excrescences, together with a general aspect of roughness, are apparent around the neck of the thigh bone.   As a whole, this pathological specimen obtained from an ancient grave shows in a very marked degree the wonderful efforts made by Nature in this instance to recover a fair amount of motion after an injury of such a serious character.   This accident is usually described by surgeons as being amongst the most rare forms of dislocation at the hip joint."

Over the body was a boat-formed deposit of unctuous earth, situated in the centre of the rubbly chalk, filling the grave.   It measured 6 feet long, 3½ feet wide, and 3 feet deep, with a narrow keel-formed bottom touching the body. This mass consisted of some greasy earth, variegated in colour, in which were small openings or cavities, and, in some places, patches in the form of con-glomerate, cemented together with a blackish bitumen-like substance, the residuum of some unknown deposit.   This cimbiform structure is very like the one in barrow No. 17 (fig. 447), and will be better understood by referring to the plan and description of that mound.   In both cases the body was placed upon the rock, under the mass of unctuous soily matter.

Two trenches were made, one on the north, the other on the south side of our central excavation, without finding anything but a small portion of an urn. This mound, which was circular in form, gave an altitude of 3 feet 10 inches, a radius of 45 feet, and was formed of thin layers of clay, divided by beds of soil.

A most interesting discovery was made in building up the vase.   In the fractured edge of one of the pieces were three grains of wheat, still connected together in the husk, indicating that they constituted one united row broken from an ear of wheat, and not separated from the chaff by thrashing.   This implies that at the time and place where the vase was made, wheat was probably also grown, and had become accidentally mixed with the plastic clay forming the substance of the vase. The husks, with the three grains, had been pressed into the walls of the vase (fig. 261), and were merely covered with a thin film of clay. In baking the vessel they had become carbonised, to which circumstance their preservation is entirely due, though, from their fragile nature, they are now somewhat damaged. They are preserved in a glass tube in the Driffield Museum, and seem to belong to a small variety.

The discovery of this proof of the cultivation of wheat in pre-Roman times in this neighbourhood, probably on the chalk hills, is exceedingly interesting.

Re-opening, April 23rd and 25th, 1869.—An extensive re-examination was made of this barrow, and into the grave beneath it, but without leading to any further result.

Though standing on a small, natural ridge, barrows Nos. 131 and 132 only rise 16 inches above the adjoining ground, and, being joined to each other, they rather resemble one single, long mound ; but most probably they are, as we have shown them on the map, twin mounds. They, however, do not stand sufficiently prominent as to have attracted the attention of the Ordnance Surveyors. They measured together 75 feet east and west, and 45 feet north and south, and the whole of the first week in May, 1869, was devoted to their examination.

BARROW No. 131

Consisted of soil and chalk grit obtained from the immediate neighbourhood, and in the centre was an oval grave (No. 1) with its longest axis east and west ; was 4 feet deep, 7 feet by 5 feet at the top, and 5½ by 3 feet at the bottom. Small sherds of ornate British pottery were found interspersed throughout, and along the bottom was a thin covering of dark matter and a small flint scraper, but no trace of a skeleton. A similar oval grave (No. 2) cut the west end of No. 1 at right angles. It measured 6 feet by 3½ feet at the top, and 5 feet by 2½ feet at the bottom, and was 3½ feet deep. The only objects found were bits of burnt wood and a small flint flake knife (fig. 261 A) chipped on its edge, which occurred at the bottom of the grave on the west side.

BARROW No. 132

Was a little larger than its companion, and consisted of similar soily matter. Near the centre was an oval grave, 5 feet deep, and measuring 6½ feet east and west by 5½ feet at the top, and 5 feet by 2½ feet at the bottom. Like the two graves in the adjoining barrow, no trace of a body was found, and beneath was a film of dark matter, close above which were piled many large flints and pieces of chalk. About a foot from the bottom a small portion of bone (which crumbled to pieces on being touched) was found sticking into the east side of the grave. Near this grave were three deposits of calcined human bones, unaccompanied by any relic.

That bodies once occupied the three graves in this twin barrow is almost a certainty, and their final destruction and disappearance may be ascribed, as in other instances, to the free access of air and water through the porous material forming the mound, rather than to the greater antiquity of the interments themselves.

No. VI.—THE PAINSTHORPE WOLD GROUP.

THE twenty-one barrows comprising this group are more scattered than those in the last, and like them they follow the western brow of the chalk escarpment, running south-south-east.

Two of the mounds were unusually rich in secondary (Anglo-Saxon) interments, having been utilised as cemeteries by a neighbouring settlement of Angles.

BARROW No. 4.

This barrow is specially interesting to the writer, as in 1860 it was the first one to excite his curiosity and to produce a desire to gain some knowledge of

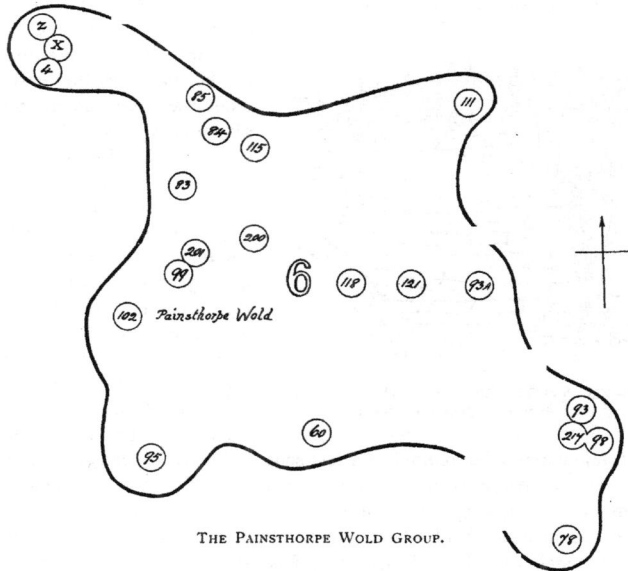

THE PAINSTHORPE WOLD GROUP.

the contents of these ancient monuments. It has from time to time been encroached upon by a chalk pit in Pudsey Plantation, by the side of the high road from Malton to Pocklington, near the cross-road called "Uncleby Stoop."* During the summer of 1860† Mr. G. Harper, the tenant of the land, in procuring chalk for repairing the roads, found numerous human bones and portions of antlers of a large deer. A few days afterwards the writer visited the place and extracted

---

* The cross-roads near the late Sir Tatton Sykes' monument, between Garton and Sledmere, is called "Sledmere Stoop." "Stoop" or "stowp" means a post; e.g., "yat-stoop," a gate-post. See "Holderness Glossary," 1877.

† A covering of trees would not then permit an opening to be made.

the leg and arm bones of an adult body from the middle of the exposed section of the barrow, and amongst the fallen debris at the bottom of the pit found broken antlers and vertebræ of red deer, also a piece of cherty rock (fig. 263), much rubbed down on one side as if it had been used for the purpose of sharpening some tool.   From the filled-in encircling trench on the east side of the barrow was obtained a stag's horn pick (fig. 264).   The accompanying rough sketch (fig. 265) was taken on November 5th, 1861.   A few weeks before, the workmen had again been quarrying chalk and found more human bones, which had fallen from the mound near *B* (fig. 265).   They also found, at *A*, in what they called a filled-up crack (pipe) in the chalk, portions of a deer antler.   The pipe eventually "worked out," and it was found that the antlers had not been in the pipe, but in an encircling trench which passed over it, just within the edge of the barrow.   A section of this trench is shown on the east side of the barrow.

On May 21st, 1862, the face of the quarry had been worked further back, and a recent fall of earth had exposed two skeletons, placed at full length, with their heads to the west.   One occurred near the left-hand margin, and was at the base of the barrow.   The other was near the right-hand margin, and a little below the base of the mound.   Being Anglo-Saxon interments, their positions are not shown in the plan.

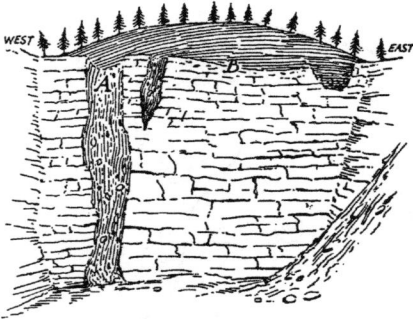

FIG. 265.— Sketch of Chalk Pit near Uncleby Stoop, made
Nov. 5, 1861, showing section of Barrow No. 4.

On June 2nd and 4th, 1870, a few trees in the centre of the barrow having been uprooted by the wind, my brother and two experienced workmen were able to explore the central grave, shown in the section (fig. 266).   An opening, 8 feet east by west, 6 feet wide, and about 2 feet from the face of the pit, was made.   Immediately after removing a few sods, a disturbed skeleton (fig. 266, No. 1) and fragments of Anglo-Saxon pottery were met with.   After descending through a stratum of clay mixed with a little soil 16 inches in thickness,* which covered the grave, and at a depth of 2 feet 10 inches from the apex of the mound, a deposit of calcined bones was reached (fig. 266, No. 2) which occupied a space about a foot in diameter.   Close to this were some pieces of unburnt animal bones.   At the same level, and only 6 inches to the south of the cremated interment, was the doubled-up skeleton of a child † (No. 3), aged about fifteen months, on its left side, with its head pointing south-east.   Near the chest of this was a food-vase (fig. 267), 4 inches high and 5½ inches across the top.   Three flint flakes occurred close by.   Near the two interments were also a few pieces of unburnt human bone. These objects occupied the upper portion of an oval grave, measuring 7 feet by

---

* This clay was eventually found to reach some distance all round, and to extend unbroken over four more graves.
† Not shown on the ground plan.

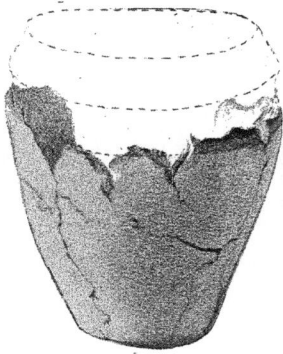

FIG. 259. $\frac{1}{3}$

FIG. 261 a.

FIG. 261. $\frac{1}{3}$

FIG. 263. $\frac{1}{2}$

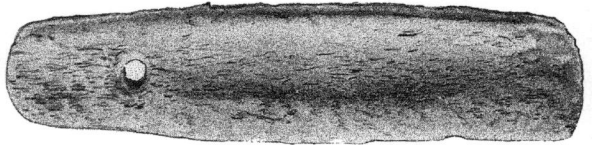

FIG. 268. $\frac{1}{4}$

FIG. 272 $\frac{1}{1}$

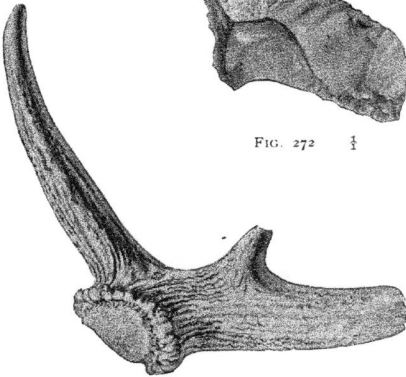

FIG. 264. $\frac{1}{3}$

FIG. 267. $\frac{1}{2}$

5 feet, which was found to be charged with soil and a little chalk, in which were several broken fragments of a drinking-cup. Detached human bones were distributed irregularly from top to bottom. At about a foot from the bottom of the grave were the crouched remains of a strongly-built man* (No. 4 in the section), on the left side, and head to the north. A spoon-shaped bone implement (fig. 268), probably made from the rib of an ox, had been placed by the side of the body.

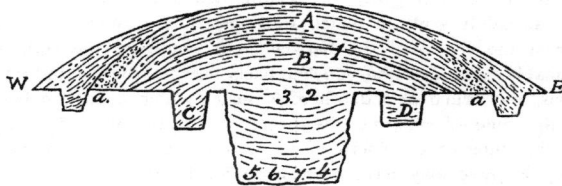

FIG. 266.—Section of Barrow No. 4. *a*—Chalk rubble cast from the encircling pit.

It measured 4¼ inches in length, and had a hole through its flat side at a distance of an inch from the narrow end. Some dark matter was observed near the vertebræ. A femoral bone measured 19 inches. On the floor of the grave, at the west end, 7 feet from the apex of the barrow, were bodies Nos. 5 and 6, in the positions shown on the plan (fig. 269). Behind the skull of each stood an elaborately-ornamented drinking-cup (figs. 270, 271), each measuring about 6 inches high

FIG. 269.—Plan of Barrow No. 4, from face of chalk quarry, showing encircling trench (*T*).

and 4½ inches across the top. Both skeletons were much decayed. Interment No. 5 was that of a youth from eight to twelve years of age. A small knife (fig. 272) of black flint occurred below the chin. Burial No. 6 contained the remains of an aged female of small stature. At the east end of the grave, at the bottom, was a third skeleton (No. 7 on the section), with head to the south, as shown in the plan. A large flake knife (fig. 273), peculiar in form, and a smaller

* Not shown in fig. 269.

one (fig. 274), were placed near the right hip. A quantity of decayed wood surrounded the bodies, being the residue of some structure which had protected the interments. As shown by the section, the unbroken bed of clay covered all the interments but No. 1.

Further Investigations.—On July 31st, 1871, having been informed that human bones were to be seen in a recently made section of the barrow caused by an extension of the quarry, and that a large jet bead (fig. 275) had been found a little to the south of the central grave, we again visited the place, and obtained the leg bones of an adult skeleton which were protruding from the mound 13 feet south-west from the centre of the barrow. On removing the soil, an extended skeleton (probably Anglo-Saxon) on its back, feet to the south-east and hands over the pelvis, was found at a depth of 6 inches. The head had been removed, probably at the time of planting the trees, or during rabbit digging. No relic accompanied this interment. South of the centre, at the point marked *a* on the plan (fig. 269), a grave may have been destroyed by the quarrymen, as the large jet bead (fig. 275) undoubtedly British, was found, and had most probably accompanied a body.

August 14th to 19th, 1876.—The whole of the trees previously growing on this mound having now been cut down and removed, the writer and three workmen devoted a week to a thorough examination of the unexplored portion of the barrow.* On the north-west side of the mound, at a point marked 1 *a, b* (fig. 269), and only about 8 inches below the surface, were the extended remains of a large-boned Anglo-Saxon, with head to south-south-east. No relic was found with them.

Interment No. 2a occurred on a film of dark matter, at the base of the mound, with its head near the western edge of the large grave, in the position shown on the plan. Near the skull was a circular impression, apparently of decayed wood, and probably the remains of some article which may have served the purpose of a food-vase. The femur measured 18 inches. No relic was obtained.

Burial No. 3a occupied the floor of the grave marked "A" on the plan, and a broad triangular flint knife (fig. 276) was found near the hips. Each femur measured 17 inches, and each tibia 13½ inches, and were apparently those of a female 25 to 30 years of age. At the feet were the remains of a child (No. 8) from 12 to 18 months old.

Burial No. 4a was at the bottom of grave *B*. It was that of an adult of medium stature—probably a female. The extreme length of femur was 16½ inches, and of the tibia 14 inches. No relic was found. Graves *A* and *B* communicated with each other, either by accident or design.

Interment No. 5a (grave C) was also on the floor of the grave, and over the body some fragments of a British drinking-cup had been thrown. Nothing more accompanied it. A femur measured 17 inches, the extreme length of a tibia was 13½ inches, and the right and left humeri measured exactly 12 inches each. This grave was only 2½ feet deep, and a passage was found to run from it in an easterly direction, a rare feature in graves. The previous excavation in the centre grave had apparently destroyed a portion of this passage at the point marked "BB."

_____

The centre grave had been explored in 1870. as previously described.

FIG. 270. ½

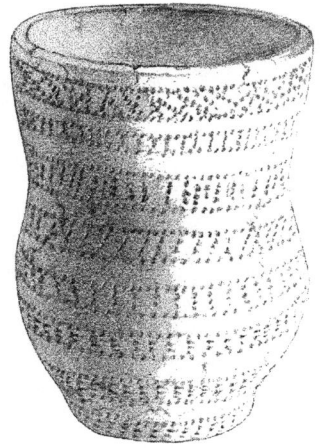

FIG. 271. ½

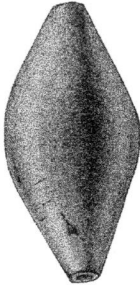

FIG. 275. ½

FIG. 273. ⅟₁

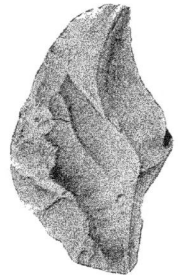

FIG. 274. ⅟₁

FIG. 276. ⅟₁

FIG. 278. ⅟₁

Burial No. 6a was only 18 inches from the vertex of the mound, partly over the passage of grave " D," where it enters the centre grave. It was that of an Anglo-Saxon female, with head to west-south-west, on its right side, knees pulled up to a right angle with the trunk, the left arm bent over the body, and the right arm doubled back with hands to face. This is not shown on the plan. A femur measured 18 inches. The skull was completely destroyed by the roots of a tree. On the chest was a circular fibula of bronze ($fig.$ 277), and at the neck were two beads of amethystine quartz, and nine coloured beads ($fig.$ 278) formed of a vitreous paste. Close within the angle formed by the body and doubled-up legs were a bronze box ($fig.$ 279), an iron knife ($fig.$ 280) 4½ inches long, and the remains of a satchel ($fig.$ 281). The box, though somewhat crushed, contained remains of thread and a corroded iron needle. The remains of the satchel consisted of portions of a woven material, a brass clasp ornamented with raised lines of plaited work, two bronze rings, and several elongated pieces of bronze, looped at each end, to which corroded iron adheres. Most of these articles are held together by what seems to be the corroded links of iron chain work.

Burial No. 7a contained the remains of a child, three or four years of age, which occurred on the floor of grave *D*, with its head towards a passage leading to the centre grave, and resembling that observed in grave *C*. A drinking-cup ($fig.$ 282) of the usual shape, ornamented over the whole exterior with nearly vertical gashes distributed without any arrangement or attempt of pattern—an unusual feature on British vases—stood behind the shoulders, accompanied by a small knife of black flint. The curved passage leading from this grave was carefully followed, and at a distance of 10 feet it entered the central grave. Its depth throughout was about 3 feet, or 1 foot less than the depth of the two graves it connected. Its width at the bottom was a little more than a foot, and its clearly defined sides of rock sloped outwards.

No. 9 is the doubled-up interment of a child, which was placed at the edge of grave *C*, a little below the base of the mound, with head to the west. A beautiful flint knife ($fig.$ 284), 3¼ inches long, was found in the mound, between the centre grave and grave *D*. It did not appear to be connected with any interment.

The five graves were all of large size, though somewhat variable; and, excepting grave *C*, each extended about 4 feet below the base of the barrow. Apparently they were all anterior to the erection of the mound, as the clay capping, previously observed, was found to have covered all the graves, and did not appear to have been cut through.

Some of the graves in this barrow possess a very rare feature. Though the writer has, in other instances, noticed a communication between two graves similar to that shown between graves *A* and *B*, yet this is the first barrow in which he has observed passages clearly connecting two graves, such as are shown in fig. 269, between graves *C* and *D* and the centre one.* There may, however, have been instances of such an arrangement in other barrows, which from not having been cut into solid rock, and consequently not being well defined, may have escaped observation. Possibly some sentimental reason actuated the provision of this connection.

---

* A somewhat similar passage was observed to connect two graves in the long barrow near Helperthorpe, see " Miscellaneous Barrows"; while I believe Dr. Schliemann noticed such a connection between some of the graves at Micenæ.

BARROWS X and Z.

During April, 1868, these two barrows were opened by the Rev. Canon Greenwell. The account of the one marked "X" on the map is taken from his "British Barrows," p. 136.

"This barrow was 94 feet in diameter, but only 2 feet 10 inches high, having within the recollection of the present occupier of the land lost some feet of its original height. At a distance of 30 feet south-by-east from the centre, there was a deposit of burnt bones—those of an adult—laid in a heap, 13 inches in diameter, upon the natural surface of the ground. With the bones was placed a bone pin, also burnt, and perforated with a large eye. At the centre was a grave, of a slightly oval form, sunk into the chalk rock to a depth of 6 feet. The longest diameter, in a direction south-west by north-east, was 6½ feet, the other 6 feet. At a distance of 3½ feet above the bottom were the pelvic bones of a horse; and at the bottom, about the middle of the grave, were two large flint stones, 1 foot apart, lying between which was a deposit of the burnt bones of an adult. Twenty-eight feet north-east of the centre, on the natural surface, was found a small polished greenstone axe, 3⅛ inches long, and 1¾ inches wide at the cutting edge; and not far from it a fragment of a drinking cup, together with some flint chippings, a round scraper, and a long flake, which showed many signs of use along one edge."

These were the only British relics found by the Canon in this barrow, but t was unusually rich in Anglo-Saxon remains, and he writes :*—

"The barrow in question had, at a long time subsequent to its original construction, been made use of for burial purposes by a community of Angles (presumably the ancient inhabitants of what is now called Kirby), who had placed in it the bodies of above 70 men, women, and children, some of whom, it would appear, had belonged to the poorer classes of the community, whilst others had certainly been persons of wealth and importance. Quite a small museum of warlike, domestic, and personal relics was furnished by the results of a fortnight's digging, and some remarkable features in connection with Anglian interments were ascertained and recorded. Of these I will, however, only mention one, viz., that contrary to usual Anglian practice, the greater number of buried persons had been interred in a contracted position, and not at full length." ‖

The barrow marked "Z" on the plan, is very small, near the northern margin of the last one, and is now hardly visible. It was also excavated by Canon Greenwell, but without any result, consequently he does not allude to it in his "British Barrows." Nevertheless, though small, it is shown on the Ordnance Map as an unmistakable British barrow.

* British Barrows, p. 135.
† These Anglo-Saxon relics are in the York Museum.

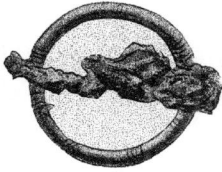

FIG. 277.   ¼

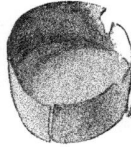

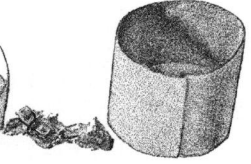

FIG. 279.   ½

FIG. 287   ¼

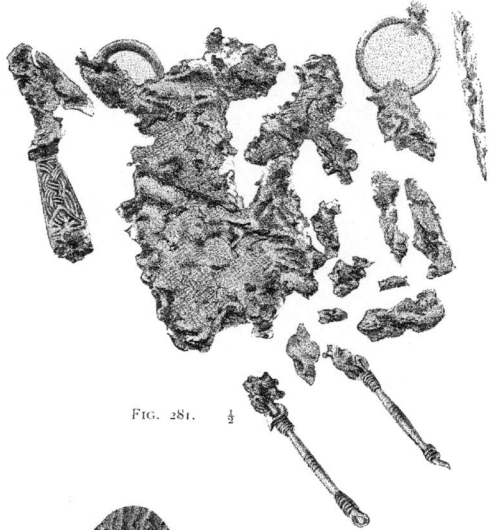

FIG. 287.   ¼

FIG. 280.   ¼

FIG. 281.   ½

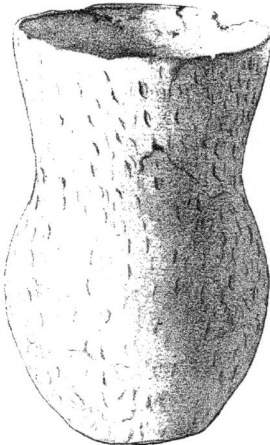

FIG. 286.

FIG. 282.   ½

FIG. 284.   ¼

FIG. 285.   ¼

BARROW No. 83

Stands in the middle of the field adjoining the south end of Slip Plantation. On May 4th and 6th, 1867, it measured 60 feet in diameter, and 2 feet in elevation. The first skeleton discovered was that of a youth from ten to twelve years of age, and was situated 4 yards north-east of the centre of the mound. It was on a thin layer of clay, a little above the base of the barrow, on its right side, head to north-east, knees pulled up, and hands to the face. At the base of the barrow, and two yards west of the body, were portions of an urn. In the centre of the mound were some large flat stones, and a number of slabs of oolitic sandstone, varying from 1 to 2 feet in width, forming a nearly circular enclosure on the ancient turf-line. Within this circle were two skeletons, side by side, with their heads not more than a foot apart, and pointing east-north-east. The most southerly one—an adult—was slightly below the base of the mound, on its left side, hands to the head, and the knees pulled up to a right angle with the trunk. The skull, though cracked by pressure, was not much decayed; but the under jaw could not be found. A femur measured 18 inches, and a tibia 14 inches. The skeleton to the north was that of a youth, probably twelve to fourteen years of age. It was close to the back of the adult, in a similar posture, except that the right arm crossed the lower part of the abdomen with the hand on the pelvis, and the left arm was stretched by its side. Near the face was a beautifully-formed saw, of black flint, $2\frac{1}{8}$ inches long (fig. 285). One side is the flat cleavage face of the flint, the other is ridged down the middle by skilful chipping. The edges, even round the ends, are finely serrated by the same delicate process of chipping, one edge being slightly more delicately toothed than the other.

Between the two skulls, and almost in contact with that of the adult, were fragments of a drinking-cup, irreparably crushed; and immediately under the knees of the older skeleton was a circular heap of cremated bones, on the north side of which was a crushed food-vase, even more decayed than the drinking-cup. A few heat-splintered fragments of a flint knife (fig. 286) were found among the burnt bones. Close to these, but on the opposite side to the drinking-cup, was a dish-shaped hole in the ground, 9 inches deep, and 12 inches wide at the top. It contained dark, greasy-looking earth, from which we took a decayed portion of *unburnt* bone. A similar hole was observed a little to the north of the two inhumed bodies, and also contained unctuous matter mixed with pieces of burnt wood. It is probable that food had been placed in the two circular cavities made in the ground, and that the cup contained liquid. Excepting a little clay near the interments, the mound was composed of surface soil from the surrounding land. From the centre of the barrow seven splinters of flint were taken, and bits of burnt wood were noticed at its base.

BARROWS Nos. 84 and 85

Were two small and nearly demolished mounds, neither of which is shown on the Ordnance Map. They both consisted of the reddish surface soil of the district, together with a little whitish loamy earth, probably obtained from the head of one of the springs at the western foot of the chalk hills. A little to the east of the assumed centre of barrow No. 84, and within reach of the plough, was a heap of burnt human bones, mixed with wood ashes. Had an urn ever accompanied this interment, it must have been destroyed by the passage of the plough long previous to our examination. A little west of the centre, and slightly below the tilled surface, was a second heap of burnt bones of a youth.

No. 85.—North of the centre of this barrow was a dish-shaped hole, containing calcined bones, wood ashes, and soil burnt red. The upper portion of the receptacle and its contents had been removed by the plough. West of the centre was a similar deposit, which had also been partly destroyed.

No relic accompanied any of the four deposits in these two barrows; neither could any indication of a grave be found. Nineteen hand-struck splinters of black flint were picked from the two barrows.

BARROW No. 115.

On June 17th and 18th, 1868, this barrow measured 50 feet in diameter, and 1½ feet in central height. A stout sod wall* ran from north to south over its eastern margin. That portion of the barrow to the west of the wall was turned over, and the ground beneath trenched, but no interment could be found. The broken half of a sandstone cobble, partly pierced on each side at the place of fracture; fragments of two urns, 4 flint knives, 2 long scrapers, 6 pieces more or less approaching the round scrapers, 5 slingstones or cores, and 82 flakes and splinters were picked from various places in the mound. A small and beautifully-formed perforated jet stud (fig. 287), was found at the base of the mound about ten feet from the northern edge.

BARROWS Nos. 200 and 201

Are about 200 yards apart, and on each was a clump of large beech trees. Fortunately those growing in the centres of the mounds had been cut down, and during July 3rd and the six following days in 1877, we were enabled to excavate 16 feet square in the centre of each, and to carefully search the ground beneath. In excavating barrow No. 200 we exhumed the remains of three beasts, which the farmer had buried during the cattle plague in the years 1866-7.† This unexpected intrusion had destroyed one interment, if not more, as we found the remains of a thin bronze cup or dish, together with the iron spike belonging to the shaft of an Anglo-Saxon spear. At the base of the mound, 3½ feet from its apex, and a little to the north of the centre, was an oval grave cut 4½ feet into the rock, and measuring 7 feet east by west, and 4½ feet north by south. On the floor of this grave were the remains of a strongly built man, on the left side, head to east, the left hand at the chin, the right hand on the left elbow, and the knees pulled up. A femur and a humerus measured 18½ and 13 inches respectively. At the west end of the grave had been placed a shoulder of a small pig and other animal food, as was indicated by their unburnt osseous remains. Between these and the feet of the skeleton, and in close proximity to

* Such erections were frequently made by the farmers on the wolds before the planting of quick-wood fences.
† Other instances of burying cattle in tumuli are recorded in these pages.

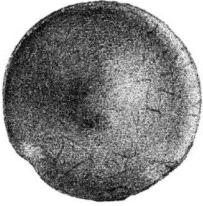

FIG. 288. $\frac{1}{1}$

FIG. 289. $\frac{1}{1}$

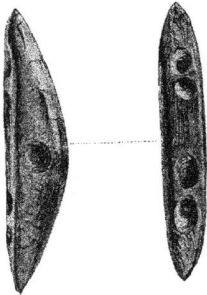

FIG. 290. $\frac{1}{1}$

FIG. 291. $\frac{1}{3}$

FIG. 293. $\frac{1}{1}$

FIG. 293. $\frac{1}{1}$

FIG. 296.

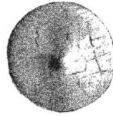

FIG. 298. $\frac{2}{1}$

FIG. 297. $\frac{2}{1}$

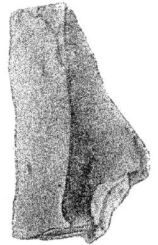

FIG. 299. $\frac{1}{1}$

FIG. 301. $\frac{1}{1}$

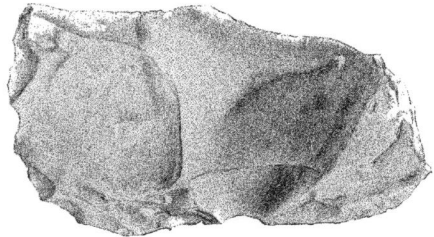

FIG. 300.

the latter, were two large circular jet buttons (figs. 288-9), and an elongated one (fig. 290). These probably belonged to some article of clothing. The grave was charged with a mixture of clayey matter from a distance, and surface soil from the adjoining land, similar to that which formed the mound, and not with the chalk that had been excavated in making it. Three other trenches were made in the sides of the mound without finding anything further.

BARROW No. 201

Measured 6 feet from base to apex. Near the centre, and 1 foot from the top, were the fragments of a crushed food-vase (fig. 291) unaccompanied by any interment. West of the centre, and at about half the depth of the mound, was a circular heap of adult burnt bones (No. 1, fig. 292), whilst between this deposit and the west side of the grave, and at the base of the mound, were two more circular deposits of burnt bones (Nos. 2 and 3). East of the centre, almost vertically under the food-vase, and about 2 feet from the base of the mound, was an elongated heap of calcined bones (No. 4), from which a portion of a flint knife and a unique bone button or dress fastener (fig. 293), both much burnt, were obtained. Close to the south side of this deposit were the fore-leg and some other bones of a young deer, unburnt. A little north-east of these, and at the base of the mound, was a circular heap of calcined bones (No. 5), white and clean, from which we picked some finger bones having an unnatural growth of bone round the edges on their inner or under sides, denoting disease. All the

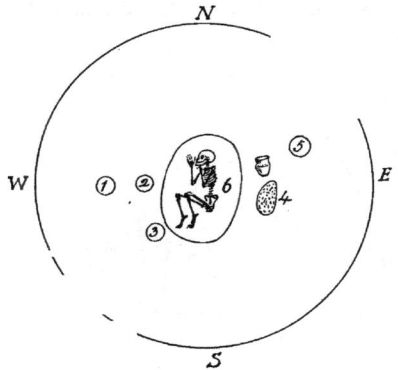

FIG. 292.—Plan of Barrow No. 201.

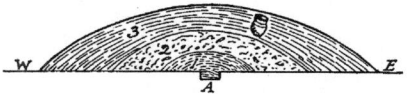

FIG. 294.—Section of Barrow No. 201.
A—Grave.   1—Soil covering the grave.
2—Chalk grit and soil.   3—Clay and surface soil.

burnt bodies were those of adults; and with the exception of No. 4, no article was found with them. In the centre was an oval grave, scooped about 9 inches only into the ancient surface soil, in which were the much decayed remains of an adult (No. 6) in the posture shown in the plan. Below was a film of dark matter, indicating the remains of a couch or wrapper, resting on the undisturbed rock.

The structure of this mound is shown in the section (fig. 294). The cremated interments Nos. 1 and 4 must have taken place as the rearing of the barrow proceeded, as there was no trace of any of the beds having been cut through.

Q

BARROW No. 99.

This low circular barrow stands in the stackyard belonging to the Painsthorpe Wold Farm-house. During four fine days in the latter part of June, 1867, we opened this barrow, and found that it had a diameter of 60 feet and an elevation of 34 inches. It consisted of the local surface soil, mixed with loamy clay brought from a distance, in about equal quantities.

We commenced by sinking a narrow trench to the base of the mound, enclosing a 20-ft. square in the middle of the barrow, after which the centre block was removed. The arrangement of the interments is shown on the plan (fig. 295), as far as could be made out from the badly preserved skeletons. South-west of the centre was an oval grave (marked A), 5½ feet east and west, 4 feet wide, with a depth of 10 inches below the base of the mound. This contained at the centre,

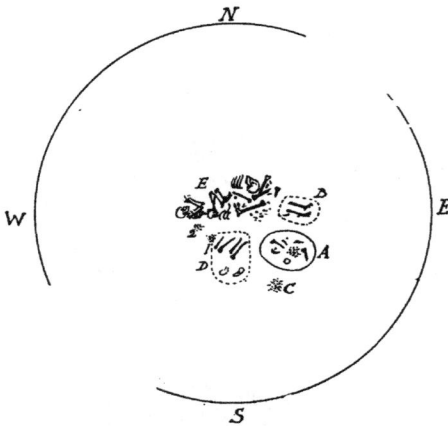

FIG. 295.—Plan of Barrow No. 99.

near the bottom, a circular heap of the burnt bones of an adult. No relic was found with this deposit, but pieces of burnt wood and many pieces of unburnt human adult bones — consisting of the thigh bones, portions of leg bones, and pieces of a skull—also many fragments of the skull of a child, were distributed throughout the grave. To the south of the grave, on the floor of the barrow, we met with a second heap of cremated bones, at C, in which was a handstruck flint flake (fig. 296), much burnt. At B, and about the base of the barrow, in a bed of foreign clay, were traces of an adult skeleton, but it was not sufficiently preserved to enable us to make out its position. A little east of this interment two jet studs (figs. 297-8) were found. Probably they had belonged to a body which had decayed, as here also were slight traces of decomposed bone. At D, and on the old surface line, were portions of the remains of two adults, also in the last stages of decomposition. Only small portions of the sides of the two skulls, and fragments of the leg bones remained. We were only able to make out that the bodies had been placed with their heads pointing to the south, and that near them, at the place marked I, were twenty-one flint flakes, varying in length from ¾ of an inch to nearly 3 inches, and in breadth from ¼ of an inch to ¾ of an inch. In addition to these, there was a flake saw (fig. 299), a rough block (fig. 300), from which some of the flakes had been struck, the end of a diamond-shaped arrowhead, and a small and very thin tool (fig. 301), chipped to a keen edge all round, and having one end obtusely pointed. There was also a fine spear head (fig. 302), 3¾ inches long and 1½ inches broad in the middle. All these are of a dark-coloured flint foreign to the neighbouring chalk. They were placed touching one another, the spear-head being under three or four flakes. About 18 inches north-west from the above (marked 2 on the plan), and 6 to 8 inches higher in the mound, were four more flakes, varying in length from 1½ to 3¼ inches, one diamond-shaped and one leaf-shaped arrow-head (figs. 303-4), 2 inches and 1¾ inches in length respectively. The two series are nearly of the same kind of flint, and from their fresh appearance it might be assumed that they had been flaked from the blocks, and some of them worked into instruments at the time the bodies were interred.

About a foot north of the heap of flints (marked 2) was a skeleton, doubled up, as shown at *E*; and close to its feet were the piled-up bones of a body which had been dismembered previous to interment. The rather slender leg bones of the first-mentioned skeleton were too far decayed for measurement, but they seemed to be those of a female of about fifty years of age, judging from the well-worn teeth. The bones of the dismembered body were unusually strong, as a femur measured 19 inches, and was exceptionally thick. It is again worthy of note that frequently the bones piled up or scattered in the grave in this way were of large size. The skull of the dismembered body was much broken, but has since been so far restored as to show that it belonged to a powerful man of about 50 years of age. Near it the whole of the bones of one hand occurred in juxtaposition, showing that after amputation the hand had been interred in the place in which it was found, the bones being held together by the ligaments. This seems to show clearly that the body had been cut to pieces and deposited before the flesh had decayed from the bones, and that the dismembered bones were not due to one interment having been disturbed by the insertion of a later one. Besides, it was clearly observed that the layers of earth forming the mound had never been broken through to make an opening for a later burial. No relic accompanied these two skeletons, unless the nearest deposit of flints (2) can be assigned to them.

Near the centre, and within twelve inches of the apex of the mound—which had been previously much lowered—were several decayed portions of the skull of a child. Many large pieces of local flint were piled in the mound, over and near the inhumed remains *D*, and the cremated deposit *C*.

We extended the southern side of the excavation towards the margin of the mound, but observed nothing further. From various places in the barrow, and at its base were picked up 20 splinters of foreign flint, and one diamond-shaped arrow-head 1¼ inches long, but not the slightest trace of pottery of any kind was found in any part of this barrow, which, considering the number of bodies that had been interred, was rather remarkable.

BARROW No. 102.

During August 13th and 14th, 1867, this barrow was opened. It stands on the summit of the western margin of the chalk hills, about 800 feet above the sea-level.* The barrow is not more than 30 feet in diameter, and but 6 to 8 inches above the plane of the adjoining ground. Consequently it is not shewn on the Ordnance Map. The first discovery was the greater portion of the body

---

* Notwithstanding this elevation the weather was so extremely hot that at times we had to protect ourselves from the scorching sun by sheltering under our conveyance, whilst a farm servant mowing thistles in the same field divested himself of all clothing, save his shirt and boots.

of an Anglo-Saxon, lying slightly below the base of the mound, on its left side, the legs much doubled up, and, as far as could be made out, having had its head within 3½ feet of the southern edge of a spacious grave, which occurred in the centre of the barrow.   The head and shoulders of this skeleton had been placed a little higher than the rest of the body, hence their almost total destruction by the plough.   A femur measured 18 inches.   A common type of an Anglo-Saxon iron knife (fig. 305), was placed close to the pelvis.   Impressions of woven cloth are clearly shown on the oxidised blade towards the point, and in one place two thicknesses are distinctly visible.   Traces of finely-grained wood also are well preserved on the tang of the blade.   A small triangular knife of flint was found in the mound, near its southern margin.

In the grave, towards the north-east side, and slightly below the base of the barrow, was a small plain food-vase (fig. 306), 4 inches in height.   One and a half inches of its upper portion consisted of a deep border resembling the usual type of cinerary urn.   Near it was a quantity of dark matter, in which we observed decayed bone and remains of teeth, indicating the body of a young person.   A portion of the lower jaw of an ox, containing three molar teeth, occurred near the vase ; and at a little distance, and about the same depth, another vase (fig. 307), in fragments, was picked up.   The grave —roughly oval in shape — measured 9 feet east and west, by 7 feet 2 inches north and south, and 3½ feet deep.   It was charged from top to bottom with gritty chalk, mixed throughout with lumps of burnt wood and detached human bones, but no animal remains occurred, except the previously-named portion of a jaw with teeth.   On the floor, in the centre of this large grave, were the crouched remains of an aged person, probably a male, on the left side, with both hands partly under the face.   A femur, tibia, and humerus measured 17½, 14, and 12½ inches respectively, and were of strong make.   Close round the head were 5 flakes of flint (fig. 308, *A,B,C,D*), arranged at about equal distances.   Nothing more was found.   A row of chalk stones had been carefully piled close behind the back of the body, and a few near the knees.   Everywhere else the material seemed to have been put hurriedly into the grave, or had been subsequently let down by the decay of some wooden covering over it.

BARROW No. 95.

On May 23rd, 1867, this mound measured 18 yards in diameter, and, partly in consequence of its having been reduced by tilling, only measured 8 inches above the adjoining ground.   Five feet south of the centre, pieces of burnt wood were observed, which led to the discovery of a shallow, dish-shaped hole in the natural surface of the land, measuring three feet in diameter, and seven inches into the rock.   It held a quantity of burnt wood, among which were a few calcined bones of apparently a young or small person.   A layer of bluish-coloured clay, brought from a distance, three or four inches in thickness, covered this cavity and its contents.

The only relics found were five flakes of flint, from the mound.

FIG. 302.   ¼

FIG. 303.   ¼

FIG. 304.   ¼

FIG. 306.   ½

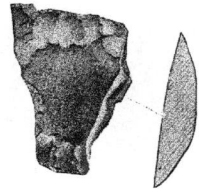

FIG. 311.

FIG. 305.   ½

FIG. 312.

FIG. 308a.

FIG. 308b.

FIG. 308c.

FIG. 308d.

FIG. 307.   ½

BARROW No. 60.

On Saturday, May 26th, 1866, we excavated this small barrow, which is situated a short distance north of the Fordham Farm-house, and only about 130 yards to the west of a narrow plantation at the end of Warrendale. Though not shown on the Ordnance Map, it measured 14 yards in diameter and 10 inches in elevation. We turned over a 17 feet square in the central portion of this barrow, and near the surface fragments of an adult body broken up by the plough were observed. On reaching the centre, one of the workmen unfortunately struck his pick into the skull of a second interment, which was found lying on the left side, the knees drawn up, both hands near the chin, and head pointing nearly due north. This skeleton was placed in a shallow grave, only 5 inches below the base of the barrow.*

A femur measured 17½ inches. About 7 inches to the west of the skull were some portions of leg and arm bones belonging to a third interment. No weapon or fragment of an urn was found in this barrow.

BARROW No. 118

Is situated in the second field west-south-west of Bradeham Farm-house. It measured about 3½ feet in central height, and had a medium diameter of about 62 feet.

From July 2nd to 9th, 1868, we turned over the whole of the barrow, and our first discovery (14 feet north-east of centre) was the bottom of a large cinerary urn, marked A on the plan (fig. 309), containing a few burnt bones. All the upper part of this urn, and most of the calcined human remains,

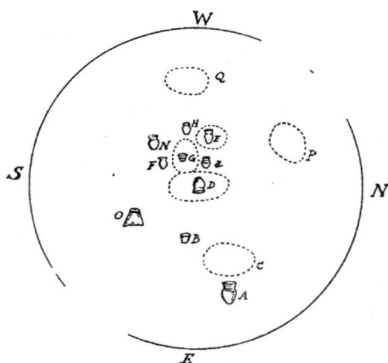

FIG. 309.— Plan of Barrow No. 118.

A, D, O—Cinerary Urns.
A, a, B, F, G, H, N—Food Vases.
The two central enclosures mark the positions of the primary graves. The other four enclosures contained the inhumed bodies.

had been removed by the plough. About six feet eastwards from the centre, and not more than five to six inches from the surface, were some unburnt remains of an infant, accompanied by a small plain cup-formed vase (B on the plan), irreparably crushed. Nine feet north by east of the centre, was an oval grave, marked C, 20 inches deep, 5 feet long, and 3½ feet in width, at the bottom of which was the skeleton of an adult, on its back. The knees and face were pressed over to the west; the head was to the north, with the right hand to the face, and the left hand upon the right elbow. A femur measured 17 inches.

Two feet north by-east of the centre, in contact with the tilled surface, was an inverted urn, D, containing the burnt bones of a young person from which was taken a heat-splintered fragment of a fine flint knife (fig. 311). This urn measured 10 inches high, and 9 inches in diameter at the top. Round the

* Possibly a re-opening might discover a body at a greater depth.

inside of the rim are four horizontal strings of twisted thong-like impressions; and one similarly-impressed line runs round the outside at the top, below which five horizontal rows of slightly oblique and somewhat split imprints given by a pointed instrument, ornamented the lower part of the border and the whole of the contracted neck. Close to the bottom of this vase, which had been damaged by the plough, was a lozenge-shaped pendant of rough jet, $1\frac{3}{4}$ inches long, pierced at one end for suspension (fig. 312). About twelve inches west of D, and on the same plane, was a food-vase (fig. 313), marked a; close to which had been placed the inhumed remains of a child, and the lower portion, with brow tine attached, of an antler of the red deer, probably a pick. The vase stands $5\frac{1}{2}$ inches in height; it is slightly oval at the mouth, the two diameters being six and five inches respectively. Three rows of circular punctures encircle the inside of the lip, and externally two grooves, ornamented with similar punctures, surround its upper portion.

Four feet to the west of a, and also in contact with the tilled surface, was a dish-shaped cavity, with sides burnt red, containing wood ashes and a few burnt bones of a young person; near to which were a few unburnt bones of a child, accompanied by a food-vase (fig. 315), marked E, having a deep border of the cinerary urn type, ornamented in herring-bone pattern, with rope impressions. It measures $5\frac{1}{2}$ inches high, and, like the last, has an oval mouth measuring $4\frac{3}{4}$ by 4 inches in diameter.

Three feet south of a, and six inches from the surface of the mound, was the flexed skeleton of a child about two years of age, and the accompanying food-vase F (fig. 316), which measures $4\frac{1}{4}$ inches high, and $5\frac{1}{4}$ inches in diameter at the top. Except that it is circular at the mouth, and has four small projections in the lower groove, its shape and ornamentation resemble vase a. Eighteen inches south of a, and seven inches from the surface, were traces of an inhumed infant only a few weeks old, together with a plain basin-shaped vase, marked G (fig. 317), $3\frac{1}{2}$ inches high, 6 inches in diameter at the top, and $3\frac{3}{4}$ inches at the bottom.* Four feet south-west from these, and on the same horizon, were the decayed remains of another infant, and near to it were portions of a food-vase marked H (fig. 318), apparently of the same size and shape as fig. 315, and with a similar deep border. Three or four inches below a dish-like hollow and the vase G, reposed an adult skeleton,† on its left side, head to the north, with the knees up, and hands in front of the face. Four inches beneath this was the body of a male,‡ from 20 to 25 years of age, having a femoral bone measuring 19 inches, lying on its left side, head to west, by the side of which lay the skull § of a middle-aged individual. Just above this was the greater portion of a medium-sized antler of a red deer, ‖ from which 4 to 6 inches of the root end had been chopped off with a rather badly sharpened tool, probably of

---

* The form of this vase is uncommon, and roughly moulded, and its texture resembles those dark-coloured vessels, frequently dish-shaped, which are rarely found whole, but not unfrequently in fragments scattered in the barrows, usually at the base, on the old surface line. We have never found them ornamented.

† Marked I in my collection.   ‡ Marked J in my collection.   § Marked K in my collection.

‖ Here we seem to have an antler from which a hammer-head has been cut, similar to fig. 152, from a barrow at Aldro', and other places. A similar antler from barrow No. 225, Group XV., has the root-end partly pierced, showing that it was probably customary to pierce the hammer-head before severing it from the antler.

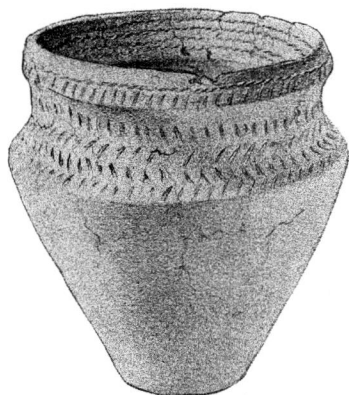

FIG. 310. $\frac{1}{4}$

FIG. 313. $\frac{1}{3}$

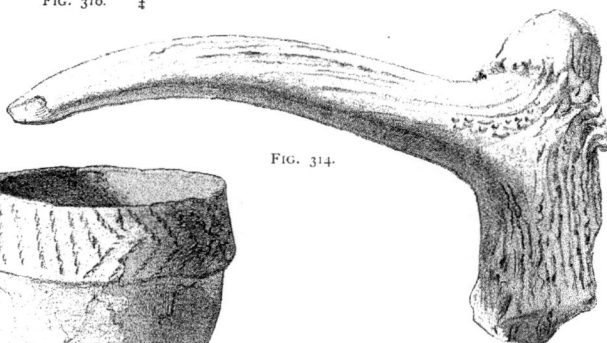

FIG. 314.

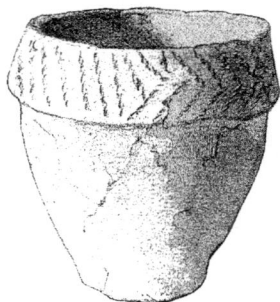

FIG. 315. $\frac{1}{3}$

FIG. 317. $\frac{1}{3}$

FIG. 316. $\frac{1}{3}$

bronze. The jagged edge of this instrument is well shown in the cuts on the antler.

Still a foot lower, and 18 inches east of the last remains, and doubled up in the same manner, was a headless skeleton,* on the right side, with shoulders pointing south-east. At the base of the mound, and close to the west side of grave D, a foot further eastwards, was the skeleton of a middle-aged individual,† minus legs and pelvis, on the left side, and head to the west. The radius measures 9⅝ inches. Close to the east of this mutilated body, and nearly vertically beneath the inverted urn, D, was an oval grave, 28 inches deep, 5 feet long, and 3 feet 10 inches wide at the bottom, in which was a skeleton‡ of an old person, on the right side, head to north, hands under the face, left knee pulled up to a right angle with the body, and the right knee—which had indications of disease in the joint—almost touching the elbows. A femur measured 18 ins. This was probably the primary interment. Close to the pelvis, just below the right femur, was a link of jet (fig. 320). Behind the head were three animal vertebræ and the grinding tooth of a young ox, to which was attached a small portion of the jaw. Close upon the thigh-bones was a large portion of a human calvarium, consisting of the occipital and the two parietal bones. The frontal bone belonging to these was found on the chest, but none of the bones of the face could be found. In the soil filling the grave above, some human finger bones, the jaw of a fox, or small dog, a vertebra, and other bones of a small animal were noticed. It is worthy of note that most of these bones, as well as the human calvarium, were well preserved and of a peculiar dark colour, quite different from those of the body they accompanied. This peculiarity we have frequently observed, and the stained and altered condition of these detached bones may be due, as elsewhere expressed, to a process of cooking, most probably for food. However repulsive the idea may be to us, in this case the human brain (admitting that cannibalism was practiced by the British, of which we seem to have much evidence) may have been cooked in the calvarium and placed in the grave.

Six feet south-west of the central grave, in a small hole cut 18 inches into the mound, clearly after its erection, was a food-vase, N (fig. 321), 5 inches high, and 6 inches in diameter at the top. Three shallow grooves surround its upper portion, the raised space between each being ornamented with short vertical gashes. Close to the north side of this vase were the doubled-up remains of a child, not more than 8 to 10 months old. Seven feet south-east of the centre grave, and also in an excavation made 2½ feet into the mound, clearly posterior to its erection, was the inverted lower half (fig. 322) of a very large cinerary urn, (O), containing burnt adult bones. No relic was found with them. A little below this urn, and rather to one side, were several animal bones, part of the jaw of a young sheep or goat, and at a distance of 5 feet southwards from these the lower jaw of a fox, or small dog.

Thirteen feet north-west of the centre, a roughly-shaped oval grave (P), cut 2 feet below the surface of the mound, contained a skeleton, partly on its back, with the head to north-east, knees pulled up to a little above a right angle with

* Marked "K." † "L." ‡ "M" in my collection.

the body, the right hand bent upwards, and the left hand lying on the right arm a little above the elbow. The femoral bones are greatly curved ; each measures 16 inches long, and belong to a person of middle age.

Fourteen feet west of the centre, in a similarly-shaped grave (*Q*), reaching to the base of the mound, were the slender bones of a person from 13 to 16 years of age, on the left side, knees up, near to which were placed both hands. The head pointed to the north, and behind it was a small triangular pendant of jet (fig. 323), upon a flake knife of dark-coloured flint (fig. 324). It will be observed that no food-vase had been deposited with any of the eight adult inhumed bodies, although one accompanied each of the seven juvenile interments, and that three of the four cremated bones had been placed in cinerary urns. The bodies in graves *D* and *G* are, most probably, primary, and nearly contemporaneous, while some of the others, as well as the cremated deposits, were intrusive secondary interments, or deposited during the erection of the mound, as none of them reached below the base of the barrow. This barrow is a good example of one of those in which later interments may from time to time have been placed.

During the excavations, several sherds of pottery, chips of flint, molar teeth of an ox, portions of the antlers of a deer, and pieces of animal and human bones were taken from the gritty substance of the mound.

BARROW No. 121

Is situated in the second field to the west of Bradeham. On September 1st and 2nd, 1868, it measured 50 feet in diameter, with a central elevation of about 16 inches. In the rock beneath the centre of the mound was a hole, measuring 2 feet 8 inches in depth, 21 inches in diameter at the top, and 10 inches at the bottom, resembling a cinerary urn. The upper half of this receptacle contained stiff unctuous earth, and the lower portion burnt wood and ashes, without any mixture of soil or trace of burnt bone.

A little to the north of the centre was a small grave containing a doubled-up and decayed adult skeleton, accompanied by a spear-head of flint (fig. 325); while a little south of the centre was a second grave, in which occurred the remains of a child, in bad preservation. Near its skull was a flint knife (fig. 326), and a small bone pin (fig. 327). Nothing more was found.

BARROW No. 111.

This barrow was examined between March 30th and April 2nd, and it was found to be about 48 feet in diameter and 2 feet in elevation, and consisted of reddish surface soil, mixed with a little gritty chalk and loamy clay brought from a distance. Close under the ploughed surface of the mound, and slightly to the east of the centre, was an oval hollow pointing east and west, 6 inches deep and 12 inches by 9 inches in width, containing burnt wood slightly mixed with a little burnt bone. On the top of this deposit were several portions of a food-vase broken up by the plough. After having been restored (fig. 328), it measures 5 inches in height, and is quite plain. At the same level, 5 feet westward, was another similarly formed depression, 6 inches deep, with similar contents ; but in this case the largest diameter ran north and south. This cavity measured 2 feet

FIG. 321.	⅓

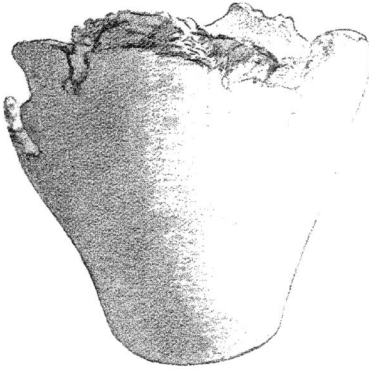

FIG. 322.	¼

FIG. 323.

FIG. 327.

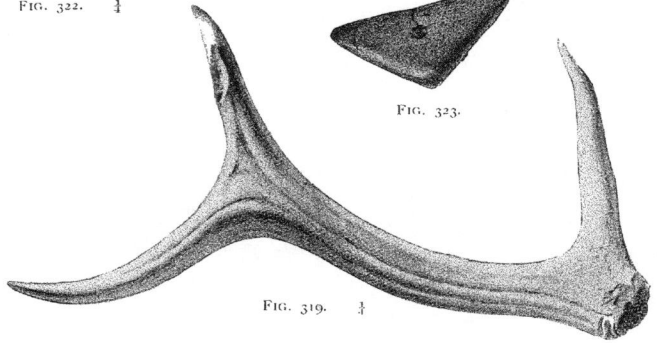

FIG. 319.	⅓

FIG. 320.

FIG. 324.

FIG. 325.

FIG. 326.

FIG 328.	⅓

by 13 inches. In the north corner stood about 2 inches of the bottom part of a food-vase of red earth. The whole of the top part had been distributed by tilling. Between the two incinerated interments, a foot nearer the base of the mound, were traces of an inhumed interment, doubled up, with head to the north. Nothing was found with it, and the bones were too far decayed to enable us to make out its position. Under the cremated body was a trough-formed grave, cut 1½ feet into the ground beneath the mound. It measured at the top 3 feet 3 inches east and west, and 2 feet 3 inches north and south; and on the bottom were the doubled up remains of a child 18 to 24 months old, on the right side, with head to the west, and the hands folded on the chest. Northwards, 12 feet from the centre and slightly below the base of the mound, were the much decayed remains of a woman on the right side, knees pulled up to a right angle with the body, and the head pointing to the east. In the corner of the angle formed by the doubled-up limbs and body were the crushed and decayed remains of a very young child, with head to north-west. No vase or other relic was found. Immediately behind the back of the adult skeleton, and parallel with it, was a shallow oval hole (probably a food repository), 2 feet 3 inches by 16 inches in depth, filled with dark earth, from which we took a dorsal vertebra belonging to a person apparently much larger than the receptacle could ever have held.

About 12 feet east of the centre, and 9 inches below the surface, was a small plain food-vase, irreparably crushed, in company with a nearly decomposed skeleton of a very young child. A few bits of animal bone, portions of two leaf-shaped arrow-heads, two small flint instruments resembling scrapers, and fourteen splinters of foreign flint were picked from the mound during the excavation.

BARROW No. 93 a.

On Saturday, May 18th, 1867, we commenced turning over a large area from the centre of this barrow, which was 2 feet in height from the original surface. Near to the centre was a deposit of burnt human bones, in a hole cut 1½ feet into the chalk rock, which measured 2 feet in length and 1½ feet in breadth. This deposit was covered with 4 inches of bluish clay, on the removal of which the half of a bone pin was observed protruding from the cremated bones. The other half was found in another part of the deposit. This pin measured 2⅞ inches long, and had a hole through its head (fig. 329). A burnt fragment of a flint knife (fig. 330) was also found among the calcined bones.

About five feet south-west of the cremated bones on the base of the mound were a few scattered fragments of an urn. Search was also made for a grave, but no trace of one could be found.

BARROW No. 93.

On May 21st, 1867, this barrow had a diameter of 15 yards. It stands a short distance from the farmhouse called Bradeham.* We first observed fragments of an urn dispersed here and there in the tilled surface soil; while at a distance

---

* The day was, for the time of year, a remarkably cold one, attended at times with showers of hail. However, we were able to shelter ourselves from the piercing north wind by fixing up with stakes several yards of thick cloth, expressly obtained and frequently used as a shelter when at work on these breezy high grounds.

of 5 feet south-west from the centre, and 8 inches deeper, were a few burnt human bones in a small hole. On the top of these rested the bottom part of an urn, the upper portion of which had been broken off by the plough and scattered amongst the soil.

At the centre was a bowl-shaped excavation, 3 feet in diameter and reaching 12 inches below the base of the barrow, over which was spread a bluish coloured clay about 3 inches in thickness; and round the upper margin of this receptacle the soil was reddened, as if by the action of fire. This excavation contained much carbonised wood—some pieces being 2 inches in thickness—together with the burnt bones of a youth; all of which probably had been deposited while hot. Not a single chipping of flint was found.

BARROW No. 98

Is situated on land marked Wayrham on the Ordnance Sheet, and was explored from May 27th to 31st, 1867. Its diameter and altitude were 48 feet and 36 inches respectively. On arriving at the spot our attention was immediately drawn to the centre of the mound by a quantity of burnt adult bones and portions of a large cinerary urn, No. 1 on the plan (fig. 331), which had been recently turned up by the plough. The surrounding earth was cleared away, and the bottom part of the urn containing more bones was found in its original position. Nearly on the same plane, and 4½ feet south-west of No. 1, was a second deposit of burnt bones of a full-sized person (No. 2 on the plan), but here the urn had been inverted over the bones, and all that remained of it was the rim, 9 inches in diameter, beautifully ornamented with herring-bone markings. Within this a few of the bones remained. No relic was found with either deposit. Interment No. 3 was a pile of burnt bones placed 5 feet north-west of the centre, and 6 feet north of No. 2. They consisted partly of bones of a child and bones of a more matured person, and were accompanied by two knives (figs. 332 and 333) of grey flint, measuring 2¼ and 1¾ inches in length, and 1 inch and ⅞ of an inch in breadth respectively. They occurred side by side at the southern margin of the bones.

No. 4, to the north-east of the centre, was a badly-crushed food vase, which stood 5½ feet to the north-east of the centre, over the north end of grave C. It has been rebuilt (fig. 334), and measures 5 inches high and 4½ inches wide at the top, and is ornamented with encircling rows of round punctures, alternating with rope-like impressions.

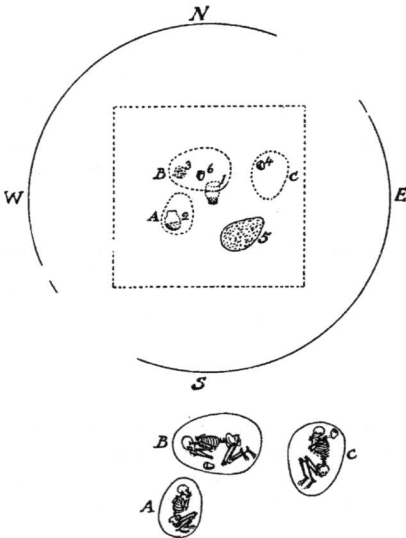

FIG. 331.—Plan of Barrow No. 98, at two feet above the base, and also of interments at the bottom of graves A, B, and C.

FIG. 329. $\frac{1}{1}$

FIG. 333. $\frac{1}{2}$

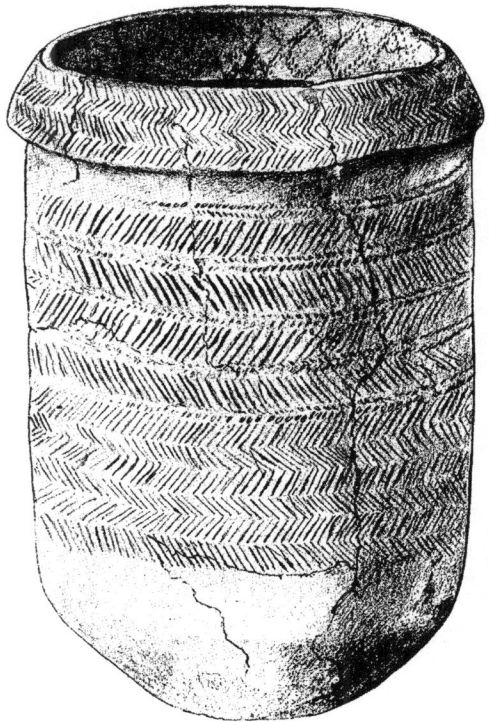

FIG. 334. $\frac{1}{3}$

FIG. 330. $\frac{1}{1}$

FIG. 332. $\frac{1}{1}$

FIG. 335. $\frac{1}{2}$

No. 5 was an oval hollow made in the mound, and at a distance of 2½ feet south-east from the central urn. Its depth was twelve inches, length 4 feet 10 inches, and breadth 2 feet 10 inches. It contained soil blackened and reddened by fire, mixed freely with burnt wood, and rather sparingly with calcined adult human bones; portions of the left side of the lower jaw and a few other bones of a child were also observed.

All the five interments were about two feet above the base of the barrow, and to all appearance had been placed there when the mound had reached that height, which was afterwards added to. No. 6 is a unique food-vase (fig. 335), which had been placed close to the west side of an irregularly-formed heap of decayed matter; but when found it was completely flattened by pressure. The vase was 2 feet north-west from the central urn No. 1, at a height of only nine inches above the base of the mound, and nearly over the middle of the grave marked B. It has been rebuilt, showing its rare shape, and probably is one type of the domestic pottery of the Britons. It measures 8 inches high, 6 inches in diameter at the top, and 3 inches at the bottom. Six feet west of the centre of the mound, and at a depth of 18 inches, a human vertebra and heel bone, and also portion of the shank-bone of an animal about the size of a sheep, were found; and in other places we picked up a few more pieces of human bone, and a small portion of the antler of a red deer. From the mound we took 28 splinters of foreign and native flint in about equal quantities; also 1 sling-stone, 3 irregularly-formed discs chipped more or less on their edges, and portions of 5 urns, all differently ornamented. One large piece is thickly marked all over the external surface with deep impressions made by the thumb. In addition to the above, a flake knife of dark coloured flint, chipped on the two edges, measuring nearly 3 inches long, was found between graves B and C, on the original surface at the base of the barrow.

A square, 20 feet across, having now been cut and removed from the centre of the barrow to the ancient turf line beneath, we commenced to probe the rock below, and discovered three oval graves (a rather unusual number) arranged as shown by the dotted lines marked A, B, and C on the plan (fig. 331). The one marked A was the first explored. It measured 4 feet long, 2 feet 7 inches wide, and was 2 feet 3 inches deep. A contracted body was found on its left side, at the bottom of the grave, with both hands to the head. It was that of a person of about 14 years of age, and probably a female. It was unaccompanied by a vase or instrument of any kind.

Grave B, with its long axis, pointing east and west, was next examined. It measured 6½ feet by 4½ feet, and was 3¼ feet deep. For the most part it was filled at the top, to a depth of 2½ feet, with beds of stiff unctuous earth, depressed in the middle, close under which, and near the centre of the grave, were the badly-preserved remains of a very young child, doubled up, with head to the west. Near these remains, were pieces of a food-vase; and a little above the bones, and more to the east, an oval knife (fig. 336), chipped on the sides to a cutting edge. It is of Yorkshire flint, and the two diameters are 2⅝ and 2 inches respectively. Beneath the clay the grave was filled with large angular pieces of chalk, and at the bottom was a strong-boned male skeleton, on the right side, head to the west, and hands to the face as shown on the plan.

From beneath its chest was taken a piece of the root-end of a very large antler of a red deer (fig. 337), about a foot long, probably used as a pick in digging the grave *B*. The only other article found was a badly-crushed food-vase, which had stood upright near the knees and left elbow. After having been restored (fig. 338), it measured 7 inches high, 20 inches in circumference at the top, and 10½ inches at the bottom. The interior of the lip is ornamented with two rows of gashes, and similar indentations decorate the upper parts of its exterior. The measurements of the thigh, leg, and arm bones are 18, 14½, and 12¾ inches respectively, and are strongly built.

The grave *C* contained at the bottom the bones of a tall female in the position shown on the plan. The leg and arm bones were exactly the same length as those of the male body, but were much more slender. A food-vase was standing at its shoulders. This was irreparably broken by the pressure of large pieces of chalk ; but, judging from the fragments, its type was quite different from the one from grave *B*. In front of the chest, and with the broad end just below the chin, was a glass-coloured flint, worked into a sharp pointed tool (fig. 339), 2 inches long, half an inch broad at the blunt end, and slightly curved. It seems most suitable for boring or drilling.

About 2 inches to the west of this article was a small lump of black matter resembling burnt wood, but apparently the residue of some other substance; and near it traces of more dark matter were observed. Slightly below the flint were portions of a decayed beaver's front tooth (fig. 340), while close by was a very fine knife of black flint (fig. 341) 2½ inches long and nearly 1 inch broad, flat on one side and ridged on the other by chipping, having also the ends rounded by a similar process. This instrument was placed across a flake of black flint (fig. 342) 2¼ inches long and 1 inch broad, and close to the west of it was a small fossil shell of *Gryphæa incurva* (fig. 343). At the lower part of the skeleton was a beautiful bone bodkin (fig. 344), with its perforated end touching the spinal column at the lumbar region, and the other end pointing to the knees. This instrument is 3 inches long, and is well adapted for piercing skins. Around the bodies in the graves we observed many snail shells *(Helix nemoralis)*, and some of the spiral shells *(Succinea putris)* mentioned elsewhere in these notes, and now rarely found in this district.

The broken state of the bones and vases in the three graves was mainly due to the large lumps of chalk everywhere in contact with the bodies, while the graves *A* and *C* were filled from top to bottom with chalk grit and pieces of chalk in a manner so much resembling the upper portion of the natural rock, as at first to cause one of our most experienced diggers to think that the ground had not been disturbed.

It is also worthy of record that all the three graves under this barrow had clearly been made previously to the raising of the mound, as part of the chalk excavated in making them had not been required for filling in, and consequently had been left on the old turf line at a little distance round the edge of the graves, and was overlaid by the undisturbed beds forming the barrow.

In filling in the excavation, we found an instrument of native mottled flint, 2½ inches long, 1½ inches wide, and about ½ an inch thick. One end is worked round, and the two edges are chipped sharp.

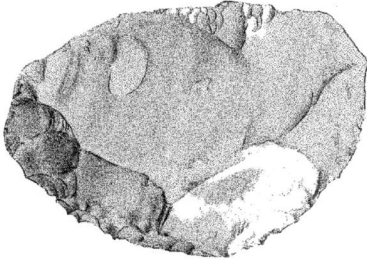

FIG. 336.   ¼

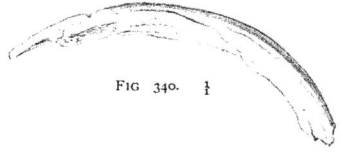

FIG. 340.   ½

FIG. 339.   ½

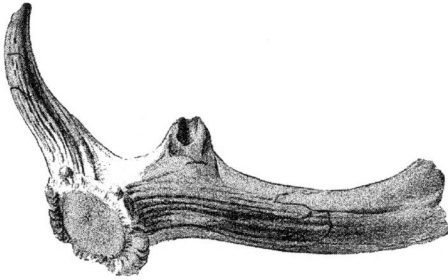

FIG. 337.   ¼

FIG. 343.   ½

FIG. 344.   ½

FIG. 338.   ⅓

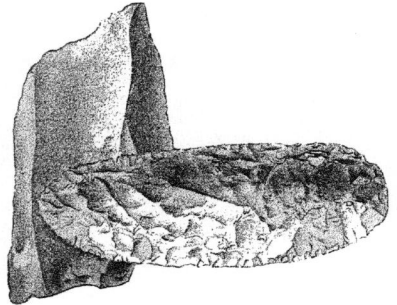

FIG. 342.   ½   FIG. 341.   ¼

BARROW No. 78

Is nearly in the centre of the second field east-north-east from Wayrham Farm-house (in the 6 inch Ordnance Sheet, No. 159).

On October 15th, 1866, its diameter was 14 yards and its elevation 12 to 14 inches. It consisted entirely of loamy soil. The only discovery was a deposit of burnt bones in a shallow hole under the centre of the barrow, mixed with pieces of burnt wood. Nothing more was found in any part of the mound. We next tested the ground below, and satisfied ourselves that no grave existed.

BARROW No. 217

Is a small and scarcely-distinguishable mound, not marked on the Ordnance Map. It was first noticed by a man who ploughed over it and observed some rubbly stone. Its centre lies 37 yards from the middle of the Barrow No. 98, and at a distance of 52 yards from No. 93.

A small hole, containing a deposit of burnt bones, with decayed pieces of wood, was all that was found. It measured 30 inches in diameter, was 10 inches deep, and had served in the place of an urn to hold the burned contents. A little gritty chalk had been procured with which to raise the mound.

No. VII.—THE GARROWBY WOLD GROUP.

This group, consisting of 18 barrows, occupies the highest elevation on the western edge of the chalk wolds (820 feet), at the base of which, over 500 feet below, are the villages of Garrowby, Kirby-Underdale, and Bishop Wilton.

The mounds, only fourteen of which are indicated as such on the Ordnance Maps, are arranged in three divisions.

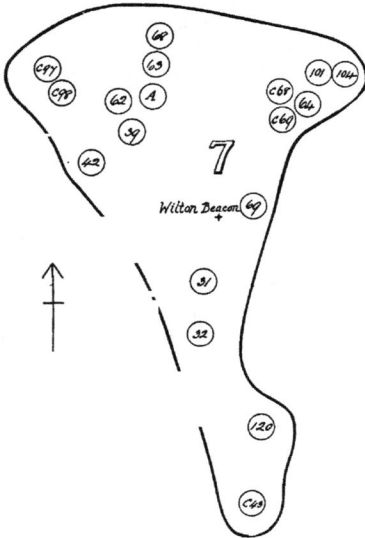

GARROWBY WOLD GROUP.

BARROW No. 104

Is about 60 yards to the north-west of the farm-house called Cot Nab, and is situated between the ramparts of the ancient entrenchments which emerge from the upper end of Deepdale. These cross the York road,* then curve slightly round the barrow, and pass along the end of the field known as "Stone-chair Close,† and enter the upper end of Hundle Dale, and lead down to a fine spring.

The original form of this barrow had been circular, and at the time of our examination, August 19th to 24th, 1867, it had a diameter of about 45 feet, and was 3½ feet from base to apex.

The first skeleton discovered (fig. 345, No. 1), was in the large central grave, marked *A*, near the western side, and at a depth of about 16 inches.

The grave was oval in form, and its measurement was 10¼ feet at the top and 6 feet at the bottom from east to west, and 7½ feet at the top and 5 feet at the bottom from north to south.

The femur, tibia, and humerus measured 18, 16, and 13⅛ inches respectively. A curved knife of black flint (fig. 346), 2¼ inches long, occurred 7 inches to the south of the well-preserved skull. Dispersed in the grave, round and above the skeleton, were fractured human bones, adult and juvenile ; and just above were two small adult tibiæ, side by side, from which the flesh must have been removed before interment. Close by was a femur, apparently belonging to the same body, the upper end of which was broken off obliquely.

About three inches beneath the interment, twelve inches to the east of the knees, were the upper end of a human femur, part of the pelvis, some scattered bones

* Known as Garrowby Street.

† The stone which gives the name to the field has been removed to the South Wold Farm-house, and placed by the side of a wall, and is now used as a stepping-stone. It is of Calcareous grit, and is probably part of the base of a large boundary cross. It is figured in "Trans. E. Riding Antiq. Soc.," Vol. IV., 1896.

FIG. 346.

FIG. 347.   ½

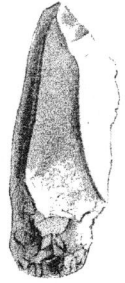

FIG. 348.

FIG. 349.   ½

FIG. 350.

of a foot, and all the bones of another foot in position ; unlike the others, the bones of this foot must have been held in position by their ligaments when buried.

The next interment (No. 2), also in the centre of the grave, was that of a male, 23 inches beneath burial No. 1, in the attitude shown on the plan (A 2, fig. 345). The femur and tibia measured 16 and 13 inches respectively, and apparently belonged to a person about 50 or 60 years of age. Close to the skull was a crushed drinking-cup (fig. 347), $6\frac{1}{4}$ inches in height and $4\frac{5}{8}$ inches across the mouth. Near this was a flake of smoky-coloured flint (fig. 348), 2 inches in length ; also two teeth and part of the jaw of an ox.

A little below the skeleton a layer of dark matter, having a laminated appearance resembling decayed leaves, extended across the grave. This might be the residue of a platform that protected the vases at the bottom of the grave. This layer was about a quarter of an inch in thickness and two feet broad, and crossed the grave from east to west, as shown in the section (fig. 355). It had a depression of at least a foot in the centre.

At the bottom of the grave, at a depth of 6 feet 3 inches from the base of the barrow, no trace of a skeleton was found, but there were two perfect elegantly-formed and beautifully-orna-mented vases,* a yard apart, on the floor of the grave. The northern vase (fig. 349) was 9 inches high, $5\frac{1}{4}$ inches

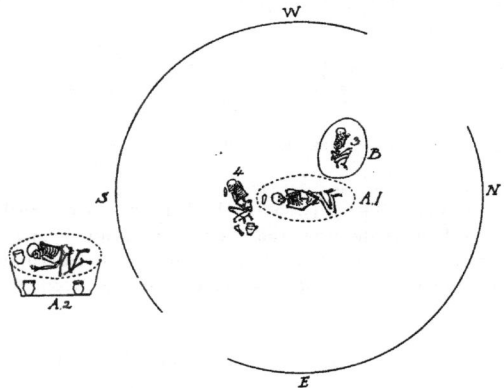

FIG. 345.—PLAN OF BARROW NO. 104.
A 2—Plan of Interments below A 1.

over the mouth, and $5\frac{5}{8}$ across the shoulders. Close by was the greater portion of the rib of an ox, in good preservation. The other vase (fig. 350) is somewhat different in shape and ornamentation, and measures $9\frac{1}{4}$ inches high, $5\frac{7}{8}$ inches across the mouth, and $6\frac{1}{2}$ inches wide at the shoulders. Excepting a little dark matter, these vases contained no trace of their former contents.

It was noticed that below interment No. 2 there were no fragments of either human or animal bone—excepting the rib accompanying one of the vases.

About 16 inches to the west of the central grave was another similarly shaped grave, marked B on the plan, measuring $4\frac{1}{2}$ feet by 3 feet 3 inches, and 2 feet deep. At the bottom of this was the doubled-up skeleton of a child (No. 3), the femur measuring $8\frac{3}{4}$ inches. This second grave had been made after the erection of the barrow, as the compact clayey beds composing the interior of the mound were cut through and the grave re-filled with mixed-up

* In Crania Britannica, p. 2, plate 16, are figured three vases from Ancient Caledonia, one of which is almost identical in form with figs. 349 and 350 as shown here.

debris.   At the base of the mound, on the southern brink of the centre grave, were the remains of a second child (No. 4), the femur measuring 8½ inches. Under the bones of the face was a flint knife (fig. 351), about 2 inches long, and midway between the chin and knees was a handstruck flake of about the same length ; around the skull were several handstruck splinters (one of which is shewn in fig. 352), all of local flint.   At the feet were the leg-bones of a pig, accompanied by a food-vase with a handle (fig. 353), the orifice only large enough to admit a finger.   This vessel is slightly distorted from pressure, and its interior differs from the flat-bottom of the ordinary food-vase by resembling the rounded form of the inside of an eggshell.

In the interior of the mound, immediately above and around the vase, were greasy-sided cavities of various dimensions, probably caused by the decay of a liberal supply of food deposited with the vase.   A scraper of native flint (fig. 354), 3 inches long, was picked up at the base of the mound, north of

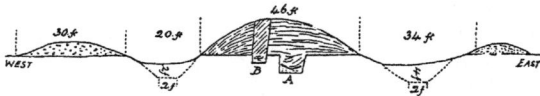

FIG. 355.—SECTION OF BARROW 104, SHOWING ENTRENCHMENTS ON EACH SIDE.
A, B—Graves.

the centre.   The section of the barrow and entrenchments (fig. 355) should show the rubbly chalk from the fosse of the entrenchment, lying upon the east side of barrow.   On the north side, a much greater accumulation was observed, proving that the entrenchment was made after the erection of the barrow.

BARROW No. 101

Is a little to the west of the last.   When excavated—July 11th, 12th, and 15th, 1867—it was found to be much lowered by agricultural operations, and measured 16 yards in diameter and 16 inches in height.   The plan and section of this barrow (figs. 356-357), show the arrangement of the three interments, each at the bottom of an oval grave.   That marked A measured 5½ feet by 4 feet, and was 3 feet deep.   It contained the skeleton of a female — apparently of middle age.   The femur and humerus measured 17½ inches and 12½ inches respectively. With it was a crushed food-vase (fig. 358), which, after being restored, measured 6¼ inches in height and 6¼ inches across the mouth.   A bronze pricker (fig. 359), was near the right elbow.   Grave B was 6 feet by 4 feet, 2 feet 8 inches deep, and contained the remains of a small person about 18 to 20 years of age. On the right side of the skull was a crushed food-vase (fig. 360), which, after restoration, measured 5¼ inches in height and 6¼ inches across the top.   This gracefully-formed vase is ornamented all over the exterior with cuneated gashes, in addition to which, in a groove a little below the rim, it is encircled by a band of eight perforated projections.   The lower end of an antler of a red deer (probably part of a pick), occurred above the skeleton at a depth of 10 inches from the top of the grave.

PLATE XLIII

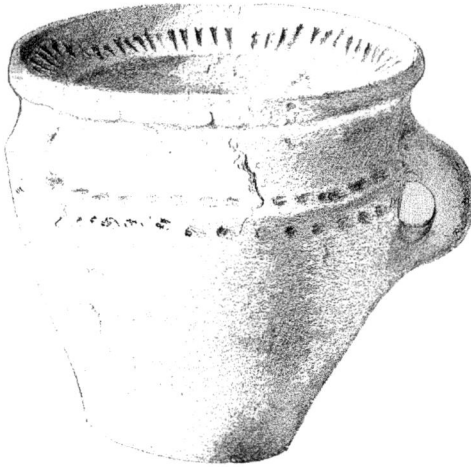

Fig. 353.   ½

Fig. 354.

Fig. 351.

Fig. 359.   ½

Fig. 352.

Fig. 358.   ⅓

Fig. 360.   ⅓

Grave *C* measured 6 feet by 3 feet 9 inches and 4 feet 3 inches in depth. In it were the remains of an aged male; the femur measuring 18 inches in length. Close to the face was a fine knife (fig. 361), of jet-black flint, 3¾ inches long and 1½ inches broad, chipped along its whole length to an exceedingly keen edge. Immediately in front of the chest was an irreparably-crushed food-vase, apparently of elegant form, which, like the vase (fig. 205), from Acklam Wold, had been provided with feet. Between the knife and vase was a tusk —probably of a boar—much shortened by wear. Several pieces of antlers of deer were taken from the boat-like mass of clay that filled the centre of the grave.

It was noticed that the other two graves also contained in the centre a similar trough-formed mass of clay, rudely laminated and depressed in the centre, as shown in the section (fig. 357), and that the mound over the three graves contained an unbroken core of hard compact clay, quite different from the rest of the barrow—which was mainly composed of local surface soil. Much of the gritty chalk which had been cast from the graves had not been put back, but remained on the old surface-line round their edges, and was under the mound, as shown in figs. 356-7.

It was clear that the three graves had been dug and the interments made previous to the formation of the clay core, as not the slightest disturbance in the barrow was noticeable.

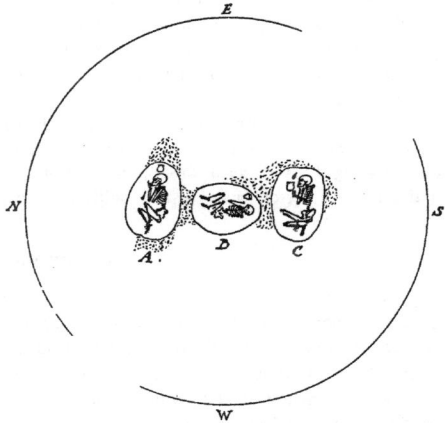

FIG. 356.— PLAN OF BARROW 101.

FIG. 357.—SECTION OF BARROW 101.
A, B, C—Graves.

In the mound were found four small flakes, 2 lumps, 1 flake knife 3¼ inches long, and a disc-formed scraper nearly 1¾ inches in diameter—all of flint. The two last-named and one of the lumps were of Yorkshire flint.

BARROW No. 64

Is not shown on the Ordnance map. It had a medium diameter of thirty feet, and an elevation of about two feet.

On June 27th, 1866, we cut out a rectangular portion 13 feet by 9 feet down to the base, but only found a chipped disc of reddish flint.

On June 30th, we noticed a little clay under the centre of the mound, which partly filled an oval grave in the rock, measuring 5 feet by 4½ feet east and west, and 2½ feet deep.   At the bottom of this was the decayed skeleton of a female, on the right side, head to the east, and legs drawn up.   A tibia—the only perfect bone—was 12½ inches long.   A portion of the leg of an animal had been placed near the skeleton, and 157 jet discs and two cylindrical jet beads were found mixed in the clayey soil just above the neck.   A quantity of this soil was taken away, and passed through a fine sieve, resulting in 47 more discs being found, making a total of 206 whole beads for the necklace (fig. 362), also a few broken discs, and possibly a few smaller ones escaped detection.   These are very circular, evenly cut, and truly bored, obviously by metal tools.   The construction of this necklace must have been a work of considerable labour.   A small bronze pricker (fig. 363), was also found.   Under the skeleton, and in the floor of the grave was a circular hole, 18 inches in diameter and 15 inches deep, containing calcined human bones.

Being under the impression that during the hurried examination of this barrow, made in consequence of bad weather, something might have been missed, on July 23rd, and 24th, 1868, the whole of the mound was again turned over, and the rock below was tested, without, however, finding anything further.

BARROW No. C 68

Was excavated on June 8th to 11th, 1874.   It then measured 66 feet in diameter, 4 feet 8 inches in elevation, and, except a thin layer of clayey matter which covered a grave beneath the centre, was made of local surface soil.   Near the apex of the mound, and vertically above the grave, were portions of a cinerary urn, which, either at the time of planting the ground some eighty years before, or during the felling of the trees the preceding autumn, had been broken up by the workmen.   The grave was elliptical in form, 2 feet deep, and measured 5 feet north-east by south-west, and 2 feet 9 inches across.   A ridge of burnt adult human bones, 30 inches in length, occupied the bottom of the north-east end.   At the southern extremity were four holes, which had apparently contained wooden stakes, forming an enclosure about the size of a large cinerary urn, within which was unctuous earth, full of cavities, unquestionably left by some decayed substance, such as food.   No relic was found with the interment.

BARROW No. C 69

Had a diameter of 60 feet and an elevation of 7½ feet.

From June 12th to 17th, 1874, the whole of it was turned over, and the ground beneath was trenched at short distances.   The plans and section (figs. 364, 365, and 366), show the nature of the barrow and the positions of the interments.   At the apex were the bones of a somewhat disturbed and broken-up adult body ("d" in the section).   At a depth of 16 inches were two cinerary urns, 9 feet and 12 feet respectively east of the centre, as shown at A and E, fig. 364.   These contained burnt bones.   The urn marked A (fig. 367) is 8½ inches high, 6 inches across the top, 7½ inches across the shoulders, and 4½ inches across the bottom.   That marked E (fig. 368) is 8 inches high, 6¾ inches across the top, 7¼ inches across the body, and 4¼ inches at the bottom.   The upper portion of each is ornamented with a

Fig. 362.   ⅓

Fig. 367.   ¼

Fig. 368.   ¼

broad belt of network, ¾ of an inch wide, produced by incised lines leaning alter-nately to the right and to the left.

Externally, the top of each urn contracts upwards from the shoulder in a rather unusual manner. Under these, and conformable with the shape of the

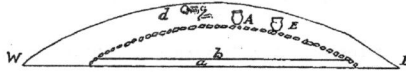

FIG. 364.—SECTION OF BARROW C 69.
a—Line of plan shown in fig. 366.
b—Line of plan shown in fig. 365.

mound, was a pavement of rough angular flints, which had apparently been gathered from the surrounding land. This was about 38 feet in diameter, and its apex was 5 feet above the base of the mound, and had not been broken through for the introduction of any of the interments beneath. Within a foot of the base

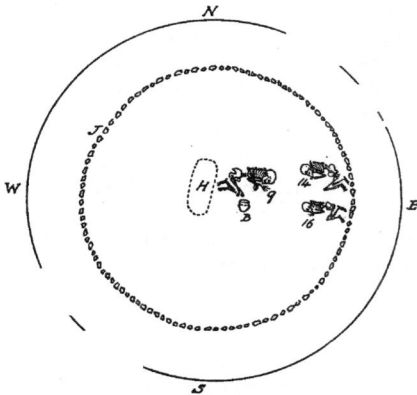

FIG. 365.—PLAN OF BARROW C 69 AT LINE *b* IN SECTION,
WHICH IS 1 FOOT ABOVE THE BASE OF THE BARROW.
H indicates position of Grave below.

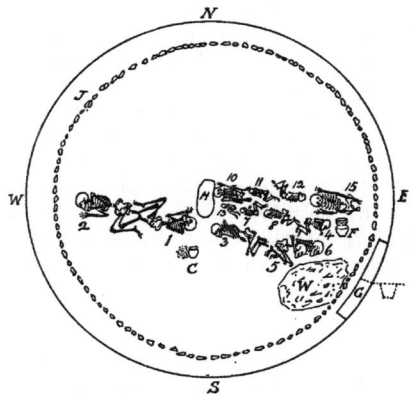

FIG. 366.
J—Ring of Stones.
H—Empty Grave.

of the barrow were three bodies of various ages, accompanied by a food-vase placed a little distance from the knees of one (No. 9), in the position shown at *B* on fig. 365. This vase (fig. 369) is 4½ inches high, 5¾ inches across the top, 6½ inches across the shoulders, and 2½ inches at the bottom. From the lip to the shoulder are two grooves, and in the smaller and lower one are four pierced projections, arranged at equal distances.

At the base of the mound, and resting for the most part on thin slabs of chalk placed closely together, were thirteen inhumed and one cremated interment, the latter is marked ."*C*" on fig. 366, and was accompanied by a badly-preserved food-vase (fig. 370), only the lower part of which was preserved. A vase (*F*) stood a little to the south of interment No. 15. This vase measures 6¼ inches across the top, 6¼ inches across the shoulders, and is 5 inches high. Figure 371 gives a fair idea of its graceful form and ornamentation.

Under the centre of the barrow was a small grave, containing rubbly chalk and a little soil, but no trace of a body. The interment at the apex, and the eight bodies at and near the base of the barrow, were those of adults, varying from middle life to old age, and were apparently of both sexes. The remaining seven inhumed bodies were those of children, probably from one to twelve years of age.[*]

There was a marked absence of instruments. Only one poor flint flake (fig. 372), serrated at the edge, was found near the skull of interment No. 14.

Body No. 9 was placed vertically over No. 10, and No. 14 above No. 15; and there was every appearance that the thirteen bodies at the base of the mound had been interred at one time. The three interments a foot above the base of the barrow (see fig. 365) must have quickly followed those beneath them, and previous to the laying of the dome-shaped pavement of rough flints, which, as already mentioned, showed no trace of having been broken through.

The mound was entirely composed of a stiff, soil-like material, with the exception of the bed of flints, and a large heap of rubbly chalk and gritty soil lying on the old surface east-south-east of the centre, covering an area marked W on fig. 366. This latter accumulation induced us to search for a grave, from which we believed it had been cast; but finally we found it had been thrown from what seemed to be the segment of an encircling trench (G on fig. 366), which, after being excavated to the length of 23 feet, had apparently been abandoned. The pavement of chalk slabs on which the bodies at the base were placed, may also have been obtained from this excavation. In the mound, and chiefly near the apex, were several flint flakes, two of which are serrated, a portion of an egg-shaped hammer-head (fig. 373), a fine barbed arrow-head, and two scapulæ and a leg-bone of some animal of about the size of a small ox.

BARROW No. 39.

Although this is omitted in the Ordnance sheet, it is twenty-two yards in diameter and 2 feet high, and is situated on Garrowby Hill Top, due north of the upper end of Worsendale Plantation, and close to the south side of the old coach-road to York. Operations were commenced by removing an oblong portion measuring 21 feet east and west, and 14 feet north and south, from the centre. In this, and mainly to the west of the centre, numerous pieces of an ornamented drinking-cup were found. At the base of the barrow, slightly to the north of the centre, was the point-end of a flint spear-head, nearly $1\frac{1}{4}$ inches long, together with a pear-shaped pebble an inch long. On the old surface line, in the middle of the barrow, was a doubled-up skeleton, greatly decayed, which, judging by the teeth, was the remains of a person considerably advanced in years. The molar teeth were greatly worn down obliquely. Near the west side of the skull was a food-vase (fig. 374), containing soil, mixed with decayed matter.

During the excavation a portion of a tooth of a horse or ox; a splinter from the long bone of a similar animal, three flint discs, nearly circular, about an inch

[*] The measurements of the long bones obtainable were as follows :—No. 3, femur 16½ inches, humerus 12½ inches ; No. 4, femur 16 inches, tibia 13 inches, humerus 11 inches ; No. 9, femur 18¾ inches, tibia 15 inches, right and left humerus 13¼ inches and 13 inches respectively ; and No. 14, femur 18½ inches, tibia 15 inches, humerus 13 inches.

PLATE XLV.

FIG. 361. $\frac{1}{1}$

FIG. 372.

FIG. 363. $\frac{1}{1}$

FIG. 369. $\frac{1}{2}$

FIG. 370. $\frac{1}{2}$

FIG. 371. $\frac{1}{2}$

FIG. 374. $\frac{1}{3}$

in diameter, chipped round the edges ; also six flakes, some of native flint and others of foreign flint, were found. Pieces of charcoal were scattered rather sparingly in the mound, but no clay was observed.

BARROW "A."

This barrow cannot at present be opened without removing and destroying numbers of a clump of fir trees, with which it is thickly covered.

On November 20th, 1883, its diameter was 60 feet, and elevation 5 feet.

BARROW No. 62.

On June 1st, 1866, we opened this barrow, situated in the south-west corner of a ploughed field, in which stands the unopened barrow A, just referred to. The small barrow, No. 62, which is not on the Ordnance map, was less than a foot in elevation, and somewhat uncertain in area.

A square, with 18 feet sides, was removed from the centre, beginning on the north side. Some fragments of a small food-vase were soon met with, accompanied by a few unburnt human bones (interment No. 1) resting on the ancient surface soil under the mound, at a depth of about eight inches. Unfortunately, the vase and interment had been previously disturbed by the plough. It was possible, however, to partly restore the vase (fig. 375), which is thickly ornamented. Towards the centre, at a distance of nine feet from the relics just named, were fragments of a leg bone belonging to another body (No. 2), which had also been disturbed by the plough. This was only six or seven inches below the surface of the barrow. On the north side of the mound, about five feet from the centre, was a grave measuring at the top 8 feet by 6 feet, cut 3½ feet into the rock. The chalk rubble which had been excavated formed a ridge by the side of the grave, which contained foreign clay only. This grave was cautiously examined, and on reaching the bottom, at the west end was a small food-vase (fig. 376), which, after being rebuilt, measured 5½ inches in height, 5½ inches across the top, and 3¼ inches across the base. As will be seen from the illustration, this very interesting vase is made up of five separate segments of clay, joined together by their overlapping bevelled edges.

The day was miserably wet, and, though well sheltered with a specially made umbrella sufficiently large to cover a small party at work, we were compelled to defer our examination.

On June 4th, we resumed work, and at the depth of three feet found a human skull (No. 3), minus the lower jaw, facing the north, in close contact with the natural wall of the grave. Near to it were the leg bones, but no other portion of the body was noticed. The upper end of one of the thigh bones was placed only nine inches from the skull. At this depth the grave was only 5 feet 8 inches in length, and about 4 feet in width, and there was a thin layer of decayed wood. About six inches below was another skeleton (No. 4), with the legs drawn up, head to the east, and raised by having been placed on a natural ledge of rock at the west end of the grave. From this the neck vertebræ curved down to the floor. The skull was very much decayed, but the teeth were sound and very little worn, and were evidently those of a young person. Upon the bones of the neck was a perfect lower jaw, with the teeth worn, which probably belonged to the incomplete skeleton above. The vase found on the first day was placed near the skull of this body. It is of common type, and has two slight grooves passing round it, and is ornamented with rude indentations.

The clayey matter filling the grave contained bits of charcoal and traces of decayed wood.

BARROW No. 63

Is in the north-east and opposite corner of the same field as the last. It is formed of alternating beds of foreign clay and local surface soil, and has a diameter of 65 feet, and an elevation of 2½ feet. From a variation of the material in the mound, and its arrangement near the centre, we were led to expect a grave below. Over this, in a line with the old surface soil, were the greatly-decayed leg-bones of an adult. All the other bones had disappeared. Dark matter was observed in the neighbourhood, and small pieces of bronze, probably portions of the upper end of a knife,* were taken from the same place.

From the barrow thirteen flint flakes and two small pieces of an urn were taken.

In emptying the grave, it was found to be filled throughout with layers of clay and soil† depressed in the centre—the clay predominating—and containing small pieces of burnt wood throughout its mass. Towards the east side of the grave, at a depth of 16 inches, was the lower portion of a food-vase. There were also thirteen flint flakes found in different places in the grave, four of which show secondary chipping. The grave was oval, measuring 8 feet north-east and south-west by 5 feet, and 4 feet deep. On the bottom, at the north-east end, were the decayed remains of a doubled-up skeleton, with the head to south, and knees pointing towards the east. A food-vase (fig. 377), crushed into fragments, had been placed between the knees; and where the skull had been, and near to this was a rude flint knife 2 inches long, and a half-moon-shaped knife (fig. 379). Under the decayed pelvic-bones was a rectangular hole in the chalk floor of the grave, 14 inches by 11 inches, and 19 inches deep. It contained a few pieces of bone, which, though much decayed, appeared to be human. The advanced state of decomposition of all the bones seemed to be due to their being in contact with a quantity of wet clay and earth, which filled the grave entirely, and capped it to the height of 16 inches.

It may be that the reason the Britons so frequently used clay—obtained often from a distance—in covering the graves of their dead was partly to keep out the wet and preserve the bodies beneath from decay. So long as the clay stopped the percolation of water and excluded the air, and was not in contact with the interment, this to some extent would be gained; but as soon as the cover of the grave, probably of wood, gave way, and let down the bed of damp earth upon the bones, decomposition seems to have been facilitated.

---

* Probably the other portions of the knife blade, not having been protected by the haft, had entirely decayed.

† I have since frequently observed this, and believe it to be due to a wooden covering over the grave which has given way, and gradually let down the soil from the mound above.

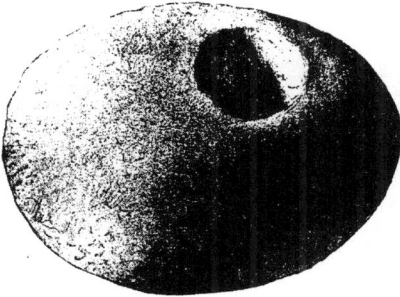

Fig. 373.   ¼

Fig. 382.   ¹

Fig. 381.   ½

Fig. 375.   ⅓

Fig. 379.

Fig. 376.   ½

Fig. 377.   ⅓

BARROW No. 68

Is only a few yards to the north of the last barrow, and at the time of opening (July 16th and 18th, 1866) differed from it but little in size. At the junction of the natural surface with the base of the mound, and near the centre, was a pile of burnt human bones. After removing these, the ground beneath and around, to the distance of 12 feet, was thoroughly searched, but nothing more could be found.

This barrow was composed of earth and loamy soil, the latter predominating at the base, round the centre. It was also noticed that the old surface was uneven, small patches here and there being 7 to 9 inches lower than in other places. I had not previously observed this, and it may have been caused by clearing the ground of gorse or brushwood previous to raising the barrow.

Nothing but pieces of burnt wood, eight splinters of flint, and a piece of an ornamented food-vase were found. These occurred in the mound, surrounding the interment.

BARROW No. C 97.

Opened October 30th and 31st, 1876.—This small mound is on the brow of Garrowby Hill, and commands an extensive view of the vale of York. In the centre was an oval grave containing the crouched remains of a juvenile from 8 to 10 years of age, on the right side, with the head to south-south-west. The right femoral bone of the body measured 12½ inches. A most elaborately-ornamented food-vase (fig. 380) was found close to the face. The densely-crowded ornamentation on this vase is most skilfully executed, and of an unusual type. Near the right elbow was a pointed instrument of flint, about 2½ inches long (fig. 381).

BARROW No. C. 98

Is situated about 100 yards to the south-east of the last, and is of medium size. On November 1st and 2nd, 1876, a portion 20 feet square was cut from the centre, and a large oval grave, extending 4½ feet into the chalk was met with. On the floor of this were the well-preserved remains of a middle-aged man, of strong build, on his back, with head to north, knees pulled up, and both hands on the left breast. A femur measured 18½ inches, tibia 15½ inches, and humerus 13 inches. Near the forehead was a food-vase, crushed into numerous pieces, but now rebuilt (fig. 382), and a quantity of dark matter was noticed near the right shoulder.

BARROW No. 42

Is situated to the south of the last, nearly in the centre of the field adjoining the north side of the top end of Worsendale Plantation. Though built somewhat upon a natural eminence, and measuring 60 feet in diameter and 18 inches high, it had not been mapped by the Ordnance Surveyors.

On September 29th, 1865, a rectangular piece, measuring 21 feet by 16 feet was cut from the centre to the dark peat-like original surface soil beneath, on which were scattered numerous small pieces of a highly ornamented drinking-cup; one portion of which (fig. 383) is decorated with a very uncommon form of impressions; also a keen-edged flint scraper, one small disc chipped half round its edge, and six splinters—all of Yorkshire flint. A tusk of a hog, a molar and an incisor of a sheep or goat, were also taken on the same level. Near the centre of the barrow were indications of the ground having been disturbed. Below these was a grave which measured 4 feet 8 inches east and west, 3 feet north and south, and 3 feet deep from the base of the barrow. At the bottom were the doubled-up remains of a young person, not far advanced in the 'teens. The bones were very much decayed; but indicated that the head had been to the east and the knees towards the south. Close to the knees was an elegantly-formed food-vase ($fig.$ 384), of an unusual type of ornamentation, measuring $5\frac{3}{4}$ inches in height and $5\frac{1}{2}$ inches across the top. The two grooves forming the neck of the vase are ornamented with zig-zag cord markings, and below are two belts of horse shoe-shaped impressions, formed by a similar cord, which encircle the body of the vase.* A piece of clay hermetically sealed the mouth of the vase, consequently when found it contained nothing but a little black powder at the bottom—probably the residue of food. Near the decayed arm-bone was a scraper-shaped knife ($fig.$ 385), and a spear-head ($fig.$ 386) of flint, $2\frac{1}{4}$ inches long, and 1 inch broad at the butt end, and neatly chipped on one side. At the bottom of the grave was some decayed wood of a reddish colour, and a few pieces of charcoal were situated close to the skull.

BARROW No. 69,

Or the "Beacon Hill" barrow, on June 20th, 1866, measured 44 feet across and only 1 foot in height, but probably originally stood two or three feet higher, with a somewhat smaller diameter. In the year 1588, it was chosen for the site of Bishop Wilton Beacon † from its elevated position, and the field in which it is situated, is still called the Beacon Field.

A little distance to the north of the barrow is an ancient entrenchment called Ewe-Gang, which crossed the ridge of high ground between the upper end of Worsendale and the upper end of Deepdale. At first, portions of decayed horizontal wooden beams, the remains of the groundwork of the beacon, were met with. Near the centre of the barrow, only about six inches under its grassy surface, was a skull and portions of an arm bone, much crushed and decayed. Close to the south side of the skull was an iron spearhead ($fig.$ 387) 11 inches long, pointing westward. A little further south were portions of two blades of a pair of iron shears, but the interment had been largely removed at the time that the beacon had been raised. This was the first instance of our finding any trace of an Anglo-Saxon interment in a British barrow.

A little more than three feet to the east of the skull, and six inches lower, was a circular hole scooped six inches into the ground, 17 inches in diameter, and charged with calcined adult human bones and bits of burnt wood; part of a bone hair-pin ($fig.$ 389) was picked from the bones, which probably represented

---

* A very similar pattern of arched ornamentation is shown on a food-vase from "Hay Top Barrow, Monsal Dale, Derbyshire," and is figured in "Crania Britannica," p. 2, plate 60. The same design, but taller, has previously been indicated (fig. 377), Barrow No. 63, and is also shown on a food-vase (fig. 932), Group XV., Barrow No. C. 89, which is ornamented with a row of horseshoe patterns round the lower part. Nevertheless, this arch-formed decoration rarely occurs in British pottery.

† See Poulson's "History of Holderness."

FIG. 380.   ½

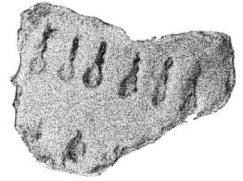

FIG. 383.   ¼

FIG. 386.   ¼

FIG. 389.   ½

FIG. 384.   ½

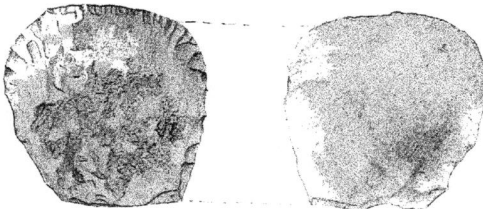

FIG. 385.   ¼

FIG. 387.   ½

a British interment. From the mound were taken four hand-struck flakes of flint. Possibly other bodies were destroyed at the time of the erection of the beacon.

Insignificant and uninteresting as this small mound must have long seemed to be, it has nevertheless been found to possess a faithful record of events, memorable in the histories of three distinct races, or nations.

BARROW No. 31.

Opened May 31st, 1865.—This barrow had a diameter of 76 feet and an elevation of 3½ feet, and consisted of clay from a distance, mixed with soil of the neighbourhood. We commenced at the top and removed a rectangular portion 14 feet by 12½ feet, but found only one end of the leg bone of an ox, pieces of carbonized wood, seven hand-struck splinters, 3 small slingstones—all of foreign flint, and probably accidently mixed with the substance of the barrow. In the centre, sunk into the chalk, was a shallow grave, at the bottom of which was the skeleton of a strong adult, on its back, with head to the south, the left arm doubled back with the hand to the shoulder, the right arm at full length by the side, minus the hand and about half the length of the forearm,[*] probably the result of some conflict, and the cause of death. This severed portion, with its hand, was found resting on the right shoulder, with the finger bones near the head.[†] The skeleton rested on a film of dark decayed matter, and under this was a layer of clay 3 inches in thickness, which appeared to have been spread on the floor of the grave previous to the interment of the body, which was covered with about two inches of clay.

The Government Surveyors, in placing a signal-post on this mound, had sunk a hole to its base, just over the legs of the skeleton.

We have since re-opened this barrow, and turned over the greater part of it, without finding any more.

BARROW No. 32

Is in the adjoining field, to the south ot the last.

On June 12th, 1865, it did not exceed 46 feet in diameter, and from repeated ploughing was not more than a foot above the surrounding ground. We cut an area 13 feet by 12 feet from its centre, and picked up numerous potsherds, belonging at least to seven different vessels ; bones, teeth, the horn-core and hoof-bone of an ox ; also teeth and tusks of a boar. There were also six flint discs chipped on their edges, three pieces of doubtful purpose, several flakes, the broad end of a leaf-shaped arrow-head—nearly all of foreign flint, also the small end of a polished stone axe. The whole of these, and pieces of burnt wood, seemed to have been scattered on the old surface-line previous to the raising of the barrow.

On the same horizon, a little south of the centre and not more than eight inches from the tilled surface of the ground, was a portion of a human skull (No. 1.)[‡] The remainder of the interment had doubtless been destroyed by the plough.

---

[*] The Indians of Brazil and Australia will sometimes cut off the right thumb of the corpse of an enemy, so that it cannot throw the shadowy spear in spirit-land. May not this body have been maimed at the time of death, by severing the right-hand, with a view to a like disablement?

[†] I have in my possession only one of these bones—the lower portion of the ulna.

[‡] No plan of this barrow is given, but I give the numbers of each interment to enable the bones, which I possess, to be identified.

Rather more to the south, and a little lower, was interment No. 2—that of a young person, though somewhat disturbed either by the plough, or someone digging for rabbits. It had been placed on the left side, with the knees up, and the head to the north. West of the centre was a dish-shaped hole, 8 inches deep and 12 inches across. It contained decayed matter, mixed with small pieces of burnt wood, but no bone. A few feet north-east of this deposit was a heap of calcined human bones (*A*), mixed with burnt wood, near which was the lower jaw of a dog, unburnt.

Near the centre of the mound was a rather extensive pavement of large angular flints, such as weather out of the chalk and are found on the surface of the land. Below this was a second pavement of a similar character, close under which was skeleton No. 3, on its back, the knees pulled up, the arms across the body, and head to the south. A food-vase (fig. 390) was near the skull.

A little to the south of the last, in a somewhat deeper grave, was interment No. 4, on the left side, with the head and legs in the same position as interment No. 3. The femur of this body measured 18 inches. The skull, as well as that of body No. 3, was much crushed and the teeth of both much worn. A keen-edged bronze dagger blade (fig. 391) was found behind the shoulders. It is 5 inches long, 2⅝ inches broad, and very thin. The handle has apparently been horn, judging from the impressions left on the blade, and had been secured by three strong round-headed bronze rivets, each ⅝ of an inch long. The two edges of the blade are worn hollow by frequent sharpening. Under and around this was some decayed matter, and about two inches from the upper end of the blade was a bone article, with two rivet holes through it, which had undoubtedly formed the pommel of the handle, as shewn in fig. 391.

The vase (fig. 390) after being rebuilt, is nearly complete, and measures 6⅝ inches in height, 7 inches across the top, and the same at half its height; it then tapers to 3¼ inches at the bottom. A few potsherds, such as were taken from the base of the mound, were mixed with the material filling the two graves. Altogether we procured fragments of eight different vases, six of which were portions of highly-ornamented drinking-cups which probably had been used at the funeral ceremony and afterwards broken and strewed around. A trace of clay in the grave was all the argillaceous matter visible in this barrow.

BARROW No. 120.

Opened July 29th and 30th, 1868.—This mound was 22 yards in diameter, and 16 inches in elevation. *Within its margin* was an encircling trench cut into the chalk rock, which was filled with soily matter. From centre to centre of the trench measured 50 feet, and the section of the trench measured 9 feet across the top, 1 foot across the bottom, and was 3 feet deep. Just west of the centre of this enclosure was a vertical-sided oblong grave (No. 1), cut 5½ feet into the chalk, and measuring, at the bottom, 12 feet north-west and south-east, by 7 feet.* On the hard floor of this grave, near the middle, was the skeleton of an adult male (No. 1), on its left side, head to the south-east, knees pulled up to a right angle with the body, the left arm by the side, with hand

---

* May this have been a pit-dwelling originally?

PLATE XLVIII.

FIG. 392.

FIG. 393. ¼

FIG. 390. ⅓

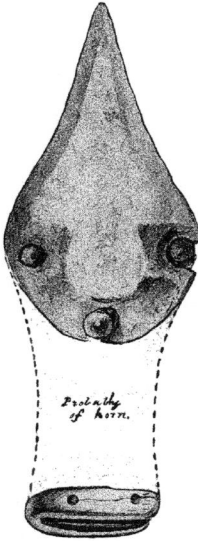

Probably of horn.

FIG. 391. ½

FIG. 394. ⅓

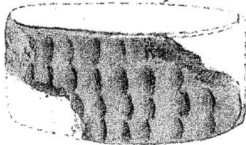

FIG. 395. ½

FIG. 396. ⅓

near the knees, and the right arm bent over the body with hand also near the knees. The femur measured 19 inches, and the skull was distorted by pressure since burial. No vase or other relic was found with this interment.

Five feet eastwards was a similar grave (No. 2), cut $4\frac{3}{4}$ feet into the rock, and measuring 8 feet north and south, by 4 feet, at the bottom of which, and rather toward the northern end, was the skeleton of a young individual (No. 2), of large stature, on its back, head to north, the knees pulled up and pressed over to the east, both hands brought up to the shoulders, bent at the wrist, and stretched across the chest, just below the chin ; a femur measured 19 inches. A small flint-flake knife (fig. 392), was found under the right shoulder. Close to the pelvis of this interment was the skeleton of a child (No. 3), about eight years of age, on the right side, legs doubled up and touching the feet of the adult, the hands to the skull, which pointed to the south-east. At the left side of the skull was a plain hair-pin (fig. 393), $2\frac{1}{2}$ inches long, made of a flat piece of bone. A sheet of loamy clay covered the top of each grave.

From 6 to 8 inches below the surface of the mound, and about 2 feet to the east of grave No. 1, was interment No. 4, of middle age and strong bone, on the right side, head to the north-west, knees pulled up, and hands to the face. In front of the face were fragments of a neatly-ornamented food-vase (the only one from this barrow), which, after re-building (fig. 394), measured $6\frac{3}{4}$ inches across the top, and 6 inches high.

Close to this vase were the ulna and radius of a pig. In the mound two flint knives were found.

BARROW No. C 43

Is a little to the south of No. 120, and at the time of opening (July 19th to 26th, 1871), had a diameter of 90 feet, and an elevation of 3 feet. We began near the western edge, and cut a strip of 30 feet wide through the centre to the opposite margin. Adjoining the circumference was an encircling fosse, completely filled with material worked off the mound by the repeated cultivation of its surface. It measured $3\frac{1}{2}$ feet deep, $4\frac{1}{2}$ feet wide at the top, and 15 inches at the bottom.

Near the centre of the barrow, and about 1 foot from its base, were a few burnt bones. At the base of the mound, on the south-east edge of an oval grave, measuring 8 feet by 6 feet, and about 12 inches to the north of the first, was a second small heap of burnt bones (No. 2), whilst 18 inches north of this, and a few inches down in the east end of the grave, was a third deposit (No. 3), measuring $2\frac{1}{2}$ feet east and west, and 15 inches across, and consisting of the calcined bones of more than one body—seemingly of different ages. Much burnt matter existed all round.

A boat-formed mass of black, unctuous, and much-burnt matter—measuring at the top 5 feet east and west, and $2\frac{1}{2}$ feet north and south—was found to occupy the centre of the grave, and was surrounded by rubbly chalk, which had been quarried from the grave and replaced. At a depth of $3\frac{1}{2}$ feet was an inhumed interment (No. 1), in the rubbly chalk, on its right side, with its back close to the northern margin of the grave, head to the west, the knees pulled up, and both hands in front of the face. The femur and humerus measured 17 inches and 12 inches respectively, and were probably those of a female.

At a depth of 4½ feet was skeleton No. 2, on the undisturbed rock in the centre of the grave, and, except that its head pointed to the east, its position was the same as that of its companion above. The femur and humerus were also of the same measurements as in the other case, but were stronger. Close behind the skull was a dish-shaped hole in the floor of the grave, 15 inches deep and 18 inches in diameter at the top, containing burnt matter partly cemented together, and enclosing a scorched human cheek-bone, and other bones (No. 4). The contents of this receptacle seemed to be connected with, and in every way resembled the central core in the grave, and both seemed to consist of embers from a funeral pyre, mixed with a little earth and chalk, and, judging from the grease-like appearance, probably a considerable quantity of flesh had been added. The whole mass was cemented together, and had to be lifted from the grave in large blocks. It seemed clear that, at least, the portion contained in the dish-shaped hole had been deposited in a glowing condition, as the lower interment, from head to pelvis, was more or less charred, and the heat had extended to the surrounding chalk.

A small portion of a drinking-cup and two bits of animal bone, unburnt, were picked from the chalk around the sides of the grave.

I am inclined to believe that the two inhumed bodies and the cremated bodies in the grave were contemporaneous, and that the embers of the latter had been interred while hot, and had been immediately placed upon the lower body, thus accounting for its burnt condition. There was no disturbance in the arched layers capping the grave above.

During the excavation we found one oval and four circular flint discs, portions of three knives, and one flake saw; also 110 potsherds, including pieces of the rims of seven drinking-cups, three food-vases, and the side of a small oblong incense-cup (fig. 395), which had been 2 inches high. With these were portions of the rib and shank-bones of an ox. The whole (except two sherds of a drinking-cup, found over the grave), were taken from the old surface-ground at the base of the mound, near the western end of the grave, where traces of fire were most distinct. These seem to mark the spot on which the funeral feast was conducted, and, judging from the number of broken vessels, and other appearances, this was extensive, and probably the very reverse of a mournful kind.

DETACHED BARROWS.

The barrows adjoining—but which are too distant to be enclosed within the lines of this group—are situated to the west, and are four in number. The two nearest, marked A and No. 104a, are situated within the western margin of a grass field at the bottom of Garrowby Hill, bounded on the north by "Garrowby Street," and on the west by "Garrowby Road." The Ordnance Surveyors have not mapped either as barrows.

That marked A is of large size, and although it is indicated on the map as a natural eminence, there is little doubt of it being, in part, artificial; and probably at one time it was known as "Mickle Head," as on the Ordnance map the ground close by still retains that name. It is far too symmetrically circular to be altogether natural, yet, as it is situated close to the foot of the escarpment, where the remains of landslips are not uncommon, it is probable that a large portion of it consists of one of those slipped masses, which have eventually been sculptured into a circular form and the apex raised. Its present nearly flat top, which is quite circular, measures 60 feet in diameter, and seems to be due to a recent mutilation, intended perhaps, for the site of some building or for holding a "folk-mote,"* rather than to enable it to be ploughed over; although at some time it has been ploughed, as shown by ridge and furrow crossing it. Its present medium height is 50 feet above the surrounding ground, while the diameter at its base is about 250 feet. It shows no trace of having been explored, and its great size has hitherto deterred me from opening it.

The large mound at Skipsea Brough has a flat top, 90 feet in diameter, whilst about half-way down its eastern side is a mass of stones and mortar.† There is also a mound on Seamer Moor, called Beacon Hill, which has a flat top 19 yards in diameter, as shown by Knox in his "Eastern Yorkshire," plate 18; and so had Howe Hill (Barrow 273), Duggleby, described in this volume. Probably these earthern mounds on which have stood the keeps of old castles—York and Pickering, &c.—were originally large British barrows or strongholds, conveniently situated on ground equally suitable for the site of a castle.

BARROW No. 104a

Is about 200 paces east of the last mound. It stands on land that has not been cultivated, and though apparently in its original form and size, is one of the smallest barrows we have ever opened.

On August 26th, 1867, it measured about 12 feet in diameter, and $1\frac{1}{2}$ feet high. Under the centre was a small grave containing a few burnt bones, and traces of what might have been unburnt bone in the last state of decay, but no relic.

The two barrows marked No. "C. 99" and "B," are situated about 6 furlongs further westwards, a little past Garrowby, in an angle formed by the York high road and "Awnham Beck."

BARROW C 99

Is called "Kity Hill" on the Ordnance Sheet. On November 3rd and 4th, 1876, its diameter was about 40 feet, and elevation 3 feet. A little west of the centre, and near the surface, were many pieces of the iron umbo of an Anglo-Saxon shield, and a flat piece of iron, probably also belonging to a shield. A little to the south-east of the centre, near the base of the barrow, were a few burnt bones, accompanied by a crushed British food-vase of red clay, since rebuilt (fig. 396). In the centre was a shallow grave, on the floor of which was an adult skeleton, No. 1, on the right side, head to east-south-east, both hands brought to front of the face, and the knees pulled up near to the right elbow. Near to the back of the skull was a bone pin‡ running obliquely over the occipital bone, with the point upwards—the position in which they were generally placed in securing the back hair. A femur measured 18 inches and tibia 15 inches, and

---

* Which probably was afterwards taken to the Garrowby New Inn, near by, and at which Court Meetings were held up to about 1856. † The remains of a Norman "keep." ‡ Now lost.

were probably those of a female. The remains of a very young child (No. 2), were found close to the back of the adult skeleton. About 4 feet to the east of the centre was a dish-shaped excavation, 30 inches in diameter, and scooped to a depth of 16 inches into the ground beneath the mound. It contained cremated bones, mixed with a large quantity of charcoal. A vase of red clay, apparently British, but irreparably crushed, was found resting on them. At the bottom of the hole, under the bones, were several pieces of another British food-vase.

BARROW B

Is a small one, adjoining the last, but is not shown on the Ordnance Map. At the time when its fellow was explored it could not be opened without destroying a crop of young wheat growing upon it.

A discovery was made a little to the south of this Group of barrows, the account of which was printed in the "Reliquary, Quarterly Archæological Journal and Review," January 1869, as follows:—

"The following are the details of a very interesting burial, accidently discovered on March 20th, 1868, on the Grimthorpe estate, about 2½ miles north of Pocklington, Yorkshire. The site of the burial is about a quarter mile to the north-east of Grimthorpe House, almost at the summit of a large knoll-formed chalk outlier, on the east side of the road leading to Great Givendale, which is but slightly detached from the southern margin of the chalk wolds. In the southern face of a chalk pit, Mr. G. Hopper, of Grimthorpe, observed the end of a small excavation, charged with soil and loose chalk, a little of which he removed with a piece of bone he found lying near, and soon came in sight of a skull. Thanks are due to Mr. Hopper for the discovery, and for having at once made known the circumstances to Dr. Wilson, of Pocklington, with whom he arranged to carefully exhume the remains the following day; and my only regret is that I was not with them. Through the kindness of these gentlemen, I possess full particulars of the find.

"First, it was found that an oval grave, measuring at the bottom about 4½ feet north and south, with a transverse diameter of 2¾ feet, had been dug to a depth of 4 feet into the chalk rock.

"'On the floor of this grave,' writes Dr. Wilson, 'the body of a young man had been placed partly on the back, with the knees and head inclining to the left side, the hands upon the breast, the lower extremities drawn up, and the direction of the head was to the south.'

"This statement agrees with Mr. Hopper's account and with what I made out from two subsequent visits to the spot.

"Dr. Wilson adds—'Three ornamented plates of mixed metal (bronze), the exterior covering of a circular shield, were lying on the breast, and under these metal plates was a considerable quantity of iron oxide in dust (probably the residue of some portion of the inner side of the shield), and decayed wood or leather.* Two semi-cylindrical plates, or half-tubes, of bronze,

---

* The form of these plates, which are little thicker than ordinary writing-paper, will be best understood from the sketch. The boss is of very unusual shape, and is ornamented with engraved lines. It measures 4½ inches by 3½ inches. The two plates are each 12½ inches from point to point, and 3¾ inches wide in the middle. They have a raised border of curious design around the outer extremity, and have, like the boss, been attached to the shield by rivets.

½-inch in diameter, and measuring respectively 11 and 11½ inches in length, which probably had been used to strengthen or adorn the slender shaft of a spear, lay, one at the head, the other at the knees, and, when found, contained the bronze nails which had fastened them to the wood, but no trace of the latter remained. A portion of an iron spear head was also found. It had been placed on the left side of the burial.'

"Two studs, each about ½-inch in diameter, and a circular plate of mixed metal, 2 inches in diameter and ornamentally impressed, were found about the chest and shoulders. The remains of an iron sword in a bronze scabbard were found by the left side, and under the shield; the much-damaged handle being close to the head of the skeleton. The low end of the scabbard is ornamented with what seems to be the conventional head of some animal, with six eyes, and the holes representing the eyes have been set with small rubies, which were all absent but one. Six or eight bone implements, measuring 3½ to 4 inches long were found distributed on the top of the interment the whole length, and others, making sixteen in all, were found below and around the remains. These, Dr. Wilson thinks, 'had been used to secure some covering or wrapper round the doubled-up body when it was placed in the grave, which was quite too small to admit the corpse in the extended position.' Two teeth of a small ox, small bits of animal bone, some of which show traces of burning, as well as five pieces of pottery, which, with one exception, were made of clay freely mixed with finely pounded flint and having a texture similar to that of a British drinking-cup, were found in the unctuous, soily matter cast from the grave; and the exceptional piece of pot was of a dark kind, very much resembling the Roman black ware.

"Though no trace of a mound was observed over the burial (the land having been under the plough for more than sixty years), the oval form of the grave, the doubled-up mode of burial, and the distribution of bits of animal bone and pieces of pottery in the matter filling the grave, closely approach the appearances observable in true barrow burials; and the bone-pin-like articles also seem to give this burial somewhat a British character. I agree with Dr. Wilson, that at the time of the burial they had most likely been used to skewer up the corpse, seemingly in some kind of skin, as evident trace of hair is observable through the whole length of one side of the sword-sheath. But that those bone articles were not originally formed for pins is quite obvious. Each has been made of the shank bone of a goat by cutting off a very small portion of the end of the joint, and scooping out the end of the bone in the form of a socket, as shown in the sketch, and the other end of the bone has been sharpened to a round or chisel-like point. That these articles have originally been shafted is proved by two or four pinholes passing through the socket end of each, and in one the pins remain in position. Possibly they were first formed and used as lance heads.

"The sword is of great beauty. It is of iron, and remains encased in its bronze scabbard in a more perfect state than usual. The extreme length of the sword and scabbard, from pommel to chape, is 31 inches; the length of the scabbard from guard to point of chape, 24 inches. The breadth at the mouth is 1⅞ inches. The guard is of bronze. The scabbard is formed of thin plate bronze, and has an encircling band of the same material to hold the upper points of the chape to its sides. The length of the chape from the band is 6½ inches. The chape, which is exquisitely formed, is of unusual beauty. It is in a remarkably perfect condition, and, being formed of bronze, is of great rarity and interest. The rubies (?) have been affixed in their places by small rivets passing through their centres."*

The various relics found with the interment are shown on the accompanying plate.

In addition to the burial just described, a previous one had been found by the workmen in a shallow grave about 10 feet to the west. It was discovered in Mr. Hopper's absence, and nothing was observed in it. The whole of the bones were in good condition, and Mr. Hopper possessed the skull which was in fine preservation, and apparently that of a female. On August 20th, 1871, and the following five days, we carefully searched the ground on the north, east, and west sides of the pit, over a considerable area, by making trenches about 3 feet apart; but only found pot sherds, and numerous pieces of animal bone, which did not seem to be connected with burials, but were mixed in the soil, more or less everywhere, and chiefly in the filled up inner ditch of a supposed camp; the south-west corner of which the chalk-pit occupies. On November 6th, 1872, I received from Mr. Hopper a card informing me that having had occasion to again procure chalk from this pit, the workmen had touched another burial, and that he had allowed it to remain for my inspection. This invitation I gladly accepted, and on the following day, Dr. Wilson, myself, and a workman proceeded to Grimthorpe. I was puzzled to account for the interment having escaped our previous search; but it appeared that our nearest trench had been carried round the three sides of the pit at a distance rather over 4 feet from its edge, and between these two was the grave which had escaped detection. This grave formed a triangle with the two previously discovered in 1868, and was about 10 feet to the north of them. It was irregular in outline, measuring 7 feet north-west by south-east, nearly 4 feet across, and contained two interments. That at the southern extremity was 3 feet deep, and was placed on its left side, with the head to the north, the knees pulled up to a right angle with the trunk, and both hands brought to the face. A femur measures 17 inches, and tibia 13 inches, and are of slender make. The interment to the north was exactly in the same posture as the last, but 6 inches nearer the surface. A femur measures 15 inches and tibia 12 inches, and are of slender build. In burying this body the skull of the previous burial had been removed some 6 inches to the east to make way for the knees of the second interment; which was placed quite over the neck and shoulders of the first. No relic accompanied either remains; but a few small bits of pottery, and some small pieces of what seemed to be burnt wood and bone were picked from the soil and chalk grit which covered the bodies and filled the grave. There was no trace of a mound.

* Most of these relics are now in the British Museum.

No. VIII.—THE CALAIS WOLD GROUP.

THIS group occupies the highest point on the Yorkshire Wolds, 807 feet above Ordnance datum.   The site affords a very extensive view over the vale of York.

It contains eighteen barrows, fifteen of which are shown on the Ordnance Map.   Twelve of the mounds are situated in close proximity to the Calais Wold Farm House.

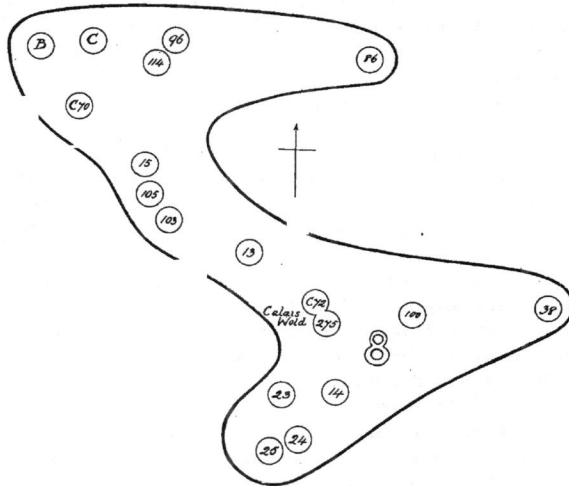

CALAIS WOLD GROUP.

BARROWS Nos. 23, 24, and 25,

Were opened during the middle of March, 1865.   They occupy the south-west corner of this group.

BARROW No. 23

Had a diameter of 70 feet and an external elevation of 5 feet, while its height above the ground on which it stood was only $4\frac{1}{2}$ feet.   This variation in the height between the ancient surface line under many of the barrows and the present surface of the land immediately near their outskirts, is partly due, as already suggested, to the subaerial denudation of the unprotected surface since the erection of the barrows, and partly to the frequent choice of a slight natural prominence for their erection.   A portion measuring 12 feet by 11 feet was removed from the centre of the mound, and a few chips of black flint were found.   An oval trough-shaped grave, 5 feet by 3 feet, situated nearly under the centre of the barrow was next emptied.   This was partly filled with clay and partly with dark mould, caused probably by the decay of organic matter.   In the material filling the grave were many cavities of various shapes, having a greasy appearance on their sides, and varying in size from 1 inch to 7 inches in diameter. Similar cavities also extended 1 foot upwards into the mound immediately above, and here, as well as in the grave, many of the cavities were connected. No trace of an interment could be found in this grave. The mound consisted of a central core, mainly of clay, with lines of dark matter and traces of fire. Several large pieces of clay were noticed, which retained all the thin laminæ of the argillaceous beds from which they had been obtained, clearly showing that some of the clay had been carried and placed on the mound in large pieces.

On April 5th, three weeks after the first opening, a further search was made by continuing the former excavation westwards, until the outer edge of the clayey nucleus was reached. The inner core measured 24 feet in diameter, and reached half way to the apex of the barrow. We next dug into the gritty chalk rock, round and under the grave, to a depth of 3 feet, but again without indication of an interment.

I have, between two pieces of glass, a portion of a leaf of a tree which was found in the grave. This had probably been buried at the time of interment, and owes its preservation to the fact that it was between two pieces of chalk.*

Re-opening, May and June, 1868.—More experience in barrow-digging led us to believe that in the former opening of this barrow we had only partly explored the grave in the centre.† On the above dates, therefore, ten days were occupied in carefully turning over nearly the whole of this barrow and testing the ground beneath. Within about 14 feet west of the centre, holes made by stakes and posts were noticed in the ground. In each of these a small upright stake was inserted to indicate their arrangement ; this proved to be in the order shown in fig. 397. On reaching the centre of the mound, the rock was observed to have been disturbed beneath, where formerly we had only excavated and removed the clay matter from the trough-shaped hollow, (believing we had reached the bottom). After a few hours digging an elliptical grave cut into the rock was emptied, the diameters measuring at the bottom 7 feet 5 inches and 4 feet 7 inches respectively, with a depth of 3 feet 10 inches.‡

On the floor of this grave, and surrounded by a considerable quantity of decayed soot-like matter, were the strong bones of an adult male, partly on its back, head to the south, and in the flexed position shown in the plan (fig. 397). A femur measured 17½ inches and tibia 14 inches. All the bones of the left hand, which are preserved, are joined together (anchylosed), and are also united to the radius and ulna. The finger bones, however, are free.

In front of the face was a crushed food-vase (fig. 398), which, after re-building, measured 6 inches in height and 6½ inches across the mouth. It is ornamented over its exterior with stamped impressions, which were no doubt produced by a knotted cord. Close to the left shoulder was a perforated axe-hammer of whinstone, 4½ inches long (fig. 399), with the decayed remains of the handle lying over the upper part of the chest. It might have been grasped by the right hand, as the finger bones were bent under, while the bones of the hand were above the decayed haft. Such

---

* Other instances of preserved vegetation are recorded in these pages.
† Other barrow diggers appear to have passed over graves in this manner in their earlier openings, and in some cases have not opened them a second time.
‡ Our previous excavation had reached to within one foot of the bottom.

FIG. 398. ½

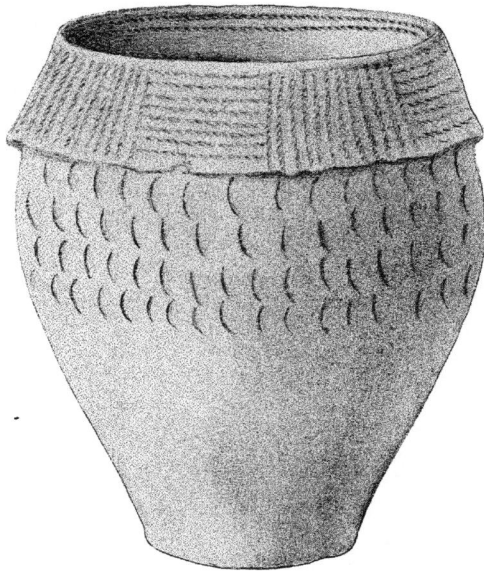

FIG. 401.

an instrument wielded by the muscular arm of a Briton would be a very dangerous weapon. The skeleton was closely surrounded by large pieces of chalk.

As the digging proceeded round the outskirts of the barrow, the post-holes were noticed at about regular distances, and formed two circles, one within the other, measuring respectively 21½ feet and 28 feet medium diameter. The plan (fig. 397) shows their number and arrangement, and also indicates that the inner and outer circles approach each other, much nearer on the east than on the west side, and also exhibits some irregularities in the arrangement of the post holes on the north side, where some of the holes measured from 12 to 15 inches in diameter, while the others often measured as little as 3 inches in diameter. They varied from 1 to 2½ feet in depth, and some were observed to reach from 2 to 3 feet upwards into the mound. Four are also shown at A, outside the circle. Plaster casts were

FIG. 400.
IDEAL RESTORATION OF BRITISH HUT.

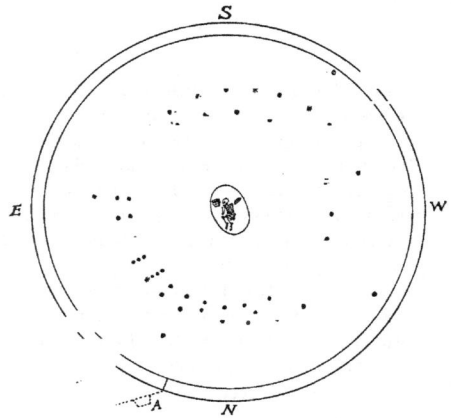

FIG. 397.—PLAN OF BARROW NO. 23.
Showing Encircling Trench and Stake-holes.
A—Section of Trench.

taken of several of the smaller holes, and although they were partly filled with an earthy deposit left by the percolation of water, it was possible to make out that some of the stakes had been roughly pointed and driven into the ground, whilst the larger—and even some of the smaller ones—had been placed in holes previously made for them, with their thick ends downwards. With regard to the purpose of these stakes, it seems clear that those forming the double ring represent the upright posts of the wattled walls of a circular hut, which would be bedaubed or plastered with clay, and probably having a conical roof, resembling the ideal sketch (fig. 400). What the space between the two walls was intended for is uncertain, but it might have been used for storing grain (as it has been already shown that it was grown in the neighbourhood at that period) and other provisions, at a time when probably a man's dwelling was the only building he possessed. Neither can we be certain as to the use of the four post-holes outside the circles. They seem too near the outer circle to be the remains of any useful enclosure, but they may have held posts or strong pegs by which the exposed roof of a dwelling was stayed and kept in position by ropes, which, from numerous impressions on cinerary urns and food vases, we know the Britons possessed. On this high land, a special support to the roof of such a building may probably have been necessary.

From the evidence it would appear that at the death of its owner a grave was dug in the floor of his dwelling, the walls and roof were pushed inwards, and over them the barrow was afterwards raised. Nothing would be more natural to early man than that he should wish to occupy in death the place of his residence or abode during life.* A filled-up fosse 100 feet in diameter, 3 feet 9 inches deep, 9 feet wide at the top and 1 foot at the bottom, encircled this barrow, and enclosed the whole of the stake holes.

A few hand-struck flakes of flint taken from the mound were the only other relics found.

BARROW No. 24

Had a diameter of 48 feet and an elevation of 2 feet. Slightly to the east of the centre were the fragments of a large cinerary urn, in a shallow hole made in the old surface ground. By pressure, this urn had been crushed into innumerable fragments, which after three long days' labour the writer succeeded in re-building, (fig. 401).† It measured 15 inches in height, 11½ inches across the mouth, 13¼ across the shoulders and 5½ inches across the bottom, ornamented with the impressions of a cord and the thumb nail of the right hand. It contained calcined bones, apparently human.‡ In removing a compact clayey covering over the urn and the dish-shaped hole in which it had been placed, fragments of carbonized wood, and several pieces resembling hazel bark were found, some of which seemed little burnt and almost free from decay, A splinter from the branch of a tree, 6 inches long and 1 inch thick, and very little decayed, was also picked up, and two carbonised seeds(?) somewhat resembling the East Indian pea, but a little larger. §

From various other parts of the mound were taken six flakes of black flint, but nothing more. ‖

BARROW No. 25

Resembles the previous barrow in size and form, and had also a dish-shaped cavity scooped into the old surface ground below it, which measured 2 feet 3 inches in diameter and 9 inches in depth. It contained calcined bones and

---

* Of such a custom, even under more refined conditions, we have historic evidence. On the authority of Diodorus, Semiramis, the wife of Ninus, the founder of the Assyrian empire, buried her husband in the palace and reared over him a great mound of earth, showing that it was also the wish of this Ninus to sleep in death where he had reigned in life.

† On being taken from the top of a high case, about four years afterwards, owing to its crumbly nature, it collapsed and fell on a brick floor, which so pulverized it as to make a second re-building impossible.

‡ A little above this was a nodule of flint, the size of a man's head, and a flat piece of chalk 10 inches square and 3 inches thick. Probably these had been placed there by the Ordnance Surveyors, as on the map this mound is marked with a triangle, indicating a trigonometrical station.

§ These were submitted to several botanists, but their identity could not be determined.

Possibly a further search might reveal a grave in the centre of this barrow.

PLATE L.

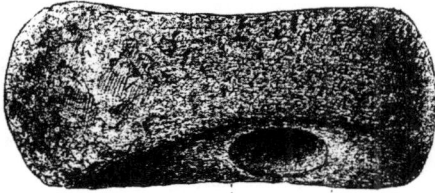

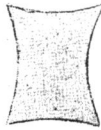

FIG. 399. $\frac{2}{3}$

FIG. 402. $\frac{1}{1}$

FIG. 403. $\frac{1}{1}$

FIG. 404. $\frac{1}{1}$

FIG. 405. $\frac{1}{2}$

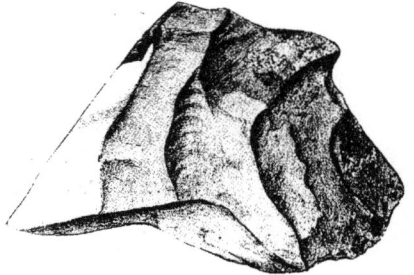

FIG. 410. ^{1}

wood ashes only, and was covered with a lenticular mass of compact clay. Only three flakes of black flint were found in the mound.

It is just possible that a grave was passed over and yet remains unexplored.*

BARROW No. 14

Stands about ten chains' length to the south of Calais Wold Farm-house. It measured 65 feet in diameter and 5 feet above the ground at its outskirts.

On July 3rd, 1864, we cut a 10 feet square from the centre, and the irregular texture of the mound indicated that it had been previously opened. Two-thirds of this barrow had been built up of mixed clay (non-local), and from the base to within a foot of its apex it consisted mainly of this material, streaked with thin dark layers of decayed vegetation, and frequently mixed with the red iron-stained local surface soil.

At the base of the barrow was a grave, containing large pieces of decayed wood, which we thought were the remains of a broken oak-tree coffin, lying east and west. At the east end were a few calcined bones and a small portion of a drinking-cup, and the conclusion was too hastily arrived at, that part of the coffin and the interment had been removed by former excavators.

Re-opening.—During the latter part of October, 1874, a cutting 20 feet wide was made from the eastern to the western margin of this barrow; and at about the centre we reached the grave which on the previous examination we thought to have been rifled. This was oval in form, measuring 6½ feet by 5 feet and slightly over 2 feet in depth. A little above the floor of the grave, close to the west side, was a heap of white calcined bones of an adult body, accompanied by a worked flint (fig. 402) nearly 3 inches long, having two keen cutting edges and a very fine point, while the broad end had a chisel-like edge. There was also a flint nodule, the size of a hen's egg, with a natural hole through the middle. On the floor of the grave at the north side were a few teeth and decayed portions of a skull of a young individual, being all that remained of the primary interment. Near these were two rude flint scrapers (figs. 403-404), the latter being a fine unfinished specimen, which had not received the usual secondary chipping round the edges.

Between the burnt bones and the fragments of the skull was a crushed food-vase (fig. 405)—probably belonging to the inhumed body—which, after rebuilding, measured 4½ inches in height, and is ornamented round its upper half with oblique chevron gashes.

The bottom and sides of the grave had been lined with oak, and most probably the top as well, as there remained some decayed wood besides that which was removed at the first opening, mentioned above, which was then thought to be the remains of an oak-trunk coffin.

From the mound were taken several discs and flakes of black flint, 107 in all, and the leg-bone of an ox, but no human remains.

---

* Unfortunately it has not been convenient to re-open this and the previous mound.

BARROW No. 100,

Is a prominent object about twelve chains to the east of " Calais Wold " Farm-house.

On June 28th and 29th, and July 1st, 3rd, and 5th, 1867, this barrow was opened, when it had a radius of 42 feet and a central altitude of 6 feet. It consisted of about three parts of foreign clay to one part of local surface soil. Some of this latter was of a reddish colour, while the clay varied from deep blue to light drab. Fragments of burnt wood were plentifully distributed throughout the 20 feet excavation, and a layer varying from one to three inches in thickness rested on the old land surface near the centre, and was found most abundant on the east and west sides. About 6 feet south-east from the centre and 4 feet in the same direction from the side of the grave which we afterwards discovered, was a large cinerary urn (fig. 406) inverted, at the base of the mound. It is freely ornamented with deep impressions made by the thumb. This urn contained no incinerated bones,[*] but about 6 inches from the south-west side, on the same level, was a circular heap (C on the plan, fig. 407) of cremated bones of a small person, and adjoining the east side of this deposit was the decayed skull of an unburnt body. From very distinct impressions left on a thin bed of clay at the bottom of a shallow excavation 4 or 5 inches below the base of the barrow, it appeared that the urn had been inverted upon a nearly circular pavement of wood, 18 inches in diameter. This was apparently made of short round pieces, varying in length,

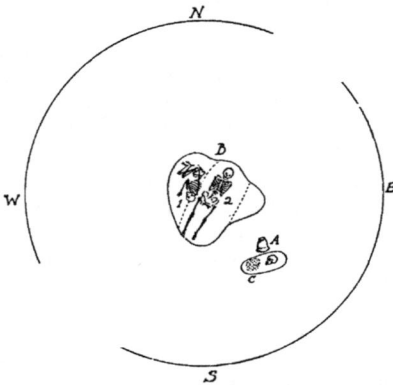

FIG. 407.—SECTION OF BARROW No. 100.

and about 3 inches in diameter, placed side by side. More impressions south of the urn, indicated the remains of a large oval receptacle of wood (C on the plan, fig. 407), measuring 3 feet 8 inches by 1 foot 7 inches, which had either contained the calcined bones and unburnt skull, or had been inverted over them.

As the digging proceeded, it was noticed that an irregularly-formed opening 8 feet in diameter at the top, but not more than 4 feet at the bottom, had been previously made a little south of the centre, to within 8 inches of the base of the barrow. At that point the previous explorers had abandoned the excavation, probably owing to their having reached a heap of chalk rubble which had been cast there by the Britons in digging the grave, which was probably mistaken for the natural rock.

At the base of the barrow was the very irregular outline of a large grave, shewn on the plan by the line B. Towards the bottom its outline changed, and on reaching the base—at a depth of 4 feet—it was oblong in shape with rounded ends, as shewn by the broken line on the plan, and measured 8 feet by 4 feet. A boat-shaped mass

---

[*] This was the first of three instances in which we have observed the cinerary urn not to contain burnt bones. Can it in these cases have served as a food-vase?

of clay and soil occupied the centre of the grave to a depth of 27 inches, and extended over the skulls of the two interments below. The first body (No. 1) was towards the north side of the grave, close under this mass of clay, on its back. It had been placed partly with the knees pulled up and pressed over to the west, the right hand on the right side of the pelvis, and the left arm doubled back with the hand bent at the third joints and placed under the chin. A femur, tibia, and humerus measured 18, 14, and 13½ inches respectively, and are probably those of a large female. Near the southern edge of the grave, at a depth of about 20 inches was a pointed instrument (fig. 408) 7½ inches long, in fine preservation, made from a leg-bone of an ox.*

At the bottom of the grave was a skeleton (No. 2) at full length, an unexpected posture, as shewn on the plan. The extreme length of this skeleton, measured as found, was 5 feet 10 inches ; but as the head was pressed considerably into the chest, the individual would probably stand nearly 6 feet in height. A femur and tibia measured 19 inches and 15 inches respectively. A dark brown substance resembling decayed bark, was noticed on the floor of the grave, near the skull and at the feet. It was not clear whether the upper interment had been placed in the grave a short time after the lower one, but it was quite obvious that all the interments were deposited previous to the erection of the barrow, as not the slightest disturbance was observed in the mound, beyond the opening mentioned, which did not reach any of the interments. Portions of three drinking-cups, fourteen flint chips, animal bones (including four molar teeth of an ox, one tusk of a pig, thirty-five splinters of bone belonging to oxen and pigs, and four pieces from some small animal), and fragments of burnt wood, were scattered from top to bottom in the grave. From the mound, and chiefly at its base within the area of our excavation, were taken seventy-seven flint flakes, one barbed arrow-head, three knives from 2 to 3½ inches in length, one large slingstone, four irregularly-formed discs, partly chipped round the edges; all of Yorkshire flint. Of foreign flint there were thirteen chips, a portion of a leaf-shaped arrow-head, and eight partly-rounded discs chipped more or less on the edges. We also found a piece of a polished stone celt, several fragments of four drinking-cups and one piece of a large urn, as well as the molar tooth of a horse, eight teeth of an ox, and sixty-eight pieces of bones of large animals, also a few from a very small animal.

At the base of the barrow there were impressions of stumps of · brushwood which had grown on the old land surface. These were observed to rise from 6 to 12 inches into the mound, while cavities, left by the roots, branched downwards.

Presumably the extended skeleton is the primary interment, and the profusion of animal bones would seem to indicate much feasting. The large number of worked flints and potsherds scattered in and around the grave also suggest a large gathering of kinsfolk on the occasion of paying the last token of respect at the grave of their departed friend, and of raising so large a mound to perpetuate his memory—

"That the princely obsequies might be performed
According to his high degree."—DRYDEN.

---

* A similarly-shaped instrument was obtained from a grave in barrow No. C. 62 (group XI), but was made from a human femur. It was also found in a similar situation away from any interment, as if accidently or purposely dropped over the interment.

BARROW No. 38

Is the most easterly in this group, and is partly covered on the western side by the outer and eastern rampart of an extensive system of British entrenchments, forming a complete oppidum with several branches (fig. 409).

On August 7th, 1865, it measured 46 feet in diameter and 4 feet in elevation. A trench was cut in the south side of the mound, in a direction east and west, which clearly showed the rubbly chalk grit, thrown from the entrenchments, to cover the western side of the stoneless mass of soil and clay which formed the barrow, to a thickness of 18 inches as shown by fig. 409 *a*. During this excavation part of the rib of an ox, a piece of the leg-bone of a smaller animal, six slingstones having many jagged edges (fig. 410), made from local flint, were found, and near the apex of the mound fragments of four kinds of pottery, some glazed and others unglazed, probably of mediæval age.

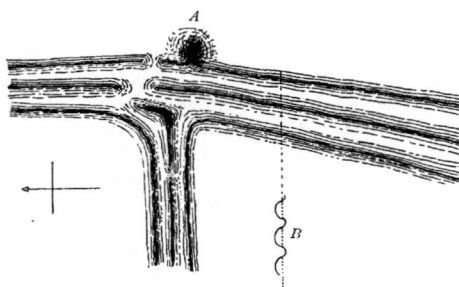

FIG. 409.—BARROW No. 38 (A) AND ADJOINING EARTHWORKS.
B—Section across Earthworks.

FIG. 409 *a*.
SECTION OF BARROW No. 38 AND EARTHWORKS.

On August 11th, a second trench was made over the centre of the mound, parallel with the first. It extended 12 feet east and west and 8 feet across. Here also the rubbly chalk from the old entrenchments was well shown overlying the western side of the barrow. It was noticed that the eastern side of the barrow, as far as the centre, had been previously excavated—probably by the late James Silburn, of Pocklington, who during 1851 or 1852 opened several barrows in the neighbourhood. Near the centre of the mound, in the area disturbed by the former explorers, and about 2 feet from the apex, two teeth of a horse (?), and teeth of an ox and a goat or sheep were taken. At the base was a quantity of wood ashes, from which a small disc of black flint, many hand struck splinters, mainly of black flint, and pieces of two vases were obtained. From the mound two other large slingstones and two splinters of local flint, six worked lumps, pieces of doubtful use, and many splinters of dark-coloured foreign flint, were secured.

The ground under the excavation was probed, but no interment could be found, neither was there anything to show that the previous explorers had been more successful.

BARROW No. 275

Is by far the largest of the three last named barrows, and is a fine example of the labour bestowed in the memory of the dead. A thick covering of large fir trees had previously deterred us from opening it.

From July 27th to August 15th, 1892, under the direction of Sir Tatton Sykes, Bart., who generously defrayed the expenses, the trees were cut down, and the writer opened the mound. It measured 90 feet in diameter and 13 feet in elevation, and must have been originally 3 or 4 feet higher, as its apex was considerably flattened and guttered by rabbit diggers and by the tenants of the farm, who at various times had buried their dead cattle on it. It was also observed that a filled-in trench, 120 feet in diameter encircled the barrow. This measured 9½ feet in width at the top, 3 feet at the bottom, and 4 feet in depth. A

FIG. 410 b.—SECTION OF BARROW No. 275.
A.—Chalk rubble.   B—Clay.   C—Local soil.

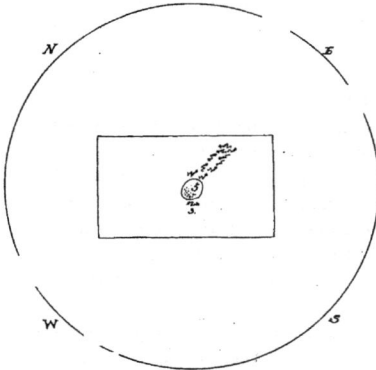

trench was made through the centre of the mound, 40 feet by 24½ feet, as shown on the plan (fig. 410 a).

About 9 feet south-south-east of the centre, and 4½ feet from the top of the mound, were the burnt bones of an adult body (No. 1 in the section, fig. 410 b).

FIG. 410 a.—PLAN OF BARROW No. 275.

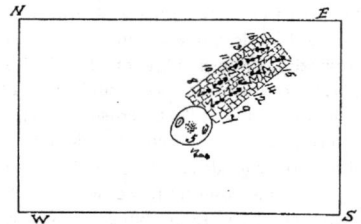

ENLARGED PLAN OF EXCAVATION IN BARROW 275.

No relic was found with them. At 13 feet east of the centre, and only six inches from the apex of the mound, was most of the upper portion of a large cinerary urn, shown at "a" in the section. It had been broken up by some former excavators. Near the centre of the mound, at a depth of 5½ feet from the summit, was a small heap of burnt bones of a youth (No. 2 in the section). No relic was found with these, but about 4 feet to the south of them, and 13 inches nearer the summit of the mound, was a barbed arrow-head of flint (fig. 410 c). At the base of the barrow, 6 feet south-west from the centre, was an adult skeleton (No. 3 on the plan, fig. 410 a), on the right side, the knees much pulled up, hands to the

x

face, and the skull pointing south-east.   A femur, tibia, and humerus measured
18 inches, 14¾ inches, and 12¼ inches respectively.   About 4 feet east of the
centre, and 2 feet above the base of the barrow, was the lower half of an adult
skeleton, (No. 4 in the section), consisting of the hips, doubled-up legs, and the
lumbar vertebræ.   The upper portion of this skeleton was absent, and to all
appearances had never been interred.   Under the centre of the barrow, a little
east of interment No. 3, was an oval grave 4½ feet in depth, and measuring 5 feet
by 4 feet at the bottom.   In the centre of this, between two large flint stones,
was a small heap of the cremated bones of an adult (interment No. 5).   We
were disappointed at finding that no relics accompanied this primary interment
under such a large mound.*   In the soily matter filling the grave were dispersed
the following detached unburnt human and animal bones:—human adult bones—one
piece of a pelvis, the head of a humerus, one heel-bone, ten short pieces of leg-
bone, two left halves of lower jaws of young persons with teeth very little worn,
fifteen pieces of skulls, three pieces of an arm-bone, two vertebræ, one kneecap,
ten portions of ribs, six fragments of fibulæ, and five bones of the hand ; children's
bones—one femur, three pieces of a skull, and a few other pieces ; animal bones—
six pieces of the antler of a red deer, one root-end of the horn of a roebuck,
and a vertebra of probably the same animal.   There were also eight small pieces
of a vase.†
     A little south-west of the grave, on the same level as body No. 4, were the
decayed remains of a child (No. 6 in the section), with its head to the south.   At
the base of the barrow, almost touching the east end of the grave, was an adult
skeleton (No. 7), on its right side, legs doubled up, hands to the face, and the
head to the east.   This and nine other adult skeletons were placed on a pavement
of flat Liassic stones, from 1 to 2½ feet in length.   These stones had been brought
from the western edge of the Wolds, a distance of not less than two miles, and
placed on the old land surface.   They covered an area measuring 12 feet east
and west, and 3 feet across, as shown on the plan.   In consequence of the 10
interments having been so closely placed together, and in several instances the
limbs of one dovetailing with those of another, and from their greatly-crushed
and broken condition, we were unable to sketch their position in detail, or even
measure their long bones.   Nevertheless, their approximate positions on the
pavement are indicated on the plan.   A few pieces of dark-coloured burnt
bones similar to those deposited in the grave were found dispersed here and
there among the 10 skeletons on the pavement.   At the left hip of interment No.
12 was a leaf-shaped arrow-head of flint (fig. 410*j*), with the point towards the
skull ; and close to and partly under the right hip were the crushed remains of
the skull of an infant only a few weeks old.   At the knees of interment No. 15
were delicately made arrow-heads *E* and *F* (fig. 410).   Each end of these is broken
off, as shown in the figures.   It was quite clear that the breakage had occurred
previous to having been placed with the bodies, and probably in compliance

---

* If large mounds indicate the interments of distinguished persons, may it be that the persons in this
barrow had become less superstitious, and less inclined to consign valuable articles to the keeping of the
dead, than the more humble and probably more superstitious persons interred under smaller mounds.
     † This cremated interment closely resembles that in Dog Hill, Sledmere, (No. 277).
     During the afternoon Sir Tatton Sykes, Bart., was present ; also the Rev. E. M. Cole, the Rev.
W. R. Jolley and Mrs. Jolley, Mr. T. Boynton, and the late Dr. H. B. Hewetson.

FIG. 410c.   ⅓

FIG. 410d.   ½

FIG. 406.

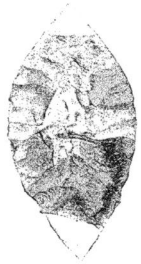

FIG. 410e.   ½

FIG. 413.   ¾

FIG. 414.   ½

FIG. 410f.

with some superstition.* That the cremated bones in the grave were the chief interment can hardly be doubted ; while, from all the appearances, it seemed evident that these, the interment at the south-west edge of the grave, and the ten interments on the pavement of flat stones at the east of the grave, had all been interred at the same time, and previous to raising the inner mound of gritty soil that covered them. The grave had been covered over with wood, and left hollow. In course of time this covering gave way and let down the rubbly chalk into the grave, and the clay above as far as the top of the grave, as shown in the section (fig. 410*b*). From the base of the mound, and in the rubbly material of the inner core, were taken several fragments of animal bones, 3 pieces of an urn, 5 flint scrapers, 1 flake saw, 2 slingstones, and 80 flakes and chips of flint.

BARROW No. C 72

Is seventy yards from the northern margin of the last barrow, and is considerably smaller. Most of the trees having been removed by the wind, it was excavated on October 23rd, 1874, when it was found to have a diameter of 25 feet and an elevation of 1 foot, being one of the smallest barrows we had hitherto opened.

In the centre was an unusually large grave (fig. 411)—possibly originally a pit-dwelling — which measured 16 feet north and south by 5½ feet across, and 2 feet deep. On the floor of this, towards the northern end, was a skeleton, on its left side, with the knees pulled up, the arms doubled with the hands near the face, and the head to the north. A femur measured 17¾ inches, tibia 14½ inches, and were strongly made. At the feet were all the bones of a young pig, with its head also to the north, and legs bent somewhat under the body. Close to this were the decayed skeletons of two small goats or sheep, on their right sides (fig. 411), and with their heads to the north.† Pieces of chalk were piled round the skeletons, forming a shallow oval trough. They all seemed to have been deposited at the same time and with equal care. A little decayed wood was observed under the goats.

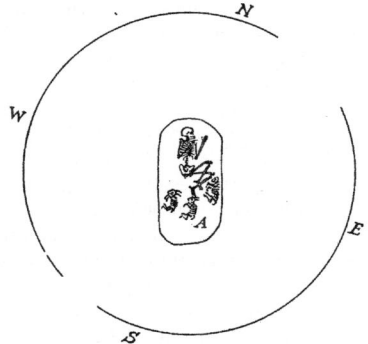

FIG. 411.—SECTION OF BARROW C 72.

The contents of this interesting grave seem to suggest a probably general belief, at that time, that the spirits of the animals would accompany that of their owner to a distant land, and there also administer to his wants and pleasures.

* A similarly broken arrow-head was found with interment " G " at Howe Hill, Duggleby, and in other barrows.

† In a mound at Dane's Graves, near Driffield, Canon Greenwell found two goats accompanying a skeleton in 1865, and in 1898 Canon Greenwell and I found in another of the Danes' graves two pigs and two goats, with a human skeleton, all buried together in a grave. In America the entire skeleton of a bison was found in a tumulus associated with human remains.—See Morehead's " Primitive Man in Ohio."

A few handstruck splinters of black flint and the tibia of a red-deer were taken from the gritty chalk filling the grave, but no tool or instrument accompanied the bodies. It was observed that no foreign clay had been used, either in the grave or the mound.

BARROW No. 13.

On the 22nd of June, 1864, with the assistance of three workmen, the writer opened this barrow. It was conical in form, without any visible trench round it, measuring about 60 feet in diameter, and rising about 5 feet above the surrounding ground. It was found to be mainly composed of layers of clay and loam brought from a distance, mixed with layers of soil procured on the spot.

A commencement was made by sinking a hole 9 feet square into the centre of the barrow. We had only penetrated about a foot below the apex, when, in the centre of the mound, we discovered (No. 1) a large cinerary urn (fig. 412),* inverted over a quantity of very white calcined human bones. No relic of any kind was found with these. About a foot to the west, and 8 or 10 inches lower, was a portion of a second urn (No. 2), standing on its bottom, and also containing a few calcined bones. All the upper parts of this urn had been broken off at some previous time—either when the later or higher interment had been made, or by some person digging for rabbits, as we found fragments of it lying in the mound separated some distance from the base of the vessel. At a depth of nearly 2 feet beneath the urn first discovered were 3 arrows and 2 spear or javelin heads, all of flint (figs. 413, 414, 415, and 416).* Unfortunately one of the workmen fractured three of them with his pick, and a small piece (belonging to fig. 413) could not be found. All these specimens were found together in a dark substance, undoubtedly the residue of organic matter ; and from the centre of this ran to the right and to the left a dark streak of the same nature, each bending in some measure round the mound. As this extended a little more than three feet in length, and was close to the arrow-heads, it was thought that it might mark the remains of the longbow. A flint knife (fig. 417), 3 inches in length, was found on the same level as the arrow and spearheads, at a distance of about 2 feet north-east from them. The excavation was continued as far as the undisturbed ground beneath the barrow, but nothing more was found, excepting a few hand-struck chips and flakes of flint, such as were met with during the whole of the excavation. Some of these may have been casually mingled with the material of which the barrow was composed, previous to and during its construction. On the natural surface under the barrow was a thin coating of wood ashes, and a few scattered ashes as well as some calcined human bones occurred in other parts of the mound. In filling in the excavation, one of the workmen picked up a small conical stud or button (fig. 418) of Kimeridge coal or jet. It has two holes that meet in a groove on its flat side.

The objects discovered in this barrow are worthy of detailed description. The cinerary urn is of reddish earth, burnt black inside. It is 11 inches in height, 9 inches in diameter at the top, and about 4 inches at the bottom. It has a lip or rim, the upper edge of which is ornamented with a row of small impressions.

* These are also figured in "The Reliquary."

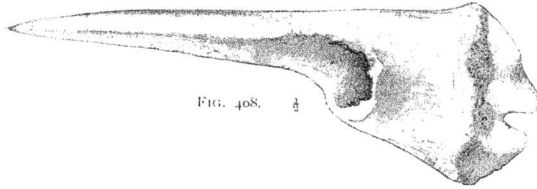

FIG. 408. $\frac{2}{3}$

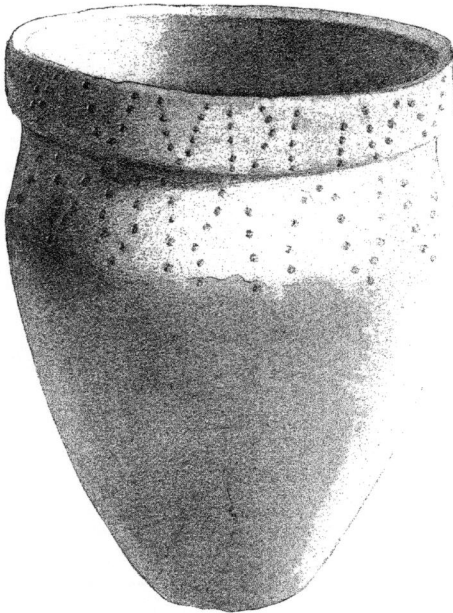

FIG. 412. $\frac{1}{3}$

FIG. 415.

FIG. 416. $\frac{1}{1}$

FIG. 417.

FIG. 418.

Vertical lines of the same kind occur on the outside, and on the neck below the rim there are zigzag lines of similar indentations. The fragments of the second urn show it to have been of a similar kind, and of about the same size. The three arrow-heads—two of which are figured (figs. 415 and 416)—are of a blackish flint, 2 inches and $1\frac{1}{2}$ inches in length respectively. The larger of the two very beautiful spear-heads (fig. 414) is $3\frac{3}{10}$ inches long by an inch broad at the widest part. It also is leaf-shaped and similar in form to the arrow-heads. It has been struck from a block of amber-coloured flint, is nearly transparent, and is most exquisitely chipped on every part of its surface. The smaller spear-head (fig. 413), to which no artist can do full justice, is $2\frac{9}{10}$ inches in length and nearly an inch in breadth at the shoulder. It is similar in shape to its fellow, but less transparent, owing to its having been struck from a block of darker coloured flint. Though hardly possible, this is the more delicate and elaborately finished specimen. The point is almost as sharp as a needle, and the edge on every side is as keen as a knife. In fact it seems impossible that the point and edges could be wrought to such perfection by chipping ; but such has been the work of the hand, there is no indication of grinding. I know of no implement more finely made. This spear-head has two notches in it, one on each side, which may have been chipped out at the time of mounting it on a shaft so as to ensure it being secured more firmly by a thong. Neither of them is thicker than a shilling in any part, nor do they exhibit the least trace of the action of fire ; but, on the contrary, they appear as fresh as on the day on which they were made. These two weapons seem far too delicate for fighting. Finally, I may mention that these beautiful objects, like most others, are not made from the flint of our Yorkshire chalk beds, which is not suitable for small articles. The flint of which they are formed is foreign to the district. Blocks of it, which have been washed out of the beds of drift, are to be met with on the coast.

Re-opening.—This is one of the mounds we opened at the beginning of our barrow researches, and I had for a long time purposed re-examining it.

August 1st, 1892, and the four following days were employed in removing a portion 18 feet square from its centre, and in most carefully searching the earth removed in our former excavation, in the hope of finding the missing piece belonging to fig. 413. In this, however, we were disappointed. Near the east side of the old opening, at about half the height of the barrow, was a dish-shaped hole (No. 1) about 2 feet in diameter and 10 inches in depth. It contained dark matter, in which were many pieces of burnt wood and carbonised stems and twigs of heather, heat-splintered portions of flint, and a very few pieces of burnt bone. To our surprise there was also a small portion apparently of a bronze knife or dagger, and two pieces of a greenish coloured glass—one piece from the neck and the other from the body of a vase.* Such a find is of rare occurrence, and the writer believes that, whatever period the glass belongs to, the deposit is

---

* Pieces of similar glass—both in kind and colour, judging from the description—were found with burnt human bones in a British, or Romano-British, cinerary urn from a cairn at Boscregan, in St. Just; and are thus described by Mr. C. W. Borlase (No. XXI., Journal of the Royal Institute of Cornwall):—"On examining carefully the agglomerated mass of bones and ashes with which it [the urn] was filled, a few rough chippings of flint and a portion of a globular glass vessel was found, $\frac{1}{8}$ of an inch thick, of an olive-greenish hue when held up to the light, but the surface was covered with a bluish-black coating of iridescent appearance." The Calais Wold specimens have almost exactly the same appearances.

of the same age.   These pieces of glass were found by the writer in separate places in the midst of the black matter, in which they must have been placed at the time of the deposit.   About one foot lower, slightly to the east, was a second deposit of black matter, very similar to the first, except that there was no glass. These two secondary interments were remarkable for the small amount of burnt bone, and seemed to have been inserted at the same time, and the extent of the incision in the mound for their reception was visible.

Close to the north side of our former opening, on a bed of loamy clay, about 3 inches in thickness and covering a little more than a square yard of the old land surface, was a jet necklace (fig. 418 a).*   It consisted of two triangular pieces $1\frac{1}{4}$ inches long, 10 circular conical-shaped studs (one of which is damaged), 2 long oval-shaped studs, 35 cylindrical-shaped beads more or less bulging in the middle (barrel-shaped), 1 tube-like bead, and 573 thin wheel-shaped discs, measuring from $\frac{1}{8}$ of an inch to $\frac{1}{4}$ of an inch in diameter ; in all, 623 beads.†   The two triangular beads are ornamented on one side with lines of small punctures produced by a fine pointed drill, leaving minute dish-shaped cavities.   The wheel-shaped discs seemed to have been produced by cutting the long cylindrical beads into thin pieces.   The beads occurred on a film of dark matter, and—though there was no trace of bone—their position seemed to favour the idea that they had been placed round the neck of a body, the primary interment, which had entirely decayed.

We carefully trenched the ground under the area of the excavation, but could not find a grave.   From the mound were taken 98 flakes, 4 slingstones, and half of a fine flint knife ground on one edge, and one very fine large hand weapon with many sharply jagged edges, the size of a man's fist‡—all of flint.

BARROW No. 103.

This barrow measures 54 feet in diameter and 1 foot above the adjoining ground, but is ˙not shown on the Ordnance Map.   A portion 16 feet square was cut from the centre, and consisted principally of bluish foreign clay.   We noticed that the barrow partly stood upon a small patch of well-rounded boulders of flint and chalk, similar patches of which are frequently observed in shallow depressions on the surface in the neighbouring fields.   In the centre was a dish-shaped excavation measuring 2 feet 10 inches over the top, and 1 foot 9 inches deep, containing burnt wood and the calcined bones of apparently a young person, in the midst of which stood a food-vase of the cinerary urn type (fig. 419).   This is 9 inches high, $6\frac{3}{4}$ inches across the top, $3\frac{1}{2}$ inches across the bottom, and is externally ornamented with punctures in two nearly vertical lines running round the border.

About 9 feet west of the centre was a second cavity of a similar form, but only 1 foot 10 inches in diameter and 6 inches deep.   This also contained wood ashes, in the midst of which was a crushed food-vase, past repair.   There were no traces of cremated bones.

---

* This is only a conjectural arrangement of the beads.

† This splendid necklace is in the possession of Sir Tatton Sykes, Bart., of Sledmere; he having very kindly defrayed the expense of opening barrow No. 275 and the re-opening of this barrow.

‡ This form of weapon was freely used at the siege of Troy (Homer's " Iliad ").

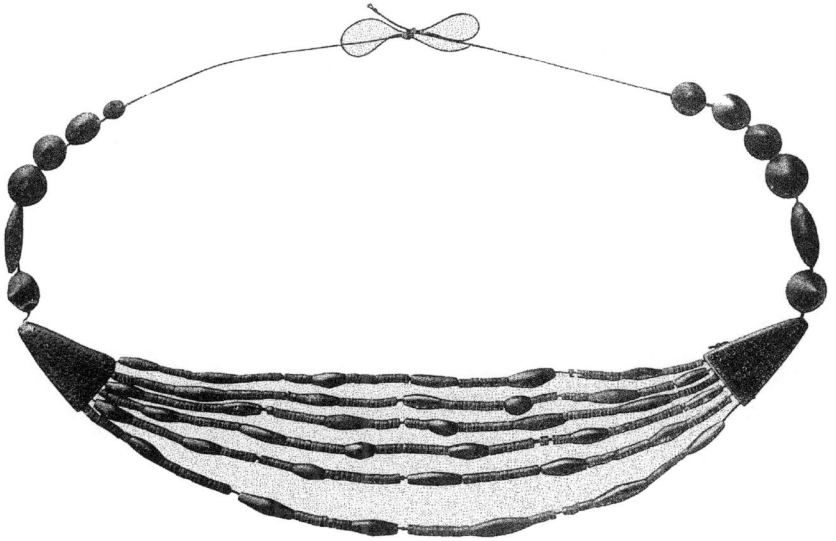

FIG. 418a.   ½

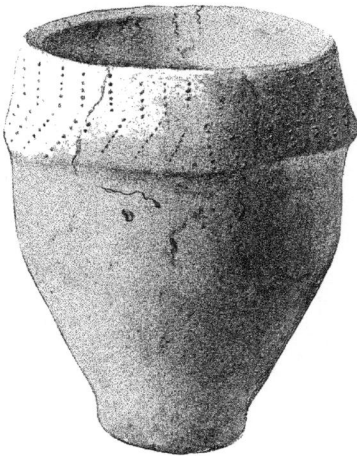

FIG. 420.

FIG. 419.

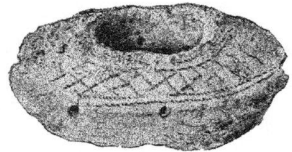

FIG. 421.   ½

BARROW No. 105.

Opened on September 20th, 1867. The tilling of the land had lowered this barrow to within 8 inches of the plane of the surrounding ground. Near its centre, and slightly below the surface, were a few burnt bones, apparently of a small person, accompanied by burnt wood and the bottom of an urn. The upper part of this vessel and the greater part of the incinerated remains had been removed by the plough. Nearly 11 feet south-eastwards from this was an oval excavation scooped into the ground under the barrow, and measuring at the top 4 feet by 3 feet, and 1 foot deep in the centre. Its sides were burnt red, and its contents were dark soil, burnt wood, and two rough pieces of freestone (Calcareous grit), showing traces of fire ; these fell to pieces on being moved. During the excavation two pieces of a large urn, ten flakes of foreign flint, and one large flake of native flint, were taken from various parts of the barrow.

BARROW No. 15.

On the 15th of July, 1864, the writer, with three assistants, opened this barrow. It had an altitude of 5 feet and a circumference of 65 yards. An opening 12 feet square was made in the centre down to the ancient turf line, in which, and near the centre of the barrow, were two circular pits about 1 foot deep, 3 feet in diameter, and 3 feet apart, each containing burnt wood and calcined bones. That to the south contained also the bottom part of a cinerary urn and an irregularly-shaped disc of flint (fig. 420), chipped about half way round its edge, and much burnt. It is probable that we had, without observing it, destroyed the upper portion of the urn during the excavation, as its rotten condition so much resembled the soil which covered it.

At the bottom of the urn, in the midst of the burnt bones, was an incense-cup (fig. 421). It is elliptical in form, $1\frac{3}{4}$ inches high ; its respective diameters being, at the base, 2 inches and $2\frac{1}{2}$ inches ; at the belly, 4 inches by $3\frac{1}{4}$ inches ; and at its contracted mouth, $1\frac{5}{8}$ inches by $1\frac{3}{4}$ inches. It shows marks of intense heat, which has given it a vitreous, cinder-like appearance. Round its greater diameter are nine perforations about a fifth of an inch in diameter, arranged at nearly equal distances ; close above these are two parallel rope-like markings, and just below the mouth a pair of similar lines encircle it, while the space between the two sets of encircling lines is filled in with chevron pattern, apparently impressed by the same tool.

The pit to the north was also carefully emptied, and we noticed among the burnt bones small carbonized shreds of woven cloth of a coarse and strong texture, which probably had been burnt to tinder at the time of cremation. The sides of the two pits were burnt red to a depth of two or three inches, showing that the calcined bones and wood ashes had been deposited while in a highly heated condition.

Throughout the excavation clay from a distance was found in abundance, mixed more or less with soil such as is now procurable from the neighbouring sub-soil, which, at the time of the raising of the mound, might have been obtainable on the surface. Only four flint chips and one leaf-shaped arrow-head were picked from the mound.

Re-opening.—During the second week in August, 1892, while engaged in opening the adjoining large barrow (No. 275), we re-opened this mound by removing an area of 20 feet square from its centre, and trenching the ground beneath to the rock in the hopes of finding a grave, which it was thought might have been passed over at the former opening. In this, however, we were dis-appointed; no further interment could be found. During the excavation one fine barbed arrow-head, one well-formed circular disc of jet-black flint 2¼ inches in diameter, one oval disc, one boring tool, two knives, and eleven flakes, one very finely serrated on one edge—all of foreign flint, were found in the barrow.

BARROW No. 86

Stands out prominently on the brow of the hill close to the north of Stone Dale. On April 1st and 3rd, 1867, it measured 2 feet 10 inches high and 60 feet in diameter, and seemed to have been much lowered and dispersed by the plough. A clear opening of 20 feet square was made to the ancient turf line, and afterwards considerably extended northwards and westwards. The barrow consisted for the most part of unbroken beds and patches of loamy clay, sparingly mixed with surface soil of various colours, dark predominating on the north and west sides, probably on account of its having been obtained from the dark Kimeridge clay which comes to the surface at the bottom of Bradeham Dale—a little to the north of the barrow. A most careful search was made under the mound within the limits of the excavation, by trenching the whole of the area into the rock below, without finding the slightest trace of an interment. During the search we picked up of foreign flint 17 splinters and 4 oval discs chipped round their edges; of native flint 8 splinters and a keen-edged flake knife (fig. 422) 4⅜ inches long, 1¼ inches broad, and ⅜-inch thick at the back, much resembling the blade of a modern English razor in shape; a portion of a polished celt, and many small potsherds. These were chiefly from the base of the barrow, where wood ashes were rather abundant.

BARROW No. 96

Is situated in the angle of some ancient entrenchments, on the western side of which a Roman road is also marked on the Ordnance maps. Extensive entrenchments and probably a Roman road also ran past this barrow east and west. On May 23rd, 1867, it only measured 24 feet in diameter, with an altitude scarcely perceptible, though at the time of the survey it had been sufficiently prominent to be placed on the map. At a distance of 7 feet south-east of the centre was a food-vase, a portion of the top of which had been carried away, probably by the plough. This vase (fig. 423) is very graceful in outline and nicely ornamented. It measured 5 inches in height and about 4 inches in diameter. Not a trace of burnt or unburnt bone accompanied it; but about 2 feet to the north and on the same plane, was a small flint tool pointed at one end. At the centre of the mound was a dish-shaped hole in the old surface line, 1½ feet in diameter and 7 inches deep, containing wood ashes and a few burnt bones, accompanied by a small pointed instrument of flint; whilst 8 feet north of the centre was an oval grave measuring 2½ feet east and

Fig. 422.   ¼

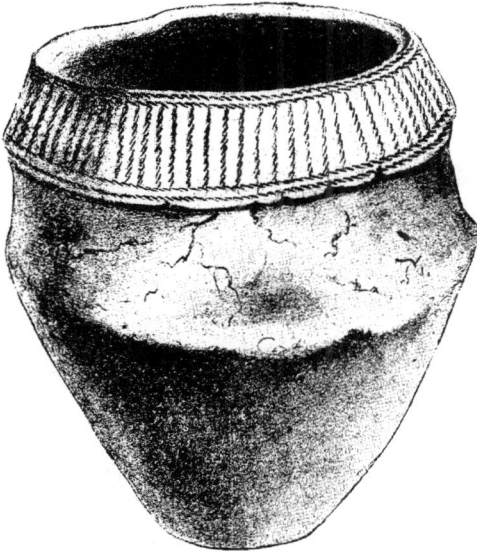

Fig. 427.   1

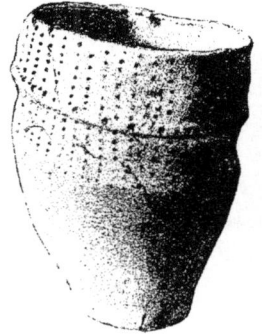

Fig 424   ¼

Fig. 426.   ¼

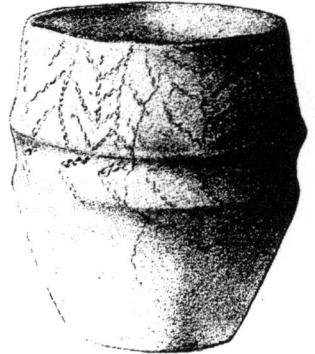

Fig. 423.   ½

west, 1 foot 4 inches across, and 1½ feet deep. All that remained in this small grave were the decayed remains of the inhumed body of a child. Some years previous to the opening of this barrow we had noticed that it had a trench round it.

BARROW No. 114

Is situated about half a mile nearly south of No. 96, partly in the York road and partly in a small clump of fir trees adjoining the north side of the road. Originally it had been circular in form, with a diameter of about 56 feet, but at some later period a considerable portion of the southern side had been removed. At the time of our opening (May 23rd, 1868, and four following days), its central elevation was 4 feet. The ground where the removed portion had been was tested, and we afterwards turned over most of the remaining mound, trenching the ground beneath as we proceeded, as far as a hedge which crossed the northern side. At the base of the mound, rather south-east of the centre, were two greatly crushed cinerary urns (figs. 424 and 425), which had stood on their bottoms in a line north and south, and nearly together. After re-building they measured respectively 18½ and and 14¼ inches in height, and 16¾ and 13½ inches across the shoulders. With the cremated bones in the southerly one were nine jet and Kimeridge coal beads (fig. 426), more or less globular in form, and varying from ¼ to ½ inch in diameter; and two small beads, seemingly made of a kind of vitreous paste, or altered by heat. These latter are the only ones of the kind found by us with British remains. The jet beads show no trace of fire. The bones from the most northerly urn are also those of an adult, but no relic accompanied them.

At the east of the centre, about 1 foot above the base of the mound, were traces of an adult skeleton of large size, doubled up, on its right side, with head within twenty-four inches of the last-named urn. About four feet to the north of this interment were traces of a second skeleton, also of large size and flexed, lying on the same horizon as the first. Though these two skeletons were in the last state of decay, and of great antiquity, I was persuaded, from their resting on 12 inches of the clayey and undisturbed lower portion of the mound, whilst above them was mixed up clay and earth—the certain indications of disturbance—that their interment was posterior to the urn burials and the erection of the barrow, and were probably Anglo-Saxon. Except a few hand-struck splinters of flint picked up from the mound, nothing more was found.

BARROW No. "C 70"

Is situated a little east of "Cot Nab," on the east side of a long plantation, the cutting down of which in the spring of 1874, enabled us to open this and other barrows. On June 18th and 19th, 1874, it measured 31 feet in diameter and 2 feet in elevation. About 6 inches from its base, and 9 feet from the centre, we took an irregular shaped food vase (fig. 427) of the cinerary urn type. About the centre of the mound, and over the middle of a large grave, was the lower half of a large cinerary urn. The upper part had been removed by surface disturbance. This urn contained the burnt bones of an adult, at the top of which was the bronze blade of a two-edged knife (fig. 428) and a small incense-cup (fig. 429). At the base of the mound were the decayed flexed remains of an adult, with the head to the west. The legs were at the north-east edge of the grave, while the trunk reached over the top, and, owing to the settling of the contents of the grave, it had broken from the legs and had been carried down fully 8 inches. We were unable to measure any of the bones and nothing accompanied them. In the centre of the grave, at a depth of three feet, was interment No. 2, on the right side, head to the east, the knees pulled up, the left arm over the abdomen, right arm doubled back with the hand under the face. The crumbled remains of a food-vase were found near the face, and a small lump of black flint (fig. 428 a) had been placed in front of the skull. Measurements of the long bones could not be taken. At a depth of 5½ feet the floor of the grave was reached, in the centre of which was the primary interment (No. 3) on its back, both hands on the right shoulder, the knees pulled up, and pressed to the south, and the head to the east end of the grave. The femora measured 17¾ inches each, the tibiæ 14¾ inches each in extreme length, and the humeri 13 inches each. The bones are those of a person of middle age. No relic accompanied them. The grave was elliptical in form, measuring 9 feet east and west and 4 feet across, and was filled with chalk and a mixture of soily matter.

BARROWS B. and C.

Each of these barrows measures from 60 to 70 feet in diameter and 5 to 6 feet in elevation, and are situated in the grass field adjoining the west end of Stonechair Close.

They occupy the centres of two small clumps of fir trees, which have so far deterred us from opening them.

"DETACHED BARROWS," &c.

BARROW No. B 2.

Opened August 3rd and 4th, 1871. This barrow is small, about half a mile from group VIII, and is partly crossed by the high road from Malton to Pocklington, near to the end of the lane leading down to Millington, and is not shown on the Ordnance map. It consisted of foreign loamy clay, but no interment was found, and during our two days' labour we only picked up three scrapers of flint and ten flakes. Probably this mound had been opened by the late James Silburn, as he opened a larger barrow by the side of the road a little nearer to Pocklington, in 1852.

ROMANO-BRITISH REMAINS.

Adjoining Group VIII, Romano-British remains have also been found. At the south-western margin of the Chalk Wolds, and about half a mile west of the village of Millington, and close to the north side of Swineridge Lane, two skeletons were discovered about the year 1858 in a small chalkpit, and between then and 1868, three more had been discovered. They extended over the pit in a line north and south, doubled up in small graves, in some places two abreast, about

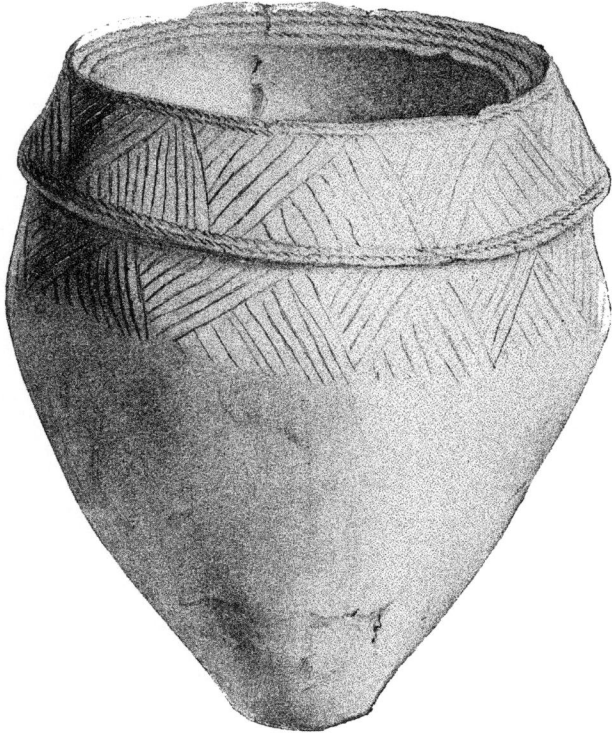

Fig. 425.　¼

Fig. 428.　¼

Fig. 428a.

Fig. 429.　½

three feet deep, and with their heads to the north. It was said that two vases were found with the first-discovered bodies. One of these (fig. 430) was given to me by the late Dr. Wilson of Pocklington. It is of a common Roman type, of a dark colour externally, measuring 4½ inches in height, 2½ inches in diameter, at the mouth, 3¾ inches across the shoulders, and 2 inches at the bottom. A hole in the side of the vase has been repaired with a plug of pewter or lead.

During the early part of 1869 we were informed of these discoveries, and obtained permission to search for more. On May 26th, during a most drenching rain which set in on our arrival on the spot, we explored two grave-like holes about three feet deep, one on the western and the other at the eastern edge of the chalkpit, but without finding any trace of an interment.

On May 29th we continued our search, and close to the southern margin of the pit found a skeleton (No. 6)* lying on the left side in an oval grave, 3½ feet by 2½ feet, and 1 foot 9 inches in depth. The knees were pulled up, the right hand brought up to the chin, the left hand on the pelvis, and the head to the north. A femur and tibia measured 16 and 13 inches respectively. Close to the west side of this skeleton were the crushed remains of a child (No. 6a), placed in a similar shallow grave, and—as far as could be made out—it appeared to be also doubled up.

On May 31st we made further search, and about 1½ feet south of No. 6 we found interment No. 7, partly on its back and partly on its left side, the knees pulled up, the right hand on the knees and the left under the head, which pointed to the north. A femur and tibia measured 19 and 15 inches respectively. The skull is of fine proportions, and seems to have belonged to a male of 25 or 30 years of age, who had been of tall stature and fine features. About 16 inches from the west side of No. 7 occurred interment No. 8, in a posture identical with that of the preceding, excepting that the knees were a little less pulled up to the trunk, and that the right arm was placed over the chest with the hand close to the left elbow. The femur and tibia measured 18 and 15 inches respectively. Close to the north of the last-named interment was another (No. 9) in a posture very similar to that of No. 7, excepting that the knees were less pulled up to the trunk. A femur measured 17½ inches and tibia 14 inches, and are apparently those of a very old woman.

It was worthy of note, firstly, that not one of the skeletons we examined was accompanied by any relic; secondly, that they all were buried with their heads to the north, their knees mainly pressed over to the east, and in oval graves just sufficiently large to admit the crumpled up body ; and, thirdly, none were more than 18 inches to 2 feet beneath the tilled surface.

No trace of a mound was observed over any of these interments, though the name of the place, "Swineridge Lane," is suggestive of the former existence of a bank or ridge of earth, somewhere near, if not on the site of, these burials.

I am informed that in working the pit at various times between 1869 and 1886, skeletons have been found, but no further pottery.

These interments are strikingly similar to those discovered in the Bessingdale Cemetery, and described in Group X.

* These numbers are retained, as I possess the parcels containing the bones, which are marked by the same numbers.

No. IX.—THE RIGGS GROUP.

This group contains fourteen barrows, nine of which are shown on the Ordnance maps. The barrows extend over a distance of two miles from north to south.

BARROW No. C. 49

Is known by the old inhabitants as the Rubbing House Hill, from a building which stood near it, which, up to about 1730, belonged to the adjacent racing stables of Raisthorpe. It is the most northerly in the group and is not shown on

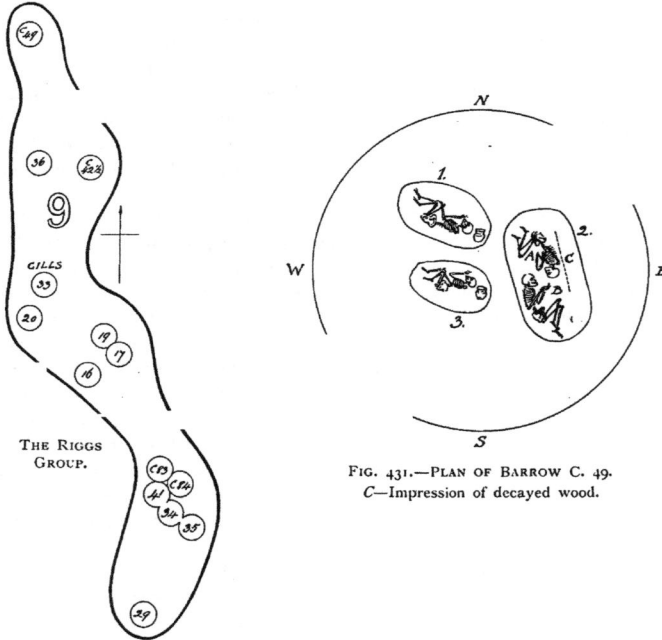

THE RIGGS
GROUP.

FIG. 431.—PLAN OF BARROW C. 49.
C—Impression of decayed wood.

the Ordnance Map, though nearly 4 feet in elevation. During the third week in July, 1872, a cut 18 feet wide was made from the northern to the southern margin. At a point 8 feet north of the centre was a grave, sunk into the chalk rock to a depth of 1 foot 4 inches. At the bottom were the decayed remains of a youth (No. 1 on the plan—fig. 431), accompanied by a crushed food vase (fig. 432) placed close to the front of the skull. On approaching the centre of the barrow we touched the end of grave No. 2, which measured 8 feet by 5 feet, and was 2 feet deep. At the bottom of this was a layer of clay about 4 inches in thickness, on which rested two decayed skeletons marked A and B on the plan, and above them the grave was filled with clay. There was no doubt that the

FIG. 430   ½

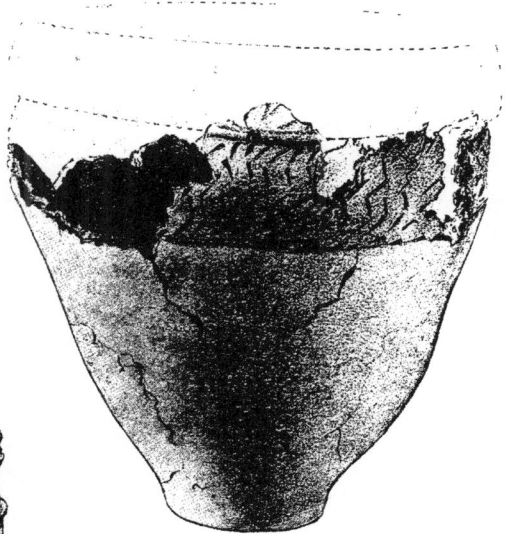

FIG. 433.   ¼

FIG. 434.   ½

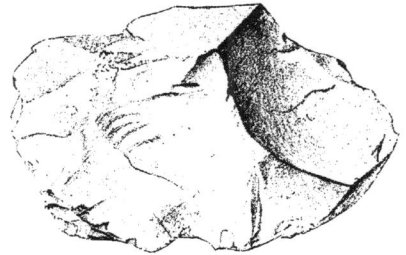

FIG. 435.

FIG. 432.

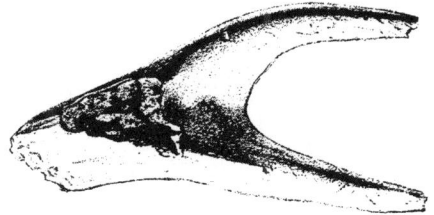

FIG. 434a.   ¼

two bodies had been interred at the same time, as there was no break in the beds above.

Distinct traces of a piece of wood, 2½ feet long and 2 to 3 inches in breadth, were observed at the east side of grave No. 2 and near the two bodies.

Five feet to the west of grave No. 2 and 2½ feet from the centre of the mound, was a third grave, of the same oval form as the two preceding, measuring 7 feet by 4 feet, and 1½ feet deep. On the floor of this were the almost disintegrated remains of a middle-aged person, in the position shown by No. 3 on the plan, accompanied by portions of an irreparably-crushed food-vase. Splinters of flint were picked up from the material filling each of the graves.

All three interments had apparently been completed previous to the raising of the mound, as there was not the slightest trace of the laminated beds in the barrow having been disturbed.

From the mound were taken thirty splinters of black flint, and four pieces of the bottom of a large cinerary urn (fig. 433).

BARROW No. 36

Is in the second field due north of Gill's Farm, and on the 6in. Ordnance map is shown a little below the first letter in "Cowdale."

Opened July 5th-7th, 1865.—Its diameter was then 60 feet and its elevation 12 inches, as measured from the apex to the old surface beneath the mound, which however, itself stood from 10 to 12 inches above the land surrounding the mound. A square of 13 feet—afterwards enlarged to 18 feet—was cut from the centre in a westerly direction. A few feet north of the centre, and only a few inches below the mound, was interment No. 1, on the right side, the legs and arms bent upwards and the head pointing west. Near the front of the skull was a small food-vase (fig. 434), tastefully ornamented with rope impressions, and containing soil only. The body at the time of interment had been placed in a very shallow grave, apparently on a bed of some vegetable substance, traces of which remained.

A few inches above the knees was a small heap of the burnt bones of a child, or very young person. Pieces of burnt wood accompanied the interment, and an impure clay encased the body and calcined bones. The femur of the inhumed body measured 17 inches, and the distance from the crown of the head to the socket of the pelvis was 2 feet 7 inches.

A little to the south of the centre, at the base of the barrow, numerous detached human bones were strewed about, and in one place a thigh and a leg bone were stuck nearly vertically downward below the base of the mound. On the old surface line, 5 feet westward from these, and placed in the same careless manner, were a detached skull (No. 2B) minus the lower jaw, and a few small bones. Round about were other human bones. We dug downwards and continued to find detached human bones. At a depth of about a foot below the surface, the tip-end of a stag's antler (fig. 434 a), cut and scratched, and a jagged edged disc-formed slingstone of local flint, nearly 3 inches in diameter (fig. 435) were picked up. Not more than 10 inches below these were the remains of an adult body (marked C), partly on its right side, with the head pointing east, the hands brought up to the face, and the knees almost in contact with the elbows.

judging from the position of the vertebral column and the ribs, this had originally been placed on its back, with the limbs drawn up and pressed over to the right side. The head also leaned to the right. On the north side of the skull was a small, well-formed food-vase, much crushed. This has since been re-built, (fig. 436). The femur and tibia measured 17 and 15 inches respectively; and from the crown of the head to the cup of the pelvis measured 2 feet 7 inches.

Under this interment was the terminal branch of the antler of a red deer, and a little lower were the remains of a young person (*D*), on the right side, with the head to the east, and the limbs in the same bent position as those of the interment above. The skull being thin, was very much crushed, as was also a food-vase (fig. 437), which stood to the north of the skull. The whole exterior of this vase is tastefully decorated with vertical zig-zag lines of broad rope impressions. The skeleton from the socket of the pelvis to the top of the head measured 2 feet 6½ inches, and the femur and tibia measured 16 and 14 inches respectively.

The remaining earth, containing many detached human bones, was carefully removed from the grave, on the following day under the direction of my brother, and at a depth of 4½ feet from the base of the mound was a third skeleton (*E*) on the hard chalk floor of the grave, on its left side, with its head to the east but facing south. The legs had been brought close to the trunk, and the hands placed in contact with the head. The femur measured 18 inches. At the south side of the skull was the bottom of a small vase, the remainder of which had so far decayed as to be undistinguishable from the soil. Near the vase was a small spoon-shaped scraper of native flint (fig. 438).

The grave, after being cleared out, was found to be circular, with a diameter of 5 feet and a depth of 4½ feet.

During the excavation we picked up from the base of the barrow a small grey flint, and two splinters, portions of the rims of two drinking cups (?), one finely marked with the impressions of a serrated tool, the other ornamented with thumb nail impressions; and portions of a jaw of a small goat or sheep, with three teeth. Two teeth of the same animal were also found in other places, as well as a splinter from the shank-bone of a larger animal, carbonized wood, and pieces of gritstone— apparently freshly broken—which may be the fragments of some tool.

BARROW "C. 42 a."

Opened July 13th, 1871, and the three following days. It measured 18 yards in diameter and 2½ feet in elevation, and was entirely composed of earth taken from the surrounding land.

A little south of the centre, and at the base of the mound, was a large cinerary urn, inverted over the calcined bones of a youth. About two yards to the west of this was a beautifully-formed flint knife (fig. 439) measuring 2⅛ inches long, $\frac{11}{16}$ of an inch broad, double-edged and finely serrated. About three feet from the urn, and near the centre of the mound, was a grave measuring 7½ feet north and south, by 5 feet, and 3 feet in depth. At its northern edge was a crushed food-vase, now rebuilt (fig. 440), rather tall in form, and much resembling fig. 450, barrow No. 34. The upper portion is ornamented with three rows of short lines of rope impressions, two rows leaning to the right and one to the left. Below these are two rows of small impressions apparently given by the end of a knotted cord.

FIG. 436.　⅓

FIG. 437.　⅓

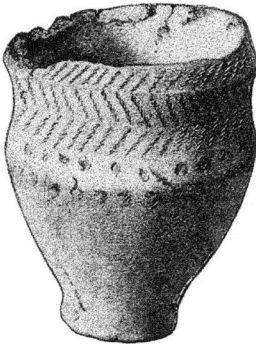

FIG. 440.　⅓

FIG. 443.　⅓

FIG. 438.　½

FIG. 439.　½

FIG. 442.　⅓

In the grave, at a depth of 2 feet, were the decayed remains of a slender person—probably a female—on the left side, the knees pulled up, the left arm bent back, with the hand on the shoulder; the right arm placed over the body; the head pointed a little to the west of north. The femur measured 16 inches. On the floor of the grave, a foot below the last interment, were the remains of a large male, on his back with head to the south, both hands to the pelvis, and legs pulled up to nearly a right-angle with the body. The femur measured 19 inches. At the right shoulder, and in several places under the interment, were impressions of decayed wood, but no relic accompanied either burial.

A boat-shaped block of earth, of the same texture as that which formed the mound above, occupied the centre of the grave.

BARROW No. 33.

Not shown on the Ordnance map, is situated in a grass paddock adjoining the front and southern side of Gill's Farm-house.

Opened June 21st, 1865.—The barrow was low and flat, and not more than 20 inches high and 40 feet in diameter. It was surrounded by a circular ditch and low rampart, the outer diameter of the latter being 84 feet, and the inner diameter 60 feet. The width of the ditch was 10 feet, and depth $1\frac{1}{2}$ feet. The ditch had not been excavated for a distance of 6 feet at the south-east side, thus leaving a natural level causeway or passage into the circular enclosure. A square measuring 16 feet each way, was removed from the centre of the mound. A little to the north of the centre, on the original land surface, was the lower portion of a large cinerary urn, containing a few human bones. The upper portion seemed to have been previously removed.

South of the centre, and on the same level, was a small heap of calcined human bones, which seemed to have been unprotected by an urn. A little below the base of the mound, near the centre, was the half of a circular chalk-boulder, 16 inches in diameter. In carefully removing this, it was found that the ground to a considerable depth was exceedingly hard. After repeated strokes with the pick, a piece of burnt bone and portions of a food-vase were brought to light, accompanied by a few calcined bones, placed in a funnel-shaped hole 12 inches deep and about 15 inches wide. Unfortunately the pick had much injured the vase, which was removed in over 50 pieces. It has since been rebuilt (fig. 441), is quite plain, and of a type and texture unusual in British vases. It is only $\frac{3}{16}$ of an inch in thickness, and its exterior has a bright appearance, as if slightly glazed. In colour it much resembles the Roman black ware, but it is not nearly so well baked, and is very different in texture from any Roman earthernware that we possess. Fragments of a similar kind of vessel are often found scattered in the barrows, and probably represent British domestic pottery. No clay from a distance entered into the composition of this barrow.

On the old land surface at the base of the barrow, were seven large sling-stones—sharp, angular, and rugged—eight splinters, one of which might have served to point a spear; 3 oblong scrapers resembling fig. 452, barrow 34, 2 or 3 inches in length, with one end of each rounded by chipping, and the other end showing a conchoidal fracture. All these are of local flint. Of foreign flint six pieces were taken.

Re-opening, Sept. 12th, 1882.—A second opening was made on this date, and very near to where we had previously taken the small vase we discovered a second one (fig. 442), accompanied by a few calcined bones in a dish-shaped hole. With the exception of a dull rough external surface, this much resembled the previous vase (fig. 441) in size, form, colour, absence of ornamentation, and texture. No other relic was found.

BARROW No. 20

Was opened on Sept. 28th and Oct. 3rd, 1864, when the diameter was 75 feet, and height 5 feet 7 inches above the immediately adjoining ground ; although it was only 4½ feet above the old surface line under it.

A square of 14½ feet sides, was cut from the centre, down to the old land surface. On this, near the centre, a grave not more than 10 inches deep had been made, extending through the surface soil to the chalk grit below. In this had been placed the body of a tall man, on the right side, with the legs and arms bent in the usual manner. The head pointed due south, facing east. Close behind the shoulders was a small food-vase (fig. 443).

Immediately above the skull were numerous greasy-sided cavities of various sizes, similar in appearance to smaller ones observed in the food-vase, which were probably caused by the decomposition of some animal substance possibly placed as food for the occupant of the grave below. Some of the sides of these cavities (fig. 444)* were marked by small impressions which might have been left by the decayed grains of wheat or other grain. In no other part of the mound did we find the least trace of these cavities.

No tool or weapon of any kind was found in connection with this interment, but under the skeleton was a thin layer of dark substance, probably remains of some vegetable matter, together with a few ashes from the funeral pyre which had been spread on the bottom of the grave, as we found in it what seemed to be a carbonized branch of heather, as well as a portion of the shell of a hazel-nut, etc. The bones were much decayed. Judging from the teeth—which alone were in good preservation—their owner had apparently reached the age of about fifty. Two slingstones roughly chipped to. about the size of a peach, a hemispherical piece about 2½ inches in diameter, and three large splinters—all of local flint—were found in separate places in the grave. Three nearly circular discs of black flint, measuring from 1 inch to 1¾ inches in diameter, chipped partly round their edges ; and upwards of fifty splinters (some with serrated edges), all of black foreign flint, were found in the mound, as well as fragments of three different vases, portions of one of which are remarkably full of small pieces of crushed flint, which had been mixed with the clay when moulding the vase.

On the north and east margins of the mound we made two small excavations without finding anything except a few splinters of flint and a small piece of an urn. The barrow consisted of red soil and drab-coloured clay brought from a distance, mixed indiscriminately with thin patches of wood ashes and soil burnt red ; and its base was clearly marked by traces of fire on the old surface line.

---

* This is a photograph of a piece taken from one of these cavities.

FIG. 444.

FIG. 441.   ⅓

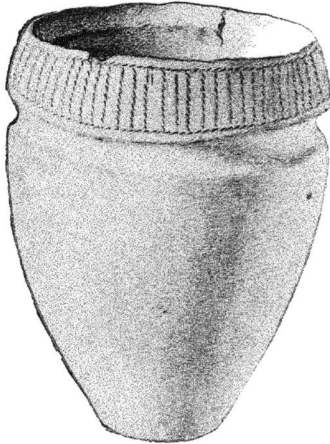

FIG. 446.   ⅓

FIG. 448.

Re-opening, July 13th to 17th, 1874.—On these dates we turned over a portion 18 feet wide from the southern to the northern margin, and tested the ground beneath as we proceeded, but, with the exception of a few worked flints, nothing more was found.

BARROW No. 16

Is one of the smallest of this group. On August 16th, 1864, it had a diameter of 19 feet and an elevation of 18 inches. A square of 10 feet was cut from the barrow, and about the centre was the contracted skeleton of a child, apparently on the old turf line at the base of the mound, on its right side, with its head pointing east. Nearly on a level with this, and about 2 feet to the south, was a link of polished jet (fig. 445),* of unknown use, the size of and somewhat like the handle of a gimlet.

This barrow had been raised over a pipe in the chalk, charged with flinty shingle mixed with a little iron-stained soil, which had become almost as firm as a mass of concrete.

BARROW No. 17

Had a diameter of 74 feet, and an elevation of 4 feet 3 inches from the undisturbed ground beneath it, on August 17th and 19th, 1864, when a square, with 14 feet sides, was carefully removed from the centre. During these two days we nearly reached the base of the barrow, and found a large slingstone or hand weapon with sharp jagged edges ; two small discs chipped on their edges, and four flakes—all, except the large slingstone, of foreign flint.

During August 27th and four following days, the south, east, and west sides of the excavation were deepened, as far as the compact surface line beneath the barrow, without finding anything but a few flakes and fragments of carbonized wood. The portion left in the middle was then carefully removed. Slightly to the south of the centre was a fine food-vase (fig. 446) of the cinerary urn type, standing on a deposit of burnt bones and wood ashes, with the top within 2 feet of the apex of the barrow. It measured 9 inches high, 6½ inches across the top, 7½ inches across the shoulders, and 3 at the bottom. The size and form of this vessel are unusual for a food-vase, for which purpose, however, it had evidently served, as it stood erect on the cinerated bones, and contained nothing but soil and apparently traces of decayed matter of various shades of colour, mixed with small particles of carbonized wood ; and in some places within it were small cavities, probably produced by the decay of some organic substance deposited in the vase. Spread over the mound, close above the vase, was a curved layer of dark matter, shown in fig. 447, consisting of wood ashes and a thin layer of a rather hard, black substance. Immediately below this was a seam of soil, burnt red, which also extended over the mound. Under the vase, and only 6 inches from the base of the barrow, was a second deposit of calcined human bones, shown at c 2 in section, fig. 447. Nothing more was found in the central core ; but a little to the north of the centre an oblong grave was found, which pointed east and west, and was entirely charged with clay and

* We have since found two other similar objects of jet.

a mixture of clay and soil.   This latter filled all the centre portion of the grave
in somewhat depressed layers and was carefully extracted in horizontal sections
about 6 inches in thickness, leaving a coating of clay adhering to the rocky
sides of the grave, giving it the trough-like appearance shown in the section,
fig. 447.   The mixture of soil and clay in the centre was very similar to that
forming the mound above, and a film of dark decayed matter separated it from
a stratum of almost pure clay clinging to the sides of the grave in a very marked
manner.   On the floor, and under the clay, was the flexed body of a young
person 12 to 15 years of age, on its right side, head to the east, and hands to
the face.   The left scapula and two neck vertebrae rested on the middle portion
of one of the femoral bones at a considerable distance from their natural position.
As this interment was 6 feet below the apex of the mound, it seemed difficult
to account for the displacement of these bones, unless it had taken place previous
to or at the time of interment.   The femur measured 11½ inches, and the skull
is large in proportion, and distorted by pressure after burial.   The grave was
22 inches in depth, and measured 6 feet 10 inches by 2 feet 10 inches.

Above the skull, and only a few inches from the top of the grave, was a
small heap of calcined bones, marked c 3 in the section, which, together with
that at the base of the mound a little
to the south of the grave, was apparently contemporaneous with the burial
in the grave, as there was not the
slightest trace of disturbance of the
strata in the mound above.   It seemed
equally clear that at some period after
the barrow had been raised to the height
shown in the section by a dark line, about 2 feet from the apex of the mound, an
incision was made to a depth of nearly 15 inches, in which were placed the burnt
bones (c 1, fig. 447) and the accompanying food-vase (fig. 446).

FIG. 447.—SECTION OF BARROW No. 17.
D—Layer of black and red clay.

The dark line just mentioned passed uninterruptedly over the vase, showing
that the burnt matter of which it was partly composed had been spread over the
top of the mound after the insertion of the vase and the accompanying incinerated
remains, and probably mainly consisted of the scattered ashes of the pyre on
which the body had been cremated.   After the last interment, the barrow had
been considerably enlarged.

Re-opening, July 2nd and 5th, 1872.—On these dates the centre and outskirts
of this barrow were again examined.

Nothing further was found in the grave, but about 20 feet east of the centre,
and ten inches above the base of the mound, was a small food-vase (fig. 448)
of elegant form, with a cover, which, as well as the sides and bottom of the vase,
is externally ornamented with branching lines of well-impressed cord marks.   It
stood alone, and measured 2¾ inches in height, 3¼ inches over the mouth, and
2¼ inches at the bottom.   The top of the cover is pierced horizontally with four
holes, at right angles, and four holes in the mouth of the vase, corresponding
with those in the cover, pass vertically through its lips, probably for securing
the cover to the vase.   A lid is rarely met with in food vases.   Further in
the mound, towards the northern margin, was a small food vase, without a cover,

PLATE LIX.

FIG. 445.   ¼

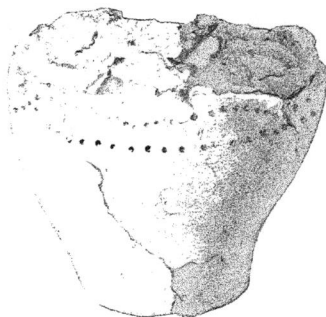

FIG. 449.   ½

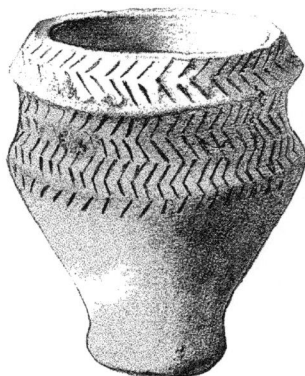

FIG. 450.   ⅓

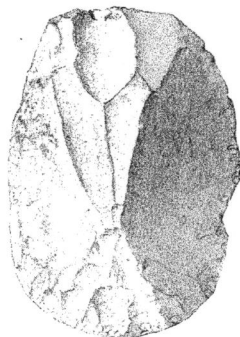

FIG. 452.   ½

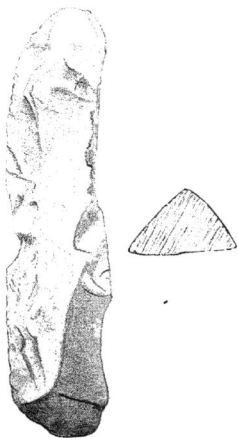

FIG. 451.   ¼

FIG. 453.

and ornamented only by two wavy lines of punctures, each passing round the upper portion of the vase like a string of loose beads. It is shown in fig. 449, with the contained soil. No trace of an interment was observed with cither vase.

A large slingstone with a sharply jagged edge, and various other forms of worked flints were picked up, but no animal bones or potsherds. Much clay from a distance had entered into the composition of this barrow.

BARROW No. 19

Is not shown on the Survey maps. On August 19th, 1864, it had a diameter of 36 feet and an elevation of 1 foot. A little south of the centre were a few calcined bones in a shallow hollow formed by piercing the surface soil to the chalk below. No relic accompanied them.

Near the centre was a grave 5 feet by 4 feet, with its sides and ends cut perpendicularly into the chalk to a depth of 18 inches. It contained nothing but clay mixed with small portions of burnt wood, the interment probably having entirely disappeared.

A small leaf-shaped arrow-head and a small flint scraper, and some rather large pieces of burnt wood, were obtained from the mound.

BARROW No. 34.

Opened June 26th, 28th, and 29th, 1865.—Through the kindness of Mr. Seymour, of York, the owner, and Mr. J. Buttle, the tenant of the land, we were permitted to explore two of a group of five barrows situated on Rigg's Farm, only three of which are shown on the Ordnance map. From long continued cultivation the diameter of this barrow was extended to 60 feet, and its elevation reduced to 20 inches. A square of 13 feet sides was removed as far as the undisturbed ground beneath. Slightly to the east of the centre a workman unfortunately damaged the upper part of an elegantly-formed food-vase of uncommon type (fig. 450), before it was noticed. It contained nothing but earth and stood on its bottom, and was only 5 inches below the surface of the mound and nearly within reach of the plough. It measures 7 inches in height, 5½ inches across the top, 6½ inches about midway, and 3 inches across the bottom. It is decorated with herring-bone markings close outside the mouth, below which is a raised rib, and below this a wide hollow or groove, ornamented with herring-bone markings. Probably an inhumed body once accompanied it, but no trace of this was found.

The excavation was extended eastwards, southwards, and westwards, and the ground below was probed.* From the mound were taken a small piece of the lip of a second vase, one chipping tool nearly 3½ inches long (fig. 451), five slingstones, nearly globular, one fine oblong scraper 2½ inches long, with one end rounded and sharpened by delicate chipping (fig. 452), and three smaller ones; also twenty-five flakes and splinters About half of the specimens are of local flint, the other half being of foreign flint.

* In two places we were tempted to sink three feet below the earth composing the barrow, without discovering anything but two natural cavities in the rock charged with loose iron-stained earth.

Re-opened, Sept. 16th to 19th, 1875. On these dates the whole of this barrow was turned over, with the result of finding one fragment of a British vase and a few splinters of bone and flint only.

BARROW No. 35

Was similar to the last in area, but had been so far reduced in the centre as not to exceed the depth reached by the plough. A portion 17 feet long by 15 feet in width was excavated, and at about 6 feet east of the centre was a dish-shaped hole about a foot below the old surface line. It contained burnt soil and wood ashes, in the midst of which was placed a cinerary urn containing calcined bones, but no relic. The urn, though much crushed has been restored (fig. 453), and measures $10\frac{3}{4}$ inches in height, $9\frac{1}{2}$ inches across the top, $10\frac{3}{4}$ inches at the shoulders, and $5\frac{1}{2}$ inches at the bottom. It is ornamented by two encircling lines near the lip, and $2\frac{1}{2}$ inches below is a second pair. The intervening space is ornamented with lines sloping to the right intersected by similar lines in the opposite direction. Below these is a slight ridge marking the widest part of the urn. No flint flake or potsherd was found.

BARROWS Nos. 41 and C. 83

Were excavated by the Yorkshire Antiquarian Club in 1849, and in 1854 were reported by Mr. W. Procter in the proceedings of the society, from which the following extract is made :—

" The next excavations of the club were made at a farm called Riggs, the property of Mr. Seymour, and situated in the parish of Thixendale. In a field called the Howefield are situated two large barrows. They are of very considerable height, about 160 feet apart, surrounded each by a separate trench. In an adjoining field to the south is a third small tumulus having an elevation of two or three feet. In the year 1844, whilst digging into the most southerly mound [No. 41], and near its base, a British vase [fig. 454], of sundried clay was discovered. It is $5\frac{1}{2}$ inches high, and $6\frac{1}{2}$ inches in diameter at the mouth, coloured with some black earthy matter, and had been deposited in a sort of circular pavement of chalk stones. The clay of the tumulus was stated to have been of an unctuous character, and to have presented an appearance of alternate striæ, varying from a reddish brown to a blue-grey. Since the period of the visitation of the club, the tenant—Mr. J. Buttle—has presented to the society a remarkably fine celt of bronze, which had been turned up in ploughing. This, and the urn presented by Mr. Seymour, are now in the Museum of the Yorkshire Philosophical Society. The adjoining tumulus [C. 83] was at least 12 feet in height, having a circumference within the wide and almost obliterated trench of 260 feet. After digging about six feet through fragments of chalk and flint, near the centre a deposit of burnt human bones, with some traces of charcoal, was reached, and separated from them by about a foot of earth was a heap of large flints, many of them exhibiting traces of the action of fire. This cairn was 2 feet in height and 5 feet in diameter, raised on a bed of clay spread on the natural chalk rock. Among the flints were traces of a grey, sooty-like matter ; and at the bottom of the cairn, beneath charred flints, were portions of a deer's horn. much decayed, and a few scattered bones of the rat."

FIG. 454.   ½

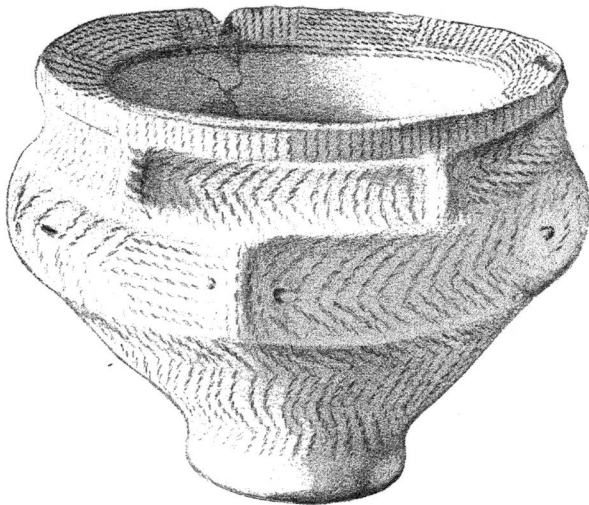

FIG. 456.   ½

BARROW No. 41

Is the southernmost of the two largest of the five barrows, and the one first-named by Mr. Procter.   Mr. J. Buttle, the tenant of the land, informed the writer that about twenty-one years previously, (this would be in 1844, the year named by Mr. Procter) his father drove a wide trench from the north side to near the centre of this barrow, to obtain soil with which to improve a piece of land, and let in the sides of the excavation to enable the plough to pass over.   A vase was then found in the mound, apparently nearly over the place where we found a body in the grave.   This vase was given to the York Museum by Mr. Seymour, and therefore must be the one of which Mr. Procter gives the dimensions.   Through the kindness of the late Canon Raine, who had charge of the archaeological collection in the York Museum, I give a drawing of this food-vase (fig. 454).

At the time of our examination this barrow had a diameter of 90 feet and a central elevation of $7\frac{1}{2}$ feet, but the encircling trench was filled in and invisible.

After working with four diggers on September 14th, six on the 20th, ten on the 22nd, ten on the 25th, seven on the 26th, and twelve on the 27th, 1865, alternately superintended by my brother and myself, we succeeded in removing from its centre a block of 40 feet square.   The ground everywhere beneath was also probed, and about the centre was an oval grave, measuring 7 feet north and south by $3\frac{1}{2}$ feet, and $3\frac{1}{2}$ feet deep.   On the floor of this, which was covered with a thin stratum of dark, sooty-like mould, was the skeleton of a young and rather small person, on its back, head to the south, the hands on each side, the knees pulled up and pressed over to the east.   The whole of the bones, excepting the teeth, were so decayed as to prevent their being removed without crumbling to pieces. Under the left arm, a little below the shoulder, was a flint knife (fig. 455) 3 inches long, pointed at one end and delicately chipped to a keen cutting edge all round. Near the right side of the skull was a large and elegantly-shaped food-vase, which, though very much crushed, has since been rebuilt (fig. 456), and measures $6\frac{1}{2}$ inches high, 25 inches in circumference at the top, and $3\frac{1}{2}$ inches in diameter at the bottom.   Two grooves, containing five stops each, arranged at equal distances, encircle the upper part of the vase, those in the lower groove being perforated laterally.   The drawing gives details of the elaborate ornamentation better than any description can, and it is only necessary to add that the straight and zig-zag lines composing the ornamentation have been produced by a loosely-twisted cord applied in various directions over the whole exterior of the vase to within an inch of the bottom.   The rim at the top is divided into eight equal parts, four of which have six lines of impressed cord-markings, and the other four divisions have impressed lines in a cross direction.   In addition, two lines of similar impressions encircle the vase close below the rim, inside, a very uncommon feature.

Above the skeleton the grave was filled with layers of clay and soil, with pieces of chalk and flint, some of large size.   From these, above the centre of the grave, we took portions of two antlers of a deer, one of which (fig. 457) had been used as a pick, as shown by its bruised and splintered point.   In making this pick, the first browtine, being at too obtuse an angle, had been cut off at the base, the second tine being left for the pick.   The other example (fig. 458), is also interesting, as it illustrates the manner in which the upper end of the antler was chopped all round—in this case apparently with a metal (probably bronze) tool—and then broken off. The sharply-defined cuts could hardly have been given with a flint axe.

A thin bed of blue clay capped the grave.

At the base of the mound were several slightly-worked flints, and a few were found in the mound. These consisted of two slingstones (fig. 459), two discs chipped round the edges, a diamond-shaped arrow-head, three flake knives, three flakes (fig. 459a) neatly notched on their edges (saws ?), five lumps of doubtful use, and twenty-eight splinters—all of black flint. Of local flint there were two flakes—one of which has a serrated edge,—one disc chipped round its margin, and two large handstruck splinters.

A section of this barrow from east to west (fig. 460), shows the position of the grave and the relative distribution of the clay, sand; and soily matter composing the mound. "A" indicates the position of the grave and the blue clay which covered it. "B" is a circular bed of blue clay, 15 inches thick in the centre, which thinned out at the margin. "D" indicates an almost central core of clay and soil, alternating in beds and patches, and streaked in numerous places with wavy dark lines covering the grave. The east side of the large portion of the mound "C" consisted mainly of sandy loam, with occasional thin seams of local soil. It formed the main part of the barrow.

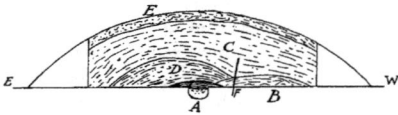

FIG. 460.—SECTION OF BARROW No. 41.

The upper portion "E" was principally of a soily nature, probably partly due to vegetation and the action of the plough. Nearly all round the margin of the bed B, and in some places a little inside it, were vertical stake-holes from 3 to 6 inches in diameter, and though all that remained was the decayed bark sticking in some places to the sides of the holes, it was clear that the stakes had been driven 12 to 18 inches into the ground under the barrow, and in three places had extended upwards nearly 4 feet into the mound, as shown at F. In various places in the bed B were pieces of partly-decayed wood, lying horizontally, as well as impressions of others of less thickness than the vertical stakes. Those preserved were of oak, ash, maple, &c. One piece of oak, about 2 feet in length and 3 inches in thickness, had a cross incision 1½ inches in depth, evidently made by a metal saw ; and on its thick end were two oblique cuts, apparently produced by the wood having been chopped from its roots by a sharp-edged metal tool. This very interesting relic clearly proves the existence at that time of a metal (bronze ?) axe and saw. The efficiency of the work produced by these tools on the piece of oak would contrast greatly with what could have been produced by tools such as the flint knife found with the skeleton in the grave. It should therefore be not too hastily concluded that metal tools were unknown because flint ones only were found.

From the bed "B" were also obtained decayed portions of the antlers of red deer ; and under it was a small natural pipe in the rock, containing dark matter with flints and pieces of chalk. Round the margin of the bed "B" was

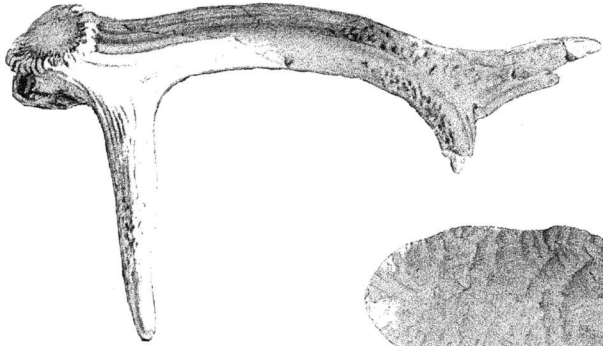

FIG. 457.   ¾

FIG. 455.   ½

FIG. 459.   ½

FIG. 459*a*.   ⁴⁄₁

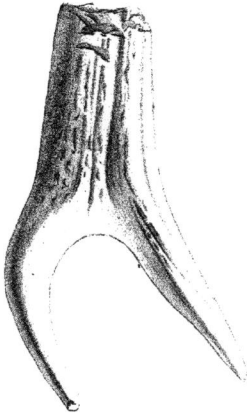

FIG. 458.   ½

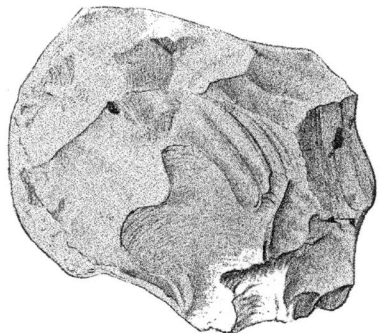

FIG. 462.   ¾

a strip of ground about 18 inches in width, stained black to a depth of several inches, which, with the stake-holes, apparently marked the limits of some enclosure. The use of such a structure we were unable to make out until 1868, when, in re-opening barrow No. 31, we discovered a series of similar stake-holes forming a complete hut circle (see fig. 397). Here also the vertical stake-holes— one of which is shown in the section (460)—and the horizontal pieces of decayed wood dispersed in the bed of clay marked B, were undoubtedly the remains of the wattled walls of a dwelling bedaubed with clay, resembling fig. 400 ; whilst the strip of dark stained ground had been caused by the drippings from the circular hut, discoloured by the decaying thatch of the roof. Possibly this thatch was formed of heather ; but it is equally probable that it was—even in those early times—of wheat straw, as we possess carbonized grains of wheat found with the primary interment in barrow No. 27 (Group V.)

In the present case the interment had not been placed in the centre of the dwelling, as in barrow No. 31, fig. 397, but a few feet outside, towards the rising

FIG. 460 a.—VIEW OF BARROW C 83, ON RIGGS FARM.

sun, and probably near the entrance.* As in barrow No. 31 also, the dwelling had been crushed inwards and covered with the mound.†

BARROW "C 83"

Stands about 50 yards to the north of the last. From June 21st to the 26th, 1875, assisted by ten workmen, alternately superintended by my brother and myself, an excavation 26 feet wide was carried from the northern to the southern margin of the mound.‡ Its diameter was 80 feet, and elevation 6¾ feet, (see fig. 460a), which is little more than half the height given by Mr. Procter when opened in 1849. The previous opening was well defined, and measured only 7½ feet by 6 feet, and was 5½ feet in depth. It seemed as if the former explorers had disturbed an inhumed body as well as the burnt bones named by Mr.

---

* Such an arrangement has been witnessed in recent times among races of low culture. Godwin Austen saw in a Naga village the grave of a man being made close to the door of a house, and the wife of the deceased was digging it.—Journal of the Anthropological Institute, Vol. XL, Nos. 1 and 2, p. 72.

† During the excavation we were visited by C. Sykes, Esq., M.P., Miss Mary Sykes, and the Rev. E. M. Cole and Mrs. Cole.   ‡ At a cost of £12 in wages.

Procter, as we observed a few pieces of unburnt human skull, leg, and other bones in the old opening.

On approaching the centre, a little rubbly chalk was noticed on the old turf line under the mound, and near its base, in the arched beds of alternating clay and soil, was a slight settling or depression, an almost sure indication of a grave. A little above the base of the mound, in the depression just named, were the antlers of a deer, too far decayed for removal. Immediately below these was the upper half of a very large antler of a deer, much crushed. It had been cut from the lower half by a blunt tool, by being chopped all round whilst held erect, with the root end on the ground. The "palm" of five terminal points of this antler were rubbed down obliquely, probably from their having been dragged along for tilling the ground.

On reaching the base of the barrow, the outlines of two large graves were noticed, in the positions shown in fig. 461. From the mound, a little above and in the immediate vicinity of the graves, were taken portions of animal bones, and several chipped balls of flint (fig. 462)—probably slingstones. About the centre, and 6 inches into the grave "A" was a small heap (No. 1) of burnt bones of an adult person, probably a female, accompanied by a few flakes of flint and a bone pin or needle (fig. 463), 6 inches long, much distorted by heat, the eye being broken. On the floor of the grave rested a small adult— also a female—in the attitude shown by No. 5 in fig. 461. The femur measured 16¾ inches, tibia 13 inches, and the humeri 12 inches each.

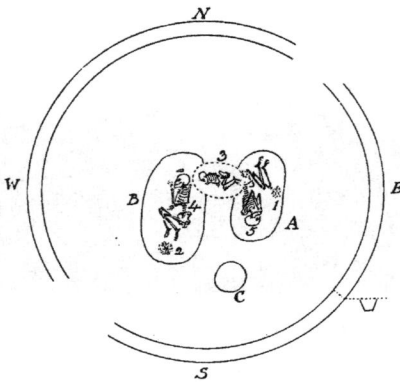

FIG. 461.—PLAN OF BARROW No. C 83.
Grave *A* measured 5½ ft. long, 3½ ft. wide, 4 ft. deep.
  „   *B*   „   7½ ft.   „   5½ ft.   „   4 ft.   „
  „   *C*   „   2½ ft.   „   1½ ft. deep.
Nos. 1 and 2 are cremated interments.

Also in grave "B," near the southern end, and twelve inches down, was another circular heap of cremated adult bones (No. 2), alone, and at the bottom were the decayed bones of an adult (No. 4), the femur of which measured 18 inches, and was strongly made. A rude flint knife (fig. 464) had been placed near the crown of the head.

Between the two graves, at a depth of twenty inches, and intruding a little way into both, were the remains of a child (No. 3) about two years of age, in the position shown in the diagram. The femur measured 6 inches only. No relic accompanied it. About five feet to the south of the graves was a dish-shaped excavation (C) made into the rock. It measured 2½ feet in diameter and 1½ feet in depth, and contained nothing but layers of clay and soily matter similar to that in the barrow above.

The cremated remains may have been those of attendants accompanying the inhumed bodies.

The encircling trench mentioned in Mr. Procter's report could not be discerned

PLATE LXII.

Fig. 463.   ¼

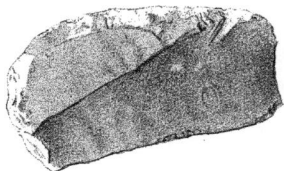

Fig. 464.   ⅓

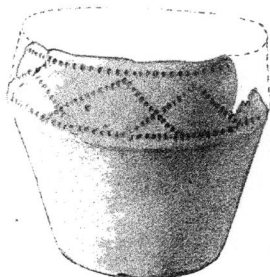

Fig. 471.   ⅓

Fig. 465.   '

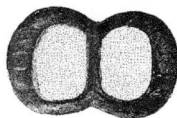

Fig. 468.   ⅓

Fig. 466.   ⅓

Fig. 470.   ⅓

Fig. 481.

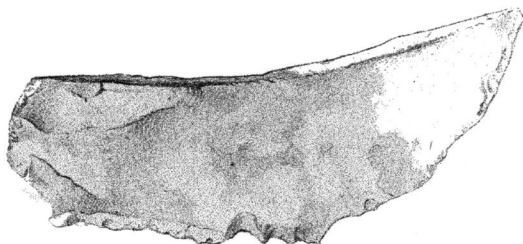

Fig. 467.

by us, but by excavating at each side of the mound it was found to be 12 feet wide at the top, 1½ feet at the bottom, and 4½ feet deep, and enclosed an area 115 feet in diameter.

BARROW No. C 84

Is situated about twenty yards from the south-south-east margin of barrow No. C 83, and is scarcely visible. It also is encircled by a filled-in trench having a diameter of about 70 feet. The elevation within is due to the selection of a slight natural rise of the ground. No burial could be found.

BARROW No. 29

Is situated on the adjoining farm called Pluckham. On May 22nd, 1865, through the permission of the late James Hall, of Scorborough, the owner of the land, we were able to explore this barrow. It measured 55 feet in diameter, and about 16 inches in height. A square of 18 feet was removed from the centre to the old turf line below, in which had been scooped two dish-shaped hollows, each 16 inches in diameter and 18 inches deep, and two feet apart. They contained burnt human bones and carbonized wood, the latter consisting of oak and hazel, of which some fine specimens were preserved. A little west of the two hollows were three-parts of a food-vase (fig. 465) in fragments, and in other parts of the mound were other fragments of the same vase; also some small pieces of two other vessels. An oval flint disc (fig. 466) measuring 2 inches by 1⅝ inches, with an average thickness of ⅜ of an inch, was found near the east side of the two cremated deposits. This form of flint tool has frequently been found with, and near incinerated remains, and may have been used in lighting the funeral pyre and afterwards placed to accompany the cremated remains.

About five feet north-east of the two shallow pits, a third and rather larger one had been made, but contained nothing but such material as formed the barrow above. During the excavation, three flint flakes 2 inches long, three undeterminable pieces, and a flake knife (fig. 467) of flint, 3¾ inches long, were taken from various parts of the barrow. After looking over some fragments of carbonised wood from various places in the excavation, we found a portion of a small stud or button of polished wood 1½ inches in length, 3/16 of an in inch in thickness, and ¾ of an inch in height at the crown (fig. 468).* It has two finely-bored perforations on its flat under side, meeting each other at a right angle, a short distance from the crown of the stud as shown in the figure, after the manner of the jet studs found with British interments.

* This is a rare instance of the preservation of an article of wood.

No. X.—THE FIMBER GROUP

CONSISTS of three barrows only, all of which had been so much reduced at the time of the Ordnance survey as to escape observation.   Probably other barrows

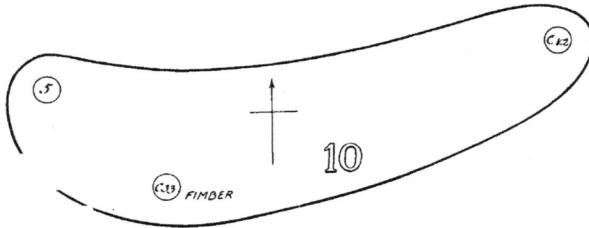

THE FIMBER GROUP.

also existed within the area which have been removed by constant tilling for a long period.

Fimber is a very old settlement, situated in the centre of a large trenched enclosure (see plan fig. 469), which was probably one of those British fortified towns (oppida) described by Cæsar as " places of refuge, viz., points naturally

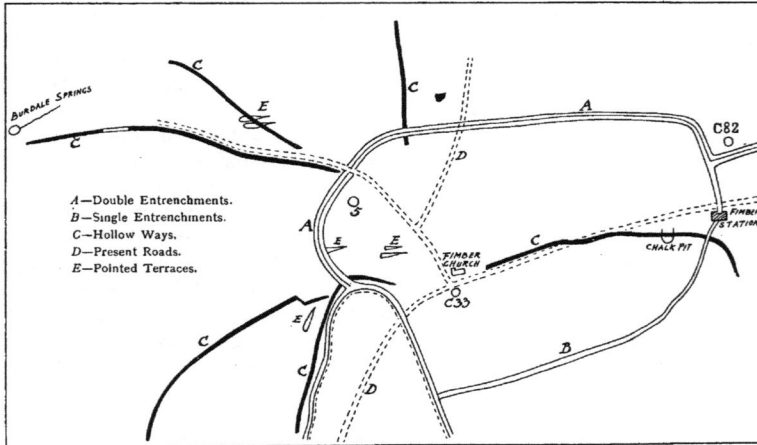

A—Double Entrenchments.
B—Single Entrenchments.
C—Hollow Ways.
D—Present Roads.
E—Pointed Terraces.

FIG. 469.—PLAN OF FIMBER AND NEIGHBOURING EARTHWORKS.

strong by reason of difficult ground, marshes, or wood, and still further secured by mounds and ditches.   To the ample area thus protected, cattle and men retreated from hostile incursions." *   In addition to this fortified enclosure, there are remains of other still more ancient earthworks (see chapter on entrenchments).

* De Bello Gallico, v. 21.

Though this group is the smallest of sixteen I have explored, it gives much interesting information in a variety of ways.

BARROW No. 5

Is known as the "Mill Hill." On August 15th, 1863, it measured 45 feet in diameter and 1½ to 2 feet in elevation, and was principally composed of angular chalk-gravel. It is situated a little to the west of Fimber, in a field called the Mortar Pits, by the old inhabitants, being near the site of extensive old pits, from which fine angular chalk-gravel, mixed with pulverized chalk, was at one time obtained and extensively used as mortar for building the stone walls and laying the floors of dwelling-houses, and other buildings in the neighbourhood.

A trench, 9 feet wide, was driven from the southern to the northern margin of the mound. The ground was noticed to be disturbed to a depth of 4 feet, in which were fragments of mediæval and other pottery, pieces of corroded iron, and teeth and bones of animals, scattered in the mound from base to apex. This gave us the impression that the mound had been rifled.

Re-Opening.—On the 19th October, 1863, a further examination was made by cutting a trench 19 feet long, 5 feet wide, and in places about the same depth, into the west side of the barrow, adjoining to and parallel with the first opening. A trench, 13 feet long and 3½ feet wide, was next made on the east side, and also adjoining to and parallel with the first opening. At the end of the latter excavation the disturbed ground was followed to a depth of 4 feet.

These openings, like the first, yielded teeth and bones, potsherds, and corroded iron, from various parts of the excavation; and in the westernmost excavation, about a foot below the surface of the barrow, we found a small buckle (fig. 470), and a small stud (fig. 471), which had been rivetted to some thin substance. Both appear to be of bronze. A few chips of flint were found. Almost everywhere were signs of the mound having been disturbed at some early period.

Four kinds of potsherds were collected, (1) a few pieces of rather small vessels, of dark composition, very similar to the Roman black ware, and free from glaze; (2) large pieces of brown colour, portions of which are glazed and somewhat resemble the common pancheons now in use; (3) many pieces of thin unglazed pottery, made of red clay, the inside of which, to almost half its thickness, is burnt black; and (4) pieces belonging to vessels of various sizes, all of which possess a beautiful green glaze, and have been made of whitish clay.

The corroded iron principally consists of nails, some of which have rather large flat heads, others with small heads similar to some now in use. There are also four bent pieces resembling the sides of buckles or staples, and four flat pieces, two of which appear to have had holes through them. The other two look like portions of knives or spears.

The animal remains are chiefly teeth of horse, ox, and goat, or small deer.

Second Re-Opening.—Increased experience led me to believe that a further examination of this mysterious mound was desirable. During May 12th-14th, 1870, a most careful search was conducted, commencing on the southern margin. At a considerable depth a well-defined excavation in the ground not previously observed was noticed extending towards the centre of the barrow. Following this towards the centre of the mound, it was observed to branch to the east and west, and also towards the north, thus forming a complete cruciform excavation' with equal arms, and charged with dirty gravel, containing numerous mediæval potsherds, broken animal bones and teeth, bits of burnt and decayed wood, and much oxidized iron, chiefly nails of various sizes, some adhering to decayed wood, apparently oak.   There was also a small bronze buckle and other pieces of bronze.

Down the centre of the cruciform excavation, at a depth of 4½ feet, was a walled cross (fig. 472), composed of two and in some places three courses of thin stones, filled in the middle with chalk gravel and a little clay obtained from a distance.* Each arm of the walled cross was about 8½ feet long, 16 inches in width, and from 8 to 10 inches high.   The stones composing it were mainly of chalk, some of which had been slightly tooled; and there were also pieces of undressed liassic and oolitic stones.   Below this, the excavation extended, and was also filled with gravel, discoloured with soily matter, containing — but in less quantities than above—potsherds, pieces of animal bone, and rusted iron nails, and, still more interesting, some fragments of a *British food-vase.*   This excavation reached

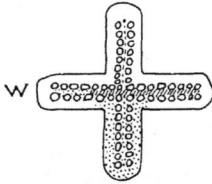

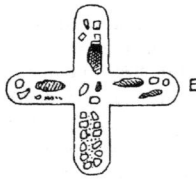

FIG. 472.   FIG. 473.

to a depth of 9 feet, and at the bottom each arm measured 10½ feet from the centre of the cruciform excavation, and nearly 4 feet in width.   On the bottom, which consisted of undisturbed angular chalk gravel, was a second walled cross, unfinished, or partly destroyed † (fig. 473), also mainly composed of rough pieces of chalk stone, with occasional fragments of liassic and oolitic rocks interspersed with clay, which seemed to have been used as mortar.   This structure measured 18 inches wide and 8 inches high where it had not been injured, and its arms were a little longer than those of the more perfect cross, situated 4½ feet perpendicularly above it.   The date of these crosses is uncertain, but they may have been used as places of assembly from late Roman, through Anglo-Saxon, to early mediæval times.   The discovery of a few flint flakes and portions of a British vase indicate the site of a barrow.   The pieces of has and oolite may have been portions of a cist, which, with its contents,. was destroyed at the time the cross-shaped excavation was made, as it completely occupied the centre of the mound.   We also noticed places where portions of the original British barrow seemed to remain undisturbed.

About a quarter-of-a-mile west of the mound just described, an entrenchment extends from Wandale over a piece of high flat land called "Lady Graves"‡

---

* The centre of the village of Fimber being the nearest place.

† During the 6th, 7th, and 8th centuries Christianity and Paganism strove with each other.   First one and then the other predominated.   Possibly this was the time when this lower cross was damaged, and some time after the upper one made.

‡ "Lady Graves," *i.e.,* Law-day graves (Gomme), the place of interment for those condemned and executed at the moot-court held on this mound, now called "Mill Hill"—and this is supported by the accidental finding of human interments at this place.

and "The Pastures," to the brow of the next hill side, called Haggdale Cliff. At the south end of this entrenchment, just on the brow of the hill forming the east side of Wandale, a labourer in digging a post-hole came upon what he thought were human bones. Hearing of this, we made a search of the place* pointed out by the labourer, and found a round hole which had been cut through the eastern rampart of the entrenchment into the ground below. This measured nearly 4 feet in diameter, and contained burnt matter, broken and split animal bones, carbonised wood, and many fragments of an uncommon kind of pottery, and some curious pieces of burnt clay. There was also the core of the horn of an ox, teeth and a tusk of a pig, some leg bones of a goat or small deer, and the end of a small whetstone of peculiar texture.

About 15 feet westwards, a similar but smaller hole was found cut through the rampart. It also contained burnt matter, a few pieces of pottery, teeth of a pig, and a few pieces of unburnt bone.

BARROW No. C 33.

The Church Hill barrow stands on the end of a natural prominence in the chalk, in the centre of the village of Fimber. Its discovery was made on June 4th, 1869, after taking down the old church, and while excavating the foundations for a new one about to be built by Sir Tatton Sykes, Bart. Traces of an earlier and larger church than the one taken down were visible. The debris of this early church was in several places 18 to 20 inches in thickness. It contained numerous small pieces of burnt wood, and, towards the western end, pieces of stained glass and a considerable quantity of melted lead, which had run into openings and cavities in the debris. Evidently this early church had suffered from fire. It had stood upon an artificial mound—apparently an oval barrow—consisting of horizontal beds of clay, interspersed with patches of loose flint stones of various sizes. These had been obtained from the surface of the surrounding land, while the clay—which at first we mistook for a natural bed of Hessle boulder-clay capping the chalk—had been obtained from a deposit filling a hole in the surface close by, and now the site of two fine meres in the centre of the village. Probably the extraction of this clay for building the barrow and bedaubing the wattled huts of that and succeeding periods† left the pits or hollows which in part now form the beds of the present meres.‡

During the very dry summer of 1826, an attempt was made to remove the mud from the most easterly mere, but when about half completed the weather suddenly changed, and a violent thunderstorm put an end to the operations by covering the bottom with about two feet of water. However, in 1884 the water was sufficiently low to enable the villagers to remove the whole of the mud which had accumulated during untold ages along its centre to the depth of three to six feet. This exposed the original irregular bottom, which much resembled

---

* During June 27th and 28th, 1869.

† Even some of the internal partitions in the old house in which the writer was born now consist of clay obtained from the locality of these meres, mixed with a little short straw; and it is known that originally the outer walls also, as well as the walls of most of the other old houses in the village, were at first entirely composed of this clay, which is found in no other place nearer than the village of Fridaythorpe, a distance of about two miles.

‡ This supposition has since been supported.

shallow pits from which clay had been, at different times, taken.   The finding—
about two feet down in the mud—of an iron spear-head (fig. 474), probably Anglo-
Saxon, would seem to indicate that this portion of the mere had not been cleansed
for many centuries.

To return to the barrow.   At the west end of the church (marked No. 1,
fig. 482), under the site of the old tower, at a depth of five feet below the present
surface and about three feet below the debris of the original church, the workmen
found some animal bones, carbonized wood, and lastly, after having dug up a
small flint axe* (fig. 475) and apparently destroyed three small vases, they made
the find known to me.   On arriving at the place I found that the workmen had
reached within a few inches of the bottom of a grave cut a little way into the
chalk rock, and after a careful search we found further portions of two food-vases
and part of a drinking-cup with a wide bottom, also small pieces of the finely-
ornamented rim of an incense-cup.   Near these were a portion of a bone pin
(fig. 476), several hand-struck flakes (figs. 477-8 show two of them), all of local
flint, a very large tusk of a wild boar† (fig. 479), and portion of the upper valve
of a Pecten (fig. 480).   Some dark matter, bits of burnt wood, splinters of bone,
and teeth of an ox and pig occurred on the floor of the grave ; whilst only a
doubtful trace of human bone remained, the body having probably completely
decayed.

A little to the south-east of the grave were indications of what proved to be
a trench, 6½ feet deep, extending due south ; but owing to the ground being
covered with building material, we were unable to follow it more than a few feet.
In the soily matter filling the trench were pieces of animal bone and many
teeth of an ox.

June 29th.—The workmen, while lowering the ground about 1 foot within the
foundations of the new church, at a point 45 feet due east of the relics discovered
at the west end, destroyed the skeleton of a full-grown individual.   On this being
made known, we examined the ground beneath, and presently found a few burnt
bones of a young person, some of which the workmen had also removed.   In
proceeding through the undisturbed portion of the barrow (which here was a
little over 2 feet in thickness, and for the most part of foreign clay), we picked
up many hand-struck pieces of foreign flint.   Under the clay was the natural
rubbly chalk surface, which seemed, at one place, to have been disturbed, and
the use of the pick brought to light the half of a fine large diamond-shaped
arrow-head, of black flint (fig. 481), which, from its fresh appearance, might have
been made yesterday.   As we proceeded downwards, a little clay was observed,
mixed, in places, with the chalk in the grave, and, at a depth of 3 feet into the
rock, and 5 feet below the floor of the old church, the bottom of an oval grave,
measuring 7 feet by 4½ feet, was reached.   On this rested the skeleton of a
medium-sized adult (No. 2, fig. 482).   The head was to the north-west, and the
interment was partly on its back, and partly on the right side ; the right arm was

---

* This is one of only three flint axes (two of which are small ones) that I have found with interments during
the whole of my barrow digging ; and Mr. Bateman, in "Ten Years' Digging," only names two reliable
instances, both found by Mr. Ruddock in the neighbourhood of Pickering.   Canon Greenwell's researches
yielded only one of small size.   Squires and Davis also, in their American explorations, found, I believe, only
one with a body.

† The tusk of the boar has been found with interments in barrows in other parts of England.

PLATE LXIII.

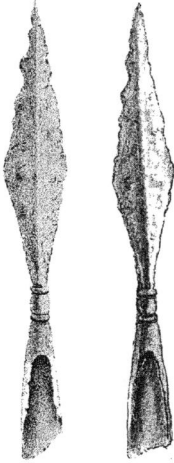

FIG. 475.   ¾

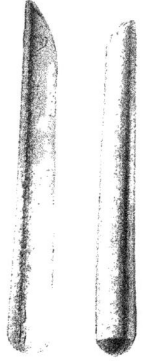

FIG. 476.   ⅟₁

FIG. 474.   ⅟₁

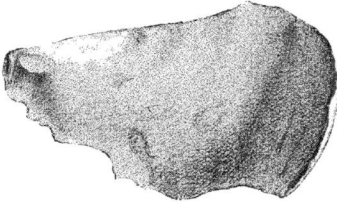

FIG. 477.

FIG. 478.

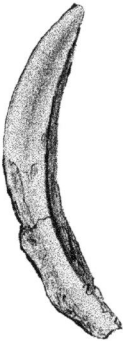

FIG. 479.   ½

FIG. 480.   ¼

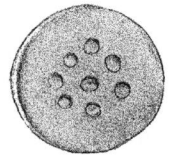

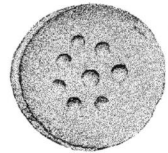

FIG. 490.   ⅟₁

doubled by the side, with the hand on the neck and left shoulder, while the left arm was bent at a right angle with the hand under the right elbow. The thigh bones were in a line with the body, and the legs were doubled back at the knees with the feet near to, and partly under the left side of the pelvis—a very uncommon position. Flat pieces of chalk were piled on the floor of the grave in the form of a trough, in which was the interment. Under it, but chiefly below the head

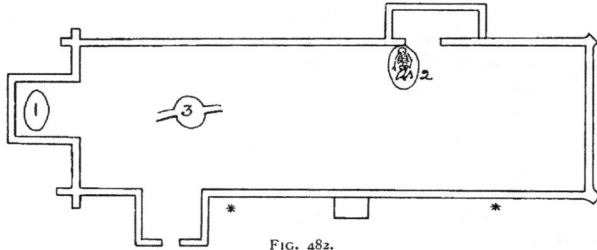

FIG. 482.

PLAN OF FIMBER CHURCH, &c.

and shoulders, was some dark matter. In front of the face stood a very elegantly-formed food-vase (fig. 483), 5½ inches high, skilfully ornamented ; and, near the forehead, were three small hand-struck splinters of flint. The femur measured 17 inches, and the tibia 14 inches, and are of rather slender make.

Again (July 22nd, 1870), the workmen, in excavating for the erection of a stove in the floor of the church, noticed an accumulation of burnt wood and fragments of pottery. The position of these is shown (fig 482, No. 3), being in a line with, and about midway between the two previous discoveries. After an examination of that portion not disturbed by the workmen, I found that there had been a dome-shaped cavity (figs. 484-5), resembling an old-fashioned beehive of straw in shape, though about twice the size. This was at the base of the barrow, and had not been injured by any previous excavation. The

FIG. 484.   FIG. 485.

PLAN AND SECTION OF STRUCTURE UNDER
FIMBER CHURCH.

bottom of this mysterious receptacle reached the rubbly chalk surface beneath the barrow, and its sides were baked and deeply reddened by intense heat. We also observed remaining portions of two clay-sided flue-holes or passages, extending about 18 inches from opposite sides, a little above the bottom of the dome-shaped structure, in a westerly and easterly direction. Within each entrance, at a point shown by an asterisk (fig. 482), was what appeared to be the decayed pointed end of an oak stake. In addition to the burnt wood, and the fragments of apparently Roman or Romano-British pottery that this place contained, there was a considerable quantity of a vitreous slag-like substance, in which were small pieces of what seemed to be fused bronze. No trace of bone was observed, but, had we been made acquainted with this find before its partial destruction, something more might have been discoverd which would have helped to elucidate the purpose it had served. I think it probable, however, that only fragments of pottery had been deposited in it.   These fragments represent three kinds of earthenware, all quite unlike any British pottery known to me, being much superior, better baked, and of a finer and somewhat different composition.   Whatever purpose this structure had served, it seems quite certain, from its position and the kind of pottery it contained, that its construction was long after the raising of the barrow, but, at the same time, anterior to the building of the first church.

Besides the discoveries made within the foundations of the present church, remains of two other bodies, probably Anglo-Saxon, were discovered while excavating for a drain close to the exterior and south side of the building.   One occurred near the east end of the porch at a depth of two feet, and near it was a small Anglo-Saxon bronze buckle (fig. 486).   The other was about the same depth, and situated nearer the east end of the church.   Not far from this body, but apparently not connected with it, and some distance below the surface, was a curious article of bronze or copper (fig. 487).   Could a full search have been made in this southern portion of the mound, possibly other Anglo-Saxon bodies would have been found, giving further proof that this British barrow, like many others, had been used as a cemetery, by the Saxons, previous to the erection of any church upon it.

There appears to be no evidence that a Christian graveyard has ever been connected with the church of Fimber.   The present burial-ground was licensed in 1877, after which, on December 18th, 1877, the first interment was that of John Cooper, an old and respected inhabitant of Fimber, 92 years of age ; and on June 15th, 1883, the writer's mother, Hannah Mortimer, who was born at Fimber, was interred in her 88th year, in the southern edge of the barrow on which the church stands.

Many churches in various parts of England are in immediate proximity to barrows, but few are known to occupy the sites of three succeeding churches and to represent the burial place of apparently four different people, viz., British, Romano-British, Anglo-Saxon, and English.   That an extended Anglo-Saxon burial-ground once existed near to this barrow seems evident from the fact that on July 25th, 1863, while making the foundations for a cottage adjoining the Wesleyan Chapel, and about 80 yards south-east of the church, the remains of six or more bodies were found.   They were not more than two feet from the surface, and some of them, as far as could be gathered from the workmen, had the legs more or less pulled up. They were accompanied by pieces of iron and fragments of pottery, most of which were destroyed at the time.   A few of the remaining ones were preserved, and seem to be Anglo-Saxon.   The remains of these interments were put in a barn, and afterwards examined by the late Dr. Clements, of Wetwang, who pronounced them to belong to small persons, chiefly females and juveniles.   This discovery produced a considerable amount of excitement at the time among the villagers, and the late Mr. S. Broadley, the owner of a small plot of ground extending from the Wesleyan Chapel towards the church, stated that he remembered while digging a little way into the subsoil, having frequently found bones and flint arrow-heads. Roman coins also have at various times been found in the ground adjoining the church barrow.

Other human remains and weapons have been found near the village of Fimber.   I remember being greatly impressed, when a boy, by my grandfather bringing home the lower jaws belonging to bodies which had been exhumed when quarrying chalk to repair the roads, at a point where the entrenchments are cut by the road to Sledmere, about 400 yards eastwards from the cross-roads near to Fimber Station.

An old labourer named Lockwood, once living at Fimber, who was for many years servant with my grandfather, remembers human bones and what he describes as an iron sword having been found many years since, where the road to Malton cuts the same entrenchments, about 300 yards northwards from Fimber station.

BARROW No. "C 82"

Is a little to the east of Fimber station, and quite near to the north side of the road to Sledmere. This mound is now almost imperceptible through its dispersal by the plough previously to its being planted with trees about a century ago. These trees, however, had been cut down a short time before we opened the mound.

On June 13th to 15th, 1875, we discovered three dish-shaped holes (fig. 488) scooped into the natural chalk gravel beneath the 10 to 12 inches of earth forming the mound. These excavations measured about 3 feet in diameter and 14 inches in depth, and contained soily matter, in which were found many small pieces of burnt wood, bits of dark-coloured pot, and a shell of a hazel nut; no trace of bone was observed.

About 5 feet to the south of the three holes, and 9 inches from the tilled surface, were the disturbed bones

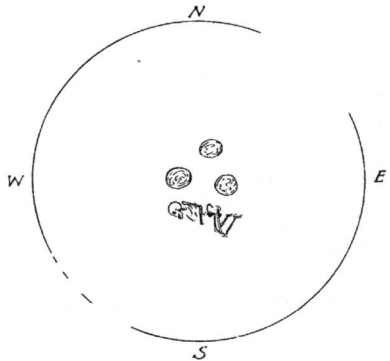

FIG. 488.—PLAN OF BARROW No. "C 82."

of a young individual, on the right side, head to the west, and legs flexed. No relic accompanied them, but a few handstruck splinters of flint were picked from the mound.

Outside this group, a little to the south of Fimber Field House, is an irregularly-formed mound, close to the north side of the high road from Wetwang to Fridaythorpe, and opposite the end of an old grass enclosure called "Bottland Trees." This mound may prove to be a barrow, and is worthy of an examination. There is also on the opposite side of the road, a thickening in the rampart of the entrenchment which crosses the road and extends down the West side of "Bottland Trees."

The approximate sites of many obliterated barrows seem to be indicated by the names of the fields in the neighbourhood. A little to the west of Wetwang are two adjoining fields; one being called Stand Hills, the other Hound Hill; and about half-a-mile southwards is a field called Mill Hill; while half-a-mile south-west and just to the west side of Painslack House is a field called Round Hill; and

2 B

again about one mile eastwards from Painslack House is a field known as Hill
Fields; and a little to the north of Wetwang are fields called Totter Hills.   Probably
numerous other sites of barrows exist and all trace or remembrance of them has
now disappeared.   Where the land has been long tilled few remain visible.

Besides the demolished tumuli there are the sites of other interesting remains,
some of which are from time to time accidentally brought to light.

Between Fimber and Wetwang, in the valley called "Bessingdale," near
the corner of a British entrenchment, at a point designated "Blealands Nook,"
where the railway crosses the green lane, is a Romano-British grave yard.   At
this place (see accompanying Plan, fig. 489) the Roman road from Malton to
Beverley crossed that from York through Bridlington to Flamborough.

The first discovery in this graveyard was made in December, 1868, in fixing
the telegraph post which stands where the railway crosses the green lane.   The
body of an adult was then removed by a workman, but no relics were observed
with it.   A notice of this discovery was published shortly in the *Malton Messenger*,
and in the *York Herald*, in which notice it was erroneously stated that the body
was accompanied by flint tools.

The second interment was discovered in March, 1873, by labourers planting
quickwood along the south side of the railway, 20 yards south-east of the interment at the crossing, and was said to be in a doubled-up position, with its head
towards the north.   Nothing was associated with it.   This discovery being made
known, I obtained the skull from the workmen, and permission from the North
Eastern Railway Company to make further search within the boundaries of the
line.   In May, 1873, several days were occupied in examining the ground between
the quickwood fence and the embankment of the line, and at the point marked *A*
a small grave-shaped hole about 2 feet deep was met with, containing dark soil,
mixed with bits of burnt wood, and a few calcined human bones, but no relics.
A body (No. 3) occurred 3 feet 10 inches deep in an oval grave, 7 feet by 8½ feet,
on its left side, the knees drawn up, both arms bent over the abdomen, and the
head pointing a little east of north; the femur, tibia, and humerus measured
respectively 16, 12, and 11 inches, and were probably those of a female.   The
right humerus was more than ¼ of an inch longer than the left one.   About
8 inches below the feet was the tibia of a stag or small ox; whilst at a depth of
3 feet under No. 3 was an interment (No. 5), on its chest, extended at full length,
except the right leg which was slightly bent at the knee; the left arm was bent,
with the hand under the pelvis, and the right arm was laid straight by the side
of the body, the head pointed in the same direction as the head of the body No. 3.
The femur measured 17¾ inches, the tibia 13¼ inches, the humerus 12½ inches,
and belong probably to a male.

A body (No. 4) was placed about 20 feet east of the last one, in a grave
similar in form and size.   It rested on the left side, with the head a little east of
north, the knees drawn up, and both the hands in front of the face.   The femur
measured 18 inches, the tibia 13¾, and the humerus 12⅝ inches.   Another (No. 6)
was 3 feet deep, much doubled up, and, except that it was on the right side, its
posture was the same as that of No. 4.   The femur, tibia, and humerus
measured 16¼, 12½, and 12 inches respectively.   About 12 feet east of the last
grave a similar one was found, but the interment had been disturbed at the

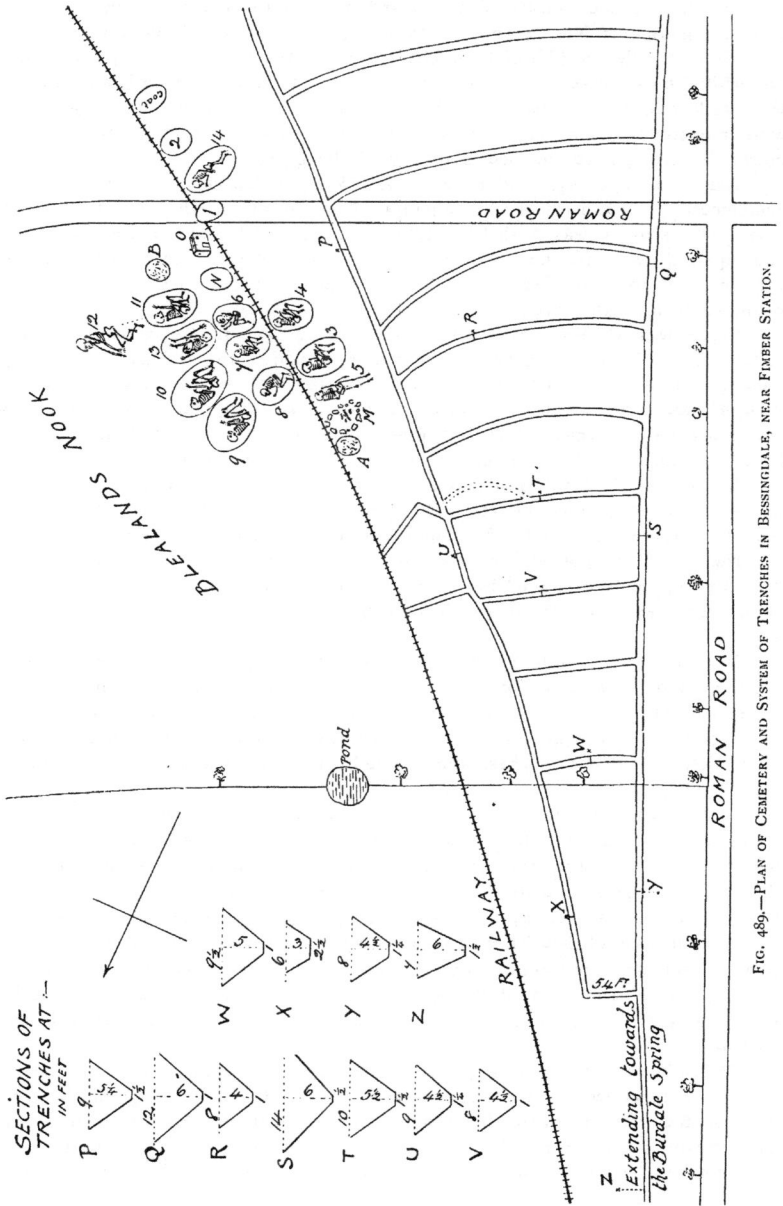

FIG. 489.—PLAN OF CEMETERY AND SYSTEM OF TRENCHES IN BESSINGDALE, NEAR FIMBER STATION.

time of planting the quickwood fence, and most of the bones had been broken. Near to interments Nos. 3 and 5 was the greater portion of the skeleton of a pig, within a rude cist (*M*) of large chalk stones. We found several places where the white chalk gravel of the valley bottom had been excavated and refilled with dark soil, freely mixed with broken and unbroken animal bones, and also with numerous fragments of many kinds of coarse Roman pottery, but no potsherds accompanied the bodies in any of the graves.

Second Re-Opening, February 20th, 1874.—A further examination was commenced in that part of the adjoining field on the north side of the line. The first discovery was a skeleton (No. 7), in an oval grave, 6 feet by $4\frac{1}{2}$ feet and $2\frac{1}{4}$ feet deep, in the position shown on the plan. The femur measured $15\frac{3}{4}$ inches; the tibia $12\frac{1}{2}$ inches; the humerus $11\frac{3}{4}$ inches; and probably belonged to a small female.

No. 8 was $4\frac{1}{2}$ feet north-west of the last, at a depth of 3 feet, and also on the floor of an oval grave. The femur measured $16\frac{3}{4}$ inches, the tibia $14\frac{1}{4}$ inches, and the left and right humeri 12 and $12\frac{1}{4}$ inches respectively, and though short were of strong make, probably those of a male. The lower jaw was curiously deformed, probably from some injury or the prolonged growth of a large abcess. The vertebræ also were much anchylosed.

No. 9 was doubled up like the last, but was on its left side, at a depth of $2\frac{1}{2}$ feet beneath the surface. The femur measured $17\frac{1}{4}$ inches, the tibia 14 inches, and the right and left humeri $12\frac{3}{4}$ and $12\frac{3}{8}$ inches respectively.

No. 10. The position of this was similar to that of No. 9, except that it had the legs a little more drawn up, the knees being within 7 inches of the chin. The femur measured $16\frac{3}{4}$ inches, the tibia $13\frac{3}{4}$ inches, and the humerus $12\frac{1}{2}$ inches.

No. 11 was 4 yards to the south-east of the previous one, in a similar position, and at a depth of only 10 inches; the femur, tibia, and humerus measured $16\frac{1}{2}$, $12\frac{1}{4}$, and $11\frac{3}{4}$ inches respectively. Immediately beneath this body was No. 12, on its right side, and in a less flexed position. The femur measured 16 inches, the tibia 12 inches, and the right and left humeri $11\frac{1}{4}$ and 11 inches respectively.

No. 13 was the skeleton of a young person, in the exceptional position of being on its back, with the head to the south, both knees were drawn up to the chest, and pressed over to the left side, the right arm was doubled with the hand by the side of the face, the left arm extended by the left side. The femur measured $12\frac{1}{2}$ inches, the tibia $9\frac{1}{2}$ inches, and the humerus $8\frac{3}{4}$ inches.

A little east of No. 11 was a dish-shaped excavation, marked "B" on the plan, 2 feet deep, containing wood ashes mixed with calcined human bones; close to which were part of the lower jaw of a deer, and a portion of the jaw of a large pig. This dish-shaped excavation had been made in a narrow filled-in trench.

Third Examination, April 25th and 27th, 1874.—On these days a considerable area was excavated at the south-eastern corner of the crossing on the south side of the railway, with the result that interment No. 14 was found in an oval grave $2\frac{1}{2}$ feet deep. Its position, excepting the arms, was almost exactly the same as No. 12. The left thigh bone was absent, and had probably been removed in digging for rabbits. The right femur measured 17½ inches; the right tibia 13¾ inches; the left tibia 13½ inches; the right humerus 12½ inches; and the left humerus 12¼ inches. Close by the ground had been much disturbed, and in several places small trenches were observed, extending north and south, or nearly so. Mixed with the soil filling these were a few fragments of dark-coloured pottery, and the teeth and bones of animals.

Just within the line of the railway, near the south side of the quickwood fence, and about 20 yards south-east of body No. 14 was a small grave, 2½ feet deep, containing the remains of a goat, all the bones being in position.

There can be little doubt that the bodies exhumed at Blealands Nook represent those buried in a Romano-British cemetery, and that many more occur under the railway, the embankment of which covers an area 41 feet wide through the centre of the cemetery. As there is nothing on the surface to indicate their existence, probably many more also remain undiscovered outside the railway, though we have examined the ground in several places. The oval form of the graves and the flexed mode of burial, except in one case, are distinctly British features, and such as we find in nearly every barrow; yet their almost constant orientation is in striking contrast to a similar number of bodies from any British barrows known to me. Out of the twelve perfect bodies eleven had their heads to north and north-east, the twelfth was to south-south-west, whilst six rested on the left side, four were on the right, one on the back, and one on the chest. In addition to the burials by inhumation, there were two (A and B on the plan) cremated. What is also exceedingly interesting is the fact that the inhumed bodies of the pig and goat had been interred with the same amount of care as had been given to the human bodies. This, however, is not the only instance of the discovery of carefully interred animal remains in this neighbourhood.*

These Romano-Britons also show an anatomical feature of interest which has been seldom noticed in any bodies from the barrows, viz., the measurements in most cases show a marked difference in length and strength between the right and left humeri. Possibly the unequal length and strength of the right arm over that of the left is the result of training in the art of using the spear and throwing the javelin. The length of the long bones shows them to have belonged to rather small persons.

No fragment of pottery was found in any of the graves, though found with numerous animal bones abundantly in disturbed ground and trenches close by. Neither, as before mentioned, were any of the bodies accompanied by relics, which, in this feature also, contrasts greatly with barrow burials and with Anglo-Saxon interments. In my opinion the graves are of Roman date. This appears further evident from the existence of a series of filled-in trenches, arranged somewhat in the shape of a gridiron near the south-west side of the graveyard (fig. 489). These trenches, like the graves, are quite invisible on the surface, but being mainly charged with rich soil, they are in a dry season indicated by green ribbon-like lines or strips in the growing corn.

The plan of these trenches was obtained by digging numerous sections during the summer of 1874, a few of which I give with measurements. They differ a

* See page 163.

little in width and depth (which may be due to the slight variations in the surface level of the land, and from the makers endeavouring to keep the bottom of the trenches level), and averaged about 5 feet in depth, and varied in width at the tops from 6 to 14 feet, and at the bottom from 1 foot to 2½ feet.

It is difficult to understand the special purpose this system of trenches served. The single trench running north-westwards from them may at times be traced by a green strip in the growing corn, extending all the way along the valley bottom to within a mile of Burdale, where a surface stream of water from a fine spring there disappears beneath the turf. I made a section of this trench in July, 1884, at a point only half-a-mile from the sinking end of this stream. The trench may have been connected with the Burdale spring, the water of which it conveyed to the series of trenches at Blealands Nook to supply a settlement there. If this surmise be correct, we have indications of a system of waterworks greatly in advance of any recent arrangement to supply this neighbourhood with good water.

These trenches, as already mentioned, were filled with dark soil, containing many animal bones and much broken Roman pottery, showing that this spot was occupied in Roman times. Besides these we found a disc of bone (fig. 490), having on one side eight small cup-shaped hollows, which may have been used as a counter in some game resembling dice. There were also found a rough pear-shaped piece of chalk (fig. 491), pierced near the small end, which had probably served as a weight or plummet ; a flat polished piece of chalk (fig. 492) with lines incised on one side ; and a sharp-pointed bone implement (fig. 493), made from the shank-bone of a goat, which has a small hole through the socket end to secure it to a handle. It is similar to several bone articles found at Grimthorpe with a late British interment, which were accompanied with an iron sword in a bronze sheath, the bronze covering of a circular shield and other articles.*

The many animal bones found everywhere in the trenched ground were chiefly those of the horse, always detached and often broken, showing that the flesh of this animal had afforded a large portion of food to the occupiers of the settlement. The series of buried trenches already described, which extend to near where the present stream disappears beneath the surface, and used for conveying water, is just such a provision as would be required at a station holding the crossing of three roads at a point where no natural spring exists. A work of this kind is what the Romans, who have always shown great care in the supplying of water to their camps and stations whenever required, would be likely to make.

Names, implying Roman origin, still linger in the immediate neighbourhood. The present road going up the hill near Fimber Station northwards in the direction of Wharram-le-Street and on to Malton is called "High Street." In the York Museum is a fine Roman cinerary urn of glass, ticketed "found near Wharram-le-Street, on the Roman road passing Fimber, in 1820, and presented by the Rev. J. W. Stillingfleet." In a straight line 1½ miles S.S.E. from Blealand's Nook, in the direction of Beverley, is a little valley called "Thorndale," which is on the line of this old Roman road from Malton to Beverley. Professor Phillips says† "Thorn is seldom far from old camps or mounds of importance." From Thorndale this old road is in places distinctly traceable in a straight line towards Beverley. It crosses Tibthorpe Wold close to the farmhouse called "Angas Farm," where,

---

* See page 150.   † "Rivers, Mountains, and Sea-Coast of Yorkshire," page 242.

PLATE LXIV.

FIG. 483.

FIG. 486. $\frac{1}{1}$

FIG. 487. $\frac{1}{1}$

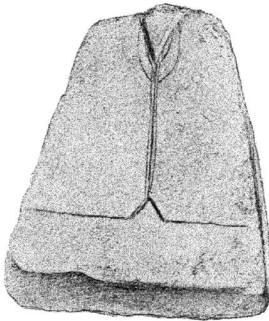

FIG. 492. $\frac{1}{2}$

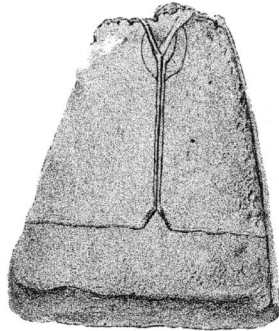

FIG. 492. $\frac{1}{2}$

FIG. 491. $\frac{1}{2}$

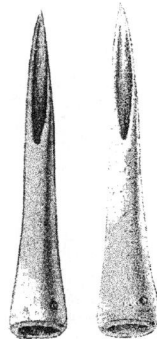

FIG. 493. $\frac{2}{3}$

in 1850, in excavating for a well on the north side of the house, several skeletons were exhumed, but their positions were not observed, neither is it known whether they were accompanied with any relics or not. About one mile S.S.E. this old road is well shown, running obliquely over the north side of Bainton Heights, in a line with Bainton and Beverley.

The existence of a Roman station near the site of the cemetery just described, is first intimated, to my knowledge, in 1847 by John Yonge Akerman, in his "Archæological Index," page 148, where he presumes Fimber to be the site of Delgovitia. This site is also favoured by Prof. Phillips,* who is inclined to Derventio being at "Stamford Bridge, and Delgovitia somewhere about Huggate, or Wetwang, and Prætorium at, or near, Bridlington." He also adds, "Roads which appear to be of the Roman period, lead from Malton towards the Wolds, as by Wharram-le-Street towards the point between Fimber and Wetwang, agreeing with the supposed position of Delgovitia on the road to Bridlington."

Several Roman coins† have from time to time been picked from the surface of the land near the crossing of the Roman roads and in other places near Fimber, many of which have not been preserved. Two from a collection picked up during the winter of 1885, near Blealands Nook, by a shepherd, are in my possession. The one is of Constantine, the other of the son of Constantine. At Cowlam, about 1860, a large quantity of Roman coins, many of which I possess through the kindness of the late C. Sykes, were found in a vase. At the same place there are extensive old foundations, which are a promising field for excavations.

Fimber is about midway between the Roman centre Eboracum and Prætorium. It is true that no trace of the ramparts of such a camp as we might expect to find at a Roman Station has as yet been discovered, but then, during the cultivation of the land and other operations of the husbandman during the lapse of fourteen centuries, it is highly probable that in this case, as in many others, such a structure has long since been swept away; though it is not improbable that the filled-up fosse of such a camp may yet be discovered; or it is possible that Delgovitia may have been more a trading or commissariat depôt from which the Roman legions were fed on their march from Eboracum to Prætorium, on the east coast, than a military camp, and that the Romans mainly occupied the site of the village of Fimber, and as suggested by the Rev. J. Wiltshire,‡ may have strengthened and made use of the extensive British earthworks which surrounded and protected this village, and which are now distinctly traceable on the surface, resembling a hugh camp, see fig. 469. In support of this view Professor Phillips in his "Rivers, Mountains, and Sea-Coast of Yorkshire, p. 246, says, "Derventio and Delgovitia may perhaps never have been marked by camps."

From the discoveries made at Blealand's Nook and other proofs, I think it may he admitted that the Romans occupied the neighbourhood of Fimber, which is on the line of the most direct road from Eboracum to the east coast, being about

* "Rivers, Mountains, and Sea-Coast of Yorkshire," pages 241-2.
† About 50 Roman coins have been picked up in the neighbourhood of Wetwang, amongst which the following have been identified by Mr. W. Fennell, of Wakefield:—1 Vespasian, A.D. 78; 1 Hadrian, 117-138; 1 Porcia Family, 130; 1 Faustina, wife of Antoninus Pius, 105-141; 3 Severus, died at York, 211; 1 Julia Mammœa, mother of Severus Alexander, 235; 1 Valerian, 254-260; 1 Posthumus, 258; 1 Claudius Gothicus, died 270; 1 Helena, wife of Constantius, 300; 1 Constantius, died at York, 306; 1 Urbs Roma, 306; 1 Constantine the Great, 306-337; 1 Magnentius, died 353.
‡ In the Proceedings of the Geologists' Association, No. 8, 1862.

midway between the two, and at a point where this road is intersected nearly at right angles by the Roman road from Malton, and therefore just where a Roman station would certainly be required. This site seems to possess a greater claim to be Delgovitia than any of the numerous places which have been previously assigned to it.

No. Xa.—THE LIFE HILL GROUP.

THIS consists of six barrows, only one of which, No. 28, had been noted by the Ordnance Surveyors. Three of these much-reduced and unshapely mounds had been planted with fir-trees for about 80 years.

BARROW No. 28

Stands on the rising ground to the north of Wetwang Station, near the southern confines of Ash Plantation, about 20 chains' length to the east of the farm-house called Life Hill.

Opened May 8th and 10th, 1865.—At the base of the barrow, rather to the south of the centre, in a contracted position, were the decayed remains of a youth

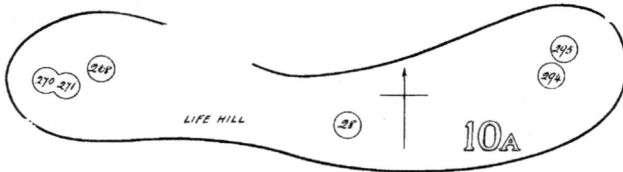

THE LIFE HILL GROUP.

(No. 1), with head to the north. At the east side, leaning on the chest, was a small food-vase of a common type (fig. 495), 5½ inches high, 5½ inches in diameter at the top, and 2½ inches at the bottom. Its ornamentation consists of two rope-like impressions passing round the inside of the lip, and, externally, the lip somewhat overhangs a shallow groove about an inch in width, at each margin of which runs an encircling band of rope markings, the lower one being immediately followed by a raised belt, and this belt by a line of similar impressions.

Occupying a small area a little north of the centre, were a few animal remains, consisting of leg bones, ribs, and pieces of a small skull; also portions of the jaw, with teeth, of a pig. To the south-west of the centre, and about 5 feet west of the human bones, was a shallow grave, containing the remains of a dismembered adult body (No. 2), consisting of leg and other bones, portions of a skull in various positions, but chiefly at some distance from each other. One large piece was high up in the mound over the south end of the grave, and was found to fit the pieces from the floor of the grave at the north end. Other human bones were also found high up in the grave. At the southern end was a heap of burnt bones (No. 3). Close to, and partly under them, were the unburnt bones, in position, of two human feet. Probably they belonged to the dismembered body, which had, possibly, been partly removed by the insertion of the cremated interment. There were also pieces of charred wood, the tooth of an ox, and a few snail shells, *Helix nemoralis*, in the grave, whilst, from the mound, more animal bones were taken, as well as fragments of two vases and three handstruck splinters of foreign flint.

Re-opening.—During the last week in January, 1869, the whole of the mound was turned over, and the ground carefully probed below. A few animal bones and potsherds, found at its base, were the only additional discoveries made. In digging near the margin it was observed that a filled-up trench encircled the barrow, 3 feet 8 inches deep, 3 feet wide at the bottom, 6 feet at the top, and enclosed a space of 70 feet in diameter.

BARROW No. 268

Was opened on July 26th and 29th, 1884. It had a diameter of 55 feet and an elevation of 18 inches. Like the two adjoining barrows, it consisted of the local somewhat argillaceous soil, but none from a distance. In the centre was an oval grave, measuring $7\frac{1}{2}$ feet north and south, by $4\frac{3}{4}$ feet, and extended $3\frac{1}{2}$ feet into the rubbly chalk below. On the floor of this was the skeleton of a young man, on its left side, knees pulled up, both arms bent upwards, and the hands in front of the face. Under the forehead was an oval disc (fig. 496), of black flint, about $1\frac{1}{2}$ inches in greatest diameter, chipped to a cutting edge half way round, the other half being left unchipped. In front of the face, and upon the finger bones of the right hand, was a large flint flake knife (fig. 497), chipped on one side and round the point to a sharp edge. A portion of the natural surface of the flint remains on one side, showing it to have been struck from a water-worn block. The right femur and tibia measured 19 and 16 inches respectively, and the humeri measured 14 inches each, and are of strong build.

BARROW No. 270

Is near an almost obliterated British entrenchment, and is only 60 feet from one of two other barrows situated in the south-east end of Belt Plantation. During the last three days in July, 1885, we found this and the adjoining barrows hardly 12 inches above the surrounding ground. The former contained an oval grave, 7 feet north and south by $5\frac{1}{2}$ feet, and 4 feet deep, which, excepting a few inches round the sides at the bottom, was charged with a boat-shaped mass of soily matter similar to that forming the mound above. Very little of the excavated chalk had been put back, it being scattered for some distance round the grave on the old surface-line under the barrow. The soil from the mound had settled into the grave, apparently, as in many other instances, in consequence of a horizontal wooden covering having slowly decayed and let down the earth. At the bottom of the grave, on a film of soot-like substance, was the skeleton of an adult, with its head to the north, partly on its back and partly on its right side, the knees well pulled up and pressed over to the west, the left arm across the body, and the right one by the side with the hand on the pelvis (fig. 498). A femur

2 C

and tibia measured 19 inches and 15 inches respectively, are of rather slender build, and belong to a person about twenty-five or thirty years of age. It was observed that the dark decayed matter under the body was the most abundant about the head and shoulders. On the chest was a heap of cremated bones of a small and probably young person. At the hips stood a fine and rather large food-vase (fig. 499), measuring 5 inches high, 7¼ inches across the top, and 7½ inches over the shoulders. The inside of the lip is tastefully ornamented with three bands of impressed cord markings, between which are two rows of pear-shaped imprints made with the closely-looped end of a cord. On the neck of the vase are two grooves, the lower containing six pierced stops. Its whole exterior is ornamented with sharply-impressed cord markings, tastefully arranged in horizontal and oblique lines. Near to it was the greater portion of the left side antler of a roebuck (fig. 500), apparently from a slaughtered animal, worked into an instrument by having all its side branches removed clearly

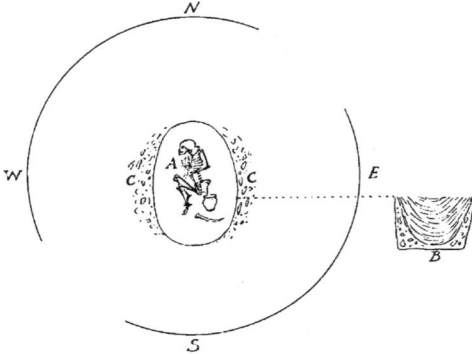

FIG. 498.—PLAN OF BARROW 270.

A—Burnt bones on front of ribs.   *B*—Section of grave in centre.
C—Chalk cast from grave.

by a sharp metal instrument. It would have served the same purpose as the two instruments from Barrows Nos. 100 and C 62, fig. 408 and fig. 533. The cremated bones, though in immediate contact with the bones of the inhumed body, had not imparted any trace of burning to them, as has sometimes been observed, notably in barrow No. C 43, which appeared to be due to the cremated bones having been deposited while in a glowing condition.

BARROW No. 271

Is fellow to the last-mentioned barrow. In the centre was a small grave measuring 3 feet north by south, by 2 feet, and about 12 inches deep. Nothing was found in it, but probably it had contained the body of a child which had completely decayed. This surmise was supported by the finding of a small ornamented food-vase of the ordinary British type standing on the west-north-west brink of the grave.

BARROWS Nos. 294 and 295.

These are two adjoining barrows in Lingwalk Wood (planted by the late Sir C. Sykes about the year 1795), a little west-north-west of the monument erected to the late Sir Tatton Sykes, Bart., of Sledmere, in 1865.

FIG. 495. ⅓

FIG. 499. ⅓

FIG. 496. ¼

FIG. 497. ½

FIG. 500. ½

FIG. 501.

FIG. 502. ¼

FIG. 504 a. ½

FIG. 505 ½

Having removed several large trees at the request of Sir Tatton Sykes, I superintended the examination of these two mounds during the first and third weeks in September, 1896.

BARROW No. 294

Was found to have a diameter of 65 feet and an elevation of 2 feet only. It had been lowered at some period before the trees were planted.

Excavations were commenced on the south side, and at a point a little east of the centre, at the base of the mound, was a crushed skull of an ox (C on the

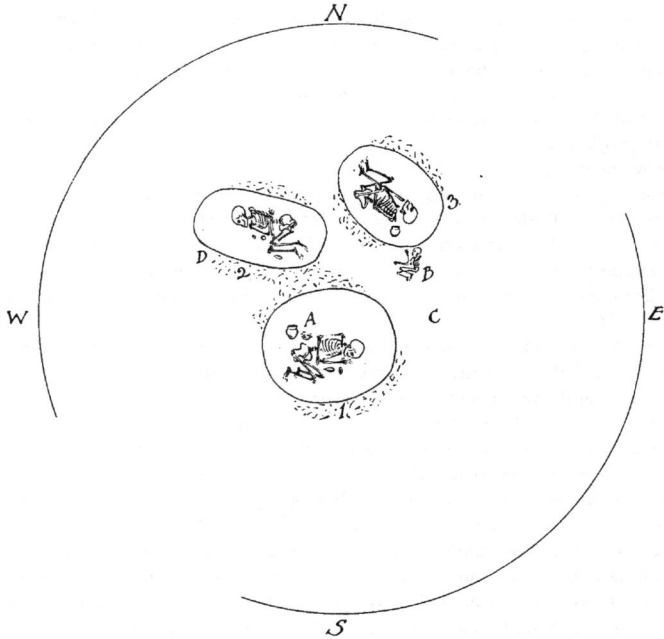

FIG. 500 a.—PLAN OF BARROW 294.

plan), minus the lower jaws, placed on its crown. The ends of both horn-cores had been broken off previous to burial; a feature observed in other instances. At the centre of the mound was an oval grave (No. 1, fig. 500a), 7 feet by 6 feet in diameter, and extending 4 feet into the chalk. On the floor of this were the remains of a tall old man on his back, with head to the east, bending slightly to the south. The knees were drawn up and pressed over to the left side, the left arm doubled with the hand near the face, and the right arm bent at a right angle, with the hand near the left elbow. Near the left elbow, in contact with the bones of the right hand (some of which were stained green) was a small bronze dagger-knife* (fig. 500b), 3 inches long and 1¼ inches in width at the broad end, pointing towards the feet. Near its broad end was a flint knife (fig. 500c). Round the skull were five or six small hand-struck splinters of foreign flint.† A femur measured 19 inches. The teeth are much worn, but none are decayed. About 6 inches above the hips was a heap of white cremated bones of an adult, "A," with which were a fine flint knife, 3 inches long (fig. 500d), a small bronze pricker (fig. 500e), and an instrument measuring 6½ inches outside the curve (fig. 500f), made of the longitudinal half of the tusk of a wild boar. This instrument is unlike the one obtained from the Duggleby Howe (barrow 273), which was also made of the tusk of a wild boar, and must have been intended for a different purpose. A somewhat similar instrument, made of the half of a boar's tusk, is figured in British Barrows, on page 56, which Canon Greenwell classes with the bone pins. The specimen (fig. 500f) cannot, however, be so placed. The pointed end of the tusk seems originally to have been purposely blunted. The other end is pierced, and the instrument may have been hafted, apparently for use by the left hand.

None of these instruments show any trace of fire, and they appear not to have passed through the funeral pile.

A few inches west of the burnt bones "A" was a large and elegantly-formed food vase (fig. 500g), 6¾ inches in diameter at the top, and 6 inches in height. From the long and slender finger bones, &c., observed in the cremated interment it seems to have been that of a female. The accompanying instruments appear also to support this view. There is no question about inhumation and cremation having been contemporaneous in this instance, and possibly the two burials were man and wife.

Grave No. 2 was 3 feet westward from the centre one, and of a more oblong form than is usual in a British barrow, its length being 7 feet by only 4 feet in width. The depth was 4 feet. On its western edge was the calvarium (at D on the plan) of a very large badger; neither the under jaw nor any other bone of this animal was found. On the bottom of the grave rested the crouched remains of a young woman (the teeth all good and very little worn), on the right side, with head to the west, as shown on the plan (fig. 500a). Femur and tibia measured 16 inches and 12¾ inches respectively, and are rather slender.

One half of a flint knife (fig. 500h), which had been broken previous to interment, had been placed near the upper end of the right tibia; and a flint scraper (fig. 500i) of medium size, and a quartz pebble (fig. 500j) about the size of a bantam's egg, occurred near the right elbow. The latter is somewhat battered at the small end, from having been used.

Grave No. 3 was 4 feet northwards from the centre one, and 3¼ feet deep. On the old surface line adjoining the east end of the grave were placed the flexed remains of a child (B) about three years old, on the right side, with head to the north. The thin walls of the skull, and even the other bones, are in remarkably good preservation. At the bottom of the grave were the doubled-up remains of an aged male (No. 3), on the right side, and head to the east. A femur measured 16 inches, a tibia 11½ inches, and are of rather strong build. The

---

* This instrument was very much decayed and split round the edges, but after having been soaked and coated with weak glue, it was well preserved, and its original appearance very little altered.

† I have observed several similar occurrences during my researches; possibly they represent charms.

Fig. 500*b*.

Fig. 500*c*.

Fig. 500*d*.

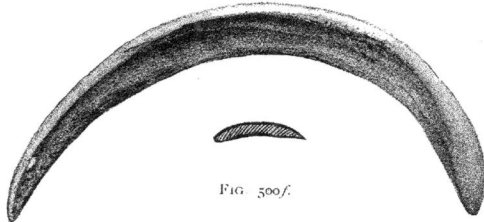

Fig 500*f*.

Fig. 500*e*.

Fig 500*g*.　½

skull is brachicephalic. The teeth are much worn, and several of the back teeth are wanting and the sockets well closed. Behind the left shoulder stood an irreparably-crushed food-vase of common type, small size, and quite plain.

Scattered from top to bottom of the grave were fragments of most of the bones of a young adult body.

It was quite clear that all the interments in the three graves had been made before the barrow was raised, as, resting on the old surface soil under the mound round the margins of all the graves, was part of the rubbly chalk which had been cast there in digging them, and had not been put back.

BARROW No. 295

Is about 70 yards to the east of the last, and has been the larger of the two. At some period previous to planting the trees which stood upon it, the centre portion had been removed. Excepting on the outskirts, we turned over and probed the whole area under this barrow without finding a grave or the least trace of an interment.

Probably one or more burials—which may have been made on the old surface line as no trace of a grave could be found—were destroyed at the time of removing the greater portion of the mound during the close of the eighteenth century. Several worked flints, a tooth of the horse, and the tine from the antler of a red deer were found on the old surface line under the barrow. About 100 yards further eastwards is a slight elevation covered with large trees, which may be a small and partly-levelled barrow.

DETACHED BARROWS, &c.

BARROW No. 122.

This circular barrow is situated about midway between Groups X.*a* and XI. It is about 65 feet in diameter and 18 inches in height, and appears to have been much reduced by long cultivation. It stands on ground called Mill Fields, close by the south side of the road to Driffield, about 300 yards east of Wetwang Vicarage. Like one of the Fimber mounds, it is known by some of the old inhabitants as the "Mill Hill."

During September 15th-17th, 1868, and three days of the following week, we commenced at the southern margin and examined nearly the whole of this mound. It consisted of darkish earth (quite distinct from the reddish-coloured natural surface soil beneath it), somewhat freely mixed with rusted nails and other pieces of iron, splintered and broken bones of horse, ox, pig, and sheep or goat; a few pieces of brass or bronze, some of which seem to be cusps or ferrules (figs. 501-2) from the ends of the scabbards of small daggers or knives, and portion of a bronze signet ring. There were also numerous potsherds of several varieties of vessels, glazed and unglazed, apparently mostly of Anglo-Saxon and Mediæval age. A silver coin of Edward IV. was found near the centre of the mound, at the depth of about 16 inches. There were also several other broken bits of bronze and iron articles, the form and use of which could not be ascertained.

Under the mound was a cross-formed excavation (fig. 503) cut 6 feet into the rock below, measuring 38 feet from north to south, and only 29 feet from east to west (as proved by our final search in 1884). The outer extremities of the northern and southern arms, notably the latter, narrowed and sloped for some distance towards the centre of the cross, in a manner resembling rude steps, considerably worn, cut in the rock (fig. 504). The centre of the cross measured 5½ feet in width at the top and 2½ feet at the bottom. It was charged with earthy matter resembling that of the mound above, and contained numerous potsherds, corroded iron, pieces of bronze or brass, fused and heat-twisted pieces of glass, and animal bones; and at a depth of 3 feet was a Roman coin of *Constantius Potus*, struck at Treves, about A.D. 335 to 350.

Scattered from one end to the other, and from top to bottom of the excavated cross, were small pieces of burnt wood. All the arms pointed about 13 degrees to the right of the true cardinal points of the compass.

July 21st and 25th, 1884, we completed the examination of the eastern and western arms—the extremity of which were only partially explored at the former opening—and found them to terminate rather abruptly, as shown by the sections, and not by a gradual slope of rude steps as in the case of the northern, and particularly the southern end. The relics discovered on this occasion were also fragments of glazed and unglazed pottery, bits of brass, a bronze stud (fig. 504a), pieces of corroded iron, rusted nails of several kinds, and a socketed arrow-head (fig. 505) of iron.

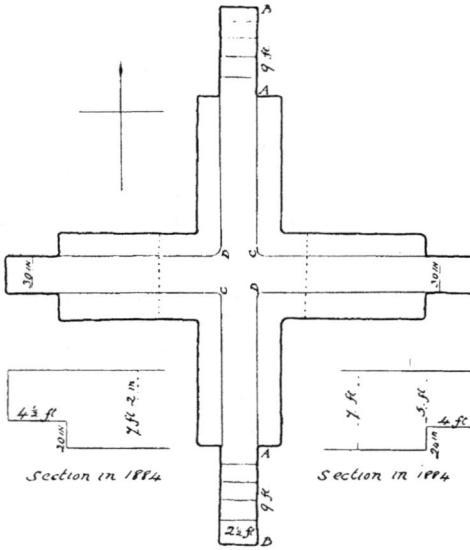

FIG. 503.—PLAN OF EXCAVATION UNDER BARROW 122.

FIG.—504.—SECTION OF SOUTHERN END OF FIG. 503.

About ¾ of a mile south of the cross, near old embankments still slightly visible, a bronze ring (fig. 506) was found in 1882. In an old gravel-pit adjoining the west side of the road to Tibthorpe, and near where the ring was picked up, several skeletons were found many years ago. Most probably the armlet, called a stone armlet (fig. 507), was then found with one of these bodies,

FIG. 500 h.

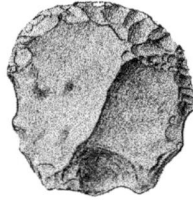

FIG. 500 i.

FIG. 500 j.

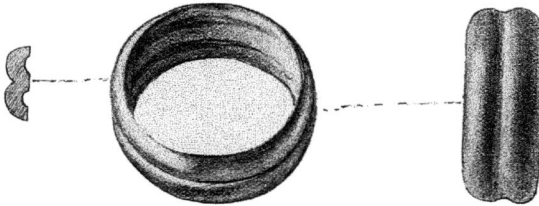

FIG. 506.   ½

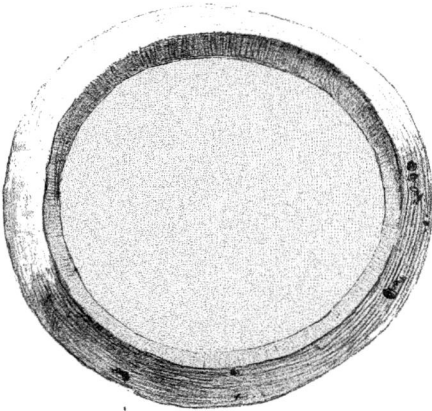

FIG. 507.   ½

FIG. 511.

FIG. 509.

a description of which was given by the late Mark Sykes, of Sledmere, in 1794, and printed in *Archæologia*, vol. xii., p. 408.   This reads as under:—

> "The bracelet [fig. 20], plate 51, p. 1,* was found upon the wrist of the skeleton of a full-sized man, about two yards underground, by the road-side in Wetwang field, in the East Riding of the County of York, by some workmen who were digging for material to mend the road.   The skeleton was laid at full length, with every bone in its proper place, and in good preservation.   Some teeth which dropped out of the skull were perfectly fresh.   In the entrenchments which divide and dissect in every direction the high wolds in that part of Yorkshire, skeletons, the heads of broken spears, arrows, and other remnants of ancient weapons and armour are frequently found."

* In *Archæologia*.

No. XI.—THE GARTON SLACK GROUP.

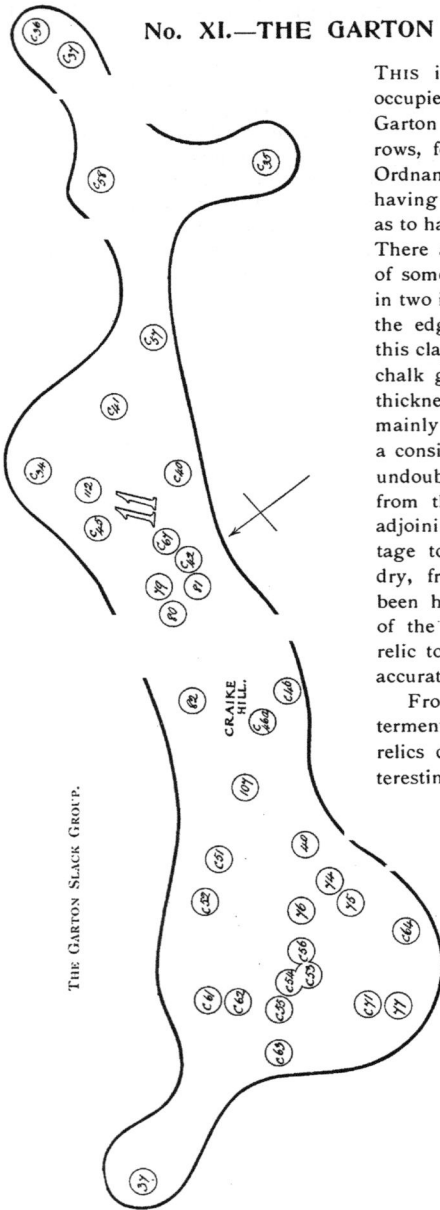

THIS is one of the largest groups, and occupies the whole of the valley known as Garton Slack. It consists of thirty-five barrows, four only of which are shewn on the Ordnance Map, the remaining thirty-one having been so far erased from the surface as to have escaped the eyes of the Surveyors. There are, probably, a few others, the sites of some of which may yet be found. Except in two instances, where the mounds stand on the edge of the drift, and are composed of this clay, they are all built of the loose white chalk gravel, which covers, to a considerable thickness, the valley bottom on which they mainly stand, mixed, in several cases, with a considerable quantity of dark peaty matter, undoubtedly obtained in the form of sods from the surface of the land immediately adjoining. This feature is a great advantage to the explorer, as the clean, white, dry, friable condition of the material has been highly favourable for the preservation of the skeletons, and enables the smallest relic to be discovered, and its position most accurately made out.

From the variety of the methods of interment, and the fine quality of many of the relics discovered, as well as from other interesting features attached to it, this group surpasses any of the other series of barrows I have explored. It is also the largest group known to the writer that is situated in a valley bottom, on low ground, being only from 50 to 100 feet above the sea; whilst Canon Greenwell remarks, in "British Barrows" (page 8), that these barrows are never, or rarely found on low ground. Probably this is partly because the low ground which was sufficiently dry for barrow-raising was also favourable for agriculture, the operations of which have obliterated most of the barrows, as in this instance.

THE GARTON SLACK GROUP.

CRAIKE HILL.

BARROW No. 37

Is a low flat-topped circular mound, situated a little to the west of elevated ground called "Garbutts." Though not shown on the Ordnance Sheet, it measured 110 feet across the centre, and 12 inches from base to apex.

On July 10th, 1865, and the three following days, a large piece was cut from the centre, the remains of fourteen bodies being found, one of which had been cremated.

Interment No. 1 was near the southern corner of the excavation, on the right side, with the head to the south-west, and occurred at a depth not exceeding that reached by the plough; consequently the arm bones, part of the skull, a few vertebræ, aud some pieces of a drinking-cup were all that remained.

No. 2 was a little to the north-east of the centre, head to the south-west, and apparently in a flexed position, on the right side, but much broken up by the plough. No relic was found with it.

No. 3 was a little north west of the centre, about 10 inches beneath the surface, on the right side, as shown on the plan (fig. 508). The femur and tibia measured 17 inches and 14 inches respectively, and are of slender make. Close behind the skull was a bone hair-pin (fig. 509), three inches long, made of the shank-bone of a goat or sheep.

No. 4, an adult skeleton, was immediately below No. 2, in a large unshapely grave, 3 feet deep, in the position shown on the plan. No relic was found with it.

No. 5 on the plan marks the place from which we took a detached skull, minus the lower jaw, near to which were a few broken human bones, probably the remains of an interment broken up by the plough. The socket end of the shoulder-blade of an ox was also picked up from this place.

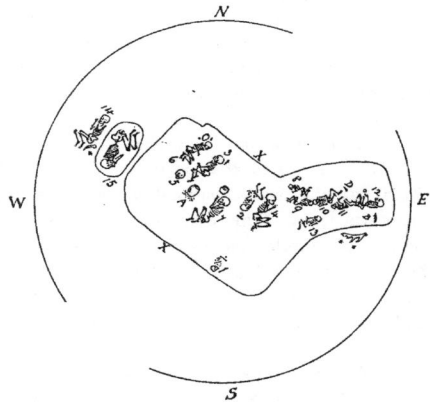

FIG. 508.—PLAN OF BARROW No. 37.
X—Area first opened.

No. 6 was vertically beneath No. 3, at a depth of 1 foot below the base of the mound, on its back, with the head pointing in the same direction as that of the skeleton above. The femur and tibia measured 19 inches and 15½ inches respectively. Close under the skull was a line of dark matter, resembling decayed wood, 8 inches long; and behind the skull, near the right shoulder, stood a highly-ornamented drinking-cup (fig. 510). Leaning against this was a beautiful flint dagger (fig. 511), 6¾ inches long. It was made of dark-coloured flint, but, through being so long in contact with the chalk gravel (which, in the main, filled the grave and formed the barrow), it is now nearly white. One edge of the dagger, near the broadest part, is covered with oxide of iron, from having been

2 D

in contact with a lump of iron pyrites, which had also stained a worked flint. Probably the two had served as flint and steel. The pyrites fell to pieces on being removed. Near the dagger, slightly to the north of the drinking-cup, was a well-formed hammer-head (fig. 513), of a hard drab-coloured stone, slightly oolitic in structure, and finely polished. A fine circular jet button (fig. 514), was also found near the cup and dagger. Its under side is flat, and shows marks of a very imperfect cutting instrument, while the upper and convex side is finely polished.

No. 7.—This interment occupied the centre of the barrow, at a depth of 12 inches. Just in front of the skull stood a handsome and highly-finished food-vase (fig. 515), 5½ inches high, 6 inches wide at the mouth, and 2¾ inches across the bottom. Two grooves occur outside, below the lip, each containing four stops placed at about equal distances. They are almost exactly alike, except that those of the lower series are perforated in the line of the groove. The under and outer sides of the lip are thickly ornamented with small herring-bone impressions, made by a notched tool, and the whole space below has irregular imprints made by a similar toothed instrument, as shown in the drawing. The vase was filled with soil, from which the rib of an animal (fig. 516) about the size of a rabbit, was taken.

A femur measured 18 inches, and was of medium substance.

" A " indicates the position of a deposit of calcined bones, on the top of which stood a well-ornamented food-vase (fig. 517), 5 inches in height and 5½ across the top. The clay forming this vase is mixed with an unusually large quantity of angular pieces of a hard dark-coloured rock, about the size of currants, shown most abundantly on the inside of the vase. Upon the bones, close under the vase, was a bone pin 2¼ inches long (fig. 518), which may have secured some kind of wrapper containing the bones.

No. 8 was scarcely a foot below the surface, in the position shown on the plan. A femur measured 15½ inches. No relic accompanied it.*

On Wednesday, July 12th, the excavation was extended eastwards, and five more skeletons were exposed to view at one time. From their positions and close proximity to No. 8, they seem to have all been interred at the same time, five of them being on the same plane, about 12 inches from the surface of the mound.

Nos. 9, 10, and 11, were in the positions shown on the plan, and the femoral bones of the two latter measured 15 inches each. Close to the elbows of No. 11, marked " D " on the plan, was a detached human foot with all the bones in position, and the lower end of a human fibula. These certainly did not belong to any of the skeletons near. The small, clean, white gravel everywhere in and beneath this barrow, enabled us to expose every bone with the greatest ease.

No. 12 occurred on its back, nearly 20 feet from the centre of the barrow. The right arm was stretched by the side, and the left arm bent over the body, with the hand near an artificially formed pounder of gritstone (fig. 519). The femur and tibia measured 18 inches and 14½ inches respectively. Close to the left shoulder was a large portion of the left lower jaw of an ox or red deer, with three teeth in it (marked " B "), and near the back of the skull was a slender

---

* Mr. Thomas Kendal, of Pickering, who had opened several barrows on the Yorkshire Moors, was present during the examination of the greater number of these interments.

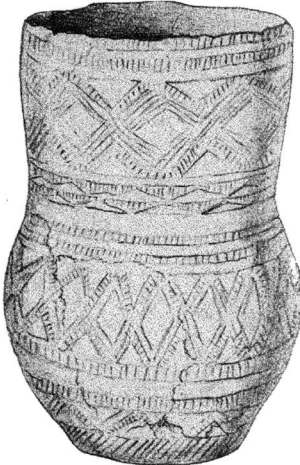

FIG 513.   ½

FIG. 510.   ½

FIG. 516.   ¼

FIG. 517.   ½

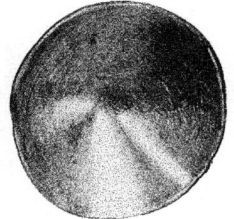

FIG. 514.

FIG. 515.   ½

FIG. 514.   ¼

hand-struck flake of black flint (fig. 520). Also, partly under the left side, and half-way between the scapula and the pelvis, was the terminal tine of the antler of a red deer.

No. 13 represents the remains of a body lying close above Nos. 9 and 10, and only a few inches from the surface, consequently it had, for some time, been gradually removed by the plough. It was clear that burials 8 to 12 had been all interred at the same time, and not more than 6 to 8 inches below the base of the barrow. Snail shells (*Helix nemoralis*), frequently accompanied the bodies.

A few animal teeth and bones were picked up from the body of the mound during the excavation.

Re-opening, May 15th to 17th, 1871.—Commencing at the eastern side of the barrow, we turned over the whole of the outskirts to the central portion previously excavated. Near the eastern margin, at a depth of about 1 foot, was a large pick (fig. 522), made of the antler of a red deer. No further discovery was made until we reached the west and opposite side of the barrow, about 17 feet from its centre. A small grave, of the usual oval form, was there discovered, in which, at a depth of 16 inches, was the skeleton of a youth, in the position shown by No. 14. The femur and tibia measured 14 inches and 11½ inches respectively. Close behind the pelvis was a brow tine of a red deer (fig. 523), this had marks indicating that it had been cut from the antler by an instrument no better than a flint saw or knife.

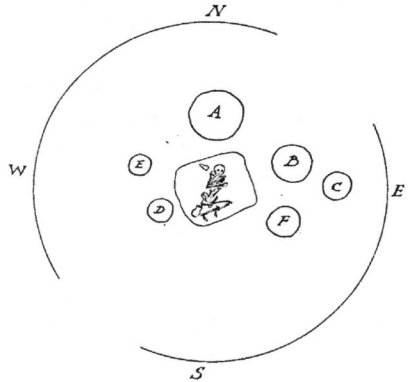

FIG. 524.—PLAN OF BARROW C. 61.

A measures 6 ft. in diameter and 3 ft. in depth.				
B	,,	4 ft.	,,	2 ft. ,,
C	,,	4 ft.	,,	1½ ft. ,,
D	,,	3 ft.	,,	8 in. ,,
E	,,	2 ft.	,,	8 in. ,,
F	,,	3 ft.	,,	2 ft. ,,

Under the last interment, on the floor of the grave, at a depth of 2½ feet from the surface, was an adult skeleton, in the position shown by No. 15 on the plan. The femur, tibia, and humerus, measured 17¼ inches, 14¼ inches, and 12½ inches respectively.

A few chains' length to the south-east of this barrow is a large gravel-pit, where the 6-inch Ordnance Map records that "British urns, weapons, and skeletons have been found."

BARROW No. C. 61

As well as Barrow No. C. 62, was opened during August 29th to September 6th, 1873. It was much dispersed, and its elevation was reduced almost to the level of the surrounding ground by cultivation. In turning it over, we observed that a slight natural eminence had been chosen for its site. The centre was occupied by a rectangular grave 7 feet by 5½ feet, by 3 feet deep. At the bottom was the skeleton of a tall male of strong build, on its back, with the head to the north-

north-east, and in the position shown on the plan (fig. 524). The femur and
tibia measured 20½ inches and 15½ inches respectively. The skull was irrecover-
ably crushed. On the left side of the chest was a fine jet button (fig. 525),
2 inches in diameter, with the top downwards. At the right shoulder was a
flake knife of black flint, exceedingly sharp, 2¾ inches long (fig. 526); and near
the pelvis, an elaborately-ornamented drinking-cup, which had been crushed into
many fragments. After rebuilding (fig. 527), it measured 8½ inches in height,
and 6 inches in diameter at the top, the same in the middle, and 3 inches at the
bottom.

The circular places marked *A, B, C, D, E,* and *F,* on the plan, indicate
dish-shaped excavations, neatly scooped into the white gravelly subsoil, and filled
with nothing but very black peat-like soil. No trace of bone, pot, flint, or anything of the kind, was observed in any of these receptacles.

BARROW No. C. 62

Was 23 yards in diameter, and had an elevation of nearly 2 feet; but from being
erected on a slight natural mound, the earth was hardly 1 foot in thickness. This
was turned completely over, and, about 13 feet north-east from the centre, in a
small hole only 5 inches under the tilled
surface, were a few calcined bones of
an adult ("*A,*" fig. 528), near to which
were unburnt fragments of the skull of
a child, and a small flake of flint. Seven
feet nearer the centre (at *B* on the plan),
and at about the same depth, were the
calcined bones of an adult. Four feet
from the edge of the grave was a third
similar deposit (*C* on the plan), so near
to the surface as to have been partly
removed by the plough. Six feet north
of the centre (at *E* on the plan), was
an oval dish-shaped excavation, measuring 6 feet by 4 feet at the top, and 2 feet
deep. This contained only black soil like
that found in the circular holes in the
last barrow.

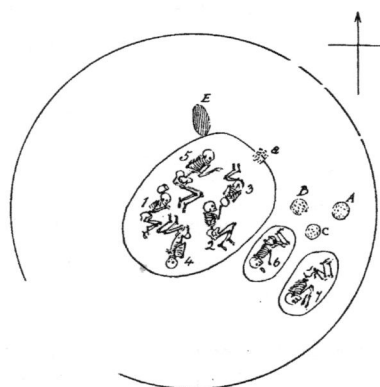

FIG. 528.—PLAN OF BARROW C. 62.

At the centre was a large oval grave, measuring at the top 13 feet by 10 feet,
and 6 feet deep. At the north-east side of this, and near the surface, were a few
burnt human bones, shown at "*a,*" and some in fragments which were not
burnt. These were the remnants of an interment which had been scattered in
tilling the land. Near the south-south-west end, at a depth of 27 inches, were
the remains of a child from five to seven years of age, with the head to the north-
east and in the posture shown by No. 1 on the plan. Owing to the unequal
settling of the contents of the grave beneath, the head and shoulders of this
interment had sunk 6 inches lower than the remainder. The femur measured
11½ inches, and the tibia 9½ inches in length.

PLATE LXIX

FIG. 518.

FIG. 520.

FIG. 523. ⅛

FIG. 519. ¹

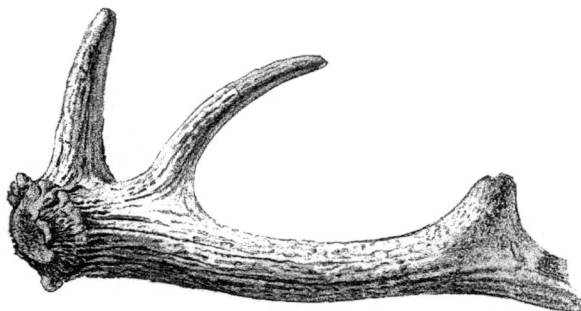

FIG. 522. ¼

FIG. 525. ½

PLATE LXX.

FIG. 530. $\frac{1}{3}$

FIG. 531. $\frac{1}{2}$

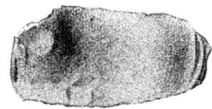

FIG. 532. $\frac{1}{3}$

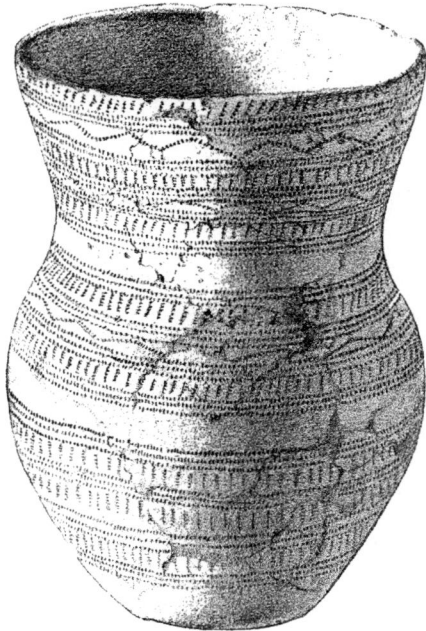

FIG. 527. $\frac{1}{2}$

FIG. 526.

FIG. 534. $\frac{1}{2}$

FIG. 533. $\frac{1}{3}$

FIG. 529. $\frac{1}{3}$

FIG. 535.

Close behind the skull was a food-vase (fig. 529), erect, 4½ inches high, by 6¾ inches in diameter at the top, and 2¾ inches at the bottom. This had six pierced stops in the lower groove. Part of the ornamentation seems to have been made by a tool having eight small notches in it. In the bottom of this vase was another small one (fig. 530), inverted, measuring 1¾ inches high, and 3¼ inches across the top. This is a very unusual occurrence, and is the first example we have found. Similar small vases, known as incense-cups, are frequently found within cinerary urns, but they have rarely been taken from the interior of a food-vase.*

Close to the left side of the skull, were two small articles of bone (figs. 531-532).

In the centre of this grave was a boat-formed mass of soily matter, while the space all round the sides was filled with the excavated gravel.

Interment No. 2 was placed with its head pointing north, and in the position shown on the plan. The femur measured 18¼ inches, and tibia 14½ inches respectively, and were strongly made. The legs and pelvis rested on the chalk gravel at a depth of 18 inches only, whilst the head and shoulders rested on the centre block of soily matter, which had settled with them to a depth of 2 feet 7 inches. No relic accompanied this interment.

No. 3 occurred a few inches under the shoulders of No. 2, with the head to the south-south-west, and on its face. On account of the unequal settling of the contents of the grave, the pelvis of this body was also 8 to 9 inches lower than the shoulders. The femur measured 16 inches, tibia 12¾ inches, and humerus 11½ inches in length, and were apparently those of a little old woman. About 10 inches lower was a dagger-like instrument (fig. 533), 10 inches long, made from a human thigh-bone. This instrument—in having been made of human bone—is probably unique. A somewhat similar instrument made of the bone of an ox was found in Barrow No. 100. It also occurred alone, as if accidentally dropped into the grave.

No. 4 occupied the south-south-west end of the grave, 3 feet down, with the head to the south-south-east, on its back, and knees much pulled up. The femur measured 16 inches, and tibia 12½ inches in length. No relic accompanied this interment.

No. 5 was reached at a depth of 6 feet. It was on the floor of the grave, at the north-north-east end, in the posture shown on the plan. The femur measured 18½ inches, tibia 14 inches, and were strongly made.†

No. 6 occupied an oval hollow, scooped 6 inches into the ground under the mound, north-east of the centre grave. In front of the face was a small knife of black flint (fig. 534).

No. 7.—This interment was on the floor of a similarly formed oval grave, south-east of the last, measuring 5½ feet by 3 feet, and 2½ feet deep. The femur measured 17½ inches, and tibia 13½ inches. The skull is of an elongated type, and probably belonged to an elderly female.

* Possibly this may have served as a cover for the food-vase.
† Interments Nos. 4 and 5 were exhumed on the 5th of September, 1873, in the presence of the Rev. E. M. Cole, of Wetwang, the late Dr. King, the late Dr. MacMillan, Dr. Evans, the late Dr. Walton, Mr. Chapman, Mr. Wake, Mr. Usworth, Mr. Scaping, Mr. Wilkinson, all of Hull, and members of the East Yorkshire Anthropological Society; also the late R. Oxtoby, and Mr. Mellor, of Hull; Dr. Wood, Dr. Ridpath, the late R. Davison, J. Sterriker, and J. Turner, all of Driffield.

From the distorted appearance of the bodies in the centre of the grave, through unequal settling of the material beneath, which could not well be shown in the drawing, it seems clear that they had been interred at about the same time; while the cremated interments and the inhumed contents of the two small graves, which were filled in with a mixture of gravel, were secondary interments. No ditch had ever existed round either of these two barrows.

BARROW No. C. 63

Is to the west of the two last, and is almost invisible on the surface. On September 11th and 12th, 1873, parallel trenches, a little apart, were driven over a considerable area, exposing a perfectly circular filled-up ring fosse, measuring 55 feet in diameter. This was $3\frac{1}{2}$ feet deep, 7 feet wide at the top, and $1\frac{1}{2}$ feet wide at the bottom.

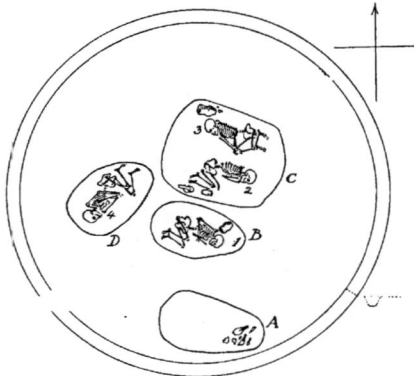

FIG. 536.—PLAN OF BARROW C. 63.

Within its enclosure were four graves, arranged as shown in the plan (fig. 536). The one marked "A" measured $8\frac{1}{2}$ feet by $4\frac{1}{2}$ feet at the bottom, and $2\frac{1}{2}$ feet deep, but contained no trace whatever of an interment; on the floor near the west end, however, were two scapulæ, an atlas, pieces of a pelvis, and portions of a skull of a red deer (?), and other splinters of animal bone. In the soil, about midway in this grave, was a piece of fibrous stone (fig. 537), one side of which is polished as if used as a whetstone. It has an oval cavity, $1\frac{1}{4}$ inches by 1 inch, and $\frac{1}{4}$-inch deep worked into it, the use for which is not certain.

Grave "B" was 4 feet in depth, measured 6 feet by $4\frac{1}{4}$ feet at the bottom, and widened towards the top. On the floor was interment No. 1, as shown on the plan. Near to the right shoulder had been placed a very fine drinking-cup (fig. 538), which when found was leaning to one side, but free from injury. It is $8\frac{1}{4}$ inches high, and measures 5 inches across the top, $5\frac{1}{2}$ inches in the centre, and $2\frac{3}{4}$ inches at the bottom. Just above the right side of the pelvis, close to the vertebrae, was a small and badly-formed flint knife or spear-head (fig. 539). Near to the front of the skull, and also by the left foot, were very small pieces of decayed matter, resembling dried putty, accompanied by a dark substance much like decayed wood. The femur, tibia, and humerus were respectively 19 inches, $14\frac{1}{4}$ inches, and $13\frac{1}{2}$ inches in length.

Grave "C" measured $6\frac{1}{2}$ feet by 6 feet, and was $4\frac{1}{4}$ feet in depth, with the sides nearly vertical. At the east end, $3\frac{1}{2}$ feet down, was a heap of human bones, consisting of two hip bones, 16 inches apart; one whole tibia, $15\frac{1}{4}$ inches long, and very broad (the other tibia was split into three pieces); a portion of a very large and strong femur and a medium-sized one, two large shoulder-blades and two of medium size, one other hip-bone, the lower ends of two other left tibia (one

PLATE LXXI.

FIG. 537.   ⅓

FIG. 539.   ¾

FIG. 544 b.   ⅓

FIG. 544 a.   ⅓

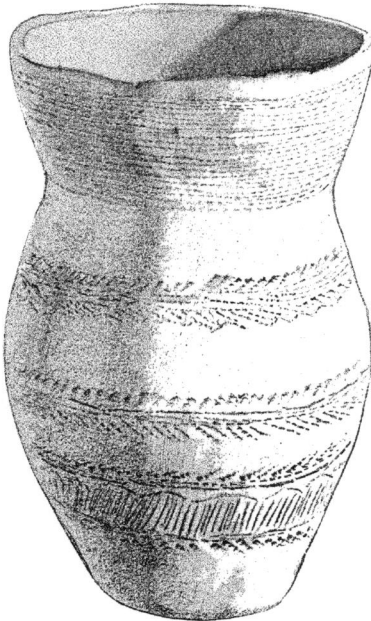

FIG. 538.

FIG. 540.   ½

FIG. 542.

PLATE LXXII.

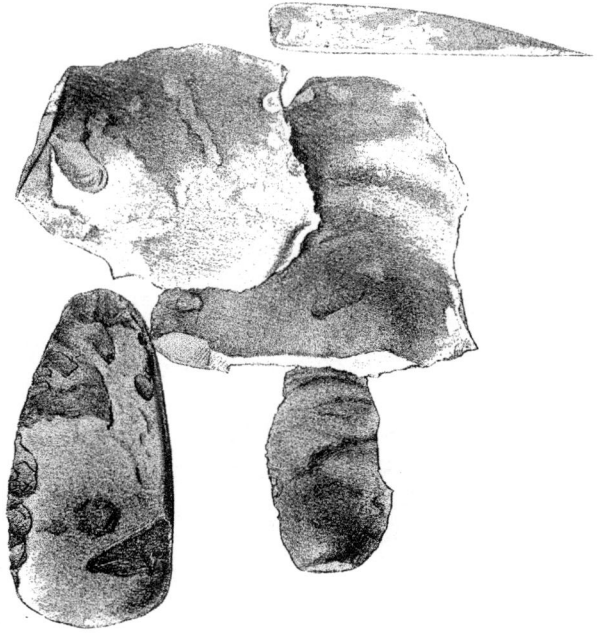

FIG. 541.   ¼

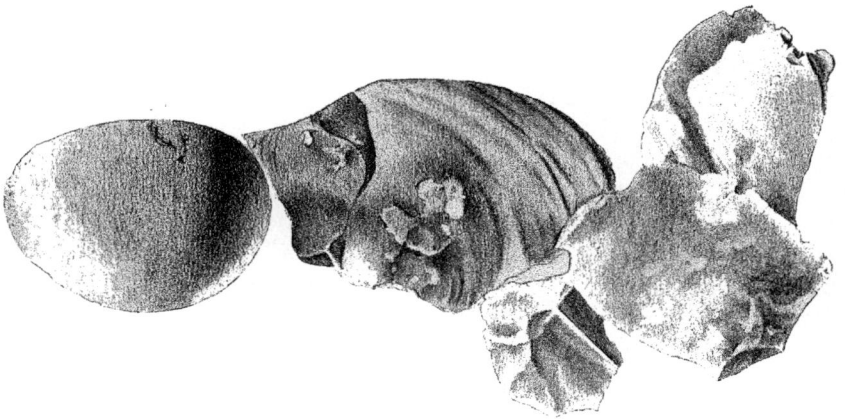

FIG. 545.   ¼

of which belongs to an upper end found in the grave at a considerable distance), the greater portions of three humeri, several pieces of bones of the fore-arm, and bits of a small skull, having a peculiarly fresh appearance. About two feet further south, and close to the side of the grave, were the front and back portions of a large skull, the upper half of an ulna, and the lower end of a tibia, close together. These various remains (not shown on the plan) seemed to clearly indicate that the bodies had been cut to pieces and part of their bones broken prior to being put into the grave, as observed in several of the barrows in Group III.

A little lower, and on the floor of the grave, was interment No. 2, on its chest (an unusual posture), with its head to the east. This was below the two heaps of fractured and dismembered human bones just mentioned. Close to the doubled-up legs was a crushed drinking-cup (fig. 540), measuring (after restoration) 7 inches high, $5\frac{1}{4}$ inches across the top, $4\frac{3}{4}$ inches in the middle, and $2\frac{3}{4}$ inches at the bottom. Near this were a bone pin, $2\frac{3}{8}$ inches long, and three large flakes of black flint; also a beautifully polished axe of black flint, $2\frac{3}{8}$ inches long, and at the cutting edge $1\frac{1}{8}$ inches broad. Fig. 541 shows these articles in the positions in which they were found. A knife of black flint (fig. 542) was found point upwards, just above the right side of the pelvis, and in contact with the lumbar vertebrae, as if worn in a garment passing round the loins. The femur measured $17\frac{1}{2}$ inches, tibia $13\frac{3}{4}$ inches, and humerus $12\frac{1}{4}$ inches, and seemed to belong to a strong male of short stature. The lower jaw had for some time before death been dislocated on the left side.

No. 3, in the same grave as the last, was in the position shown. The long bones, though too much injured to admit of measurement, were observed to be of a slender build, and probably those of a female, whose age, judging from the teeth, might be about forty at death.

Behind its head had been placed an elegantly-formed drinking-cup (fig. 543), which was also leaning and crushed when found. After being rebuilt it measures $7\frac{3}{4}$ inches high, and has a diameter of $5\frac{1}{4}$ inches at the top, 6 inches at the widest part, and $2\frac{3}{4}$ inches at the bottom. Close to its base were three flakes of black flint ("A" and "B," fig. 544), and the remains of a decayed bronze pricker. Four flakes of black flint occurred in a line upon the vertebrae, at the farther end of which was a small yellow pebble. Fig. 545 indicates the position in which they were found. This pebble is nearly the size of a hen's egg, and one of its ends is slightly battered.

Considerable quantities of burnt wood appeared above this double interment. Distributed in the grave, from a depth of about one foot down to the bottom, besides the two heaps placed above the head, were fragments of human bone, consisting of pieces of the skull of a child, and adult bones, pieces of a very thick skull, ribs, several pieces of splintered leg and arm bones, a sacrum, portions of pelvis, vertebrae, half of the left lower jaw, and many bones of the foot. It should be emphasised that these detached bones exhibit less decay and differ in external appearance from the bones of the best preserved skeletons in the same grave, and that this may be due to their having been subjected to a process of cooking.

Grave "D" measured 6 feet by $4\frac{1}{2}$ feet at the bottom, and was 3 feet deep. Nothing accompanied the interment (No. 4) which occupied the floor of the grave. The femur measured $17\frac{1}{2}$ inches, tibia 14 inches, and humerus $12\frac{1}{2}$ inches.

BARROW No. C. 51

Is on a low natural ridge of water-worn chalk gravel, and at the time of opening was much dispersed by the plough.

Opened September 13th and 14th, 1872. Long trenches were dug in various directions, exposing an irregularly-formed ring fosse, so completely filled with soily matter as to be quite invisible on the surface. Its diameter was 14 yards north and south by 10 yards, and in section was 3½ feet deep, 2 feet wide at the bottom, and 7 feet wide at the top. In the centre of this enclosure (which, like other examples met with, had been formed previous to the erection of the mound, and not for the purpose of encircling the barrow, as was frequently the case) was an oval grave 7 feet by 5 feet, and nearly 2 feet in depth, containing two interments, one close upon the other. The uppermost was on its right side, with the knees pulled up, the left arm bent over the body, the right arm doubled back with the hand on the left breast. The head was to the north-east. A femur measured 18 inches, tibia 14¾ inches, and humerus 13 inches in length. The skull was dolichocephalic, and belonged to a person of middle age. Behind the skull, near the left shoulder, was a crushed food-vase (fig. 547) on its side. It is of elegant shape, and ten finely-pierced stops are arranged in the lower encircling groove. On the floor of the grave was interment No. 2, with its flexed legs to the east, close under the shoulders of No. 1, and with its arms bent over its body. Strange to add, the head, vertebræ of the neck, and right scapula had been severed from its shoulders and placed close to its pelvis, near the head of No. 1 and almost in contact with the food vase. The lower jaw of this brachycephalic skull was not to be found.* A femoral bone measured about 15½ inches, and was that of a young person of probably not more than fifteen years of age. In addition to all the bones belonging to the arms of these two bodies, there was a detached human ulna lying close by the head of No. 2, and about one foot to the west, were a humerus and a radius, and some other portions of human bone, clearly remains of a small dismembered adult body placed there at the time of interment. No stone tool or other article accompanied either skeleton.

On the northern side of the barrow, in the upper portion of the material filling the encircling trench, was a small collection of burnt bones, which must have been deposited some time after the completion of the barrow, and the filling-in of the encircling fosse.

BARROW No. C. 52

Stands on a portion of the apex of the same ridge as the last barrow, and about 170 yards to the west, and, like it, was nearly obliterated.

September 15th and 16th, 1872, were devoted to its examination, and led to the discovery of a circular fosse which enclosed the interments. It was 77 feet in diameter, and in section was 6 feet at the top, 1½ feet at the bottom, and 2½ feet deep. This, too, was invisible on the surface, from having been filled with dark

---

* Other examples are given in these pages, and Mr. Bateman in his "Ten Years' Diggings," page 76, mentions the discovery of two human crania placed side by side, near a drinking-cup, but no trace of the lower jaws or any other parts of the skeleton could be found.

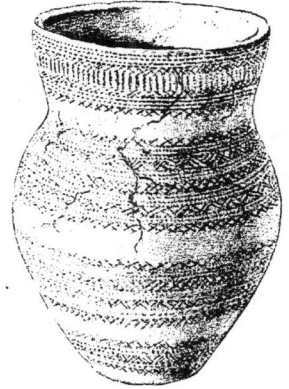

FIG. 543.   ⅓

FIG. 543.   ½

FIG. 547.   ¾

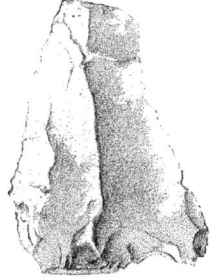

Fig. 552

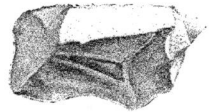

Fig. 550.   ½

Fig. 553.   ½

Fig. 555.   ½

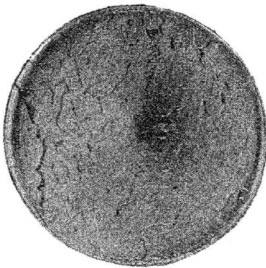

Fig. 556.

soil. The accompanying plan (fig. 548) shows the form and arrangement of the graves within this enclosure. The one marked A was 2½ feet deep, and measured 6½ feet by 4½ feet, and, like the two adjoining graves to be presently described, was charged with the excavated gravel, more or less mixed with black soily matter. At the bottom were the decayed remains of a young female (No. 1), in the position shown, the femur and tibia measuring 16 inches and 12½ inches respectively. Close to the right side of the face were two handstruck splinters of flint (fig. 549), and between the feet was the bronze point of a pricker or awl (fig. 550).

The next grave (B) was 18 inches from the north end of the last, and much larger; the sides measuring 7½ feet. At its eastern side, and not more than 15 inches down, were the remains of interment No. 2. A femur measured 18½ inches and a tibia 16 inches in extreme length, and are those of an old person. No relic accompanied this burial.* The third interment was immediately beneath No. 2 at a depth of 3½ feet, and on the floor of the grave. It was much decayed, and the ribs and vertebræ had disappeared. A rude flint knife (fig. 552) occurred near the right elbow, and a similar one (fig. 553) under the face, and near the front of the skull was a small and rudely-formed lump of dark flint (fig. 554).

The western side of the grave was found to be still deeper, and at a point about 10 inches below the floor of the eastern portion we found the remains of an aged female (No. 4), with head to the south. The femur,

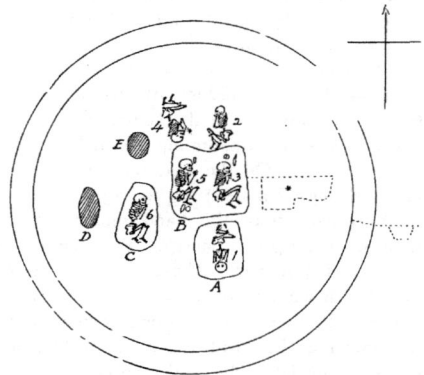

FIG. 548.—PLAN OF BARROW C. 52.
*—Section of Grave.

tibia, and humerus measured 16 inches, 12½ inches, and 11½ inches respectively. Close beneath this was interment No. 5, on the floor of the grave, with its head to the north, and close under the legs of No. 4. The femur measured 18¾ inches and tibia 14 inches in length, and are those of an old and strong-boned male. A fine flint dagger (fig. 555) was in contact with a stud or button of jet (fig. 556) a little to the south of this double interment. The edges of this fine blade near the butt end are deeply serrated to enable it to be better bound to its handle. On the floor of the grave, at each end of this double burial, was some decayed matter much resembling old mortar in appearance.† Under the left side of the skull of interment No. 5 was a fine flint knife of rare type with a chisel end (fig. 557), the under side of which is free from chipping, and quite flat, except a large bulb of percussion produced in detaching it from the parent block of flint.‡ The third grave

* On the plan this interment, as well as No. 4, is for clearness shown at the end of the grave, but both were found vertically above Nos. 3 and 5.
† An analysis of this gives: moisture 3·5, organic matter 6·5, silica 16, iron and trace of phosphate 2·5, carbonate of lime 71·5.
‡ Mr. Bateman found a similar but smaller one in Nether Low, see "Ten Years' Diggings," page 52.

2 E

(at C on the plan) was about 18 inches from the west side of the last. It measured 7½ feet by 4 feet, and was 2½ feet deep. On its floor was a doubled-up skeleton (No. 6), a femoral bone of which measured 18½ inches. No relic accompanied it.

About 2 feet to the west of this grave was an oval hole (marked D), which measured 4 feet by 2½ feet, and 1½ feet deep; and about the same distance from its north end was a similar hole (E on the plan) measuring 2 feet by 1½ feet, and 1¼ feet in depth. These contained a dark soot-like matter, in some places having a greasy, bituminous appearance, but there was no trace of burning.

BARROW No. C. 53

Is one of a line of four barrows, situated about 100 yards from each other. They were nearly obliterated, and had, up to our examination (September 16th, 1872), escaped observation.

It had a diameter of about 60 feet, and it consisted entirely of dark soil, mostly the product of decayed turf and surface soil, probably gathered from the vicinity. In the centre was a trough-formed grave, rounded at the ends and concave at the bottom, measuring 3 feet deep, 7 feet east and west, and only 2 feet across. On the bottom, with its head to the west end of the grave, was a large skeleton (male?) on its right side, with the knees pulled up and right arm doubled back with the hand under the chin. The left arm was bent, with the hand on the right humerus. The femur measured 18¾ inches, tibia 15 inches, and humerus 13½ inches. Close beneath the legs of the skeleton were the flexed legs of a youth from 8 to 12 years of age, lying on the left side, with the head to the east and the arms in the same posture as those of its companion. In contact with the crown of its head was a small handstruck splinter of black flint (fig. 557a). Close to the left side of the forehead were a portion of the coil of an ammonite (fig. 558) and a spindle-formed article of jet (fig. 559) 1½ inches long, with grooves round its circumference. Possibly these had been used as charms. At each side of the skull was a bronze ring (figs. 560-1), each 1½ inches in diameter, but one, a portion of which is wanting, is narrower than the other. The position in which these were found seemed to indicate that they had been worn in the lobes of the ears at the time of interment.

About 8 inches from the front of the face was an elegantly formed food vase, which unfortunately was broken by the workman's pick. It is now restored (fig. 562), and measures 5½ inches in diameter at the top and is 5 inches in height. In the lower encircling groove are four pierced stops, at equal distances. Between this vase and the skull was a mass of decayed matter of a porous texture, probably the remains of a food deposit, from which we picked the tooth of a young ox. A piece of yellowish ochre-like substance (a little darker in colour than that from tumulus No. 40), about 2 inches in diameter, occurred partly under the knees of the youth, and may have served for painting the body. The two interments seemed to have been buried at the same time.* None of the gravel excavated in forming

---

* More than 20 years previous to our examination, an oak-tree coffin, containing three interments, was discovered in removing a tumulus at Sunderlandwick, proving the contemporaneous interment of three bodies in the same receptacle.

PLATE LXXV.

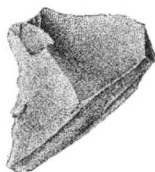

FIG. 557 a.

FIG. 557. ¼

FIG. 559. ¼

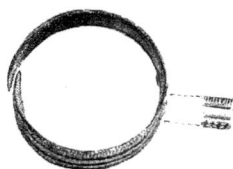

FIG. 560

FIG. 561.

FIG. 558. ¼

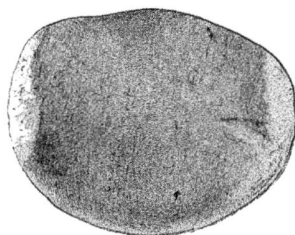

FIG. 564. ½

FIG. 562. ⅓

FIG. 563.

the grave had been put back. The bodies were entirely covered by black mould, from which a flint flake and a portion of the shank-bone of an ox were taken. No trench existed round this barrow.

BARROW No. C. 54

Was opened on September 23rd, 1872. In size and material it was very like the last. At the base of the mound, near the centre, about 7 inches above the natural chalk-gravel (consequently on the surface of the ancient turf-line), was an adult skeleton on the left side, head to the north-west, the left arm at full length, with the hands clenched by the side of the pelvis. The right arm was bent with the hand on the lower part of the body, and the legs were pulled up to a right angle with the trunk. A femur measured 19 inches, tibia 16 inches, and humerus 14 inches. All the bones were sufficiently soft to be crumbled between the fingers. About 5 feet east of the interment was an oval hole, reaching slightly below the old turf-line, filled with black, greasy-looking soil, and contained no trace of bone. From the barrow a small flint-knife, and a broad, flattened, kidney-shaped, water-worn boulder of grit-stone (fig. 564), 4½ inches long, 3½ inches broad, and 1⅜ inches thick, each end rubbed to an obtuse edge or face, was taken.

The only relic with the interment was a food-vase (fig. 563), standing near the left shoulder. It measured 4½ inches high, 6¼ inches across the top, and is ornamented over the whole exterior with cord-like impressions. Round the neck are two grooves, the lower one having six unpierced projections at equal distances.

BARROW No. C 55.

On September 28th and 30th, 1872, the southern margin of this barrow was excavated towards the middle, through black vegetable mould, to a depth of 16 inches. On approaching the centre a quantity of excavated gravel was found on the old turf-line. This indicated a semi-circular grave, with the straight side to the north north-west, measuring 8 feet by 5 feet, and 2½ feet deep. At the bottom was a male skeleton on its right side, in a much contracted posture, the knees being brought up to within 9 inches of the chin. The head was to the north north-east, the right hand at the pelvis, and the left arm bent with the hand on the knees. The femur measured 18½ inches, tibia 15½ inches, and humerus 13½ inches. One large and one small splinter of flint had been placed at the crown of the head.

This grave was entirely filled with dark mould, from which one splinter of animal bone and a small piece of a British urn were taken. It was clear that a small steep-sided mound had at first been heaped over the grave.

About 5 feet towards the north-west margin of the barrow was a long oval grave, pointing north and south, and measuring 8 feet by 4 feet, and 4 feet deep. At the bottom of this was the skeleton of a young adult, and, with the exception of being on the left side and having the right hand in front of the face, it was nearly in the same position as that in the adjoining grave. The femur, tibia, and humerus measured 18 inches, 14½ inches, and 13 inches respectively. A vertical line of black matter was noticed at each side of the interment to a height of 12 inches, apparently the remains of wood which had been placed round the body in the form of a cist.   No splinters of flint were found in this grave.   Unlike the previous grave, this was filled, in the main, with the gravel obtained in digging it, and a portion of the excavated gravel, not put back into the grave, occurred at its north side on the original surface line, and, like that excavated from the previous grave, was covered by the mound, clearly showing that both graves had been made previous to the raising the barrow.

The interments were enclosed by a shallow ditch 30 yards in diameter.   The fact that a large proportion of graves here were charged with soft peaty turf fully bears out the theory expressed by Sir Thomas Browne in his "Hydriotaphia," when, referring to the sepulture of the ancients, he writes that they "wished that their bones might lie soft and the earth light upon them."—See Bateman's "Ten Years' Digging," p. 124.

BARROW No. C 56,

Opened October 2nd and 4th, 1872.   This barrow was even more obliterated than the three last.   At a point which most probably had been the centre of the mound was a large oval grave.   It measured 10 feet north and south by 5½ feet, and was 5 feet deep.   On the floor were the remains of a female about twenty years of age, lying on the back, with head to the north-east.   The legs were closely doubled to the thighs, with knees but slightly pulled up.   The right arm was straight by the side, and the left was bent with the hand on the lower part of the right breast.   Across the right humerus, just above the elbow, was the bronze point of a small bodkin (fig. 565), the decayed handle of which was visible in the form of a small heap of black matter.   Two small rude handstruck splinters of flint occurred close to the skull.   A femur measured 18 inches, and tibia 14 inches, and are of slender make.   Previous to depositing the corpse, a few inches of loose gravel had been put back into the grave, making a trough, which had been lined with some soft and perishable material, indicated by the presence of dark matter.   The upper part of the grave had been entirely filled with gravel, similar to that which had been excavated from it.   Close by were two dish-shaped holes, 18 inches deep and 3 feet in diameter at the top, one near the south-west side and the other near the east.   Like many others in the barrows of this group, they contained nothing but black soil.

About 12 feet south-west of the assumed centre of the barrow was a second grave, in the same direction as the first, and, with the exception of being two feet shorter and 2½ feet shallower, and containing dark peaty soil only, resembled the first.   At the bottom was a large adult male skeleton, on the left side, the left arm doubled with the hand in front of the face, and the right arm bent with the hand on the middle of the left humerus.   The legs were in the same posture and the head in the same direction as those of the female in the adjoining grave.   The femur measured 18½ inches, tibia 15 inches, and humerus 14 inches.   Small pieces of burnt wood were found in all the graves.

This mound also had stood within a deep ring fosse, about 25 yards in diameter.

PIT-DWELLING.

About 100 yards to the west of the last barrow (C. 56), a very slight rise on the surface led to the discovery of a pit-dwelling. After being carefully cleaned out, this measured at the bottom 8 feet 8 inches north and south, and 5½ feet east and west. The sides all round sloped outwards. Its depth was 4¾ feet, one-third of which passed through soil, the remainder through rubbly chalk. Fig. 566 gives a restored section of this dwelling. In form and size the sunk portion is very like some of the large graves. Slightly to the east of the centre of its floor (which consisted of the even surface of an undisturbed stratum of the chalk rock), was the residue of a fire, marking the hearth of this ancient pit-dwelling. Strewed on the fireplace were many splinters of animal bones, those of the red deer being most numerous. About 10 inches above the floor were the lower ends of

FIG. 566.—Ideal Restoration of Pit-Dwelling near Barrow C. 56.

two humeri of the urus, measuring 4⅝ inches across the joint. Unlike the horizontal roofing of the passage-dwellings in connection with barrows Nos. 80 and 110, these pit circles were most probably roofed with the branches of trees, meeting together over the centre, and thatched with grass or heather.

BARROW No. 74.

Opened September 5th, 7th, and 12th, 1866. This barrow had been considerably dispersed by the plough, and was not more than 12 to 14 inches high. It consisted entirely of dark mould resting on the water-worn chalk-gravel of the valley bottom. A little south of the centre, and at the base of the barrow, was a crouched adult skeleton (No. 1), on the right side, head to the east, the left hand in front of the face and the right hand on the hips. Remains of decayed wood, a little over 1 inch in thickness, were parallel with the left tibia, and extended a little past the knee. The femur, tibia, and humerus measured 17½ inches, 14¼ inches, and 12½ inches respectively. In the centre was a slight change in the appearance of the gravelly ground beneath. This indicated an oval grave, which measured 6½ feet east and west, by 3¼ feet, and 3½ feet deep. The infilling consisted of the white chalk-gravel which probably had been excavated in making it. On the floor of this grave was the skeleton of a youth about 14 years of age (No. 2), on the same side, and with its head in the same direction as No. 1, but otherwise differing slightly by having the knees less pulled up, and the left hand down on the pelvic bones, while the right arm was stretched with the hand between the knees. Under the right side of the skull was a fine knife of black flint (fig. 567), 2¾ inches long, delicately chipped to two keen cutting edges. Close to the legs, midway between the knees and feet, stood a large and unusually sound food-vase (fig. 568), 5½ inches high, 6½ inches across the top, and containing the greater portions of two ribs of a small animal, clearly indicating its use as a food-vase and the kind of food it had contained.* The femur measured 14 inches, and humerus 9¾ inches.

* In barrow No. 37 a food-vase contained the rib of a small animal.

A thin seam of dark matter was observed on every side of the body. In the gravel just above the body were one small splinter of animal bone and five very small hand-struck splinters of dark grey flint. Fully 10 feet west of the centre, on the old turf-line, were the remains of an infant, in the same position as the two previous bodies. Seven splinters and three lumps of flint were taken from the earth surrounding this interment, but except those from the grave not a fragment of worked flint was observed in any part of the barrow.

<h2 style="text-align:center">BARROW No. 75.</h2>

The 8th, 10th, 17th, 19th, 21st, 26th, and 27th of September, 1866, were devoted to the examination of this barrow, which measured 90 feet in diameter, 3¼ feet in elevation, and consisted entirely of stiff earth. An opening, 18 feet square, was first made in the centre, but only teeth and part of the jaw of a pig, teeth of an ox, some pieces of human bone, and worked flints were found. Just at the base of the barrow, and near the centre, were indications of a grave, and rather south of the centre, was a very small heap of burnt human bones, marked A in the plan (fig. 569), and about 8 inches vertically beneath these was the well-preserved skull of a young woman. This skeleton was on the top of the chalk grit, the ancient surface soil having been removed, close to the south side of an oval grave, in the posture shown in the illustration (No. 1, fig. 569a), with both hands together in front of the face. The femur measured 17 inches, tibia 13¾ inches, and humerus 12½ inches. In front of the face was a crushed food-vase (fig. 570), which, after being rebuilt, measures 5⅜ inches high, 6½ inches across the top, and 3 inches at the bottom. It is of common shape, ornamented externally from top to bottom with horizontal rows of vertical impressed lines, given apparently (except one row of vertical gashes), by a notched instrument, and two rows of similar markings encircled its upper edge. A bluish-coloured chipped flint (fig. 571), 2 inches long, which may have served the purpose of a spear-head or knife-blade, was close to the left knee; and the point of a bronze pricker (fig. 572), accompanied it. In excavating in the north side of the grave, at the west end, there was the base of a stag's horn; and just beneath it, at a depth of 16 inches from the top of the grave, was a long heap of burnt human bones, marked B (fig. 569a), measuring 20 inches east and west, and 8 inches across. Mixed with them were some heat-splintered pieces of a flint knife (fig. 573), and a few inches to the south of them was a fine globular food-vase (fig. 574), which could only be removed in fragments. It is now put together, and measures 5 inches in height, 6 inches in diameter at the top, and 2⅜ inches at the bottom. Externally two grooves run round its upper part, the lower one containing four projecting pieces of clay, unpierced; and the interior of the lip, as well as the upper exterior half of the vase, is well ornamented with horizontal rows of rope-like impressions; below which oblique thong-like markings form an encircling chevron.

As we proceeded downwards, chippings of flint, small splinters of stag's-horn, and the upper end of the scapula of an ox were picked from the soil and gritty chalk filling the upper part of the grave, and at the depth of 2 feet 8 inches was another inhumed adult female (No. 2), with the feet close on the top of a circular

FIG. 570.

FIG. 576.

FIG. 568. ¼

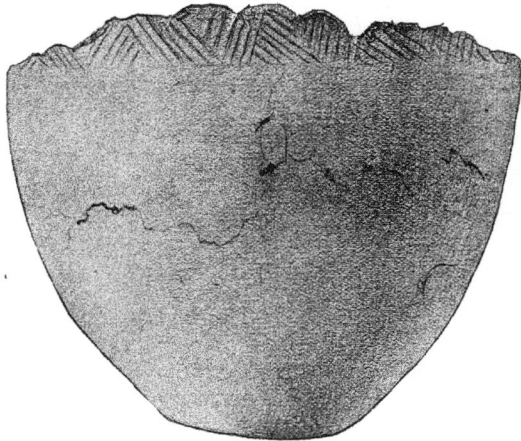

FIG. 577. ½

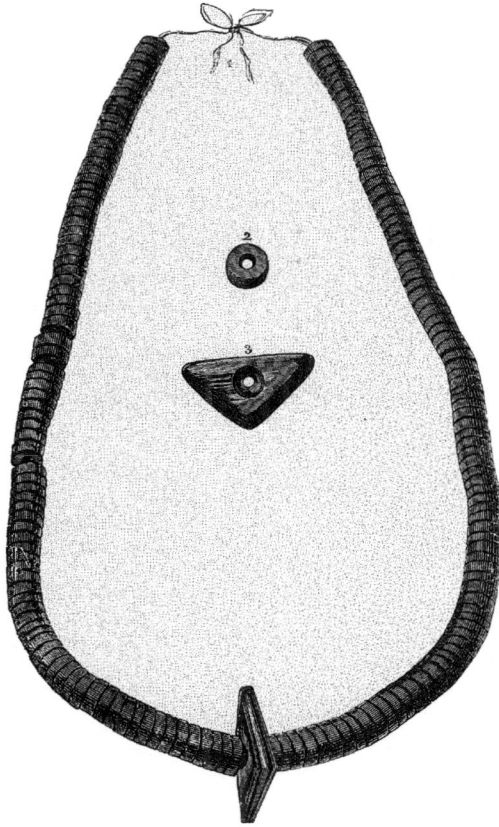

Fig. 575.

Fig. 575 b.

Fig. 574.

heap of burnt human bones, as shown at *C* in the section of the grave, with the head to the west; in fact, almost in the same posture as the one previously found on the brink of the grave, except on the reverse side. The length of the femur is $17\frac{1}{2}$ inches, tibia $13\frac{7}{8}$ inches, and humerus $12\frac{1}{8}$ inches. This female wore a necklace (fig. 575), formed of small perforated jet discs, and a triangular piece of the same material, measuring on the longest side nearly 1 inch. It was pierced in the middle to be threaded as a pendant or centre-piece. Behind her shoulders was a small pricker of bronze (*d*, fig. 575), inserted in a short wooden haft, resembling the handle of a bodkin, which crumbled to pieces as soon as touched, except a very small piece which yet adheres to the metal. A food-vase, 4 inches high, $5\frac{1}{8}$ inches in diameter at the mouth, and almost similar in form and ornamentation to the one first described, stood on its bottom a few inches from the forehead of the body. The burnt bones, *C*, at its feet, are those of an adult. No relic was found with them.

After carefully removing this double interment, we found the grave to still continue downwards, and the chalk rubble was larger than that above, and more free from soil; and wood-ashes were found more

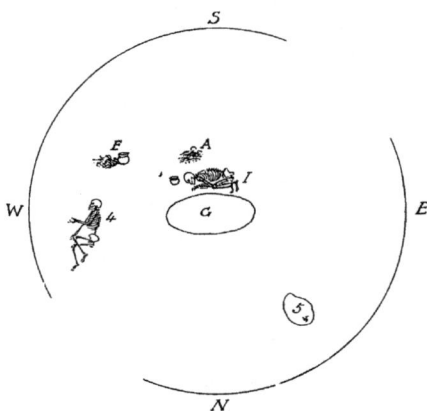

FIG. 569.—PLAN OF BARROW 75.

FIG. 569 *a*.

SECTION OF GRAVE IN BARROW 75.

and more plentiful as we proceeded downwards. At the west end, fully 3 feet 8 inches from the top of the grave, was the lower end of a stag's horn, and at the east end, at a depth of $4\frac{1}{2}$ feet, was another very fine and similar piece.

Nothing more was found but wood-ashes, until, at a depth of 6 feet from the base of the barrow, we reached the bottom. Here, on the floor of the grave upon a thin film of dark and decayed matter, which failed to yield any trace of its original form or nature, was the crouched skeleton of a strong-boned and middle-aged man (No. 3 in the Section), on its right side, and, like the two preceding ones, with its head due west, the left hand reaching to near the knees, and the right hand bending under the chin. The massive long bones measured, femur $17\frac{7}{8}$ inches, tibia $14\frac{5}{8}$ inches, and humerus $12\frac{5}{8}$ inches.

A magnificent and most elaborately ornamented drinking-cup (fig. 576), $8\frac{3}{4}$ inches high, 6 inches in diameter at the mouth and centre, and $3\frac{1}{2}$ inches at the bottom, stood close behind the shoulders.   Fig. 576 shows its form and ornamentation better than any description.   No other relic was found.   The grave, as already stated, was oval, measuring 8 feet east and west, and 4¾ feet across, but at the depth of 3 feet it suddenly shortened to about 6 feet in length, and measured nearly the same at the bottom.

We next drove the eastern side of the excavation within a few feet of the margin of the barrow, testing the ground beneath as the work proceeded, and at a point 21 feet due east from the centre of the grave, just 9 inches below the surface of the barrow and 18 inches from its base, was a large skeleton (No. 4), with the head almost due south in the attitude shown in the plan.   No relic accompanied it.   We could only secure the skull in many fragments.   The femur measured 19½ inches and humerus 13¾ inches.

September 21st.—On working round to the south side we touched a heap of burnt bones of a youth, accompanied by a small and badly preserved food-vase (fig. 576A in plan) of common shape and decoration, situated on the same plane as the last burial, and 17 feet distant from the middle of the grave.   No bone or flint instrument accompanied them.   At the close of this day's labour most of the southern side of the barrow, to within a little distance of the margin, had been turned over to the gritty rock below.   Three pieces of burnt human bones were found scattered on the ground, under the barrow, 20 feet south of the centre, clearly showing that they had been dropped previous to rearing the mound, and most likely belonged to one of the heaps of cremated bones found in the grave.

On September 26th and 27th we turned over the north and west sides of the barrow, carefully testing the ground below, and at a spot 22 feet north-east from the centre, found a small elliptical grave (No. 5), 14 inches below the base of the mound, measuring 34 inches north and south, and 22 inches east and west.   At its northern end, on a level with the base of the mound, was the greater portion of the head of a dog, and below this the grave was filled with dark unctuous earth, at the bottom of which were slight traces of decayed bones, seemingly those of a child, which had almost disappeared, while the compact head-bones of the dog were in good preservation.   This burial brings to the writer's mind, a passage in " Prehistoric Times," page 409, by Sir John Lubbock (Lord Avebury), who on the authority of Crantz and Egede, relates that the Esquimaux " lay a dog's head by the grave of a child, for the soul of a dog can find its way everywhere, and will show the ignorant babe the way to the land of souls."

From the centre and side excavations, and chiefly near the base of the mound, we obtained two oval discs of flint, one nearly 3 inches long, and both having one end rounded by chipping, and the other end showing the rough conchoidal fracture; 175 flakes and splinters; 9 sling-stones; 12 irregular lumps; 8 pieces of British pottery; besides teeth of the ox and other animal bones.   The two burials at the brink of the grave, one by cremation and the other by inhumation, as well as those in the grave, may be regarded as primary, and probably contemporaneous burials deposited before the erection of the barrow; but the three found away from the centre are doubtless secondary.

PLATE LXXVIII.

FIG. 565. ¼

FIG. 572.

FIG. 567. ¼

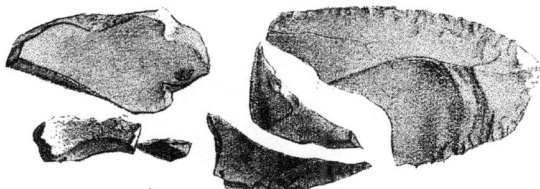

FIG. 573.

FIG. 571.

FIG. 575 a.

FIG. 579.

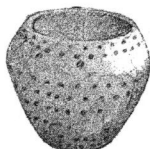

FIG. 588. ½

FIG. 582   FIG. 583
⅓   ¼

FIG. 576 a.   ½

FIG. 581

BARROW No. 76.

On September 18th, 1866, we observed another slight, and in the main natural eminence, situated about 200 yards north of barrow 74. In turning over an area of 20 feet square, we discovered the lower half of a very large cinerary urn (fig. 577), near the centre. The upper diameter of the portion remaining measured 15 inches. It stood erect, on its bottom, and was quite full of burnt human adult bones, mixed with burnt wood and a little soil. The upper portion of this urn had been cut away by the passage of the plough. Nothing more was found in the mound.

BARROW No. 77

Is at the extreme east end of the same field as the three last barrows, and close by its eastern side is a single entrenchment, which at the time of our examination (October 1st, 1866) was almost obliterated. By making a narrow cutting we obtained a section of the fosse of the entrenchment, which measured 5 feet at the top, 1 foot at the bottom, and 2 feet deep. The barrow was about 55 feet in diameter, and formed entirely of black earth to a height of 14 to 16 inches. We turned over an area of 30 feet by 19 feet in its centre, and trenched the ground below as we proceeded. During this operation we picked up 125 hand-struck flakes of flint, eight slingstones, seven oval discs of various sizes chipped more or less round their ends; seven irregular lumps, and thirteen fragments of pottery. The head of a dog or fox, teeth and part of the jaw of a red deer (?), human bones, consisting of a femur, portions of a skull, and some vertebræ, were also observed. The latter seemed to be the remains of an interment near the centre, which had been disturbed and broken whilst digging for rabbits, the mound being trenched and guttered in some places to a depth of 2 feet below its base.

BARROW No. C 71.

This mound was opened August 6th, 7th, and 8th, 1874. It measured about 60 feet in diameter, 18 inches in elevation, and had been erected on a slight natural mound. Operations were commenced on the southern margin, and continued without any discovery until reaching the centre, and here was an oval grave measuring 9½ feet east and west, 6½ feet across, and 4 feet 10 inches in depth.

The plan (fig. 578) shows the disposition of the various interments. No. A 1 was 4 feet down in the centre grave. Its femur, tibia, and humerus measured 17 inches, 14½ inches, and 13 inches respectively. Close below, and resting on the floor of the grave, were portions of the remains of four bodies, two being children (Nos. 4 and 5), whilst those marked Nos. 2 and 3 were adults. No. 2 was minus head, right humerus, and left femur. Only the heads and trunks of Nos. 4 and 5 remained. The only trace of No. 3 (which, if ever an entire interment, had apparently been placed with its head towards No. 2)—was one tibia. Two fibulae and the whole of the bones of two feet were found close to the north side of the two juveniles. A femur, tibia, and humerus of No. 2, measured

2 F

19 inches, 15 inches, and 13 inches respectively. A crushed food vase (fig. 579) stood upon the right side of the chest. The four skeletons on the floor of the grave appeared to have been interred at the same time, and were those of two adults and probably two of their children. The mutilation of the bodies and the injury done to the food-vase might in this case have been caused by the re-opening of the grave for the insertion of the body marked No. 1. If so, the fragments of two adult skulls and other human bones found in the grave round and above No. 1 most probably belonged to these mutilated remains below. Altogether this grave seems to afford the strongest evidence yet observed by the writer of the injury and displacement of the primary interments by an intrusive burial. During the exhumation of the central bodies the two diggers who had been set to work from the northern margin to the centre came upon a grave (marked B on the plan) at a point 19 feet north of the centre. This grave was only 3 feet deep, and hardly large enough to admit the crouched body (B). The femur, tibia, and humerus of this measured $17\frac{1}{4}$ inches, $13\frac{1}{4}$ inches, and 12 inches respectively. Midway between the two graves was a third (C on the plan), at the northern side of which, and only 20 inches from the surface, was an interment (C No. 1) on its chest. Its femur measured 17 inches, and tibia 14 inches. A little to the south, at a depth of $3\frac{1}{2}$ feet, and on the floor of the same grave, was a second skeleton (C No. 2), the femur, tibia, and humerus of which measured 17 inches, $14\frac{1}{2}$ inches, and 13 inches respectively. Under this

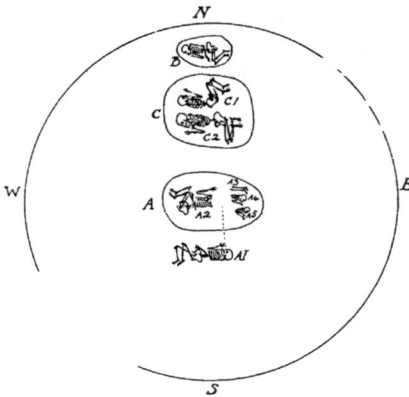

FIG. 578.—PLAN OF BARROW C. 71.

was a considerable quantity of a soot-like substance. Wood ashes were observed in all the graves, and in the centre one several bits of burnt human bones were found. Except the urn with No. 2 A, no relic accompanied any of the interments. In the mound were a few animal and many dispersed human bones.

BARROW No. C. 64

Stands mainly on the green lane, with its northern side reaching into the adjoining field, a little west of Craike Hill. Though the extreme elevation of this mound was not more than 18 inches, it covers a considerable, yet indefinite, area, due to the surface having been tilled.

September 30th and the greater part of the first week in October, 1873, were occupied in excavating the central portions of the mound (fig. 580), which was entirely of a dark brown soily nature, resting (wherever no excavation beneath existed) immediately upon the clean white chalk-gravel which fills the valley bottom. In the mound were a great many broken animal bones and bits of pot, the latter mainly Roman, though a few were British. Also near the centre of the mound was the greater portion of the humerus* of an adult, near to which, and about 18 inches below, were a few animal bones. Under the barrow, slightly to the north of the centre, was a narrow trough-like excavation, marked *W* on the plan, 50 feet long, and varying from 2 feet to 3¼ feet deep, charged with earthy material mixed with dirty gravel. Midway between the centre and the west end of this trough, at a point marked *A* on the plan, was a circular deposit of burnt matter, containing bits of burnt bone and a bronze ring (fig. 581), two inches in diameter; also a bone pin or pricker (fig. 582), pointed at both ends. At the extreme west end, the

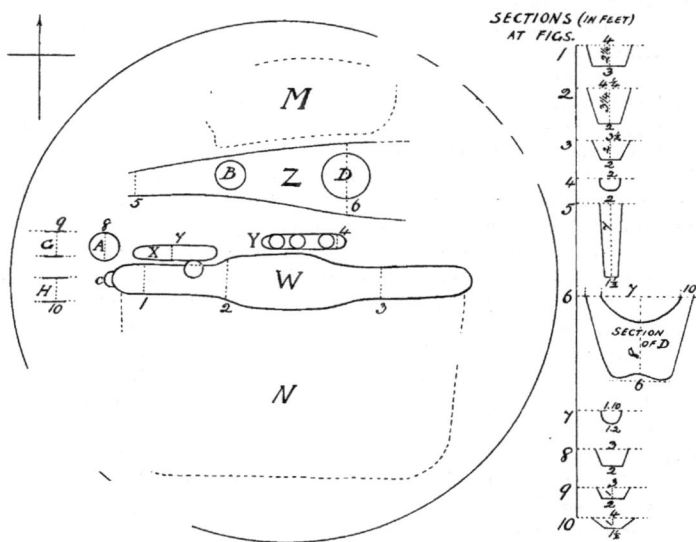

FIG. 580.—SECTION OF BARROW C. 64.

G, H—Ends of two other Trenches (?).　　*M*—Area excavated in 1874.　　*N*—Area excavated in 1875.

projecting half-circle (*C* on the plan) marks a shelf or stepping into the trough. Close to the north side of the long excavation were two small troughs of nearly equal dimensions, being each about 1 foot deep, 9 feet long, and 2 feet wide. The one to the west, marked *X*, contained nothing but soil. The other, *Y*, had three dish-shaped cavities, scooped 6 inches below the bottom of the trough, but no trace of bone was observed in them.

The circular dish-shaped excavation, marked *A A*, at the west end of the small trough *X*, contained dirty gravel and a little soil resembling that in the adjoining trench.

A few feet north of these two trenches was a yet larger one, *Z*, which

* This humerus and fragments of the British vase probably belonged to a British interment in the barrow, which had been destroyed in making the excavations to be described.

was also filled with soil mixed with dirty gravel. We carefully emptied 38 feet of its length without finding either end, and, as shown on the plan, it is unequal in width. At some period after the filling-in of this trench, a circular hole (D), 7 feet in diameter and 3½ feet deep, had been made, at the bottom of which was a stratum of five to eight inches of burnt wood, soil, and bones, mostly burnt to powder. A few feet westwards was a similar receptacle (B), 4 feet in diameter, and about the same depth as its fellow. It was filled with a similar deposit of burnt matter, bits of bone, and at the bottom a considerable quantity of burnt bone reduced to powder, from which we took a small piece of bronze, a Roman bronze coin of " Nero Cæsar Augustus " (date about A.D. 58-60), and the greater portion of a rude bone pin. In the mound, over the last-named excavations, we found a well-shaped bone pin (fig. 583), and in places small pieces of a British urn. All the trenches were mainly charged with dirty gravel and soil, in which were dispersed many sherds of Roman pottery, bones of various animals—horse, pig, sheep, &c., but those of the horse predominating. The mound above the trenches also contained many animal bones and potsherds.

August 12th, 1874, a renewed search was made by excavating that portion of the margin just within the field to the north of the lane. It was found that opposite the east side of the trench Z, a large pit, with sloping sides, varying from 5 to 7 feet in depth, the extent of which we did not make out, had existed at this side of the mound, but had become filled up with soil, mixed with bones of ox, pig, sheep or goat, and horse, as well as numerous pieces of apparently Roman pottery, mainly dark in colour, and one piece of Samian ware. Some small pieces of very thin glass,* much resembling ordinary window glass, were found adhering to the under side of a piece of black pottery. Soil reddened by heat, carbonised wood, and other traces of burning, were observed in several places; as well as some bits of burnt bone and a few corroded nails.†

Hoping to obtain some further information as to the purpose of this strange mound, on September 16th to 19th, 1875, its southern side was examined, and the ground beneath was found to have been disturbed to varying depths, particularly on the east side of the mound. Fragments of pot, shells of the common mussel, and animal bones similar to those found in other parts, split and blackened boulders (apparently by heat) of various sizes, were picked from the disturbed ground under the mound; also portions of two hand millstones, one of which has a cup-like cavity in the grinding surface near the edge, 1½ inches deep and 3 inches in diameter, with a groove leading from it to the edge of the stone. A flint arrow-head was also found. The potsherds and bones were not so numerous as on the northern half of this mound, but one piece of a well-marked British food-vase, ornamented with incised lines, was noticed.

---

* *The Antiquary* for June, 1894, p. 263, described some Roman window glass from the Silchester excavations, which seems to be very similar to the above.
† Possibly this was the site of a Romano-British pit dwelling.

BARROW No. 40

Was opened in September, 1865, when it measured 60 feet in diameter and 15 inches in height. A start was made by carefully removing a 16 feet square from the centre of the barrow to its base, whereon, and near the southern limit of the excavation, was the skeleton of a young and slender person, with a very small skull (fig. 585). Close above the left hand were two yellow quartz pebbles, about the shape and size of a hazel-nut, and upon the elbow was the scapula of a pig. At the back of the skull was a rather rudely-worked knife of black flint (fig. 586), 3 inches long, apparently adapted for the left hand, and a small disc of baked clay (fig. 587), similar in texture to a small vase found near it. There were two holes through it near the centre, probably to enable it to be secured to the dress to serve as a button. There were also two lumps of yellow ochre, each about the size of a walnut, the sides and corners being clearly rounded by use.* In front of the skull, near the left hand, were portions of two boar's tusks. But the most remarkable feature was that the lower jaw was removed from the skull, and there was a small food-vase (fig. 588) inserted with its mouth between the upper jaw, touching the palate. The displaced jaw was found uninjured, on the chest, teeth downwards, about 3 inches below the bottom of the vase, as shown in the sketch (fig. 585). The vase is of fine brown-coloured clay, mixed with a little pounded quartz. Eight horizontal rows of circular punctures, $\frac{1}{8}$ of an inch in diameter, ornament its exterior. These penetrate to a depth of $\frac{1}{16}$ to $\frac{3}{16}$ of an inch, and seem to have been bored by a tool. At two opposite sides of the vase, a little above its greatest diameter, are a pair of holes, about $\frac{1}{8}$ of an inch in diameter, drilled completely through the sides, probably for the purpose of suspending it by a string. In the soil within the vase were some fragments of bone belonging to some small animal, and near the vase was a portion of the skull and two teeth from the lower jaw of a sucking pig.† Two feet south-east of these, on the same level, was a small scraper of flint.

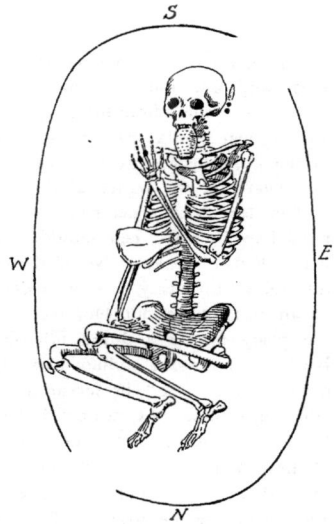

FIG. 585.—INTERMENT IN BARROW No. 40.

About 5 feet north of the skeleton was a grave measuring 8 feet long by 4 feet wide and 4 feet deep, on the floor of which was a layer, 8 inches thick, of loose gravel and soil, containing several detached human and animal bones. On this was a skeleton on its left side, with both hands in front of the face and the

---

* One of these the writer presented to the late Miss Sykes, of Sledmere, who, with a lady friend, was present and witnessed the exhumation of the bodies.

† Determined by Mr. E. T. Newton, F.R.S.

knees towards the elbows.   The head pointed north, and was rather lower than
the rest of the body.   At the feet was a human skull minus the under jaw, placed
upon some detached arm and leg bones, and a perfect lower jaw was found a little
below this deposit.   Above the skeleton in various places up to the brink of the
grave, human and animal bones were scattered, the former consisting of portions
of a lower jaw, several vertebræ, and the lower end of a humerus.   The latter
consisted of part of the lower jaw and bones of the foreleg of a young pig ; also
two leg-bones of two small animals, and portions of some large ribs, probably
belonging to an ox.   In various places at the base of the barrow were some teeth
of a sheep or goat, the tooth of a pig attached to a small piece of jaw, a portion
of the tusk of a boar, and part of the rib of some animal.*

BARROW No. 107.

This interesting barrow was explored during November 11th, 12th, and 14th,
1867, and was found to have been erased by agricultural operations to within
10 inches of the adjoining ground.   Under it was a ring-trench enclosing a central
area 35 feet in diameter, filled with dark soil, but not like the peaty mould found
in the five centre graves shown in fig 589.
Nearly in the centre of this enclosure was a large grave ("B" on the plan)
4½ feet deep, and measuring 10 feet by 8 feet at the top.   A section shows a large
boat-shaped mass of peat mould occupying its centre from top to bottom, surrounded
with filled-in gravel.   No skeleton or deposit of cremated bones was found, but
throughout the peaty mass were detached adult bones and the portion of the leg-bone
of an ox ; and about half way down the grave, close to the north side, between
the peaty matter and the filled-in gravel surrounding it, were a human lower
jaw, a humerus, a radius, two ulnæ, a scapula, some vertebræ, ribs, and finger
bones, all in good preservation.   With the exception of the calvarium and the
left thigh bone, the scattered contents of this grave consisted of nearly all the
bones of a middle-aged male of about 5 feet 11 inches in stature.   The arrangement
of these bones could hardly be due to secondary interments, as, had such been the
case, there would not have been the distinct and separate positions of the peat
and gravel in the grave.   Possibly the confusion in which the bones were found
was due to the body having been placed on a platform of wood at the top, or
at some distance from the bottom, of the grave, which on decaying gave way,
and let down the bones and the peat into different positions.
Interment "A" was in an oval grave scooped only 8 inches below the base
of the mound, and measuring 5 feet by 3 feet 10 inches.   It seemed to be that of
a male from thirty-five to forty years of age.   The femur, tibia, and humerus
measured 18 inches, 14½ inches, and 13 inches respectively.
At F, in a similar hollow to the last, was the skeleton of a small adult, aged
about sixty years, and probably a female, in the position shown in the sketch.
The femur, tibia, and humerus measured 17 inches, 14 inches, and 12½ inches
respectively.

---

* We have preserved some of the pieces of carbonized wood taken from both the grave and the mound
above, and we also possess the three skulls, which have been sufficiently built up for comparison, and have
since been examined by Dr. Wright.

At *C* were the remains of an infant at about the same depth as the two last, but in a much smaller excavation.

The circular dish-shaped hole marked *D* on the plan was 3½ feet in diameter, 3 feet deep, and filled from top to bottom with pure peat soil, but no trace of a body or of calcined bones was observed. A similar earth entirely filled the graves *A*, *C*, and *F*. The grave "*E*" measured 8 feet by 5 feet, was 2¼ feet deep, and its west end cut into the encircling trench. Unlike the other graves, it contained no peat-mould, but only chalk gravel slightly mixed with soil, in which were pieces of burnt wood and four teeth of an ox. At the bottom, on the undisturbed gravel floor, were the decayed remains of a bronze-equipped adult, whose life-period

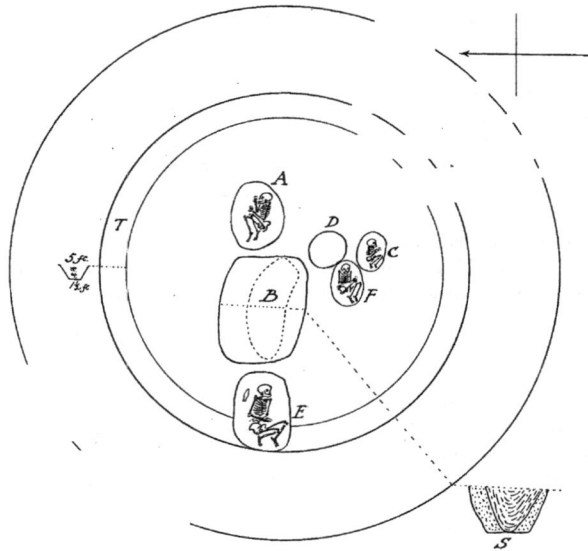

FIG. 589.—PLAN OF BARROW NO. 107.

B—Bottom of Grave.   *S*—Section of Grave.   *T*—Trench.

had been about fifty years. Owing to decay, the position of the left hand cannot be shown in the sketch, neither can the length of the long bones be given. All the under side of the skull had gone, and the upper part was very soft. About 7 inches from the right side of the skull were the remains of a very beautiful bronze knife-dagger (fig. 590), with rounded point, and therefore probably never used as a dagger. The pommel of the handle is of bone (fig. 590*a*), and has been secured to its place with two rivets. From traces of the handle remaining on the blade, it seems to have consisted of two pieces of horn held together by forty-two rivets of bronze, varying in length from ¼ to ⅜ of an inch, and ⅛ of an inch in thickness, and two curved strips of bronze 2⅞ inches long, ⅛ of an inch wide, and ⅟₁₆ of an inch in thickness. When found these rivets were in four rows just as the decayed handle had left them. The blade is $5\frac{5}{8}$ inches long, $2\frac{5}{8}$ inches broad at the shoulders, and is about $\frac{1}{17}$ of an inch in thickness, except all round the margin, where it is ground to a keen cutting edge. It has been secured to the handle by the end rivet of each row. The extreme length of this very beautiful specimen is 8 inches. It occurred parallel with the skeleton, with the point to the east. Close under it were three curved pieces of bronze (fig. 591), in the shape of a horseshoe; fig. 591a shows the actual size and ornamentation. The largest piece measures $10\frac{1}{2}$ inches in length, is $\frac{1}{2}$ an inch broad, and $\frac{3}{20}$ of an inch in thickness, and skilfully ornamented with incised lines. Both ends are pierced with a circular hole $\frac{1}{8}$ of an inch in diameter, and at some time during its use part of one hole had apparently been broken off and a second one bored. The two smaller pieces measured in length $9\frac{1}{2}$ inches and 10 inches respectively, and seem to have been formed of nearly square bronze wire about $\frac{1}{18}$ of an inch thick. One of them is ornamented by indented lines crossing it; the other is plain. The ends of each wire are twisted, as if for fastening to something. These curved pieces of bronze may have formed a bow or handle for a small vessel of wood,* probably containing food, which, with the dagger-knife placed upon it, was buried with the body. A little decayed wood was observed, and, jndging from the span of the supposed handle, the vessel would be about $4\frac{3}{4}$ inches in diameter.

This skeleton, clearly a secondary interment, was the only one accompanied by any relic. Bits of burnt wood were observed in most of the graves, but no fragment of pot or chipped flint was found during the excavation.

BARROW No. 82,

Though not shown on the Ordnance Map, was, at the time of our visit (February 13th, 15th, and 18th, 1867), 2 feet high, and had a slightly elliptical outline, being 34 yards north and south, by 30 yards east and west. It consisted of gravel and peaty earth. About 7 yards south of the centre, 10 inches below the tilled surface (at " A " on the plan, fig. 592), were the remains of a child, with its head to the east. A little south-east of the centre were two deposits of burnt adult bones (B), 3 feet apart and 10 inches below the base of the barrow. Near the centre was a circular grave, 11 feet in diameter at the top, and 4 feet 8 inches deep, with sides sloping inwards to the bottom, the contents of which will be described in their probable order of deposition. A circular heap of cremated adult bones (E on the plan), occurred at the bottom of the grave in the centre, without any accompanying urn or instrument. Close to the south side of this were pieces of decayed wood, evidently the remains of a trough-shaped receptacle about 2 feet long and 1 foot wide, which might have contained food, in place of the usual food-vase ; or it may have served some other purpose. Close to this was a decayed antler of a red deer, standing on the root end. Fully $2\frac{1}{2}$ feet vertically above the incinerated remains rested the inhumed body of a strongly-built adult male (D). The femur, tibia, and humerus measured 18 inches, 15 inches, and $13\frac{1}{8}$ inches respectively. Close under its badly-crushed skull were four small chips of dark-coloured flint

---

* It has been suggested that these may be the remains of a torque.

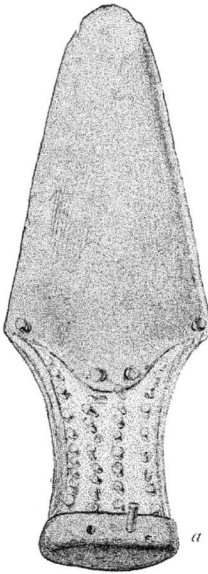

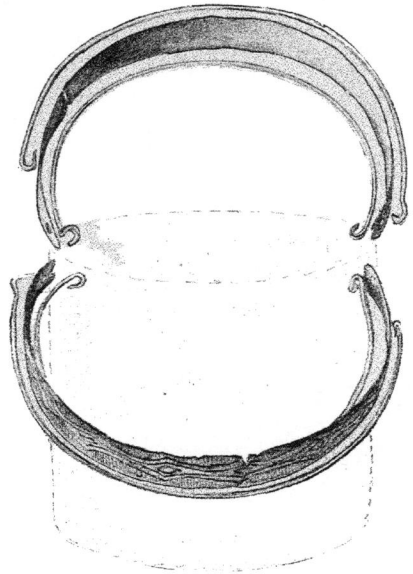

FIGS. 590 and 590 a.   ½   FIG. 591.   ½

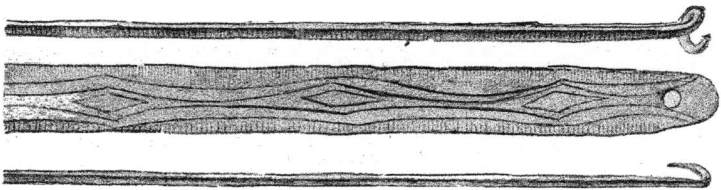

FIG. 591 a.

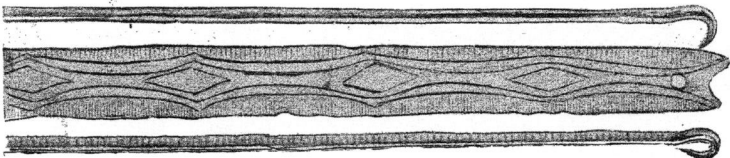

FIG. 591 a.

(fig. 593, *a*, *b*, *c*, and *d*), in a row, reaching from the left parietal bone to the chin. A film of dark matter adhered to the skeleton.

At the top of the grave, corresponding with the base of the barrow, was a second heap of cremated adult bones (*C* on the plan), accompanied by a plain food-vase (fig. 594), and near the west side of the burnt bones, and a few inches north of the vase, was a dish-shaped cavity in the in-filling of the grave, 16 inches across, charged to the brim with a peculiar homogeneous coloured matter, probably the decayed remains of a store of food, as two small splinters of bone were found in it. The grave was filled from top to bottom with gravel and black peaty soil,* mixed with detached human bones. These consisted of a few burnt pieces, unburnt dorsal and lumbar vertebræ, a piece of a skull, the

right half of a powerful lower jaw, bones of the toes and feet, finger-bones, the lower end of a radius, a portion of a fibula, and many pieces of ribs. Ten inches below interment "*D*," and near the western edge of the grave, were nearly all the bones of a foot, lying together. There were also thirteen splinters of animal bone, a small vertebra, and a few snail shells (*Helix nemoralis*). We followed every sign of disturbance in the ground under the barrow without making any further discovery. Only one sling-stone and one flake of flint were found in the mound. Possibly the centre grave had, in the first instance, been a roofed pit-dwelling, and, after the death of its owner, had been used as a grave.

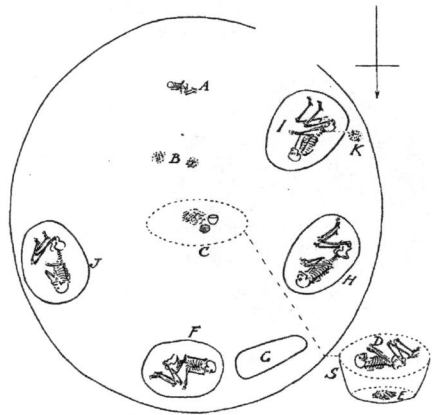

FIG. 592.—PLAN OF BARROW NO. 82.

S—Section of Grave under *C*.

Re-Opening.—On October 13th and 14th, 1874, we cut four concentric trenches round the outskirts of this barrow, as in the previous opening only the centre portion was explored, and 24 feet from the northern margin of the central grave were the crouched remains of a middle-aged male, about thirty years of age. It occupied the bottom of an oval grave (*F*), measuring 5½ feet by 3½ feet, and 2½ feet deep. Two flakes of dark flint were placed near its feet, and close to the

* This dark turf-soil, found nearly everywhere at the base of the barrows situated in this valley, is worthy of special notice, as it seems to be due to floods, as we do not find this peat soil under barrows on higher ground. This indicates that in early times the intermittent springs (gypseys) have periodically flooded the valley bottom to a greater extent than at present. Partial flooding happens now after a prolonged rainy season, and this condition of things would be more frequent, and of much greater extent one hundred years ago, before the time of artificial drainage in Holderness, by which the surface water is now more quickly removed. Mr. W. Jackson, the tenant of a portion of the land in this valley, told the writer that he had heard his father relate that at times he had had to ride in a cart drawn by a horse to enable him to pluck up and remove the stakes of the sheep nets out of the water, most of the ground being submerged for a time.

2 G

right knee were two splinters, apparently of the leg-bone of an ox. The right femur, left tibia, and left humerus measured respectively 17½ inches, 14½ inches, and 12¾ inches, and one of the fibulæ had an abnormal growth at the upper end.

The grave "G" measured 7 feet by 2 feet 10 inches, and was 2 feet 4 inches in depth, but contained no trace of an interment.

Grave "H" measured 6½ feet by 4½ feet, and was 2 feet in depth. The skeleton it contained had been placed on its chest, with legs and face towards the south-west. The femora measured 18¾ inches each, the tibiæ 15⅛ inches each, and the humeri 13 inches each. The upper ends of the fibulæ are abnormal in form, and all the bones, which are those of an old person, are strong and rugged in outline.

Grave "I" measured 5½ feet by 5 feet, and was 3 feet in depth. On the bottom were the small and slender remains of an old woman, doubled up. The skull is in good preservation, with all the sutures closed. Several of the teeth had been removed previous to death, as the alveoli were closed ; and, what was very remarkable, several loose teeth were placed below the chin, which possibly were those extracted during life and preserved for interment with their owner. There were no open sockets in the jaws. Under the skull were fragments of string or fine rope (fig. 595), a little thicker than coarse worsted, made of two strands, each being of a fine fibre resembling flax, and well twisted. There were also small portions of both woven and knitted textures, apparently made of strands of the same fibres as the small pieces of

FIG. 595.—CORD FROM BARROW 82.

rope. Remains of this nature are exceedingly rare with British interments.*

The femora measure 14¾ inches in length each ; the tibiæ 11½ inches, and the humeri 10½ inches. In the grave, about 12 inches above the pelvis, was a heap of clean white calcined bones (marked K), apparently of a young individual.

Grave "J" measured 5½ feet by 4½ feet, and only 1 foot 8 inches in depth. At its base was a skeleton, on the right side, with head to the north. The femora were 18 inches each, the tibiæ 14¾ inches, the right humerus 13 inches, and left 12¾ inches. The whole of the bones were strong, and apparently those of a middle-aged male.

Over this interment, and mixed with the soil in the grave, were a collar-bone, an atlas, a cervical vertebra, and an astragalus from another body. These had a bleached appearance, as if boiled or otherwise treated before burial.

Except the two flint flakes in grave "F," no relic accompanied any of the inhumed interments.

---

* From the account of the opening of Silbury Hill, in 1849, ("Diary of a Dean," p. 13), fragments of a variety of string with two strands, about the size of whipcord, were taken from the centre near the base of that Hill.

PLATE LXXX.

Fig. 593 c.

Fig. 586.   ⅓

Fig. 593 b.

Fig. 604.   ¼

Fig. 593 a.

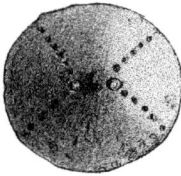

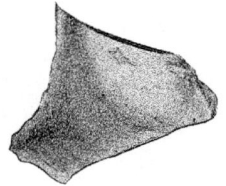

Fig. 593 d.

Fig. 587.   ½

Fig. 600.   ½

Fig. 594.   ½

Fig. 599.   ½

BARROW No. C 46,

Though having quite the form of a partly-demolished barrow, is, in the main, a low convex natural mound on the surface of the western flank of Craike Hill, which consists of drift, sand, and gravel.

On June 26th and 29th, 1872, parallel trenches two feet apart were made over the greater portion of its surface, sufficiently deep to enable us to ascertain that no previous excavation had reached lower. Our only discovery was the skeleton of a middle-aged male, of strong bone, 2 feet below the surface and 28 feet south of the assumed centre. It was laid in a small grave almost at full length, partly on its back and partly on its right side. The head was to the south, and both hands were placed together at the outside of the right femur. A piece of iron resembling a stout nail, 3 inches long, was found near the upper end of the left thigh-bone. The femur, tibia, and humerus measured 18 inches, 14½ inches, and 13 inches respectively. The mode of interment and form of the grave much resembled that of an Anglo-Saxon. The skull, however, which is in good preservation, is more brachycephalic than any Anglo-Saxon skull hitherto discovered by the writer.

A somewhat similar find was made by Mr. J. Horsley, the then tenant of the farm, in a similar natural rise on the north-west skirts of Craike Hill, at a little distance from that just described, in excavating for gravel, when one or more skeletons were destroyed by the workmen.

BARROW No. 80.

About the year 1850, when the Eastburn rabbit warren was brought into cultivation, this barrow had its top cut off to more readily permit the passage of the plough.

On December 7th, 1866, its base measured 103 feet in diameter and 3 in elevation. The mound was found to consist of a mixture of gravel and peat soil, and at its base the old peaty surface-soil was 3 or 4 inches in thickness, sharply separating the gravelly subsoil below from the mound above. It was also noticed that the old surface, indicated by the stratum of black mould, stood about 10 to 12 inches above the present surrounding land, due, apparently to denudation. A start was made near the eastern margin, and almost the whole of the mound was turned over. About 23 feet east of the centre, and at the base of the mound, two large boulders were found together, one a sandstone, the other Carboniferous Limestone. On removing these we emptied what seemed to be a small grave (B on the plan, fig. 596). It was filled with gravel, reddened in places, probably by fire, and mixed with a greyish material, apparently the remains of some decayed substance; and round its sides was dark matter, and pieces of burnt wood. It contained nothing except traces of decomposed matter under the two boulders at the north end. From this oval receptacle, which was 2½ feet in depth, a trough (A, fig. 596), extended towards the centre of the barrow, but did not reach below its base, and about the bottom of this, large pieces of burnt human bones were scattered.

On December 10th, 17th, and 19th the excavation was extended westwards, and the ground beneath was trenched at short intervals. At a point 10 feet north-east of the assumed centre, and within reach of the plough, were the flexed remains of an elderly person, in the position shown by No. 1 on the plan. The skull was irreparably crushed. The humerus, the only perfect long bone, measured 13 inches. A small dish-shaped hole (*C*), about 25 feet north of the centre, 2 feet in diameter, and 12 inches deep, containing reddened gravel, had been scooped into the ground beneath the mound ; and in the barrow above was a piece of a human skull, 4 inches in diameter, and both human and animal bones were found in other places.

A second hole (*D* on the plan), also filled with chalk-gravel, mixed at the bottom with dark matter, was found about 25 feet south of the centre.

Returning to the trough-like excavation; this was found to be slightly wider towards the west, and also showed more traces of fire. It contained increased quantities of large pieces of calcined human bone, especially towards the west end. Here, within the trough, masses of flint were found burnt to the whiteness of porcelain, and part of the gravel was burnt red. Occasionally a few detached and apparently unburnt human bones were found, consisting of a scapula, a lumbar vertebra, and a few others, but no animal bones. Masses of calcined human bones and chalk-gravel were found throughout the length of this trench, and the cremated remains of not fewer than six adult bodies were identified, portions of which were burnt black, whilst others were quite white and much contorted by heat. The incinerated bones were in large pieces, just as the fire had left them, and not broken into small pieces as when found in cinerary urns or in small heaps in the mounds. Near the centre of the trough three nearly complete skulls, though calcined and much contorted, were apparently in the position the bodies had occupied in this crema-

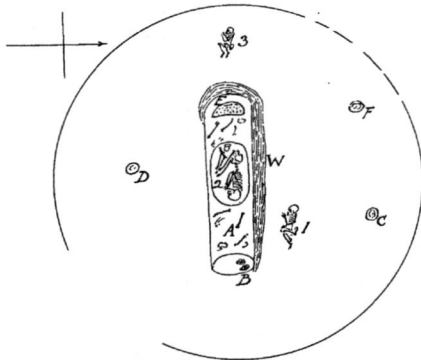

FIG. 596.—PLAN OF BARROW 80.

Showing Crematorium (*A*) and position of Interments.
2—Interment below the Crematorium.   *W*—Peat-wall.

torium. Under this trough, about the centre of the barrow, was an oval grave (fig. 596, No. 2), 16 inches in the ground below the old turf-line, and measuring 5½ feet by 4 feet. At the bottom were the strong bones of a young man (No. 2 on the plan). The femur, tibia, and humerus measured 18¾ inches, 15¼ inches, and 13 inches respectively. The skeleton rested on a thin layer of dark matter, and was covered with gravel reddened by heat from the furnace above, and mixed with dark matter. At its feet was a crushed vase, probably a drinking-cup, of an unusual type (fig. 597). This has been rebuilt, and measures 9 inches in height, 5¾ inches across the top, 6½ inches in the middle, and 4¾ inches at the bottom. This unique vase is very heavy for its size, which may be partially due to an admixture of powdered pyrites in the clay of which it has been made. Pieces of pyrites are not uncommon in the beds of clay at the base of the chalk, on the western side of the Wolds, from which the material for this vase was probably taken.

A little over 5 feet to the west of the grave, but within the trough-like furnace, was a semi-circular hole (E on the plan), extending 18 inches below the bottom of the trough, and 2½ feet in diameter, containing the burnt bones of a young person, mixed with charcoal and burnt gravel. Deep trenches were cut across the bottom of the trough without finding anything further.

It seemed quite clear that the inhumed body No. 2 was the chief interment, which had been placed in a shallow grave, and that on this being filled in, the very simple and effectual crematorium was erected over it, possibly for cremating the bodies of those sacrificed at the funeral. It was also plain that this furnace had been made previous to raising the barrow, as on the original surface-line a wall of decayed turf sods, capped with gravel, 2 feet wide and about 2 feet high, defined its north side, and its southern extremity consisted of a sharp-topped ridge of white chalk-gravel, supported on its south side by a large wedge-shaped mass of decayed peaty sods, as shown in the section (fig. 598).

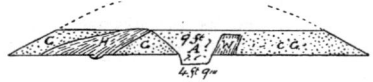

FIG. 598.—SECTION OF BARROW 80.
(From north to south.)

G—Gravel.   C G—Chalk-gravel.   H—Peat-soil.

About 30 feet north-north-west of the centre was a small heap of burnt bones (F on the plan), about 2 feet from the base of the barrow, and 22 feet west of the centre, and within reach of the plough, was interment No. 3, as shown on the plan. The humerus measured 11¼ inches, and belonged to an aged person, probably a female, of slender build. Animal bones, including those of ox and pig, were found in various places in the mound, but it is remarkable that not one worked flint was found during the whole of the excavations.

ANGLO-SAXON REMAINS.

About 200 yards north of the last barrow, and 300 yards west of Garton Station, the labourers on the Malton and Driffield Railway discovered, on November 3rd, 1865, a human skeleton, close to the north side of the railway, at a depth of 10 or 12 inches. I visited the place on the same date, and one of the workmen who exhumed the body described it as being on its left side, head to the north, with the legs slightly bent, the left arm at full length by its side, and the right arm doubled back with the hand near the head. Behind the skeleton were seven iron spearheads. The largest (fig. 599) had a ridge along the middle, and was 7 inches long. The other six varied in length from 5½ inches to 3½ inches (fig. 600). They were found in a row, reaching from the back of the head to the hips. All the specimens have sockets for inserting shafts, and in two cases the impressions of wood are visible within the sockets. A portion of the skull, which is preserved, is that of a young individual.

Thinking this skeleton might be accompanied by others, the ground all round was well trenched, but nothing further was discovered.

ROMANO-BRITISH REMAINS.

At about 500 yards to the north of the last skeleton, several cremated interments have since been discovered, and destroyed by the workmen in obtaining
clay from the Garton brickyard.   These remains were sometimes found in large
plain pancheon-shaped urns, of a coarse texture, dark coloured, and freely mixed
with white grit resembling pulverised quartz.   They were generally found, however, in small holes in the ground, about 2 feet deep, and sometimes covered
with a pavement of stones.   A quantity of dark matter and bits of burnt wood,
accompanied the burnt bones.   The urns were all broken and dispersed by the
workmen, and as the discovery was not made known to me until some time
after, I was only able to obtain a few fragments.   No accompanying relic was
recorded.

On May 13th and 14th, 1884, two workmen were employed to cut a series
of long narrow trenches immediately adjoining the south side of the brickyard,
but no further remains were found.

Since then the workmen at the brickyard have found other similar deposits,
which they also destroyed, except a few pot-sherds and some bits of material
resembling slag, found with the pottery, given to me some time afterwards.

BARROW No. 81

Is situated a little south-east of Barrow No. 80, on a low natural ridge of limited
extent.   On December 24th, 1866, it measured 84 feet in diameter, and 18 to
20 inches from base to apex, being composed of dark peaty soil and chalk gravel,
in about equal proportions, alternating in layers and patches.

About 9 feet south of the assumed centre, and in a shallow oval grave, slightly
below the base of the barrow, one of the workmen struck his spade into the front
part of a human skull, luckily only leaving an incision in the frontal bone.   Six
to 9 inches of clean white chalk gravel, which everywhere covered and surrounded
this skeleton, were then carefully removed, and exposed the remains of a female
(fig. 601, No. 1), probably about 25 years of age.   Figure 602 gives the exact
attitude in which it was found.   The femur, tibia, and humerus measured respectively 17¾ inches, 14 inches, and 11½ inches in length.   The remains were in
excellent preservation, and all the bones in position, except those of the left foot,
which, previous to interment, seemed to have been severed at the instep.   It was
clear that the other portion of this foot had been amputated previous to burial,[*]
as not a trace of the missing bones could be found ; but where they ought to have
been were two worked flints (fig. 603, a and b).   One is a small double-edged
knife, very sharp ; the other is a mere hand-struck splinter.   About an inch below
the back of the skull was a bone pin (fig. 604), 3½ inches long, placed in a position
strongly suggestive of having secured the back hair at the time of interment.
It is made of the longitudinal half of the shank-bone of a goat or sheep.   Close

---

* Potter's "Grecian Antiquities," Vol. I., p. 210, says, "The hand of a murderer was cut off, and
interred in a place separate from the body." May some similar custom explain this missing foot, and
the interment of detached feet, met with in Barrow No. 37, and elsewhere?

in front of the teeth,* and almost in contact with them, was a flint scraper (fig. 605), 2¾ inches in length.   One end is 1½ inches broad by ⅜ of an inch thick; the

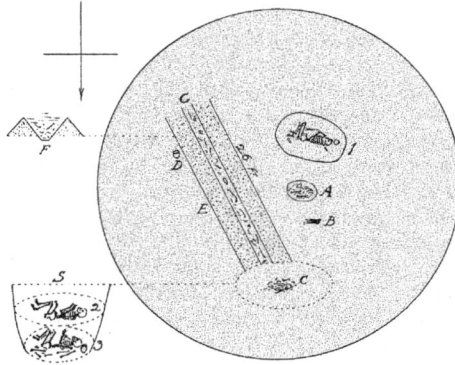

FIG. 601.—PLAN OF BARROW 81.
S—Section of Grave under C.   E—Crematorium.   F—Section of Crematorium.

other end is ⅝ of an inch broad by ⅜ of an inch thick.   One side is made slightly convex by having been rudely flaked.   The other and flat side, which was placed upwards, is just as it was struck from the parent block.

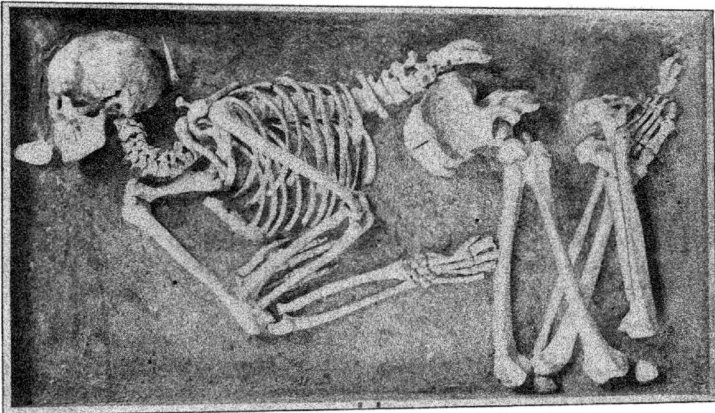

FIG. 602.—BRITISH BURIAL (NO. 1) IN BARROW 81.

Being desirous of possessing this skeleton in its entirety, we obtained a quantity of stiff, mortar-like material, scraped from the adjoining high-road, with which we covered the remains, in order to keep all the bones in position.   We then passed

* Canon Greenwell found a similar flint scraper touching the teeth of a skull.—"British Barrows," p. 555.

three broad pieces of sheet iron under it without displacing any of the bones.
The remains were then lifted on a prepared board, and conveyed to Fimber. After
being carefully cleaned, the skeleton was mounted in a glass case (fig. 602), and
now, with its relics, and part of the ground on which it was found, forms a
highly-interesting relic in the museum at Driffield.

On january 9th and 28th, and February 11th and 13th, the return of favourable
weather permitted us to renew explorations, and, near the centre, a little above
the base of the barrow, and 5 feet north of interment No. 1, was a scattered heap
of dismembered bones (fig. 601, A), consisting of those of a child from five to seven
years old, and part of those of an adult, including the skull, some of the long
bones, two shoulder-blades, and some of the vertebræ. The skull of the child
was broken into many pieces, and scattered in the heap. A flint knife (fig.
606), 1¾ inches long, and 1 inch broad, was found at the western edge of this
deposit, and about 16 inches westward from the knife were all the bones of a full-
sized foot (B on plan). These could not possibly belong to the missing foot of
interment No. 1, as they included the heel and ankle bones, which had not been
severed from that skeleton. A portion of the lower jaw of a sheep or goat was
found in the barrow.

A little north-east of the bones of the foot was a trough, in the mound,
(fig. 601) similar to that in the last barrow. A small portion of the south-east
end had been destroyed by digging for rabbits, and by the dispersal of the
mound through agricultural operations. At this end of the trough, on the
bottom, were several pieces of two plain British vases, of a very fragile kind,
owing to their having been made of clay, too freely mixed with small chalk
gravel, which, on baking, was partly converted into lime.

The trough was perfect for a length of 26 feet north-westwards, and filled
with gravel, burnt red, mixed with calcined human bones, and large pieces of
oak charcoal, some of which were several feet long, and were placed horizontally.
The bottom of the trough reached a little below the base of the mound, and in
it, from end to end, was a continuous stratum of incinerated adult and juvenile
bones, broken and splintered by the action of fire. In one place several pieces
of a skull were stained green, probably from having been in contact with some
bronze article which had decayed.

In this barrow no peat wall assisted to form the trough-like crematorium, as
in the previous barrow. Each side consisted of a triangular bank of clean chalk
gravel, which was distinctly covered on the outer sides with the material forming
the mound. At the north-west end of the trough was the outline of an oval
grave, and near the top were some of the bones of a dismembered body, in a
heap (C), and under the pelvic bones of this were several calculi, varying in
size from a small pea to a bean.* A little beneath these bones was interment
No. 2, that of a young female, in the position shown in fig. 601. The femur,
tibia, and humerus measured 15¾ inches, 13 inches, and 11¾ inches respectively.
Upon the chest was a small jet stud or pendant (fig. 607), with two pairs of
small holes bored into it. Close below the elbows of interment No. 2 was the
humerus of a child, and in the soil covering the interment were detached adult

---

* The presence of these calculi seems to prove that the bones of this dismembered body had been
covered by flesh, when deposited.

Fig. 608.   ⅓

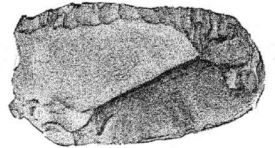

Fig. 597.   ½

Fig. 606.

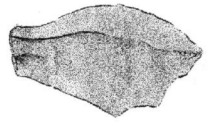

Fig. 603 a.

Fig. 603 b.

Fig. 609.   ½

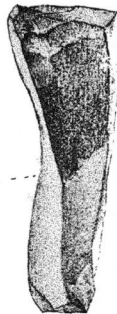

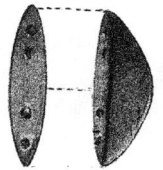

Fig. 605.   ½

Fig. 607.   ½

vertebræ, a sternum, portions of a skull, finger-bones, bones of the foot, a portion of femur, and part of a lower jaw; also some small bones of a juvenile. A few fragments of a drinking cup were also found. Further down, pieces of both animal and human bones occurred all through the grave to the bottom. On the floor, at a depth of 26 inches, was interment No. 3, the femur and tibia of which measured 17 and 14 inches respectively. At the feet and along the back of this were many detached human bones, consisting of a tibia, femur, humerus, two fibulæ, a pelvis, various small bones, portions of a skull, and a perfect lower jaw, all belonging to a person of not less than thirty years of age. In the jaw, the first right molar was absent, and the alveolar cavity closed, showing that the tooth had been removed some little time previous to death. The jaw had apparently never held more than fourteen teeth. These were six molars, two bicuspids only (instead of four), two canine, and four incisors.

The femur, tibia, and humerus from the dismembered bones accompanying body No. 3 measured 17½ inches, 14 inches, and 12½ inches respectively. Nearly all the detached bones were unburnt.

Close behind the shoulders was a crushed drinking-cup, of rather uncommon type (fig. 608). It measures 7½ inches high, 5¾ inches across the top, the same across the middle, and 3¼ inches at the bottom. The outline of the grave, 7 feet by 5½ feet, was sharply defined, and showed clearly that the grave had been cut through the mound and the north-west end of the trough, and refilled with the mixed-up debris. This is one of the most definite secondary graves we have met with, and clearly proves that the Britons practised inhumation for some time after cremation.

Near the east side of the trough, 7 yards east of the centre of the mound, at "*D*" on the plan, was a small hole, containing fragments of a large, plain, shallow, dish-shaped vase, resembling in form and size fig. 248, Barrow 110. No remains accompanied it.

BARROW No. C 42.

On May 2nd and 3rd, 1871, an opportunity occurred to test a slight mound about 100 yards to the east of No. 81. It was discovered that the centre of the mound contained traces of a rabbit type which had been erected when the surrounding land was Eastburn Warren. The only relic discovered, proving the original purpose of the mound, was a partially-destroyed deposit of cremated bones of a full-grown person, at a depth of 2 feet, and a little way from the centre.

BARROW No. 79

Is in the corner of four cross-roads, about 200 yards south of Garton Station. During 1850 and 1851 the eastern side to the centre was carted away to form a new road, consequently all the chief interments were destroyed. As far as the late Francis Jordan, the tenant of the land at the time, remembered, six or seven skeletons were found, but no relic was noticed.

During several days in the middle of November and the beginning of

2 H

December, 1866, our examination was conducted.* The greatest height of the remaining part of the barrow was 5 feet. It was composed of chalk gravel and peaty soil, arranged as in most of the mounds in the neighbourbood. Previous to its being used as a gravel-pit, its diameter and elevation must have been about 120 feet and 10 feet respectively. The old excavation for gravel was emptied, reached 6 feet below the base of the barrow, and had totally destroyed the centre grave. A central portion 75 feet in diameter was turned over, and the ground beneath was trenched.

The first skeleton discovered was 10 feet south of the original centre, 2½ feet above the base of the barrow, and 10 inches from the tilled surface. It was on its back, the head pointing west, the knees up and pushed over to the south, the right arm at full length by its side, and the left arm across the body with the hand touching the knees. The femur, tibia, and humerus measured 18 inches, 15 inches, and 13 inches respectively. No relic was found.

About 12 feet south-west of the centre, and 2 feet from the base of the barrow, was the skeleton of a child (No. 2), on the left side, the legs closely doubled up, both hands to the face, and head pointing east-north-east. Close to its feet was a small and crushed food-vase. The femur, tibia, and humerus measured respectively 8½ inches, 7½ inches, and 6 inches. Fully 23 feet due south of the centre, in a grave clearly cut through the barrow to its base, were three skeletons. The first (No. 3), was apparently an aged female of slender bone, placed on the left side, head to the north-east, both hands bent under the chin, and the legs closely doubled up to the body. A femur measured 16 inches, tibia 13 inches, and humerus 11½ inches. Close under this was interment No. 4, on its right side, the knees pulled up, the right hand over the pelvis, and left arm across the chest. The skull was missing, but the lower jaw was found at the feet, teeth downwards. The femur, tibia, and humerus measured 16½ inches, 13½ inches, and 12¼ inches respectively, and were of strong make, and probably those of a short male. A flake of black flint was near the left shoulder, and close in front of the chest, near the left hand, was a small boulder (fig. 609), one face of which was chipped to an obtuse and slightly-jagged edge, and had possibly been used as a hand weapon. A few inches under this interment were most of the long bones of a child (No. 5), six to eight years of age, upon which was a skull, on its side, with the under jaw a little apart, and above was the remainder of the long bones, but no portion of the pelvic bones or shoulder blades was found. We could not account for the missing head of the adult and the missing bones of the child. A few snail shells were observed near the bones.

About 19 feet to the west of the centre, and about 20 inches from the base of the barrow, was the skeleton of an aged female (No. 6), in a flexed position, on the right side, with head to the south-west, and much crushed. The femur, tibia, and humerus measured respectively 14½ inches, 11½ inches, and 10½ inches. A splinter from a polished greenstone axe was found at the base of the mound.

Thirty-five feet south-west of the centre, at the foot of the mound, was interment No. 7, a heap of calcined bones of an adult, and on the same plane, a

---

* At times in the presence of Sir Tatton Sykes, Bart., the late Miss Sykes, and several lady visitors.

little to the south, and about 30 feet from the centre, were the incinerated remains of a second adult body (No. 8). About 2½ feet above these were the decayed bones of a fox or dog. Under the mound was a circular filled-in V-shaped trench 4 feet deep, a little within its circumference.

A few animal bones were observed in the mound.

BARROW No. C 67.

On May 29th and 30th, 1874, not a trace of the artificial portion of a mound was visible. A slight natural elevation of the grouud alone suggested the probable site of interments and induced us to make a series of long narrow trenches across. At a depth of less than a foot white chalk gravel was reached, where the slightest disturbance was distinctly visible. As a result, eight interments were found. The first one observed had been broken up by the plough. Judging from portions of the lower jaw, it was that of a young individual and probably a male. No relic was found with it.

Interment No. 2 consisted of the remains of an infant, about 4 feet south of the last, 12 inches from the surface, and close upon the legs of an adult. The head was to the east and the legs doubled up.

No. 3, probably a female, occurred a couple of inches beneath No. 2, on the right side, head to the north-north-west, the legs pulled up, and the arms apparently over the body. A femur measured 16½ inches. All the small bones had decayed.

No. 4, apparently the chief interment, was 5 feet south of the two last, and occupied an oval grave measuring 3 feet in depth, 6¼ feet east to west, and 4 feet north to south. It rested on the right side, head to the east, both arms doubled with the hands partly under the head, the legs drawn up with knees touching the elbows. A femur measured 16 inches, tibia 13¼ inches, and the humeri 10¾ inches each, and were those of a person about fifteen years of age. Three small knives or spearheads of foreign flint (fig. 610, a, b, and c), all close together and with points towards the feet, were found partly upon the bones of the hands near the chin.

Interment No. 5 was found 6 feet south-east of the last, on its chest, head to east-north-east, knees towards the south, and the head twisted with face to the north. The femur and humerus measured 16¾ inches and 12 inches respectively, and are probably those of a female. It was placed on the floor of a small and nearly circular grave, 16 inches deep.

Over this interment, and only a few inches from the surface, were two vases much broken by the plough. That marked b is a food-vase (fig. 611), 3¼ inches high, and 4½ inches across the top.

Interments Nos. 6 and 7 occupied a grave situated 13 feet north of the last, and measuring 6 feet by 3 feet, and 2 feet deep. The upper burial, a child about two years old, was flexed, on its right side and head to south-south-east. The other, immediately below, was that of a boy about five years old, and was on the right side, the arms on the body, and the femora at full length, with the legs bent sharply back at the knees. The two skulls were much crushed and decayed.

Near them was a small food-vase (fig. 612), ornamented inside and outside to a depth of 1¼ inches below the lip.

Burial No. 8, also that of an infant, was in a small shallow grave between Nos. 5 and 7, and rather to the east of them. It also was flexed, on the right side, with the head to the north. Nothing was found with it.

BARROW C 40

Is not more than 10 or 12 inches above the surrounding surface of the land, and has an irregular outline due to agricultural operations. It covers a large area.

On March 6th and 8th, 1871, we found a round-ended grave measuring 7 feet by 4 feet, and 3 feet deep (grave A) near the centre, dug into the chalk gravel beneath. At the bottom was the skeleton of a large male, on its back, with the head to the south end of the grave. The right arm was doubled with the hand under the chin, and the left arm was bent over the body, while the pulled-up knees and the head* were pressed over to the east. The femur, tibia, and humerus, measured 19¼ inches, 15½ inches, and 13¾ inches respectively, and are very strong. Close to the skull was a food-vase of the common type (fig. 613), measuring 4¾ inches high, 6 inches across the top, and ornamented on its upper half with five horizontal rows of peculiar impressions. Two similar rows pass round the interior of the lip. Several minute splinters of dark-coloured flint (fig. 614) were placed round the skull, evidently intentionally. Near the opposite end of the grave, at about half its depth, was a small deposit of burnt human bones, and from other places in the grave two pieces of unburnt animal bones were taken.

About 4 feet to the east was a second grave (B), similar in form to the first, but at right angles to it. At a depth of 3½ feet were the crushed remains of a child, about three years of age, with the head to the west. The posture of this body resembled that in the preceding grave. Close beneath, on the floor of the grave, was the skeleton of an adult in good preservation, also with its head† to the west and near the child's head. It was in a flexed position, on its right side, with both hands brought under the chin. A femur, tibia, and humerus measured 17 inches, 14¾ inches, and 12 inches respectively, and were rather slender. A small crushed food-vase (fig. 615) stood close to the right of the two skulls, and after rebuilding measured 5 inches high and 5¾ inches in diameter at the top. It is very similar to the last, and the same or a similar tool has been used in its ornamentation. Close upon the feet of the adult skeleton was a heap of bones, consisting of several pieces of a skull, the upper and lower halves of a femur with opposite ends placed together, and the upper end of a tibia split in two. Immediately to the south of the two graves, at a depth of not more than 12 inches, was a double interment (Nos. 5 and 6), consisting of the remains of an old person and a child. The former was partly on its right side with the head to the east, the legs bent to a right angle with the body. The right arm was bent back with the hand in front of the face, and the left arm was bent over the body with the hand on the elbow. The child, excepting being on its left side and with its head to the west, was in the same posture as the adult. The feet of both skeletons touched. Behind the

* Cephalic Index, about 72.   † Cephalic Index, 84·5.

FIG. 610 a.

FIG. 610 b.

FIG. 610 c.

FIG. 615.

FIG. 614.   FIG. 614.   FIG. 614.

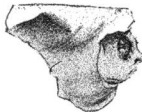

FIG. 614.   FIG. 614.

FIG. 611.

FIG. 612.

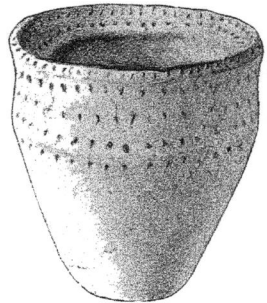

FIG. 613.

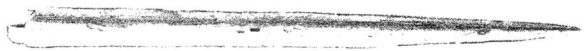

FIG. 617 c.

FIG. 617 b.

FIG. 617 a.   ⅟₁

pelvis of the adult were portions of the bottom of a British food-vase; all the upper part having been destroyed by the plough.

No other relic accompanied any of the interments.

BARROW No. C 45

Is a little to the west of barrow C 44, and close to the north side of a British entrenchment, which extends from the hills, down the middle of Garton Slack to the springs at Elmswell. On the surface this entrenchment is visible in places only by a low rampart and an almost filled-in ditch on the south side.

On March 11th, 12th and 13th, 1871, this barrow was found to be enclosed by a filled-in circular ditch, 18 yards in diameter and 5 feet deep. Many years previous to our examination all but a small portion of the southern side of this barrow had been removed by persons obtaining gravel, of which it had largely been made. In the portion remaining, nearly at its base, and almost midway between the southern side and the encircling trench, were the remains of a male, lying on the left side, with the head to the west, both hands brought to the head, and the knees pulled very close to the chest. The femur measured 19 inches, and tibia 15 inches in length. About 4 yards east of the skeleton was a small round hole containing burnt human bones and wood ashes. No relic accompanied either interment.

BARROW No. 112.

This mound had been erected on a natural rise on the surface. It was opened on April 6th, 10th and 13th, 1868, when its diameter was 70 feet, and its elevation reduced to 2 feet, from repeated ploughing. In the central area was a filled-in circular ditch 40 feet in diameter, 5 feet deep, and 9 feet wide at the top, and 2 feet at the bottom. Within this enclosure (fig. 616) were the remains of three infants, in small graves, from 2 to 2½ feet from the top of the mound. The relative positions of the graves are shown at 1, 2 and 3 on the plan. Hardly anything remained but a bone pin in each, (a, b, and c, fig. 617), which probably had been used to fasten up the body in a wrapper. These pins measure 4 to 5 inches in length.

About the centre of the mound, 8 to 10 inches below its base, were the remains of an adult (No. 6), head to the south, with the arms pushed out in front, but the hands doubled back. The femur and tibia measured 16½ inches and 14¼ inches respectively. Under it were the decayed bones of an infant,* but in this case no bone pin accompanied them. Close to the east and the west sides of interment No. 6, and about the same depth, were portions of two other adult skeletons, which had been partly dispersed, probably by digging for rabbits. Near them were portions of a food-vase, underneath which were pieces of burnt bone and a white punch-shaped flint (fig. 618), burnt white, 3½ inches long.

From the surface the split half of another bone pin (fig. 619) was taken. In the upper part of the circular fosse were four interments, as shown at 4, 5, 7 and 8 on the plan, which had evidently taken place after the trench had been three-parts filled. At No. 4 was the skeleton of a young child, close to which were a

---

* No. 6a not shown on the plan.

few burnt bones of a small person (*a*).   At No. 5 was an adult skeleton, possibly
that of an Anglo-Saxon, with the head to south-east, in the posture shown in the
illustration.   The femoral bones measured 16 inches each.   No. 7, also possibly
an Anglo-Saxon, was placed on its right side, with the head to the west.   The
femur measured about 18½ inches, tibia 14¾ inches, and humerus 13 inches.   About
16 inches north-west of the skull were traces of the bones of an infant.

No relic accompanied either of the three last interments, all of which were
about 18 inches below the tilled surface, and at a depth of about 10 inches in
the trench.   No. 8, evidently an Anglo-Saxon interment, was found 10 inches
below the surface, and was not doubled quite so much as the other skeletons; its
head was to the north.
The femur measured 18
inches, tibia 14¾ inches,
and humerus 13 inches.
Two corroded iron objects,
one, apparently the re-
mains of a knife, 5 inches
long, and the other pro-
bably a sharpening, iron
(fig. 620), occurred across
the lower part of the
skeleton just under the
bones of the forearm—the
position of the belt in
which they had probably
been carried.

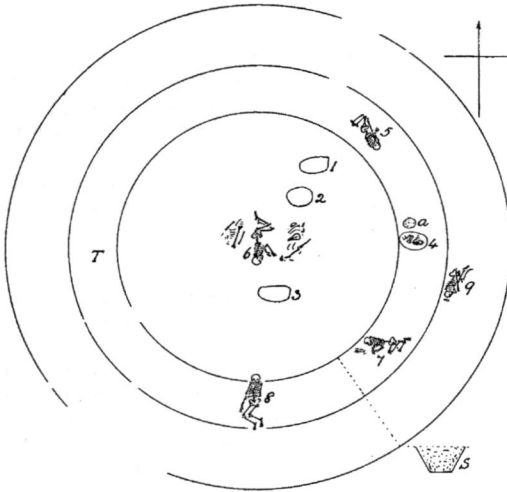

FIG. 616.—PLAN OF BARROW NO. 112.

T—Trench.   *S*—Section of Trench.

*Re-opening, April 26th,
1872.* — Having subse-
quently found a consider-
able number of Anglo-
Saxon interments about
200 yards to the north,
we decided to search the
extreme margin of this
barrow for further remains, and discovered another skeleton (No. 9).   It was
about 20 inches from the surface, in the position shown on the plan.   The femur
measured 14 inches, tibia 11¾ inches, and humerus 9½ inches in length, and were
those of an individual about 10-14 years of age.   Near the skull were some leg
bones of a small pig, but no other relic was discovered.   The close doubling-up
of the remains much resembles a British interment, but from the shape of the
very small grave in which it was placed, and the type of the skull, it is probably
of Anglo-Saxon age.

BARROW No. C 34

Is close to the south side of the Malton and Driffield Railway, about 200 yards
to the west of the Garton gate-house, at the Green Lane crossing.   It is now
almost obliterated.

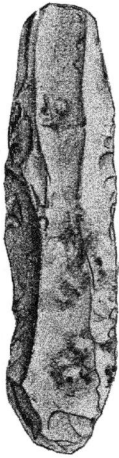

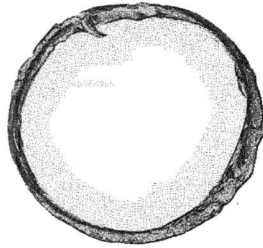

FIG. 623.

FIG. 622.   ½

FIG. 620.   ½

FIG. 626.   ½

FIG. 625.   ½

FIG. 618.

FIG. 624.   ½

FIG. 627.   ¹⁄₁

FIG 630.   ½

FIG. 628.   ¹⁄₁

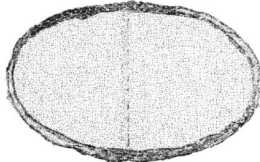

FIG. 632.   ¹⁄₁

FIG. 631.   ¹⁄₁   FIG. 619.   ¹⁄₁

FIG. 633.   ¹⁄₁

FIG. 629.   ½   FIG. 636.   ⅓

FIG. 634.   ¹⁄₁

March 7th, 8th, and 9th, 1870, were devoted to its examination. The lower portion of a nearly-demolished trough-like crematorium, 15 feet in length (shown on the plan, fig. 621), similar in construction to that in Barrow No. 81, extended nearly east and west, and contained a few white calcined human bones, mixed with chalk gravel reddened by fire. To the north of the trough, in the mound, were portions of leg bones and scapula of an ox, unburnt.

ANGLO-SAXON CEMETERY.

Near the northern margin of the barrow, at a depth of 2½ feet, was the skeleton of an Anglo-Saxon (No. 1), about seventeen years of age, on its right side, head to the west, as shown on the plan (fig. 621). At the feet were the remains of a child (No. 2), about two years of age, head to the east, with the legs dovetailed into those of its companion. Accompanying these interments was an iron hoop, 3½ inches in diameter, and half an inch deep (fig. 622), with traces of wood on the inside. Probably this is the rim or binding from the top of a wooden vessel.* Its position is shown by the letter "b" in the illustration, and "a" indicates the position of some unjointed animal vertebræ, the residue of food, while "c" represents the position of an angular plate of bronze (fig. 623), found near the chest of No. 2, each side measuring about ⅞ of an inch. It had been rivetted to some small article, the dark decayed remains of which were found close to the chest of the child. Pieces of animal bone and a portion of the rim of a hard variety of earthenware were found just above the two skeletons.

The position of No. 3 is shown on the plan. Its femur measured 19 inches, tibia 15¾ inches, and humerus 13½ inches, and belong to a powerful man of about 6 feet in height. Across the lower part of the vertebræ was an iron knife (fig. 624), 7¼ inches long, with portion of the wooden handle still attached. At a right angle with the knife was a sharpening iron (fig. 625), 6 inches long, with its lower part almost in contact with the end of the knife. Part of the wooden handle was also attached to this article. These instruments had probably been placed in a girdle, as there were some pieces of decayed iron, much resembling portions of a buckle, close by them. Some square pieces of bronze rested on the lower vertebræ, and dark matter and small bent pieces of bronze, probably the remains of a small leather pouch or wallet, were found at the fifth vertebra. Between the left hip and the ribs was the shoulder-blade of a sheep or goat, which had, apparently, been deposited with flesh on it at the time of interment, and a little to the north was a cup-shaped hole (*d*), 2 feet wide at the top and reaching 18 inches below the burial, in which were portions of vertebræ and leg bones of an ox.

Interment No. 4 is probably that of a female about seventeen to twenty years of age. Its mode of interment will be best understood from the sketch. Over the chest was a slender iron knife (fig. 626), 4½ inches long, and close to the doubled-up leg was the shank-bone of an animal. A small disc of bronze (fig. 627), pierced in the centre, and a flattened bead of amber-coloured glass (fig. 628), were found near the breast, but their exact positions were not made out.

* The silver edging or rim of a leather cup was found by Mr. Bateman. See "Ten Years' Diggings," p. 28.

Interment No. 5 occurred on its left side, with an iron knife (fig. 629), 8¼ inches long, close under it, near the elbow, and with the point towards the head. Small pieces of oxidized iron were also found near the lumbar vertebræ. The femur measured 18½ inches, and tibia 15 inches; they are very strong, and probably those of a male. Nearly in the same posture was interment No. 6, also accompanied by an iron knife (fig. 630), 4¾ inches long, with the point towards the head. Just within the bend of the left arm was a bronze buckle (fig. 631),* and a small bronze article (fig. 632), with one end spatulate and the other end split, through which is a small bronze rivet, probably to secure it to a handle. There were also pieces of iron (fig. 633), among which was the blade of a bodkin (fig. 634), and dark-coloured matter. Upon the bones of the left foot were several vertebræ of a small animal.

The femur of interment No. 6 measured 16½ inches, tibia 14¾ inches, humerus 12½ inches, and seem to belong to a female.

The depth of these interments varied from 2½ feet to 4 feet, and for a distance of forty yards they mainly occupied the northern fosse of a British double entrenchment, which divides at this spot and encloses the barrow. This entrenchment leads from the chalk hills on the north-west to the Emswell springs, about three-quarters of a mile to the east of the barrow. The frequent method of interment was apparently to place the body in the hollow by the side of the rampart, without digging a grave, and then to cover it sufficiently by filling in the fosse with soil, mixed with broken animal bones and potsherds. A skeleton was usually found either on its side or back, with the knees pulled up. It was interesting to observe that an accumulation in the trench more than 2 feet in depth had taken place previous to the interments. As this accumulation would take place but slowly, it indicates a considerable antiquity for the earthworks.

On September 1st, 1871, excavations were again commenced, and at a depth of 3½ feet, close to the position occupied by the skull of interment No. 3, was the skeleton of a female (No. 7), from 17 to 20 years of age. In front of the abdomen had been placed a wooden bucket (fig. 636), of which two iron hoops, measuring respectively 6½ inches and 5¾ inches in diameter, remained. The smaller one was about six inches above the other, and the two seem to have been united by four upright pieces of iron of which nothing but rust remained. On the outside of these hoops, to the west, were several pieces of ribs, apparently of a sheep, and in front of the skull were other animal bones. On the right shoulder was a silver buckle-fibula (fig. 637), and on the chest were two small decayed hemispherical pendants of very thin bronze, and a circular gold bulla (fig. 638) with a garnet set in white paste in the centre, and surrounded by ornamental embossed lines. About the neck were 13 beads of glass, amethyst, and other materials (fig. 639). A bronze pin (fig. 640), 1½ inches long, pointed at one end and flattened at the other, was found under the skull. Close by was an ear-ring of silver (fig. 641), and at the lower part of the body was a similar one, but slightly larger (fig. 642).† One large bead was found in the soil eight inches above the interment. Upon the ankles were the following articles :— a cylindrical bronze box (fig. 643), to which was attached a bronze ring

---

* Similar to one figured in Wright's "Celt, Roman and Saxon," p. 409.
† Probably the position of the last ring, as well as the displacement of a few teeth and beads, were due to the scratching and gnawing of mice.

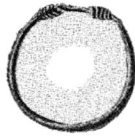

FIG. 642. ½

FIG. 641. ½

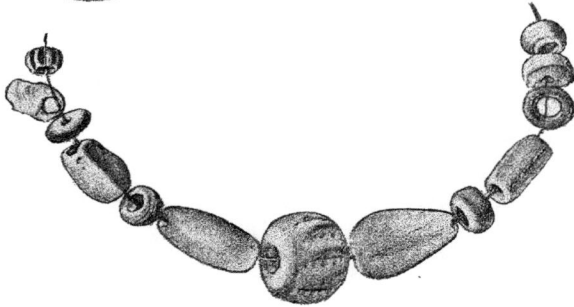

FIG. 639.

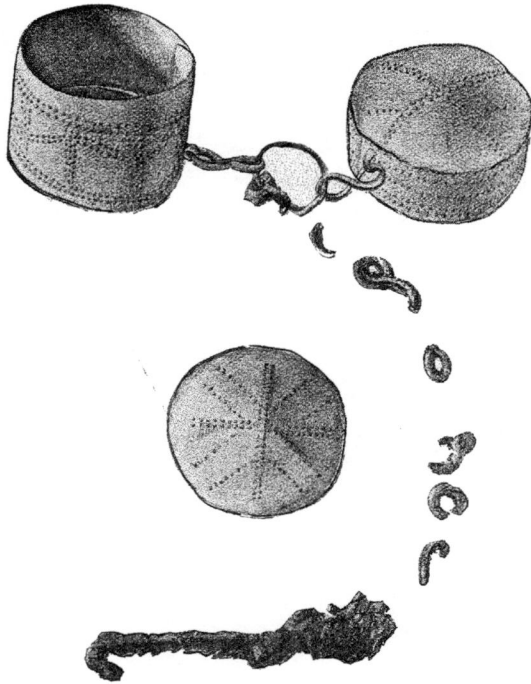

FIG. 643. ¼

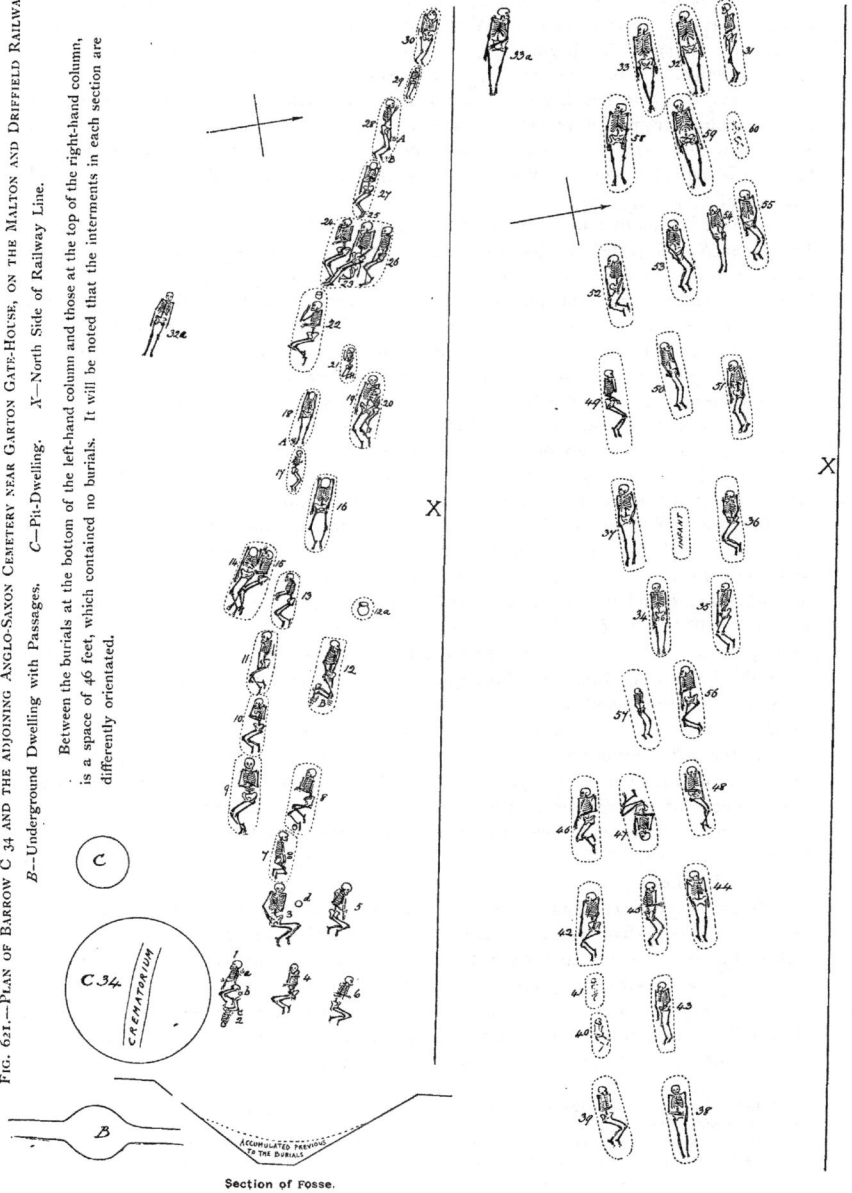

FIG. 621.—PLAN OF BARROW C 34 AND THE ADJOINING ANGLO-SAXON CEMETERY NEAR GARTON GATE-HOUSE, ON THE MALTON AND DRIFFIELD RAILWAY. B—Underground Dwelling with Passages. C—Pit-Dwelling. X—North Side of Railway Line.

Between the burials at the bottom of the left-hand column and those at the top of the right-hand column, is a space of 46 feet, which contained no burials. It will be noted that the interments in each section are differently orientated.

Section of Fosse.

and two S-shaped links connecting the lid and box. To these were attached several portions of iron links. With these was found an iron hook, a bronze buckle (fig. 644), a flat bronze ring 1¾ inches in diameter (fig. 645). There was also a spoon-like article of iron (fig. 646), and fragments of a bone comb. The bronze box is 1¼ inches high and 2 inches in diameter, ornamented with dotted lines punched from the inside. There was also a chipped piece of thick blue glass (fig. 647), and two circular pieces of similar glass (figs. 648-9), which may have ornamented a box or wallet, and a spindle whorl of chalk (fig. 650), and another of bone (fig. 651).

A large ox tooth and a sherd of hard greyish pot were found above the skull. Interment No. 8 rested on its right side. An iron knife (fig. 652) was found on the right arm just above the elbow, and an iron buckle (fig. 653) occurred near the lumbar vertebræ. Several animal bones were found near the right pelvis, and a plain globular vase (fig. 654) stood near the feet. This measured 5¼ inches in height, and 4¼ inches across the top.* Owing to the unequal settling of the contents of the grave, this vase had shifted from its original vertical position.

Interment No. 9 consisted of the remains of an adult male. The femur measured 18 inches and tibia 14½ inches. Close to the skull were pieces of ribs and a scapula of a sheep or goat, and across the lowest lumbar vertebra was a small iron knife (fig. 655), and near it a small iron buckle, both in bad preservation. A marine shell (limpet) was found near the skull.

Interment No. 10 was in a small grave, 3 feet 4 inches by 2 feet, as shown in the plan. The femur and humerus measured respectively 16 inches and 11 inches, and were those of a strongly built youth, 14 to 17 years of age. An iron knife (fig. 657) was found on the lower vertebræ with its point to the feet, and near to it was a small buckle (fig. 658), also of iron. On the left ribs was a bridle-bit of iron (fig. 659) and a similar, but smaller, one (fig. 660) rested on the opposite side. Near the latter were four iron rings (fig. 661), 1⅝ to 1½ inches in diameter. Close by were two iron buckles (figs. 662-3). The rings of the larger and stronger bit measured 4 inches, and those of the smaller 3¼ to 3½ inches in diameter.†

At the left shoulder was a small bronze buckle (fig. 664), and the iron points of a bodkin with a little decayed wood attached to it (fig. 665). On the feet were many pieces of the ribs of a sheep or goat (?) and two ox ribs. Near these were several small clasps of bronze (fig. 666) accompanied by decayed matter, apparently the remains of a small box or wallet, which had accompanied some food, as indicated by animal bones.

Interment No. 11 consisted of the remains of apparently a short male about twenty to twenty-five years of age. The leg bones measured 17½ inches and 13½ inches respectively, and were of strong build. At the left elbow was an iron knife (fig. 667), with the point towards the skull, and on the right side of the lower vertebræ was a small iron buckle (fig. 668). At the feet were traces of decayed wood, a pointed iron article (fig. 669), and some small clasps of iron, which probably had belonged to a small wooden box.

---

* In form this vase closely resembles one from an ancient Teutonic pagan cemetery at Selzen, in Rhenish Hesse, figured in Thos. Wright's " Celt, Roman, and Saxon," p. 427.

† It is interesting to observe that in this interment is all the metal work necessary for two snaffle bridles with martingales, and that they differ but little from those in use at the present day.

FIG. 637.

FIG. 638. $\frac{1}{1}$

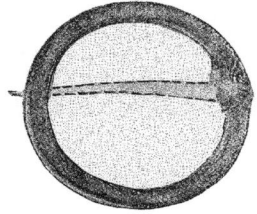

FIG. 645. $\frac{1}{2}$

FIG. 644.

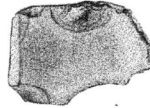

FIG. 647.

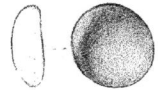

FIG. 648.

FIG. 640. $\frac{3}{4}$

FIG. 646.

FIG. 649.

FIG. 652. $\frac{1}{2}$

FIG. 650.

FIG. 651.

FIG. 654. $\frac{1}{2}$

Fig 653.

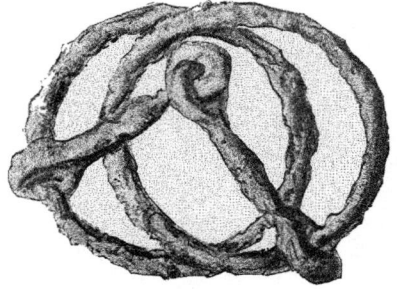

Fig. 659. $\frac{1}{2}$

Fig. 653 *a*.

Fig. 658. $\frac{1}{1}$

Fig. 655 $\frac{1}{2}$

Fig. 657. $\frac{1}{2}$

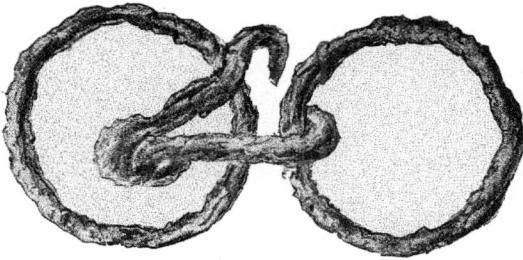

Fig. 660. $\frac{1}{2}$

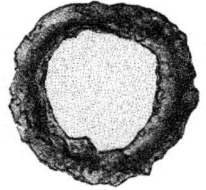

Fig. 661. $\frac{1}{1}$

Fig. 661. ^{1}

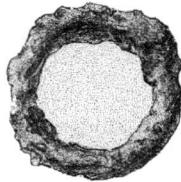

Fig. 661. $\frac{1}{1}$

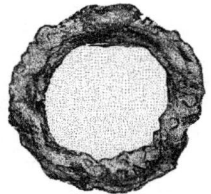

Fig. 661.

Interment No. 12 was found 4 feet to the north of the last, and is that of a female of about 26 years of age. An iron object (fig. 670) was found above the feet. This was possibly the framework of a satchel, to the end of which had been attached two S-links of bronze, pieces of corroded iron, and several iron rings—apparently part of a chain. At the knees were animal bones similar to those found with interment No. 10, which no doubt had been deposited with the flesh on them.

Partly under the iron object (fig. 670) was a finely-cut bone comb of beautiful workmanship, which, though broken into numerous pieces through the unequal settling of the contents of the grave, has been restored as shown in fig. 671. Close by were a few fragments of a smaller comb. Upon the breastbone was an almond-shaped pendant of dark material resembling jet, surrounded by gold (fig. 672). Near the right shoulder was a circular bronze buckle (fig. 673), and below the chin were nine beads of different materials (fig. 674).

No. 12a consisted of a fragmentary vase, 3 feet north-west from No. 12, on the original bottom of the fosse, 4½ feet deep at this point. The vase had been packed round with medium-sized boulders, and with it were pieces of unburnt animal bone, burnt wood, and traces of fire. A very fine white powder was probably disintegrated bone ash.

Interment No. 13 occurred about 2 feet north-west of No. 11, in an exceptionally small grave, 4 feet deep. In this instance the grave had been cut below the bottom of the old trench, into the gravel. The femur measured 17¼ inches and tibia 14 inches in extreme length. Close to the hips was an iron knife (fig. 675) with the point towards the skull, and behind the shoulders were apparently the remains of a sharpening iron (fig. 676), and between this and the knife was a small iron pricker (fig. 677). Each bore traces of a wooden handle. Close by was an iron buckle (fig. 678), and upon the left shoulder was a thin piece of bronze together with dark matter. Near the knees were two pieces of animal bone.

Interments Nos. 14 and 15 occurred together at a depth of 20 inches, and pointed somewhat more to the north-west than any of the preceding. The skull of No. 14 was pushed forward on to the chest. The femur and tibia measured 19½ inches and 16¼ inches respectively, and seemed to be those of a male about twenty years of age, as some of the wisdom teeth are not fully developed.

No. 15 was placed on its right side, with the legs arranged with those of No. 14, in a manner clearly indicating that the two interments had been made together. A femur measured 17 inches and a tibia 13½ inches. Close to the left hip of No. 14 were a knife and a sharpening iron (figs. 679, 680), placed together, with the points in opposite directions. At the waist of No. 15 was a small bronze buckle (fig. 681); a piece of the shank-bone of a sheep or goat was near the hips, and another piece near the skull.

Interment No. 16 occupied a grave 3 feet deep, situated 5 feet from the last. The skull was pressed on to the chest, probably due to the body having been interred with its shoulders raised. The femur measured 18 inches, tibia 14½ inches, and humerus 13 inches, and appeared to be those of a male of middle age. A knife (fig. 682) and another instrument (fig. 683) had been placed together upon the right hip, with their points to the left. Near the right side of the loins was an iron buckle belonging to the girdle (fig. 684).

Interment No. 17 consisted of the remains of a boy, not more than eight or nine years of age, in a grave hardly 15 inches deep, and with the head raised to within 10 inches of the surface. The femur measured 13 inches, tibia 10 inches, and humerus 9¼ inches.

No. 18 was also that of a juvenile, from seven to ten years of age. It occurred at full length, in a shallow grave—the first exception to the flexed mode of interment observed in this cemetery. Owing to the shortness of the grave the body had been placed with the head and shoulders raised against the end, and, like Nos. 14 and 16, the skull had been forced forward upon the chest. The dimensions of the leg bones were somewhat greater than those of the preceding body. At the right side of the pelvis was an iron buckle (fig. 685), and on the outer edge of the left hip was a knife (fig. 686) with the point towards the skull. Near the feet, at "A" on the plan, were several portions of the ribs of a small animal.

Interments Nos. 19 and 20 consisted of the remains of a middle-aged female, on its back, and a child (No. 20) from four to five years of age, with its head resting on the left breast of No. 19. The femora measured 17 inches and 10½ inches respectively. Just behind the shoulder of No. 20 were portions of plates and clasps, pieces of bronze (fig. 687), decayed matter, and a piece of iron resembling a lock or clasp (fig. 688). Probably all belonged to a small casket. Lower down was a small iron buckle (fig. 689). On the upper portion of the slender breastbone was a circular fibula of bronze (fig. 690), with an iron pin. The bronze had imparted a greenish hue to the bone. At the right side of the skeleton was an iron knife (fig. 691) pointing outwards. At the right knee was a small iron buckle (fig. 692), and at the ankle a ring of bronze, 1 inch in diameter (fig. 693). Between these were found eleven beads of different materials and colours (fig. 694); the most interesting being a hollow, fluted, spindle-shaped bead of thin silver (fig. 695). This measures 1 inch in length, half an inch in diameter in the middle, and has been made by uniting two halves. The beads had been strung when buried, as they were found in a line with their axes in one direction. Just below the skull was a large bead of amber (fig. 696), which had probably been worn in the ear.

Interment No. 21 was not more than 15 inches below the surface. The femur measured 14 inches, and tibia 12¼ inches in length, and are those of an individual not more than ten or twelve years of age. No relic accompanied this interment.

No. 22. This interment was 2 feet deep, in an exceptionally long grave, the other graves being generally too short for the adult interments. The femur and tibia measured 17 inches and 13½ inches respectively, and are those of a middle-aged female. At the head stood a plain food-vase of dark clay (fig. 697), much resembling the one with interment No. 8 (fig. 654). On the left side, just above the shoulder, was a large flat bead of blue glass (fig. 698), marked with white rings, and under the right side of the skull was another bead (fig. 699), smaller than the other, and entirely blue. The position of the two isolated beads points to their use as ear ornaments, and the small rings by which they were probably suspended may have decayed. A flat ring brooch with a bronze acus (fig. 700) was found at the right breast. Close to it, under the bones of the right hand, was a double comb of bone (fig. 701). We may remark that this comb, as well

FIG. 662.　¹⁄₁

FIG. 663　¹⁄₁

FIG. 664.　¹⁄₂

FIG. 665.

FIG. 666.

FIG. 667.　¹⁄₃

FIG. 668.

FIG. 670.　¹⁄₂

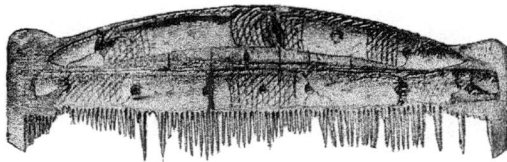

FIG. 669.
¹⁄₂

FIG. 671.　¹⁄₂

FIG. 672.　¹⁄₁

FIG. 673.　¹⁄₁

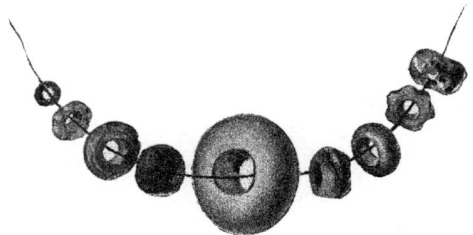

FIG. 674.　¹⁄₁

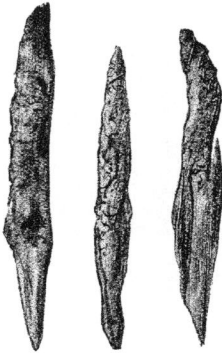

 PLATE LXXXVIII.

FIG. 679 $\frac{1}{2}$

FIG. 680. $\frac{1}{2}$

FIC. 682. $\frac{1}{2}$

FIG. 675.   FIG. 676.   FIG. 677.
$\frac{3}{4}$ $\frac{3}{4}$ $\frac{1}{1}$

FIG. 684.

FIG. 685. $\frac{1}{1}$

FIG. 681. $\frac{1}{1}$

FIG. 678. $\frac{1}{1}$

FIG. 683. $\frac{1}{2}$

FIG. 687.

FIG. 686. $\frac{1}{2}$

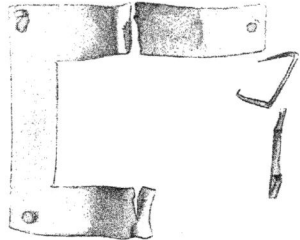

FIG. 688. $\frac{1}{1}$

FIG. 689. $\frac{1}{1}$

FIG. 691. $\frac{1}{2}$

FIG. 690.

as that found with interment No. 12, had been toothed after all the pieces of the comb had been rivetted together, this being clear from the fact that the saw used for the purpose has slightly indented the two side pieces of bone at the base of the teeth.

Interments Nos. 23, 24, 25, and 26 were in one grave, and, from every appearance, had been interred at the same time, being all closely arranged on the same plane, and no disturbance was visible.*

Interment No. 23 was that of a youth, twelve to fourteen years of age, and was crushed under No. 25. The femur measured 16 inches, and tibia 12 inches. Nos. 24 and 25 seemed to be males, of large stature, and of about middle age. Under the skull of the former, were an iron buckle (fig. 702), and a knife (fig. 703), pointing in the same direction as the skull; and at the waist, on the right side of No. 25, was an iron buckle (fig. 704). Their femora measured the unusual lengths of 20 inches and 21½ inches, and tibiæ 16 inches and 17 inches respectively. No. 26 was probably the remains of a female, from twenty-five to thirty years of age. Though somewhat slender, the bones were those of a proportionally tall person. The femur measured 19 inches, and tibia 15 inches. No trace of a deposit of food was found with this interment.

No. 27 had its skull much pressed forward on the chest. The femur and tibia measured 18 inches and 14 inches respectively. On the right breast was a small, beautifully-formed, circular buckle of bronze (fig. 705), with a bronze acus.

No. 28 was less doubled than usual. The femur measured 16 inches, and tibia 13¼ inches in length, and seemed to be those of a middle-aged person. Near the right elbow, and between the loins and extended left arm, was an iron knife (fig. 706), with the point towards the feet. On the right shoulder was a ring-shaped buckle, of bronze (fig. 707). At the place marked "B" near the feet, were pieces of iron (fig. 708), apparently belonging to a small casket; and a splinter of animal bone, probably remains of food. In front of the hips, close to and upon the hand of the extended left arm (A), were portions of the leg bones of a small sheep or goat. The bones were not separated at the joints, showing that the flesh was upon them when buried. The depth of the grave, which was rather larger than usual, was 2½ feet.

Interment No. 29 consisted of the remains of a child about eighteen months old, which was placed at full length, with the face pressed over to the left. On the right side of the neck, close below the position of the right ear, was a single small blue bead (fig. 709).

No. 30 was placed with the face downwards—quite an exceptional method—and at full length. Owing to the shortness of the grave the head was pressed backwards towards the shoulders, and the feet and lower part of the legs were pushed upwards towards the opposite end of the grave. The femur measured 17½ inches, and tibia 14 inches in length, and were apparently those of a person of about thirty years of age. On the left side was an iron knife (fig. 710), and at the right side, close to the upper edge of the hip bone, was an iron buckle (fig. 711). Between the left elbow and the trunk were the shoulder-blade and some ribs of a small animal.

---

* Had they been put in at various times, the bones of the first interments must have been displaced by those of subsequent date.

At this point the line of interments was cut through and destroyed by the construction of the railway during the years 1848 to 1852. The late Mr. Baines, the inspector of the line, informed the writer that he remembered several skeletons being found, many of the skulls being placed on the fence posts and smashed to pieces by the navvies. It is not remembered that any relics were observed.

We returned to the side of the barrow where the first skeletons were discovered, and excavated 46 feet eastwards from Nos. 1 and 2 before reaching interments Nos. 31, 32, and 33.

Touching the outer side of the right thigh-bone of No. 31, and midway between the hips and the knee, was a thin piece of iron (fig. 712), 4½ inches long, ¾ of an inch wide, and rounded at the ends. A similar piece of iron (fig. 713), but half-an-inch shorter, occupied a similar position with the left femur. With the latter was a bent article of ¼-inch iron wire (fig. 714), 4 inches long and flattened and pierced at both ends. Through each end of these pieces of iron was a nail, about 1½ inches long, and each exhibited traces of wood upon it. Possibly these iron objects belonged to some wooden article.

No. 32 was apparently the remains of an elderly slender female. The long bones were of the same dimensions as those of the preceding body.

No. 33 occurred in the middle of the fosse, but under it were about 18 inches of dark-coloured soil, which had accumulated between the time of making the entrenchments and interring the body. Mixed with the lower portion of this accumulated matter were many pieces of split animal bone and pottery.

Body A No. 32a was outside the fosse west of the barrow, and about 35 feet south of the No. 22, and 18 feet from the western margin of the barrow. It was placed at full length, on its back, head to the west, and so near the surface that all the upper part of the bones had been carried away by the plough. No relic was found.

Body B, No. 33a, like the previous one, was outside the fosse. It was about 36 feet south of Nos. 31, 32, and 33, and about 60 feet from the eastern margin of the barrow. It was found in a shallow grave, and unlike any of the others, was accompanied by the tire of a wooden box or coffin. At the left shoulder, and near the left knee, were the two hinges of the lid (fig. 715), and at the right side about the hips was the iron fastening of the lid (fig. 716), while at the head and feet were square iron clasps (fig. 717), and three other small hook-shaped pieces (fig. 717a), which had bound the coffin at the corners. This skeleton was much decayed, and the long bones could not be measured.

On November 6th and the following six days we commenced 20 yards east of the interments Nos. 32 and 33, and worked towards them. Nearly the whole of these occurred with feet to the east.

At a depth of 20 inches was interment No. 34, at full length, as shown on the plan. The femur measured 18¼ inches, tibia 15 inches, and humerus 13 inches, and were probably those of a male from 25 to 30 years of age.

No. 35 was about the same depth and parallel with the last, at a distance of about 3 feet. It occurred on its right side and was bent at the knees. The femur and tibia measured 18¼ inches and 14½ inches respectively. The right humerus measured 13½ inches, while the left measured 13 inches only, and was otherwise visibly smaller. They were thought to be those of a male from 60 to 70 years

FIG. 692.   ⅟₁

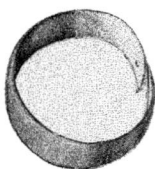

FIG. 693.   ½

FIG. 695.

FIG. 696.

FIG. 694.

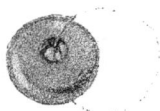

FIG. 699.

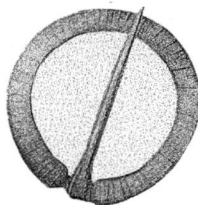

FIG 698.   ½

FIG. 697.   ½

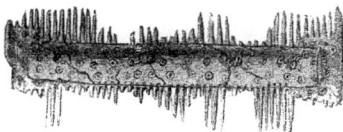

FIG. 700.   ⅟₁

FIG. 701.   ½

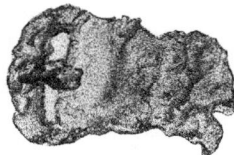

FIG. 702.   ⅟₁

PLATE XC.

FIG. 703.   ½

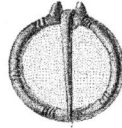

FIG. 707.   ¼

FIG. 711.   ½

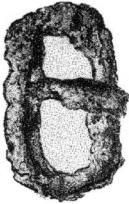

FIG. 704.   ¼

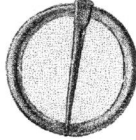

FIG. 705.   ¼

FIG. 709.   ¼

FIG. 706.   ½

FIG. 710.   ½

FIG. 708.   ⅓

FIG. 712.   ½

FIG. 713.   ½

FIG. 714.   ¼

FIG. 717 a.

of age. The skull, which was in good preservation, is preserved, together with many others from this graveyard.

Interment No. 36 occurred at a depth of four feet, on its chest, with the knees pulled up and the head twisted on its right side. In consequence of this grave being filled with pure chalk gravel, the bones were in sufficiently good preservation to be removed, and they are now arranged in a glass case (fig. 718) in the posture in which the body had originally been deposited. Up to the date of exhuming this skeleton we had only discovered three Anglo-Saxon interments in this posture, and but one British.* The femur measured 16½ inches, tibia 13¾ inches, and humerus 12½ inches. Nothing accompanied this interment, but to give it additional interest as a cabinet specimen and to illustrate the positions of some of the articles found with many of the interments in this cemetery, we have placed with it the relics from No. 8, arranged as found with that burial.

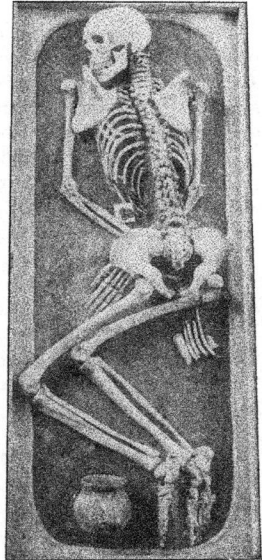

FIG 718.—ANGLO-SAXON INTERMENT (BURIAL 36) FROM NEAR BARROW C. 34.

Interment No. 37 was to the west of the last, and at a depth of two feet, and was apparently that of a middle-aged person. The femur measured 17½ inches and tibia 14½ inches. The body was very short and the chin square at the end. To facilitate our work we excavated at 64 feet east of No. 35, and at the same time worked the two lengths westwards, as the numbers on the plan will show.

Interment No. 38 was two feet deep, and was at full length. The femur and tibia measured 18 inches and 15 inches respectively.

No. 39 was parallel with, and five feet to the south of the last, and at about the same depth. The knees were pulled up and the bones were greatly decayed, owing to the body having been covered with soil.

Interment No. 40 was that of a very young child, and occurred at a depth of about two feet.

No. 41 was also that of a very young child, and occurred at a depth of two feet. The head was to the west, but the position of the body could not be made out owing to the decayed condition of the bones.

No. 42 was about three feet to the west of the last and at the same depth, and was also in a doubled position. The femur measured 19½ inches, tibia 15½ inches, and humerus 14 inches, and are those of an old person.

No. 43 occurred about five feet to the north of No. 41, and at a depth of about 2½ feet. The femur measured 18 inches, tibia 14 inches, and humerus 13 inches.

No. 44 was at the same depth as the last, and was at full length on its chest, with face twisted to the north. The femur measured 14 inches, tibia 11½ inches, and are those of a boy from 8 to 12 years of age.

* Since the above example other British interments have been found lying on the chest.

No. 45 occurred at the same depth as the last, and only two feet to the north of it. The femur measured 18 inches and tibia 13½ inches.

No. 46 was found about 18 inches to the east of No. 42, and at the same depth.

No. 47 was 3 feet north of the last, and at about the same depth, but, unlike any hitherto found here (except the child, No. 2), its head was to the east, and the knees were pulled up. The skull is preserved.

No. 48 contained the remains of a short but very strongly built male, and was about 3 feet to the north of the last, and at about the same depth. The femur measured 17¾ inches, and tibia 13½ inches. The arm bones were peculiarly twisted.

No. 49 was in a grave 3 feet deep, 8 feet long, and 18 inches wide at the bottom, and the sides of the grave—as in every other case—were nearly vertical. The unusual length of this grave was curious, as the body had been placed in a somewhat contracted position. The bones, as usual, were much decayed, and the long bones could not be measured with accuracy.

No. 50 was at a depth of 2½ feet. Near the left knee were portions of some small iron clasps (fig. 719), which had bound the corners of a small box, as wood adhered to them.

No. 51 occurred at the same depth as the last. The femur measured 19 inches, and tibia 15 inches.

No. 52 was at the same depth as the last, and the long bones were exactly of the same length as those of No. 51.

No. 53 was found at a depth of 2 feet 10 inches. The femur measured 19½ inches, and tibia 15½ inches.

Nos. 54 and 55 formed a double interment. The former was at full length and at a depth of only 12 inches. The femur measured 15½ inches, tibia 12½ inches, and are those of a small person. No. 55 was immediately beneath No. 54, on the floor of the grave, at a depth of 3 feet. The femur measured 18½ inches, and tibia 15½ inches. Both the interments were in the centre of the grave, and had apparently been deposited at or about the same time.

The whole of these graves were from 2 to 6 feet distant from one another.

On March 11th, 12th, and 13th, 1872, further search was made and more skeletons were found.

No. 56 is that of an aged female, with most of the molar teeth absent. The femur measured 18 inches, and tibia 14 inches. The grave in this case was only 4¾ feet long, 1½ feet wide, and 2 feet deep, with a concave bottom.

No. 57 was 2 feet south of the last, and facing it. It was the skeleton of a juvenile of five or six years of age. The grave was only 12 inches deep, but measured 5 feet by nearly 2 feet in width.

No. 58 occurred at a depth of 2½ feet, and was that of a small female, the femur and tibia measuring 15½ inches and 12½ inches respectively.

No. 59. A full-sized male, at full length, on its back. Length of femur 18 inches, and tibia 14 inches. The grave was 2 feet deep, and like the others in shape.

No. 60. A child's grave, but the position of the body could not be made out.

It will have been noted from the descriptions of the bodies discovered in this

PLATE XCI.

FIG. 715.   ½

FIG. 716.   ½

FIG. 715.   ½

FIG. 716.   ½

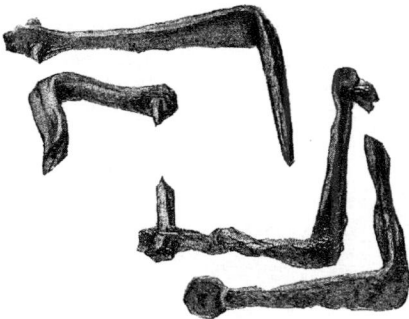

FIG. 719.   ⅟₁

FIG. 719.   ⅟₁

FIG. 717.   ½

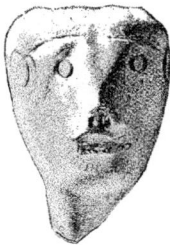

FIG. 720.

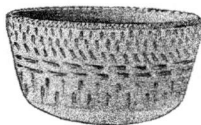

FIG. 724.

FIG. 725.   ⅓

cemetery that no sword, spear, or shield was found. Though the interments were undoubtedly of both sexes, all appeared to be those of civilians, judging from the relics discovered. All the knives were small and adapted for domestic purposes. According to Aylett Sammes (" Britannia Antiqua Illustrata," p. 413), the Saxons had two sets of weapons, a greater and a lesser. The long seax (knife), they wore by the side. The other, called the small seax, or hand-seax, was either worn in the scabbard or else in a separate sheath. The knives found in this cemetery seem to have been usually carried at the waist, probably enclosed in a sheath and stuck in the girdle.

A reference to the plan will show that the orientation of the bodies to the west of the barrow is not quite the same as that of those to the east of the barrow, and that between the two lines of interments there is a space of 46 feet without any burial. Also, those to the west were generally accompanied by relics, whilst those to the east of the barrow had none, except some bits of iron with No. 33a. Small pieces of burnt wood, which we observed in all the graves to the west, were seldom observed in those to the east. Though all are remarkably narrow, there is a marked difference in the length of the graves, those to the west being in all cases so short as to cramp up the body, whilst those to the east were quite long enough. Other peculiarities exist. In the eastern division eighteen of the twenty-eight bodies had their hands at the lower part of the body, whilst in the western portion only eleven of twenty-nine bodies are shown with their hands in this position. The positions of the arms also differs in the two divisions of this cemetery.

To account for the differences in the two sections of the graveyard, we must either suppose (1) that they belonged to two distinct periods—the interment to the west being earliest, those to the east probably occurring at the dawn of Christianity, when the burial of relics was, to a great extent, discarded,—or (2) they all may be of transition age, when paganism and Christianity co-existed, and places of interment, though near, were kept distinct. There is one other feature of note: none of the bodies had been destroyed and broken up to make place for others, as observed by the Rev. Bryan Fawsett, during his excavations in Anglo-Saxon cemeteries in the south of England. This, and the regularity of the interments, as shown on the plan, would seem to indicate that each grave was banked up, or otherwise kept distinct. Most probably this cemetery, and other Anglo-Saxon remains discovered in the vicinity, belonged to a small Anglian settlement in the neighbourhood. Traces of the habitations of such a community have been discovered in a field half a mile east of this cemetery, and a little to the south of the beautiful spring at Emswell. Whenever the ground is tilled, foundations of rude dwellings and quantities of broken Anglo-Saxon pottery are found. In the spring of 1872, Mr. Hopper's shepherd, while attending the sheep, collected a bushel-basket full of these fragments for me, some of which are placed in the Museum at Driffield. He also picked up a bronze buckle and pieces of bronze, and the head of a rude earthenware image (fig. 720), of small size.

2 K

BRITISH REMAINS.

During November, 1871, while testing the ground closely surrounding Barrow No. C 34 for Anglo-Saxon remains, it was observed that at about 40 feet east of its circumference (at *B* on the plan), the gravelly subsoil showed traces of fire. This burnt gravel filled a circular hole (fig. 721), with arms pointing north and south. Half of this was emptied, and lines of burnt wood, running in various directions, and at different angles, were noticed from top to bottom. A quantity of dark matter was observed round the sides, and the gravel there was burnt red,

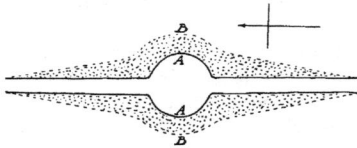

FIG. 721.--PLAN OF DWELLING AND PASSAGES.
A A—Bottom of Dwelling, 5½ feet across.
B B—Top of Dwelling, 9½ feet wide.

similar to that at various places in the centre, near the lines of carbonized wood. After emptying the hole, an underground dwelling, 7 feet 4 inches deep, 9½ feet in diameter at the top, and 5½ feet at the bottom, was discovered. The entrance passages sloped from the surface at an inclination of one in three, and each measured about 24 feet long by 2 feet wide at the bottom.* The entrance to each passage would doubtless be very small, and might have been closed and hidden from view by a covering of brushwood, &c.

From the deeply-reddened chalk gravel mixed with wood ashes, it seems evident that this dwelling had been destroyed by fire. The burnt matter on the sides probably indicated that the habitation as well as the passages had been lined with something to exclude the damp, whilst the streaks of charcoal running obliquely into the midst of the interior showed that beams of wood, probably placed horizontally, had originally covered the excavated dwelling and its passages. The supporting beams having been weakened by fire, gave way, and were pressed down by the superincumbent gravel and turf.†

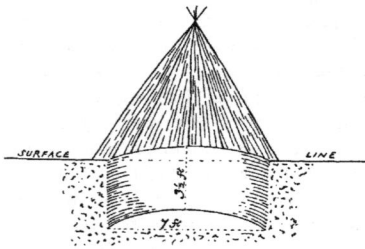

FIG. 722.—SECTION OF PIT DWELLING NEAR BARROW C 34, WITH RESTORED ROOF.

PIT DWELLING.

On the opposite side of this barrow, and about 40 feet from its margin (*C* on the plan), was a circular pit-dwelling, 7 feet in diameter and 3½ feet deep. Its sides were nearly vertical, and no trace of an inclined entrance existed. Fig. 722 gives a section with an ideal restored roof. It contained nothing but gravel and dark soily matter, probably the accumulation of many ages, and no trace of fire was noticed. It much resembled the one near Barrow C. 55, and doubtless was roofed in the same manner with branches of trees placed on end all round it and meeting at the top.‡

---

* This dwelling is similar in construction to the one described in Barrow 110, page 103.

† This had happened also to the passage-dwelling connected with Barrow No. 110, page 104.

‡ Probably others may be found in the neighbourhood; and, as mentioned elsewhere, the large graves in barrows 82, 120, C. 36, C. 72, C. 41, and others, may first have served as a dwelling for the living.

BARROW No. C. 41

Is situated about a quarter of a mile south of the last barrow, and at the date of opening—March 21st, 1871—was scarcely distinguishable on the surface. In the centre was an oval grave, measuring at the bottom 10 feet east and west by 7 feet. At a depth of 4½ feet were the doubled-up remains of a female of middle age (fig. 723), on the left side, with the head to the east. The left arm was doubled back with the hand under the head, and the right arm was bent over the abdomen. A femur, tibia, and humerus measured respectively 17½ inches, 14¾ inches, and 12½ inches, and are rather slender. Close to the face stood a small and rudely-ornamented vase (fig. 724), resembling an incense-cup, which measured 2½ inches in height, and 4½ inches in diameter at the top. Also near the crown of the head was a food vase (fig. 725), with a handle on one side, and ornamented over the whole exterior with rude cuneated gashes. It measured 6½ inches high, and 5½ inches across the top. The disturbed position in which this skeleton was found* was probably due to the unequal settling of the contents of the grave beneath, after the burial of the upper body, and indicated an interment still lower. This surmise proved to be correct, as on reaching to the depth of 6 feet we found

FIG. 723.—SECTION OF BARROW C 41.

the skeleton of a once powerful man, of about middle age, on the left side, and head to the east, as shown in fig. 723. The long bones were 19 inches, 15½ inches, and 13¾ inches in length respectively, and are much stronger than those of the interment above. No instrument or food vase accompanied this skeleton, but close to the crown of the head, on the floor of the grave, was a heap of broken bone (scapula, ribs, and fore-leg) of a young pig, evidently a food offering. Close above the hips were the two bones of the forearm of a slender person, with many finger bones in position, and part of the left temporal bone of a human skull. A mass of sods and light earth filled the centre of the grave, touching the lower body and reaching to the top. Between this and the sides all round was the replaced chalk gravel.

BARROW No. C. 57.

On March 29th and 30th, 1873, this mound measured about 70 feet in diameter and 18 inches high. It was irregular in form, and had the appearance of a small natural hillock. In the centre was an oval grave 5 feet by 4 feet, and 3 feet deep. On the floor of this was a doubled-up skeleton, on its left side, with head to the west, the left hand under the head and the right hand to the chin. The metacarpals and phalanges were very small. The femur, tibia, and humerus measured 15½ inches, 13 inches, and 10⅝ inches respectively, and seemed to be those of an old woman. The skull is in good preservation, and all the sutures are closed. Not a single tooth remained in the lower jaw, and the

* Not shown in the sketch.

alveoli were all closed.   Exactly over the skull, at a depth of 18 inches, was a small heap of burnt human bones.   Approximately at right angles with the grave just described, and in contact with its west end, was a second grave, of smaller dimensions, and only 2 feet deep.   On the floor of this were the remains of a child, from four to six years of age, on the right side, the head to the north, the right hand on pelvis and left hand on the right elbow.

Seven yards north-north-east of centre, and from 4 to 5 inches deep, were a few broken adult bones, indicating a skeleton with its head to the centre of the mound.   This, however, had been almost destroyed by the plough.

Six yards east-north-east of the centre was a small grave only 12 inches deep, in which were the decayed remains of an infant, on the left side, with the knees pulled up, and the head to the south.   Behind the hips was a hand-struck flake of black flint, and in front of the face were three small pieces of a British urn.

In the mound, west of the centre, were a few pieces of animal bone.

BARROW No. C. 58.

Opened july 11th and 12th, 1873,   This barrow stands on a slight natural rise in the field, which, from repeated. tilling is almost levelled.   A considerable portion of its area was excavated, and near the centre was a small hole containing a few burnt adult bones ; but no relic accompanied them.   A portion of a large flake-knife picked up at some distance from the interment was the only article found.

BARROW No. C. 35

Is the most southern of this group, and stands in How Hill Field, a little to the north of Eastburn House.   About the year 1857 the late F. Jordan, of Eastburn, lowered this barrow fully 3 feet, and about twelve years previous to that the late Bethel Boys, the then tenant of Eastburn, opened this mound, but with what result the writer has been unable to ascertain.   Some years afterwards (in 1860) Dr. R. Wood, of Driffield, observed a British food-vase with a plant growing in it, in a cottage window at Kirkburn, near to this Barrow.   On making enquiry he was told by the woman in the cottage that her husband, some time before his death, found it at Eastburn.   The Doctor procured this vase which had probably been taken from Barrow C. 35, and kindly presented it to the writer.   Its ornamentation and form is shown in fig. 726.   On its upper portion are three well-marked grooves, the middle one having had the unusual number of eleven pierced stops. Four of these had been removed, on one side, probably at the time the hole was bored in the bottom of the vase by the cottager.   It had also been covered with a thick coating of red pigment, patches of which, after several washes, are still visible.

On August 20th and 26th, 1870, the diameter of this mound was found to. be 90 feet, and elevation 3 feet.   An 18-feet square was removed from the centre, and on reaching its base the natural ground beneath was found to be considerably above that surrounding the barrow.   A previous excavation running 17 feet east and west and 10 feet across, and irregular in depth, but not exceeding 5½ feet, had been made.   Probably this had removed an interment and the vase just referred to, as we only found pieces of wood and a few hand-struck splinters of black flint.

BARROW No. 268.

THIS mound is named "Mill Hill," and stands on the slope of the southern bank of the Kirkburn stream between the site of the village of Eastburn and Battleburn Cottages.

On June 24th, 1884, it measured about 40 feet in diameter and 4½ feet in elevation, and had a depression in the centre, which might have been caused by a former opening. By the old inhabitants of the neighbourhood it is known—like several other similar mounds near old settlements—by the name of Mill Hill. A 15-feet square was cut from the centre, and the natural ground beneath was found to consist of 3 feet of clay, resting upon chalk gravel. Through this clay and into the chalk gravel beneath was a roughly-cut trench, 3½ feet deep by about 3 feet wide, running north and south the whole width of our excavation and beyond, and from about the centre of the mound a similar roughly-formed trench was observed to run east and west. The mound was of surface soil obtained from the neighbouring land.

From the portion of the mound and the trench which we examined we took teeth and bones of horse, ox or red deer, sheep or goat, and pig; glazed and unglazed pottery, partly mediæval and a little Anglo-Saxon and Romano-British;[*] a few nails, some pieces of corroded iron, part of the thick stem of a seventeeth century tobacco pipe, and a spindle whorl.

The result of this examination seems to show that this mound may have been used for some time as a Moot Hill. Scarcely a mile away is a similar mound, with a similar dish-shaped depression in the centre, in a grass field at the west end of the village of Kirkburn, close to the south side of the road leading to Tibthorpe. It is also known by the old inhabitants as the Mill Hill.[†]

BARROW No. C. 36

Is principally a natural hillock of chalk gravel, which we examined during the first days of September, 1870. In the centre was an egg-shaped grave, measuring 11 feet by 6 feet, and 5 feet deep, with the narrow end to the west. Close to the west end of this, and 2½ feet down, was an undisturbed heap of bones, consisting of three ribs probably belonging to a deer, eleven entire ribs of a large ox, an adult human fibula, and the metatarsal bones of a human foot in their relative positions. At the same depth, but about 3 feet southwards, were portions of the bones of the right side of the skull of an old person. No relic accompanied these deposits, and no trace of an interment was found on reaching the bottom of the grave. We could only assume that an interment had probably been placed on the floor of the grave and had entirely decayed. Mr. Hopper, the tenant of the land, assured us that the mound had not been disturbed during the previous fifty years.

---

[*] The pottery much resembles that from the Fimber Cross under Barrow No. 5.

[†] Drake's "History of York," p. 221:—"The Mayor and Aldermen of York met at the Miln," which may be a shortened form of Mill Hill.

BARROW No. C 37.

OPENED September 5th, 6th, and 7th, 1870. It was much displaced by agricultural operations. Its diameter was 90 feet, and elevation only 12 inches. At a point 21 feet north-north-east of the apparent centre was a small hole about 18 inches deep, containing several pieces of a large cinerary urn, which at some time had been broken and greatly scattered by persons digging for rabbits. It had held the burnt bones of an adult, among which were three molar teeth of an ox, also burnt. Near the urn were some broken animal bones, unburnt, and a curious tool (fig. 727), made of the root end of an antler of a red deer. The small end of this instrument had originally been worked into nine points, but during use one had been broken away at the base and was rounded off. The point end of these tines had been broken off and the opposite end of the instrument fractured, apparently by fire. Its original length was probably about 6½ inches. Sir J. Evans, to whom I sent this specimen, wrote: "The stag's horn implement is very curious, and seems to me to belong to the same class as the so-called combs. It has been suggested that their use was for unravelling the ends of the sinews of fibres while in course of being plaited together. I have never seen anything that exactly matches your specimen."

About 5 feet east of centre, in a grave 7½ feet by 4 feet and 2 feet deep, were the decomposed bones of a slender young person. The head was to the south, and the knees pulled up and pressed over to the east. Close to the right shoulder, enclosed in dark decayed matter, was a small flake of black flint, on which was a bronze pricker (fig. 728), handle and blade being of one piece of metal,* a very rare feature. Under the middle of the left humerus was a small scraper of black flint (fig. 729). From the surface soil above this grave were found two pieces of Roman(?) pottery, and on the surface of the mound close by was a portion of a large cross-shaped bronze fibula, which had very likely belonged to an Anglo-Saxon interment destroyed by the plough.

About 30 feet north-east of the centre, in a small hole about 7 inches deep, were portions of a second cinerary urn and some cremated bones, but the upper portion of this urn and most of the bones had been removed by the plough.

The whole area of this mound was examined, but yielded nothing further.

BARROWS Nos. C 58 and C 58a

Stand close to the east side of Emswell, in a small grass paddock which has never been under the plough. They are about 80 yards apart, and on the 6-inch Ordnance Survey Map are shown as mounds.† Each measured about 30 feet in diameter and 3 feet high, and was closely surrounded by a shallow fosse. They are probably of later date than British.

On October 22nd, 23rd, and 24th, 1873, a large square was cut from the centre of each, and the ground below was probed. About the centre of the easterly

---

* A similar pricker, with a bronze handle was found with a plain axe and a dagger, all of bronze, accompanying an inhumed body, in a barrow at West Kennet.—"Crania Britannica."

† Probably these are the "Nast Hills" mentioned at page 130 of Best's "Book of Farming." (*Surtees Society Publication*).

FIG. 726. $\frac{1}{2}$

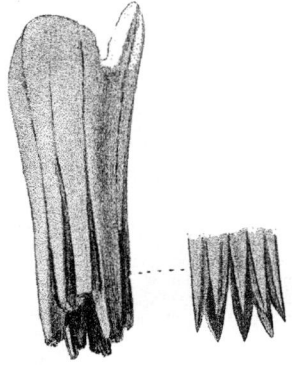

FIG. 727. $\frac{1}{1}$

FIG. 732. $\frac{3}{4}$

FIG. 728. $\frac{1}{1}$

FIG. 729.

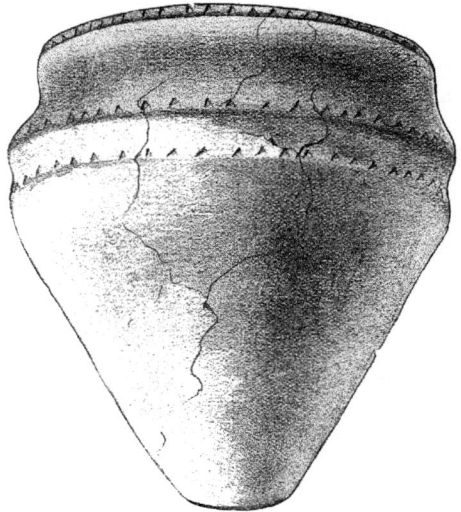

FIG. 730. $\frac{1}{4}$

mound, in a shallow hole below its base, were many fragments of plain pottery of a dark brown colour outside, and brick-red inside. These have since been built up into nearly a vertical half of apparently a cinerary urn (fig. 730), 11½ inches high and 10½ inches in greatest width. It contained a little fine bone ash. In the mound were several fragments of undoubted Roman pottery, as well as others of more recent date ; many pieces of animal bone, pieces of corroded iron, and a thin piece of bronze 2½ inches long and half an inch broad.

The mound to the west (No. C. 58a.) was of a more clayey nature than its fellow, and the subsoil beneath it was clay and not chalk gravel. In the mound were a few pieces of pot, splinters of animal bone, a small piece of rusted iron, and a corroded brass coin, probably Roman, pierced at one side as if for suspension.

Under the centre of the barrow was a small hole, in which were a few pot-sherds and what seemed to be a little powdered bone ash, but nothing further to indicate its age or use.

BARROW No. C. 59a

Is a little to north of Emswell, and has given the name of Mound Sikes to the field in which it stood.* It was opened by the late Lord Londesborough, on October 29th, 1851, and the following description of it is given.† "At Little Driffield, in a field in the occupation of J. D. Conyers, Esq., is a hill of great height for the circumference. It is composed entirely of sand. On the removal of most of the mound nothing was found to indicate its artificial formation except a few pieces of pottery (from appearances Roman) and some bits of much-corroded iron."

The writer, in 1871, re-opened the remaining part of the mound, and tested the ground on which the removed portion had stood, but nothing conclusive could be ascertained as to its age.

The large primary graves in several of the barrows in this group may originally have been pit dwellings, whilst those which contain several interments seem to show that at the death of the head of a family one or two others at least were buried with him.

The immolated bodies sometimes consist of one or more children and one or more females (most probably wives), and not unfrequently of others also, which, judging from their different mode of interment, may have been attendants. Probably when inhumation was most honourable the attendants were cremated ; and when cremation was in great esteem the attendants were inhumed. The former existence of such a custom would fully account for the two contemporaneous modes of interment often found in the same grave.

* Best's " Book of Farming," p. 38.
† Proceedings of the Society of Antiquaries for 1851-2.

DETACHED BARROWS.

BARROW No. C. 59b.—BEST'S GRAVE.

One mile north of the last mound is "Best's Grave," a small mound 30 feet in diameter and 4 feet high, in the centre of a small clump of trees called Spellow Clump. This is in the field now called Dog Hill, a name given in Henry Best's Book of Farming 138 years before the erection of Francis Best's grave-mound, and, therefore, most probably derived from the then existence of a British barrow or some artificial mound, since removed, as there is nothing natural on the surface to give the name of Dog Hill.* "Francis Best was buried in this private vault (Best's grave) in 1779, and Rosamond (Constable) his widow, in 1786, the service being read in Little Driffield Church."

This raising of a mound over a vault erected in unconsecrated ground is most interesting. Elsewhere I refer to two more instances in this neighbourhood.

MILL HILL.

A place half way between Emswell and Garton, near the south-western corner of the four cross-roads, is known by the name of Mill Hill. This clearly indicated that a mound once existed there. This site is equally as good and commanding as the site of the Driffield Moot Hill. Probably its site is now occupied by the Garton Vicarage and grounds, which have removed all surface trace of the hill.

Sites of other mounds are also indicated on the Ordnance Maps by such names as Middle Hill, near Eastburn Warren Farm, and by Clay Hill Fields, close to the north of Tibthorpe; also probably by Shackle Hills, Winter Hills, and Hunger Hills, just north of Garton, and others where there is now no special or marked feature on the surface to suggest such names.

ANGLO-SAXON REMAINS.

On rising ground about three miles to the north of the Garton Slack group, an extensive Anglo-Saxon cemetery was accidentally discovered in the following manner. The memorial to the late Sir Tatton Sykes, Bart., having been completed, workmen were employed to level the adjoining ground by removing part of the entrenchment known as the Double Dyke,† which passes close to the north side of the monument and extends east and west for several miles. On May 18th, 1866, while removing part of the central rampart, six skeletons were discovered close together at the base of the rampart, in the postures shown by Nos. 1 to 6 on the plan (fig. 731). This discovery was made known to the writer by Dr. Wood, who was passing when the workmen had three of the skeletons partly exposed. On the 22nd, the writer, with two assistants, visited the workmen, and carefully exhumed each body as soon as discovered. No. 7 was not more than 16 inches deep, and about 2 feet

---

* Barrow No. 276, near Sledmere, is called Dog Hill.

† The dykes near the monument have been cut through by the green lane, which is the site of a Roman road from Blealands Nook towards Bridlington and Flamborough.

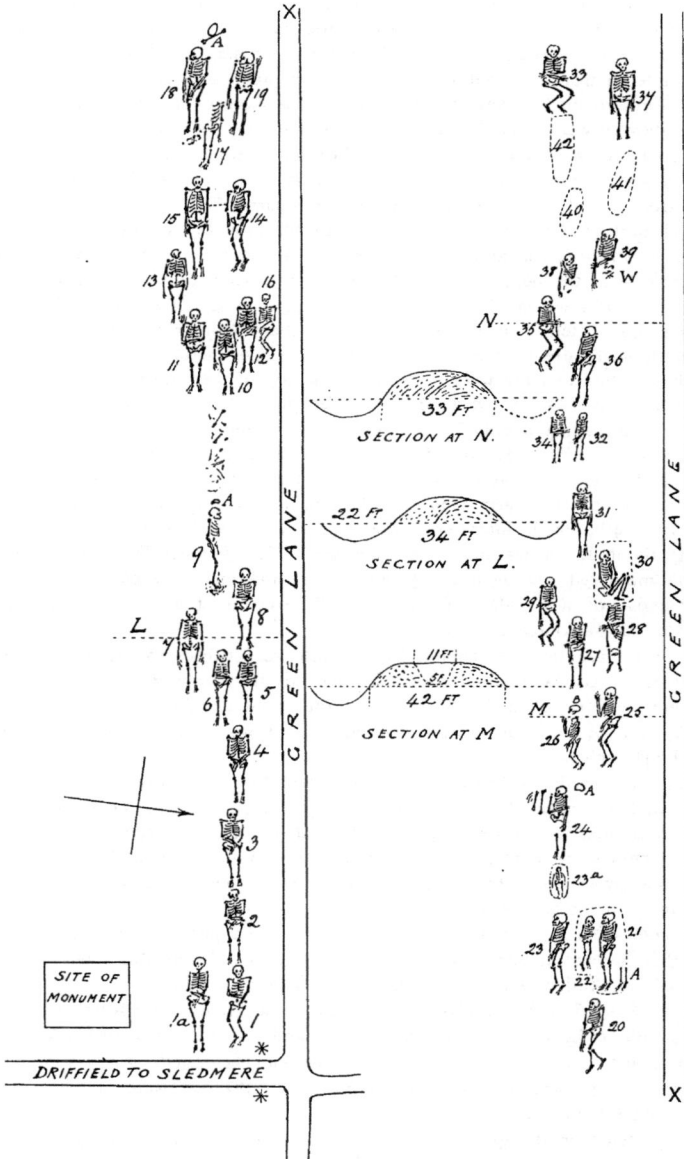

FIG. 731.—PLAN OF ANGLO-SAXON CEMETERY NEAR SIR TATTON SYKES' MONUMENT.

The top of the left hand column joins the bottom of the right hand column at X. Total length of the graveyard, 63 yards.

above the base of the rampart. The femur and humerus measured 16½ inches and 12 inches respectively. No. 8 occurred at the base of the rampart, a section of which at this point showed that the ditch on the north side was first excavated, and that the material from the southern ditch was cast upon and partially covered that from the northern ditch. Near the left knee was a piece of burnt wood, and about 18 inches above it were a small piece of dark-coloured pot and a splinter of grey flint. A femur measured 16½ inches, a tibia 13½ inches, and a humerus 12¾ inches.

No. 9 was found on its left side, at the same depth as the last, and also on the old iron-stained surface-soil, under the rampart. The arm, as well as the femur and part of the pelvis, had been removed, probably by rabbit-diggers, as we found a left humerus and a femur broken, about 12 inches above the body. Near the skull, at the point marked *A*, was the calvarium of a juvenile, and upon the feet and ankles was a piled-up heap of human bones, minus the head. These had either been interred at the same time as the body, or had afterwards been put in with such great care as to touch its bones without disturbing them. Potsherds and bits of bone were found near the top of the grave.

May 24th, 1866.—For a distance of ten feet from the last skeleton the ground was much disturbed, and only broken bones were found.

No. 10 occupied a grave one foot below the base of the rampart. Close under the legs, and also a little above them, were portions of the skull of a child. The femur, tibia, and humerus measured 18 inches, 14 inches, and 13¼ inches respectively.

On June 4th, 1866, interments Nos. 11, 12, 13, and 16 were exhumed, all occurring about 12 inches under the rampart. The femur, tibia, and humerus of No. 16 measured 17½ inches, 13½ inches, and 12⅝ inches respectively, and are probably those of a female. From the soil covering these bodies we took a fragment of dark-coloured pottery.

No. 14 represented the remains of a youth from twelve to fourteen years of age, and rested a few inches below the base of the rampart. Under its right elbow were portions of a bone comb, of the common Anglo-Saxon type and ornamentation. A piece of burnt wood was taken from under the skull. A femur measured 14¾ inches.

No. 15 was vertically below No. 14, at the bottom of a grave, 7 feet by 2 feet 4 inches, and 15 inches below the base of the rampart. The femur, tibia, and humerus measured 18 inches, 14½ inches, and 13 inches respectively, and are those of a person of middle age. Near the skull was the tarsal bone of an ox, while in the grave above the interment were other bones, apparently of the same animal, and a tooth of a goat or sheep.

June 20th.—No. 17 had been partly removed, apparently in digging the grave for No. 18. A femoral bone was 17 inches in length. Above this interment were portions of the skull of a child and part of the rim of a vase.

No. 18 was 16 inches under the rampart, in a grave scarcely long or wide enough to admit the body. The femur, tibia, and humerus measured 19½ inches, 15½ inches, and 13½ inches respectively. They had belonged to a person about sixty years of age, and are of great strength. At the feet were portions of the skull and other bones of No. 17.

No. 19 rested on the gritty subsoil, in a grave cut 10 inches below the bank. Though a femur measured 17 inches, and all the long bones are rather massive, the skull is that of a youth whose wisdom teeth were not developed. The teeth of a pig were found in the grave close above the interment, and higher up were teeth of sheep, tusks of a pig, a vertebra of an ox, and a few detached human bones.

No. 20 consisted of the remains of a young person, the right and left upper back molars having only just cut through the jaw, whilst the under ones were not visible. It was 20 inches below the rampart, in a remarkably short grave. The femur, tibia, and humerus were 18 inches, 14¼ inches, and 13¾ inches in length respectively. In the grave, at various depths, were a human calvarium, left femur, arm and leg bones, and the greater portion of a lower jaw, all belonging to a disturbed adult interment; also a large portion of the under jaw and fragments of the skull of a juvenile, as well as the femur and shank bone of an ox. Over the pelvis and feet of this skeleton, and varying from 10 to 14 inches above them, were variously-shaped pieces of oxidized iron, probably from a coffin, to one of which was attached decayed wood.

June 25th.—No. 21 was about two feet from the last, and one foot below the rampart. A femoral bone measured 18 inches. Above the skeleton were teeth of an ox and sheep. Just to the right of the lower part of this interment were the bones of two small human legs (at *A* on the plan), a tibia of which measured 10 inches.

No. 22 is the skeleton of a child not more than two or three years of age, which had been interred at the same time as No. 21. Above and below this double interment were several detached bones, apparently belonging to the legs marked *A* on the plan.

No. 23 was the remains of an adult, apparently a female. Close upon the head and chest rested the decayed remains of an infant, a humerus of which measured three inches only. A thin layer of dark matter was noticed just above the child. The adult femur measured 16¾ inches, tibia 13¾ inches, and humerus 12⅝ inches.

Over the three last described bodies, about midway in the rampart and two feet above the interments, was an iron knife (fig. 732), and at a short distance a piece of Anglo-Saxon pottery.

June 27th.—No. 23a was the skeleton of a child in a small grave sunk two feet below the base of the rampart.

No. 24 was an adult, both femora of which were missing, and in their place were a few rib bones, showing that the body had been disturbed subsequent to interment. A tibia and humerus measured 13 inches and 11¾ inches respectively. Close to the right side of this skeleton were a femur, humerus, and some vertebræ of another body, and on the left side of the head, at *A*, was an adult skull, palate upwards, and minus the lower jaw.

No. 25 was slightly below the base of the rampart, on its right side, with the knees somewhat pulled up. The femur, tibia, and humerus measured 18, 14, and 13 inches respectively.

A section of the rampart over body 25 showed a hollow up the middle for some distance, due to the material cast from the two ditches being insufficient to form a united ridge, as in the case of other sections where the two ditches come closer together.

No. 26 was that of a youth in a similar attitude to the last. The femur measured 12 inches and tibia 9½ inches.

No. 27 was 16 inches below the rampart, in a grave too small for the body. The femur, tibia, and humerus measured respectively 18 inches, 15½ inches, and 13 inches, were of slender build and probably belonged to a female of middle age.

No. 28.—This headless body rested 10 inches below the base of the bank. A large calvarium was found upon the legs, and probably is a portion of the missing skull. The femur measured 19 inches and tibia 15½ inches. In the grave above were pieces of the shoulder-blade and the leg-bone of an ox, and some small pieces of Anglo-Saxon pottery.

No. 29 was discovered in the writer's absence on the 7th August, at the base of the rampart.

No. 30 is remarkable for its extremely flexed position and close resemblance to a British interment. The femur, tibia, and humerus measured 16 inches, 13½ inches, and 12 inches respectively, and are those of a middle-aged person. The top of the right femur was much enlarged.

No. 31 was on the same plane as the last. A small piece of iron, resembling the point of a pricker or the tongue of a buckle, was found in contact with the left shoulder-blade. The femur and tibia measured 16¾ inches and 13½ inches respectively, and are those of a person from 40 to 50 years of age.

No. 32 represents the remains of a child, occurring a few inches above the base of the rampart. The femur, tibia, and humerus measured 10½ inches, 8¼ inches, and 7¾ inches respectively.

No. 33 is the most westerly interment found. Its knees were pulled up. The femur, tibia, and humerus measured 16 inches, 12½ inches, and 11¾ inches respectively. The teeth were much worn.

No. 34 was discovered on the 10th August, in the writer's absence. It was the skeleton of a youth.

No. 35 (August 11th) was at the base of the rampart. The femur measured 17 inches and tibia 13¾ inches.

A section of the rampart at this point measured 33 feet across, and showed the north ditch to have been excavated first, and that the material cast from the two ditches had been sufficient to fill up the space between, so as not to leave an opening down the centre of it, as observed across body No. 25, where the distance between the two ditches was 42 feet.

No. 36 rested on the same plane as the last. The femur, tibia, and humerus measured respectively 16¼ inches, 13¼ inches, and 12¼ inches, and are probably those of a female of about 70 years of age.

No. 37, and the two following, were also at the base of the rampart. A femoral bone measured 16½ inches.

Nos. 38 and 39 were both minus the legs and the greater portions of the pelvis. A humerus of the former measured 11¾ inches, and of the latter 12½ inches. From the soil within the lower jaw of No. 38 was taken the common sea shell, *Fisurella*. About a foot above No. 39 were the leg and pelvis bones which had been later removed from the body. Close by this skeleton were the remains of an infant (marked *W* on the plan).

Nos. 40, 41, and 42 are the places from which bodies were removed by the workmen in my absence. A spear-head (fig. 733), and an arrow-head (fig. 734), were picked up separately from the northern side of the rampart by one of the workmen, but there is no evidence that they ever accompanied an interment.

The late Miss Sykes, of Sledmere, frequently attended these excavations, and informed the writer that her father, the late Sir Tatton Sykes (to whom the adjoining monument had just been raised), remembered that when the rampart of the entrenchments was cut through, near this place, in levelling the present high road from Sledmere to Garton and Driffield, about the beginning of the last century, about ten or twelve skeletons were found. Mr. Major, the present tenant of the land, also informed the writer that, about 1860, while putting down posts and rails, a skeleton was found on each side of the road, close to the present quickwood hedges, at the points marked * on the plan.

During May 30th and 31st, 1872, three excavations were made in the rampart on the east and opposite side of the road,* the first being about 30 yards from the road. Near the centre of the rampart, about 2 feet from the top (*i.e.* half way down) was the skeleton of a large male of middle age, at full length, on its back. A femoral bone measured 19 inches. The next opening was 50 yards from the road, and exposed the skeletons *A* and *B*. One was only 18 inches deep, and about the same distance from the base of the rampart. It was that of a middle-aged male, extended, on its back, with the right leg a little pulled up. About 3 feet to the south of the last, and 6 inches lower, was interment B, also on its back, with the legs pulled up a little, and both hands on the pelvis. The bones were slender and probably those of a female of about forty years of age. All the interments had their heads to the west, like those on the west side of the road.

The third excavation was made 70 yards from the road, but no interment was found, though fragments of animal bone were noticed. About 300 yards eastwards from the road a considerable length of this rampart had been recently removed and spread on the land by Mr. Crust, the tenant of the farm, exposing a good section,† but no human remains were observed. In the grass field a little further eastwards the entrenchments are in good preservation.

The cemetery just described has much in common with the eastern division of the Garton Slack cemetery, and probably it was in use about the same time. Very few of the skeletons were accompanied by relics, and no trace of cremation was observed. Indeed few examples of cremation have as yet been discovered in any of the Anglo-Saxon graveyards of this immediate neighbourhood. As in the Garton Slack cemetery, all the interments here seem to be those of civilians, inhabitants of an adjoining settlement (close by the old Roman road from York to the east coast), traces of which have from time to time been brought to light, viz., numerous Anglo-Saxon potsherds, portions of buckles and fibulæ of bronze, and traces of foundations of primitive dwellings in the adjoining fields, especially to the north of this graveyard. The skeletons were also much more disturbed than those in " Garton Slack," partly owing to intrusive interments, but mainly to recent disturbances by rabbit diggers.

It may be noticed that all the bodies had their heads to the west. Twenty-eight were at full length, one was greatly doubled up, nine more or less doubled up,

* These are not shown on the plan, fig. 731.

† For this Section and others, see chapters on Entrenchments.

whilst the positions of the remainder could not be ascertained. These interments, like those in Garton Slack, had been made mainly along the centre rampart and ditch of a line of British entrenchments, which must, in both instances, have been the common burial place, as the remains exhumed were those of all ages, from the infant at its mother's breast up to an aged grandsire.

BARROW No. 274.

This detached barrow, which is not shown on the Ordnance Map, is situated near the farmstead called "Warren House," close to the east side of the road from Garton to Sledmere, about half-a-mile north of Sir Tatton Sykes' memorial.

Opened November 10th and 12th, 1891. Owing to its having been much dispersed by the plough, this barrow measured 75 feet in diameter, and only 16 inches from its apex to the undisturbed ground beneath it. The ground outside the limits of this mound was over 12 inches below the ancient turf line under it, due most probably to denudation and the tilling of the land.

There was an oval grave under the centre of the barrow, measuring 7 feet north and south and 4½ feet across, and reaching 4 feet into the rock. The grave was principally filled with the chalk which had been obtained in making it. At the bottom were the remains of an adult body, on its right side, the head to the south, the knees drawn up to a right angle with the trunk, the right arm doubled by the side with the hand bent over the upper portion of the chest. The left arm was bent at a right angle, with the forearm over the abdomen, and the extended hand upon the right elbow. The two femora, tibiæ, and humeri measured respectively 18½ inches, 15¼ inches, and 13½ inches each. The skull, vertebræ, and ribs were decayed. Judging from the teeth this person at death was probably about thirty years of age. The dark residue of decayed wood was observed in contact with most of the bones of the skeleton. A crushed food-vase, which had been placed upright near the right shoulder, was the only accompanying relic. After having been repaired, it measured 4¾ inches in height, 6 inches across the top, and 7 inches at its unusually broad shoulders, round which is a very narrow groove, and along this groove at equal distances are five unpierced projections, each with a vertical depression up the middle. Fig. 735 shows its form and ornamentation. This vase* is of a peculiar type; but no two are exactly alike.

* It is possessed by Sir Tatton Sykes.

No. XII.—THE DRIFFIELD GROUP.

THIS includes only nine barrows,* and all have been much injured by surface improvements. It is quite probable that several others have been entirely removed and forgotten. The site of one may be indicated by the name of Cross *Hill*, a plot of open ground close to the east side of the National Schools, now

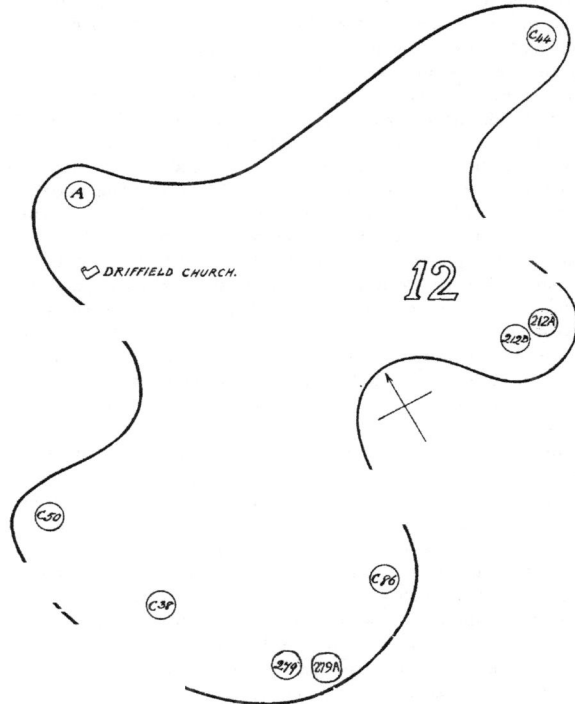

DRIFFIELD GROUP.

used as a market. Two of the barrows are remarkable for containing many interesting remains of a much later date than the erection of the mounds. One of these,

BARROW No. C. 38

Is situated near the northern side of the Gypsey Race, a little before it enters the Driffield Trout Stream, at Halliman's Wath Bridge. This barrow was opened by the late Lord Londesborough, in October, 1851, and a description of

* Moot Hill (marked " A "), has not been opened.

it is given in the Proceedings of the Society of Antiquaries for 1851-2, from which the following has been taken.

"Not far from the first barrow [an unproductive mound at Little Driffield, No. "C 59A" Group XI.], is another [No. "C 38"], of about the same diameter, but not more than 4 feet high, although several persons can recollect its having been much higher previous to the enclosure of the land. It is situated in a field upon part of the farm called Kelleythorpe or the Greets, skirted on two sides by the Beverley and Market Weighton roads,* and is in the occupation of Mr. Thomas Hopper. The individuals before mentioned spoke of quantities of bones having been turned up by the · plough when the hill was brought into cultivation, which were reinterred. This proved to be correct, for at a very slight depth in the centre were found the disturbed remains of several skeletons. On the south side of the cutting, a few inches from the top, was a large sandstone flag, in a slanting position, and on coming to the natural bottom was another, but of much larger size, laid flat, and a small one standing upright. At the west end, a little to the south, was a fourth, much in the same position as that first discovered. The hollow sound emitted by the largest of the stones on being struck favoured the opinion that it might be a cover to a vault, which, on clearing away the earth from its edge, was found to be the case,† for at one corner was a hole, just of sufficient size to admit a hand and arm, by which means the side of the interior could be felt. As the stone was more than seven or eight men could remove, a tripod, or set of tackle poles and windlass were borrowed from Mr. Hopper, by means of which the lid was raised, but again lowered to its original position till Monday.

"The removal of the surrounding soil was again resumed, and, on the south side, was discovered a very large skeleton, close to the fourth stone before mentioned [No. 3a, fig. 736]. It lay in the usual contracted position, on the left side, and about 20 inches from the outside of the cist, but was unaccompanied by any weapon or ornament. Towards the east end were traces of an extensive fire, the chalk gravel having evidently been subjected to intense heat, which had turned it to a brick-red colour.

"The day being far spent, the work was suspended till the following Monday.

"On Monday the operations were resumed, and in a short time on the north side was discovered a considerable mass of bone, which on examination proved to be those of two skeletons [No. 5a] laid one upon the other. The bones were so interred that it was impossible to distinguish to which they belonged. One of the skulls was in excellent preservation, the other much crushed and broken. Just above the whole head was an urn of coarse British pottery [see fig. 737, and plate 20 fig. 9 in the Society's Proceedings], ornamented with rows of large perforations. Also a flint spearhead neatly formed and chipped [fig. 738]. Amongst the bones of the hand, belonging to one of these skeletons ‡ was a curious piece of

* Mr. J. Brown, late of Driffield, informs me that he remembers a gravel-pit in the south-east corner of this field, a short distance from the mound, in which many human bones were found, and adds that he has seen skulls protruding from the side of the pit.—J. R. M.

† See Lord Londesborough's plan of interments in this barrow, copied into this volume, figs. 736 and 740.

‡ Most probably the upper one—an Anglo-Saxon.

FIG. 734.   ½

FIG. 739.

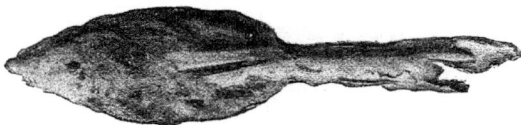

FIG. 733.   ½

FIG. 739.

FIG. 735.   ½

FIG. 739.

FIG. 737.

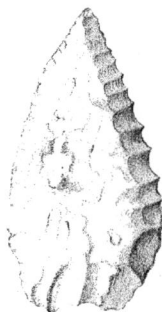

FIG. 738.   ¼

FIG. 739.

bone of about $1\frac{1}{2}$ inches long and $\frac{3}{8}$ of an inch thick [fig. 739], with a small projection in the middle. On one side of this projection was a hole, through which had been fastened a small hollow iron ball [*a*, fig. 730], the size of a marble, to which had been attached a thin strip of wood and iron, as if the metal had been fastened between two sides of thin wood. This ran in a straight direction from the little ball at the top (plate 20, fig. 2),* but, with the exception of the bone, to which the whole had been attached, and part of the ball, corrosion had completely destroyed it, for on being touched it crumbled into dust. What it had been could not be conjectured, but from the position in which it was found it seemed as if the bone had lain across the hand, and the part suspended from it had passed between the fingers in a straight line. There is every

FIG. 736.—PLAN OF CENTRE OF BARROW No. C. 38.
As opened by the late Lord Londesborough.

probability that the individual to whom the urn and flint spearhead belonged had been of an earlier date than the vaults,† as the urn which was within 6 inches of the grave had a long thin stone of the same description placed over it, with one end resting on the top of the large stone, evidently for the purpose of protecting it when the soil had been thrown on the vault. The iron would indicate a still more recent date, but whether it belonged to the topmost of the two skeletons was impossible to determine.

" Having completely removed these two interments and a considerable quantity of the surrounding soil without meeting with anything more, preparations were made to investigate the contents of the vault.

* Of the Proceedings of the Society of Antiquaries.
† More probably contemporaneous.—J.R.M.

"The tackle poles being fixed, the lid was again raised and deposited on one side, displaying the contents of the tomb, which was entirely free from soil, so that everything could be seen at a glance [fig. 740] exactly in the position in which it was placed when interred. This rude sarcophagus was sunk in the ground till the top of the sides, which were formed of four slabs of sandstone, came on a level with the natural surface, and was paved with small irregular pieces of the same stone. The dimensions were, on the north side, 3 feet 9 inches, on the south 4 feet 2 inches, on the east 2 feet 5 inches, and on the west 2 feet 11 inches, and 2 feet 6 inches deep.

FIG. 740.

PLAN OF CIST IN BARROW No. C. 38.

On the floor lay a skeleton of large size (the thigh bone measured 19 inches), placed in a similar position to those before mentioned, with the knees drawn up and lying on the left side, the hands bent towards the face. On the bones of the right arm was laid a very singular and beautiful armlet [fig. 741]* made of some large animal's bone about 6 inches [exactly 5 inches] long, and the extremities which were a little broader than the middle, neatly squared. In this were two perforations about half-an-inch from each end, through which were bronze pins or rivets with gold heads, most probably to attach it to a piece of leather which had passed round the arm and had been fastened by a small bronze buckle [?], which was found underneath the bones. Immediately behind the vertebræ, and as if it had fallen from the waist, was a small bronze dagger [fig. 742] in a wooden sheath, having a handle of the same. Round the neck were three large amber beads† [figs. 743-4] of conical form, having the under side flat, and which was pierced by two holes running upwards in a slanting direction till they met at the centre. At the lower end of the vault, between the extremity of the spine and the feet, was a highly-ornamented drinking cup‡ [fig. 745], completely covered with rows of marks and indentations, each row being divided by ridges or bands. About the centre of the pavement

---

* May 10th, 1884. This armlet or bracer, which is of fine grained greenstone, and not of bone as described, also the bronze dagger (fig. 742) which accompanied it, were shown to the writer by the late Sir Wollaston Franks, of the British Museum, who had a few days before purchased them at the sale-room of Messrs. Christie & Manson, who were disposing of Lady Londesborough's collection. Canon Greenwell figures a similar bracer in "British Barrows," p. 42; and in the "Proceedings of the Society of Antiquaries of Scotland for 1882-3, p. 454, is figured an identically similar one, 4½ inches long, except that it had not gold-headed rivets. It is described as a polished bracer of felstone, found with an urn (food-vase), 6 inches high and 6 in diameter at the mouth, from a cist on the farm near Evanstoun, Ross-shire. Also at page 455 is an account of the finding of another bracer of a similar kind. Canon Greenwell gives several other instances as a foot-note in his introduction to "British Barrows," p. 36. I believe the Kelleythorpe find is the only one in Yorkshire —J.R.M.

† These were probably studs, like the one of amber found in a barrow on Acklam Wold (fig. 213).—J.R.M.

‡ More of the type of the fine kind of food vase.—J. R. M.

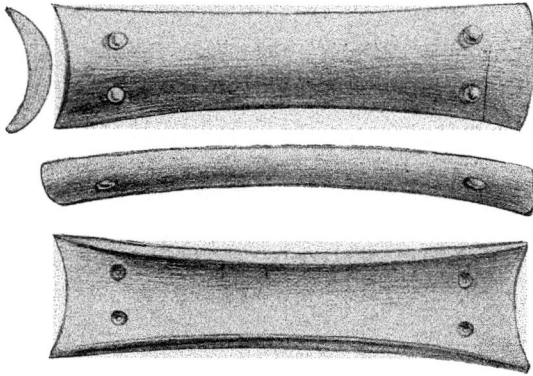

FIG. 741.   ⅔

FIG. 742.

FIG. 748.   ½

FIG. 745.

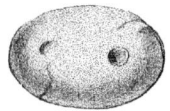

FIG. 743.

FIG. 749.   ¼

FIG. 749.   ¼

FIG. 744.

in front of the body was the upper part of a hawk's head and beak.* A mass of what seemed to be linen cloth lay under the entire length of the skeleton, but the interstices were so filled up with animal matter as to give it the appearance of leather. There was however a portion about 2 inches long and three-quarters of an inch wide laid across one of the thigh bones, which showed the texture of the fabric very plainly, and from the quantity of these remains it is very likely the body had been wrapped in linen from head to foot. The skull was in a much worse condition than several others which had been found, the whole of the facial bones being decayed. It is of a very peculiar round form, and quite different from any other belonging to this tumulus. The contents of the cist having been thoroughly examined, attention was next turned to the traces of fire before alluded to. It covered a space of about 5 feet in diameter and fragments of bone belonging to different skeletons, more or less burnt, were met with throughout the extent of the fire. In the centre of the burnt gravel, and where it was evident the heat had been most intense, lay a skeleton at full length, the vertebræ and middle portions completely calcined, but the extremities not so much destroyed. Quantities of charcoal were met with, both above and below the bones. The red gravel formed a conical heap, and it was evident that the fire had subsided before the earth had been placed over it, as there is no appearance of the latter having been subjected to any heat.

" Portions of two vases of Romano-British or Saxon pottery were found scattered over the north and eastern parts of the barrow. Being at a considerable depth, it was remarkable they should have been so much disturbed, which must have been caused by the depositing of a later interment, but there was nothing to prove which were the remains of the individual last interred. The number of interments in this tumulus had been very considerable, the remains of ten different skeletons having been exhumed during the investigations. The head of one is peculiarly long and narrow, and near it was found a circular fibula of bronze (fig. 9 in the next page).† This was at the west end, but several other skeletons being close together and at all angles, nothing satisfactory could be made of them. There was also a rude flint spearhead and a joint of some large animal's backbone turned up in the same place. The mound having been all nearly turned over, and to every appearance being on the outside of the deposits, all the bones were collected and placed in the vault. The lid was again lowered to its former position, and after placing the other stones round it in the manner they were found, the remainder of the day was occupied in filling in and restoring the hill to its former shape."

Re-opening.—On October 1st to the 10th, 1870, I examined the greater portion of this barrow, and in the centre, at the depth of 18 inches, touched the covering stone of the previously discovered cist, which I removed to Driffield.‡ This covering-stone measures nearly 6 feet by 4 feet, and is 7 inches in thickness.

---

* Mr. Bateman in "Ten Years' Diggings," page 80, says: " Two instruments of flint and the lower mandible of a hawk were found between two bodies;" supplying the third instance in which is recorded the remains of this bird in tumuli.

† *i.e.*—In the Proceedings of the Society of Antiquaries ; it resembles that (fig. 809) found with my interment No. 26.—J.R.M.   ‡ It is now in the front of the Museum in Lockwood Street, Driffield.

The relative positions of the interments which I discovered in this barrow are shown on the plan (fig. 745*a*).

No. 1 was that of a youth from eight to ten years of age, on its back, with the legs bent and the knees pressed over to the right, the left arm over the chest, and right hand under the chin. The head was to the west. It was 30 feet east

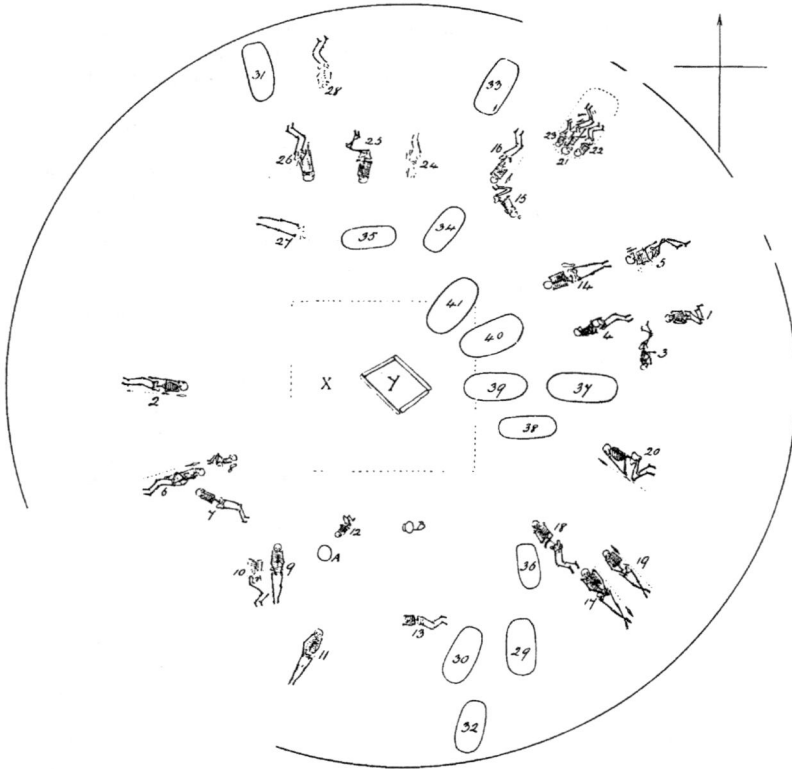

FIG. 745 *a*.—PLAN OF BARROW NO. C. 38.

X—Area excavated by the late Lord Londesborough.

from the centre of the mound, 18 inches deep, in a shallow grave too small to hold the body without cramping it, as indeed was the case with most of the bodies in this barrow. This is a frequent feature in Anglo-Saxon graves.

No. 2.—This occurred 22 feet west of the centre, 2½ feet deep, and was partly on its back with the head to the east. The right arm was stretched by the side, the left arm bent over the chest, the knees slightly pulled up and pushed to the right, and the head inclined in the same direction. At the left side of the head

FIG. 746. $\frac{1}{4}$

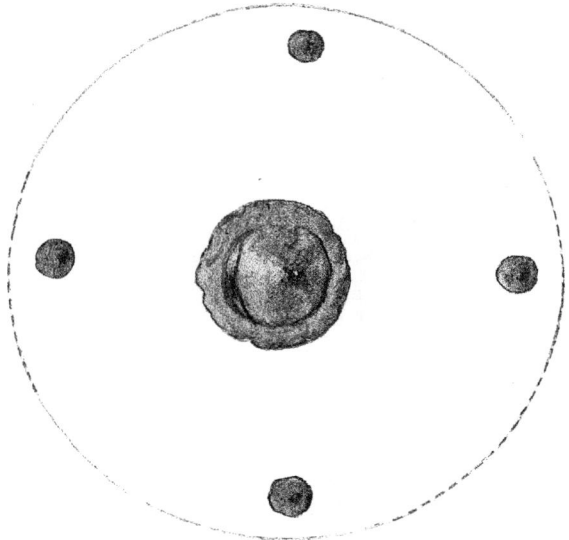

FIG. 749 a. $\frac{1}{8}$

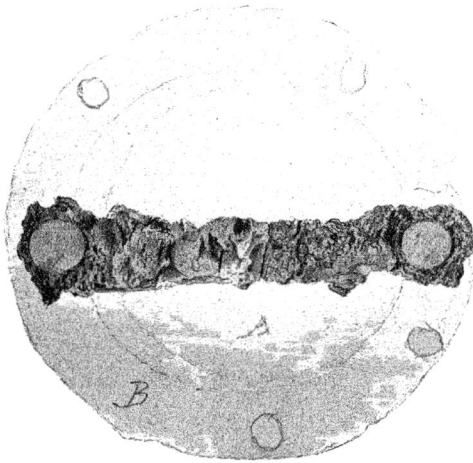

FIG. 750.

FIG. 754. $\frac{1}{2}$

FIG. 747. $\frac{1}{4}$

FIG. 751. $\frac{1}{2}$

FIG. 752. $\frac{1}{4}$

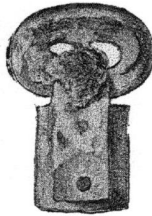

FIG. 753. ¼

FIG. 755. ½
(Front View.)

FIG. 755. ½
(Back View.)

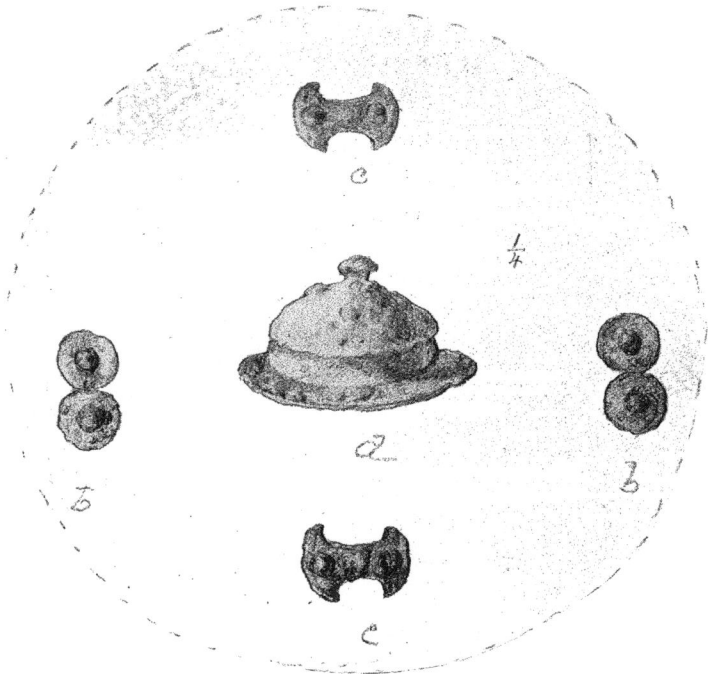

FIG. 757.   ¼

FIG. 587.   ½

FIG. 760.   ½

was an iron spearhead (fig. 746), 18 inches long, and at the feet was the iron spike belonging to the lower end of the shaft (fig. 747). The distance from the extreme ends of the two showed the spear to have been 6 feet 3 inches in length. Upon the bones of the left hand was the iron boss or umbo of a shield (fig. 748), with traces of wood adhering to it, while four iron studs (fig. 749) with flattened heads about 2 inches in diameter, occurred on four sides of the boss, at a distance of about 10 inches from its centre, as shown in fig. 749a. They indicated the shield to have been about half an inch thick, made partly of wood, and probably circular. Under the boss was the iron portion of the handle of the shield (fig. 750), through each end of which was a large bronze-headed iron rivet by which it had been secured to the boss. At the left elbow, with the point to the shoulder, was an iron knife (fig. 751), and near the lumbar vertebræ were two small iron buckles (figs. 752-3). The femur measured $17\frac{1}{2}$ inches, tibia 14 inches, and were evidently those of a strongly-built man.

No. 3.—This was found about 26 feet east of the centre, and hardly 20 inches from the surface. The bones, though small, were those of an adult, lying on the right side, with the head to the south. Near the bent knees were several pieces of Anglo-Saxon pottery. Probably this was a female interment.

No. 4 was 18 feet east-north-east of the centre, in a grave the same depth as the last. The skeleton was partly on its left side, head to the west-south-west, the left arm at full length by the side, and the right arm bent over the body. On the upper part of the hips was an iron knife (fig. 754), with the point towards the feet, and at about the middle of the body was a bronze buckle with an iron tongue (fig. 755), and a bronze tag which had been rivetted to a strap. This also was in all probability a female interment.

No. 5.—Twenty-eight feet north-east by east of the centre was a grave $2\frac{1}{2}$ feet deep, in which rested the remains of a strongly built male, partly on the back and partly on the left side. The head was to the west-south-west, the legs bent, the right arm at a right angle over the body, and the left arm down by the side. A little above the right elbow was the iron umbo of a shield (fig. 757a), and on opposite sides of this were two broad-headed iron studs (bb) touching at their edges, and between these were two double crescent-shaped pieces (cc), through each end of which was a rivet. Remains of wood adhered to most of the rivets, indicating that the shield was made partly of wood, not more than half an inch in thickness. The relative positions of the boss and the studs are shown in fig. 757, and the broken line represents the probable outline of the shield. Fig. 758 illustrates the form of the iron handle. The entire spear having been too long for the grave, the shaft had been broken and the blade (fig. 579) and the spike (fig. 759a) were placed together at the left shoulder, as shown on the plan (fig. 745a). They measure respectively 16 inches and $6\frac{1}{2}$ in length, and from the socket of each protrudes a part of the shaft. On the lower part of the body and near together were a small iron knife (fig. 760) and a buckle (fig. 761), a flat oblong piece of bronze, notched at the ends (fig. 762), two silver-plated rivet heads (fig. 763), and an irregular piece, with four pear-shaped perforations, made of bronze and plated with silver on one side (fig. 764).

No. 6 was found about 23 feet west-south-west of the centre, and at a depth of only 12 inches. It was on its back, with the knees slightly flexed, the right arm at full length, and the left arm bent across the body.   The head was to the centre of the mound and pressed over to the right.   On the chest and near the left hand was an iron umbo (fig. 765), terminating in a button-like top. On the right elbow was an iron knife (fig. 766), pointing towards the feet, and by the right shoulder a spearhead (fig. 767) 12½ inches long, pointing to the head.

No. 7 was close to the side of No. 6, but with the head and knees pressed in an opposite direction ; the head pointing to the west-north-west.   It was only 6 inches from the surface of the mound.   On the upper portion of the chest was a fine bronze cruciform fibula (fig. 768), 5½ inches in length, and upon the right shoulder was a flattened ring fibula (fig. 769), 1¾ inches in diameter, with a portion of the iron pin, much rusted, attached to it.   Close to the right thigh was an ornamented strap of bronze (fig. 770), and near the left knee a portion of the shankbone of an ox.   This interment was much damaged by the plough.

No. 8, the remains of a boy from ten to twelve years of age, was fully 4 feet nearer the centre than the last, but was at twice the depth.   It was on its right side, with the legs pulled up, and both hands together between the knees and chin.   Its head was towards the centre of the barrow.   Nothing was found with it, except a portion of the rib of an animal near the hips.

No. 9 was 16 inches deep and 20 feet south-south-west of the centre, at full length, with the head to the north and both hands on the pelvis.   The femur measured 17 inches, and was that of a person of middle age.   No relic accompanied it.

No. 10 was close under No. 9, and its head, left thigh bone, and part of the right arm had been removed, probably at the time of interring No. 9.   It was partly on its left side and partly on its back, with knees brought up and pushed to the left side.   Both hands were on the pelvis.   The head had been towards the north.   Near the hips were two small iron buckles (fig. 771) three pieces of bronze (fig. 772), and some decayed matter, while just above the left hip was an iron knife pointing to the feet (fig. 773).

No. 11 was a little to the south of the last, 28 feet from the centre of the mound, and 13 inches deep.   It was in the same posture, and with its head nearly in the same direction as No. 9.   The femur measured 16½ inches.   Nothing accompanied it, and the whole of the bones—like those of nearly all the other interments—were in bad preservation.

Nineteen feet south-south-west of the centre was a cup-like hole (A on the plan), 2 feet deep and 18 inches in diameter at the top.   It contained burnt wood and soil, but no trace of bone.

No. 12 was 15 feet south-west from the centre and 18 inches deep, and was the interment of a child from one to two years of age.   It was on its back, legs doubled sharply back at the knees, with both arms over the body, and the head—which is one of the only three that we had so far found worthy of preservation—pointed to the south-west.

Sixteen feet south of the centre, and 15 inches from the surface, were portions of a wide-mouthed Saxon vase (B on the plan), which, at some time, had been broken and some of the pieces removed, probably by rabbit diggers.   This is now restored (fig. 774), and measures 7¼ inches in height and 7½ inches across

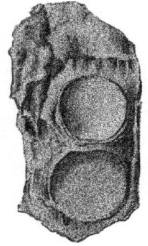

FIG. 763.

FIG. 765.　½

FIG. 762.　¹

FIG. 759.　¼

FIG. 761.　¼

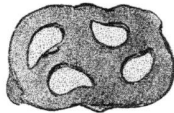

FIG. 764.

FIG. 759 a.　¼

FIG. 768.　¼

FIG. 766.　½

FIG. 767.　½

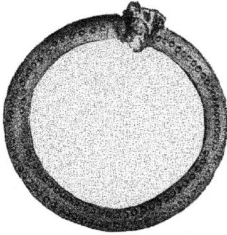

FIG. 771.　⅓　　　　FIG. 771.

FIG. 769.　　　　　FIG. 770.　¹⁄₁　　　　　FIG. 773.　½

FIG. 772.　⅓　　　　　　　　　　　　　　　　　　　　　　FIG. 789.　¹⁄₁

FIG. 772.

FIG. 774.　¼

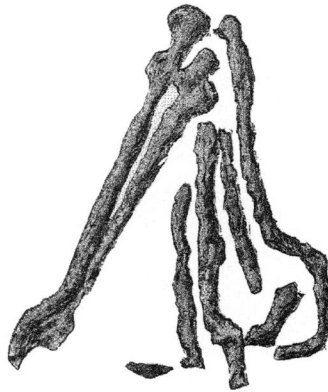

FIG. 777.　⅓

FIG. 775　½

FIG. 776.　¼　FIG. 778.　¼　FIG. 779.　⅓　　　　FIG. 781.　⅓　　　　FIG. 780.　¼

the top). It bears strong marks of fire on its lower half, and seems to have been a cooking-pot. Nothing was found with it.

No. 13 was 23 feet south of the centre, and had its head removed by the plough. It was that of a youth, six to eight years of age, on its back, with the head to the west, and the knees slightly bent. The right hand was brought under the head, but the position of the other arm was not clear.

No. 14 was fully 19½ feet east-north-east of the centre, and the upper part of the face had been taken away by the plough. The head was to the west-south-west, with the legs at full length, and both arms over the body. Near the left hip was a large portion of the lower jaw of a deer, and a bone pin (fig. 775), 5 inches long, and grooved round the upper end. It was found in an oblique direction over the lower part of the pelvis. It may have secured some wrapper covering the body at the time of burial. This interment, like nearly all the others, had the head a little higher than the trunk.

No. 15 was 23 feet north-north-east of the centre, with its head to the south-east, in a contracted grave, 3 feet deep. It was much doubled up, and placed on its right side, the right arm being at full length, and the left bent at a right angle over the body. The femur measured 17½ inches, tibia 14½ inches, and humerus 12½ inches. They were probably those of a secondary British interment, and not Anglo-Saxon. Portions of a small crude urn, resembling British ware, which crumbled to pieces on being removed, were found at the front of the skull.

No. 16 was 24 feet from the centre of the mound and 18 inches north of interment No. 15, and about 2 feet deep. It was on its back, with the left hand on the hips, the right hand on left shoulder, and the knees slightly pulled up. A femur measures 17½ inches, and tibia 13½ inches. There was an iron spearhead, 11½ inches long (fig. 776), at the right shoulder, an iron buckle (fig. 777), near the top of the sacrum, and an iron knife (fig. 778), on the inside of the left arm, just below the elbow, and pointing to the shoulder.

No. 17 was 30 feet south-east of the centre, at a depth of 2 feet, on its back, with the head to the north-west. Both hands were on the upper part of the pelvis, and the legs were crossed just below the knee. A small iron knife (fig. 779), was placed across the lower part of the chest, with the point to the right. An iron spearhead (fig. 780), occurred with its point to the feet—an exceptional position. No trace of an umbo of a shield, or anything else, was found.

No. 18.—About 22 feet south-east of the centre, and hardly 10 inches from the surface, was the skeleton of a young female, on its back, with both hands upon the chest, and the knees pulled up and pressed over to the right side. The head was to the north-west and pressed over to the left side. At the knees was a splinter of animal bone. Under the lower portion of the hips were the corroded remains of several iron articles (fig. 781), which seem to have been strung together at one end, and probably suspended from a girdle. The lower ends of some of these, though almost crumbled away, were observed to be bent. Just above the pelvis was a bronze buckle (fig. 782), with an oblong piece of the same metal, silvered on one side. A portion of coarse woven fibre adhered to this specimen, as well as to many others. Near the right wrist were several decayed pieces of an ivory ring, and round the neck were fifty-five amber and glass beads, of various sizes and shapes, forming a beautiful necklace, measuring 2 feet in length (fig.

783). At each shoulder was a flat ring fibula (figs. 784-5), with traces of iron pins attached, each measuring fully two inches in diameter. At the right shoulder were two flat pieces of bronze (fig. 786), which seemed to have been rivetted to the opposite sides of the end of a strap, and two small pieces of bronze with decayed matter on the chest. A bronze hairpin (fig. 787), was found behind the head, with the point to the right shoulder. Attached to the upper end of the pin was a ring of bronze wire, about ½ an inch in diameter. A perforated ball of ivory or bone (fig. 788), considerably fretted in consequence of its nearness to the surface, was found at the left side of the skull. This ball is 1¾ inches in diameter, and the perforation is ½ an inch in diameter. It differs from the spindle whorl, and was found on its edge as if it had been interred on the end of a staff or walking-stick. At a distance of about 16 inches from the feet of the interment, and on the same plane, was an iron knife (fig. 789), which had, most probably been separated at some time from this or some other interment.

No. 19 was 2 feet east of No. 17, in a grave 2 feet below the surface, and, except the left hand was on the chest, its posture was in every way like its companion, No. 17, the legs being crossed below the knees. The femoral bones measured 18 inches each. On the loins was an iron buckle, resembling fig. 793, and, by the left side of the pelvis, an iron knife (fig. 790). A small spearhead (fig. 791), was at the left shoulder, with the socket-end towards the feet.

No. 20 occurred at a depth of 14 inches, and was 20 feet from the centre of the mound. It was on the right side, legs and left arm being doubled up to a right angle with the body, and right hand on the knee. The femur measured 17 inches, tibia 14 inches, and humerus 13 inches in length. An iron spearhead (fig. 792), was found in front of the face, an iron buckle (fig. 793), on the upper lumbar vertebræ, and an iron knife (fig. 794), at the left elbow. From the mound many fragments of British vases, flakes of flint, and a fine leaf-shaped arrowhead of flint were picked up. As the farmer was anxious to sow the land, we were now compelled to postpone further inquiry. No sign of a coffin was found in any of the graves.

From March 30th to May 6th, 1872, we renewed our examination, and explored the remaining and western part of this mound. At a point 30 feet north-north-east of the centre we reached a grave containing interments Nos. 21, 22, and 23. This comparatively large grave only measured 6 feet in length, 2 feet 4 inches in width, and 2 feet 3 inches in depth. From the internal arrangements there was reason to believe that the three bodies had been buried at the same time. Their relative positions are shown on the plan.

No. 21 was a female of medium stature, and nineteen to twenty-two years of age. The femur measured 16¼ inches. Close to the back of the head—which was separated from the neck and pushed a little from its place by the unequal yielding of the contents of the grave—was a small piece of bent iron. On the breast was a short necklace (fig. 795), consisting of eight amber beads, five yellowish ones of vitreous paste, one disc of bone three-quarters of an inch in diameter, pierced near the circumference, and a cylindrical piece three-quarters of an inch long and half an inch in diameter, cut from the legbone of a bird. Near the left shoulder was a small iron buckle (fig. 796). By the side of the left thigh was the point of a bodkin (fig. 797) and a pair of shears (fig. 798) 7 inches long

FIG. 786.

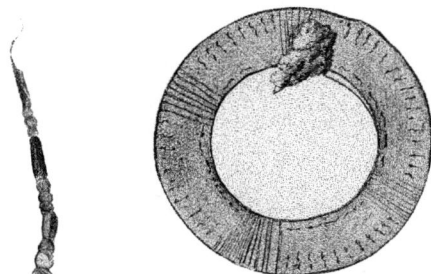

FIG. 784.

FIG. 788.

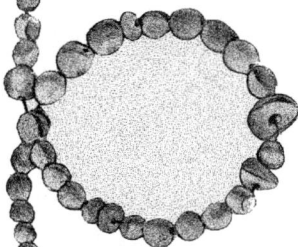

FIG. 783.

FIG. 782.

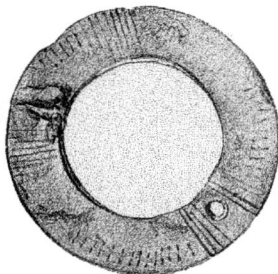

FIG. 785.

FIG. 793.　¼

FIG. 796.　¼

FIG. 787.　¼

FIG. 792.　½

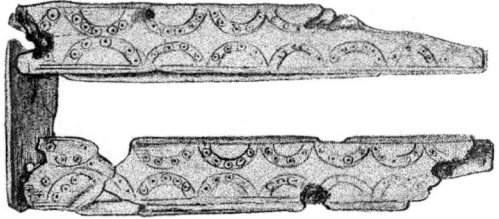

FIG 800.   ¼

FIG. 797.   ¹⁄₁

FIG. 791.   ½

FIG. 794.   ½

FIG. 790.   ½

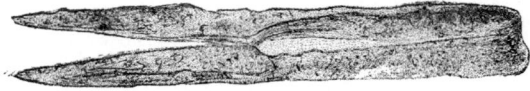

FIG. 798.   ½

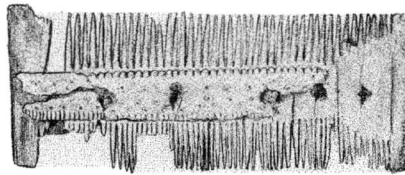

FIG. 799.   ¾

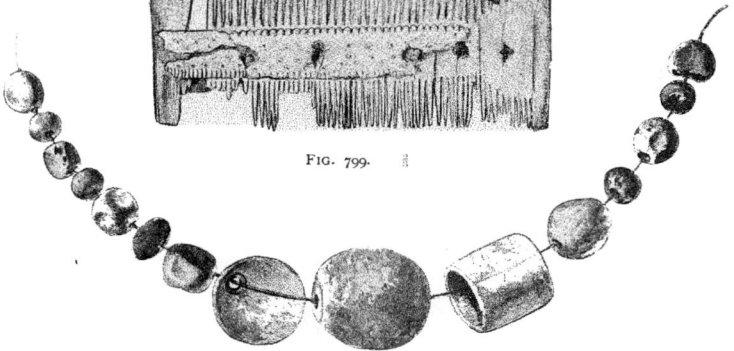

FIG. 795.   ¹⁄₁

Both were of iron, and pointed towards the feet. In contact with these was a double-cut comb (fig. 799), one row of teeth being finer than the other. It was enclosed in a sheath of bone (fig. 800), which appears to be unique in form. The two sides of the case are rivetted to the ends of a short piece of bone, from which they open and shut to admit the comb. Near the right ankle was a rectangular plate of iron (fig. 801), 3 inches by 2 inches, and $\frac{3}{16}$ of an inch in thickness, through each corner of which was a stout iron rivet, $1\frac{1}{4}$ inches long. It stood on its long edge, with the rivets pointing from the body.

No. 22 was close to the south of the last, and was that of a child about five years of age. Near its head was a small clasp of iron, on which traces of wood were visible, and on the neck under the chin was a quantity of dark matter resembling decayed leather, and the remains of a damaged instrument of bronze. This latter consisted of several cylindrical or drum-shaped pieces, inside which were small tongues of bronze arranged in a row on their ends, side by side, (fig. 802). From the position in which they were found they seem to have been fastened together by a thin flat piece of bronze. This article much resembled the one with interment No. 6 in Cheescake Hill barrow, C 44, which is more fully described later.

No. 23 consisted of the remains of a child about three years of age. No relic accompanied it.

No. 24.—This interment had been almost completely destroyed by the plough, only bits of the lower sides of the bones remained. The relics with it were also much injured. Those of iron consisted of a pair of shears in fragments (fig. 803), and the greater portion of a steel for striking a light (fig. 804). Those in bronze were two flattened ring fibulæ (figs. 805-6), the greater part of a hairpin (fig. 807), and some thin strips for the end of a strap (fig. 808). There were also an amber bead and small pieces of a double-cut comb of bone.

No. 25 occurred with its head about 25 feet from the centre of the mound, and about 16 inches down. The femur measured 17 inches, tibia $14\frac{1}{2}$ inches, and humerus $12\frac{3}{4}$ inches, and seem to be those of a male of about forty years of age.

No. 26 was 30 feet north-north-west from the centre, at a depth of $2\frac{1}{2}$ feet. The femur and humerus measured 16 inches and 11 inches respectively, and are apparently those of a female twenty-five to thirty years of age. On the right shoulder was a flat ring fibula of bronze with an iron acus (fig. 809), and near it was a circular brooch or bulla of white metal (fig. 810). It is very thin, and is ornamented with embossed lines of curious design. About the neck were twenty-four beads of variously-coloured vitreous paste (fig. 811), the colours (white, blue, red, purple, and yellow) being artistically blended in each bead, forming a graceful and uncommon pattern. At the left side of the waist was an iron knife (fig. 812), and near the elbow fragments of wood and two pieces of bronze. Close to the left hand was a corroded ring of iron, three-quarters of an inch in diameter, from which a piece of iron an inch long projected at right angles to the ring (fig. 813).

No. 27.—Seven feet nearer to the centre were the extended leg-bones of a large skeleton about 16 inches beneath the surface. During life the left tibia and fibula had been broken about four inches above the foot, and had afterwards grown together, causing the left leg to be fully one inch shorter than the right

2 N

one. All the other parts of the skeleton had been removed at some previous time, probably by rabbit-diggers.

No. 28 was near the northern margin of the mound, at a depth of 16 inches. It had been greatly injured by rabbits burrowing into the mound, and the legs were the only undisturbed portions of the body. The accompanying articles were a bronze hairpin (fig. 814), and an armilla (fig. 815) 2½ inches in diameter; also two flat pieces for the end of a strap (fig. 816), an iron knife (fig. 817), an iron ring 2 inches in diameter (fig. 818), and a small bronze buckle (fig. 819).

From various parts of the mound were taken one spearhead, one leaf-shaped arrowhead, and several other articles of flint; a portion of a stone axe, sherds of British and Anglo-Saxon pottery, a lead slingstone (fig. 820), and a Roman coin.

No sharpening iron, such as was found with several bodies in the Garton Slack cemetery, accompanied any of the knives buried with these interments.

Further Excavations.—On December 9th and 10th, 1887, a few weeks after the commencement of the construction of the Driffield and Market Weighton Railway, which encloses the whole of this barrow, the labourers in obtaining gravel from its southern side, discovered graves Nos. 29 and 30, in each of which was an adult skeleton at a depth of about 3 feet. From the length of the graves—which the writer saw after the navvies had emptied them—the bodies must have been doubled-up, one, as far as could be ascertained, with its head to the centre of the mound and the other with its feet to the centre.

In looking over the soil which had been cast out from grave No. 29, portions of an iron knife, two halves of a fine ring fibula of bronze (fig. 822), and a massive solid silver buckle (fig. 823), each having traces of an iron tongue, were picked up; whilst from the material removed from the grave No. 30 we obtained part of an iron knife (fig. 824), a bronze article of doubtful use (fig. 825), small bits of the same metal, two of which form a hoop—probably a ferrule belonging to the haft of a knife—(fig. 826), also four amber, four glass, and five earthenware beads (fig. 827) belonging to a necklace.

During the following week six more graves (which are numbered and shewn on the plan) were found by the workmen, but the skeletons in them were so carelessly removed that afterwards their positions could not be ascertained.

An iron spearhead was found in No. 33, and some small pieces of bronze had been taken from some of the other graves. Probably several other relics were removed unobserved.

Again, some weeks afterwards, a workman employed to obtain gravel from the sides of the excavation in the mound found five more skeletons, in graves, situated, as far as we could make out, in about the positions shown by Nos. 37 to 41 on the plan. The articles found with these were taken charge of by Mr. Rigby, the contractor, and consist of two or three knives and two spearheads, all of iron, and two fine bronze fibulæ somewhat similar in shape and showing traces of gilding. By the kind permission of Mr. Rigby, these are shown in figs. 828-9.* There were also most of the fragments of a double-cut comb, resembling fig. 799, several glass and amber beads, and a large globular bead of crystal, as well as two flat ring fibulæ resembling fig. 809, and portions of

* The latter is now in my possession.

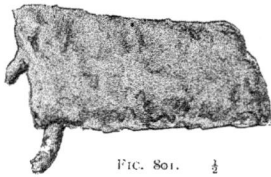

FIG. 801.   ½

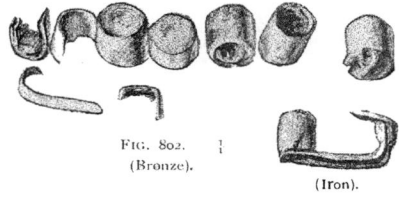

FIG. 802.   ⅟₁
(Bronze).

(Iron).

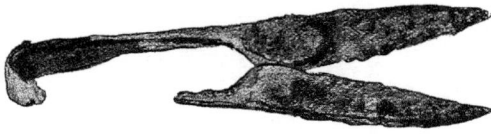

FIG. 803.   ½

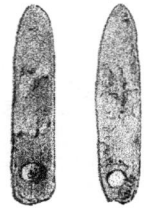

FIG. 808 a.

FIG. 808.   ⅟₁

FIG. 804.   ½

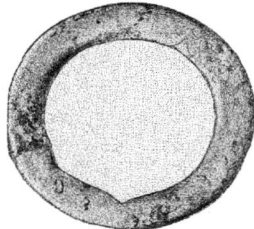

FIG. 805.   ⅟₁

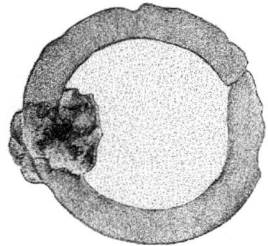

FIG. 806.   ¼

FIG. 807.   ¼

FIG. 809.   ⅟₁

FIG. 815.   ¼

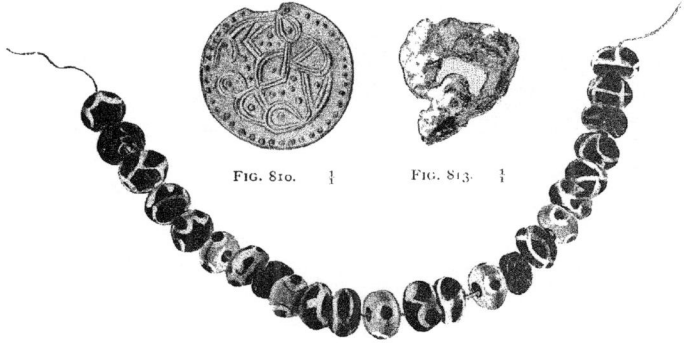

FIG. 810.   ⅓   FIG. 813.   ⅓

FIG. 811.   ⅓

FIG. 812.   ½   FIG. 816.   ⅓

FIG. 814.   ½

FIG. 817.   ½

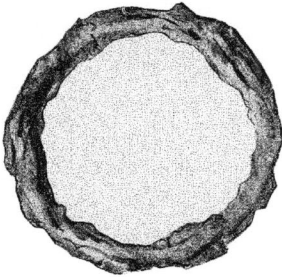

FIG. 818.   ¼

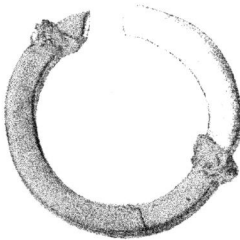

FIG. 819.   ⅓

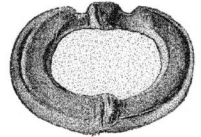

FIG. 822.   ⅓   FIG. 820.   ⅓   FIG. 823.   ⅓

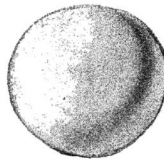

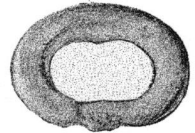

clasps and buckles of bronze. There were likewise portions of buckles and rings of iron.

Though the workmen had been told to give to Mr. Rigby any ornaments, &c., found, doubtless several small articles were removed unobserved, consequently these five bodies appear to have been rather rich in relics. They escaped our notice in the first instance, as we did not think it necessary to search the whole of the area excavated by the late Lord Londesborough. With the ten bodies named by him, there have been recorded in all fifty-one inhumed and two cremated interments from this barrow. Of those found by Lord Londesborough three to five seem to have been British; all the others were Anglo-Saxon. Previous to his Lordship's discovery, several shallow interments must have been destroyed by rabbits and by the lowering of the mound by cultivation.

An epitome of the eventful history of this barrow may now be given. A slight natural mound of chalk gravel had first been selected as a dry and suitable site for the last resting-place of an ancient Briton, who was securely placed within a substantial sarcophagus of heavy slabs of oolitic rock, conveyed, we know not how, from a considerable distance.* Over this a considerable mound was raised. Long ages after, it was possessed by an alien race—the Anglo-Saxons—who in turn used it as a burial place. It has now been entirely swept away, and the material of which it was composed has been spread north and south to form a pathway along which the modern steam-engine will for a time move. Thus does change follow change as the centuries roll by.

BARROW No. C. 50

THIS barrow also was opened by the late Lord Londesborough in 1851, as shown by his description, and by a letter to Mr. Akerman which is copied from the Journal of the Society of Antiquaries:—

" Piccadilly, Nov. 28, 1851.
" Dear Mr. Akerman,
" I send you an account of the opening of some tumuli in the East Riding of Yorkshire, under my direction, in the autumn of the present year, and will thank you to lay the same before the Society of Antiquaries at some early meeting.
" I am happy in this opportunity of adding to the information which the Society has already acquired on the subject of the primeval remains of our native land, and I am
Yours very sincerely,
LONDESBOROUGH. "

" October 17th, 1851. In a field in the occupation of Mr. Hopper, of Kellythorpe, and situated behind the King's Mill, near Driffield, is a large mound (No. C. 50), which forms a very conspicuous object, being from 7 to 8 feet above the ground on the east side, where it is evident the soil has been taken to form the hill. On the west side it is but slightly elevated above the adjoining ground, with which it is connected by a neck or ridge. On its summit was discernible a slight depression or basin. At the base it measured nearly 20 yards in diameter.

---

* Filey Brig is the nearest place from which they could have been procured.

" A cutting was made in the centre, 4 yards by 5 yards. The soil lay in the most irregular manner, in small heaps of different kinds interspersed with fine gravel. On going lower down the chief composition was stiff clay.

" At about 3 feet from the top traces of bone were discovered, but, as it was getting dark, further research was deferred till next morning.

" *October 18th.* At six o'clock the following morning, the work was resumed and the traces of bone followed, which proved to be those of a skeleton lying in the usual contracted position, with the hands bent up towards the face from the elbow. It lay nearly due east, with the face looking to the south. The skull was much crushed, but the other bones appeared to be in a very fair state of preservation. Immediately above the skull was a rude spearhead of flint [fig. 830], which was all that accompanied this body. There seemed every probability that this was the original interment from its proximity to the centre and the undisturbed soil appearing immediately under it. A considerable surface having now been bared, without any indications of more burials having taken place, the sides were pulled into the cutting, but nothing more was discovered."*

Re-opening.—This mound is largely a natural formation of chalk gravel and clay, in the form of a long barrow, with the broad end to the east. It measured 90 feet in length, 51 feet across the west end, and 66 feet across the east end, which was the only part that had been a little artificially raised.

On July 29th, 1872, and the three following days, the writer removed the sods from the greater portion of the surface of this mound, and tested the ground beneath from end to end. It was observed that the previous opening was only about 9 feet square and 7 feet deep, and that the grave had been found and bottomed.

About 16 feet north of the centre at the east end of the barrow, and about 3 inches below the surface, were many portions of a food-vase of a common British type, near to which were portions of the leg and rib bones of an ox, and a very beautiful barbed arrowhead, $1\frac{1}{2}$ inches long and $1\frac{1}{16}$ inches in greatest breadth (fig. 831).

From the artificial portion of the mound, near the centre, we picked up three flakes and two knives of dark-coloured flint. The largest knife is tongue-shaped, nearly 2 inches long, and chipped to a keen cutting edge all round. At the west end of the mound was a piece of Anglo-Saxon pottery.

BARROW No. C. 86

Is situated on elevated ground about half a mile to the south of Driffield, and close to the west side of the railway opposite Poundsworth Mill.

On October 26th and 27th, 1875, it was in very old grass, measured 90 feet in diameter, and from frequent ploughing in early times had been much dispersed and reduced to 2 feet in elevation.

A portion measuring 30 feet north and south, and 8 feet across, was excavated, and about the centre of the mound was a small oval, trough-like grave, nearly 2 feet deep, containing the doubled-up skeleton of an adult, much decayed, on its right side, with the head to the west. No measurements could be taken of the

---

* It is said that a looker-on picked up a fine arrow-head, but did not make it known to the explorers. He afterwards showed it to Mr. J. Browne, the Driffield antiquary.—J. R. M.

FIG. 824.

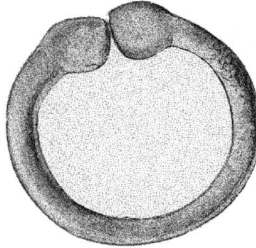

FIG. 825. $\frac{1}{1}$

FIG. 826.

FIG. 828.

FIG. 829. $\frac{1}{1}$

FIG. 827.

FIG. 833.　¼

FIG. 837.

FIG. 830.　½

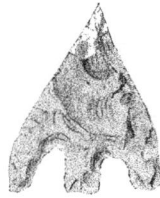

FIG. 831.

FIG. 834.　½

FIG. 840.

FIG. 836.

FIG. 836.

FIG. 835 a.

long bones. Close to the chest had been placed an ornamented food-vase, which from being in contact with some large lumps of chalk above was crushed into many pieces. After being restored (fig. 832), it measures 6½ inches in height, 6¾ inches across the top, and 2¾ inches across the bottom. A few flakes of flint were taken from the ground near the interment. Close to the northern edge of the grave, and opposite the interment, was a large human calvarium. There were no traces of the lower jaw or any other portion of this second burial.

BARROWS Nos. 212a and 212b.

These are two small adjoining mounds, for the most part natural, and consisting largely of fine chalk gravel. They are close to the north side of the canal, opposite Chesnut Cottage, about half a mile east of Driffield River Head.

During the Spring of 1880, the Rev. Canon Horace Newton, the Vicar of Driffield, removed the upper portions of these mounds to obtain material for raising some low swampy places in the same field. In doing this the workmen came upon human bones, and made the discovery known to the writer. On the same day (March 23rd, 1880), accompanied by an experienced workman, I made a careful examination of the westerly mound, and discovered three interments arranged as shown in fig. 833. No. 1 was in a shallow oval grave. Nos. 2 and 3 also occurred in an oval grave about 3 feet deep.

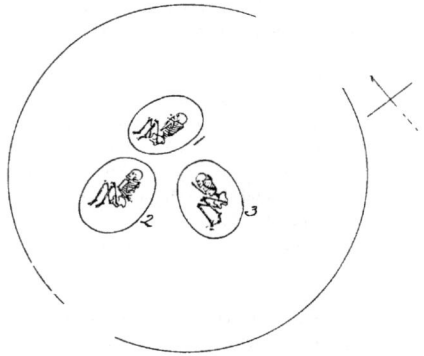

FIG. 833.—PLAN OF BARROW NO. 212 a.

They were of medium stature, but the long bones were too far decayed to admit of measurement.

No. 212b is near the east side of the last. It contained an oval grave in the centre, 2½ feet deep, in which were two medium-sized skeletons, back to back. The one on the north side of the grave was on its right side, with the knees well pulled up, the left hand near the face, the right hand over the lower part of the body, and the head to the north-east. That at the south side was partly on its back and partly on its left side, the knees drawn up, the right hand on the lower part of the body, the left arm doubled with the hand to the face ; and the head was in the same direction as that of its companion. No relics of any kind were found with any of the bodies in these mounds.

All the skulls were in bad preservation, but it was observed that they much resembled those from Swine Ridge, near Millington, Grimthorpe, and from Bessingdale, between Fimber and Wetwang, and probably are of about the same age, viz., Romano-British. There was also a great similarity in the shape of the graves and in the mode of disposing the bodies.

BARROW No. C. 44

Is known as "Cheesecake Hill." The following account, written by the late
Dr. Thurnam, when Curator of the York Museum, is copied from Akerman's
"Remains of Pagan Saxondom," 1855, p. 13 :—

"In a field near the railway, about a mile to the east of Great Driffield, and
between that town and the village of Nafferton, is a large flat mound of
earth, which has long been known by the name of Cheesecake Hill. The
field—which is one of those called The Meadows—formed part of the
ancient common of Driffield, the enclosure of which did not take place
until the middle of the last century, viz., 1742. The tumulus is nearly
circular, much in the shape of an inverted saucer, but of very irregular
form, having a diameter of about 90 feet, with a very gradual descent
to the circumference, beyond which the ground, for the most part, rises
as if by a natural undulation.

"The sepulchral character of the tumulus now to be described was not at all
suspected till the spring of 1845, when the upper part of its eastern half, to
the depth of about 2 feet, was removed by the owner (the late Rd. Jennings,
of Driffield, solicitor), for the purpose of filling up some hollows in another
part of the field. In removing the earth, several human skeletons—from
ten to fifteen, as now stated—were discovered at a depth of 2 feet.

"The workman who was employed at this time informed me that the skeletons
were found lying in all directions, usually at a distance from each other
of about 6 feet.

"The bodies would appear to have been deposited without any precise method,
and, in some cases, had been interred in a confused manner, with the
head bent on the chest, and the knees drawn up. With most of them
were found either weapons of iron, or ornaments of the person. Amongst
the weapons were a large spearhead, two knives, and, it is said, an
arrow-head, of iron [fig. 834].* Near the skull of one skeleton was the
umbo of a shield [fig. 835], in itself not of unusual form, but with peculiar
appendages in the shape of three flat circular discs of iron, each about
2 inches in diameter.

"These, as I am informed, were found arranged round and near the umbo,
one having corresponded with the forehead, and the two others with the
ears of the skeleton. Each is furnished with a projecting pin or rivet of
iron in its centre, by which it had probably been attached to the board
which had formed the body of the shield. Among the ornaments were
several clasps and fibulæ of bronze, of both cruciform and circular shape,
with beads of various kinds, particularly of amber and glass. There were
also tweezers of bronze [fig. 836], and, what is unusual, a pair of scissors
of iron [fig. 837].† There must also be named a circular plano-convex
disc of bone, about 1½ inches in diameter, having a slight central perforation, ornamented on the convex side with concentric rings, and, on the
flat side, rough and unpolished. The various articles were presented by
Mr. Jennings, the owner of the property, to the Yorkshire Philosophical

---

* Probably a javelin, as it seems too large for an arrow.—J.R.M.
† These are probably of later and accidental introduction.—J.R.M.

FIG. 832.   ½

FIG. 835.

Society. These objects have been briefly described by Mr. Wellbeloved in the Journal of the Archæological Association, Vol. II, 1846, p. 54. Several vases of coarse earthenware, of a common Anglo-Saxon type, some of them described as containing charcoal and bone ash, were also found. The remaining part of the tumulus was explored [by several members of the York Antiquarian Club], in the last week of August, 1849, when the greater portion was levelled and examined. It would appear to have been less rich in sepulchral deposits than the eastern section, previously removed. Eight skeletons, several of them accompanied by weapons and ornaments, were, however, uncovered. In describing the skeletons, and the articles found with them, they will be enumerated in the order in which they lay, beginning with the north side.

" No. 1. A skeleton extended west to east, feet to the east. Stretched across the body, with its point to the right hip, was a large iron knife, the broad blade of which measures upwards of 8 inches in length. Near the left were two fine spear-hoads [figs. 838-9], also of iron, the one about 14 inches, the other 8 inches in length, having their points directed upwards towards the head. The skeleton must have been that of a man of rather more than average stature, the femur measuring $18\frac{3}{4}$ inches, the tibia 15 inches in length.

" No. 2. This skeleton was of much smaller size, probably that of a female, and would seem to have been interred in the same grave with the preceding, the upper part of the body having been laid on the lower part of the other, but in a sitting posture, with the skull raised and facing the east. The thigh bones were extended, those of a leg forming a right angle with them. Around the neck were five beads, a large one of amber and four cylindrical ones of baked clay or vitrified paste of a brown-red colour marked with veins. By the side of the left leg was a round iron spike [fig. 840], about 4 inches in length, which had probably been attached as a ferrule to the lower end of the shaft of the larger spearhead found near the shoulder of the preceding skeleton. In these two interments we may perhaps recognise the remains of an Anglo-Saxon warrior, with those of his wife deposited literally on his knees.

" No. 3. A female skeleton of moderate size extended, the head to the north. Around the neck was a necklace of amber, glass, and vitrified paste, there being no fewer than forty to fifty beads of various sizes. Lying near each shoulder, near the clavicles, was a round fibula in the form of a flat ring of bronze, of about 2 inches in diameter and only slightly ornamented. The pins of the fibulæ had been of steel, and attached to the rust were traces of the clothing of a very coarse fabric. Round each wrist would appear to have been an armlet of small beads, chiefly of glass and amber. By the side of the right leg, above the knee, was a small iron knife [fig. 841], the blade about 3 inches in length, attached to which were traces of a wooden handle. In a corresponding situation with regard to the left leg was another knife of the same length, but altogether of more delicate proportions and better workmanship. A considerable part of the wooden handle remains separated from the blade by a thin plate of bronze. Adjoining these were the remains, as at first supposed, of a pair of scissors. The handles of these instruments are clumsy rings of iron, 2 inches in diameter.* The shafts or blades, if they may be so called, were broken into many portions, but would appear to have been 6 inches in length, round, and tapering towards the end, and not thicker than a quill pen. About 2½ inches from the rings the blades seem to have separated from the handles by small shoulders. What may have been the use of these instruments seems very doubtful, but whatever this may have been, they had probably been worn in a pouch or pocket, or in some other way suspended from the girdle. On each side of the waist were several broken clasps, tags, and other small articles of bronze, which probably formed part of the girdle and other fastenings of the dress. A small buckle and ring were also found.

" No. 4. This skeleton was also that of a female, younger than the foregoing one, immediately adjoining which the body had been deposited, stretched at full length, on the west and rather to the south of the other. They were possibly mother and daughter or sisters who had been interred in the same or closely-adjoining graves. In this instance, however, the position of the skull was reversed, the head being to the south, the feet to the north, the latter of which were crossed at the ankles. Not very far from the right shoulder was a circular fibula, formed of a concave disc of bronze, of more than 1½ inches in diameter, presenting traces of what appeared to be gold foil on the interior surface, which may possibly have had an additional setting of glass or paste [fig. 842]. Round the neck was a less number of beads of the same as were found with the preceding skeleton. Corresponding to the breast were a pair of remarkably fine cruciform bronze fibulæ, each of which is nearly 5 inches in length [fig. 843]. Portions of bronze clasps, &c., were also found, but there were no remains of steel implements.

" No. 5. A male skeleton of large size, nearer the surface than the preceding one, the depth not being more than 18 inches. The body had been laid at full length, the feet to the south. No objects of any kind were found with this skeleton, the legs of which appeared to have been previously disturbed.

" No. 6. The skeleton apparently of a female, with the head directed to the north-north-west, the face being turned towards the east. This skeleton was situated more to the west than any of the others. From a part of the skull being found 7 or 8 inches below the rest of its body, and one of the thigh bones being in a nearly perpendicular position, it is probable that this skeleton had likewise been disturbed. The only object found in this instance was a knife on the left side, of a similar description with the larger of those with No. 2.

" No. 7. This skeleton lay at some distance to the east of and at right angles with that last described, the body having been deposited from east-north-east to west-north-west. The skull and upper portion of the bones had been removed when the eastern part of the mound was levelled.

" No. 8. A skeleton lying north-north-west to south-east, the feet to the latter point. The face had been turned towards the east, and the arms apparently crossed on the breast. The bones of the right leg were flexed at right

---

* These seem more probably to have been something resembling the articles from Barrow C. 44, and shown in fig. 854, and not scissors.—J. R. M.

FIG. 839.

FIG. 841.

FIG. 842.

FIG. 842.   FIG. 842.

FIG. 844.

FIG. 838.   ¼

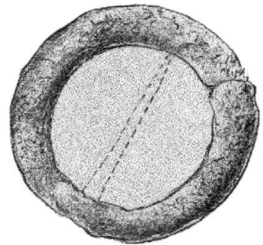

FIG. 847.   FIG. 848.

Fig. 843.   ½

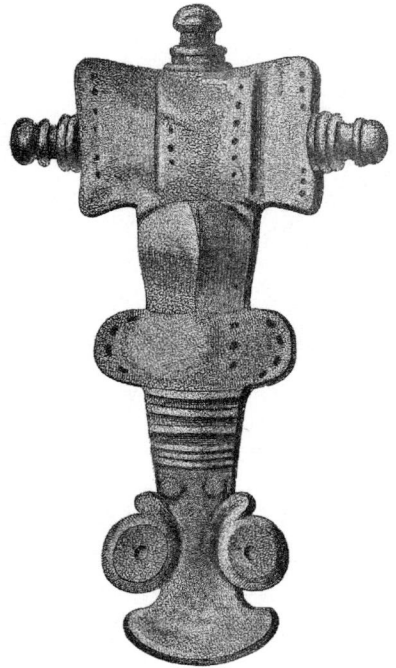

Fig. 843.   ½

Fig. 843.   ½

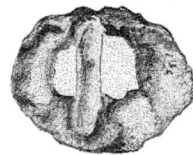

Fig. 849.

Fig. 850.   ½

angles with those of the thigh.   Under the skull was a small clasp of bronze not more than half an inch in length, and a similar object with one side of the clasp of the same material, were found about 3 feet from the east.

" The excavations were extended to the western limits of the mound at several points, without finding any other remains, but as a portion is still un-levelled a few additional interments may at some future time be discovered. In each case the skeletons lay at a depth of little more than 2 feet below the surface, and were uniformly covered by a stratum of stiff clayey soil, contrasting strongly with the very fine rolled chalk rubble and yellow sand of which the natural subsoil in this locality consists, and in very shallow graves or rather hollows in which the bodies appear to have been laid. Between the adjacent skeletons were vacant spaces of varying and often considerable extent.   There appears reason to suppose that the south part of the mound in which the four last-described skeletons were discovered had previously, and perhaps at some remote period, been disturbed and any objects accompanying them removed.   In the course of the excavations various articles were found, which must have either been accidentally buried or, as appears more probable, dispersed in such previous explor-ations.   Among these was a knife [fig. 844] like those found with skeletons Nos. 3 and 4, an iron buckle, the joint of a pair of scissors, and a small fibula and portion of a clasp, both of bronze.   The most interesting of these scattered objects were relics of a preceding race—the early Britons. These consisted of a fragment or two of British pottery of the finer kind, and a beautifully-formed arrowhead of flint [resembling fig. 831], remarkable as containing a fossil, (*Terebratula semisulcata*), very rarely, if ever, as observed by Professor Phillips, found in the flint of Yorkshire.*   These objects point to early British occupation on the spot, and appear to indicate that this cemetery was formed on or near the site of early tumuli of the stone period."

Re-opening.—October 18th, 1871, and the following workable days to the end of the month, were spent in examining this mound, which had remained in the form left by Dr. Thurnam.   We removed the grassy surface and carefully searched almost every foot beneath, from the centre to the circumference.   Fig. 846 is a plan of the interments discovered.

Near the centre was a shallow oval hole " *C* " 3 feet in diameter, containing burnt matter, and about 10 feet to the east was a shallow grave-like hole "*D*," with dark earth of a greasy nature, but no visible remains of an interment.†   Fifteen feet north-east of the assumed centre, and close under the turf, was a doubled-up skeleton (fig. 846, No. 1), on the right side, head to the south and both hands in front of the face.   It had been considerably crushed at the time that the upper portion of the barrow was removed.   No relic accompanied this interment, but the absence of relics may be taken as negative evidence, whilst its doubled-up position is strikingly British.   The bones were too far decayed to be measured.

No. 2 was in a shallow grave 17 feet east-south-east of the centre, and is that

* This flint is not from the Yorkshire chalk, but from a boulder from the drift.—J. R. M.
† Probably these places were observed at the time of carting the mound away and were rifled of their presumably British contents.

of a middle-aged Anglo-Saxon female. The body had been deposited on its back, head to the west-north-west, the legs slightly bent at the knees, the left arm extended by the side and the right bent at a right angle with the hand on the left elbow. On each breast was a flattened ring fibula of bone or ivory (figs. 847-8).* At the right side of the skull, just above the right shoulder, was an iron buckle (fig. 849) and a decayed strap of thin bronze. On the upper part of the breast was a straight piece of iron wire (fig. 850) 3 inches long, and some very thin bits of bronze, probably the remains of a breast ornament, which crumbled to powder on the attempt to move it. From under and above the neck we took 84 beads

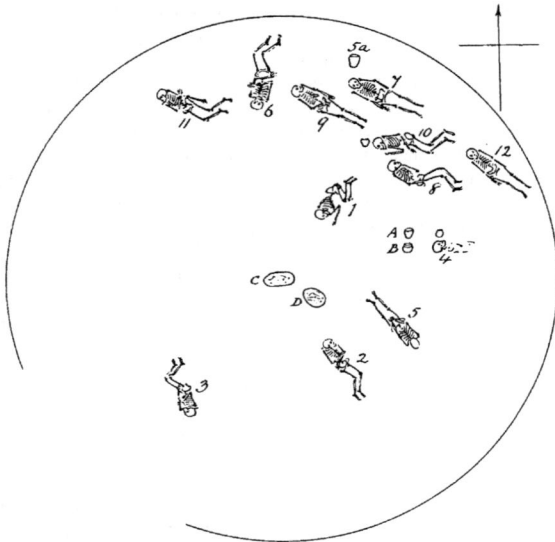

FIG. 846.—PLAN OF BARROW C 44.

(fig. 851) of amber, glass, and a kind of paste, variously shaped and coloured. Upon the lower part of the waist, and partly under the flexed right arm were a bronze clasp (fig. 852) and a small strip of bronze (fig. 853), surrounded by decayed matter ; and between the left hand and left side of pelvis were thin bits of crushed bronze and more dark matter. Close under the left knee was a small iron knife (a), a buckle (b), a ring 3¾ inches in diameter (c), and a pair of bent key-like irons (d) 8 inches long.† Some small strips of bronze (e) occurred within the centre of the ring. Fig. 854 shows the position in which they were found.

No. 3 was 30 feet south-west of the centre, at a depth of 2 feet. It was on the

---

* In Akerman's " Pagan Saxondom," plate xxxvi, a similar one is erroneously described as a spindle whorl.

† Probably similar to those discovered by Dr. Thurnam, with bodies No. 3, which he took to be portions of scissors.

FIG 851

FIG. 856.   ½

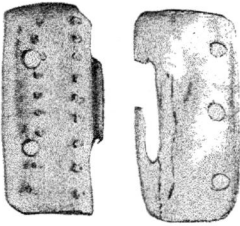

FIG. 852.

FIG. 853.   ¼

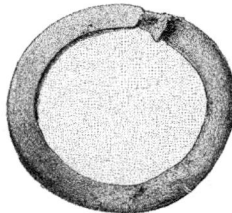

FIG. 857.

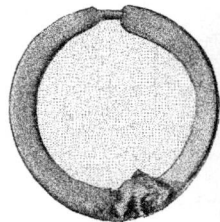

FIG. 858.

PLATE CIX.

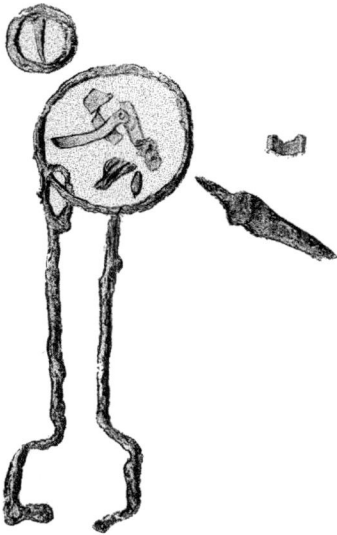

FIG. 859.   ½

FIG. 854.   ⅛

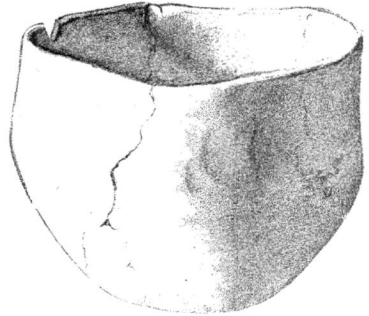

FIG. 861.   ½

FIG. 860.   ½

FIG. 862.   ½

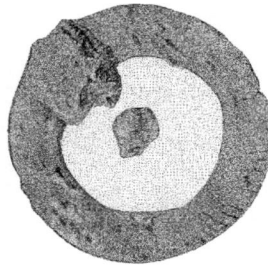

FIG. 867.

FIG. 863.

FIG. 864.

left side, with the head to the south and the knees slightly bent. Close by the
left thigh, with the point to the pelvis, was an iron knife (fig. 856), and near the
neck were two ring fibulæ of bronze (figs. 857-8.) At the time of Dr. Thurnam's
explorations an adjoining skeleton had been removed, and this one had been
disturbed. The long bones were too far decayed to admit of measurements
being taken.

No. 4 was 23 feet east-north-east of the centre, and close under the turf. The
head pointed to the west, but nearly every other bone had been removed by the
previous explorers. Close to the forehead stood a vase of dark texture (fig. 859),
measuring 4¼ inches across the top, and 5¼ inches in height. Two feet to the
west of the last interment two small food-vases (figs. 860-1), marked A and B
on the plan, stood together, and only 6 inches from the surface. Near the vases
was a small iron knife (fig. 862), which had been disturbed, and there was every
appearance of some interments having been removed from near these vases by
the previous excavators.

No. 5 was extended on its face, 18 inches below the surface, and 20 feet
east-south-east of the centre. The feet pointed to the centre of the mound, and
both arms were bent with the hands under the abdomen. Beneath each shoulder
was a flat ring fibula of bronze (figs. 863-4), 2 inches in diameter, resembling those
found with No. 3, and about the neck were a few beads (fig. 865). An iron knife
(fig. 866), was under the lumbar region, with the point to the head, and near it
was an iron buckle (fig. 867). With the decayed bones of the right hand was
a small bronze ring (fig. 868), standing on edge—a position which seemed to
show that it had been worn on the finger at the time of interment. It fell to
pieces when touched. Under the feet was a cruciform fibula (fig. 869), 5½ inches
long, face downwards, with the broad end towards the head. Its position seemed
to indicate that it had secured the lower end of a garment or wrapper, in which
the body had been interred.

No. 5a had been cremated, as, at about 45 feet north-north-east of centre,
near the margin of the mound, and at a depth of 18 inches, was the bottom of
a cinerary urn, containing a very few burnt bones, rather finely pulverised, but
no relic. The upper portion of the urn had been previously removed.

No. 6 was 32 feet north of the centre, and 2 feet down. Its head was directed
to the south-west, with the hands on the lower part of the body, and the knees
slightly pulled up. On each shoulder was a flattened ring fibula of bronze (figs.
870-1), nearly 2 inches in diameter. The pin of the one on the left shoulder had
been of iron, while the other was of bronze. The two fibulæ differ also somewhat
in ornamentation. On the breast were 92 beads (fig. 872), in contact with a
crescentric article (fig. 873), which was on the upper part of the chest. The shell
of this—which had partly crumbled into green dust—had been made of very thin
bronze. Its lower and convex edge had been set round with a row of hollow,
drum-shaped studs (?) of bronze, standing on their ends, about ¼-inch in height
and ¼-inch in diameter; and near its upper edge was what resembled the iron
acus of a brooch, 4 inches long. These drum-like studs were close together, and
the interior of each contained the remains of an arrangement of small thin strips
of bent bronze, resembling those in fig. 802. This internal arrangement seems
unnecessary, had it been intended for ornamentation only, and probably it served

some other purpose.* At the right side of the hips was an iron buckle. This interment was that of a female of medium age and stature, and, like all of the interments in this barrow, was much decayed.

No. 7 was 43 feet north-north-east of the centre, 2½ feet down, with the head to the west. At the left side of the pelvis was an iron knife, with the point towards the head ; and on the left side, at the waist, was an iron buckle. The bones, which were greatly decayed, were probably those of a man.

No. 8 was 36 feet north-east of centre, and hardly so deep as the last. It had been interred on the left side, with head to the west, and the legs slightly bent. Upon the chest, towards the right shoulder, was a cruciform fibula of bronze (fig. 874), 5 inches long, with its small end to the left shoulder. Near to the head were seven beads, some thin bits of decayed bronze, and a small bronze ring which crumbled to bits when removed. These were, probably, ear ornaments, as shown by figs. 875-6.

No. 9 was 38 feet north of the centre, and at about the same depth as the last. It was an extended body, on its back, with the head to the west-north-west. On the shoulders were two fibulæ (figs. 877-8), resembling those from No. 6, and close to the one on the right breast were five small beads (fig. 879). The bones were those of a medium-sized female.

No. 10 was three feet to the east of No. 9, and a little lower ; otherwise it was arranged as shown on the plan (fig. 846). On the upper part of each breast was a ring fibula (figs. 880-1), and below the chin were pieces of thin bronze (fig. 882), some showing traces of gilding. Probably they were the remains of a brooch, as the bronze catch for the acus remained. Unfortunately, this portion of the interment was accidentally disturbed, and part of the relics damaged by a workman's spade. Above the hips was a bronze buckle (fig. 883), fixed to a bronze strap. At the right side of the head were a few beads, comprising 6 amber and 7 long spindle-formed bugles of paste (fig. 884) ; also a double-cut bone comb, in bad preservation. Close to the right side of the head were the fragments of an irreparably crushed food-vase.

No. 11 was 44 feet north-west of the centre, 2½ feet deep, and nearly in the same position as the last. Unfortunately, an unskilful digger was at work at this point, and disturbed portions of the left side of the head and the chest before it was observed. A ring fibula (fig. 886), and hairpin 3½ inches long (fig. 887), were also disturbed and slightly damaged. As only one fibula was found after a very careful search, its fellow may have been crushed to powder. A beautiful necklace was found on the left side of the chest. This ornament was most probably worn round the neck in three links, as shown in fig. 888. It consists of 219 beads. Three of these are of crystal, one being nearly globular and ¾-inch in diameter ; the other two are cylindrical in form, and measure ⅞ of an inch in length and over ½-inch in diameter, and are cut round the circumference into numerous facets ; 141 are of amber, measuring from ⅛ of an inch to 1 inch in diameter, two are of glass and the remainder are made up of five cowry shells (*Cyprœa Europœa*) about ¾ of an inch long, 2 long bugles, 39 small single, double, and triple beads of vitreous paste, and 10 of baked earth. Large as this necklace now is, it must

---

* Probably these articles were the remains of musical instruments.

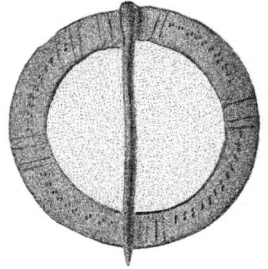

FIG. 87c.   ¼

FIG. 868.

FIG. 865.   ¼

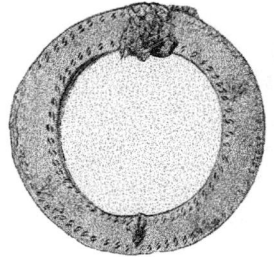

FIG. 871.

FIG. 866.   ½

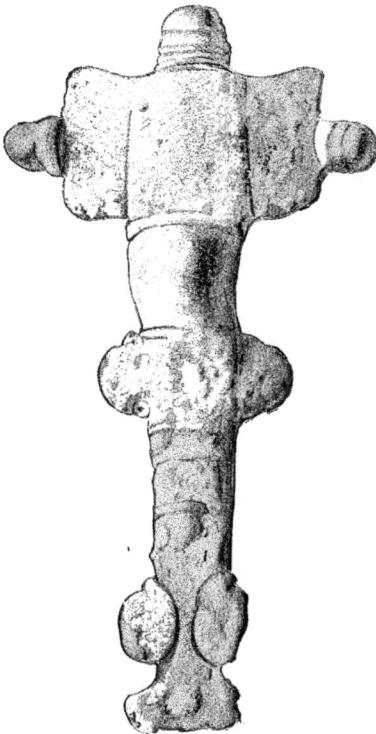

FIG. 875.   ¼

FIG. 876.   ¼

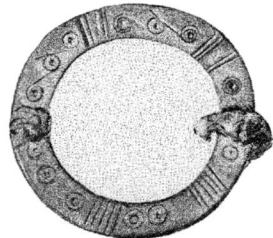

FIG. 869.   ¼

FIG. 877.   ¼

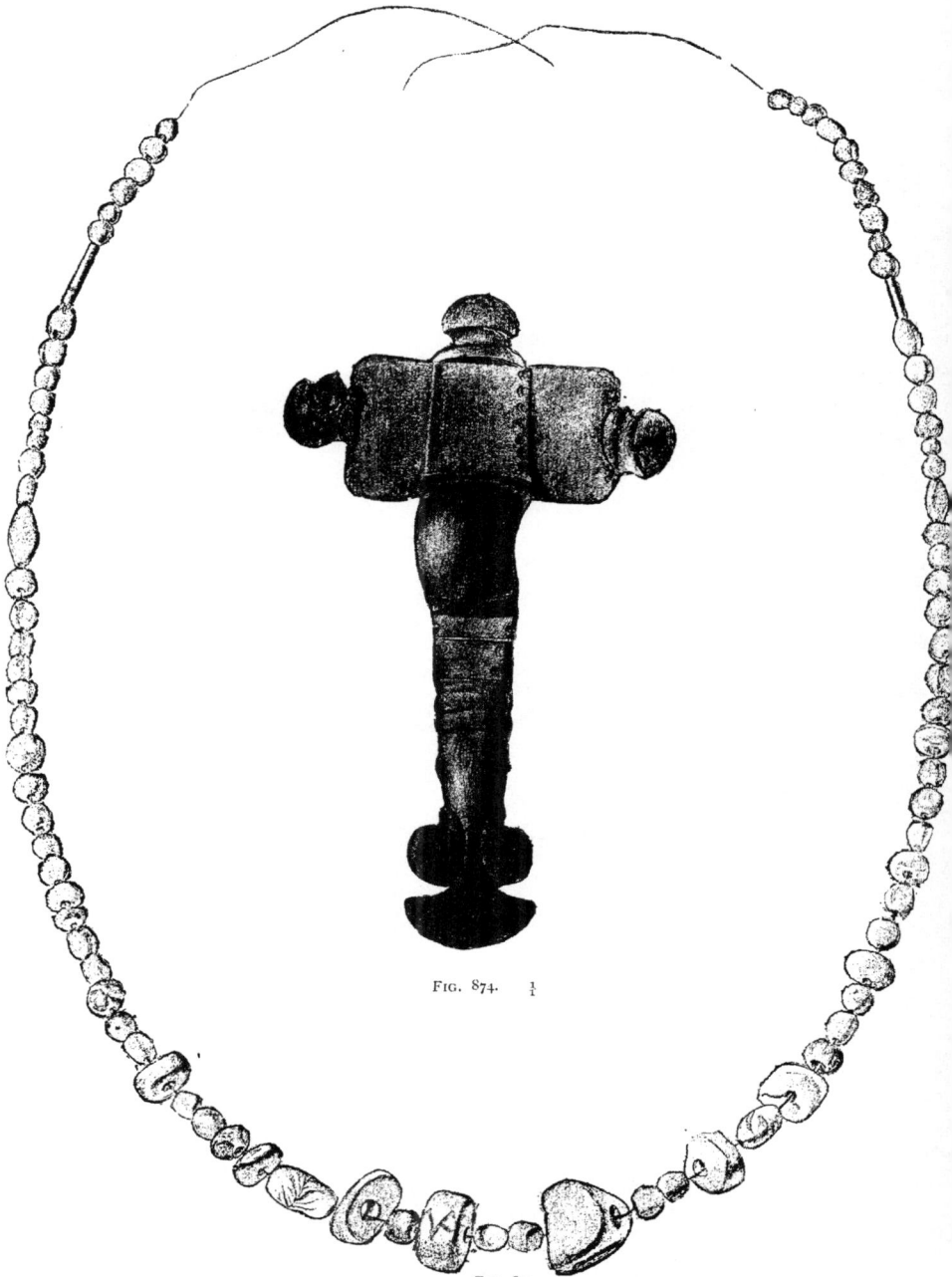

Fig. 874. $\frac{1}{1}$

Fig. 872.

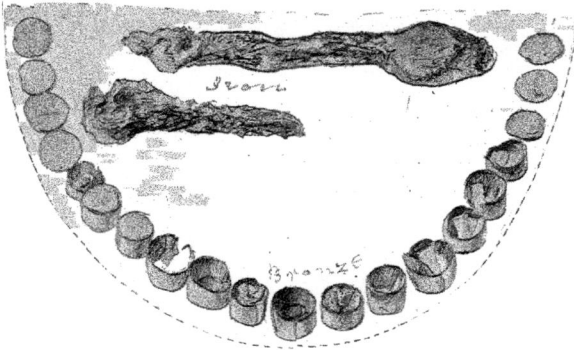

FIG. 873.   ⅓

FIG. 879   ⅔

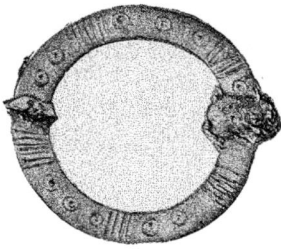

FIG. 878.   ⅔

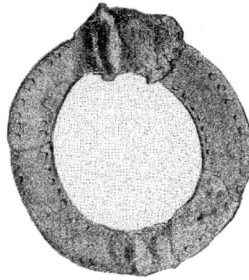

FIG. 880.   ⅓

FIG. 882.

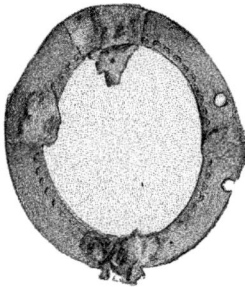

FIG. 881.

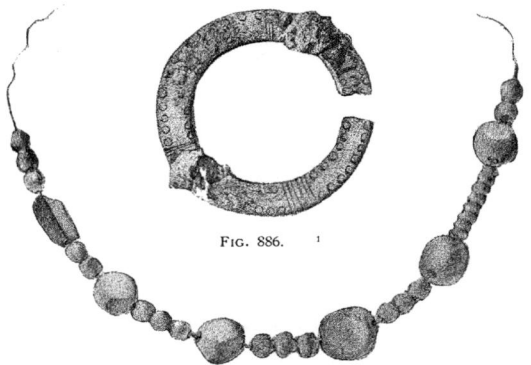

FIG. 886.   ¹

FIG. 884.   ⅓

originally have been considerably longer, as, although every possible precaution was taken, several of the delicate bugles and small cowries were destroyed in extracting them from the tenacious earth, and very probably a few of the very small amber and other beads may yet remain in the soil.

Near the lumbar vertebræ were two pairs of bronze clasps (figs. 889-890) and an angular loop with three rivets (fig. 891), which had secured it to some strap or belt. Behind the body, and half way between the hip and the knee, were two crooked irons, 6 inches long, some pieces of bone, and a hoop of ivory or bone, 5 inches in diameter. Two or more articles seem to have been placed one upon another, and fig. 892 shows their position as sketched at the time. This circle of bone may have been the rim of a leather or wooden drinking-cup, or other vessel.

No. 12 was 4 feet to the east of No. 10, 2 feet deep, on its back, with its head to the west. No relic was found.

The bad preservation of the interments in this mound was due probably to the damp nature of the earth in which they occurred. The number of females was somewhat remarkable. Though we found no animal bones indicating deposits of food, such may have decayed, as the presence of four food-vases shows the survival, at the time the interments were made in this mound, of the old British custom of supplying the body with food.

Altogether about 35 inhumed bodies, and one or more cremated ones have been observed in this barrow, and probably many more were removed unnoticed by the workmen when the upper portion of the mound was removed in 1845.

Of the 12 bodies discovered by the writer, 11 are undoubtedly Anglo-Saxon, belonging to a time long after the raising of the barrow, since all the graves were shown to be sharply cut into the compact mound. The flint arrow-head and the fragments of British pottery seem clearly to indicate the dispersion of a British interment at some early time, probably when the Anglo-Saxon bodies were interred. The doubled-up body of No. 1, the dish-shaped hole (C) in the centre containing burnt matter, and the empty oval grave (D), 10 feet to the east of the centre, point also to British interments.

Other pagan interments of more or less interest have from time to time been made within the area of this group. About half a mile west of the last barrow, close to the south side of the railway, several interments—apparently Anglo-Saxon— were found about 1876 during the excavation for a short railway siding to the Driffield Cake Mill. Some were accompanied by bits of iron, portions of Anglo-Saxon pottery, part of which, with two skulls, the writer procured from the workmen. There were also traces of one or more cremated interments. It is not improbable that in the future further discoveries will be made in this locality.

During January, 1876, whilst excavating the foundations for a wall at the gas-works, eight or more skeletons were found at a depth of about 2 feet, with their heads in various directions. No relic was observed by the workmen, who smashed up the bones in a most careless manner, and would not be likely to notice small objects. The bones were much decayed, but some fragments of the skulls preserved seem to resemble Anglo-Saxon crania. About 1820, whilst excavations were being made for the foundations of a house on the north side of the new road in Driffield, the workmen found two human skeletons, which appeared to have been interred at an early period, and probably belong, with the eight found near the gas-works, to an extensive Anglo-Saxon graveyard.

Further discoveries were made in 1882, during the excavations for the new drainage works, when for some distance along the Scarborough road, near the east end of Bridge Street, more than a dozen skeletons were found scarcely 2 feet deep, lying in various directions in the middle of the road. These were all broken to pieces by the workmen while excavating the very hard ground, and no relics were obtained. Probably the road at this point runs over an Anglo-Saxon cemetery, which may have extended to Moot Hill, near to and in which Anglo-Saxon remains were found about the year 1858 by the late Mr. Gibson, the owner, whilst removing part of Moot Hill to fill up an old chalk-pit close by. An Anglo-Saxon sword and other relics were then found and afterwards shown to the writer by the late Mr. Harrison, of the Buck Hotel, Driffield, who had obtained them from the workmen.

In digging the new drainage works in Shady Lane, the workmen removed two or more skeletons, probably Anglo-Saxon, as the undisturbed portion of one of them, which the writer saw, showed that the body had been in a more or less flexed position, with head to the north. No relic was observed.

FURTHER ANGLO-SAXON REMAINS.

In the latter part of May, 1893, whilst levelling two small fields adjoining the King's Mill Road, Driffield, for the purpose of a recreation ground, the workmen came upon several human skeletons in the gravelly subsoil. At first nothing was found with them, and very little notice was taken of the circumstance. Afterwards, some food-vases were discovered, which were broken and many of their fragments disposed of before the find was made known to the writer. The vases were mainly of a semi-globular shape (fig. 893), varying, after restoration, from 4 to 6 inches in height, and about the same in diameter. With the exception of one vase they are all of a dark colour, and free from ornamentation. The exceptional one (fig. 894) is quite of another type, and of a dull red colour. Altogether there were about twelve skeletons found, at depths varying from 10 to 18 inches, and extending over an area of about 50 by 60 yards. They consisted of the remains of children as well as of adults, placed with their heads directed to various points of the compass, and, as far as could be made out, in some cases their legs were doubled up.

No cremated bodies were found, and, with the one exception, all the vases seem to have been of the Anglo-Saxon food-vase type. Yet in the midst of this undoubted Anglo-Saxon burial ground was a grave from which the workmen took many handstruck flint flakes, some horse teeth and other bones. I possess two of the teeth, which are large ones, and twenty of the flakes, about half of a circular knife, ground to the edge, and an axe-shaped knife chipped on the sides. The flakes show no trace of fire, but the two knives had been burnt and may have accompanied a cremated British interment, the bones of which the workmen had not noticed. There was a very slight rise observed on the surface, which seemed to indicate the site of a barrow, in and around which the Anglo-Saxon interments had been placed. As the ground was being lowered only about 6 inches in some places, and in no case more than 18 inches, probably many interments were passed over unobserved, and further discoveries may be expected at some future time.

FIG. 888. $\frac{2}{3}$

FIG. 887.

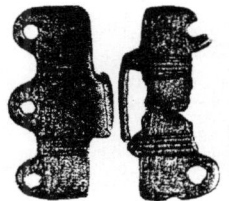

FIG. 889. $\frac{1}{1}$

FIG. 891.

FIG. 890.   1

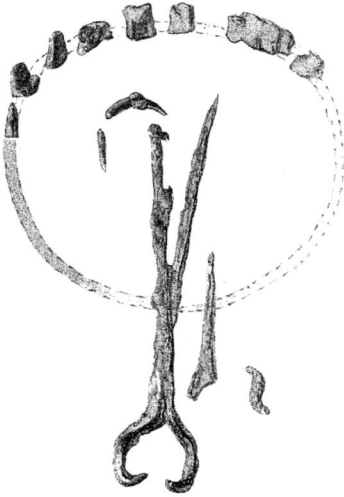

FIG. 892.   ½

FIG. 893.

FIG. 894 a.   ¼

FIG. 894.   ½

From the preceding account of the discoveries of numerous Anglo-Saxon bodies in the neighbourhood of Driffield, it would seem that they were mainly of the pre-Christian period.[*]

BARROW No. Ia.

Called Moot Hill, was probably used as such long after it had been raised as a memorial to some ancient Briton. It stands on the western brow of a low escarpment of chalk, near the east side of the stream at the north end of Driffield. It seems to have been formed mainly of chalk. The eastern side only remains, the western portion having been removed about the year 1856 by Mr. Gibson, the owner of the land, to fill up a large chalk pit close by. Before that time it was circular in form, with a diameter of about 90' feet, of considerable height, and had a ditch and rampart, part of which remains, close round its circumference. The late J. Browne, during his long residence in Driffield, took great interest in investigating the origin and purpose of this mound, and wrote to me as under :—

> " I was the first to discover that it was a Moot Hill, its name having been corrupted into Mundal Hill, and in several old documents it is written "Mude Hill" and "Mud Hill." At the time Mr. Gibson, the owner of the field in which the mound is, levelled part of the mound, I watched the operations. It had no doubt been a British burial ground, and used first by the Druids from which to deliver their laws, and afterwards by the Anglo-Saxons to hold their "moot courts' on. They are also called 'Hills of Pleas.' This hill used also to be called Fairy Hill, the belief being, when existence of fairies was believed in, that they inhabited this sort of hill."

Mr. Browne has also kindly supplied me with the following list of relics discovered by the workmen at the time of the excavation :—A bronze celt, bits of corroded swords and spears, a small pocket sundial, evidently used, Mr. Browne thinks, to carry in the pocket before the common use of watches and clocks, and several small English silver coins. With the exception of the celt, all the articles are of mediæval date. Whether the bronze celt had accompanied a British interment or not, there can be no doubt that this mound was raised by the Britons. The portion now remaining is covered with a rich sward, but at some future time the writer hopes to obtain permission to explore it and discover further British remains.

BARROW No. 278

Is called Howe Hill, and, viewed from the north, appears to stand on rising ground, and has an imposing appearance. It has a flat top, and at some time may have been used as a moot-hill. It is situated at the north corner of the site of the village of old Sunderlandwick, in a grass field close by the north-west side of the road, which runs south-west from the Beverley road through the centre of the site of the old village.

[*] If the village of Wansford be derived from Wodnesford, as suggested in "The Saxons in England," by J. M. Kemble, vol. 1, p. 344, we have in the name of this village evidence of the worship of Woden then lingering in the neighbourhood, whilst the villages of Goodmanham and Fridaythorpe, a short distance away, are also names that may indicate places of former pagan worship.

The barrow has been disturbed and put out of shape by persons digging for rabbits, and by the uprooting of the large trees which once grew upon it. Two trenches form a right angle round the margin of its southern half. Its present diameter is, roughly, 75 feet, and its elevation 8 feet above the old surface line, though, in all probability, it was originally 6 or 8 feet higher.

During the last five days in September, 1892, we employed five labourers in removing from the centre of this mound the upper portion of an area measuring 26 feet by 25 feet, with the result of only finding three small flint scrapers, three knife-like articles, nearly one hundred flint flakes and chips, and one fragment of a British vase. It was found to consist entirely of loamy soil mixed with a little bluish clay, and we observed that at some early period a small opening had been made from the top, a little west of the present centre, and had been carried down to the base of the mound. This opening had removed, at least, a cremated interment, portions of which we observed scattered in the disturbed area.

During the middle of October we renewed our examinations, and, a little to the north-west of the centre, found three circular dish-shaped holes scooped out of the old surface line. They each measured about $2\frac{1}{2}$ feet in diameter at the top, and varied from 9 to 12 inches in depth. They were arranged with a space of about 4 feet between them,* and nearly in a straight line north-east by south-west: The two to the south-west contained cremated bones and dark-coloured matter, mixed with small pieces of burnt wood only. The one to the north-east contained dark-coloured soil and burnt soil only. At about 2 feet south-east of the central hole, and at an elevation of 3 feet in the mound, stood erect a small food-vase (fig. 895). It has an unusually broad bottom, stands proportionably low, and it is otherwise somewhat exceptional in form by having in one place a bulge in the rim outside the mouth of the vase, resembling an attempt at a rudimentary handle. This vase had been enclosed in a small cist of wood, traces of which were very distinct. Nothing was found with it, and no trace of an interment was visible. Probably an accompanying body had entirely decayed.

After completing our excavation, and most carefully trenching the ground under the mound, we were surprised to find no trace of a grave.

BARROW No. 279

Is a small and mainly natural rise in the gravelly subsoil, not more than a foot in elevation, situated near the east side of the road between Almanwath Bridge and Sunderlandwick Bar. There are in this neighbourhood several natural elevations of irregular shape. It was the remarkably circular form of the present one that attracted our attention. In the centre was a shallow grave containing at the bottom the decayed bones of an adult body, on its left side, with the knees drawn up, and head to the east. Nothing accompanied the interment.

BARROW No. 279a.

This is the approximate site of a barrow which once stood in the stack-yard at old Sunderlandwick, about 300 yards south of No. 279. The late J. Browne, of Driffield, gave me the following particulars of the discovery made at the time

---

* Three similarly-arranged holes were found under Barrow No. C 39, in Group I.

of the removal of this mound, an account of which he supplied to the newspapers at the time, and with which—as well as a sketch of the wooden sarcophagus—he also furnished to Mr. Thomas Wright, the antiquary :—

> " In August, 1856, on levelling this tumulus, a large oaken coffin was found in the centre, lying due east and west. On raising the lid it was found to contain three skeletons. Two of the skulls were towards the east and one towards the west ; the bones were very much decayed. No warlike weapons or domestic implements or personal ornaments could be discovered. The coffin was formed out of one split piece of wood, being the lower part of the trunk of a massive oaktree. The cavity to hold the bodies had been scooped out in a concave form, or probably it had been burnt out by the action of fire. It was about 6 feet in length and about 4 feet in breadth, and resembled a rude boat with square ends.* The bodies were covered by two large portions of the same wood, which were very black and much decayed.
>
> " Amongst the surrounding soil were quantities of ashes, which still retained a peculiar fiery smell. The mound was only about half cut through, and may still contain other interesting archæological remains."

No portion of this mound now remains, and we are unable to find its exact site.

Extract from the " Driffield Times," January 12th, 1895 :—

> " INTERESTING DISCOVERY.—A man named D. Adams, working in Mr. T. G. Marshall's brickyard a few days ago, found a small vase, at a depth of over 4 feet in the clay. The vase was got out practically unbroken. It has been turned upon a wheel, and though without ornamentation is a splendid example of early pottery. It is formed of a blue-grey clay, and has evidently been burnt in a kiln. It stands 5 inches high, on a foot, and has a flanged mouth, and is 4 inches across at the widest part of the belly. Most probably the vase is a Roman one, and has been placed in the ground along with the ashes at a burial after cremation. The find is the more interesting since this is perhaps the only evidence of the Roman occupation found in the town." †

---

* This coffin was given to York Museum, and may now be seen there with others.
† The vase is now in the Museum at Driffield.

No. XIII.—THE HUGGATE WOLD GROUP.

THE twenty barrows in this group are raised along the side of a British track leading towards the east coast, and much resemble the linear arrangement of Group No. 1, the barrows of which also appear to be along an old line of

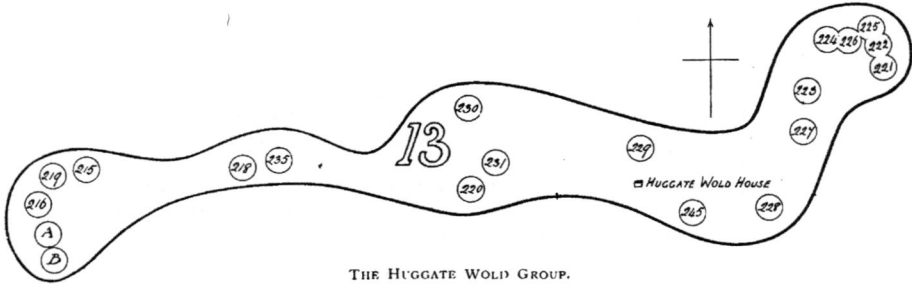

THE HUGGATE WOLD GROUP.

communication. Mounds so arranged are not infrequent, and they form readily recognised landmarks. The barrows now under description extend 2¼ miles east and west, and seven out of the ten of those to the east (fig. 893) are arranged

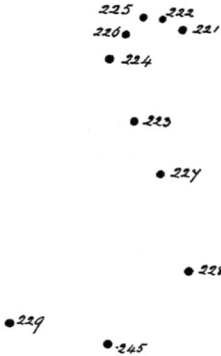

FIG. 893.—PLAN OF BARROWS IN GROUP XIII.
Copied from the 6-in. Ordnance Map.

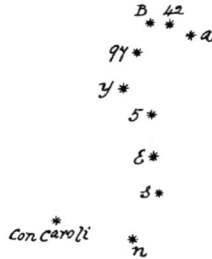

FIG. 893 a.—"CHARLES' WAIN."
Copied from Proctor's Star Map.

after the plan of the group of seven stars forming Charles' Wain in the constellation Ursa Major. The arrangement of some of the groups of barrows in the form of constellations is very striking. I have dealt fully with this subject in the Transactions of the East Riding Antiquarian Society, vol. 3, 1895, p. 53, and in the Proceedings of the Yorkshire Geological Society for 1897, pp. 201.

Barrow No. 221 and the following nine barrows are situated at an elevation of 675 feet above the sea level.   They were opened during thirteen fine days from March 5th to 19th, 1882, under the alternate supervision of my brother and myself, and at times by both of us.   They had been lowered and distributed by tilling, and varied from 55 to 65 feet in diameter.

It was known that several of these barrows had been opened by the late Jas. Silburn, of Pocklington.*   Mr. Henry Silburn, of Pocklington, has kindly supplied the following extract from the late Jas. Silburn's catalogue of relics discovered in the Huggate Wold barrows :—

> "No. 14.   Urn from a barrow at Huggate Wold, October 27th, 1851.
> "No. 16.   Jet ornament from a barrow on Huggate Wold, October 27th, 1851.
> The two are now in the British Museum."

BARROW No. 221

Is the most easterly of the group, and was only 18 inches high.   We removed a portion of the centre, 25 feet square, in which was observed an old excavation about 10 feet by 9 feet.   This early opening was over a grave in the centre, which had been completely emptied.   All the way down we found broken bones and portions of a very thick skull of a large person.   We also obtained a large hand-struck flake of local flint (fig. 894).   There was also

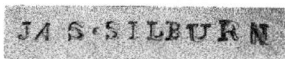

FIG. 895.

a slip of lead (fig. 895) with "Jas. Silburn" stamped upon it, but no date.   This was on the smooth white chalk floor of the grave.

The grave was oval, and measured 6½ feet east and west, by 5 feet across, and reached 3½ feet below the base of the barrow.

BARROW No. 222

Was 2 feet high, and had also been previously excavated, as a disturbed area of 10 feet east and west by 5 feet was clearly visible.   This old opening extended in one place about 3 feet below the base of the barrow, but whether the excavators had emptied a grave, or had been tempted to follow a "pipe" in the rock (part of which remained on the side of the excavation) we were unable to determine, as no trace of a disturbed burial was observed.

About 3 feet south of this, on the old surface line, was a heap of burnt bones extending 2½ feet north and south by 9 inches across.   They seemed to have been placed in a wooden receptacle, decayed traces of which remained.   About 8 feet north of this was an adult body, doubled up, on its left side and with head to the south.   It was about a foot below the base of the mound, in a hollow scooped through the surface soil into the rubbly chalk below.   At the back of the skull (fig. 896) was a disc of flint (fig. 897), ¾-inch in diameter, and chipped

---

* While opening a barrow on the adjoining farm (Blanche), on February 24th, 1852, Silburn unfortunately took a severe cold, and died on the 17th of April in the same year, at the age of 26 years.

round the edge. At the crown was a sharp-edged flake (fig. 898) of black flint, 1¼ inches long, whilst in front of the face was an elongated scraper of flint (fig. 899), 1½ inches long and 1¼ inches broad.

This interment was so far decayed that little more than impressions of some of the bones remained.

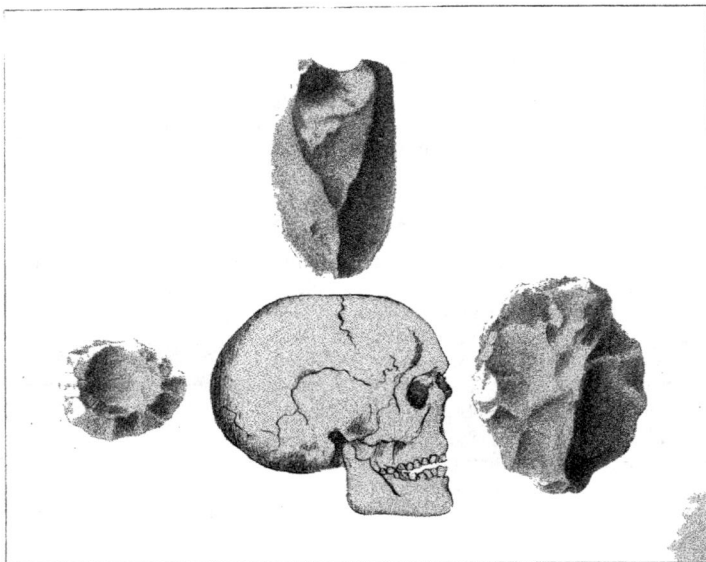

FIG. 896.—SHOWING THE RELATIVE POSITIONS OF THREE WORKED FLINTS AROUND THE SKULL IN BARROW NO. 222.

BARROW No. 224

Was about 30 inches in elevation. All the original surface under the eastern half to the centre was reddened and blackened in consequence of having been the site of a large fire. About 8 feet east of the centre, and occupying a circular area about 4 feet in diameter, were many calcined human bones (B, fig. 900), from more than one body, as the heads of three adult humeri and portions of others were observed. These calcined bones—like those from Garton Slack barrows Nos. 80 and 81—were in much larger pieces than those found in urns, or in holes in the ground, which, after burning, seem to have nearly always been reduced to a small size. They were mixed with burnt chalk and soil reddened by fire, and extended from the base to near the apex of the mound. Much of the burnt chalk occurred in large brecciated masses.

Outside the area containing the calcined bones, the chalk grit and surface soil, which, in the main, formed the barrow, were in places burnt and reddened by fire, clearly showing that much of the material had been heaped upon the ashes of the funeral pyre before they had cooled. No trace of the action of fire was observed on the western side of the mound.

On the original surface at the centre of the barrow was the skeleton of a large adult male of middle age, on its back, head pointing nearly to the north, the arms doubled, with hands to each side of the head (A on the plan). The legs were closely bent back with the heels to the hips, a very unusual position (fig. 900). The femur, tibia, and humerus measured $19\frac{3}{4}$ inches, $16\frac{1}{2}$ inches, and 14 inches respectively. At the right side of the skull was a knife of black flint (fig. 901), with the point downwards. It has been made from an outside flake, some of

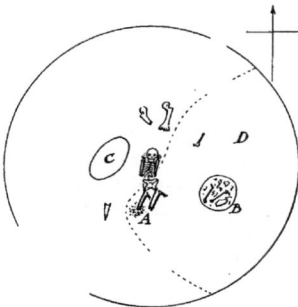

FIG. 900.—PLAN OF BARROW NO. 224.
D—Site of Fire.

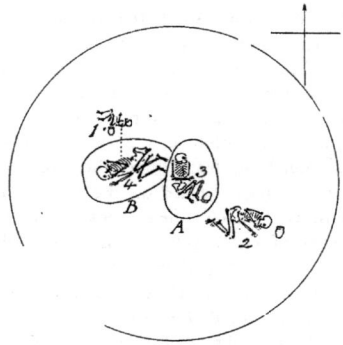

FIG. 902.—PLAN OF BARROW NO. 225.

the outside of the original flint nodule being still left along the middle of the convex face. It has been carefully chipped along both edges and at the round point, but not at the broad end, which shows the bulb of percussion. It is 3 inches long, and $1\frac{1}{8}$ inches wide. The edges are quite sharp and unbroken. A small handstruck chip of flint was near it. In contact with the right knee, mainly under it but partly at the west side, was a heap of burnt adult bones. About 2 feet west of the skeleton was an oval grave (C), $3\frac{1}{4}$ feet deep, and measuring at the bottom $2\frac{1}{2}$ feet south-south-west by north-north-east and 1 foot 9 inches across. It contained rubbly chalk, burnt soil, and bits of carbonised wood, but no trace of an interment.

The barrow was mainly composed of chalk grit and soil, from which we took unburnt pieces of a human skull, leg and arm bones, and a femur, also the femur and portions of the skull and other bones of an ox, &c.

BARROW No. 225

Had an elevation of about $2\frac{1}{2}$ feet, and—with the exception of a little gritty chalk which had been cast from the two graves in the centre—consisted of loamy clay brought from a distance, and local surface soil.

The greater portion of this mound was turned over, and reaching the centre, the outlines of two graves became visible (fig. 902). Over grave B, on a level with the base of the barrow, was a crushed food-vase (No. 1, fig. 902), accompanied by the decayed remains of an infant. The vase resembles in type the one from barrow C. 54, Group XI. It is tastefully ornamented from top to bottom with delicate cord marks, and with impressions from a finely-notched tool.

On the same horizon, but over the south-east corner of the grave *A*, stood an inverted cinerary urn of unusual type (fig. 904), containing calcined bones of an adult. This urn measured 10 inches high, 9¼ inches across the top, and 4 inches across the bottom. On the same level, but a little south-east of grave *A*, was the skeleton of an adult (No. 2), and a short distance from the front of the skull was a food-vase (fig. 905) of common type and ornamentation.

Grave *B* measured 6 feet east and west, 3½ feet across, and 2½ feet deep, and at the bottom were the remains of an adult (No. 4). The femur, tibia, and humerus measured 18¼ inches, 15 inches, and 12¼ inches respectively.

At various depths in grave *A*, were the fractured portions of a large brachycephalic skull, and other bones of a large individual, a fragment of the skull of an infant, a portion of the leg-bone of an ox, and an antler of a deer (fig. 906), which is cut and worked with the apparent intention of making a hammer-head from it, as the two brow-tines are removed and the aperture for the haft has been begun on the two opposite sides.* On the rocky floor of this grave were the flexed remains of a small and apparently young person (No. 3), with pieces of chalk piled round the body. The femur, tibia, and humerus measured respectively 15½ inches, 13 inches, and 12 inches. This grave measured 7 feet north and south, 4½ feet across, and 4½ feet deep. A boat-shaped block of clayey matter occupied the centre to a depth of 2½ feet.

It was observed that grave *B* had first been made and covered with a little loamy clay, over which had been cast gritty chalk obtained in making grave *A*, and above this unbroken beds of loamy soil formed the mound.

BARROW No. 226

Also possessed a central elevation of about 2½ feet. It principally consisted of loamy clay brought from a distance, and the surface soil of the neighbourhood. Near the centre was a large circular grave (*A*, fig. 907), over the south side of which, and about 1 foot above the base of the barrow, was an irreparably-crushed food-vase (No. 1 on the plan). Close to the south-east side of this was a knife of semi-transparent flint, 2½ inches long (fig. 908). It seems to be worn on its edges by use. Near to these, and on the same horizon, were traces of a skeleton (No. 1), which had almost decayed† through being in contact with unctuous clay, which extended some distance into this portion of the grave in a boat-shaped mass.

Under interment No. 1, at a depth of 10 inches, was an adult skeleton (No. 2), on its right side, the knees up, the hands in front of the face, and head to the south. The position of this interment was puzzling. Its trunk was nearly horizontal on the southern side of a ridge of chalk grit which occupied the grave all round the sides, whilst the legs and part of the hips were bent 18 inches

* This is interesting, and shows that in this case, and probably also in others, the method was to pierce the hammer-head previous to detaching it from the antler. when it would not be so liable to split in the process of boring.
† Its position cannot be shown in the section.

FIG. 895. $\frac{1}{3}$

FIG. 901. $\frac{1}{4}$

FIG. 903.

FIG. 904. $\frac{1}{4}$

FIG. 905. $\frac{1}{3}$

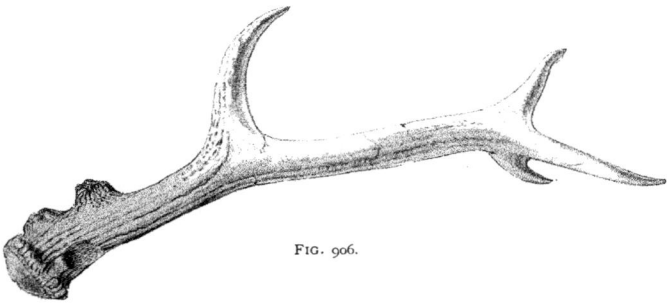

FIG. 906.

downwards, between the chalk edge and the core of clayey matter which almost occupied the centre of the grave from top to bottom. This central core measured at the top 6¼ feet south-east by 5½ feet across. The femur measured 17½ inches, and the tibia 14 inches, and the whole of the interment was covered with a thick film of soot-like matter, though none was observed under the bones.

The black matter which covered the bones of No. 2 was in the form of a hollow, extending a little outside the southern edge of the grave, apparently showing this interment, and No. 1 above it, to be intrusive, and consequently subsequent to the filling-in of the large grave beneath.

At a depth of 3¼ feet from the base of the mound was the bottom of the grave, on which rested two medium-sized adult bodies (Nos. 3 and 4), possibly man and wife. They were 1 foot 9 inches apart, with their heads to the south-east and facing each other, the legs pulled up, and at about equal distances from the centre of the grave. No. 3 was on its left side with the hands to the head, while No. 4 was on its right side with the hands to head. Pieces of chalk were piled round them, forming shallow hollows, and rough chalk was in contact with the

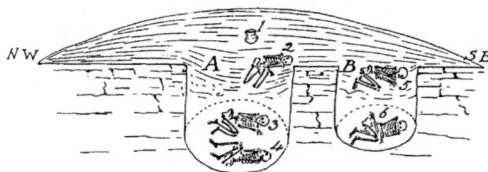

FIG. 907.—SECTION OF BARROW NO. 226.

bones, hence their greatly crushed and broken condition. The teeth were worn, the front right lower molar was decayed, and belonged to an old person— probably a male. The skull was crushed and distorted.

The grave was circular, measuring 7¼ feet in diameter at the bottom and 9½ feet at the top. The longest diameter of the boat-shaped mass of clay ran lengthwise, with the two bodies below.

A little to the east of the centre was a second grave (B), in the upper part of which was a punch-like article (fig. 909) of black flint, 3¾ inches long and about 1 inch thick. At a depth of 18 inches was the skeleton of a youth (No. 5), from eight to ten years of age, on its left side, the knees pulled up and hands to the face. The skull was towards the east. On the abdomen had been placed a large circular flake of local flint (fig. 910). Remains of decayed wood, 2 feet long and 1 to 1½ inches wide, extended from about the feet to near the head, along the south side of the body and resting upon the leg bones. Immediately below was a second interment (No. 6), on its back, the knees pulled up and pressed over to the south, the right arm under the loins and the hand towards the knees, the left arm with the elbow near the knees, and the hand on the abdomen. The head pointed in the same way as that of the interment above it, and was pressed over in the same direction as the knees. This is the skeleton of a young adult male, with the back molar teeth just cutting. The femur measured 18½ inches. The grave was 6 feet east and west, and 3 feet 9 inches across.

BARROW No. 223

Had an elevation of 2½ feet. In the centre was a grave measuring 7 feet north and south, 4½ feet across, and 3½ feet deep. The late Jas. Silburn had made a very small excavation in the centre of this mound, and had emptied the southern half of the grave, but the northern half had not been disturbed. At the north end, on the floor, were the leg bones of an adult, much decayed, and near the feet were the bones of a very young child. The remainder of the adult skeleton had been removed by Mr. Silburn, who left a slip of lead (similar to fig. 895) with "Jas. Silburn" stamped upon it. Broken-up human bones, and a vertebra of a red deer were found in that portion of the grave which had been previously opened.

About 2 feet from the east side of the grave, and 1 foot above the base of the barrow, was an inverted food-vase (fig. 911). It measures 4½ inches high, 4¾ inches across the top, and 2½ inches across the bottom. Nothing accompanied it.

BARROW No. 227

Was 50 feet in diameter, and only 1½ feet high, though visible at some distance. We turned over a portion measuring 22 feet square, and frequently trenched the subsoil to the chalk rock below. At a distance of 4 feet to the north of the assumed centre was a deposit of burnt human bones and wood ashes, occupying a hole 15 inches deep and 2 feet 10 inches in diameter, which had been made below the base of the barrow, through the surface soil into the chalk rock. From all appearances, the calcined bones had been interred whilst hot, as the sides of the cavity had a reddened appearance to a depth of an inch. This hole was covered over with a brown loamy clay, but no clayey matter was found in any other part of this barrow.

BARROW No. 228

Was 40 feet in diameter, and is not shown on the Ordnance Survey Map. We commenced on the east and west sides, turning it over to its base, and terminating in the middle. The portion thus excavated was 26 feet square, and only 15 inches deep, having been much reduced by agricultural operations. An interment (No. 1) of a middle-aged strong-boned male, was found as shown on the plan (fig. 912), with its trunk sunk into the grave, and the thigh and leg bones on the natural surface at the brink of the grave. The skull and trunk had settled down somewhat,* together with the gritty material which filled the grave, fully 7 inches lower than the bones of the legs, which rested on firm ground. The skeleton was on its left side, doubled up, with the head to the south-east. The vertical section of the barrow shows its position approximately. A terminal tine from the antler of a red deer was found just above the skull of No. 1.

The gritty chalk was removed from the grave, and fragments of three broken-up skeletons—two adults and a youth—were found to be dispersed from one side of the grave to the other, to a depth of 1 foot. At the east end, at a depth of 14 inches, was a second entire doubled-up skeleton (No. 2) of a middle-aged person,

* After the manner of the subsidence in the Barrow No. 226.

PLATE CXVI.

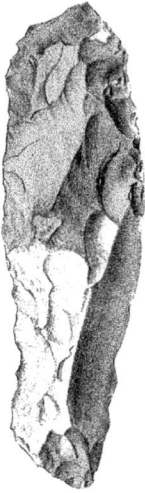

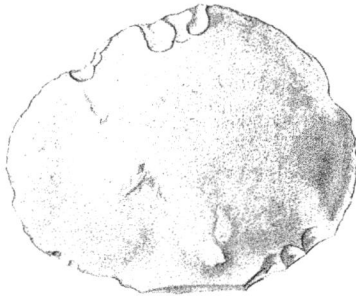

FIG. 910.

FIG. 908.   ¼

FIG. 909.

FIG. 913.   ⅓

FIG. 911.   ⅓

FIG. 914.   ¼

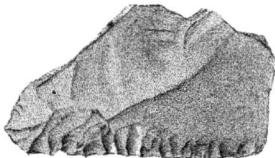

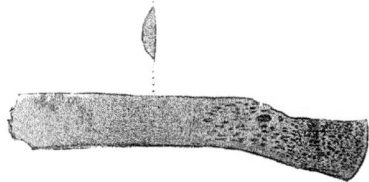

FIG. 916.   ¼

FIG. 917.   ½

with the head to the west, on its left side, with the left hand up to the face and the right arm extended as shown in the section. A thigh, leg, and arm bone measured respectively 17 inches, 14 inches, and 12 inches. Two pieces of an urn were found near this skeleton. The grave measured 9 feet east to west, and 5½ feet across.

Below No. 2, at a depth of 3 feet, was No. 3, the skeleton apparently of a female, on its back. It seemed as if at the time of interment the knees had stood up vertically, but the bones had subsequently fallen down, bringing the thigh bones upon the leg bones. The skull was to the south-west, and the lower jaw had dropped 5½ inches from the upper jaw. A femur measured 17 inches, and tibia 14 inches.

Near the skull was a food-vase of common form (fig. 913). It measured 6¼ inches high, 6¾ inches across the top, and 3 inches across the bottom. Its upper part is ornamented externally with five encircling belts of nearly vertical gashes, each half an inch long. At the west end of the grave, and at the same depth as the last, was interment No. 4, on its back, with the legs doubled and the head pointing nearly west. The femoral bones measured only 13 inches in length, and were those of a young person.

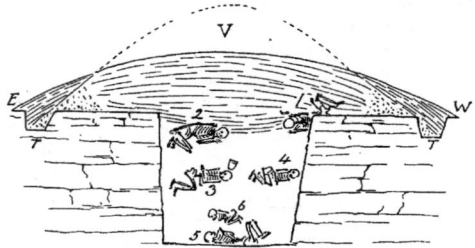

FIG. 912.—SECTION OF BARROW NO. 228.

V—Probable original height of Barrow.

T—Trench, 2½ ft. wide at the bottom.

Still lower was interment No. 5, at the bottom of the grave. This was on its left side, the legs doubled up, the head pointing north-east, and was apparently that of an aged female, the teeth being well worn, but not decayed. The tibia measured 14¾ inches, and humerus 12½ inches.

About 10 inches in front of this skeleton were the fragile bones of a child (No. 6). Bits of decayed wood, like charcoal, accompanied these bodies, but nothing more.

At a distance of 8 feet from the southern side of the grave, and at the base of the barrow, was interment No. 7,* probably a female, with its back to the inner side of a trench which encircled the whole of the interments. It was on its left side, the legs doubled up and the head towards the south-west. The encircling trench was followed part of the way round, and from the chalk rubble, with which it was mainly filled, was obtained a portion of the antler of a red deer, and three bits of other bone.

The section of the barrow and trench (fig. 912) shews that the chalk had been cast inwards, and formed part of the mound.

* Not shown in the section.

BARROW No. 245

Was opened on September 11th, 1882.   It is not shown on the Ordnance Survey sheet, though its elevation was not less than 16 inches.   Some light blue foreign clay was spread over a considerable area at and near its base.   Under the centre of the mound the old surface line was covered with burnt earth and wood ashes. Within this area, and also on the same level, was a scattered heap of burnt human bones, unaccompanied by any relic.   From the mound one scraper and four other worked splinters, all of black flint, were taken.   We noticed an old excavation a little south of the centre, about 4 feet square, and reaching to the chalk rock.   Probably this was evidence of a previous opening.

BARROW No. 229

Is about 150 yards north-west of Huggate Wold House.

During six days intervening from April 19th to 30th, 1882, we examined the barrow and found it to have a diameter of 66 feet and a central elevation of 5 feet.

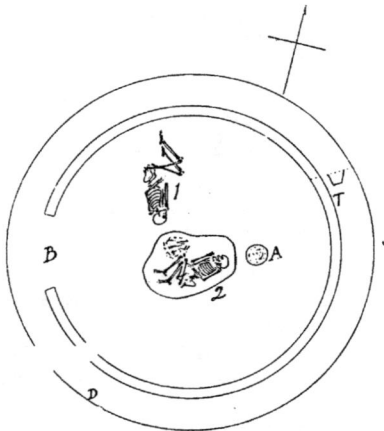

FIG. 915.—PLAN OF BARROW No. 229.
T—Trench.
B—Break in the Trench.

It was crossed north-west by south-east, by a quickwood fence.   The western and smaller portion (26 feet) was grass ; the eastern and larger portion (40 feet) was under tillage.   A piece 30 feet by 24 feet was removed, and about 4 feet east of the centre of the mound, and at about half its depth, were a few burnt human bones (A on the plan), near to which was a fine scraper of black flint, chipped round the edge (fig. 914).   Two feet north of the centre, and 9 inches below the base of the barrow, was an adult body (No. 1, fig. 915), within 3 feet of the northern edge of the grave afterwards discovered, head to the south, on its right side, the left arm doubled back with hand to the neck, and the legs doubled up.   Nothing accompanied it.   The femur and humerus measured respectively 17 inches and 12 inches.

At the centre was an oval grave nearly east and west, measuring 6½ feet by 5 feet, and 2 feet 7 inches deep.   At the bottom were the remains of a young person (No. 2) resting in precisely the same flexed position as No. 1.   The femur, tibia, and humerus measured 17¼ inches, 13½ inches, and 12½ inches respectively. At the knees was a pile of broken human bones, consisting of portions of leg and arm bones, which, after being joined together, measured as under :—femur 19 inches, tibia 15¼ inches, humerus 14¼ inches.   There were also many pieces of skull and pelvic bones, detached vertebræ, and other broken human bones, all of which belonged to a person of large size.   In the midst of these was a rib of some animal, possibly a red deer. Throughout the gritty soil filling the grave were detached and broken human bones, some belonging apparently to the same large body as those found at the knees of No. 2. Amongst them were observed three clavicles, two of which were of large size, two cervical vertebræ (anchylosed), and other human bones ; also part of the end of the antler of a red deer, a vertebra and parts of a rib, possibly also of a red deer. The grave was wider opposite the knees, as shown in the plan, apparently in order to admit the heap of dismembered and broken bones, which seemed to have been deposited contemporaneously, as some of the bones were under the others upon the knees. Whether the broken bones belonged to a previous interment broken up at the time of burying No. 2 or were those of persons sacrificed at the grave, is somewhat uncertain. The discovery of animal bones along with the broken-up human bones would seem to favour the latter supposition, and suggests the probability that cannibalism was practiced at the funeral feasts.

A circular trench, which was concealed within the barrow, enclosed the interments. Its exterior diameter was 25 feet, and its depth varied from $1\frac{1}{2}$ feet to $2\frac{1}{2}$ feet, and in width at the top from $2\frac{1}{2}$ feet to $3\frac{1}{2}$ feet. It contained rubbly chalk, and from it the horn-core of an ox, three small potsherds of doubtful age, and bits of burnt wood, were taken.

On the west side of the circular trench was a break, 9 feet wide, which had not been excavated.

After the completion of both the interments—which were probably contemporaneous—a small mound of soil and gritty chalk was raised, 2 feet high, within the trench. Afterwards a covering of blue clay, varying from 9 to 15 inches in thickness, had been brought from one of the dale bottoms $1\frac{1}{2}$ to 2 miles distant to the west, and added to the mound. Finally the adjoining surface soil had been used for the completion of this large barrow.

During the excavations we picked from the mound pieces of a large skull, half the lower jaw of a small individual with teeth much worn, and other adult bones, portions of a child's skull and half a lower jaw, together with other bones— probably those of a disturbed body—also animal bones, half the lower jaw of a sheep or goat, potsherds, chipped flints, one (fig. 916) a keen-edged knife, and, a little above the grave, half of a large celt of greenstone. Amongst the animal bones was found the greater portion of a bone knife (fig. 917). This had been made by rubbing flat the longitudinal half of a bone from the leg of a red deer.

BARROW No. 230

And the following two mounds had previously been opened by Mr. Thomas, of Boston, Lincolnshire, during November, 1881, and the following particulars of his discoveries were obtained from one of the workmen and a young farmer in the neighbourhood who accompanied and assisted him.

Mr. Thomas turned over a portion of this barrow, measuring 47 feet east and west by 6 feet north and south, and discovered two skeletons a little below its base near the centre. They were together, on their right sides, one with its head to the north, the other with its head to the south. Behind the shoulders of one was a fine spearhead of black flint (fig. 918), of the unusual length of $3\frac{7}{8}$ inches, and a somewhat similar one (fig. 919) placed at the feet of the other body.   These specimens are now in the British Museum, and I am indebted to the kindness of the late Sir Wollaston Franks for allowing my daughter to make drawings.

During the last week in April, 1882, we re-opened the barrow and tested the ground beneath.   It had consisted of a central core mainly of bluish clay brought from a distance, over which was a covering of yellowish-brown loamy soil.   We also observed near the centre some dispersed burnt human bones, showing that Mr. Thomas had probably removed a cremated interment also.

BARROW No. 231.

In our re-opening of this mound in May, 1882, we only observed scattered burnt bones and wood ashes belonging to a cremated interment, which had been removed by Mr. Thomas.   Our inspection also failed to discover any trace of a grave having ever existed under this barrow.

My brother picked up a leaf-shaped flint arrowhead at a distance of about 30 yards from the mound.

BARROW No. 220.

On February 25th, 1882, we re-examined this barrow by turning over the greater portion, during which we took from the mound the larger and apparently freshly-broken portion of a fine spearhead of black flint (fig. 920).   This specimen is very thin and most beautifully chipped on both sides.   Whether or not Mr. Thomas obtained the other portion we were not able to ascertain, neither do we know what further discovery he made in this barrow.   Possibly the large cinerary urn which he took from one of the three mounds was found here.

The very fine weather which had prevailed for some time now changed, and put a stop to our work until the 5th of March.

BARROW No. 235.

On August 4th, 1882, this barrow measured 35 feet in diameter and 16 inches in height.   In the centre was an oval grave 18 inches in depth.   A film of dark soot-like matter covered the bottom, from which we took a small but beautifully-chipped knife or spearhead (fig. 921), of black flint, $1\frac{3}{4}$ inches long, with one side flat, and the other ridged from having been skilfully chipped from both edges, leaving it only $\frac{7}{10}$ of an inch wide, and very sharp all round, and pointed, with a well-defined bulb of percussion at the butt end.   With it was a short flake of similarly-coloured flint.   About 12 inches north-west from these was another short handstruck flint flake.   There was no trace of bone, the interment having probably completely decayed.

In the mound—which consisted almost entirely of the loamy subsoil adjoining it—we found nineteen flakes and five pieces of black flint, and three long flakes of light-coloured flint from the neighbouring chalk.

FIG. 918. $\frac{1}{1}$

FIG. 919. $\frac{1}{1}$

FIG. 920. $\frac{1}{1}$

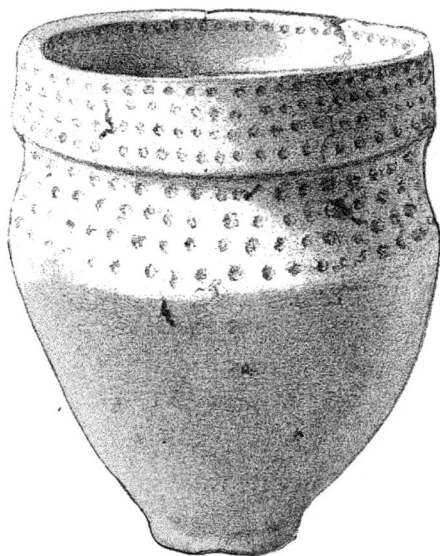

FIG. 921. $\frac{2}{3}$

FIG. 923. $\frac{1}{4}$

FIG. 924.

BARROW No. 218

Had a diameter of 48 feet and an elevation of 2 feet.

On February 24th, 1882, we turned over the major portion of this mound, and near the centre found a small basin-like hole scooped into the ancient turf-line, 13 inches in diameter at the top, and 9 inches deep. It was well formed with smooth sides, and contained wood-charcoal, with a few burnt human bones, thus serving the purpose of a cinerary urn.

Over the interment was a lenticular bed of bluish clay, about 18 inches in central thickness, and reaching some distance all round. The nearest point from whence the clay could be obtained is not less than $1\frac{1}{2}$ miles. Over this was soil obtained on the spot, which raised the barrow to its final height.

BARROW No. 215

Had but a slight elevation, and is not shown on the Ordnance sheet.

February 20th, 1882, we turned over a portion of this mound, 24 feet square, and near the centre, at a depth of 15 inches, was a deposit of wood ashes $2\frac{1}{2}$ feet in diameter, in which was a quantity of the burnt bone of an adult and a few bones of a very small animal. The deposit was 4 to 5 inches in thickness, and below, the reddened earth indicated the site of a fire.

Just above, and in contact with the wood ashes and calcined bones, was the bottom of an urn. The rest had been broken and carried away by the plough. One piece of burnt bone is stained green by oxide of copper from the decomposition of some bronze article.

The day was mild and spring-like. The owner of the land, Mr. Jessop, commenced to sow oats at the other end of this 50-acre field, the land being then in fine condition. The weather almost to the end of this month was a most remarkable contrast to that of February of the preceding year, when every farmer was kept from field work by the frost and great quantity of snow on the ground.

BARROW No. 216.

On February 22nd and 23rd, 1882, this mound was about 55 feet in diameter, but probably originally it did not exceed 35 feet. Its elevation was about 2 feet, and consisted almost entirely of the tough reddish subsoil of the adjoining land. The greater portion of the barrow, down to the undisturbed ground beneath it, was turned over. In the centre was a large oval grave, measuring 8 feet east and west by 7 feet across, with a depth of 5 feet from the apex of the mound. A cinerary urn (fig. 923), measuring 15 inches high, 12 inches across the top, and 3 inches across the bottom, ornamented round the rim with star-like impressions, stood in the centre of the grave, with its mouth within 1 foot of the apex of the barrow. It was half filled with calcined adult human bones. On the top of these was a flint spearhead or knife (fig. 924), $2\frac{1}{2}$ inches long, and a globular article of jet $\frac{3}{8}$ of an inch in diameter, bored through from the flattened ends, giving it the appearance of a bead (fig. 925). It is also pierced on one side with two holes a little apart and inclining towards each other, so as to meet at a short distance below the surface, after the manner of the boring of the jet buttons (fig. 188).   At a depth of 3 feet from the apex of the mound were the decayed remains of a small and probably young person, on the left side, the legs doubled up, and head to the north-north-west.   In front of the face were the remains of a crushed and decayed food-vase, which had been in part ornamented with impressions made by the end of the thumb.   At the feet was a keen-edged flake knife of black flint, 3 inches long and 1¾ inches broad (fig. 926).

This interment had been placed in a shallow grave, which had been cut partly into the large central grave and partly into the undisturbed rock at its north-north-east side, apparently not long after the making of the large grave, as that portion of the body which reached over and rested on this grave had sunk some inches lower than the remainder.

Interment No. 2 was a little west of the centre of the large grave, at a depth of about 3½ feet from the top of the mound.   It was that of a child, five to six years old, with the legs pulled up, on its right side, and the head in the same position as No. 1.   The chief interment (No. 3) was in a shallow trough-shaped hollow situated in the centre of the grave, and was that of a large adult, on its right side, in the usual flexed position, with its head to the west.   At the back of the head had been placed a drinking cup, which we found crushed into numerous pieces ; but after being rebaked and rebuilt it stands 7¼ inches high, measures 5¼ inches across the top, and 2½ inches across the bottom (fig. 927).   The whole exterior is ornamented with impressions produced by a notched tool, and arranged in horizontal bands separated by belts of short vertical lines alternating with sets of oblique lines.

All the skeletons were in contact with the wet soil—resembling that in the mound—which occupied the grave in the form of a boat-shaped mass.   They were consequently in the last stages of decay.   Not a tooth remained belonging to any of the bodies and only a few bits of the skulls and other bones were sufficiently firm to bear touching.   It was therefore impossible to take any measurements.

BARROW No. 219

Is shown on the Ordnance sheets a little to the north-east of the last.   It is now only just distinguishable.   On February 21st, 1882, we opened the mound, with no other result than finding that this slight elevation was due to one of those peculiar filled-up "pipes" in the rock.

The two barrows marked *A* and *B* have not yet been opened.   The former adjoins a cottage, and is now thickly covered with fir trees.   The latter is so far obliterated that its site is now doubtful.

FIG. 925. ¼

FIG. 926.

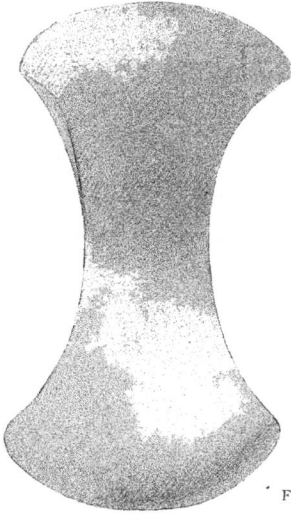

FIG. 928.

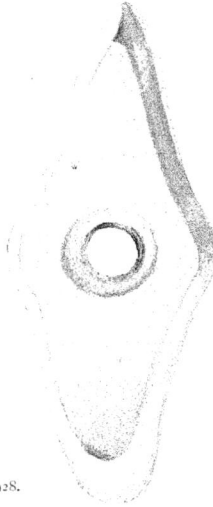

FIG. 929. ½

FIG. 927. ¼

FIG. 931. ¼

FIG. 930.

)

No. XIV.—THE HUGGATE AND WARTER WOLD GROUP.

THIS series of barrows branches off from the last group at an angle of about 75°, and probably it also skirts an ancient British track-way running along the western side of the Wolds, in a direction nearly north and south. It consists of nineteen circular barrows, sixteen of which are shown on the Ordnance Survey Map, and the positions of the other three have been marked by the writer. Many of these barrows were opened in 1851 by the late James Silburn, and through the kindness of his brother I am able to again give an extract from his catalogue of the relics found :—

> "No. 1. Large urn, found in a barrow at Warter Wold, July, 1851 [probably a cinerary urn].
> "No. 2. Very small urn, found at the same time, and placed with the other [most probably an incense-cup].
> "No. 3. Urn, from Warter Wold, found with a skeleton, November 13th, 1851.
> "No. 5. Urn, found inverted in a barrow on Warter Wold, November 13th, 1851.
> "No. 8. Urn, from a barrow on Warter Wold, December 31st, 1851. Urn, much broken, from a barrow on Huggate Pasture, October 16th, 1851.
> "No. 15. Stone axe-head, from a barrow on Huggate Pasture, October 16th, 1851."

Most of the above articles are now in the British Museum.

The barrow marked "A" is the most northerly of this group. It was opened in 1851 by Silburn, and also in the autumn of 1881 by Mr. Thomas, of Boston, but, so far as we have been able to ascertain, in neither opening was anything found, and I believe that any further examination would be equally disappointing.

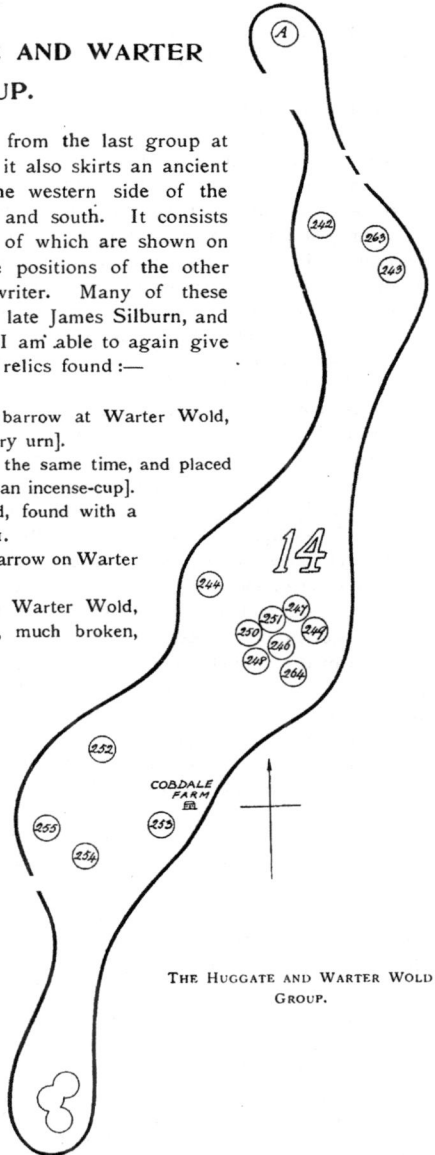

THE HUGGATE AND WARTER WOLD GROUP.

BARROW No. 242

Is on Huggate Pasture. It was opened by Silburn on October 16th, 1851, and was the one from which he took the axe-head (No. 15 in his list), of which, through the kindness of the late Sir Wollaston Franks, I am able to give the accompanying illustration (fig. 928). Silburn also found a broken urn, and these are the only relics named from the Pasture mounds. We opened the barrow during three days in the middle of August, 1882.*

It had a diameter of 60 feet, and an elevation of 3 feet, and consisted of the local loamy soil, mixed in the centre, at the base, with a little clay from a distance. We removed a portion, measuring 29 feet east and west, and 25 feet across, from its centre. In this, Silburn's excavation of about 9 feet square was clearly visible, extending from the centre westwards. This small excavation had, however, enabled him to find the grave in the centre, and by emptying about two-thirds of it he had reached the interment at the bottom. The north side of the grave had not been excavated, and from this we took portions of a large antler of a red deer (fig. 929), which showed deep cuts and scratches by a very poor cutting instrument. At the bottom of the grave, towards the south end, was a heap of bones belonging to a stout-framed adult. These were part of the interment Silburn had discovered and put back into the grave. No portion of the skull was observed ; most probably it was found in good preservation and taken away by him. Under the bones, between two pieces of chalk stone, was a slip of lead, with "JAS. SILBURN" stamped on it. Undoubtedly the broken urn and the stone axe-head, mentioned in Mr. Silburn's catalogue, were found with this body. The grave was oval, measuring 7 feet east and west, by 5½ feet, and penetrated the compact chalk rock to a depth of 4½ feet below the base of the barrow. Near the east corner of our excavation, 18 feet from the centre of the grave, and at the base of the mound, were the remains of a cremated body, but nothing accompanied it. From the barrow we obtained a great number of flakes, and rough chips of flint, five large slingstones, three scrapers, two knives, and one piece of no particular shape, all of Yorkshire flint. Many flakes, one knife, and one beautifully-shaped barbed arrow-head, all of foreign flint, were also found, as well as five potsherds belonging to different vessels.

BARROW No. 263

Is situated in the field adjoining the south-east side of Huggate Pasture, and near to the last barrow. On Aug. 17th and 18th, 1883, we cut a rectilinear piece measuring 32 feet north and south, and 24 feet across from its centre. The barrow had been much altered in shape by the plough, and consequently was not more than 2 feet high. In the centre was a grave containing the bones of a large man, disturbed by an opening made by Silburn. This excavation measured about 12 feet square, and the ground beneath and around the grave had everywhere been probed to the undisturbed rock, in a very thorough manner, not always adopted at that period.

---

* Soon after the commencement of our research we were visited by C. Rooks, the pasture shepherd, who, although quite deaf, had held this office many years. After viewing us for a short time with intense curiosity, he thus accosted us,—"What ah ya' deeain'? Ah ya' guvvament chaps? Ah ya' lewkin' fo' munney? Yoo'll fynd nowt. Ther was sum chaps dug inti't thotty year sin'. They meead a greeat hooal at wad ha' tecan me up bi heear-a-way," (meaning nearly to his ears), "bud they fand nowt."

BARROW No. 243

Is not shown on the Ordnance Survey. On August 17th, 1882, it was so far reduced by the action of the plough as to be scarcely visible on the surface.

Apparently in the centre, in a shallow hollow scooped through the thin surface soil to the chalk rock, and only just below the reach of the plough, was an adult skeleton, much crushed, on its right side, the head to the south, the right arm doubled, with the hand in front of the face, the left arm bent over the body, and the knees pulled up. Nothing was found with it.

From the mound we took three worked flints.

BARROW No. 244

Is the most westerley of a small group of eight. Though shown on the Ordnance Map, it was, at the time of our examination (August 18th, 1882), so far reduced by cultivation as not to have been previously observed by Mr. Simpson, who had rented the land for many years.

Near the centre was a small oval grave in the rock, reaching about 16 inches below the apex of the barrow. At the bottom was the greater part of a doubled-up adult skeleton, on right side, head to the south, the right hand to the head. Most of the leg bones had been removed by diggers for rabbits, and replaced at some distance from the position they had originally occupied in the grave. At the feet were the remains of a very young child, with the head to the north-west. The narrow excavation made by rabbit-diggers was plainly discernible.

The following barrows (Nos. 246 to 251), are in the centre of this group.

From September 25th to October 13th, 1882, we examined them, and they all showed evidence of early openings, most probably by Silburn, during 1851-2; and No. 250 was afterwards opened by a nephew of Mr. Simpson, the tenant of the farm.

These barrows have been otherwise mutilated. About thirty years ago Mr. Clarkson, the then tenant of the land, marled the field in which the mounds were situated, and caused a pit for obtaining the chalk to be made close to each of Barrows Nos. 248, 249, and 251, so that he might obtain material from the mounds with which to soil the sides of the pits, and be able, afterwards, to partly fill them up with the remaining portions of the mounds. Barrow 246 had a diameter of 36 feet and an elevation of 18 inches. In the centre we observed an old excavation, about 6 feet square, by which the northern side of the grave had been entered to a depth of 1 foot, but which had not reached the interment at a depth of 2½ feet. A pavement of large flints covered the top of that portion of the grave which had not been disturbed. This oval grave measured 7½ feet east and west, by 5½ feet across, and reached 2½ feet below the base of the mound. Towards the west end, a little short of half the depth of the grave, were scattered three points from an antler of a red deer—probably broken picks,—part of the jaw, with two molar teeth, of a pig, detached human bones, three flint flakes, three fragments of a food-vase, and a bone pin, 4¾ inches long (fig. 930). Several detached human bones were also taken from the grave. At the east end of the

grave, near the upper part, was a quantity of burnt wood. At a depth of 2½ feet
was an adult skeleton, on the left side, the knees pulled up, both arms being
slightly bent, with both hands just in front of the lower part of the abdomen.
The head was to the east. A femur, tibia, and humerus measured 17 inches,
13¼ inches, and 12 inches respectively. This skeleton was much contorted and
its bones displaced, apparently from the subsidence of the contents of the grave
below, and by pressure from above.

A portion of the rim of a food-vase—of which we had previously found
fragments in the upper part of the grave—was found on the chest, in contact
with the left arm bone. About 12 inches below this interment was a heap of
burnt bones of an adult body, unaccompanied by any relic.

BARROW No. 247

Had a diameter of 55 feet and an elevation of 2½ feet, and, like the previous one,
was made entirely of the neighbouring surface-soil. In the centre was an old
excavation, about 9 feet square, by which the former explorers had, apparently,
emptied a small grave ; but there was no trace of their having discovered an
interment.

About 6 feet south of the centre, and on the old surface-line, was an inverted
food-vase (fig. 931), but there was no evidence of an accompanying interment.

BARROW No. 248

Measured 50 feet in diameter, and 2½ feet in height. It stood close to a pit in the
chalk. An old opening had been made in the centre, about 7 feet square, the
south side of which was within a few inches of a cinerary urn (fig. 932), inverted
at the base of the mound. It measured 10 inches high, 8 inches in diameter at
the top, 9 inches across the shoulders, 8¼ inches across the middle, and 4 inches
at the bottom. Below the mouth is a border 2 inches deep, ornamented with a
reticulated pattern formed by incised lines running obliquely to the right, crossed
with similar lines running at a similar angle to the left, at about ⅜ of an inch
apart. It was nearly filled with the calcined bones of an adult. From the mound
we took 17 flakes and chipped flints, and a fragment of a vase.

BARROW No. 249.

The upper part of this barrow had been cut away to soil the sides and bottom
of a marl-pit close to its west side. The remaining portion measured 2 feet high,
and had a diameter of 60 feet. A small opening had also been made in the
centre of the barrow, the south-west corner of which just missed a crushed food-
vase (A on the plan, fig. 934), found within 8 inches of the present surface of the
mound. It shows no trace of ornamentation, and has since been repaired (fig. 933).
About 5 feet south-east of this old excavation, and at the base of the mound,
were several pieces of a dark-coloured vessel, resembling those from Barrow
No. 110, and others. Two and a half feet north-east of the edge of grave C,
and at the base of the mound (at A A), was a circular heap of burnt adult bones.
No relic accompanied them.

The grave, *B*, contained the remains of an adult, of powerful build, in the position shown on the plan. The femur, tibia, and humerus measured 18½ inches, 14½ inches, and 13¼ inches respectively. A thick film of decayed wood, the grain being distinctly perceptible, covered the skeleton from the head to the feet, and curved up the grave, at the north end, to the top, showing clearly that it was the remains of logs which had covered the top of the grave, and which, in decaying, had been pressed down upon the interment at the bottom. At the north-east end the grain of a piece of wood ran cross-wise under the longitudinal piece, evidently the remains of a support for the covering pieces. The grave measured 5½ feet by 3½ feet, and was 18 inches deep.

In the grave *C* was a deposit of burnt adult bones, at a depth of 2 feet below the base of the mound, in the position shown at "*a*" on the plan. It measured 2 feet 2 inches by 9 inches. At the bottom was the skeleton of a young female, in the posture shown. The femur, tibia, and humerus measured 15½ inches, 12½ inches, and 11¼ inches respectively. Just above the left humerus, and close to the side of the grave, was the point of a small bronze pricker, placed vertically (fig. 935), and close to it a bone stiletto (fig. 936), 3 inches

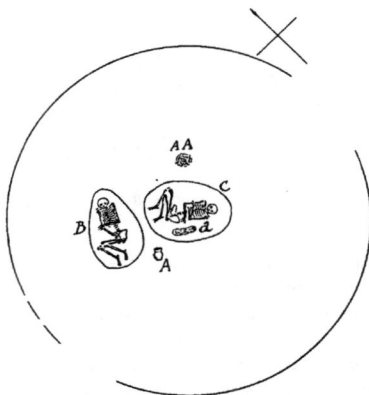

FIG. 934.---PLAN OF BARROW No. 249.

long, with their points upwards. The point end of the latter is stained green through having been near the pricker. Close to the left femur was a bone spatula (fig. 937), 5¼ inches long, made from a longitudinal splinter from the shank-bone of some animal.

Many large detached adult bones were found mixed in the gritty material filling the grave, but mainly near the two interments. There were also pieces of burnt human bone scattered throughout the grave, and among the bones of the inhumed body, principally on the chest, burnt human bones, fragments of handstruck splinters of flint, and snail shells were noticed. These pieces of burnt human bone, presumably portions of the cremated body in the upper part of the grave, seem to be proof of the contemporaneity of more than one interment in the same grave. The grave measured 6¾ feet by 4¾ feet, and 4¾ feet in depth.

We took from the mound the cutting end of a celt of grey stone, twenty-nine hand-struck splinters of black flint, and three of Yorkshire flint.

BARROW No. 250

Equalled in dimensions those of No. 248. The grandson of the present tenant of the land, and two young friends from Manchester, during August, 1881, cut into the centre of this barrow and obtained a medium-sized cinerary urn, containing burnt bones. The urn was taken to Manchester, and is said to have been repaired.

In the centre, under the excavation just named, was an oval grave, measuring 6 feet north and south, by 3½ feet, and 3¾ feet in depth.   In this grave was a boat-shaped mass of stiff soil, similar to that in the mound, filling the grave all round at the top, but narrowing inwards to 1 foot in width at the bottom, as shown in the section (fig. 938).   The wedge-shaped spaces between the sides of the grave and this were filled with rubbly chalk.   This rubbly chalk, probably obtained whilst digging the grave; had been put back and piled between the sides of the grave, and a coracle-shaped coffin of wicker-work, containing the body interred ; then the grave was roofed with timber placed horizontally.   Afterwards the roof gave way, and allowed material to settle into the hollow space left by the decay of the coffin and its contents.   This would account for the boat-shaped mass of clayey material so often observed in the graves.

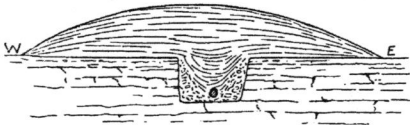

FIG. 938.—SECTION OF BARROW NO. 250.

At the bottom of the grave was an adult skeleton, partly on its back and partly on its right side, the arms doubled, with the hands to the face, the knees pulled up, and the head to the south.   Between the knees and the head stood a food-vase (fig. 939), measuring 5 inches in height, 6¾ inches across the top, and 3 inches at the bottom.   The femur, tibia, and humerus measured 20 inches, 16 inches, and 14 inches respectively.   About 16 feet from the centre of the mound, and 12 inches from the surface, was a small vase or incense-cup (fig. 940).

From the mound we took four pieces of animal bone, fragments of an urn, twelve chips of black flint, and two of local flint.

BARROW No. 251

Was the largest of the group, having a diameter of 75 feet and an elevation of 18 inches.   A rectangular piece, 45 feet north and south, by 29 feet across, was cut from the centre.

An old cutting, 7 feet by 4 feet, was perceptible, extending from the apex to the base, in which the previous explorers had discovered an interment, the broken-up bones of which we found.   This excavation was over a grave which had not been previously noticed.   It measured 6½ feet north-east and south-west, by 4¾ feet.   On the floor, at a depth of 18 inches from the base of the mound, were the remains of a strong middle-aged male (?), on its back, the head to the north-north-east, the knees pulled up, the left arm bent, with the hand on the chest, the right arm doubled up by the side, with the hand on the neck.   The knees and face were pressed over to the west-north-west. Between the left humerus and the right side of the chest was a small heap of burnt bones, apparently those of a child, and between the right elbow and the drawn-up knees was a crushed and badly-preserved food-vase.   This has been one of the largest vessels of the food-vase type I have met with.   A partial restoration (fig. 941), shows it to have measured 5½ inches in height, 9 inches across the top, and 3¼ inches across the bottom.   Immediately below the lip are two

FIG. 932.   ¼

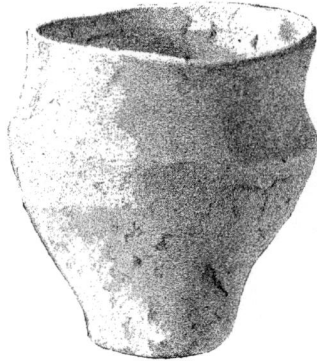

FIG. 933.   ·⅓

FIG. 937.   ½

FIG. 935.   ¼

FIG. 936.   ¼

FIG. 939   ½

FIG. 940.   ½

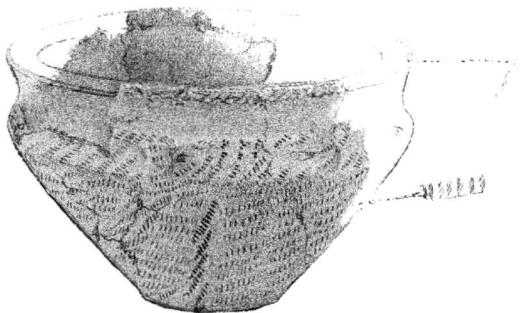

FIG. 941.   ¼

broad grooves, the lower one having had six or seven pierced stops at about equal distances. The top of the rim is ornamented with five impressed lines of small cord-markings, and nearly the whole of the vase, externally, is tastefully covered with stout lines of rope-like impressions running at various angles, apparently without any designed pattern. A quantity of soot-like matter rested on the skeleton, and the bones were so much crushed and damaged by large flints placed upon them, that no measurements could be taken. Above the flints the grave was filled with soil similar to that composing the part of the mound above; and appearances indicated that these flints were not in contact with the body at the time of interment, but had afterwards sunk into the grave.

The barrow consisted of an inner mound of loamy soil, in which were lines of dark matter, the result of the decay of turf. On the top of this mound, and probably some time after its erection, there had been heaped 3 feet of stiff soil, containing many small angular flints, mixed with foreign clay. Nearly 14 feet south-east from the centre, at a depth of 4 feet from the apex, and 2 feet from its base, was a crushed food-vase (fig. 942), measuring, after restoration, 4¼ inches in height, 4¾ inches across the top, 5¼ inches across the shoulders, and 2 inches at the bottom. It is quite plain. We found distributed in the mound a beautiful little barbed arrow-head of flint (fig. 943), the lower jaw of a sheep or goat, one small vertebra, and five other pieces of animal bone; also two pieces of an urn, eleven splinters of Yorkshire flint, and nineteen splinters and two cores of black foreign flint.

BARROW No. 264

Had a diameter of 60 feet and elevation of 3½ feet, and is partly on the road from Huggate to Warter, and partly in the adjoining field. It contained a central core mainly composed of large pieces of flint gathered from the surrounding land, mixed with rubbly chalk and a little of the local loamy surface soil. In the barrow, mainly about the centre, were numerous broken and detached bones of an ox, and a few adult human bones, six flint chips, and a fragment of a drinking-cup. Beneath the centre was a large and well-shaped oval grave, south-south-west by north-north-east, 10 feet 5 inches by 7 feet at the top, and 9 feet by 5 feet 3 inches at the bottom. The depth was 5 feet 5 inches.

At the base of the mound, 2 feet 9 inches outside the southern edge of the grave, was an adult skeleton, on its right side, the knees pulled up, the right arm doubled back with the hand to the face, the left arm bent to a right angle over the chest, with the hand near the right elbow. The head pointed to the west. A femur, tibia, and humerus measured 18 inches, 15¼ inches, and 13 inches respectively, in their extreme lengths.

Close within the south end of the grave, only a few inches below the base of the mound, stood a drinking-cup (A), 6 inches in height, accompanied by the decayed bones of an infant. It is the fourth example we have found which has a true handle. Being in contact with rubbly chalk and rough flints, it was much crushed, but has since been restored. Its original form and ornamentation are well shown in fig. 944.

At a distance of 1 foot outside the northern edge of the grave, and 1 foot above the base of the mound (at B), was a fine food-vase (fig. 945), 5¼ inches high, 6¾ inches across the top, 6 inches at the shoulders, and 3 inches across the bottom. The ornamentation round the inside of the lip consists of three rows of gashes about half an inch long, arranged in herring-bone pattern; and similar gashes form three belts which, alternating with three bands, each consisting of three incised lines, pass externally round the upper half of the vase. This vase also was accompanied by the remains of a child. Whether these interments were made at the time of the filling-in of the grave and the erection of the mound, or some time afterwards, could not be satisfactorily determined. Scattered in the grave almost from top to bottom were numerous broken and detached bones, teeth, and the horn core attached to part of the skull of an ox, indiscriminately mixed with detached and broken human bones. There were also seventeen fragments of a broken drinking-cup, one large flake, and one large slingstone (fig. 946),

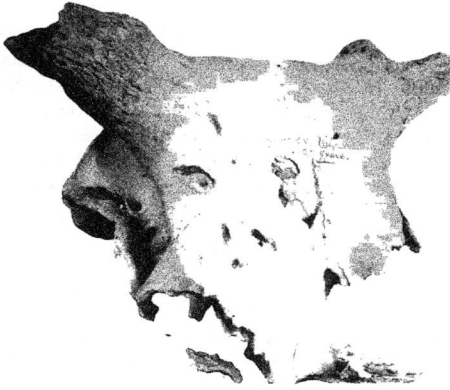

FIG. 947.—SKULL OF OX FROM BARROW No. 264.

both of local flint. Besides these, at a depth of 2 feet, and near the centre of the grave, was the greater portion of the skull of an ox (fig. 947), the frontal bone of which had been fractured.* Though the lower jaw was absent and the ends of each horn-core had been roughly broken off, no attempt had been made to obtain the brains by splitting open the skull, which would seem to indicate that the skull had been deposited as food for the occupants of the grave.†

Immediately below the skull, at a depth of 2 feet, was the nearly entire skull of a person of rather fine features, and apparently in the prime of life— probably that of a female. A little to the north of this was a small heap of calcined bones of a young person, accompanied by a flake knife of dark-coloured flint (fig. 948). At the bottom of the grave, in the centre, was a confused

* Similar instances have been observed by other explorers. In a barrow near Silbury, opened in 1849 by John Merewether, D.D., F.S.A., Dean of Hereford, "The heads of two oxen lay side by side in a grave at the depth of 5 feet, in very perfect condition. In each the centre of the forehead had been fractured in a circular hole."—"Diary of a Dean."

† We find the following remark by Bateman :—"This, the fifth instance of the intentional burial of the head of the ox, goes far to prove the existence of some peculiar superstition or rite of which no notice has reached modern times."—"Ten Years' Digging," p. 130.

PLATE CXX.

FIG. 942. ⅖

FIG 945. ½

FIG. 943. ⅓

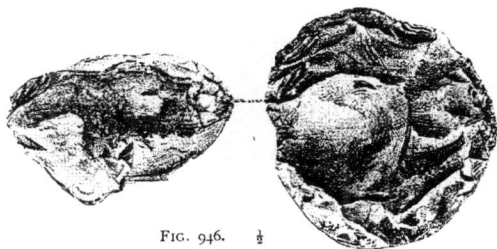

FIG. 946. ½

FIG. 944. ½

FIG. 946. ⅓

heap of the bones of a powerfully-built man of middle age. A careful examination fully convinced us that the disarrangement of the bones was due to the body having been interred cross-legged in a sitting position, and protected by a small wooden enclosure, decayed traces of which remained.* As the body and the wooden protection decayed, the bones dropped, some one way and some another, the skull rolling a little distance to one side, as found. At the same time the earthy matter gradually settled down upon and became somewhat mixed with the bones. The femur, tibia, and humerus measured 19 inches, $15\frac{1}{2}$ inches, and $13\frac{3}{4}$ inches respectively. The sacrum was anchylosed to the adjoining vertebra.

Over the grave, almost to the top of the barrow, and down into the grave to the depth of 4 feet, were numerous large flints, and some ox bones. From the indiscriminate mixing of the detached and broken animal and human bones in this grave (all of which had apparently been purposely placed there), it would seem that the broken-up human bones were those of a person or persons sacrificed at the funeral feast and deposited in the grave as food, along with the remains of the two oxen.

From October 13th to 20th, inclusive, 1882, the three following barrows were opened :—

BARROW No. 252

Had a diameter of 45 feet, and an elevation of $2\frac{1}{2}$ feet. An area of disturbance 12 feet by 7 feet was observed in the centre, above an oval grave, which had been emptied, excepting about 18 inches at the east end. It measured 8 feet east and west by 5 feet across, and was 4 feet in depth. In the grave, at various depths, were many broken bones of a disturbed body, and at the bottom was a slip of sheet lead with "JAS. SILBURN" stamped on it. Beneath the undisturbed portion at the east end was a quantity of decayed wood, along the floor of the grave, and extending about 10 inches up the end of the grave. This was, probably, the remains of a lining of wood. At about half the depth of the mound, and 12 feet south of the centre, were two discs of chalk (figs. 949-50), about $\frac{3}{4}$ of an inch thick, one measuring 4 inches and the other $3\frac{1}{2}$ inches in diameter, and each is perforated in the centre with an aperture $\frac{3}{4}$ of an inch in diameter. In consequence of having been embedded in damp ferruginous earth, more than $\frac{1}{8}$ of an inch of their surface was in a soft condition, so that, if they were ever ornamented with incised lines, all trace of such must have been removed. Their use is uncertain.† No trace of an interment accompanied these discs. From the mound we took a large angular slingstone of flint (fig. 951), nine flakes of Yorkshire flint, two scrapers and seventy-six flakes of foreign flint, and five fragments of a food-vase.

BARROW No. 253

Measured 58 feet in diameter and $2\frac{1}{2}$ feet in height. It had been carefully opened by Silburn, by making two large cuts about 1 foot apart, reaching from near the

---

* "Journal of the Anthropological Institute," vol. xi., p. 437-8, gives an account of Chilian graves being covered with branches and the bodies placed in a sitting position. This is similar to what is sometimes indicated in British interments.

† Some curious pieces of chalk, of a somewhat similar nature, but deeper, and ornamented by incised lines, were found by Canon Creenwell in a barrow in the parish of Folkton, on the Wolds. See *Archæologia*, Vol. 52.

western .to the eastern margin of the barrow.   He had emptied two graves, and we observed the remains of two disturbed bodies, some of the long bones of which measured as follows :—femur 20½ inches, tibia 16½ inches, and a small femur was 18¼ inches.   At the bottom of the most westerly grave he had again placed a tablet of lead with his name stamped upon it.

We took from various parts of the mound thirteen sherds of British pottery, two chipped slingstones of black flint, a tooth of an ox, thirty-six splinters and worked flints, mostly of the black variety.

BARROW No. 255

Was not quite so large as the last, and had also been explored by Silburn.   In the centre was an oval grave, from which had been removed an adult skeleton, many of the bones of which he had put back into the grave.   We found, in the soil filling the grave, a large and fine knife, of greyish coloured Yorkshire flint (fig. 952).   Excepting a few flint flakes from the mound, nothing further was found.

BARROW No. 254

Is now almost unrecognizable, a slightly raised portion round its circumference only remaining.   It is shown on the Ordnance Maps as a medium-sized mound, and must, therefore, have been con-siderably larger at the time of the Survey.   Probably it is one of the many mounds on the Wolds which have been removed and spread over the land at various times during the last fifty years.

In the apparent centre, and almost within reach of the plough, were two adult skeletons (Nos. 1 and 2, fig. 953), each accompanied by a fine drinking-cup, and on the lumbar vertebræ of No. 1 was a bronze pricker (fig. 954).   The femur and tibia of this body measured 18½ inches and 13½ inches respec-tively.   Those of No. 2 could not be measured with certainty, but the two humeri were about 12½ inches each.   A pointed stake-hole, 9 inches deep and 2 inches in diameter, and filled with burnt soil, was observed near the knees of No. 1.   The vase at the hips of No. 1 was crushed down on its side, but has been rebuilt (fig. 955). The one near the head of No. 2 had its top cut off by the plough.   It was irrepar-able, but it had been similar in form to the other, though somewhat differing in ornamentation.   The two bodies had been placed at the west end of an oblong grave measuring 10½ feet by 5 feet, which had been formed by merely remov-ing the 7 or 8 inches of surface soil to the rubbly chalk beneath.   The east

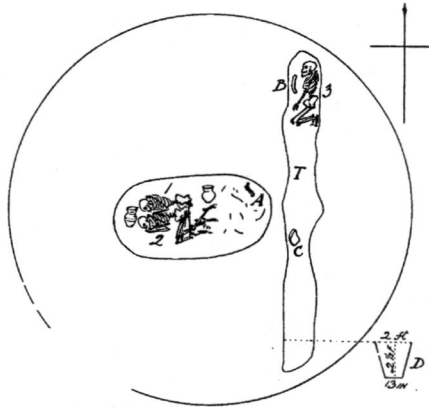

FIG. 953.—PLAN OF BARROW No. 254.

A—Bones of human foot.

B and C—Portions of vase.   T.--Trench.

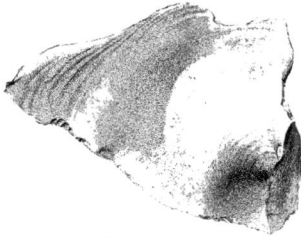

Fig. 948.   1

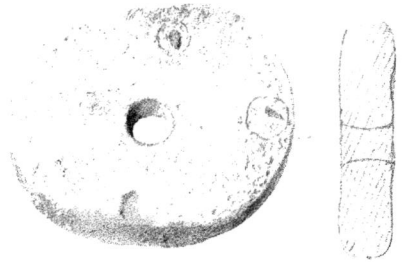

Fig. 949.   ½

Fig. 950.   ½

Fig. 951.   ½

Fig. 952.   ¼

Fig. 956.   ¼

Fig. 955.

end of this shallow grave was from 4 to 6 inches deeper than that on which the interments were. Over the whole of the bottom of the grave were traces of burning in the form of wood ashes and soil reddened by heat, clearly indicating the site of a fire, or the covering of the bottom of the grave with matter obtained from the remains of a fire. We also found two or three handfuls of calcined human bones mixed with burnt soil distributed over the greater part of the east end of the grave. Whether or not these had been disturbed and scattered by any earlier opening or at the time of the removing of the barrow we were unable to ascertain. Upon the edge of this burnt matter, and at about the same depth as the interments at the east end, were the undisturbed bones of a human foot, indicating the presence of an inhumed body at the east end of the grave also. Probably this was destroyed at the time when the mound was removed ; or Silburn may have made a small opening in its centre, and on finding a skeleton concluded there was nothing more.

About 20 inches from the east end of the grave was a narrow trench with sloping sides, 30 feet long, 2½ feet deep from end to end, 2 feet wide at the top, and generally about 13 inches at the bottom. It was charged from end to end with chalk rubble and soil resembling such as would be obtained in excavating it ; and in the centre portion—notably opposite the end of the grave—there were traces of fire, the chalk rubble being burnt red and mixed with burnt wood, pieces of which have been preserved. At each end the trace of fire had disappeared. At *B* and *C* in the trench were large pieces of dish-shaped pottery, of the type of that from barrow 110 (fig. 248) and others. We also picked up four fragments of unburnt animal bone from other parts of it. Opposite the end of the grave there was a slight curved recess in the eastern side of the trench, showing marks of fire. Can this centre part have been a receptacle in which a body was burnt—a rude crematorium ?

At the north end of the trench, and about 10 inches from the bottom, was an adult skeleton (No. 3) in the posture shown in the ground plan of the barrow. It had been roughly squeezed into the narrow trench, was minus its entire right arm, no trace of which was observed. It could not have been removed after interment without breaking up the body, neither could it have decayed, as all the other bones were sound and in very good preservation.[*] The skull is a fine specimen. Had the upper arm been missing, it might have been accounted for by the supposition that it had been removed by some subsequent excavation. The femur, tibia, and humerus measured 17 inches, 14 inches, and 12 inches respectively. It was interesting to have the grave, the trench, and the bodies therein on view together, and it seemed clear that the whole had been arranged in position at the same time, or at least before any part of the mound was raised over them.

The three barrows at the north end of this group we were not permitted to examine. They are in a grass paddock, and Mr. Richardson objected to have the sward removed. It is believed that they were all explored by Silburn.

---

[*] Herodotus, book iv., c. xlii., in describing the customs of the Scythians, says " They sacrifice every hundredth captive to the god of Mars. Having poured libations upon their heads, they cut their throats into a vessel, and with the blood besmear the scimitar of Mars. Whilst this is doing above, the following ceremony is observed below :— From the human victims they cut off the right arms close to the shoulders, and throw them up in the air. This ceremony being performed on each victim severally, they depart. The arms remain where they happen to fall ; the bodies elsewhere."

No. XV.—THE BLANCH GROUP.

THIS interesting series contains twenty-eight barrows, two of which
have not been opened. Most of them are nearly parallel with those
of the last group, about two miles to the east, and on equally
elevated ground. The barrows are crowded together in
two groups, the prevailing mode of interment in each
being strikingly different.

Several of the barrows were opened by
Silburn, and the relics discovered
are thus described
by him :—

" No. 6, Urn from a barrow at Blanch, October 20th,
1851. No. 7, Very large urn found inverted
and filled with bones, calcined, from a barrow
at Blanch, October 20th, 1851. No. 9, Urn
from a barrow at Blanch, February, 1852.
No. 10, Urn from a barrow at Blanch, February 24th, 1852. No. 11, Urn found in the
same barrow with the above. No. 12, Early
British sword found with a skeleton,* and an
urn (very rude) that was destroyed by the
finders, on a farm at Blanch, June, 1851.
The teeth of some animal accompanied the remains. Several skulls and bones were found
with the urns."

BARROW No. 2

Is isolated, on the brow of the north hill-side of Ox
Lands Dale, a little to the north-east of Huggate.
On July 12th, 1863, it measured 13 yards in diameter
and 1½ feet in height, and was surrounded by a nearly
filled-in trench. Near the centre of the mound, and
only a few inches below the surface, were two tines from an
antler of a red deer, the lower jaw of a dog, and three
pieces of an urn. A little below these was a doubled-up
adult skeleton, with the head to the west. A femoral bone
measured 19¼ inches. Close to the feet was the bronze blade
of a knife (fig. 956) having two keen cutting edges and a

* Most probably Anglo-Saxon.—J.R.M.

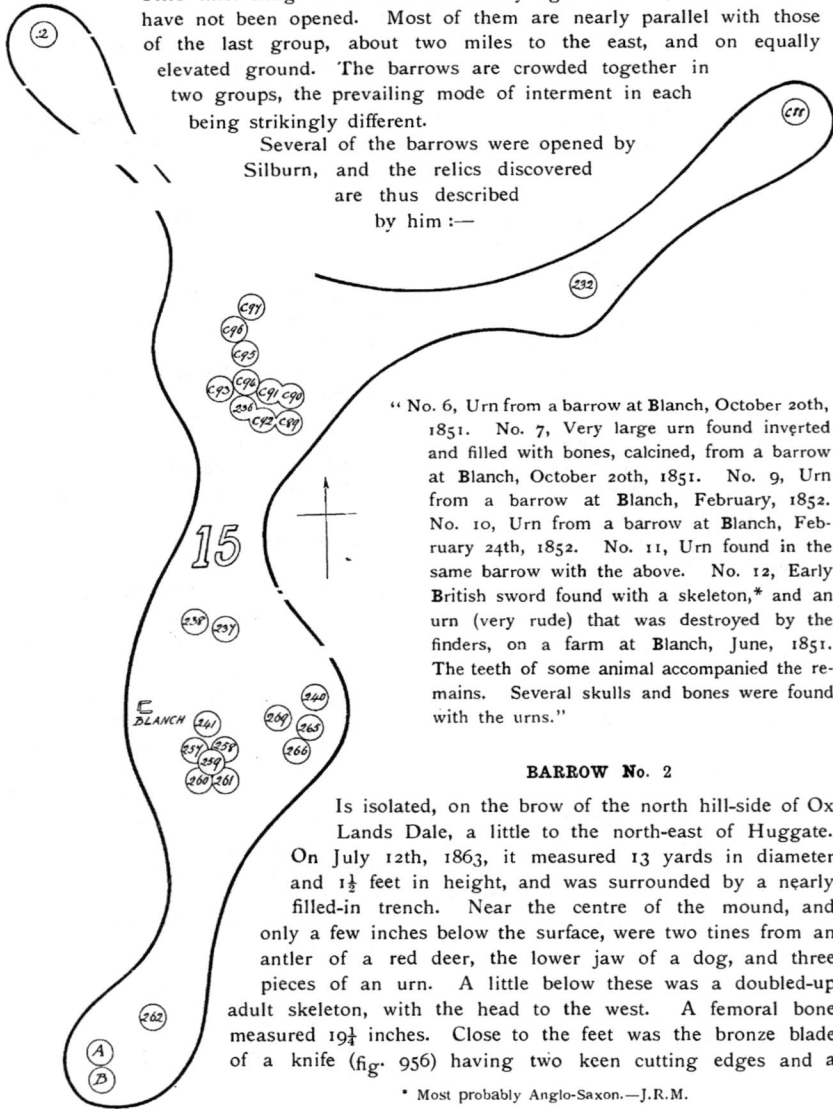

Fig. 954.　¼

Fig. 959.

Fig. 961.　⅔

Fig. 958.

Fig. 962

Fig. 957.　½

Fig. 965.　¼

Fig. 960.　½

Fig. 963.　¹⁄₁

Fig. 964.　¾

broad chisel point.   At the tang end of the blade is a hole for rivetting it to a haft.   This hole is bruised and elongated in the direction of the length of the blade, evidently from the half of the knife having been frequently struck with a mallet while being used as a chisel.

A few feet west of the skeleton was a small grave in the rock 4½ feet deep, at the bottom of which were cremated bones.   With these were many snail shells (*Helix nemoralis*) and the point end of a beautifully-made bodkin of greenstone (fig. 957).

BARROW No. C. 89

Is one of ten closely associated barrows, nine of which were opened during the early part of May, 1876.   Not one of these is shown on the Ordnance sheet.   No. 89 was about 50 feet in diameter and not more than 15 inches in elevation.   A trench had originally encircled it.   In the centre was a large irregular grave cut into the chalk rock, in which were the cremated bones of a youth, placed in the midst of a quantity of charcoal.   On the northern side of this deposit were three flint flakes burnt and splintered (figs. 958-9), a small food-vase (fig. 960), and fragments of a pierced hammer-head of grey stone, which had been much broken by the heat of the funeral pile.   These fragments have been put together, as shown in fig. 961.   On the south side of the deposit was a bone pin with a hole in the broad end (fig. 962).

BARROW No. C. 90

Measured about 40 feet in diameter and 12 inches in height.   A little to the west of the centre were the cremated bones of a small person (No. 1) occupying a small dish-shaped hole extending 15 inches below the base of the mound, and measuring 20 inches in diameter at the top.   The sides of this were reddened, probably by the introduction of the hot embers.   Accompanying the bones were three small burnt flakes of flint (figs. 963-4).   Rather to the south of the centre was a large crushed cinerary urn, inverted (fig. 965).   It contained nothing, but was found to be on the northern side of an oval grave, which measured 5½ feet east and west and 3½ feet across, and 3¼ feet in depth.   Along the floor of this was a shallow trough containing the calcined bones of a large adult.   This deposit (No. 2) measured 2 feet 6 inches in length* by 10 inches, and varied in thickness from 2 to 4 inches.   On the west end of these bones was a flint knife (fig. 966), and a few splinters of burnt flint were found in the debris.

BARROW No. C 91

Was slightly larger than the last.   The interment had been placed on the original surface under the centre of the mound, and consisted of burnt bones, accompanied by a small food-vase, which was irreparably crushed.

BARROW No. C. 92.

This mound was not quite so large as the preceding one.   We took from its base, a few feet south of the centre, the lower portion of a food-vase (fig. 967) which accompanied a few burnt bones of a child (?).   A little to the west of the

* Nearly the length occupied by a doubled-up body.

centre was a basin-shaped excavation, with burnt sides, which was 3 feet in diameter at the top, and extended 15 inches below the base of the mound. At the bottom were the burnt bones of a full-grown person with a very thin skull, and possibly also some bones of a child. Above these was a quantity of charcoal, mixed with burnt soil.

BARROW No. C. 93

Was a little larger than the last, and had been enclosed by a circular trench. In the centre was a nearly circular grave, measuring 4½ feet deep and 6 feet in diameter at the top, and 5½ feet at the bottom.

The only interment consisted of the calcined remains of a large individual, placed in an elongated heap on the floor of the grave. No urn or instrument accompanied this deposit, which was almost free from wood ashes and soily matter, and remarkable for the white porcelain-like appearance of most of the bones.

Close under and surrounding the bones was a film of yellowish matter, seemingly the residue of some decayed substance.

BARROW No. C. 94

And the following three were the mere sites of barrows which at some previous time had been carted away. More material having been removed from their centres than from the sides, they had the appearance of hollows with slightly raised borders. Under the centre of No. C. 94 was a dish-shaped hole about 2½ feet in diameter, and extending 12 inches into the old surface ground. At the north side of this was a crushed and damaged cinerary urn (fig. 968). It contained an incense cup (fig. 969) and burnt bones, apparently those of an adult female, whilst a few were those of a child. To the south of the cinerary urn was a flint drill (fig. 970) and an irreparably-crushed food-vase with an unusually broad base. It had been placed on its bottom, but had fallen to one side through the settling of the soil.

BARROW No. C. 95

Yielded nothing. Probably a small interment of cremated bones had been destroyed at the time of the removal of the mound.

BARROW No. C. 96

Was not reduced so much as the last barrow. Near the centre, at its base, on the natural surface soil, was an interment of burnt adult bones, mixed with soil and a few pieces of burnt wood. This elongated deposit measured 2 feet east and west and 9 inches across.

Two flint knives were picked from the old surface line below the mound.

BARROW No. C. 97,

Like several of the previous mounds, was hardly visible from the surrounding ground. Its centre seemed to have been deeply cut away, and nothing was found.

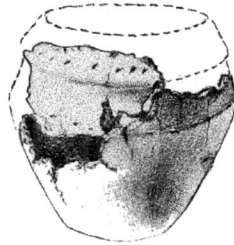

FIG. 969. ½

FIG. 967. ⅛

FIG. 966.

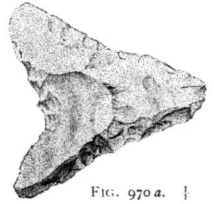

FIG. 970. ⅓

FIG. 970 a. ⅓

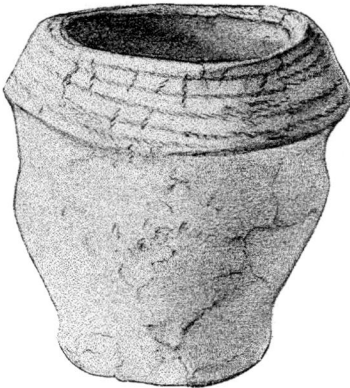

FIG. 972. ½

FIG. 968. ¼

FIG. 974. ⅓

FIG. 976. ⅔

FIG. 973. ⅓

FIG. 975. ¼

BARROW No. 236

Was opened August 5th [and 7th, 1882. It is the largest of ten adjoining barrows, and though it measured 45 feet in diameter and 2 feet in height, is not shown on the Ordnance map. At the centre was a shallow, dish-shaped excavation cutting through the old surface soil to the rock below. It contained burnt soil, in which was a little charcoal and a few calcined human bones, from which we took a portion of a burnt bone pin and a small flint flake. From the mound fifty-three chips and tools of black flint, and twenty-four of local grey flint were taken. One (fig. 970a) is chipped into a peculiar shape.* A small axe roughly chipped into form ready for grinding, was also found. Several worked flints were picked up on the outskirts of this and the preceding nine mounds.

BARROW No. 237

Is one of twelve closely-adjoining barrows in this group, at some distance from those just described. During the week ending August 14th, 1882, this and the following four barrows were opened. They were filled in afterwards. The diameter of barrow No. 237 was 60 feet, and elevation 2½ feet. It had an oval form, in consequence of the frequent passage of the plough, with its longest axis north and south—the direction of the old high-ridged lands. It stood on a slight elevation, and appeared to have been made entirely from local material.

About 5 feet north of the centre, and 8 inches above the base of the mound, was the flexed skeleton of a youth (No. 1, fig. 971), twelve or fourteen years of age, on its right side, and head to the west. About 4 feet south of the centre, in a slight hollow in the ancient surface soil, was the greater portion of an adult

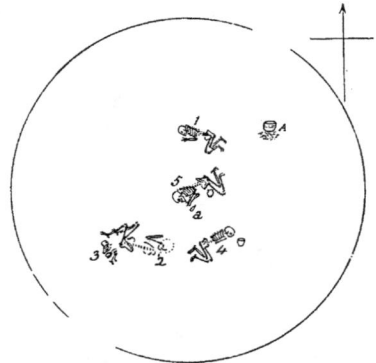

FIG. 971.—PLAN OF BARROW No. 237.

skeleton (No. 2) on its right side. The femur and tibia measured 18 inches and 14½ inches respectively. The skull, which had been to the east, was broken up and the greater portion of it removed, most probably by diggers for rabbits. Near where the head had been were some bones of a very small animal, and a small flake of dark flint. At the feet was the skeleton of a child about three years of age (No. 3), on the left side, and the head to the north; and a little east of No. 2, and a few inches above the base of the mound, was the skeleton of a second child (No. 4), about four years of age, on its right side, and head to the east. In front of its chest was a crushed food-vase (fig. 972), which had been much displaced through the burrowing of rabbits. Near the centre, in a shallow

* A considerable number of this type have been found on the land.

hollow reaching the gritty chalk sub-soil, was an adult skeleton of middle age (No. 5), partly on its right side and partly on its back, and head to the south-west, both hands to the face, and the legs gathered up with knees at a right angle with the trunk. A femur and tibia measured 18 inches and 14 inches respectively. Between the knees and right elbow was a crushed food-vase (fig. 973), and in front of the face a small scraper of grey flint (fig. 974). The vase is 6½ inches high, 7 inches across the top, 7½ inches wide at the shoulders, and 3¼ inches across the bottom. Cord-like impressions adorn the inside of the lip and the upper half externally. About 5 feet north-east of No. 5, and about 6 inches above the base of the barrow, (at A on the plan), stood a small food-vase (fig. 975) quite uninjured. It measured 3¾ inches high, 5½ inches across the top, and 2¾ inches across the bottom. A few inches above this was a deposit of animal bones, including some from a pig and a few from a much smaller animal. Probably these and the vase were the remains of a food offering. We found a sandstone boulder (fig. 976) in the mound, battered nearly all over from having been used as a hammer-stone ; four flakes and one large lump of black flint ; also a tooth of a deer, a tusk of a pig, a shank-bone of an ox, a leg-bone of a goat, and a humerus, probably of the same animal.

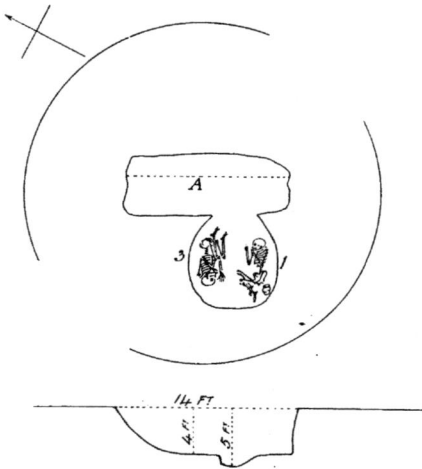

FIGS. 977 AND 978.

PLAN AND SECTION OF BARROW NO. 238.

BARROW No. 238

Is not shown on the Ordnance Map, and is hardly visible on the surface. Slightly to the east of the centre was a large filled-in excavation, as shown at A on the plan (fig. 977) and section (fig. 978). It measured 14 feet by 6 feet, and varied in depth from 4 to 5 feet. From the soil and gritty material filling it * we took two vertebræ of a red deer and splinters of other bones. Irregularly scattered at the bottom was a little burnt wood and other dark matter, but no trace of an interment. Connected with the west side of this hole was an oval grave, 7 feet by 5 feet and 6 feet deep. Near the south side of this, and about 20 inches below the base of the mound, was an adult skeleton (No. 1) with a crushed food-vase (fig. 979) at its feet. The femur, tibia, and humerus measured 19 inches, 15 inches, and 13 inches respectively. The vase is 6 inches high, 8 inches across the top, the same at the shoulders, and 3½ inches at the bottom. The inside of the lip and the upper external half are ornamented with short broad impressions made by a small cord, which seems to have been wound round some small

---

* Probably it represented an underground habitation, resembling that in barrow 241, to be presently described.

PLATE CXXIV.

FIG. 979.

FIG. 989. ¼

FIG. 980.

FIG. 983 ½

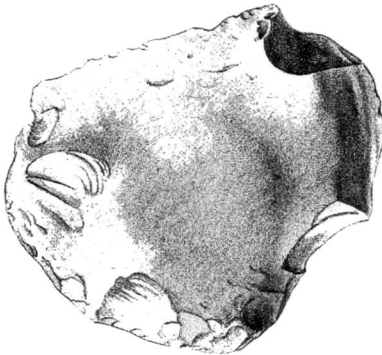

FIG. 988. ½

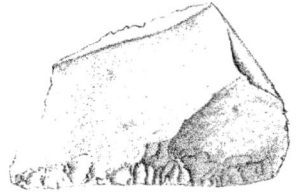

FIG. 981. ½

FIG. 982 ½

FIG. 986. ¼

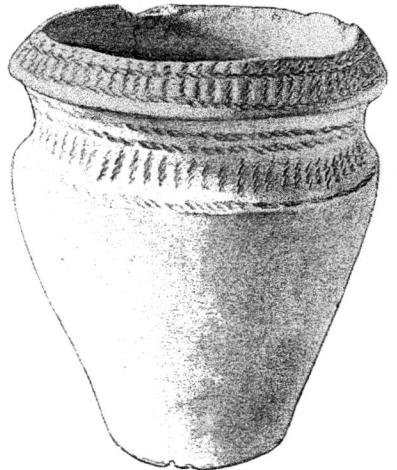

FIG. 985.

article, such as the blade of a bronze pricker. Beneath this skeleton, and as far as the bottom of the grave, were pieces of animal bone and dismembered human bones, consisting of the greater portion of the frame of a large adult (No. 2, not shown in the plan). The bones had evidently been disjointed before they had been placed in the position in which we found them. The front part of the skull with the facial bones was near the east end of the grave, whilst the back of the skull was near the west end. The bones of the legs and arms were separated, the two fibulæ being some distance from the tibiæ, and at different depths in the grave, and the vertebræ and other small bones were scattered everywhere. Each femur measured 19 inches. None of the long bones seem to have been broken previous to their having been placed where we found them. Possibly these bones belonged to a body disturbed by the introduction of a later interment.

On the bottom of the grave was a doubled-up adult skeleton (No. 3, fig. 977). A femur measured 17½ inches, and a tibia 13½ inches. Near the chin was an oval jet button (fig. 980), and in front of the skull was a triangular flint knife (fig. 981). If the large excavation may be considered to be part of a pit dwelling, this grave had been dug so as to communicate with it.

BARROW No. 240

Had the appearance of having been much lowered on the south-west side, and one of the labourers employed on the farm told me he remembered assisting to cart a portion of it away fifty-five years previously, for the purpose of making ponds on the estate. At the time I opened this barrow—August 13th, 1882—it had a diameter of 60 feet and an elevation of about 2 feet. A rectangular piece 30 feet by 24 feet, was cut from its centre, and exposed an oval grave scooped through the ancient surface soil to a depth of 10 to 12 inches in the gritty chalk below. In the grave were the remains of a large adult male, on its back, the head to south-south-west, the knees pulled up and pressed over to the right side, the left arm at full length by the side, with the hand under the left hip. The right arm was doubled back with the hand bent along the shoulder. A femur and tibia measured 18¼ inches and 14½ inches respectively. The right humerus measured 14⅛ inches, and the left humerus 13½ inches. A beautifully-chipped flint knife, 3¼ inches long (fig. 982) was found close to the right shoulder, the point being towards the right knee, and with the flat side upwards.

From the mound were taken two teeth of an ox, two knives and eight flakes of flint.

BARROW No. 241

Had a diameter of 35 feet and an elevation of 18 inches, and is not shown on the Ordnance map. Towards the base was a long heap of excavated chalk grit, and presently were indications of disturbance in the ground beneath, extending over a considerable area. Following this line of disturbance to a depth of 1 foot, and obtaining from different parts three teeth of an ox, pieces of animal bone, flint chips, one small barbed arrow-head (fig. 983), and a little burnt wood, we defined the northern three-fourths of this excavation, the plan of which is shown at fig. 984. We next commenced to empty the northern end, and immediately

ound the greater part of the jaw of a large ox, with the teeth in position, but too
far decayed to be removed without falling to pieces, though the teeth were in
good condition. Near it was the upper part of a cylindrical mass of black matter
and burnt wood, 17 inches in diameter and 16 inches deep (*A*, fig. 984), in the
centre of which, at the bottom, was an inverted cinerary urn (fig. 985), containing
pearl-like calcined bones of a young individual. With them was a bone pin
(fig. 986), which, at the head, shows a small indentation, probably the result of an
attempt to pierce it. The urn is rather small but well shaped. The black deposit
surrounding it seemed to have been enclosed at the time of the interment, in a
cylindrical receptacle of coarse basket work, which left impressions on the plastic
soil forming the sides of the
cavity. We then followed
downwards and southwards
the other portion of this excavation, which became narrower and shallower as we
proceeded, but only a few
small pieces of burnt wood
were found near the bottom.

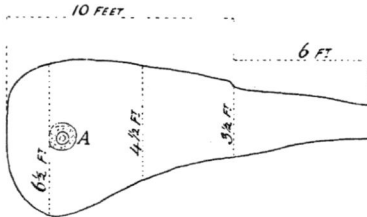

FIG. 984.—PLAN OF DWELLING UNDER BARROW NO. 241.

The excavation now as-
sumed the form given in fig.
987, and it seemed quite clear
that it had been a habitation
previous to its becoming a
resting-place for the ashes of
the dead. The underground
plan of this dwelling much
resembles the one in Kemp
Howe, Cowlam (barrow No.
209*a*), described in the Journal
of the Anthropological Insti-

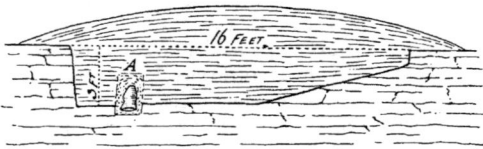

FIG. 987.—SECTION OF BARROW NO. 241.

tute for May, 1880, and under
the head of "Miscellaneous Barrows" in this Volume, but was not so deep. It
would most probably be roofed by rafters resting along its sides and meeting over
the centre, after the manner of a modern roof. The entrance was an inclined
passage from the south. The dimensions given on the plan are those taken at
the bottom. The side sloped gently outwards. There was no trace of a burnt
roof, or the covering of the sides, to indicate its destruction by fire. Probably
this dwelling was abandoned immediately after the death of one of the occupants,
the roof of the dwelling being pushed in and covered with a mound.

BARROW No. 257.

This and the four following and adjoining barrows were explored from
August 6th to the 14th, 1883. None were then more than 12 to 18 inches above
the surrounding ground; but judging from the areas covered by their base, they
had measured from 60 to 80 feet in diameter, and had no doubt originally been
of considerable elevation. At various times these mounds had been lowered to

supply material for agricultural improvements. Mr. Marshall, the tenant of the farm on which they were situated, informed the writer that his father had removed and spread on the adjoining land eight hundred cart-loads from one of these mounds alone; and another had been almost entirely removed to soil a garden. Since then the plough has further lowered them.

In the centre of Barrow No. 257 was a shallow grave, adjoining which—and only 2 feet from its north-west end—was a cylindrical hole in the ground, 2 feet in diameter and nearly 3 feet deep. It was charged with dark soil containing a quantity of charcoal in small pieces, from which we took one piece of calcined human bone. Both graves seemed to have been previously disturbed. Two handstruck chips of local flint found, near the graves, were the only relics found.

BARROW No. 258.

Slightly to the north of the centre of this barrow was an oval grave measuring 6 feet north and south by 4 feet across. On the bottom, at the south end, was a confused heap of human bones, broken in a former opening. Under these was a slip of lead, with "Jas. Silburn" stamped upon it. The broken fragments of the skull were of great thickness, and apparently belonged to an aged person. Two dorsal and two cervical vertebræ were firmly anchylosed. Nearly 18 inches south of the grave, and on the old surface line, were traces of a fire, consisting of burnt wood occupying a circle 4½ feet in diameter and 3 inches thick. Between this and the grave was a large tine from the antler of a red deer.

BARROW No. 259

Contained a shallow grave in the centre, in which were some broken bones of a strong man, the remains of a former opening. The only measurable bone was a tibia, 15¾ inches in extreme length. No trace of the skull remained. Probably it was found in good preservation and taken by Silburn at the time of his exploration of this barrow, and may be the one he thus alludes to in his catalogue: "No. 3, urn found inverted on a farm at Blanch, together with a perfect skull, October 20th, 1851." The grave had been shallow, but as the natural surface had been disturbed to some depth all round it, its length and breadth could not be ascertained. We took from the base of the barrow near the grave the tooth of an ox, four flint chips, and two scrapers.

BARROW No. 260

Had also been previously opened. Near the centre was a shallow grave containing the re-placed and broken-up bones of a disturbed interment, and a little to the south of the centre was a large oval excavation, 3½ feet deep, 10 feet north and south, and 6½ feet across at the bottom, which was on a firm bed of undisturbed rock. No trace of bone, pot, burnt or decayed matter of any kind was observed in any part of this hole. Possibly it had served as a pit dwelling, and not as a grave.

From near the centre of the mound we picked up one broad flint knife 2½ inches in length, chipped on one side to a sharp edge, and two scrapers, all of Yorkshire flint.

2 T

BARROW No. 261

Like No. 259, had a shallow grave in the centre, containing some fragmentary bones of an adult skeleton, the residue of a former opening. Round the grave we found one oval knife (fig. 988), measuring 2¼ inches in its greatest diameter, with a sharp edge on one half of its circumference; two scrapers, three flakes—(all of Yorkshire flint); the tooth of an ox or red deer, and a portion of the front tooth of a horse.

It should be mentioned that the five barrows last described had been opened by Silburn in a very careful and creditable manner.

BARROW No. 265.

This barrow, on September 12th, 1883, was 50 feet in diameter and 1 foot in height. In the centre, 8 inches from the apex, were a few cremated bones mixed with wood ashes and burnt soil, accompanied by one flake of black flint (fig. 989) unburnt. These were over the centre of an oblong grave, measuring 6 feet east to west by 3½ feet, with a depth of 20 inches at the west end and 14 inches at the east end. On the floor of this, at the latter end, was an adult skeleton (No. 1), head to the west, on the right side, the left arm bent to a right angle over the chest, with the hand near the right elbow, while the right arm was stretched by the side of the skeleton with the hand turned along the left femur. The knees were brought up to form nearly a right angle with the body. The extreme lengths of a femur and a tibia were 17½ inches and 14¾ inches respectively. The right humerus measured 12¾ inches, while the left humerus measured 12⅝ inches only, and was of less substance. At the feet was a crushed food-vase in a very decomposed condition. The vase (fig. 990) measures 5 inches high, 6 inches across the top, and 3 inches across the bottom. Lines of cord impressions, variously inclined and carelessly distributed, cover its whole exterior. It possesses a handle, and is, as far as our researches go, unique in having a bottom in shape between a square and a cross. Under the skeleton was a film of dark matter, evidently in part the residue of decayed wood, which had left its impression on a thin layer of soil upon the floor of the grave. The west end of the grave deepened a little, where, partly under the interment just described, were the dismembered bones of two youths (Nos. 2 and 3) of about the ages of 13 and 15 years respectively. They were in the greatest disorder. One skull had its base upwards, the other being in a reversed position, the lower jaw being a foot distant from either skull; and none of the leg bones were articulated. These remains were accompanied by portions of a food-vase placed in two heaps a foot apart. A fragment needed to complete the vessel could not be found anywhere. The confusion of the bones might be due to the bodies at the bottom having been placed sitting on their hips—as in a few other instances—with a covering of wood above them, on which had been placed another body in a recumbent posture. In time these would fall in by decay.

From the mound we took one slingstone, eleven chips of native flint, three pieces of an urn, a tooth of a red deer, and four pieces of animal bone.

FIG. 993.   ¼

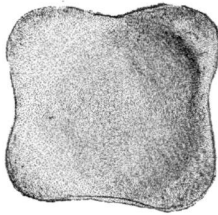

FIG. 990.   ½

FIG. 994.   ¹⁄₁

FIG. 991.   ¼

FIG. 992.   ¼

BARROW No. 266

Was similar in size to the last, and was examined on the following day. In the centre was a rectangular grave 20 inches deep, with the sides measuring a little over 3½ feet. In the centre of this was an elongated heap of cremated adult bones, accompanied by a broken food-vase (fig. 991), placed close to the north side of the bones. This measures 4¾ inches in height, 5½ inches across the top, 6 inches across the shoulders, and 3 inches at the bottom. Two grooves encircle the vase a little below its mouth ; the lower and smaller one contains four pierced bosses. The inside of the lip and the external upper half of the vase is most delicately ornamented with impressions made by a small and rather closely-twisted cord. From the mound seven flint flakes were taken.

BARROW No. 269.

This barrow had been, at some time, completely removed, excepting a ridge round its circumference, and the ground beneath its centre had been excavated to obtain chalk, leaving no trace of an interment.

BARROW No. 262

Is some distance from the last, and quite separated from the twelve barrows just described. Being of small dimensions, it is not shown on the Ordnance map. On August 15th, 1883, we discovered near the centre, and about 10 inches from the surface, two flat pieces of iron, apparently of late introduction and of modern workmanship. About 10 feet east of the centre stood a small food-vase of the cinerary urn type (fig. 992), part of the upper edge of which had been carried away by the plough. Just below were a few cremated bones of a young person.

One-half of a large flint scraper was picked from near the centre of the barrow.

BARROW No. 232

Is a detached mound at the opposite end of the group, and is not shown on the Ordnance map. On May 4th and 5th, 1882, its diameter and elevation were about 40 feet and 1 foot respectively. In the centre were two oval graves. The one slightly to the south of the centre measured 5½ feet east and west by 4 feet, and 19 inches deep. On the floor of this was the skeleton of a young female (the back lower molar just cutting), on the right side, the knees pulled up to a right angle with the trunk, with both arms doubled with the hands to the head. The femur, tibia, and humerus measured 17½ inches, 14¼ inches, and 12¼ inches respectively. Several of the small bones of the hand were inside the skull, and probably were taken there by mice. Behind the skull, which was to the east, were two rudely-worked flints, one (fig. 993) of light colour, 2 inches long, and probably a knife ; the other (fig. 994) of black flint, 2½ inches long, and in form resembling a rude spear-point or drill.

The grave a little to the north of the centre was also oval, and measured 5 feet 6 inches north and south by 4 feet 5 inches across, and was 2 feet in depth.

It contained the remains of a child from 12 to 18 months old, doubled up, on its left side, with the head to the south.

A few potsherds and bits of animal bone were found in the mound, which consisted entirely of the red loamy subsoil of the neighbourhood. A similar material filled the two graves. No trace of clay from a distance was visible.

BARROW No. C 88

Is situated about three-quarters of a mile north-east of the last, and about one hundred yards to the north of Christ Cross, which is an earthen entrenchment with four arms, each about 12 to 14 yards long, pointing nearly to the four cardinal points of the compass. This had been constructed by digging two parallel trenches at a little distance apart, and casting the material between them in the form of a ridge.*

On May 12th, 1876, this barrow was found to be much dispersed by the plough, and it did not measure more than one foot in elevation. We turned over the greater portion of the mound, and a few bits of burnt bone were all we observed. Probably they were from a previously-disturbed cremated interment, as we have been informed that Silburn, in his explorations during 1851-2, opened this mound, but with what result is not known. The two barrows marked A and B, we were not permitted to open.

* I possess the dimensions and a plan of this cross, taken when in better condition than now.—See chapter on "Embankment Crosses."

its

iich
ilar

nent
linal
ches

u

rved.
have
)und,

;.—See

BARROWS NOT GROUPED, &c.

THE following descriptions are of barrows, &c., that have come under my notice, outside the area of the groups already described.

BARROW "A"

Is situated on the southern limit of the parish of Helperthorpe. On the old 6 inch Ordnance sheet No. 144, it is shown in the top left hand corner as a twin-barrow, near the bend in the Green Lane, in a field called "Cross Thorns."*

During the years 1851-2, the upper portion of this barrow, to within 1 foot of its base, was carted away by Messrs. L. Clarkson and R. Ash, tenants, and spread on the land as marl. It mainly consisted of chalk and chalk rubble.

The barrow was opened by Canon Greenwell in the Autumn of 1866, when he turned over a considerable portion of it, and emptied a large grave (No. 1 on the plan, fig. 995). This grave alone took two of Canon Greenwell's workmen two days to reach the bottom. The writer was present the latter half of the first day, and was shown a rectangular piece of jet (fig. 51 in "British Barrows"), which had been found in the grave.

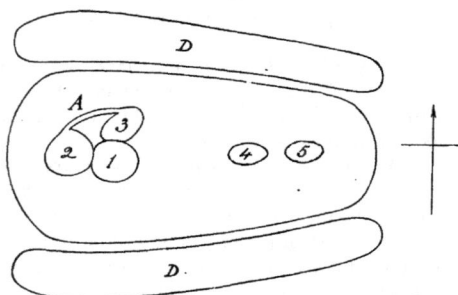

FIG. 995.—PLAN OF BARROW "A."

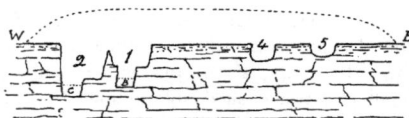

FIG. 996.—SECTION OF BARROW "A."
The broken line shows the probable original height of the mound.

No trace of an interment was found in the grave, or in any other part of the mound. In "British Barrows," p. 53, Canon Greenwell refers to the mound as follows :—

> "Besides these instances, there were found in a disturbed (?) barrow at Helperthorpe two flat beads of jet, which had formed part of a necklace. They are ornamented with a pattern consisting of minute punctured holes on the surface, and are similar to many which have been discovered in other parts of Britain."

* Probably derived from the cross excavation in Barrow No. 210, a little distance to the south.

In describing a neighbouring barrow (XLIX.) brief reference is again made to this barrow :—

"A true long barrow once existed, not very far from the barrow under notice, which presented features analogous to those of the ordinary wold mounds of that character."

And in a foot note, on page 489, of the same work we find :—

"Also, at the east end of a long barrow, removed several years ago, near Helperthorpe, the same peculiar deposit of calcined chalk was observed, having amongst it some broken bones. The calcined matter was so novel in its appearance that the people of the neighbourhood preserved specimens of it about their houses, thinking it was some petrified substance, on account of the resemblance it bore to the concretions formed by springs highly charged with carbonate of lime."

Re-opening.—In February, 1868, we commenced a re-examination. Though the base of the mound only remained, it was readily observed to be a long barrow, measuring 96 feet, nearly east and west; 42 feet across the east end, and 48 feet across the west end.

At about half the depth of the grave referred to above (No. 1 on the accompanying plan) it suddenly narrowed (as shown in section, fig. 996) to less than half its width, and the southern half of this narrowed portion was 16 inches lower than the northern half, as shown by the broken line *B* in the section. In the material filling the grave, we found a lump of foreign black flint, about the size and shape of half a brick. Its chipped and battered sides suggest that it may have been used as a mallet in digging the grave.

Adjoining the west side of this grave, was a second one, the east side of which Canon Greenwell's workmen had entered to a depth of about 4 feet. After having carefully removed the contents of this second pit, we were surprised to find that it contained no interment, and was of the same form as the previous one. Its shape at the top was a rough circle, 11 feet in diameter, whilst at a depth of 9 feet it suddenly contracted to 7½ feet in diameter, in the manner shown at 2 in the section.

From this point the western portion was sunk 18 inches further, and at this depth its southern half, like the bottom of grave No. 1, was also excavated 18 inches lower than the northern half (as shown by the broken line *C* in the section), thus making the southern portion of the grave No. 2 12 feet in depth. Except the slight entrance previously named, there was no trace of this pit ever having been opened. It was filled, to within about 2 feet of the top, with the broken chalk such as would be obtained in making it, on the top of which was chalk grit mixed with soil.

About 5 feet into the grave were portions of a femur, part of a fibula, and another leg bone of an ox, mixed with the broken chalk.

Grave No. 3 was next found in close contact with the north side of grave No. 1. It was 6 feet in depth, and measured 7½ feet south-south-west by north-north-east, and 6½ feet across; the sides were perpendicular. Unlike the two previously named graves, the broken chalk which it contained was mixed with ferruginous soil, obtained in sinking the grave, probably from a small pipe in the rock.

At about 1 foot from the bottom of this grave, in separate places, were portions of the upper jaw of a dog, containing teeth; also pieces of animal bone, but no human remains. Unlike the two former graves, the floor was smooth and unbroken; but, as in the other cases, no trace of an interment was to be found.

A thin stratum of dark coloured matter rested on the floor of the grave, from which we took two pieces of the lower jaw, with teeth, of a large dog, also pieces of burnt wood, and three small fragments of a British vase. We did not observe any appearance of this pit having been previously explored.

It will be observed, by referring to the plan, that these three pits were connected by contact, and also by a curved trench (A) about 16 feet long. The trench measured 2½ feet in depth, 3 feet wide at the top, and about 1½ feet at the bottom, on which were two pieces of a rib of some animal. This connection between two graves is of very rare occurrence. Barrow No. 4, Group 5, is the only other well defined instance we have met with.

About 25 feet east of No. 1 was grave No. 4, oval in form, measuring 6 feet north and south, 4½ feet across, and 2½ feet in depth. Like No. 3, it was filled with gritty chalk, mixed with a little soil. In this, at the north end, and about 16 inches down, was a small heap of burnt human bones, apparently of a young person. A little to the south of this deposit were the unburnt, or only slightly burnt, humerus and ulna of a person of medium size. At the bottom were a few wood ashes and a thin covering of dark matter, in which were some snail shells.

Quite 11 feet to the east of the last grave, was a similar oval one (No. 5). In its upper portion were traces of burning. Below were two small pieces of burnt bone, and a small hand-struck splinter of black flint. Nothing remained on the floor but a little dark matter, a small quantity of burnt wood and some shells of the common snail (*Helix nemoralis*).

Between graves No. 1 and 4, at a depth of about 10 inches (probably the original land surface) was a considerable area covered with wood ashes.

Noticing a slight depression on each side of the barrow, we proceeded to excavate, and discovered two large ditches running the whole length of the mound. They were filled with soil, and were trough-shaped, 6 feet in depth, 12 feet wide at the top, and 3 feet at the bottom. The material obtained in excavating them was most probably used to raise the barrow.

The singular form of graves Nos. 1 and 2, and the absence of an inhumed body in any of the five graves, is a remarkable feature. Graves Nos. 1 and 2 were admirably adapted for placing inhumed interments in a sitting position, the feet at the bottom of the grave and the hips resting on the ledge above.

The preservation of the detached and broken bones found scattered in the graves might have been due in part to water percolating freely through the loosely arranged chalk ·and rubble in which· they occurred, and probably partly by the bones being hardened by cooking. Bodies placed as suggested above, and therefore exposed to conditions favourable to decay, would be far more likely to disappear than would the pieces of bone placed in the upper part of the grave.

BARROW 209.—KEMP HOWE.

"KEMP HOWE"[*] is about one mile south of the last barrow, and is one of the few barrows on the "Cowlam Farm," six miles north of Driffield, which was not opened by the Rev. Canon Greenwell. At the time of his researches this

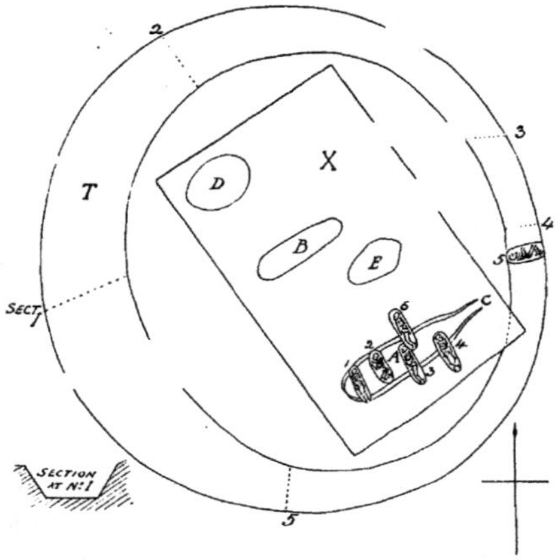

FIG. 997.--PLAN OF BARROW No. 209.   *X*—Area excavated.   *T*—Trench.

No. 1	Section of the Trench is	21 ft. wide at the top,	12 ft. at the bottom,	and 8 ft. deep.
No. 2	,,	,,	14 ft.	,,	,,	and about 6 ft. deep.
No. 3	,,	,,	8 ft.	,,	,,	,, ,, 4½ ft. deep.
No. 4	,,	,,	7 ft.	,,	,,	and 4½ ft. deep.
No. 5	,,	,,	10 ft.	,,	,,	and 2½ ft. deep.

Diameter of the Mound, inside of the Trench, from N.W. to S.E. 100 ft.
,,   ,,   ,,   ,,   from S.W. to N.E. 86 ft.

mound was covered with a clump of old fir trees. Previous to the planting of these, a moiety of the south-east side of the mound had been carted away, leaving it somewhat unshapely and its original limits difficult to determine. But a three-

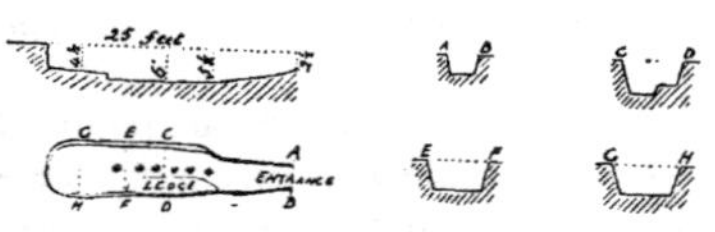

FIG. 997 *a*.

PLAN AND SECTIONS OF CAVE-DWELLING.

weeks' free use of the pick and shovel during July and August, 1878, enabled me to obtain the original plan of this remarkable barrow.

At the time of opening, it measured 4½ feet from base to summit, and the natural surface of the ground beneath it stood fully 1 foot higher than the present surface of the land for some distance round its margin. It was formed entirely of chalk rubble and soil, mainly obtained from an encircling trench, which on the north-west side was very deep and wide.

We turned over the whole of this mound except its outskirts. Near the north-west margin there was an excavation (*D* on the plan, fig. 997) extending

* There is a "Kemp Howe" near Brackenboys, in Penrith—see "Rude Stone Monuments," page 13. There is also a "Kemp Howe" in Scotland—see "Early Fortifications," by D. Christison, p. 268.

8 to 10 inches below the base of the mound, and measuring 8½ feet by 6½ feet, the floor of which was covered with a film of dark matter, in which were small bits of burnt wood. No relic, nor the slightest trace of an interment was observed. A little west of the centre (at *B*) there was a still larger excavation, 18 inches deep. It contained rough chalk, but no trace of an interment. East of this was a third excavation (*E*), oval in form and 3 feet deep.

Like the previous one it was filled with chalk and contained no relic or trace of a skeleton. The digging of these had preceded the erection of the mound, as there were no indications of it having been cut through. These excavations were doubtless graves, the bodies having entirely decayed.

This was not, however, the case with the secondary and comparatively recent interments of six adult skeletons, found at the south-east side of the mound, 1 foot to 2 feet below its base. Though unaccompanied by any relic, the very narrow form of the graves and the extended and but slightly flexed position of the interments alone showed them to be Anglo-Saxons.

Below these secondary graves was an older and far more interesting excavation. Its form and position is shown on the plan at *A*. At first it was thought to be a huge grave, but as the work proceeded appearances indicating it to have served some other purpose were visible. Its filling-in was peculiar. It consisted of broken chalk, surface soil, and burnt wood, presenting altogether a very unusual arrangement. Along its centre for a distance of about 15 feet were six carbonized uprights of wood, 6 to 9 inches in diameter, at about equal distances and in a row. Wood ashes were also found on the sides and bottom, and scattered in the material filling the excavation.

Also along the centre many of the large flat pieces of chalk stood on their edges, and at various depths were portions of animal and probably human bone, burnt as well as unburnt, and many fragments of a reddish urn. It was observed that the east end of this excavation became narrower and shallower. It now seemed evident that it was a habitation. Its form, as shown on the accompanying plan, was oblong, with a ground floor 25 feet by 4½ feet; and its greatest depth was 6 feet. To its east end was a passage 11 feet long, gradually sloping to the surface.

On the south side, commencing at the inner end of the passage and extending inwards for about 12 feet, was a ledge or rock-seat, about 13 inches above the opposite side of the floor, as shown by the dotted lines in the plan and section. The whole width of the floor at the south-west end, for a distance of about 6 feet, was 10 to 12 inches above the centre and lowest part of the floor. The roof of the cave had most probably been formed of horizontal timber, supported by strong uprights of the same material, and then covered with a mound of earth and stones. The roof eventually gave way and the superincumbent earth and stones slid into the dwelling, several of the large flat stones, as mentioned before, remaining on their edges.

The abundance of wood ashes affords unquestionable evidence of the dwelling having been burnt. The preservation of the remains of the six uprights was due entirely to their having been completely charred. The fragments of red pottery are quite plain and belong to three or more vessels, which were probably used for domestic purposes.

2 U

The roof of the cave must have fallen in long previous to the Anglo-Saxon interments, as where the skeletons were found, partly over the cave and partly upon the undisturbed rock, not the slightest distortion was visible, which would have been the case had not the filled-in portion under the bodies become firm. Near the south side of the dwelling, at about the base of the mound, were several broken human bones and pieces of a dark-coloured urn. Probably these belonged to a disturbed Anglo-Saxon burial.

We also found in the mound, between the graves *E*, *B*, *D*, a considerable quantity of detached animal and human bones; the latter indicated three or more individuals; a few of the bones showed traces of fire. There were also several small pieces of a dark plain urn.

From a little south of the grave *D*, one of the workmen picked up a large jet stud (fig. 998), of British type, but having been found in material, part of which had fallen from above, its original position was not made out. Considerable interest is attached to the cave-dwelling being within the encircling ditch of the barrow, and had not this side of the mound been previously removed, a section would have shown whether the cave was posterior to, or contemporaneous with, the erection of the barrow.

FIG. 998.
JET BUTTON FROM BARROW No. 209 a.

BARROW No. 210.—COWLAM CROSS.

This small mound is in the north-east corner of the field in which " Kemp Howe " is situated, and about 800 yards to the north of Cowlam Church. It measured 50 feet in diameter and 20 inches in height, but was at one time of greater elevation. Near the top we found the half of an adult human tibia, which probably belonged to an interment broken up at the time of excavating the cross (to be described presently). Many pot sherds, bits of animal bone, and corroded iron, were also obtained.

Under the mound was a cruciform excavation (fig. 999), with the arms pointing almost exactly to the four cardinal points of the compass. It was roughly cut 7 feet deep into the solid chalk rock, and the centre corresponded with the centre of the mound. We carefully cleared out the middle and the southern arm of this excavation, and removed the material from the outer extremities of the three other arms, and found the whole filled with soil resembling that in the mound above, and containing, mixed promiscuously, large pieces of chalk; numerous pot sherds, glazed and unglazed; animal bones; teeth of the horse; corroded iron, consisting of an arrow head (fig. 1,000), nails (?) &c. There was also the broken corner of a small trough of hard sandstone, closely resembling a portion of a similar sized trough made of chalk, from the Fimber cross. The Cowlam cross contained no trace of a platform of dry walling at the bottom, as was observed within the Fimber example.

About 4 miles north of this point a similar structure to the Fimber cross was discovered, of which the following account by C. Monkman is given in the *Malton Messenger* for 1866 :—

THE HELPERTHORPE CROSS.

" Between Weaverthorpe and Helperthorpe, in the great Wold Valley in the East Riding, there are several low, irregularly shaped mounds in the grass fields adjoining the high road. What these mounds were has long been a puzzle, and during the visit of the Rev. Canon Greenwell (in 1866) and the other archæologists to the Wolds, it was resolved to see if these mounds were places of sepulture.

The work was placed in the hands of Mr. W. Lovel, of Helperthorpe, and this gentleman selected one of the largest on the farm of Mr. G. Quickfall. It was soon found that the mound was not sepultural, but that it was

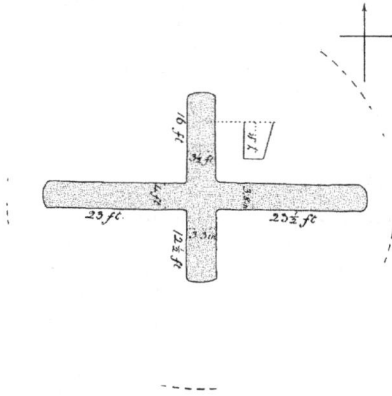

FIG. 999.—PLAN OF CROSS IN BARROW NO. 210.   FIG. 1000.

composed of various stratifications. The section in the centre, at 4 feet deep, showed the curved lines of the original hollow, and above this, portions of British pottery, bones of deer, ox, dog, and swine, were found. At a higher level was another dark line, not hollowed, and above this large quantities of pottery, of undoubted Roman make, were found. Still higher, paved floors, as if of the hearth, showing signs of burning, and part of a large vessel, very like Anglo-Saxon ware, and an unmistakable Anglo-Saxon bead, were met with ; and nearer the present surface the glazed pottery of mediæval times was found with iron nails and other objects. The work was discontinued when it was found the mound was not a place of sepulture. One gentleman (Mr. W. Lovel) who recently accompanied the Rev. Canon Greenwell in the Wold tumuli investigations, has since been engaged in further examination of the Helperthorpe mound, with very surprising and quite novel results. Mr. Lovel has laid bare a perfect cruciform structure, as perfect in many parts as the day the walls were built. This can only be compared to two tanks 21 feet long each, crossing

each other at right angles, thus forming a perfect cross, each limb of which
is walled up at the end.   The structure is formed of chalk walled in clay,
the walls being "faced" inwards and left rough outside, being wide at
the bottom and about a foot wide at the top, and have never been
higher than now, nearly 2 feet.   The space enclosed by these walls consists,
about 6 inches at the bottom, of a peculiarly black unctuous matter, not
charcoal nor not peat.   Analysis must determine what it is.   The rest of
the space is filled with hard-beaten yellow clay, quite to the top of the
wall.   The limbs of the cross are not graves and not flues—indeed, from
the narrowness of the walls, no superstructure has ever been there.   The
building stands in a circular hollow at about the natural surface, and is
cavered with 3 feet of forced earth, which abounds in Roman pottery [?] and
various animal bones.   Several antiquarians have visited the place, but no
one has seen any similar construction, and the purpose for which it has
been reared is not known.   There seems no question but that the "cross"
is of Roman date [?] from the quantity of pottery surrounding it.   The
building will be carefully covered over to await the inspection of the
archæologists. . . . . It is intended that drawings and measurements shall
be taken.   There are several other mounds on Sir Tatton Sykes' estate
which resemble the one opened."

BARROW No. 277.

This barrow is in "Willie Howe Plantation," adjoining the south side of a
long line of double entrenchments running east and west, about 300 yards west
of "Kemp Howe," and 2 miles north-east from Sledmere, close to the north
side of the old coach road-from York to Bridlington.   It is not shown on the
6-inch ordnance map.   It was opened during the first week in September, 1892,
and had a medium diameter of 55 feet, and an elevation of 4½ feet.

We cut a piece from the centre measuring 35 feet north and south, and 24 feet
across.   It consisted entirely of surface-soil, and the local rubbly chalk subsoil;
there was no foreign clay.

Near the centre, at a depth of 14 inches, was interment No. 1, on its left side,
head to the south-south-west, the legs drawn up towards the chest, arms folded,
the left hand under the chin, and the right hand upon the left elbow.   At the
hips was a flint flake knife (fig. 1001), and at a little distance (evidently displaced
by rabbits, which had burrowed under the skeleton), was a beautiful jet ring (fig.
1002).   The skull was greatly distorted.   It probably belonged to a tall female
of about forty years of age.   A femur measured 18½ inches.

About 1 foot immediately below No. 1 was interment No. 2, with its head in
the opposite direction, on the right side, the knees pulled up towards the face,
and the arms folded with both hands on the chest.   The bones of this skeleton
were too much injured by the roots of a large fir tree to be measured, but they
belonged to an adult person, probably a male, of about forty-five years of age,
judging from the teeth.   Near the back of the skull were the decayed remains
of a small food-vase.   Both these interments were apparently secondary, as
neither reached within 2 feet of the base of the mound; and appearances showed
that an incision had been made in the mound for them.

About 24 inches south-east of the two interments was a comparatively small oval grave, 2½ feet into the ground under the barrow. It measured 4½ feet nearly north and south, and 2½ feet across. No trace of bones was found at the bottom, but, there were evidences of an interment, probably of a child. In the material filling the grave, were four detached bones of a human foot, portion of a rib, and the joint end of the leg bone of a red deer (?), all unburnt, and comparatively little decayed; and the presence of numerous pieces of charcoal and three fragments of a dish-shaped vase in the grave seems to indicate that an unburnt interment had at one time occupied it.

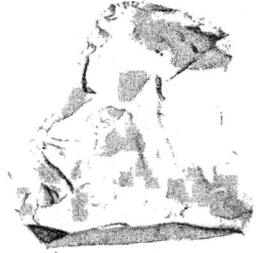

FIG. 1001.

Over the grave, for a breadth of 4 feet, and extending fully 12 feet to the south-east of it, were traces of burning. The old surface-soil, to a depth of 2 to 3 inches, was baked as hard as a brick, and upon this were wood ashes and burnt human bones scattered throughout the whole length. Over these was chalk rubble which had evidently been cast upon the fire, the heat having partially converted it into lime, producing a breccia which was very hard and difficult to excavate, resembling that in the neighbouring

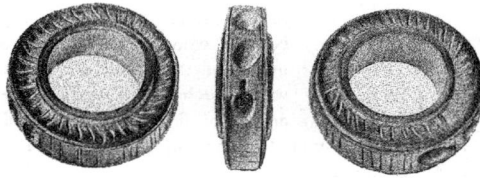

FIG. 1002.

long barrow "A." It had, apparently, been a crematorium for several bodies. From the mound we took a small, sharply-jagged slingstone of flint, a broad flake knife, and a pounding-stone of quartzite about the size of a large apple.

ROMAN HYPOCAUST AT DRIFFIELD.*

A remarkable underground structure was discovered 2½ miles east of the last barrow, on elevated ground, about 1 mile south-west of the village of Langtoft, and 7 miles north of Driffield.

On November 15th, 1875, Mr. Wilson, of Langtoft-field, while making stake-holders for a sheep-fold, found that his gavelock suddenly sank into the ground. This very unusual occurrence induced him to dig, and, at a depth of about 18

* See the Journal of the Anthropological Institute, February, 1878.

inches, he came upon some flat chalkstones forming the roof of a hollow trench. The trench was neatly walled in with two parallel walls of chalk, built without any mortar or cement, about 13 inches apart, 5 feet in length, and 2 feet in height (fig. 1003).*

It contained nothing but 1 or 2 inches of dark sooty matter on the bottom, in which were a few small pieces of burnt wood. Two days later, Mr. Wilson made the discovery known to me, and I at once visited the place. It is situated on the northern brow of an elevated chalk range running nearly east and west.

I observed that, for a short distance, a similar branch, running north at right angles to the original opening, had not been explored. After personally examining this passage, which was also roofed with slabs of chalk, and contained a stratum of dark matter at the bottom, I found that, after a distance of about 5 feet, it entered a somewhat circular cavity, excavated 4 feet in the chalk rock, about 3 inches lower than the passage.

The cavity measured 3 feet in diameter at the bottom, and 5 feet at the top; its sloping sides were formed by the rock, and there was no trace of any covering stones, as in the passages. On the bottom was an accumulation of the dark substance already mentioned, fully 6 inches thick, containing portions of carbonised wood, a small piece of iron, and fragments of three Roman vases, some of which were much flaked and splintered as if by the action of fire. The remainder of the cavity was filled with rubbly chalk, mixed with soil, in some places showing traces of burning, containing portions of burnt animal bones.

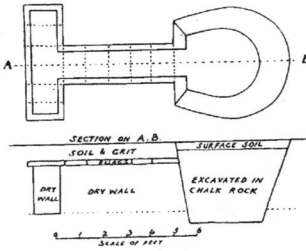

FIG. 1003.

PLAN AND SECTION OF HYPOCAUST.

The walls of the passages of the structure showed evidence of the action of fire. The surface soil, of gritty texture, 18 inches in depth, contained potsherds of a bluish colour, and unburnt animal bones, amongst which were recognised teeth of a pig, sheep or goat, and portions of the horn-core of an ox.

The following day the walls, which averaged 12 inches in thickness, were pulled down, and it was found that the heat had been sufficiently intense in certain places to pass through the wall and redden the packing of soil behind.

A similar structure to this was discovered, in the summer of 1874, on one of Lord Hotham's farms, at Etton, near Beverley, in the occupation of Mr. Whipp. The discovery was made known by Dr. Stephenson, of Beverley. It was visited at the time by the late Mr. C. Monkman, of Malton, and by him described, in the "Malton Messenger," as a "Bortontinus (?) formed of two parallel walls of chalk and sandstone, 11 feet in length, and about 2 feet high, the hollow space or trough being nearly 2 feet wide, and showing many traces of charcoal and burning. The roofing was of slabs of sandstone, bearing marks of fire. Mixed in the soil over and around it were a large quern or millstone, animal bones, and many fragments of pottery, seemingly of Roman date." These, the account

* A model of this is in the Museum, at Driffield.

goes on to say, "are deposited at Lord Hotham's mansion at South Dalton." Mr. Monkman adds, "this structure was discovered while ploughing, and the opening was unfortunately carried on through motives of curiosity alone, and its true form was not satisfactorily made out."

From Dr. Stephenson's account, however, and that of others who saw it when first discovered, I find that there were clear indications of a third arm running in a northerly direction, and ending in a dish-shaped excavation in the rock.

These descriptions show clearly that the Etton find was in every way similar to the one since discovered on Langtoft Wold, except in point of size, the Etton one being the larger. Whatever may have been the use of these structures, the fragments of pottery found in them seem to fix their date somewhere between the first and fifth centuries.

Most likely these rudely constructed underground flues were used as hypocausts for warming dwellings of the Romanised peasantry of the neighbourhood.*

BARROW No. 272

Or the " Beacon Hill " barrow is the site of " Ruston Parva Beacon." It is situated on elevated ground about half a mile to the north-west of Ruston Parva. On September 20th and 21st, 1886, it measured about 70 feet in diameter and 2 feet in elevation ; and had originally been several feet higher, as an old inhabitant remembered assisting in removing its upper portion, which was carted away and spread on the surrounding land many years previously. At the base of the barrow, near the centre, was a long heap of cremated bones, which had been interred in a hollow log of wood with rounded ends, about 3 feet in length and 14 inches in width, well shown by impressions in the plastic soil, and by the remains of the decayed wood. The heap of bones was rather large and probably consisted of the remains of more than one body. No relic accompanied them. Several splinters and flakes of flint were picked from the mound.†

Adjoining is the grave of Richard Laybourne, who died on the 29th of October, 1820, aged 77 years, and was buried on the 1st of November, 1820.

Captain G. Hebblethwaite Boynton, was buried in a paddock near Haisthorpe Lodge, Haisthorpe, in the spring of 1888. Afterwards, on December 4th, 1895, his body was exhumed and re-interred in Bridlington cemetery.

I believe these are the last instances in East Yorkshire of a survival of the very ancient custom of a person being buried in his own inheritance.

At Nafferton, nearly 2 miles to the south of barrow No. 272, many urns and

---

* Since the above discovery, the late General Pitt-Rivers, whilst excavating a Romano-British village at Woodcuts, in Dorset, from 1888 to 1891, found several similar structures, which he unhesitatingly named hypocausts.

† In the adjoining field, to the west of this barrow, is the grave of Richard Laybourne, covered by a small clump of trees, now fenced round with iron rails. Laybourne was a landed proprietor at Nafferton, who preferred to sleep peacefully on his own land in his own fields. In his will, dated 15th July, 1819, he gives the following directions respecting his desire to be buried in his field :—" I direct that my body may be decently interred in a grave to be dug 8 feet deep in a field belonging to me, called " Windersome," in the township of Nafferton, and such grave to be 20 or 30 yards southwards of George Purdon's gate in th. said field, and it is my wish that so much of the Burial Service of the Church of England as the circumstances will admit may be performed at my funeral, my direction in this behalf being solely on account of the little regard which is paid to the ashes of those who are interred in the customary places of burial, and not on account of any want of attachment to the doctrine and discipline of the Reformed Church of England, by law established, of which I profess myself a sincere member."

other Anglo-Saxon relics were found by Mr. Longbottom when excavating clay in the brick-yard between the Church and the Pottery, during 1850 to 1855. They were disposed of and no trace of them remains.

Also about 2 miles northward of the Beacon, shown on the Ordnance survey close to the south-east side of the village of Kilham, several Anglo-Saxon urns and other relics were from time to time discovered in a chalk pit during the first quarter of the last century. In the York Museum is a portion of this find, consisting of several fibulæ, both cruciform and circular, beads, clasps, buckles, armlets and other articles, evidently from an extensive Anglo-Saxon graveyard, a portion of which may remain undisturbed.

The following communication, made by the late Thomas Cape, of Bridlington, to Mr. John Cole, of Scarborough, may have reference to this cemetery :—

DISCOVERY OF ANTIQUITIES AT KILHAM IN 1824.

From the *Scarborough Repository* for 1824.

" A party of us lately met at Kilham, and had a grand field day of it. We commenced operations in a field called " Tuft-hill," where some fragments of urns, part of a quern, &c., had been found not long ago. A trench, recently opened, showed us distinctly where the remains were laid. We found the original earth of a light sandy nature, but alternately crossed by veins of a rich black soil. In the latter we discovered many pieces of urns, fragments of half burnt bones, part of another quern, &c., but could not succeed in procuring a whole urn. In many instances the urns were placed on an irregular pavement of white stones with a covering of the same materials. The place appears to have been a cemetery. We next went to a sand pit, where we had formerly been successful, and after a little digging, discovered a human skeleton, about 3½ feet below the surface, with the skull to the north-west and the legs crossed. Near the lower part of the body was a brass [bronze ?] buckle, with a plate or loop, apparently for the purpose of being rivetted to a strap or girdle ; and within a few inches of the same place, an iron ring, much corroded. Close by the breast was a fine piece of neatly-worked brass about 5 inches in length and varying in breadth from 1 to 3 inches, with a kind of hook or catch on the nether-side. Near the upper part of the right arm we found a pair of brass clasps and another pair on the wrist of the same arm. About the neck and shoulders we picked up several beads of glass and amber of various sizes. All the brass was in excellent preservation. The person when living had been of a moderate size."

BARROW No. 280

Is situated about 200 yards to the south of Marton Hall.

On May 29th and 30th, 1893, I conducted the opening of this mound, by an invitation from Ralph Creyke, Esq., the owner, for the inspection of the members of the East Riding Antiquarian Society. It measured 45 feet in diameter and 2½ feet in elevation, and it had probably been several feet higher. It mainly consisted of boulders mixed with a little soil.

About 8 feet south of the centre, near the base of the mound, were the much crushed and decayed remains of an adult with the head to the north. About 9 feet north of the centre were a few decayed bones of a second adult interment, the position of which could not be made out. In the centre between the two interments was an oval grave (fig. 1004). It measured 11 feet east and west by 8 feet at the top, and 7½ feet by 4 feet at the bottom; the depth beneath the mound being 4 feet. Over the top of the grave were two finely-chipped flint knives, each about 2½ inches

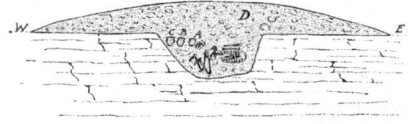

FIG. 1004.—SECTION OF BARROW NO. 280.

long, and over one hundred chips and worked flints were found in the mound. In the western end of the grave, at a depth of 16 inches, was a heap of burnt

FIG. 1005.   ¼

FIG. 1006.   ¼

FIG. 1007.   ¼

bones of a child, among which were portions of a bone pin and a flint flake knife (fig. 1005), 2½ inches long, both much burnt. Accompanying these was a food-vase (fig. 1006) measuring 6 inches in height and 6 inches across the top; round the shoulders is a row of short gashes, and the sides are ornamented from top to bottom with long oblique incised lines, forming a reticulated pattern. At the west side of this vase was a second one (fig. 1007) near which was a flint knife (fig. 1008), about 2 inches long, showing no trace of fire. This elegant vase measures 6 inches in height, 7 inches across the top, 8 inches at the shoulders, and only 3 inches across the bottom. It has two grooves round its upper portion, the lower one containing four large perforated stops. Three lines of rope impressions encircle the inside of the lip, and externally, from the top of the lip downwards to the shoulders of the vase, are nine similarly impressed

FIG. 1008.   ¼

lines, while below these are two rows of oblique lines in herring-bone pattern, forming a belt about 2 inches in width all round. Lower still are three impressed lines similar to those inside the lip. All these impressions have been

2 X

given by a two-strand cord, about $\frac{1}{10}$ of an inch in thickness. At the west side of the second vase stood a third one (fig. 1009),* near to which was a worked flint. This vase is 5 inches in height and measures 6 inches across the top; two grooves pass externally round its upper portion, the lower one has four small projecting pieces of clay arranged at about equal distances round the vase. The whole exterior, as well as the inside of the lip, is covered with short gashes arranged

FIG. 1009.   ¼

in herring-bone pattern round the vase. Near to the central vase were small pieces of the decayed bones of a child, sticking to the sides of boulders, which had greatly crushed the vases.

It seemed that each vase had probably accompanied a child, one having been cremated, the other two inhumed, and all buried close to each other at about the same time. The inhumed ones had nearly disappeared.

A little distance from the vases were several small splinters of the leg bones of some large animal, which were in a remarkably sound condition. On the floor of the grave were the remains of a large male, about forty-five years of age, partly on its back and partly on the left side, with the head to the east, the knees pulled up to about a right angle with the trunk, the right arm doubled with the hand behind the head, and the left hand resting on the neck. The right femur measured 19 inches, indicatiag a person of about 6 feet in height, and was of strong make. No relic was found with this interment.

BARROW No. 281

Known by the name of "Hedon Howe," is situated about 1 mile to the west of the village of Langton on the Eddlethorpe Estate of Sir Tatton Sykes, who kindly defrayed the cost of the examination. It stands on elevated ground sloping to the north. The medium diameter is 50 feet, and its elevation above the surrounding ground is about 8 feet. In September, 1893, during seven delightful days of the most beautiful summer which England has experienced for many long years, I excavated almost the entire area of this barrow. The first difficulty was the uprooting of several old thorn trees and the roots of two large ash trees which, until about twelve years ago, grew on its summit. The mound was found to have been made up of slabs of Coral-Rag, of various sizes, and friable hazel-coloured soil (both obtained from the vicinity, the latter preponderating on the top and sides of the mound, whilst the former was predominant in the centre, and round the five cists to be presently described. Over and round the central cist, were two deposits consisting of several leg bones, vertebræ, and other bones of a young ox, mostly with their articulating surfaces in position, indicating that they had been buried with the flesh on them. Scattered in the mound were a

* All the relics from this barrow were given by Ralph Creyke, Esq., to the York Museum.

few flakes of flint and many pot sherds of a large round-bottomed dish-shaped vessel, with overturned lip, resembling fig. 248, of dark red clay. Some of the fragments are more burnt and blackened than others. This kind of British vessel seems to be the only one at all suitable for cooking purposes. There were also numerous detached bones of an ox, pig, red-deer, dog or fox, and probably of the badger. Besides these there were a few scattered burnt and unburnt human bones.

Towards the northern margin of the barrow was a stone cist, No. 1 on the plan (fig. 1010), measuring about 5 feet in length and 3 feet 6 inches in width internally. The covering stones were broken and the soil above had settled down and filled up the cist, but a careful removal of this exposed the disturbed bones of an adult of middle age lying on the flagged floor. The calvarium was in the

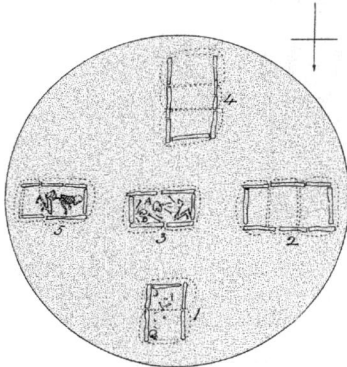

FIG. 1010.— PLAN OF BARROW 281.   FIG. 1011.   ½

northern corner of the grave, whilst the leg, arm and other bones occurred mixed up at the east end of the grave, near to which was a leaf-shaped arrow head of flint (fig. 1011) minus the point.

On the floor of the cist, also, were the skulls and other remains of two foxes and one badger. As one end of the cist had been removed, these animals may, at some early period, have found an entrance into the cist, and have occupied it, thus accounting for the displaced positions of the human bones.

The next cist, No. 2, on the ground plan, measured internally 9½ feet in length, 5 feet in width at the west end, and 4 feet at the east end. The covering stones had fallen in and only the lower half of the outer-end stone remained in position, the upper portion having been broken off and removed. Except two or three very small pieces of bone nothing was found in the cist.

Cist No. 3· was in the centre of the barrow, and measured 6 feet in length by 3 feet 3 inches in width. Near its southern side, but a little higher in the mound, was a food-vase, in fragments, which has since been rebuilt (fig. 1012), accompanying some cremated bones of an adult. At the west end, on the flagged bottom, was the flexed skeleton of an adult male, about 70 years of age, a little disturbed (A on figs. 1010 and 1013), placed on the right side, with the head to the west. At the east end of the grave were the displaced bones of a second individual (*B*) about 60 years of age, a female having a thin and pointed chin. There was also the greater part of the left arm-bone of a third skeleton, and a

FIG. 1012.   ¼

section of the right lower jaw with all the molar teeth, indicating the person to have been about 25 years of age. These remains are well shown in the accompanying photograph (fig. 1013), kindly taken at the time by Miss Walker, of

FIG. 1013.—INTERMENT IN CIST NO. 3 IN BARROW NO. 281.

Burythorpe. The femur of interment *B* measured 16½ inches; the femur and tibia of *A* measured 16 and 13 inches respectively. It is difficult to account for the great displacement of the bones of interment *B*, as in this case it seemed almost impossible for any burrowing animal to have entered the cist.

At the southern side of the mound, close above the northern end of cist No. 2, were the decayed bones of a small child, accompanied by a small and elegantly formed drinking-cup (fig. 1014). The covering stones of cist No. 4 had also broken and fallen in it. It measured 9 feet 4 inches in length, and varied from 4½ to 5 feet in width. No trace of any interment was found in it. A fifth cist was situated on the eastern side of the barrow, measuring 6 feet in length by 3 feet 6 inches in width. At the bottom was a skeleton of an individual about 30 years of age, on the left side, the legs drawn up, and the head in contact with the slab at the west end. The covering stone of the cist was broken into two pieces; the smaller one, which had slipped some distance inwards, had then fallen obliquely against the end of the cist and so protected the skull from the pressure of the material above. The larger portion of the cover-ing slab had settled down on the bottom of the grave in a horizontal position. On removing this stone, we found that it had flattened and crushed the trunk and limb bones of the skeleton below. No instrument or pot sherd was observed. A femur was the only bone we were able to measure, its length being about 18 inches.

The three other crania from this mound, which are, however, incomplete, are even more dolicocephalic, but of the same general type as that from the last cist.

The occurrence of five cists is of considerable interest. Their size, formation and arrangement are exceptional in character in East Yorkshire.† They are also of greater length than usual, the sides consisting of from two to four slabs, but in no instance had more than one stone been used to form the end. Each cist had been

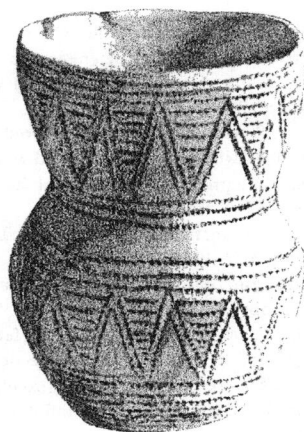

FIG. 1014.

covered with two or more stone slabs, all of which had fallen in. Judging from the side-stones, the height within the chambers had been from 3½ to 4½ feet. The slabs forming these cists were not large, none exceeding 5 feet by 4 feet, and not more than 3 to 5 inches in thickness. Their thinness and the somewhat brittle nature of the stone may probably account for the covers of all the cists having fallen in, having been unable to resist the pressure of the mound above.

The outer ends of all the cists, except the central one, having been placed near the outside of the barrow, had been removed or partly removed, probably by persons digging for foxes or rabbits.

---

† Cists arranged in the form of a cross are somewhat common in Ireland. Mr. E. Cornwall thus writes:—"The long passage and the tricameral arrangements round a central octagonal chamber gives in general outline the appearance of a cross, which shape, judging from the internal arrangement in most of the cairns on Sliabh na Caillight, as well as at New Grange and Dowth in the same county, appear to have been the favourite form adopted by our pagan ancestors in the construction of the tombs of their great people."—"Tomb of Ollamh Fodhla," page 32.

For a circle of cists, some of which are arranged in the form of a Manx cross, see "Manx Antiquities," pages 101 and 114.

As to the age of the cists, it was clear that they all had been made previous to the raising of the mound, by fixing the lower edges of the upright slabs 10 to 12 inches into the old surface. There was not the slightest indication of any cutting have been made in the barrow for the introduction of any of the cists. Moreover, the slight stratification of the material composing the barrow was unbroken above all the cists. It was also observed that outside each cist (especially round the centre one, so as to form a slight inner mound) stones of various sizes had been piled to keep the sides of the cists from falling outwards; this would not have been necessary had the four outer cists been later insertions in the barrow.

<h2 align="center">BARROW No. 284</h2>

Stands in a grass field, about 50 yards from the south side of the Gypsey Race, in the valley bottom, near the village of Wold Newton, about ¾ of a mile west of Willie Howe,* and about ½ a mile east of the place where the aerolite fell on December 13th, 1795.

The mound measures about 83 feet in diameter, and 12 feet in elevation. Its top had been much flattened and its circumference increased by rabbit diggers, &c., so that probably its original height would be from 15 to 18 feet, and its diameter not more than 75 feet.

By instructions from Sir Tatton Sykes, Bart., I employed, during the latter half of August, 1894, eight or nine labourers daily in excavating this barrow—the filling-in being done afterwards. Commencing a little within the eastern margin, an opening was cut westwards through the centre of the mound, measuring 60 feet east and west, and 30 feet across; and at short distances we probed the ground beneath as we proceeded. The barrow stood on the edge of a thin bed of peat, resting on chalk gravel, which had been formed by the periodic overflow of the Gypsey Stream, and the lower and greater portion of the mound consisted mainly of this peaty soil, as shown in the section (fig. 1015), with an occasional patch and streak of white gravel gathered from the surrounding ground, which increased in thickness from the barrow northwards to the stream. This peaty matter, it was observed, covered nearly the whole basal area of the mound to a thickness of 5 to 6 feet, in the form of a raised platform.

Its upper portion consisted of local white chalk gravel, streaked with patches of peaty soil. Seven feet south-east of the centre, at a depth of 6 feet, was a small heap of the cremated bones of a child (No. 1, fig. 1015); two unburnt pieces of a very thick adult skull were found, 14 inches north of this deposit, but no other remains.

About 18 feet south-south-east of the centre, and upon the ancient turf-line, were the remains of five skeletons (Nos. 2 to 6), close together, and much crushed. They represented three adults, one youth, and one child. One of the former (No. 2), was on the right side, with the knees drawn up, head to the north-west, the arms bent, with both hands under and near the chin. A femur and tibia measured 16 inches and 12 inches respectively, and seemed to belong to a young

* This barrow was opened by the late Lord Londesborough in 1857, and his Lordship believed it had been a twin barrow. It was re-opened by Canon Greenwell, in 1887, but in neither instance was any interment found.

female.* The positions of the others were not ascertained, excepting that their heads were in various directions; and that the skull of one had been smashed into many pieces, which had been placed some distance from each other, apparently at the time of interment. They belonged to a thick skull of an adult male, and were in much better preservation than any fragments of the other skulls which they accompanied. With these skeletons were the skull and a few other bones of a young pig.

No relic accompanied them, except two small pieces of a food-vase, but in the mound, immediately above them. were numerous bones of frogs and toads,† in heaps varying in size from an orange to a medium-sized melon.

About 9 feet east of the centre, and at a depth of 8 feet, was interment No. 7, on the right side, with the knees drawn up, the head to the west, the left arm bent with the elbow on the chest, and the hand near the chin. The right arm was stretched at full length, and the hand near the knees. The femur and tibia measured 17½ and 14½ inches respectively, and seemed to be those of a male. In this case a leaf-shaped arrow-head (fig. 1016), was on the pelvis, also, in

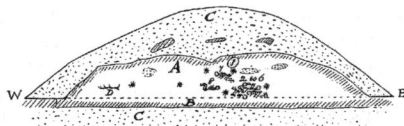

FIG. 1015.—SECTION OF BARROW NO. 284.
1—Cremated Interment.   A—Peat soil.
B—Peat surface under the Barrow.   C—Fine chalk gravel.
D—Antler of red deer.   *—Nests of bones of frogs, &c.

FIG. 1016.   ⅓

several places, a little above the body, were innumerable bones of frogs and toads, in heaps similar to those observed over interments Nos. 2 to 6.

A little east of the centre, at a depth of about 9 feet from the top, and 3 feet from the base of the mound, were the remains of interment No. 8, on the right side with knees pulled up, the head pointing east-south-east, both arms were bent, with hands near and under the head. The femur, tibia and humerus measured 15½, 12, and 10¾ inches respectively, and seemed to be those of a female of middle age. Like all the other interments, there were many bones of frogs and toads in the mound above it, but there were none in close proximity to any of the skeletons.

During the excavation we collected one sandstone pounder, one large sling-stone of flint with many sharp edges, sixty-three hand-struck splinters of flint, and three pieces of a thick, well-baked, cinerary urn, the clay having been freely mixed with pounded flint. Nearly 28 feet west of the centre, at a depth of 5 feet, was a large and nearly complete left antler of a red deer. It evidently belonged to a slaughtered animal, as a portion of the skull was attached to it. Near the antler, as well as in several other places, more heaps of the bones of frogs and toads were found. In the mound, at all depths, were many fragments of broken

* This skull is preserved, and is considerably prognathous.   † Determined by Mr. E. T. Newton, F.R.S.

bones of the following animals, determined by Mr. E. T. Newton, F.R.S., of the Jermyn Street Museum.—

BONES FROM BARROW NO. 284.

Man	...	...	Irish Elk ...	... *Cervus giganteus*
Ox ...	...	... *Bos taurus*	Water Vole	... *Microtus amphibius*
Pig ...	...	... *Sus scrofa*	Sheep and Goat, uncertain	
Roe-deer ...	... *Capreolus caprea*	Black Grouse	.. *Tetrao tetrix*
Dog and Wolf	... *Canis*	Bird (tibia)	...
Horse	...	... *Equus caballus*		

Twenty-five to thirty feet south and west of the centre were four shallow trough-shaped hollows, measuring about 6 feet in length, 15 to 18 inches in width at the top, and scooped about 10 inches into the white chalk gravel under the barrow. They were from 3 to 4 feet apart in a slightly curved line. These hollows were filled with peaty soil only, not the slightest trace of bone or anything could be found.

It seems strange that after the most careful search in the clean, white, gravelly subsoil no primary grave or central interment was discovered. The interments numbered 7 and 8, were deposited after the barrow had been raised 3 to 4 feet above the base; whereas those numbered 2 to 6, on the old surface line, seemed too far from the centre to have been those for which this large mound was raised.

It is very unusual to find so large a mound raised on such low, wet ground, as this spot must then have been.

In referring to the section (fig. 1015), it will be observed that the nests of small bones are almost confined to the neighbourhood of the interments, and entirely to the peaty portion forming the lower half of the barrow. About a pint of these bones was sent to Mr. E. T. Newton, who kindly examined them. He determined them to be mainly those of frogs and toads, with a few of the water vole, field vole and field mouse. As these nests of bones must have represented several hundreds of these animals, how came they there? Either they were gathered and deposited in the neighbourhood of the interments, or the animals may have crawled into holes made by rats or other burrowing animals in the peat. The skulls of the animals were rarely present.

ROMAN COINS.

On May 12th, 1897, a hoard, consisting of one silver and sixteen bronze Roman coins, with two pieces of bronze, probably portions of the handle of a box or leather bag, were found in deepening a drain on "Copper Hall" farm, Skerne, three miles south-east of Driffield. The drain was originally cut about the year 1835; and from its appearance whilst deepening it in 1897, it is probable that the greater portion of this hoard had been removed when the drain was first cut, leaving only a portion of the broken handle and the coins found in 1897. ·

As the farmhouse close by was built about the time the drain was originally cut, it is probable that its name "Copper Hall," originated from a find of coins. The late Lord Londesborough obtained the seventeen coins last found.

PART II.

ANGLO-SAXON REMAINS, BRITISH
EARTHWORKS, &c.

ANGLO-SAXON REMAINS AT LONDESBOROUGH.

On Londesborough Wold, near the summit of the hill, about three-quarters of a mile north of the village of Londesborough, is a chalk pit. In quarrying here at various times from 1870 to 1895, the workmen have met with many Anglo-Saxon graves, apparently containing inhumed interments only. These were in several instances accompanied by glass and amber beads, bronze fibulæ, bronze and iron buckles and iron knives, as well as earthenware vessels. All of these, however, have been dispersed, and now their whereabouts is uncertain.

On May 27th, 1895, the members of the East Riding Antiquarian Society visited Nunburnholme and Londesborough. To add to the interest of this visit Mr. Chowen, the estate agent, employed two labourers to excavate near the margin of the chalk pit, where bodies had been previously found. A skeleton was discovered

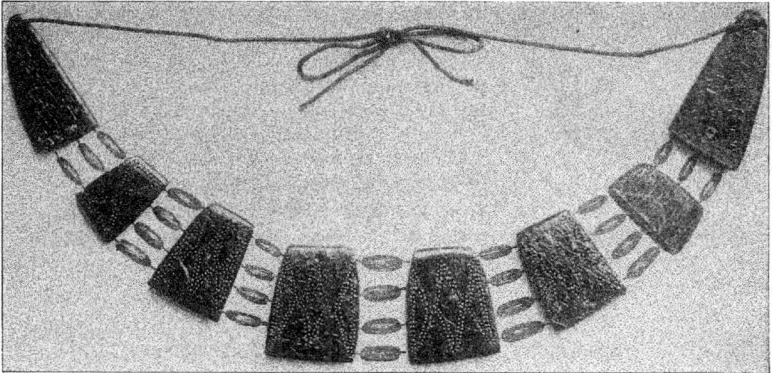

FIG. 1017.—IDEAL RESTORATION OF JET NECKLACE.

at a depth of about 2 feet, on uncovering which two bronze clasps were found at the loins. Behind the skull stood a plain semi-globular earthenware vessel of dark colour. On the breast was a fine cruciform fibula of bronze, face upwards; and a little below this were two more small bronze clasps, which had doubtless secured some part of the dress. The body was partly on its back, and left side, with the knees slightly pulled up, the head to the east, and probably was that of a female. The relics were taken to the Rev. Canon Wilton, at the Londesborough Rectory.

BRITISH REMAINS AT MIDDLETON.

Whilst a workman was digging for sand, in October, 1901, at Middleton-on-the-Wolds, in Mr. T. Broadley Soanes' garden, he struck a human skull. This was at a depth of 3 feet. The remainder of the skeleton was afterwards discovered, and had apparently been buried in a doubled-up position. With the skeleton were seven large flat pieces of jet, evidently part of a necklace, a restoration of which is given in fig. 1017. One of the broad pieces and all the smaller beads

2 Y

shown in the illustration were not found, having probably been overlooked by the workmen. I obtained the specimens from Mr. Soanes.

About six or eight years previously, a British drinking-cup, now at Middleton Hall, was found in a sand pit, owned by Col. A. Brooksbank, situated a short distance eastwards. Through the kindness of Col. Brooksbank, I am able to give an illustration of this, see fig. 1018. It is an uninjured specimen of one of the best types, and measures 7 inches high, 4½ across the top, 5 inches across the middle, and 3 inches at the bottom. As far as can be ascertained nothing was found with it, but it is probable that the labourers removed an interment without noting it.

On August 26th, 1902, the Rev. H. D. Blanchard, the vicar, informed me that Mr. Soanes had found another skeleton close by the spot where the jet necklace was found. On my arrival at Middleton the following morning, I found that a workman had destroyed half a skull and the greater part of a drinking-cup, before he was aware of the find. The other portions of the skeleton and the remainder of the cup I uncovered and secured. This interment had been that of a youth from ten to twelve years of age, placed on his right side, the knees drawn up, and the head to the south. The drinking-cup, which has been rather a large one and well ornamented, had been placed close behind the skull.

FIG. 1018.   ¾

ROMAN (?) REMAINS AT NORTH GRIMSTON.

On June 16th, 1902, one of Lord Middleton's labourers named Binge, while planting posts for a fence on the south side of the most easterly of three old chalk pits, which run in a line east and west along the chalk escarpment, came upon human bones, two iron swords, bronze and iron rings, fragments of other bronze and iron articles, and portions of a jet ring.

The place referred to is about a quarter of a mile due north of the farmhouse named Luddith House, on North Grimston Brow. Fortunately these specimens were soon afterwards procured and taken charge of by Mr. Parsons, his lordship's agent, through whose kindness I have had the privilege of inspecting them. Afterwards, Mr. Fraser, the forester, accompanied by Binge, and equipped with a pick and spade, conducted me to the site of the find.

The post-hole was small, and could not possibly have exhausted the contents of the grave which it had entered. The sods were therefore removed from an area which it was supposed would include the grave, which was found to be only 16 inches in depth. On the bottom there still remained the greater portion of a human skeleton in an advanced state of decay. Many of the ribs and other small bones had entirely disappeared. The interment had been placed at full length, on its back, with the head to the south, the face being pressed to the right side.

Along the left side, from the hips to the feet, were several leg bones of a pig, and a skull of the same animal, apparently indicating that an entire animal had been interred.*

We also took from the grave a piece of a jet article, three rings, and several small pieces of iron, which had been broken when the swords were removed. Several of these fragments appear to be portions of the iron scabbards of the two weapons; but the use of the rings and other pieces of metal is uncertain. There were also portions of the longitudinal half of a thin bronze tube, which, judging from the presence of a bronze rivet about an inch long in the ends of two of the pieces, seem to have been fixed to the rounded edge of a piece of wood.† Besides these, the labourer had, in the first instance, picked up similar pieces; and he had also removed all the bones of the right leg.

The blade of the sword is about 30½ inches in length, with a medium breadth of about 1¾ inches. It has a double edge, and, as far as can be made out from the lower end of the scabbard, is pointed. The part of the handle which remains is 3½ inches in length, the pommel having been broken off and lost. There is

FIG. 1019.

no trace of a crossbar to serve as a hand-guard. The blade of the short sword is 20 inches long from pommel to point, and the width of the blade (except at the point) is about 1¾ inches, with a ridge down the centre.

Its bronze handle, which is 4½ inches in extreme length, is a beautiful piece of work, the pommel being in the form of a human head and shoulders, with uplifted arms, while representations of legs form the guard and the lower end of the handle, the grip representing the body. These articles are shown in the accompanying figures (1019 and 1019a). The rings and other pieces of iron, as well as the rings and half tubes of bronze, suggest the equipment of an equestrian, supplied with two swords.

The scabbards have been of iron, judging from the preserved fragments previously mentioned. The pieces of jet are portions of a ring 2 inches in diameter. A ring of red amber more than 1½ inches in diameter, similar in shape to the one of jet which had been interred with this body, was found with an interment in a grave under a small mound on Arras, near Market Weighton, by the Rev. E. W. Stillingfleet, in 1817. ‡ Mr. Daniel Wilson, in "Prehistoric Annals of Scotland,"

---

* This is not the only instance of the burial of a pig with human remains. I have found it accompanying the interments of the ancient Britons, the Romano-Britons, and the Anglo-Saxons. Such practices at one time appear to have been universal.

† These pieces appear to have formed a half tube of bronze, resembling two half tubes of bronze found with a sword, the bronze facing of a shield, and other articles, accompanying a doubled-up body in a grave at Grimthorpe, near Pocklington in 1870, and now in the British Museum.

‡ See "Crania Britannica."

p. 302, writes, "When found with the spear and sword, the ring (mainly referring to jet and amber)* may indicate the grave of the warrior, priest, or lawgiver."

As such relics are our only record of this early period, it is very desirable that they should be recorded, and preserved in safe keeping. All the decayed fragments of the skull procurable have, as far as possible, been put together (fig. 1020); and Dr. Wright, of the Birmingham University, has kindly supplied the accompanying photograph and the following description:—

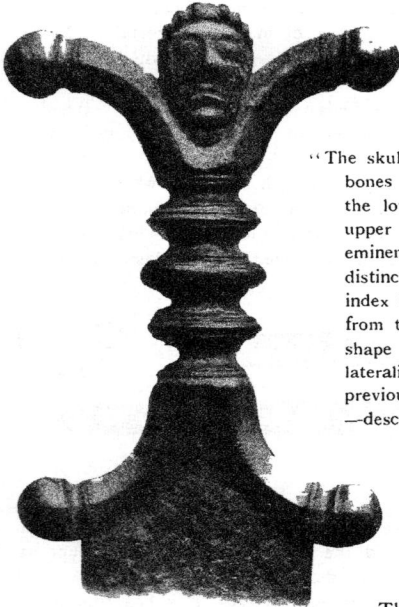

"The skull is fragmentary; the basicranial and facial bones have all disappeared with the exception of the lower jaw and the alveolar portions of the upper jaws. The calvarium is long, the parietal eminences tolerably well marked, and there is a distinct bulge of the occipital squame. The cephalic index is approximately seventy-three. As viewed from the norma verticalis, the calvarium has the shape of a long pentagon. From the norma lateralis the contour—with the exception of the previously-mentioned bulge of the occipital squame —describes a uniform curve of a medium height. The lower jaw is massive; the angle of the jaw is "square"; the chin is well marked. The teeth have been all present at death, and are considerably worn. The skull is that of a male, of forty to fifty years of age."

FIG. 1019 a.

The preceding description gives no clue to the period to which this interment belongs, as this type of skull is represented in my collection of ancient British skulls, both of the bronze age and the early iron age; also in the Romano-British and the Anglo-Saxon skulls. We have, therefore, to rely almost entirely on the mode of interment and the articles found. Mr. C. H. Read, of the British Museum, who has examined the two swords, and an iron spear-head, which was found about thirty years before, near the same place, writes, on June 29th, 1903 :—

"I safely received the spear-head. It is in a good state, and, although there is no clear evidence, apparently it may well belong to the two swords that I still have here. I should think that you might, roughly, put the swords and spear as at the beginning of the Christian era."

According to this, the interment may be either of the Romano-British period, or of the early iron age. I am somewhat inclined to the former, in view of the ornamentation of the sword hilt, and the fact that the body had been placed in

* I possess several similarly-shaped rings of stone.

the grave at full length. I know of no instance in East Yorkshire of an interment of the early iron age in which the body is other than much flexed. Some support may be given to this view by the fact that the remains of two detached Roman villas* have been discovered 1 mile and 1½ miles respectively north of this interment. On the other hand, the pieces of the bronze tubes have been apparently almost

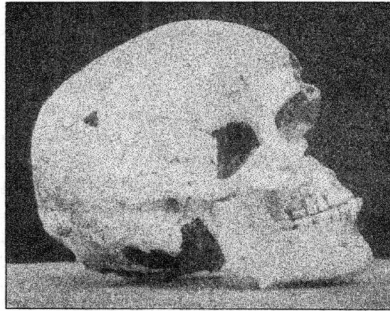

FIG. 1020.

identical in form and size, as the two half tubes found in connection with an iron sword, the bronze facings of a circular shield, and other articles that accompanied a doubled-up body in a grave at Grimthorpe, which almost certainly belonged to the early iron age.†

It is very desirable that the uncertainty as to the age of this very interesting discovery should, as far as possible, be removed by excavating in the immediate neighbourhood, under proper supervision, for further remains.

* See " Transactions of the East Riding Antiquarian Society," vol. x., p. 74.
† See the " Reliquary," for 1869, vol. ix., p. 180.

BRITISH CHARIOTS FOUND IN BARROWS,

CHIEFLY IN EAST YORKSHIRE.

NOT until towards the close of my work amongst the barrows, viz., in 1887, had I the good fortune to find any remains of a British chariot, although such had been found on the Wolds. The first two discoveries of this kind of which I have any knowledge were made by the late Rev. E. W. Stillingfleet, Vicar of South Cave, during the years 1816-17.* One of these was at Hessleskew, and the other at Arras, both places being about three miles east of Market Weighton, and both were with inhumed interments. One chariot was accompanied with the bronze boss and iron rim of a shield,† and with the other were the skulls of two boars and the bones of two small horses. Both chariots were accompanied by rings, buckles, and two snaffle-bits, belonging to the horses' bridles—one of iron, the other of iron coated with bronze. Portions of some of these objects are in the York Museum; the others are, as far as I know, lost. The wheels from the Hessleskew barrow measured rather more than 2 feet 11 inches in diameter; and the diameter of the iron hoops covered with copper, which had encircled the naves, was very nearly 6 inches. The wheels from the Arras barrow were only about 2 feet 8 inches in diameter, and the iron hoops of the naves were about 5 inches in diameter.

On December 15th, 1879, the guard to a North Eastern Railway ballast train informed me that he was present at the finding of the large shap granite boulder in the ballast pit of Seamer Station, near Scarborough, which is now set up in the station-master's garden at Seamer. It was found at about half the depth of the face of the pit, and about one-third the distance from the Scarborough end of the pit. He also said he was present when the remains of what he called a small horse and cart were found in the pit, about the year 1862. On being questioned, he stated that the horse and cart were found in a quantity of dark soily matter, which, as far as he could remember, filled a hole 4 to 5 feet in depth, that had been dug into the clean gravelly material forming the upper part of the pit. He added that one of the workmen made his long smock-frock into a sack by tying up the neck, in which he carried away the bones and bits of iron, and afterwards sold them. The hoops of the wheels were broken and much rusted, and all the wood had disappeared.

This appears to be a discovery worthy of being recorded, as it seems to have been nothing less than a British interment, consisting of the remains of a chariot, with the bones of the horse and probably those of the charioteer, which would not be recognised by the workmen.

In 1875 a fourth discovery was made by two labourers digging for chalk at Arras. A very small barrow was then encroached upon, under which a grave had been sunk into the chalk rock. It was circular, 12 feet in diameter, and 3 feet deep.‡ At the bottom was a skeleton, accompanied by the remains of a

---

* See "Account of the opening of some barrows on the Wolds of Yorkshire," by the Rev. E. W. Stillingfleet, B.D., in the Proceedings of the Archæological Institute at York, in 1846, p. 26.

† I do not know that these have been figured, or that they are now in existence.

‡ "British Barrows," by Canon Greenwell, p. 454.

chariot. The iron hoops of the wheels measured about 3 feet in diameter. The hoops of the naves were of bronze, or were plated with bronze. Accompanying these were two bridle-bits of bronze, or plated with bronze; and a circular mirror of iron, 8 to 9 inches in diameter, the handle of which is slightly ornamented with bronze.[*]

A mirror of iron was found with the chariots discovered by the late Rev. E. W. Stillingfleet in one of the barrows on Arras, which he opened in 1816.[†]

The fifth discovery was made by Canon Greenwell in a barrow on Westwood, Beverley, in 1875,[‡] and consisted of the hoops of two chariot wheels, about 3 feet in diameter, and what was almost certainly an iron bit or bits.[§]

Still later, the remains of a chariot were found in No. 13 of the "Danes' Graves," which I excavated during the first fortnight in July, 1897. These (fig. 1021) consisted of the iron hoops of the wheels and naves, and rings of bronze and iron belonging to the chariot and the trappings of the horses. In the grave with these were two adult skeletons, probably the remains of the owner of the chariot and his charioteer.

This appears to be the sixth instance of the discovery of remains of a British chariot in East Yorkshire. Reference should be made to two more, though they are somewhat doubtful finds.

FIG. 1021.—PLAN OF CHARIOT BURIAL IN GRAVE.
C— Outline of Grave.
D—Outline of Mound.

At the commencement of my barrow digging one of the labourers (John Gilbank, of Wetwang) told me that when a boy he was engaged by Mr. R. Holtby, of Haywold, near Huggate, as a yearly servant, and that he remembered assisting to cart away some howes (barrows) and spread them on the land. In doing this the iron tyres of two small wheels and many bones were found in one of them, all of which were carted away with the soil.

The other probable find was in 1888, during the construction of the Driffield

<hr>

[*] In the British Museum there is a similar mirror, but of bronze, 8 to 9 inches in diameter, which was found in the Parish of Keverne, Cornwall, in 1833. There are also some almost identical circular-shaped bronze mirrors, 7 to 8 inches in diameter, from the Egyptian and Assyrian tombs.

[†] "British Barrows," foot-note, p. 455.   [‡] "British Barrows," p. 456.

[§] The two last finds are now in the British Museum.

and Market Weighton Railway, in a deep cutting in the chalk between Middleton and Enthorpe stations. One of the navvies—a Driffield man—told me that on undermining the side of the cutting and letting down a mass of rock into the ballast waggon, a quantity of bones and rusted iron were observed, mixed with the stones and soil, which they tipped over the end of the embankment. No further notice was taken of them, except that he put two or three pieces in his pockets. He gave me the pin, or bolt (fig. 1022), but had lost the others. It is $5\frac{1}{2}$ inches long; the middle portion is of iron, $3\frac{1}{4}$ inches long and half-an-inch square, to

FIG. 1022.

which are fixed two ends of solid bronze, one being in the form of a flattened ring. Its greatest diameter is $1\frac{1}{2}$ inches, and the hole through it is sufficiently large to admit the end of one's little finger. About half-an-inch below this aperture, but diagonally opposite to it, is a second perforation, nearly a quarter of an inch wide. The edge of the ring is ornamented with zigzag ridges within sunken furrows. The other end of the pin resembles the head of a horse or dog. At each end of the pin one side is considerably worn, the other being only slightly worn. This article seems to be similar to two articles called "lynch-pins" from the so-called "King's barrow" on Arras, figured in "Crania Britannica," and thought to be connected with the yoke for the horses. It is also similar to one found on the estate of the Duke of Northumberland at Stanwick, and figured in the Journal of the Archæological Institute for 1866, vol. xxxi., plate 4, fig. 2. It is described to be an iron pin mounted at both extremities with bronze, supposed to have been attached to some part of a chariot. Length, $6\frac{3}{8}$ inches; diameter of ring, 1 inch.

The tyres of two chariot wheels were sold at Mr. Bernard Clarkson's sale, at the White Horse Inn, in Coppergate, York, in March, 1832.* In the catalogue one is described as having been taken from a British tumulus near Market Weighton, and is marked in pencil in the margin of the catalogue as having been sold for 2s. This wheel probably belonged to one of the chariots found on Arras by the late Rev. E. W. Stillingfleet, as I believe Mr. Clarkson joined in the excavations and obtained a portion of the objects discovered there. The other is described as a chariot wheel found at Kirkham,† but nothing more is known of this find, and there is now, I believe, no trace of the whereabouts of any remains of these two wheels.

* I possess a catalogue of this sale.
† Mr. Clarkson resided at Kirkham Abbey in 1829, according to a list of subscribers in Oliver's "History of Beverley."

In the North Riding the late Thomas Kendal, of Pickering, about the year 1849, found the remains of a British chariot, in a barrow close to the Cawthorne Camps, north of Pickering, the wheels and other parts of which are now in the possession of Thomas Mitchelson, Esq., of Pickering. I well remember Mr. Kendal naming this find to me many years ago, and he much regretted that he was not able to sketch, so as to give the shape and position of the chariot. He described the mound as being mainly composed of light-coloured sand, and said that the position, and, in the main, the form of the chariot was clearly visible. The tyres of the wheels were well preserved, whilst the pole (which had measured about 7 feet) and other woodwork was shown by dark lines of decayed wood, clearly defined in the clean light-coloured sand. It is much to be regretted that so good an opportunity of obtaining a restoration of the chariot was lost.

On April 2nd, 1894, I interviewed Mr. Thomas Dowson, of Pickering, who was Kendal's foreman in all his barrow-digging. Though he was about seventy-eight years of age he retained a vivid recollection of the barrow openings at which he had assisted. He fully confirmed what Kendal had told me about the chariot, and added that the mound is situated very near the south-eastern corner of the most easterly of the three Cawthorne Camps, and that at the time its height would be a little over 3 feet. One of the chariot wheels was pressed down nearly flat, and the decayed wood of the spokes, which numbered only four, was shown very clearly. The other wheel stood upright, and nearly reached to the top of the barrow. The diameter of these wheels, judging from the tyre now preserved, was about 3 feet; and from preserved portions of the tyre of the naves they seem to have been hooped with iron plated with thin bronze. Mr. Dowson said the pole reached eastwards about 7 feet from the body of the chariot, and at the terminal end were decayed hooks and rings of iron and brass (bronze).

In reply to further inquiry, he said there were no human or animal bones, or any other article, with the chariot, which seemed to have been placed on the old surface line under the barrow. Unless the interment was a cremated one, simply placed in a heap at the base of the barrow, and not observed by Mr. Kendal, I am inclined to think that the owner of the chariot may have been buried in a grave somewhere under the mound, and that after his body was covered up the chariot was placed upon or near the grave, and then covered with the mound. If so, the grave yet remains unexplored, and the mound should, if possible, be traced and carefully reopened.

This chariot is the only one I know of as having been found in the North Riding of Yorkshire. It is, however, highly probable that in both Ridings others have been accidentally unearthed by persons who were ignorant of the nature of the finds.

Chariots have been found in various districts throughout England,[*] Scotland,[†] and Ireland; but in no district of the same area have a greater number of them been found than in the barrows of the East Riding of Yorkshire. They have

---

[*] Fragments of a chariot were found at Hampton Hill, by Sir R Colt Hoare. —*Archæologia*, vol. xxi.

[†] Another chariot was found in a barrow at Ballindalloch, in Moray (Wilson, " Archæology of Scotland," p. 456). Another in Aberdeenshire, and one at Inverary—the latter with four large jet knobs with iron pins Thurnam's " Round Barrows," *Archæologia*, vol. xliii.).

been found also throughout Europe,* and three hundred years before Christ chariots were extensively used by the Gauls.

In every instance the remains are those of the two-wheeled war chariot, which probably was drawn by two horses, and which I believe is the only kind that has ever been found in connection with an interment.

At what period the chariot was first introduced into the British Isles, and whether by the Phœnicians, Gauls, or other nation, may probably never be ascertained. That it must have been at a period long previous to Cæsar's invasion is evident from the great numbers which were then brought together to oppose him, and from their remains having been found in tumuli so widely scattered throughout the country.

The chariot, according to the Greek historians, was invented by the goddess Minerva. The war chariot had only two wheels, which revolved upon an axle, as in the modern carriage. The pole was fixed at the lower extremity to the axle, and at the other end was attached the yoke, either by a pin or by a rope. It was generally drawn by two horses. The oldest war chariots of which we read are those of Pharaoh (Exodus, xiv., 7). All the Eastern nations used them at a very early period.†

The following is an abridged account from " Crania Britannica," pp. 96 and 99, by Dr. Thurnam :—

> " Diodorus tells us that the Britons, preserving primitive modes of life in their
> wars, used chariots, as the ancient Greeks did in the Trojan war. This
> Northern war-chariot is named " Essedum " by Cæsar, and " Covinus "
> by Mela and Tacitus. Each chariot carried two men, a driver and a
> chariot-soldier. The charioteer had, by practice, such command of the
> horses that he could, even when on hilly ground, run along the pole, raise
> himself on the yoke, and retreat with the greatest speed into the body of
> the car, which he drove with extraordinary swiftness and skill. The war-
> chariots formed an important division of the British armies, and were
> brought into battle in great numbers—as by Cassivelaunus against Julius
> (54 B.C.) and in subsequent engagements, up to as late as the wars of the
> Caledonian Britons with Severus. Cæsar refers to the 4,000 essedarii of
> Cassivelaunus, all which remained to him, as a small number."‡

By Dion it is implied that the chariots were of small size, when he refers to them as drawn by small swift horses. Mela says that the axles were armed with scythes, but Dr. Thurnam justly remarks that no traces of such an appendage have been found with those remains of chariots which have been exhumed. The body of the chariot was probably open, or but slightly enclosed, both in front and behind, so as to allow free ingress and egress. At the sides, however, the antyx seems to have been sufficiently elevated to protect the

---

* From France, M. Gustave Chauvet announces the discovery in a tumulus known as the " Gros
Guegnou," on the right bank of the Charente, of a bronze chariot, curiously ornamented, and similar to those
which have been found in Scandinavia and Micklenburgh. The body was in a vaulted recess, and on either
side were wheels, with detached circular and spherical ornaments, bronze and iron nails, and two Gallic urns.
The discovery of another chariot is reported from Septaux (Marne). The skeleton of a boar, with a knife
embedded between the ribs, was found in front of the right wheel. The weapons, horse-bits, and rings enclosed
in the tumulus appear to indicate their Gallic origin.—*The Antiquary*, No. 63, vol. vi.

† " Chambers' Encyclopædia."   ‡ " Cæsar," B.C., lib. v., c. 19.

charioteer and essedarius from the wheels, and was filled, as is likely, with painted wood, or with wicker-work,* as we know was the case with the carriages of another Celtic people—the Cimbri—and at a later period with those of the Irish.

The diameter of the wheel was 2½ feet in an example from Hamden Hill, Somersetshire, and 2 feet 8 inches and 2 feet 11 inches in others from Arras; the spokes in these instances being said to vary from 12 to 16 (?) in number.

The British chariot was much prized at Rome in the time of Julius, Augustus, and their successors. Thus Cicero, writing to his friend Thebatius, who was serving with Cæsar in Britain, advised him to capture an essedum and return it to Rome.†

The number of spokes in the chariot wheels from Arras, mentioned by Dr. Thurnam is unusually great, and is probably a mistake. In the Rev. E. W. Stillingfleet's original account of the Arras find, there is, I believe, no mention of the number of spokes in the wheels. I fear so small a nave as 5 to 6 inches in diameter, which must have had an axle of wood passing through it of comparatively large size, would have been weakened by the insertion of so many as sixteen spokes.

Dr. Schliemann,‡ who illustrates and describes a small wheel of lead, with four spokes of lead, writes :—

> " It may be an ex-veto. But there can hardly be a doubt that this wheel was copied from those wheels existing at the time it was made. Wheels with four spokes were also in use at Mycenæ, for they are seen in three chariots represented on the tombstones of the royal sepulchres, as well as the chariot represented on one of the gold rings."

Dr. Schliemann adds :—

> " I also found at Mycenæ two wheels of bronze and six wheels of gold with four spokes. In the Swiss lake dwellings at the station of Corcelettes were found two ornaments of bronze in the shape of a wheel with four spokes, and two others of gold with six spokes ; also an ornament of tin, and another of bronze, in the form of wheels with four spokes, at the station of Auvernier. We see also wheels with four spokes on two miniature bronze chariots found at Berg in the bed of the river Spree, and of which one is in Professor Virchow's collection, the other in the Royal Museum at Berlin ; and also on two other chariots of bronze, one of which was found at Ober-Kehle, the other near Drossen in Prussia."

He further adds :—

> " The Trojan wheel of lead he figures is unlike the wheels of Homer's chariot of the gods, which had eight spokes round the axle."

In addition to the sculpturing on the Royal tombs and the wheel-shaped trinkets just mentioned, I found in 1897, behind a skull in one of the Danes'

---

* In the " Iliad," Homer says that a wicker seat was fixed on the axle of the car, and at the siege of Troy both the Grecian and Trojan chariots had wicker seats.

† " Cicero," E. P., 7 (55 B.C.).   ‡ " Ilios, City and Country of the Trojans," p. 565.

graves, a bronze pin (fig. 1023), with a head in the form of a wheel with four spokes.   And there was etched on a disc of bronze the figure of a wheel, also showing four spokes.   The writer has seen a model of a chariot from Crete, or Cyprus, in the York Museum, showing four* horses abreast, attached to the pole of the chariot, each pair of horses by one yoke.   A driver stands in the middle of the chariot, and close by him stands another person.   The wheels in this case are shown to have eight spokes.

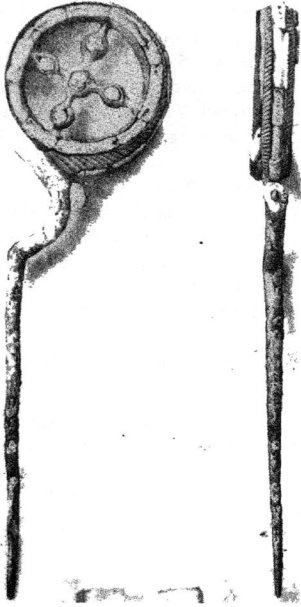

The numerous sculptured representations of the Egyptian chariot in the British Museum show the wheels in most cases to have four spokes; and in a few instances six.   The Assyrian war-chariot is generally shown with six spokes in each wheel, and the bullock carts with eight spokes in each wheel.†

The question as to whether the chariots found in Britain were of native manufacture or were imported by Phœnician or other traders, must for the present remain unanswered.   As we have not so far found any appearances of a transitional stage of development, between the Bronze Age and the apparently sudden introduction of iron and its accompanying greater advance in mechanical skill and the decorative arts, ‡ I am strongly not in favour of their independent native origin.

As far as we can gather from the scanty remains we possess of the British chariot, its shape may have been very similar to the sculptured representations of the Egyptian chariot.   It was therefore, most likely, first brought to Britain from the east, probably by Phœnician and Gaulish traders, considerably advanced in the arts and civilisation.

FIG. 1023.   ½

* Achilles' chariot was drawn by three horses.

† Cæsar in speaking of the Britons says: "Their mode of fighting with their chariots is this: first they drive about in all directions and throw their weapons and generally break the ranks of the enemy with the very dread of their horses and the noise of their wheels; and when they have worked themselves in between the troops of horse, leap from their chariots and engage on foot.   The charioteers in the meantime withdraw some little distance from the battle, and so place themselves with the chariots that, if their masters are overpowered by the number of the enemy, they may have a ready retreat to their own troops."—"Cæsar's Commentaries," Book iv., Chap. xxxiii.

‡ Accompanying the chariots at Arras and Hessleskew were beautiful ornaments of bronze, jet, amber, and ivory, and a ring of gold.

ANCIENT ENTRENCHMENTS.

A KNOWLEDGE of the position and extent of old earthworks is of assistance in picturing the appearance of the neighbourhood in early times, and aids our perception of the manners and customs of the former occupants of the land.

Of these structures Thomas Wright* remarks:—"Among the monuments of a remote period which it is most difficult to class, are the earthworks and entrenchments which are found in considerable number in every part of the island."

I propose to divide the earthworks of East Yorkshire into three distinct classes, each of which I believe to belong to a separate period.

The first is the extensive labyrinth of entrenchments called, in East Yorkshire, dikes, double dikes, and treble dikes. They appear to have once covered the whole of the Wolds. They also intersect the moorland hills, and are found between the Tees and the Swale in the North Riding of Yorkshire, and similar earthworks are numerous still further north. John Collingwood Bruce, in the preface to his work on the Roman Wall, refers to an assistant of his measuring eighty British strongholds to the north of the wall.†

The old writers believed the vallum was first made, and the wall, as a more effectual barrier.‡ Recent researches seem to support this view. The "Antiquary" for December, 1897, page 362, refers to the turf wall (entrenchment) at Birdoswald, as passing right across the area of the fort. In other words it is older than the existing stone walls and forts, as shown by excavations made in 1897 by Mr. F. Haverfield, M.A., F.S.A.

They are also very abundant in Wiltshire, Berkshire,§ and Devonshire;‖ while numerous entrenchments traverse Cambridgeshire, some of which are known as the "Devil's Ditch," the "Eight-mile Ditch," the "Fleam Dyke," &c.¶ In fact, they are found on most of the high and dry ground in all parts of England. They also exist in Scotland.

It is observed, however, that even where man has held his hand, the action of time and tempest have greatly lowered these ancient earthworks, and they are now fast disappearing.

The accompanying map, copied from the 6-inch Ordnance Survey sheets, includes an area of 75 square miles of the mid-wolds of East Yorkshire, and shows the arrangement of 80 miles of these dykes or earthworks, probably nearer their original plan than can now be obtained from any other part of the island.

As to the date of their construction, and the purpose they served, there is more uncertainty than there is about any other class of ancient earthworks.

---

* "The Celt, the Roman, and the Saxon," p. 86.

† The vallum, which runs nearly parallel a little to the south of the wall, is of the same type of earthwork (excepting a berm or platform about 20 feet broad on one, and often on both sides of the centre ditch) as those on the Yorkshire Wolds we are now discussing; and, if made by the Romans, it has been constructed mainly on the plan of the much older British entrenchments. After a week's inspection of this vallum, during July, 1896, in company with the Rev. E. M. Cole, of Wetwang, whose knowledge of British earthworks is well known, I am convinced this vallum was not originally an auxiliary to the Roman Wall, but a work anterior to it, and for a time independent of it.

‡ Per Lineam Valli, by G. Neilson, p. 7.

§ See "The Archæological Journal," vol. v., foot-note pp. 280-1.

‖ Ditto, vol. xxxi. p. 339.   ¶ Ditto, vol. xi. p 210.

Dr. John Burton, of York, and Francis Drake, the York historian, in a paper[*] published in the " Philosophical Transactions of the Royal Society " for 1747, p. 541, endeavoured to show that all the entrenchments in the neighbourhood of Millington, Huggate, and Garrowby-Hill, were of Roman age, being part of the defences of the long-lost Delgovitia, which they attempted to show was at Millington.   Drake, in speaking of Millington, says :—

> " That this was really the Delgovitia so long sought after I think is beyond
> contradiction."

And in reference to that portion of these earthworks on Garrowby-Hill, he writes :—

> " On the top of that mountain, as I may well call it, begins a series of such
> enormous works for fortification, as the like is not to be met with in the
> whole island."

Later, Sir Richard Colt Hoare says:—

> " In no part of our county [Wiltshire] have we a greater assemblage of this latter
> species of antiquities [entrenchments], which are evidently connected with
> the Britons and their villages; for, on referring to our map, you will per-
> ceive two lines of banks and ditches running nearly parallel from north to
> south, and uniting their branches at the British settlement on Westdown
> Hill, and tending afterwards to the strong fortress on Chidbury Hill.   On
> the north side of the camp you will see also a connection, by means of
> ditches, between two other British villages, which is also continued to a
> third at Lidbury.   In short, whether they are considered as boundaries of
> territory or covered ways of communication, they are evidently the works
> of the Britons, and therefore deserving of the antiquary's notice.   I can
> entertain no doubt that some of these were lines of boundary and defence;
> for their modes of construction warrants such a purpose; whilst for the
> same reason I cannot but consider others as covered ways, or roads of
> communication from one British village to another." [†]

Professor John Philips, in 1855, writes as follows in reference to the Yorkshire dykes:—

> " Imperfectly as we understand them, much information regarding the life of the
> ancient Britons is derived from the numerous and extensive earthworks
> which they constructed for defence, for the enclosure of cattle, and perhaps
> for the separation of districts.   Such are the dyke at Flamborough, the
> great mounds between the Swale and the Tees, and the numerous banks
> and trenches on the Wolds.   If it be asked for what reason these are
> regarded as British rather than Saxon works, we must reply that wherever
> the system of these earthworks can be studied, so as to bring into one
> point of view the probable abode, way of life, mode of burial, the result
> is in favour of the British claim.   This may be exemplified on Acklam
> Wold, where the double and even treble dykes extend widely over the Wolds,
> embrace the springs, and enclose many large and small sepulchral tumuli,
> which contain only British remains." [‡]

---

* Accompanied by a map.   † Sir R. Colt Hoare on South Wiltshire, Station 6, Eversley.
‡ " The Rivers, Mountains, and Sea Coast of Yorkshire," p. 215.

He adds:—

"The word 'dike' has the general meaning of a fence, or a mark of division."

Canon Greenwell, in his introduction to "British Barrows," page 111, writes as follows:—

"The very extensive and strongly-constructed defensive arrangements, so abundant on the Wolds, enclosing, in many instances, large tracts of country within their lines, are strongly indicative of a combination which necessitates a union of very considerable bodies of men; and there is every reason to believe that these works and the barrows were constructed by the same people." *

Further on he adds (p. 125):—

"I cannot assent to the view which would attribute the Wold entrenchments to the Anglican invaders. . . . . There is nothing which has ever been found, so far as I know, in connection with the entrenchments of the Wolds enabling us to attribute them with certainty to any time or people. . . . . We must, I think, look to some other people than the Angles for the invaders who erected these works; and we seem naturally brought to regard the brachy-cephalic occupants of the round barrows as the probable constructors."

The following extract is from Major-General Pitt-Rivers' paper on the "Danes' Dyke" at Flamborough and on the "Earthworks of the Yorkshire Wolds," read at the York Meeting of the British Association in 1881, and printed in the "Report," p. 690 :—

"General Pitt-Rivers showed, by means of a large map, that many of the entrenchments on the Wolds and north of the Derwent valley appeared to have formed part of a connected system for the defence of the ground from the westward. First, the entrenchment known as the Danes' Dyke, which cuts off Flamborough Head, was obviously an entrenchment intended to secure the promontory from an attack from the west. Next, the Argam Dyke was a work parallel to the last, and probably formed the next position which the invaders took up as they advanced inland."

The North Wolds are traversed by entrenchments which run along the top of the chalk escarpment overlooking the Derwent valley; and several entrenchments on the northern and southern Wolds run along the hills in a position to command the valley to the north-westward. General Pitt-Rivers made a cutting partly through the Dane's Dyke in the autumn of 1879, to ascertain if possible the date of its construction, and in so doing found evidence of the manufacture of flint implements, both before and after the construction of this entrenchment. This result shows (he believed) that the Dyke was not later than the Bronze period—

"That is to say the period of the tumuli on the Wolds, which Canon Greenwell has shown to have belonged to the early Bronze Age—an age in which flint continued to be used for many ordinary purposes."

---

* My observations do not lead me to this conclusion.—J.R.M.

Later, the Rev. E. M. Cole gives a paper on these works, with map, in the
" Yorkshire Geological and Polytechnic Society's Proceedings " for 1888, p. 45.   His
extensive knowledge of these earthworks causes him to speak somewhat cautiously
of their age and purpose.   After quoting from General Pitt-Rivers' paper, he
makes the following remarks :—

> " The tumuli and entrenchments were doubtless to a certain extent contem-
> poraneous, though instances can be pointed out where an entrenchment has
> evidently been diverted for the purpose of avoiding a tumulus.   If, therefore,
> any preference as to age must be given, it should be in favour of the
> tumuli."

Neither does he fully support General Pitt-Rivers' views that these works were
" the defence of the ground from the westward."   Mr. Cole further remarks :—

> " After the enclosure of the Wolds at the beginning of the present [19th] century, the
> land was brought more into cultivation, with the result that many of the old
> entrenchments were destroyed by the plough.   The site of such may yet
> be traced by the experienced eye, though the process of identification is
> sometimes slow."

He then adds :—

> " Were the entrenchments on the Wolds the work of the Britons or the Romans ?
> I have no hesitation in saying of the former, for one reason, and that
> is a good one, that there is not a straight line amongst the whole lot.
> They may look straight on paper, but not on the ground itself."

Canon Atkinson, in his " Memorials of Old Whitby," (1894), page 61,
speaking of the entrenchments, says :—

> " Passing by the great defensive work at Eston Nab, and the almost more
> interesting though smaller hill forts, such as those at Castle Lidington,
> East Castle Hill, Grisby Castle Hill, and other places ; the way in which
> all the tongues of lofty moorland which stretch down in their grand elevation
> into the valley of the Esk on its southern side, creating the Cleveland dales
> by the fact of their own being, are scored across with single lines or by a
> more compound work of fosse and vallum (doubled or trebled in some
> instances), is both remarkable and significant ; and what they reveal seems
> to be not merely that they were intended to be defensive against attack
> from the south, but (what is more to our present purpose) that they were
> constructed at such cost of effort and toil and perseverance as could have
> been available only as the result of concert and combination on the part
> of a not scanty population, united alike in toil of construction and in the
> resolution to defend a series of works which has to be measured by miles
> rather than by furlongs merely."

He then adds :—

> " I make no attempt here to assign even an approximate date to these earthworks
> further than assuming that they are probably co-eval with the early section
> of the grave-mounds."

That a great number of entrenchments were in far better preservation in this
neighbourhood at the close of the 18th century than now, is indicated by the

following extract from a paper by the late Sir Mark Sykes, of Sledmere, in "Archæologia," vol. xii., 1795 :—

> "In the entrenchments which divide and dissect in every direction the high Wolds of that part of Yorkshire (Sledmere and Fimber), skeletons, the heads of broken spears, arrows, and other remnants of ancient weapons and armour, are frequently found."

These skeletons and weapons, however, belong to intrusive Anglo-Saxon interments, which have been made in the ramparts of the entrenchments, and are of later date. Even, since the writer was a boy, many of the entrenchments, passing from hill to hill, have been removed by the labours of the husbandman, and many of the ramparts which then stood out in bold relief are now razed to a level with the natural surface of the land, with the ditches filled in ; their former existence being now only traceable on the surface by the line of rubbly stone from the ploughed-down ramparts, and the green bands in the growing corn caused by the additional depth of soil in the filled-up ditches.* Certainly the last two centuries have erased the greater portion of the entrenchments which once existed, and time has quite obliterated their history. Still, a careful examination of the magnitude and structure of those remaining, of the methods adopted in connecting one section with another, and of the arrangements which were originally made to give ingress and egress to the interiors of the ditches and to the areas enclosed within their lines, will probably assist in partly making out the purpose for which they were constructed.

It is found that the entrenchments have traversed the high grounds of the Yorkshire Wolds in every direction, forming a network over the surface connecting hill to hill and valley to valley.† This arrangement seems to consist of three or four main lines, each consisting of two to four ramparts—sometimes more—generally extending nearly east and west. Along these main lines, as at Fimber, Aldro, Millington Wold, &c., are enclosures of considerable area ; whilst from them, in every direction, and at all angles, are numerous branch lines of single, double, and even treble dykes. These either connect two trunk lines or lead down to springs of water, and to the once numerous swamps of Holderness and the Vales of York and Pickering.

By examining the connections and numerous bifurcations of this great system of earthworks, we observe that‡ they are provided with means of ingress and egress, and that they are linked together in such a manner as to show that they were constructed on a pre-conceived plan of great magnitude. Enlarged plans of a few of these connections are given on figs. A, B, C, D, E and F, plate A, from which it will be observed that access from one line to another has been of importance.

A further reference to the map will show that another prominent feature in their construction is the great number of parallel ditches and ramparts frequently displayed in crossing a neck of high ground from the narrow end of one valley to

* About one mile south of North Burton, on the Wolds, some fields have the name of "Nine Dykes," on the 6-inch Ordnance Survey, No. 127 ; but no trace now remains of the Dykes.
† For similar works in Scotland, see D. Christison, on "Early Fortifications in Scotland," pages 356 and 363.
‡ Omitting a few of the single ones, indicated on the map, which we have termed V-shaped hollow-ways, and which the writer believes to be anterior to those now being described.

that of the adjoining one, as at Huggate Pasture (fig. *E.e.*, plate C), Garrowby
Hill top, and other places. Also from the side of a valley over the high ground to
the narrow end of the nearest adjoining valley, as on Acklam Wold and other
places.*

In such instances these entrenchments often consist of three or four parallel
ditches and four or five ramparts, as on Garrowby Wold, near Cot Nab, and other
places, and in some instances as many as six parellel ditches and seven ramparts
occur, as on Huggate Pasture. It is also noticeable that on entering the narrow
end of a valley they often divide and separate, one portion fringing the brow of
the hill on one side of the valley, and another portion passing down the bottom
of the dale, as on Huggate Pasture and other places.

They seem to have been mostly excavated on one side of the valley, along
the brow of the hill side ; and apparently ran least of all along the bottoms of
the valleys or dales, the dale bottom serving in lieu of a ditch. In a few instances,
however, remains of these works are yet traceable along the bottoms of the valleys,
as in Back Dale, and Milham Dale (fig. *G.g.*, plate C), both near Thixendale.
Sometimes they are shown running out of the narrow end of a branch valley, or
up the sides of a main valley, at various angles. Many of them also can yet be
observed crossing the high plateau grounds in every direction; though they are
fast being obliterated. These plateau and valley bottom entrenchments have suffered
very much more from the tilling of the land than those on the crests of the
untilled and barren hill sides, and this, probably, partly accounts for the greater
number of entrenchments now visible in the latter position.

Digressing for a short time from the limits of the map to the moors on the
north of the Wolds, it is found that the arrangement of these earthworks is
somewhat different. In crossing the high ground from Troutsdale to the Vale
of Pickering, leading towards Scarborough, they appear to have been made less
use of for enclosing ground than on the Wolds, and they are more in the form of lines
of hollow ways of great dimensions. Fig. *Z*, plate C, shews a section of Oxmoor
Dyke, on Scamridge, taken by the writer on June 22nd, 1891, at the limestone
quarry, shown half-way on the northern edge of the 6-inch Ordnance Map, No. 92.
In the face of this quarry there is a clearly exposed section (north-west by south-
east) of the north-west foss of this entrenchment, which shows the shape and size
of the foss, and that the upper side of one of the beds of limestone forms its floor.
At this point the depth of the ditches from the summit of the ramparts seems
to have originally varied from 10 to 12 feet.

About a mile further eastward is a still finer series of entrenchments, consisting
of six ramparts and five ditches, which run obliquely over the high ground for
three-quarters of a mile in a southerly direction, and then divide. One portion
passes along the brow of the east side of Scamridge Slack, into Netheby's Dale;
the other branches to the south and west, and enters the narrow end of Kirkdale.
The centre rampart of this line along the greater portion of its length is generally
unusually broad and flat.

One third of a mile further eastwards, close to Cockmoor Hall, is the most
remarkable group of all (fig. *D.d.*, plate C), running nearly parallel with the two
previously-named groups. For a short distance there are yet remaining as many

* This is a striking feature on the moors in the neighbourhood of Scamridge.

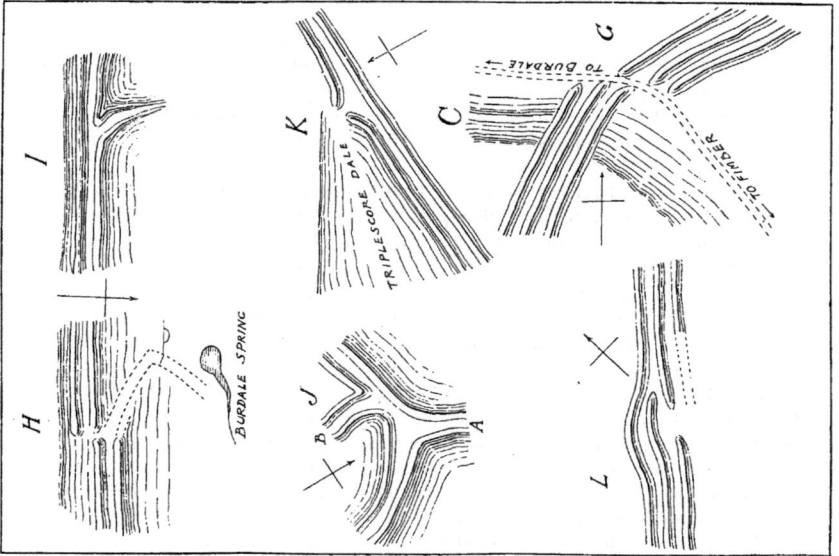

I

H

BURDALE SPRING

K

TRIPLESCORE DALE

C

TO BURDALE

G

TO FINDER

B

J

A

L

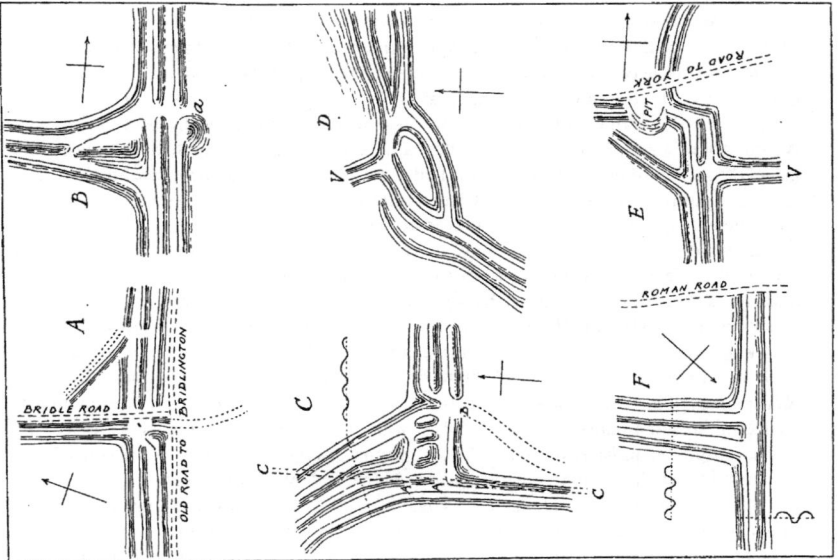

B

a

A

BRIDLE ROAD

OLD ROAD TO BRIDLINGTON

D

V

C

c

c

E

PIT

ROAD TO YORK

V

ROMAN ROAD

F

as eighteen adjoining ramparts and seventeen ditches, running parallel with one another. As mentioned elsewhere, this group encloses two tumuli, which have proved to be, as in other instances, older than the entrenchments. The ditches and ramparts of the western half of this group of earthworks are not so broad as those of the two previously-described groups, the ramparts of which are unusually wide.

The two last described series of parallel lines are connected by a trench running east and west between them, a few hundred yards from the brow of the southern side of Troutsdale. These three very elaborate lines of covered ways on Scamridge Moor come from Troutsdale, and proceed southwards across the elevated ground into the ends of valleys, which lead to springs of water and to the low and once swampy land between the Moorland Hills and the chalk Wolds.* Thus they may have served (as on some parts of the Yorkshire chalk Wolds), as covered ways for escape.

Returning to the area of our map, from plates B and C it will be observed that there is a great resemblance between the two, and that the original shape of the ditch seems to have been strictly constant in form, while the shape of the rampart has been mainly so. The present outline of the rampart is, with few exceptions, more or less that of a convex ridge. The original width of the ditches at their bottom is much more uniform than that of the ramparts. As shown by the descriptions, a few of the middle ramparts are much broader and have flat tops, as on Millington Ling and several other places. In some instances this may be accidental, but probably in others the ramparts were often originally so designed.

In rare cases, such as the entrenchment nearly one mile north of Cowlam Church, the central rampart for a few hundred yards is so much broadened or widened as to leave a hollow up its centre (see fig. "Q," plate B); while one mile westwards a similar longitudinal hollow (fig. "R"), exists in the north rampart of the same line of earthworks, nearly opposite Collingwood House.† Again, about 4 miles further west, in the same entrenchment (which here runs on the brow of the southern side of York Dale, near Fimber Station), are traces of a similar feature. In each case these hollows seem to have been purposely so constructed, and they may have served as places of concealment. The entrenchments which enclose Fimber, show all along the north side of the enclosure a "berm," or level platform, from 20 to 25 feet in width, between the outer rampart and the central ditch, as shown by fig. C.c., plate C. This feature is continued, to some extent, for about half-a-mile after the entrenchments leave the Fimber enclosure and enter York Dale on their course eastwards. I know of no other instance of such a regular and well-defined platform existing between the ramparts in East Yorkshire. This berm may have been a special provision in an entrenchment enclosing a settlement—such as Fimber was—in places along the sides where an attack might be most expected. And it seems strange that there is no such berm on any side of the similar enclosures on Aldro and Millington Ling.

There still remain, along the sides of these long lines of entrenchments, inlets, or entrances, through the outer ramparts into the adjoining ditches. Plans of a few of these are shown enlarged on plate A, from which it will be observed

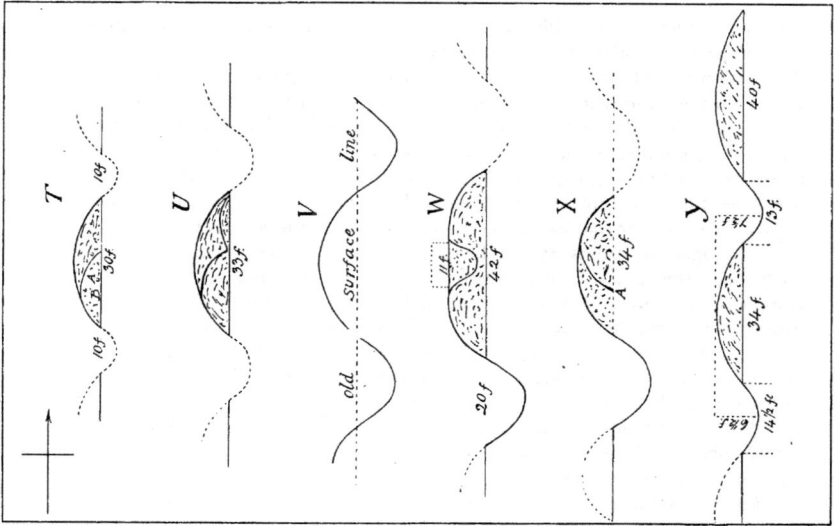

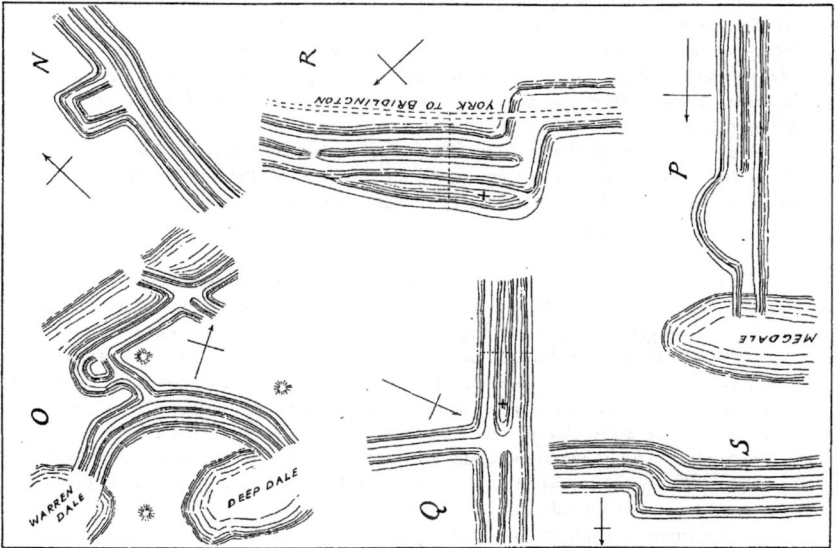

that they differ considerably in arrangement.   Fig. *G* represents approximately
one of the main gateways, through the ramparts and ditches, that once protected
the north-west side of the village of Fimber.   The present road to Burdale now
passes through this gateway.   When I was a boy these ramparts were unmolested
and of a considerable height.   In 1870, I excavated and obtained a section of the
filled-in outer ditch, which was 7 feet in depth, measured from the natural surface
of the land, and in August, 1899, I dug a section at the eastern side of this enclosure
one mile from the previous section, and found the outer ditch to reach 7 feet
3 inches below the natural surface of the land, with a width of 14 feet at the
top, and only 21 inches at the bottom.   Fig. H shows an opening or entrance
made like the gateway just referred to by a short and peculiar break in the
entrenchment, which runs along the brow of the southern hill-side facing Burdale
Station, just opposite to a fine spring of water in the valley bottom.   The writer
has noticed in other places similar entrances passing into the ramparts, and they
are clearly shown to be part of the original design.   Fig. I. represents an opening
into the same line of entrenchments, about half-a-mile further north-west, leading
a little way down the hill-side towards the valley bottom.   About half-a-mile
further northwards is a similar one, and both these are also part of the original
plan of the entrenchment.

Fig. *J*. is the plan of a gateway a few hundred yards to the east of Fimber
Station, which the writer took, with many others, in 1862.   This is at the entrance
of "Triplescore Dale," and seems to commence near the valley bottom, and run
up the hill-side into the entrenchments that sweep round the brow of the promontory,
bounded on the north by Triplescore Dale, and on the west by Bessingdale.
At this point, there is also an opposite entrance from the brow of the hill-side.
Being in an old plantation, this hill-side ingress is yet in good preservation.
Many similar short hollow ways are here and there observable on the untilled
hill-sides leading from the valley bottom, entering the entrenchments which run
along the brows of the hill-sides.

Fig. *K*. This gateway enters the same entrenchments as does fig. *J*, and
about half-a-mile eastwards from it, on the portion of the earthwork which runs
eastwards in the direction of "Life Hill" farm house.   It leads from the entrenchments into the narrow end of Triplescore Dale, giving the two a well-designed
connection.

Fig. *L* represents an entrance a little west of Weaverthorpe Pasture farmhouse
(6-inch Ordnance Sheet, No. 144), about one mile east-north-east of Cowlam, on
slightly rising ground.   It is an ingeniously contrived entrance.   Let it be observed
that, various as these entrances are, the writer knows of no gateway flanked by
slightly-curved wings, like those in the small Romano-British camps at Cawthorn
and traceable in Danes' Dyke, near Flamborough; or traversed with a short
straight bank or a circular mound like those in most of the hill forts in the North
of England.*   This is remarkable and may indicate a different purpose and probably
an earlier date for the entrenchments now being described, and also that the gateways
into them were *not* intended to be defended.

Furthermore, in places along the line of entrenchments are small camp-like
enclosures (fig. *N*., plate B), which, if these entrenchments were, in part, used also as

---

* See " Military Antiquities," by Major-General Roy.

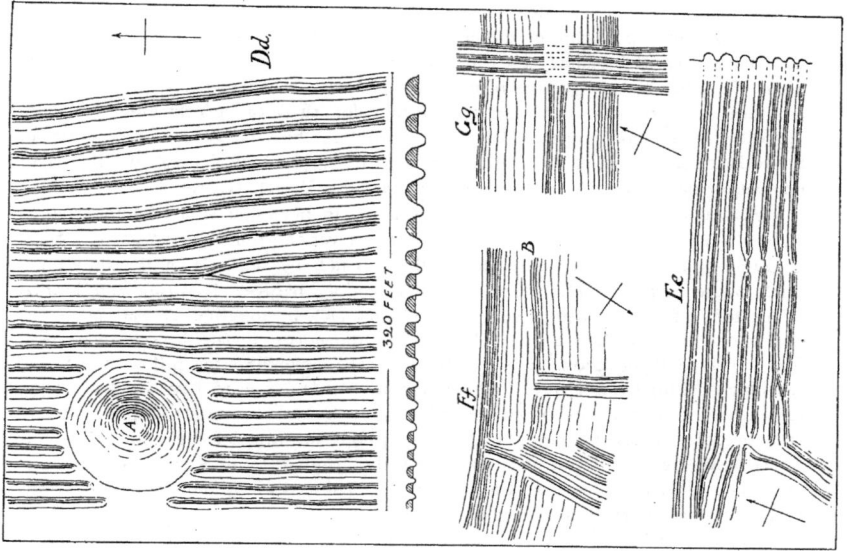

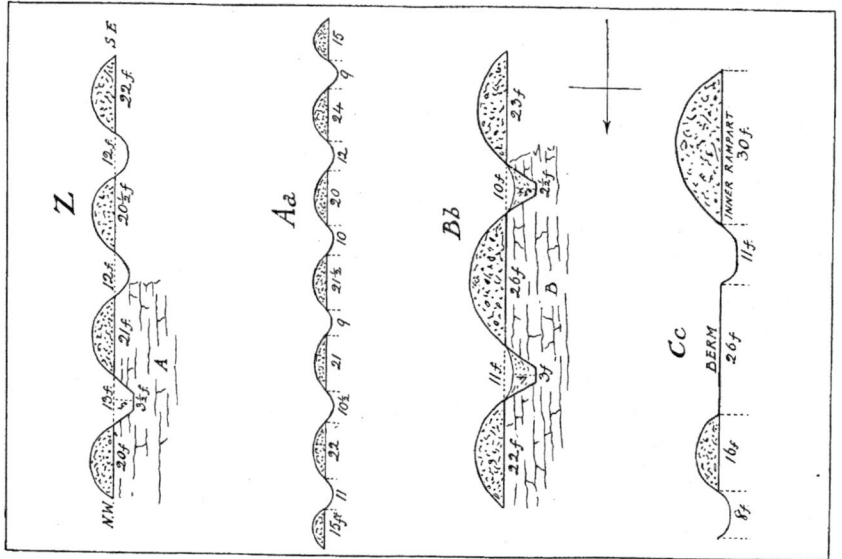

lines of communication, may have served as small wayside halting and even hiding places for cattle passing along the ditches from one locality to another. The still further multiplication of ditches, as on Huggate Pasture and other places, may have served, in some cases at least, to meet additional requirements of this kind. In other places, the foss of the entrenchments is widened for a short distance as shown on Garrowby Wold (fig. *P*), a little before these earthworks enter Megdale, opposite the end of Hundle Dale, which adjoins the first field to the north of Stonechair Close. This and similar places are noticed by Drake, in his paper on Delgovitia, previously referred to, and named " Watch Guards."

Several of the lines of entrenchments have, in places, a short double bend at right angles. The deviation from a straight line varies from 20 to 50 yards. Such a feature (fig. *S.*) exists at the foot of the hillside, by the side of the railway, a little to the east of Kipling Cotes railway station, between Beverley and Market Weighton. There is also a similar bend (fig. *R*) in the line of entrenchments nearly one mile north-east from Sledmere, by the north side of the old coach road from York to Bridlington, called " High Street," ascending the hill a little before reaching Collingwood House.[*] Two similar bends seem to have existed in the entrenchments a little west of the late Sir Tatton Sykes' Memorial; and this feature is noticeable in several other places throughout the area of the map. There is rarely any irregularity on the surface of the ground to necessitate in the least any such deviation from a straight line.[†] These not infrequent sharp bends may, therefore, have been constructed for the purpose of limiting the sight along the ditches (see figs. *S* and *R* along the entrenchments).

The varied and complicated modes of connecting diverging lines are well shown in figs. *B, C, D,* and *E,* plate A, made by me between 1863 and 1865, from the four corners of the rhomboidal enclosure, including about 130 acres on Millington Ling. A similar union of lines is also shown by figs. *O* and *Q,* plate B, and many others were undoubtedly once visible.

Judging from several rows of small pits—which the writer believes to be lines of unfinished dykes or ditches[‡]—existing on several of the wild uncultivated moorland hills, it would seem that, on planning the direction which the entrenchments were to take, workmen were, in some instances at least, placed in a line at distances of 10 feet to 12 feet apart, and after so far penetrating the ground as to make the pits—and often a slight bank—these workmen, from some cause or other, discontinued their work. Hence the productions of the rows of regularly-placed pits and slightly-raised banks (unfinished entrenchments) which have so long perplexed alike the antiquary and the geologist ; the former naming them pit-dwellings ; the latter believing they were the sites of mining shafts or lines of natural sinkings of the surface.

The six sections (plate B) of a portion not exceeding a quarter of a mile in length, of the central rampart of the entrenchments which pass close to the Sykes monument, situated between Sledmere and Garton, were taken by

---

[*] Now pulled down.

[†] The vallum along the Roman Wall near Birdoswald makes a most extraordinary bend to the south, so as to have the camp in a sort of nook in the north. As yet this is unexplained ("Antiquary" for October, 1896, p. 289). There is also a double bend in the Roman road near Violet Grange, between the Tees and the Swale, for which the nature of the ground does not suggest any reason ("Archæological Journal," vol. vi. p. 217).

[‡] See "Archæological Journal," September, 1895.

the writer during 1866-7, when a considerable length of the central rampart was being removed, and many Anglo-Saxon interments were discovered in it.* These show that in some places first one side of the rampart and then the other had been cast up. This proves clearly that different lengths of the ditches were excavated by separate gangs of workmen, in advance of each other. The observations made in these sections also show almost certainly that metal tools of no mean kind had been used in their construction, as in digging the ditches hard rock had often to be penetrated, and it is shown in the structure of the rampart that the material from the ditches had been cast, in a workmanlike manner, to a considerable distance, apparently much as it would have been if excavated and cast there by the tools now in use for such a purpose.

The enormous amount of labour bestowed on the construction of these very extensive earthworks will be more readily comprehended when we find that within the area of the map alone we have been able to trace no fewer than 80 lineal miles, the lines themselves varying in strength from one rampart and one ditch to seven ramparts and six ditches, as on Huggate Pasture (fig. Aa), where we have the finest entrenchments in number of ramparts and lateral development now extant in East Yorkshire. The great system of earthworks included within the area of the accompanying map represents the most laborious work ever undertaken and executed within its limits.

The question of the original use of these earthworks is not easy to answer definitely, but that they were, as expressed by most of the writers previously quoted, defensive works, at least in part, I agree with.

I do not agree with General Pitt-Rivers that they were made by a body of invaders, landing on the east coast and protecting themselves, firstly by the Danes' Dyke,† and next by the "Argam Dyke," as a connected "system for the defence of the ground from the westward." I incline rather to the views of Sir R. Colt Hoare and those of John Phillips, and believe them to be the works of a numerous settled people who had, for some short time at least, possessed the district. To make this district more secure, they found it necessary to construct these vast entrenchments, as a protection to themselves and to their cattle; probably more against the sudden incursions of freebooters, than against a conquering foe.

They would, in many cases, serve as enclosures for family or even tribal boundaries and tribal settlements, and were admirably adapted for keeping cattle. Some of the enclosures, such as those at Fimber, Aldro, and Millington Ling, correspond well with the "oppida," or Ancient British fenced camps or settlements described by Cæsar as :—

> "Places of refuge, points naturally strong by difficult ground, marshes, or wood ;
> and still further secured by mounds and ditches. To the ample area thus
> protected, cattle and men retreated from hostile incursions." ‡

---

* See description at the end of Group XI.

† I am inclined to believe that the "Danes' Dyke" may have been an independent work, probably of a later period, to protect the promontory from the west.

‡ Bell. Gall., v. 21. As a proof of the early existence of such a practice, Homer's Iliad gives a graphic description of a cattle-lifting raid (Book XL, lines 765 to 780). A cattle-lifting raid, with other deeds of plunder, is described as having been figured on Achilles' Shield, Book XVIII. line 595, showing that in those times such acts of violence were neither infrequent nor considered dishonourable.

The foregoing is a good definition which Cæsar gives of their use and construction.*

Miall, in his "Illustrated English History," p. 13, thus writes :—

> "The Britons avoided the swamps and woods of the Vale of York and Holderness
> as places of settlement, but kept near them for their requisite supply of game
> and fish, and probably as places of safe retreat in time of danger ; their
> permanent settlement being on hilly ground."

Whatever was the purpose of their construction, it is clear that they were the works of a settled community, who spared no amount of labour to enclose their pasture—and probably, to some extent, tillage—lands, and to protect their homes and their herds by the most substantial boundaries and ways of communication then known.   At the Peak, south-east of Whitby, an entrenchment, with a considerable ditch and rampart, crosses the moors from the south, and runs past the Ravenscar Beacon and close to an upright boundary stone at the brow of the cliff, and can be traced a considerable distance down the sloping cliff towards the sea beach.

A reference to the accompanying map and to the figures of sections will further assist in showing the arrangement and great extent of these entrenchments, and the way in which line has been joined to line, better than any written description can do.   The black lines are the portions shown on the 6-inch Ordnance Map, No. 160, and parts of Nos. 159, 161, 142, 143, and 144, published in 1852 ; whilst those shown in red are restored portions which have been from time to time carefully traced out by my brother, myself, and the Rev. E. M. Cole, during a period of not less than forty years.   There is scarcely a yard of the whole entrenchments within the area included in the accompanying map that has not been visited and inspected—and some portions several times over—by one or more of us.   Numerous sections, many obtained by excavating the ditches and ramparts, have been made.   At the same time plans of the well-preserved points of connection and intersection were prepared, which would now be difficult to obtain.

The thin double black lines on the map, and the thick black line shown at pages 186 and 381, denote the remains of hollow ways, which mostly appear to radiate from a centre, and are sometimes crossed and cut by the entrenchments (see B, fig. Ff, plate C).   By this and other appearances the writer believes them to belong to an older system of earthworks, to be referred to later.

The age of the entrenchments can only be ascertained approximately, as even tradition is silent.   Unlike the tumuli, nothing has ever to my knowledge been found within their banks to give the least clue to the people who raised them. Sir R. C. Hoare and John Phillips consider them of British date.   Canon Greenwell, General Pitt-Rivers, and Canon Atkinson unhesitatingly refer them to the ancient Britons of the Bronze period; and though the Rev. E. M. Cole is more guarded, he believes they "were doubtless to a certain extent contemporaneous;" but adds,

* Destined for more than temporary protection, they were a complete labyrinth of hollow ways, forming expanded enclosures, which covered and protected, rather than defended, nearly the whole area of the Yorkshire Wolds.   From much evidence we possess, it seems almost certain that at one time most of the elevated grounds in England were similarly enclosed.   No better protection could have been desired in lawless times for protecting cattle against plundering expeditions.

"instances can be pointed out where preference in age must be given to the barrows."

In fourteen instances (all of which are alluded to in the account of the opening of the barrows) where the two have come into collision, the barrows have always been more or less cut or mutilated by the entrenchments[*] in a manner which shows clearly that the latter are the more recent. In one instance, in particular, the barrow had been desecrated in a most ruthless manner (see fig. 89, barrow 127, page 51), clearly the work of a later people than those who raised the barrows to protect their dead. In other parts of our Wolds, beyond the limits of my map, I have also observed several instances where the entrenchments encroach on the barrows.

When planning these earthworks, it would seem that, in many instances, certain barrows had been chosen as points to mark the direction the entrenchments should take; hence the not infrequent collision of the two and the mutilation of the barrow.

The same relative age holds good on the moorland hills. The famous Scamridge Dykes close to Cockmoor Hall, on the moors north of Ebberston and west of Scarborough enclose two barrows. These entrenchments run near to the margin of the barrows, but not under them, as I proved in July, 1894, by an excavation cut right across the southern half of the barrow to the undisturbed old surface line under it (fig. *Dd*, plate C), and showed that no ditch existed under the barrow.[†]

Though no mean tools of metal must have been used in excavating these very extensive earthworks, their construction is—at least for the most part—pre-Roman, being in several instances crossed by what are believed to be portions of old Roman roads.

The Roman road from York to the sea coast at Bridlington and Flamborough runs at a little distance almost parallel to the side of a line of these entrenchments from Garrowby, by Fimber, Sledmere, Cowlam, Octon, and Thwing—a distance of twenty-five miles.

Near the Sykes monument on the high ground between Sledmere and Garton, the southern branch of the Roman road from York to the east coast cuts obliquely through a line of treble entrenchments, which can be traced for miles in opposite directions, close by the side of the site of this branch of the Roman road, but in no way belonging to it.

From the facts we have so far been able to gather, it is probable that the introduction of these earthworks took place in late British times after the erection of most of the barrows of the Bronze age. Possibly their completion did not long precede the introduction of the chariot.

That the two were—at least, for a short time—used contemporaneously would

---

[*] Canon Greenwell gives a similar instance; he says: "Barrow lxxi. was placed just to the west of one of the entrenchments so abundant on the Wolds; and it had apparently been constructed at an earlier period than the mound [entrenchment] which formed part of the defensive work, for the side of the barrow appeared to have been partly cut away at that point."—"British Barrows," page 274.

Dr. Thurnam says "on Salisbury Plain the entrenchments make a decided curve in order to avoid the tumuli."

Also it has been observed that the entrenchments in Berkshire wind round barrows, and it is remarked "They always do when the two works come together."—"Archæological Journal," Vol. v. p. 281.

The same holds good in the North Riding and along the Roman wall.

[†] This figure also shows that sufficient space was left between the barrows and the ends of the ramparts, so as to give an entrance into several of the ditches, from the sides of each barrow.

seem almost certain from the following extract from " Britannia Antiqua," illustrated by Atlett Sammes, p. 198:—

> " The Britons, through secret and by-paths sallied out upon them [the Romans] with their chariots, and, having made great slaughter, again retired through *hidden ways*, and only known to themselves, returning to their main body."

From a long study of these earthworks it is clear that every necessary feature had been thoughtfully woven into their design, suggesting that they had been copied from a matured plan of such earthworks previously worked out and existing in some other land. Yet regarding their existence in other parts of the world, history seems almost silent. Lieut. General Pitt-Rivers says of them, " I have read with attention all the writings that were accessible to me upon the obscure period of history to which these entrenchments may have belonged. Some are by scholars of great ability, who would not have failed to bring to light evidence relating to them if it was to be found in ancient chronicles and the works of ancient authors. But these writings served chiefly to convince the reader that nothing definite is to be expected from such sources."[*]

Dr. J. W. Foster, in his " Prehistoric Races of the United States of America," p. 351, says, " The mound-builders erected an elaborate line of defence, stretching for many hundred miles, to guard against the sudden eruption of enemies."

This seems to refer to an extensive series of earthworks resembling our British entrenchments. Possibly, also, such may be alluded to in the following lines, where Achilles tells Agamemnon :—

> " For though I here with warlike Trojans fight,
> 'Tis not to vindicate my private right,
> Since they by impious thefts have ne'er detained
> My oxen, horses, or on Phthia's land
> Destroyed my fruits ; secured by *craggy ways*,
> O'er pathless mountains and tempestuous seas,
> I fear not what invasions they can make."
>
> "Iliad," v. ii. p. 2 ; a.v. 152.

Be these "craggy ways" an allusion to such earthworks or not, we can hardly believe that they were confined to this island alone. Probably reference to such earthworks by the ancient writers have been partially overlooked and not correctly rendered by the translators. Let us, therefore, hope that some passage may yet be found which will give some information on their origin and use during early times in other parts of the world, and so approximately indicate the time and place of their origin.

---

* Vol. III., Excavations in Bokerly and Wansdyke.

ANCIENT HOLLOW=WAYS.

OLDER than the entrenchments are the Ancient Sunk Roads, remains of which are yet traceable in several places in the Wold area. They seem to have been covered ways, mainly connected with and leading to primitive settlements. Three of the least obliterated series of these sunk ways are shown by the thick black lines on the map. Their present appearance is that of a very shallow hollow, 5 feet to 8 feet in width, running mainly along the steep and untilled hill-sides. These are the result of the filling-in of a V-shaped ditch on sloping ground.* Where the ground has been tilled and the surface is level no hollow remains, and, as a rule, no trace is visible except at times in the growing corn, when the

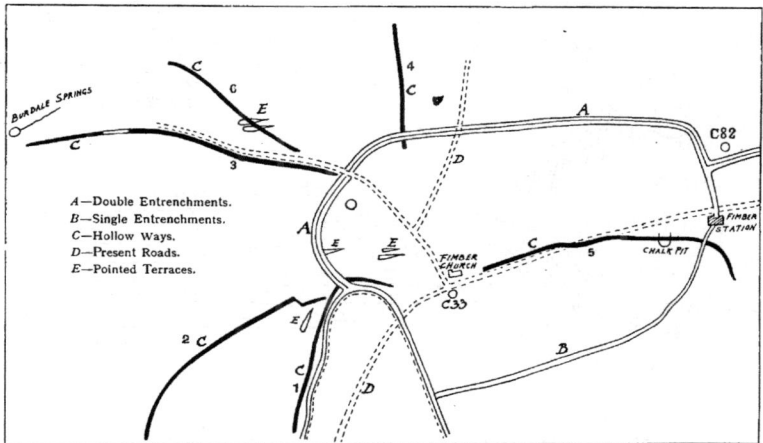

FIG. 1024.—Plan of Earthworks, &c., near Fimber.

direction of the filled-up ditches is distinctly seen in the different growth of the corn.

The black lines on the accompanying plan (fig. 1024), show six of this class, to which I have given the name of " Hollow-ways," converging towards the village of Fimber. Wherever the ground has been long tilled no trace of these hollow-ways remains; but it is probable that they all approach as near to the village of Fimber as the western end of No. 5 has been traced to; and possibly a similar track, all surface trace of which has been removed by long cultivation of the land, ran southward between Nos. 1 and 5. In an excavation near the church I found the end of such a trench pointing in that direction.

* During the wars with France and America, between 1774 and 1814, when wheat reached the price of 126s. 6d. per quarter and oats 2s. 6d. per stone, many of the steep hill-sides in this neighbourhood were tilled for a time, and very probably many interesting surface features were then entirely removed.

Between 1863 and 1880 I obtained many sections by cutting across these hill-side ledges at different points, and in every case there were found to be V-shaped trenches (see Sections 1 to 6, fig. 1025), 3 feet to 4½ feet deep, and measuring from 8½ feet to 16 feet wide at the top, and from 18 inches to 3 feet at the bottom. The excavated material from these trenches now slightly raises the natural contour of the hill-side along their lower edge, and originally may have been sufficiently

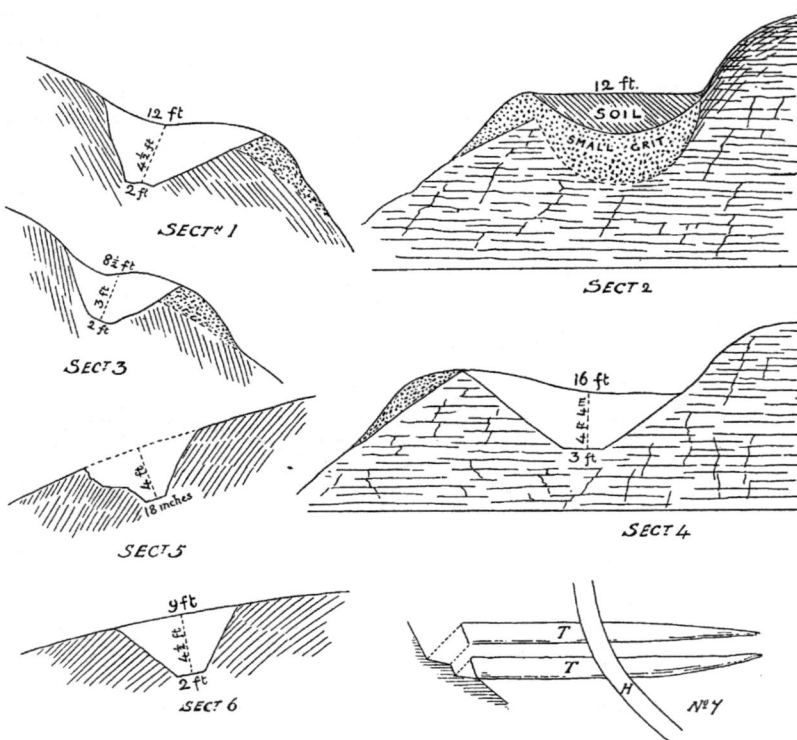

FIG. 1025.—The Numbers of the Sections compare with the Numbers on the Plan (Fig. 1024).

high to hide a tall man passing along the bottom. The lower halves of these trenches were found to be filled with small chalk grit which has been slowly removed from the hill-sides above by rain and frost, and the upper portions consisted of soil. A short description of these typical hollow-ways will throw some light on their use, show the uniformity of their plan, and enable their positions to be made out on the 6-inch Ordnance Map.

Fig. 1 is visible for three-quarters of a mile, running midway along the south-west side of "Rain Dale," and about a chain's length below the entrench-ments, locally called double dyke, which extends along the brow of the hill-side.

At its bottom we observed two or three inches of grit, hard and compact as if having been frequently walked upon.

No. 2 branches from No. 1 at a point on the 6-inch Ordnance Survey Map, indicated by the letter " e " in Rain Dale. It crosses the east end of " Wan Dale," and is visible midway between the northern side and the western termination of this dale.

No 3 is distinctly shown for a short distance equally dividing the hill-side called " Hagdale Cliff." It faces the south side of the railway, mid-way between Fimber and Burdale stations, and can be seen from the train. From here it is traceable in places as far as Burdale, in the form of a ledge, and is well shown terminating there on the south-west hill-side, near a fine spring of water (about 2 miles from Fimber), to which it probably led, there being no other spring of water for some considerable distance.

No. 4 strikes nearly due north from Fimber, then swerves more easterly towards the old settlement of Towthorpe, but only begins to be distinctly traceable on the surface at the southern end of " Big Dale," on the eastern hill-side, where it is cut across by a double dyke running vertically up the hill-side in the direction of Sledmere. On June 8th, 1863, the section (No. 4, fig. 1025) was taken about 200 yards north of the entrenchments, and on August 29th, 1865, an excavation was made into the north rampart of the entrenchments, and showed a similar section of this hollow-way extending under the rampart, clearly proving it to be the older.

No. 5, except being seen at times as a green strip in the growing corn, can only be traced by excavating, all surface configuration having been removed by tilling. In tracing its position we made more than 20 sections, and the one nearest the village was taken a few yards north-east of the most easterly mere, in the grass field close to the north side of the road to Sledmere, and its position on the 6-inch O.S., is near the letters "se" in Manor House. From this point it runs eastwards close to the north side of the road to the bottom of the hill, a distance of one-sixth of a mile, or one inch on the 6-inch map. It then crosses the road obliquely and runs by the south side of the road, where it is cut by a chalk pit, from the opposite sides of which the section (No. 5, fig. 1025) was taken. It then gradually ascends the hill-side, and on reaching a point opposite Fimber station it is crossed by the entrenchments shown on the plan, but now almost entirely obliterated. From here it sweeps round " Cole Nab," and was found extending one-sixth of a mile, and probably might be traced further.

No. 6 rises obliquely, the ground sloping to the south. Cultivation has levelled these trenches, but at times they are distinctly visible in the crops. Section 6, fig. 1025, represents one of the three taken, in all of which was found fragments of Roman, or Romano-British pottery, but in no case below half the depth of the trench. This sunk-way possesses additional interest by crossing two narrow terraces (Section 7, fig. 1025). At this point an excavation was specially made across this track, and one of the terraces at the point of intersection, with the view of proving which was the oldest, and the section seemed to show that the terrace had been made first.

The hollow-way was shown to be pre-Roman by the fragments of Roman pottery in all the three excavations, which, however, were not found below half its depth, indicating that the road had been disused, and half filled up by slowly

accumulating debris, before the potsherds had found their way into it. The three
hollow-ways marked Nos. 1, 3, and 4 are sharply cut by the old entrenchments
which enclose the village of Fimber, and No. 5 appears to afford similar evidence,
proving that they are older than the entrenchments.

They have, at some remote period, been excavated, and almost certainly used
as foot-roads, leading in nearly every direction to and from small and probably
rudely entrenched settlements. In a wild and wooded district these narrow sunk-
ways would be safe and sure guides by day and by night. The site of one of them
is now occupied by the little village of Fimber, and the demolished barrow on
which three succeeding churches have stood, was probably within the area of this

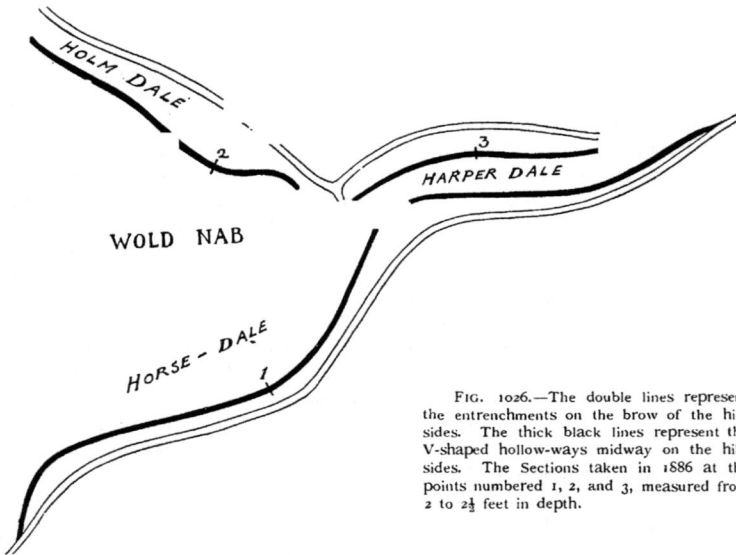

FIG. 1026.—The double lines represent
the entrenchments on the brow of the hill-
sides. The thick black lines represent the
V-shaped hollow-ways midway on the hill-
sides. The Sections taken in 1886 at the
points numbered 1, 2, and 3, measured from
2 to 2½ feet in depth.

enclosure. Indications of such an enclosure yet remain in places. They would
likewise assist the hunter to approach unobserved any animal in the vicinity
he wished to capture. Lastly, they unquestionably denote the fixed settlement of
a community in pre-historic times, earlier even than the period of double dykes.

The second series of this class of hollow-ways is shown (fig. 1026) running
along the sides of three valleys (Holme Dale, Horse Dale, and Harper Dale),
mainly at their point of junction, a little north of the village of Huggate. From
the central part of this system runs a branch line for a considerable distance
about half way up one side of each of the three valleys. The one going in a
S.W. direction along the south side of Horse Dale is, after running some distance,
cut and covered by a line of double entrenchments. This hollow-way, however,
can be traced as far as Huggate Pasture, proceeding in the direction of Millington

Springs, the nearest place where a permanent supply of spring water would be obtainable.

The third series of this class of earthworks is situated on the northern edge of the chalk Wolds, opposite the village of Birdsall. Not so many of its trenches are visible as in the case of those of the two sets just described, probably partially due to the land being more accessible to the plough. Those that are traceable seem to converge to a point near Aldro.

HABITATION TERRACES.

PROBABLY older than the hollow-ways are the terraces or platforms, which are pointed at one end. These must not be confounded with the cultivated garden terraces which are so common in the immediate vicinity of old villages, the work of the Roman and mediæval ploughs.

. A few of the old pointed terraces or ledges are yet visible on several of the steep hill-sides of the Yorkshire Wold valleys, and many others which have once existed have now been erased by natural or artificial causes. They are quite distinct from any other form of earth-works, and where they remain perfect in outline are remarkably alike in shape and in size. They are unlike the garden terraces, being generally found away from the immediate sites of old villages, and are mostly on that side of the valley which faces the morning or the mid-day sun, at about one-third the distance from the foot of the slope, and are parallel with the course of the valley. They occur in some cases as single platforms, in others as double platforms, whilst sometimes there are three (fig. 1027), or even more terraces, running parallel one above another. One end of each terrace is always of full width, while the other end runs out to a fine point ; and it is also worthy of note, that when two or more are found arranged like steps, one above the other, they invariably have their wide ends in the same direction. When well preserved, they are found to have a breadth varying from 15 to 21 feet, and a length of 100 to 200 yards. I know of no written allusion to this peculiar form of terrace, which is seldom found mapped even on the Ordnance sheets, except occasionally as entrenchments. From 1863 to 1865 I took the measurements of several of the most perfect of them. The positions of some of them are shown on fig. 1024, and on the coloured map.

One is 135 yards in length, with an average width of about 6 yards. It is in Rain Dale, near Fimber, and is situated a little above the foot of the hill-side, facing S.E.

Another is slightly to the east of that described above, and though partially obliterated at the time of our examination, seemed to have its broad end cut across by the British entrenchments which encircle the village of Fimber.

Two others are on the S.E. side of Rain Dale, a few feet one above the other. They had been a long time under the plough, and were partly effaced. An excavation made across them showed an accumulation of soil, in some places $1\frac{1}{2}$ to 2 feet in thickness, at the bottom of which were pieces of animal bone, and several fragments of coarse pottery, much resembling the dark variety rarely found whole, but not unfrequently in fragments, in British barrows.

Another two also occur together, on the north side of the railway, between Fimber and Burdale. They are cut obliquely by an old filled-in hollow-way, one of six radiating from the village of Fimber. The great age of these two terraces is shown by their being intersected by the hollow-way, as this contained fragments of Roman pottery in all the three sections which we dug across it, but in no case was the pottery found lower than half its depth, indicating that this road had been disused and half-filled up by slowly accumulating debris, before the potsherds found their way into it. This indicates that it was constructed in pre-Roman times, while the terraces are still older. Outside Fimber are many similar terraces on the sides of the valleys, some being in good preservation (see map). One of these is well shown on the hill-side, close by the south side of the road from Raisthorpe to Thixendale. It is cut across by a chalk pit, and the section thus obtained clearly shows that the form of the terrace is due to material having been removed from its upper to its lower side, and

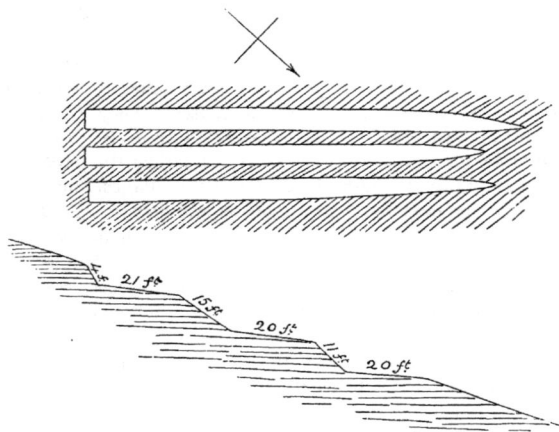

FIG. 1027.--Plan and Sections of Habitation Terraces.

there can be no doubt of its artificial construction. Two fine examples, one above the other, curve round the N.E. end of Brubber Dale, about a mile and a half to the north of Fridaythorpe. They are about ten yards above the valley bottom, and face the rising sun. There is a further series of three terraces situated on the western hill-side of Wad Dale, about one mile N.N.W. of Weaverthorpe. At the time of our visit, October 5th, 1863, the east end of Wad Dale plantation covered the ground, and the terraces were sharply defined.* Many others occur on the untilled hill-sides. It has been suggested by Mr. Stackhouse that the somewhat similar terraces he observed on the hill-sides in the South of England had been made by the Britons as advantageous stations for placing their war-chariots before a battle, from which they might swoop down upon their enemies with greater force. But it seems to me that for such a purpose their form and position is quite unsuited, indeed almost

* These have since been obliterated by the plough.

impracticable ; and I think that these simple hill-side terraces could hardly have been made for any other purpose than as sites for primitive dwellings. Their narrow ledge-like form and situation, on ground generally difficult to approach, would make them pleasant and somewhat secure positions for habitations such as would be erected by a few early hunters. At that time this neighbourhood would be more or less a wooded district, and, it is fair to presume, sufficiently well stocked with game to supply a scanty population, whose wants were few.

Mr. Foote, of the Indian Geological Survey, has discovered similar pre-historic artificial terraces in India.† The abstract of Mr. Foote's paper states that

> "In December, 1885, he re-visited Bellamy, and looked up the localities where he had found the celts, both chipped and polished. Mr. Foote's reasons for regarding many of the localities at which he got numerous celts and other implements as old settlements or village sites of the celt makers, are the following :—Whenever the celts and other implements were found in large numbers, the hills on which they were found showed many signs of human habitation. Many small terraces have been raised among the great blocks of granitic gneiss of which all the hills but one consisted. Many of the terraces were evidently constructed with reference to the convenient proximity of rock shelters, and in most cases they lie on the eastern flanks of the hills, where they obtain shelter from the blazing afternoon sun. On the terraces and flats are large quantities of flakes produced by the manufacture of the implements, and implements in all stages of completion."

These artificial terraces are most probably imitations of natural ledges, such as are on the hill-sides in other parts. In the early ages man would select these natural platforms as secure and suitable places for his dwellings, and where nature had not placed them he would with his own hands provide them. They were among the first earthworks constructed in this neigbourhood.

There is abundant evidence that man did occupy natural hill-side terraces in early times. During the summer of 1885, Mr. W. Horne, of Leyburn, discovered on a natural terrace on the limestone escarpment called "Leyburn Shawl," ancient interments, one of which was accompanied by a curious article of bone, which had probably served to secure a skin garment. He also found bones of the reindeer and the red deer, chipped flints, fragments of rude pottery, and numerous sandstone boulders, reddened and cracked by fire, which he believes to be pot-boilers. There is also a carefully-constructed cairn on this terrace, which has been examined.

Probably these artificial terraces and the neolithic barrows are the oldest earthworks of which any trace remains. But that these barrows are in any way contemporaneous with the terraces, or with the two other classes of artificial earthworks just described, I have no evidence, and the possibility of obtaining such evidence becomes daily more difficult.

* "Journal of the Anthropological Institute," vol. xvi. No. 1, p. 72.

CULTIVATION TERRACES.

Quite distinct from the Habitation Terraces referred to in the previous pages are some parallel strips of land of varying length, one above another, on hill slopes in the vicinity of old villages. These usually run parallel with the hill sides. At Croombe, near Sledmere (fig. 1028), and at North Grimston, are good examples. They owe their existence to the action of the plough, which has removed the soil from the upper to the lower side of each strip of land, eventually producing a ledge with a steep bank on its upper side. These terraces were once bounded by fences, as shewn by very old ash and other trees in places still standing at irregular distances along their margins. The terraces possibly date from the Romans, and were probably continued in use until mediæval

FIG. 1028.—Terraces at Croombe.

times. Thomas Wright * alludes to terraces of this character, and says, "it is not improbable that they may have been the work of the Roman plough." He also mentions that they have been noticed in many other parts of the country ; in fact they were doubtless at one time common throughout the kingdom.

EMBANKMENT CROSSES.

THE explorations of the barrows in the neighbourhood of Fimber and Sledmere have revealed the interesting fact that the early Anglo-Saxon settlers not only, occasionally, used some of the British barrows as graveyards, but that they also utilized several of them as Moot-Hills. A British barrow, conveniently situated near an Anglo-Saxon settlement, was chosen as a place on which the people gathered to conduct secular and religious matters. After embracing the Christian faith, they seem to have often excavated in their Moot Hills a large and deep trench in the form of a cross (fig. C, plate D), reaching through the mound. Seven examples of these have come under my observation. These sometimes extend 5 to 7 feet into the rock below ; and always with the arms towards the four cardinal points of the compass. The trenches have invariably been filled in with a mixture of soil and rock, in which are pot sherds, animal bones, and corroded pieces of iron. Sometimes, along the bottom, a cross is built, of two to four horizontal courses of stones† (fig. C on the plate), walled with clay.

Many of these mounds now bear the name of Moot-Hill, Mall-Hill, Mill-hill, Gallows-Hill, and Hangman-Hill or Hanging-Hill.

* "The Celt, the Roman, and the Saxon," p. 209.
† Most probably these cruciform trenches were made to give sanctity to the mound, to induce fair dealing, and to stamp with reverence and make binding all matters transacted thereat.

PLATE D.

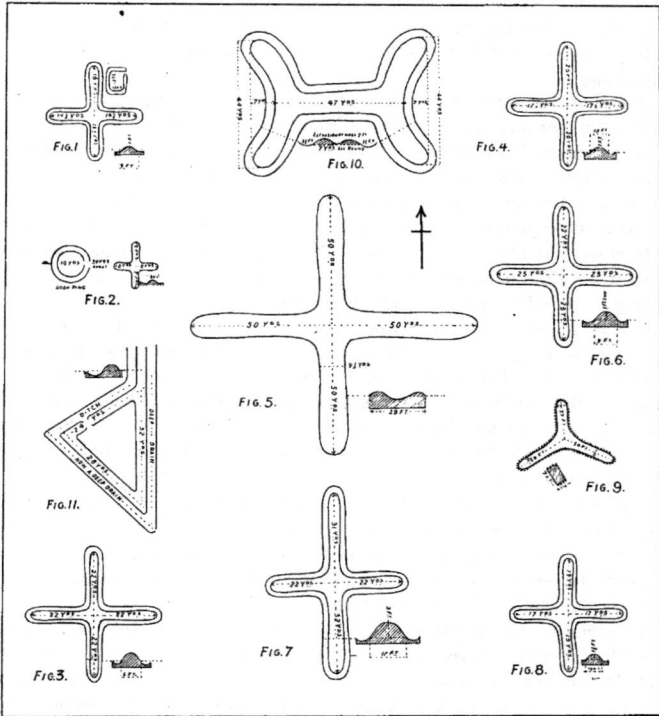

Plans and Sections of East Yorkshire Embankment Crosses.

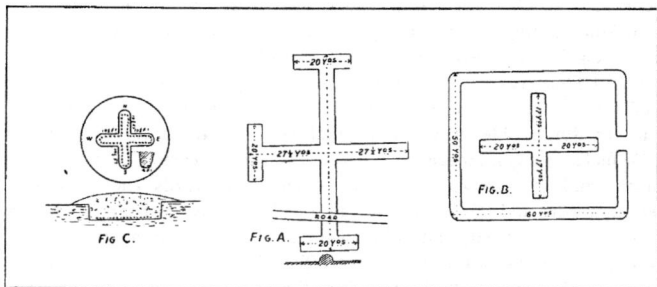

Plans and Sections of other Embankment Crosses.

Besides the crosses excavated in some of the circular moot-hills, described in the account of the Barrows Nos. 5, 122, 210, and 268, there are others consisting of two ridges of earth and stones, crossing each other, generally near their centres, at right angles.

It seems to me not improbable that these embankment crosses were used by the early Christian converts for a purpose similar to that which the circular moot-hill served their pagan fore-fathers. It would naturally strike these early converts that where a fresh or additional Moot-hill was needed, an embankment cross would be equally suitable and more striking than the concealed cross under the circular mound, and consequently it would, at times, be constructed. There are eleven of these structures, as shown on the plate D. The two first are near some traces of old settlements on small plots of dry ground which stand 2 feet to 4 feet above the swampy ground in Kelleythorpe Hogwalk.

No. 1 is about two miles south-west of Driffield Church. The arm to the north measures 16 yards, and the three others measure 14 yards each from the centre of the cross. The width of each arm is 3 yards, with an elevation of 1 foot.

Between the northern and eastern arms is a low four-sided bank, enclosing an area measuring 13 feet by 12 feet, to which reference will be made later.

No. 2.—This cross I discovered as recently as June 16th, 1895. It is situated about a quarter of a mile south-east of No. 1. Its southern and northern arms measure 7 and 9 yards respectively, the eastern and western 8 yards each. Their width is 2 yards, with an elevation of about 1 foot. Thirty yards from the terminal end of the western arm is a low circular bank (fig. 2a) enclosing an area nearly 10 yards in diameter. An apparent break in this ring opposite the western arm of the cross seems to indicate an entrance.

No. 3 is known by the name of Christ Cross. It is on high ground half-a-mile to the north of the site of the ancient village of Haywold, about 7 miles south-west of Driffield. I first examined this structure about the year 1863, before it had suffered from the demolishing action of the plough. At that time, each of the four arms measured approximately 22 yards in length, a little over 3½ feet in height, and 8 feet in width. A ditch about 18 inches in depth ran close round each arm, the material from which had probably assisted to raise the cross. My last visit was on May 8th, 1895, and I was sorry to find that the cultivation of the land during the intervening years had almost entirely erased this structure, and that even the practiced eye could observe little more than the outline of its site.*

No. 4.—This cross is on low and sheltered ground at the foot of the northern edge of the Wolds, in a grass field near "Coke Farm, now the dog-kennels, close to the south side of the village of Birdsall, about 14 miles west-north-west from Driffield. Its southern and northern arms measure about 14½ yards each in length, and its eastern and western arms 15½ yards each. They are about 12 feet in width, and 1 foot in elevation. This cross appears to be more recent than the old high-ridged lands upon which it seems to stand.†

No. 5.—This structure is called on the Ordnance map the "Old Bield." It stands on high ground slightly within the northern verge of the Wolds, near

* About one mile north-north-east of this cross is a field called "Beadygraves."
† The second field east of the cross is called "Steenhowe," indicating that a mound once existed there, which was probably made use of in connection with the cross.

Whin-Moor Farmhouse, on "Whin" or "Tween-Moor,"‡ about 12 miles north-west of Driffield, and a little south of East Heslerton. Its northern and southern arms measure from the centre of the cross 45 yards each, and the eastern and western arms 50 yards each in length. Their elevation does not exceed 2 feet, but their width varies from 9 to 10 yards. This unusually great width seems to be due to the fact that the cross originally consisted of two parallel mounds (see section of fig. 5), with a deep trench between them, whereas in nearly all other cases there was a single mound with a ditch on either side. In this example, from its mode of construction, there is no trace of a ditch round the outside of the cross, and as the ground seems never to have been ploughed, there is no likelihood of one having been obliterated. At the points marked with a " * " on the plan (fig. 5) stand some very old ash trees, and in several other places along the arms of the cross are marks where others have been. There are other old trees and banks indicating an early settlement near to it, and probably this and other crosses were planted with trees after their original use was abandoned. About one-eighth of a mile south-east of this cross is a mound or barrow (now planted with fir trees and called the "New Bield"), which measures 45 feet in diameter and about 3 feet in height. Very probably this mound, though originally a British Barrow, was afterwards used in connection with the cross. Whilst a little to the south-west the fields are called Lady Hills (meaning Law-day Hills, according to some antiquaries), and probably derive their name from the use once made of the cross and mounds near it.

No. 6.—This example is 8 miles north of Driffield, on high ground just to the north of the site of the village of Swaythorpe, near Thwing. Each arm measures about 23 yards in length, and the elevation is 18 inches, with a breadth of 9 feet. A partially filled-in trench is distinctly visible on both sides and round the end of each arm of the cross. This cross stands on old grass land which seems never to have been ploughed, but close past the terminal end of its western arm some old high-ridged lands run north and south. This would seem to indicate that the cross is older than the old raised lands which run close by the side of it.

No. 7.—On the 6-inch Ordnance Map this cross is shown on "Wharram Hill," (also "Worms Hill"), nearly half-a-mile east of Burton Carr House, two miles south-east of the village of Burton Agnes, and seven miles east of Driffield. It has unequal arms. Its north and south branches measure approximately 31½ yards and the other two 22 yards each. About midway on the western arm, is the decayed stump of a sycamore tree, probably 200 to 300 years old. The cross is a large and massive structure, and the large ditch round it still remains open to a depth of from 2 to 3 feet.

No. 8, which is not shown on the Ordnance Map, is 1¼ miles south of No. 7, near High House Farm, Gransmoor, close to the left-hand side of the road to Lissett. It differs from the previous one in having its eastern and western arms each only two yards shorter than the northern and southern ones, viz., 17 yards each. The two last-named crosses, though on small naturally-raised islands in the carrs, are on ground only 25 feet above Ordnance datum line.

No. 9.—This unusual shaped structure is 15 miles north-north-east of Driffield,

‡ This name is given on the O.S.

close by the south side of the line, nearly opposite Cayton Carr House, between Cayton and Seamer railway stations. It is not shown on the 6-inch Ordnance map. It consists of only three banks of earth, respectively 16½ yards, 12½ yards, and 16½ yards in length, radiating approximately from a centre. Each of these arms is 4½ feet high, with a medium width of 7 feet. The sides are faced all round with a nearly vertical wall of stones—chiefly boulder stones—embedded in a little clayey earth, evidently to protect the banks. There is, at present, no trace of a ditch round the outer margin of any of the arms. On its summit are some elders and other trees of considerable age. It is built on the southern edge of " Holme Hill," close to several other small and slightly raised plots of ground —little islands*—of but a few acres in extent, surrounded by the low swampy ground of Osgodby and Cayton Carrs.

No. 10 is situated 1½ miles west of the village of Brandesburton. On the Ordnance maps it is named the "Old Bield" and "Bield Hill," and the adjoining field to the west is named "Butts Hill." The ground here is only 10 feet above Ordinance datum. The middle embankment of this structure measures 47 yards down the centre, east to west, whence it curves outwards and forwards in the form of a crescent, increasing the length of the structure to the extent of 7 yards at each end, thereby making its extreme length 61 yards, and its width 7 yards.

The diameter of the western crescent is 44 yards and that of the eastern crescent 45 yards. All round it is a shallow ditch 2½ yards wide, the material from which has been used to form the embankment which is now nearly 2 feet above the surrounding ground. Like the "Whin Moor" Bield cross (fig. 5), the embankment has a hollow along the centre, probably due to the material from the surrounding ditch (see section) not being sufficient to raise the centre of the rampart. This structure seems to partake of the form of a cross and crescent combined, and most probably it has served a purpose similar to that of the four-armed embankment crosses previously described.

No. 11.—This triangular embankment is near the south side of the village of Brandesburton, about 150 yards from the northern foot of Coneygarth Hill, and about 1½ miles east of structure No. 10. The ramparts of the three sides of the enclosure measure 24, 28 and 32 yards respectively, and are surrounded by a ditch on the outside, the material from which has been used to raise the ramparts.

On the north, near the western corner, are appearances of an entrance from which is now traceable a raised causeway (very little above the ordnance datum line), across the low swampy ground between this earthwork and "Coneygarth Hill." "Coneygarth Hill" is one of a chain of sand and gravel banks, running from north to south, and then curving eastwards; and, though its elevation is only about 25 feet above Ordnance datum line, it seems to have been terraced round, and in early times occupied as a dwelling-place, with which the triangular enclosure was possibly connected, as a place of meeting.

The eleven structures referred to all occur within a radius of 15 miles of

---

* In draining the ground a short time ago, on the north-west side of one of these islands, the trunk of a remarkably tall elm tree, 60 feet long, was discovered at a depth of 18 inches, lying horizontally, with one end touching the island, the other reaching straight into swampy ground as if to serve the purpose of a bridge.

Driffield, and are all that I know of at present, but possibly a few more exist unnoticed, and almost certainly several others have been totally destroyed.

These structures would appear to be almost confined to East Yorkshire; I know of none in North Yorkshire. As to their presence in the south of England, the late General Pitt Rivers, on October 26th, 1894, wrote:—

> " In reply to your letter, I am not aware that there are crosses in this part of
> the country of the kind you describe. I have seen one of these crosses
> in Yorkshire, but I have seen nothing like it here."

A few such, however, do exist in other parts of the country. I have met with the descriptions of seven similar structures which have been observed.

In St. Margaret's Park, Herefordshire, is a cruciform mound of this class (fig. *A*, plate D), with the four arms to the cardinal points. The terminal end of its northern, southern, and western arms are traversed by a short cross bank giving them the shape of the letter " T "; its eastern arm is straight. This is a very rare form of cross, and is occasionally found engraved on gems.

It is described as a "longitudinal half-round embankment, 15 feet wide at the base and about 4 feet high. Its extreme length is about 68 yards (giving 34 yards to each arm), and it maintains the shape throughout, except where it has been cut through by a temporary roadway. That it is of considerable antiquity is evident from the decayed stumps of oaks still visible, felled ages ago, together with more recent ones.—" Gentleman's Magazine," 1853, part 2, pp. 387-9, and " Archæological Journal," vol. xxiii., p. 268.

A cruciform earthwork, similar to the above, was described by a gentleman of the name of Moggridge, at the Ludlow Meeting of the Cambrian Archæological Association, in August, 1852, as existing near Margam, Glamorganshire (see " Gentleman's Magazine," October, 1852, p. 405); and at the Edinburgh Meeting of the British Association, in 1871, an account of a similar raised cross, situated upon a hill at Gringhitic, near Peebles, and measuring 26 yards from opposite extremities, was read by J. Wolfe Murray. No excavation has been made, and nothing, except its existence, was known about it.

Two others are noticed by W. H. Tregellas, in the Journal of the Archæological Institute, vol. xxii., p. 268, one near Cæsar's Camp, Wimbledon (referred to by Mr. T. Stackhouse, in his lectures), the other a large example on the top of a mountain at Margam, Port Talbot, South Wales. Mr. Tregallas writes as follows respecting the structures:—

> " The subject of cruciform tumuli is one of much interest. The notices which
> exist of such remains are, I believe, few, and the subjects of them appear
> to be of very uncertain origin."

And further on he adds:—

> " Nothing, so far as I am aware, seems to be known positively, at present, of the
> origin or history of these singular remains, except that they are doubtless
> of great antiquity."

Through the kindness of a friend, I am able to give a plan (fig. *B*, plate D) and short account of a very fine example, from Wiltshire, enclosed in a square

3 D

embankment, with an opening for access on the east side, copied from " Ancient Wiltshire," vol. 2, p. 43. Sir R. C. Hoare, writes :—

> " Before I quit this interesting eminence [Shipham], I must not omit to take notice of a very singular little earth-work, situated on the same ridge of hill, but nearer to the village of Banwell. Its form proclaims it to be Roman, but I cannot conceive for what use it was destined."

In the " Archæological Journal," vol. xi., p. 225, is a description of a somewhat similar structure, near the Maiden Way, in the angle formed by the White Line River, passing through the Parish of Bewcastle. It is called the "Shiel Knowe," and is thus described :—

> " The 'Shiel Knowe' appears to have been a very extensive cairn, rising to a considerable height in the centre, and having three ridges or barrows running from it at smaller elevations, and diverging towards different points. The centre cairn is 22 yards on the slope on the north-west side, and the ridges or barrows about one-half of that height. The ridge or barrow running to the south-west is about 100 yards long, the ridge to the south-east is about 140 yards long, and the ridge to the north about 380 yards long. They are now covered with green turf and heather, but stones show themselves in abundance." *

For what purpose these embankment crosses have been constructed history is silent, but they are traditionally called Bields by the country people, who believe they were made to give shelter to the cattle grazing in the open country. This is the only opinion I have heard expressed as to their purpose, except Canon Atkinson's suggestion that they may have been boundary marks before the parishes were enclosed. There is little evidence, however, to support either of these views, except that at times cattle would be observed to occupy, during stormy weather, the sides of the cross where there was the most shelter, just as they would make use of a clump of trees or a stone wall—hence probably the origin of their country name " Bield," a shelter. I feel fully convinced that none of the examples under review were originally constructed for shelter for cattle.

None of the crosses with four arms appear to me to have been made within many centuries of the present time. Had they been frequently constructed and in general use to shelter cattle up to the enclosure of the parishes, we should have had several of them remaining on our bleak hills. Besides, had they been made originally to shelter domestic animals, the deep and dangerous ditch would not have been left open close round the sides and end of every arm of the cross, as is the case with all, except that on Tween or Whin Moor (No. 9), which now shows no trace of a lateral trench. Neither would the arms have been always directed to the four cardinal points of the compass. Again, most of them (Nos. 1, 2, 6, 7, 8, 9, 10 and 11) are built on a small plot of but slightly raised ground, in low, swampy districts (only Nos. 3, 4 and 5 being on high ground), where

---

* Mr. Noake in his " Worcester in the Olden Times," page 110, gives the following entry from the Corporation books of that city, which seems clearly to refer to a similar embankment cross :—" In the year 1625. For mending the stocks at the *Grass Crosse*, for whipping of divers persons, and carting of other some, and for halling the goome-stoole to the houses of divers scouldinge people."—The " Archæological Journal," vol. xiii., p. 262.

Also—The " Antiquary," for October, 1900, p. 316, mentions a *turf* cross, one foot high, 2 feet broad, and 80 feet one way and 70 feet the other way. It is situated at Bedd-y-Gwydelel.

in early times but very little, if any, cattle could be kept. And even if kept, no shelter would seem to have been needed in low places, at that time surrounded, most probably, by forest and brushwood. Furthermore, No. 2 cross seems to have been too small and too low a structure to ever have afforded any shelter for cattle.

These raised cross-shaped mounds are nearly always found near the sites of old settlements, to which they undoubtedly served some useful purpose. The fact that their ground plan and orientation are similar to those of the excavated crosses found under some of the moot-hills, strongly suggests the idea that they may have been raised for open-air meeting-places, either for conducting and settling parish and other matters, or for religious gatherings. This view appears to be strongly supported by the enclosed* cross (fig. B) from Wiltshire.† This structure seems as if it may have been a very fine example of one of these primitive law-courts, but little adapted for the shelter of cattle.

The very rare form (fig. 9) with but three arms‡ was most probably used for a similar purpose as those with four arms, from whence secular and religious laws were promulgated to a little community settled on the small islands—or possibly on pile dwellings which may have existed in the carrs down to the 8th and the 10th centuries.§

Thus the deep ditch (a great objection to the theory of their having been in the first instance made to shelter cattle), closely outlining the arms of most of these crosses now becomes a useful adjunct by forming a boundary trench (a Thing-brink),‖ acting as a protection to the judges in their places of office from the attacks of the often disappointed and angry clients; for these moot-courts often ended in a conflict between the contending parties.¶

It will be observed that Nos. 6 and 7 are only 1¼ miles distant, in a straight line, and that Nos. 1 and 2 are so very near to each other that it seems evident that each pair belong to the machinery of a moot court, other examples of which are known. Mr. G. L. Gomme, in "Primitive Folk-moots," page 265, gives the following from the "New Statistical Account of Scotland," iv., p. 455 :—

> "At Mouswald, in Dumfriesshire, are two mounds, one called Styal, about 288 feet in diameter, and the other called Deadmangill. Tradition has handed down that at one place malefactors were tried and executed at the other." ·

---

* Probably many of these embankment crosses were at one time enclosed within a fence of brushwood or wattlework.   † See the "Archæological Journal," vol. xxiii., p. 269.

‡ At Somersby, near Horncastle, in Lincolnshire, is a three-armed or triangular stone cross on the top of a tall graceful column (shaft) 15 feet in height, which Alfred Primmer figures and describes, as quite unique, in his "Ancient Stone Crosses of England," p. 80.

§ That the meeting at the cross was most essential in giving judgment is shown by the following extract from "Primitive Folk-Moots," by Mr. G. L. Gomme :—"The sayd Sixteens hath not any authority to make any orders, or to set any amercements touching ye commons, except there be and do meet at ye Crosse nine of ye sayd Sixteens at ye time, and those nine may pinn ye rest of ye Sixteens."—"Archæologia," xxxv., 472, 1809.

‖ "That day men went to the 'Thing-brink' and spoke their pleadings. Also Egil and Thorstein with their whole troop went up to the 'Thing-brink' and sat them down where they were wont to sit."—"The Story of Egil Skallagrimsson," by Rev. W. C. Green, p. 187.

¶ At a meeting at Coveshoo in 822, two dukes were slain.—"Primitive Folk-Moots," p. 58, by Mr. G. L. Gomme.

He also, at p. 273, adds :—

"It will have been noticed that with many of the Moot-hills and Law-hills just
    enumerated is associated another hill or place connected with the gallows.
    No doubt the erection of the gallows complete the machinery of the ancient
    assembling places. The local judges adjudged the wrongdoer and saw
    him executed forthwith."

The remains of such a system are numerous in East Yorkshire, and only
require investigation. At Fimber, as well as the "Mill Hill" (fig. C), we
have the site of a second hill, indicated near the present village School, by
the name of "Hanging Hill" (meaning Gallows Hill), and Hanging Hill is
connected with several other villages.

Near the many settlements in this neighbourhood, there yet remain two
adjoining mounds, which, in all probability have, in most instances, served as
Moot and Gallows hills. We have Gallows-hill at Pockthorpe, Gallows-hill at
Brompton, near Scarborough, and other places. There are two artificial mounds
in a grass field close to Emswell,* two at Wold Newton, and two in a field
between the Priory Church, Bridlington, and the Quay. These two examples are
named butts on the Ordnance Sheet, probably from having been used as spear or
archery butts in later times. There are also two at Wetwang, one near to and
on opposite sides of the Vicarage, that on the east side having a large excavated
cross reaching from the centre to near the circumference of the mound, in the
direction of the cardinal points of the compass. That these law mounds have
had something to do in giving the name to this village is, I believe, pointed out
by my friend, the Rev. E. M. Cole, the Vicar of the Parish, in his "Scandinavian
Place Names in the East Riding of Yorkshire." Wetwang, apparently, has been
derived from "Voetti," "witness," and "Vangr," a field—i.e., the witness-field,
or place of justice.

Numerous other instances of two neighbouring mounds could be mentioned.

Presuming that the embankment-crosses served the same purpose as did the
circular Moot-hill, we seem to have in the Kelleythorpe example, near Driffield,
all the machinery of the most complete arrangement for carrying out the jurisdiction
of such a primitive court of justice. We have the larger cross (No. 1), within
two arms of which are traces of a building, possibly a temporary shelter for the
Moot-priest when giving judgment in cases brought to his primitive law court.
We also have, at a short distance, another cross, accompanied by a circular
enclosure—possibly a doom-ring, in which the condemned may have been
confined until he was executed on the small cross-shaped gallows-hill close by—
thus promptly ending the punishment of the accused.

---

* In the autumn of 1873, I opened these mounds, and found portions of Romano-British, or Anglo-
Saxon pottery, and what seemed to be traces of a cremated interment in the centre of each mound,
whilst, mixed in the mound, were animal bones, bits of iron, and fragments of Roman and Anglo-Saxon
pottery.

TABLES OF BARROWS, INTERMENTS,

AND

ARTICLES DEPOSITED WITH INTERMENTS.

GROUP I.

Table of Barrows, Interments, and Articles deposited with Interments.

No. of Barrow	BURNT — No. of Body	Urn, Dish-shaped Hole, or Circular Heap	UNBURNT — No. of Body	Description	In Grave or Body of Mound, or at Base	Primary or Secondary Burial	On Back, Right, or Left Side	Direction of Head	Bone or Stone Tools with Bodies	Bronze Implements	Worked Flints; Pot Sherds; Detached, Unburnt, Human and Animal Bones scattered in the Grave	Food Vase	Cinerary Urn	Incense Cup	Drinking Cup	Bodkins, Pins, Buttons, or Ornaments	Clay from a Distance, and Dish-shaped Cavities without Burnt Bones	Detached Bones, Relics, &c., from the Body of the Mound, not with Interments	Remarks
1	...	1	1	?	Base	P.	?	...	Flint flake	Fragm't.	...	2	...	...	...	...	Much.	22 worked flints.	Body extend
		Heap		Child	Mound	S.	B.	N.W.	Flint flake	...	...	...	...	...	...	...		Bits human bone, many flint flakes.	
C 39	...		1	Male	Grave	P.	...	N.W.		Dagger	...	...	...	...	...	...	Large quantity 3 U.	52 worked flints.	
C 73	1	Wood cist	...	Adult	Grave	P.	...	...	(Stone hammer & flint knife)	...	...	...	...	...	...	...	Quantity.	Flint flakes.	
233	...		1	No. 1 — flint find	Side	P.	?	...	...	...	...	1	...	...	...	...	Large quantity little cl'y		
			1	No. 2 — interment	Grave	P.	R.	E.	...	Dagger	...	...	...	...	...	...		Few flints.	
234	...		No i[nterment]	No. 1	Mound	S.	?	?	...	...	...	...	...	...	...	...			
			1	No. 2	Grave	P.	?	W.	...	...	...	...	...	...	...	...			
			1	No. 3	Grave	P.	?	W.	...	...	...	...	...	...	...	...			
6	...		4	Heads of children	Grave	?	?	?	...	...	...	...	...	...	...	...			
			2	Adult	Grave	?	?	S.E.	...	...	...	...	...	...	...	...	No clay.		
			1	Adult	Grave	?	?	S.	...	...	...	...	...	...	...	...			
			1	?	Grave	?	R.	?	...	...	...	...	...	...	...	...			
				Child	Grave	?	?	...	...	...	...	...	...	...	...	...			
7	1	Grave	...	?	...	P.	...	...	...	...	{Splinters of animal bone & 2 bits of bone}	1	...	...	...	...	None.		

18	1	Heap	...	?	Mel	S.	...	...	2 flint spears, 4 flint arrows, 3 stone pounders and flint flakes	...	Rib of an ox, many rat bones	2	...	...	Bones & teeth of the ox, pig; skulls and other bones of three small dogs or foxes; also flint chips and other animal bones.
	6	...	Bodies	Adults	Grave	P.	B.	Various	...	...	...	...	...	Much clay in the mound.	Detached bones.
22	1	...	...	Adlt	Grave	S.	R.	N.N.W.	Bone pick	...	Pot sherds	1	...	...	...
	1	...	...	Adlt	Mound	S.	?	?	...	...	...	1	...	...	...
	1	...	...	?	Mound	S.	L.	E.	...	...	...	1	...	...	...
	1	Hole	...	Alt	Mel	P.	?	?	...	...	...	...	...	...	...
21	1	Heap	...	?	Grave	S.	R.	S.W.	Worked flint	...	Tine of red deer, sherds of drinking cups, many broken bones	1	...	A little clay.	
	1	...	...	Adlt	Bse	P.	?	?	...	...		1	...		
	1	...	...	Infant	Grave	P.	R.	?	...	...			...		
	1	...	...	Adult	Grave	P.	?	?	...	...			...		
	1	...	...	Infant	Grave	P.	B.	S.E.	...	...	Child and other human bones	1	...		
	1	...	...	Female	Grave A	P.	L.	N.N.E.	...	...			...		
	1	...	...	Infant	de A	P.	L.		...	...			...	1 U	
	1	...	...	Female	Grave B	P.			...	...			...		
106	1	...	...	Adult	Grave	P.	R.	E.	15 worked flints	...	Detached human and animal bones	1	...	1 U	Human calvarium, many flint chips, and some pot sherds; human and animal bones.
	1	...	...	Adult	Grave	P.	R.	S.	...	...			...		
43	3	...	Skulls	Adults	Mel & Grave	?			Flint knife	...	Unburnt human & animal bones and 15 worked flints	...	Bone pin	...	{This deposit similar to some on Aldro.
72	1	...	...	Adult	Grave B	P?	R.	S.W.	1 Flint knife	...	4 pieces urn, 7 flint flakes	...	...	...	
	1	...	...	Adult	Grave D	P	R.	S.W.	...	...			...	...	...
1 A	...	Long heap	A	?	Grave A	P?			...	...		...	...	...	...
1 C	...	Round heap	C	?	de A	P?			...	...		...	...	...	...
73	1	Hole	...	Adult	...	P. ?	?	N.W.	1 Flint knife	...		1	...	1 U	Pot sherds. {The hot ashes had scorched the legs of the body.
	...	...	...	...	Grave	P.	?		...	...			...		

GROUP I.—continued.

No. of Barrow	Burnt: No. of Body	Burnt: Urn, Dish-shaped Hole, or Circular Heap	Unburnt: No. of Body	Description	In Grave, or Body of Mound, or at Base	Primary or Secondary Burial	On Back, Right, or Left Side	Direction of Head	Bone or Stone Tools with Bodies	Bronze Implements	Worked Flints; Pot Sherds, Detached, Unburnt, Human and Animal Bones scattered in the Grave	Food Vase	Cinerary Urn	Incense Cup	Drinking Cup	Bodkins, Pins, Buttons, or Ornaments	Clay from a Distance, and Dish-shaped Cavities without Burnt Bones	Detached Bones, Relics, &c., from the Body of the Mound, not with Interments	REMARKS
44	...	...	...	...	...	...	...	...	...	...	...	...	...	...	...	...	A little.	Worked flints.	No inter
213	...	...	1	...	...	:P.	?	...	...	...	...	...	...	...	...	...	Part clay	...	No inter
214	1	...	...	...	Base	P.	...	...	...	...	...	...	...	...	...	...	...	...	
3	...	Heap	...	Child	Base	P.	...	...	...	...	3 lower jaws & other bones, all burnt	...	...	...	...	Bone bead	...	Animal bones.	
214½	...	...	1	Adult	Grave	?	?	W.	1 Worked flint	...	...	...	...	...	...	Bone article	...	...	
	...	...	1	Child	Grave	P.	R.	...	...	...	...	...	...	...	...	...	...	...	
211½	...	...	1	Youth No. 2	Grave	P.	L.	E.	2 Flint flakes	...	Animal and human bones	...	...	...	1	...	...	...	
	...	...	1	Adult No. 3	Grave	P.	?	N.E.	1 Axe-hammer	...		...	...	...		...	...	...	
	...	...	1	Child No. 2	Base	?	?	S.W.	...	...		...	...	...		...	...	...	
	...	...	1	Child No. 3	Base	?	?		...	...		...	...	...		...	...	...	
276	1	Heap	...	Adult	Grave 1	P.	...	...	...	...	Many human and animal bones, also 11 pot sherds	...	...	...	...	...	...	A human foot.	A human
	...	...	1	Youth No. 4	Grave 2	?	R.	S.W.	...	...		...	...	...	...	...	...	...	
	...	...	1	Infant No. 5	Grave 2	?	R.	N.E.	...	...		...	...	...	...	...	...	...	
	...	...	1	Adult No. 6	Grave 2	?	R.	S.W.	...	...		...	...	...	...	...	...	...	
	...	...	1	Adult No. 7	Grave 2	?	L.	E.	2 Worked flints	...		...	...	...	...	...	...	...	

INTERMENTS — UNBURNT — ARTICLES DEPOSITED WITH INTERMENTS — Vessels of Pottery

DETACHED BARROWS adjoining GROUP I.

No.	Heaps				Grave/Mound	P.	R.	Direction	Implements	Bones		Pins	U	Remarks
7a	...	1	...	AdultM.	Grave	P.	R.	E.S.E.	...	...	...	...	2 U	Animal bones, pot sherds, & flint flakes.
	53	...	...	(Of all ages)	...	...	...	...	...	...	...	...		
	...	1	A	Infant	Mound	P.	L.	N.E.	...	...	...	3 bone pins	...	
	...	1	B	Youth	Mound	P.	R.	E.	2 Horn picks	...	...	...	...	
	...	1	C	AdultM.	Grave	P.	L.	N.N.E.	Worked flints	Bones of ox, 2 beaver teeth, 8 boar tusks	...	1 bone pin	...	At the top of the mound was a + excavation and great quantities of Anglo-Saxon and medieval pot sherds and portions of iron articles.
	...	1	D	AdultM.	Grave	P.	R.	W.	Flint knife	...	...	...	...	
	...	1	E	Child	Mound	P.	R.	W.	...	...	...	...	...	
	...	1	F	Youth	Grave	P.	L.	S.W.	...	...	1	...	Clay in the form of an arch	
	...	1	G	AdultM.	Grave	P.	R.	N.E.	1 hammer head of stag's horn, 1 flint arrow, 1 flint axe	...	...	...	...	
	...	1	H	Child	Grave	P.	R.	E.	...	...	...	...	...	
	...	1	I	Adult	Grave	P.	R.	E.	...	1 Calvarium	...	...	...	
	...	1	K	AdultM.	Grave	B.	B.	E.	...	...	...	...	...	
	...	1	L	Youth	Mound	?	?	N.	9 Flint flakes	...	...	...	...	
	...	1	M	AdultM.	Mound	?	B.	S.W.	...	2 very small infants	...	...	...	
291	...	1	...	Adult	Grave	P.	R.	W.	6 Flint chips, Small piece of wood	...	...	...	1 U, 1 clay U	2 arrow heads, many flint chips
292	...	1	...	Trace base mound		?	?	...	...	...	...	...	...	
293	...	...	...	Nothing		...	...	...	...	...	...	...	...	
26	64	67								3	13 0 0 2	7	10 U	

See Summary at the end of these Tables.

3 E

GROUP II.

Table of Barrows, Interments, and Articles deposited with Interments.

No. of Barrow	No. of Body (Burnt)	Urn, Dish-shaped Hole, or Circular Heap	No. of Body (Unburnt)	Description	In Grave or Body of Mound, or at Base	Primary or Secondary Burial	On Back, Right, or Left Side	Direction of Head	Bone or Stone Tools with Bodies	Bronze Implements	Worked Flints; Pot Sherds; Detached, Unburnt, Human and Animal Bones scattered in the Grave	Food Vase	Cinerary Urn	Incense Cup	Drinking Cup	Bodkins, Pins, Buttons, or Ornaments	Clay from a Distance, and Dish-shaped Cavities without Burnt Bones	Detached Bones, Relics, &c., from the Mound, Body of the Mound, not with Interments	Remarks
45	1	Dish	…	…	…	…	…	…	…	1 Instrument burnt	…	…	…	…	…	…	…	Worked flints.	
46	1	Heap	…	…	Grave	P.	…	…	…	…	…	1	…	…	…	…	…	Worked flints and pot sherds.	
47	1	Heap	…	?	Grave	P.	?	?	1 Flint knife	…	2 Worked flints	1	…	…	…	Bone pin	Clay	Worked flints and 3 Flint flakes.	
48	1	Urn	…	?	Base	P.	?	?	1 Flint tool	…	…	…	1	…	…	…	Clay	Pot sherds and flints.	
70	…	…	1	(Young) (Female)	Grave	P.	B.	S.E.	…	…	23 Flint flakes	…	…	…	…	2 Jet studs	…	30 … flints.	
71	1	Urn	…	…	Grave	P. ?	…	…	…	…	Horn of roe-buck and bones	…	1	…	…	Bone pin	None	8 Worked flints and pot sherds.	
71	1	Urn	…	Child	Mound	?	…	…	…	…	…	…	1	…	…	Bone pin	None	…	
65	…	…	1	No. 1 Adult	Grave	P.	B.	W.S.W.	1 Flint disc	…	Many human and some animal bones	…	…	…	…	…	None	Human and animal bones.	
65	…	…	1	No. 2 Adult	Base	P.	R.	W.S.W.	1 Bone tool	…	…	…	…	…	…	…	None	Human and animal bones.	
66	…	…	1	No. 1 Child	Mound	S. ?	?	W.S.W.	1 Flint knife	…	…	…	…	…	…	…	None	Human and animal bones.	
66	…	…	1	No. 2 Adult	Mound	S. ?	?	?	1 Flint spear	…	…	1	…	…	…	…	None	Human and animal bones.	
66	…	…	1	No. 3 Child	Mound	?	?	N.N.W.	…	…	Human bones	…	…	…	…	…	None	Human and animal bones.	
66	…	…	1	No. 4 Youth	Grave	P.	R.	E.	…	…	…	…	…	…	…	…	None	Human and animal bones.	
67	1	Heap	…	Infant	Grave	P.	…	…	…	…	…	…	1	…	1	…	Clay	18 Worked flints, animal and human bones.	
67	1	…	…	Adult	Grave	P.	B.	E.	4 Flint flakes	…	…	…	…	…	…	…	Clay	Human and animal bones.	
127	1	Urn	…	Adult	Mound	?	…	…	…	…	…	…	1	…	…	…	Clay	Human and animal bones.	Snail shells the bones mice in the grave.
127	…	…	…	…	Mound	?	…	…	…	…	…	…	…	…	…	…	Clay	Human and animal bones.	
10	8		12							1		3	4		1				

Table of Barrows, Interments, and Articles deposited with Interments.

No. of Barrow	BURNT — No. of Body	Urn, Dish-shaped Hole, or Circular Heap.	UNBURNT — No. of Body	Description	In Grave, or Body of Md., or at Base.	Primary or Secondary Burial.	On Back, Right, or Left Side.	Direction of Head.	Bone or Stone Tools with Bodies.	Bronze Implements.	Worked Flints; Pot Sherds; Detached, Unburnt, Human and Animal Bones scattered in the Grave.	Food Vase	Cinerary Urn	Incense Cup	Drinking Cup	Bodkins, Pins, Buttons, or Ornaments	Clay from a Distance, and Dish-shaped Cavities without Burnt Bones ᴜ	Detached Bones, Relics, &c., from the Body of the Mound, not with Interments	Remarks.
116			1	No. 1	Youth	Grave A	P.?	R.	S.	Flint flake.	Pricker	Animal bones.							Portions of 5 vessels; a very large quantity of various animal bones; 105 flint flakes, and 11 worked flints	A vase with a cover to it; a vase with a handle; and an incised cross at the bottom.
			1	No. 2	Male	Grave B	P.	L.	N.E.		Dagger					1		Clay		
			1	No. 3	Adult	Grave C	P.	L.	N.E.			Several human bones in the grave				1				
			1	No. 4	Youth	Grave C	P.	L.	N.				1			1				
			1	No. 5	Youth	Grave C	P.	R.	N.E.			in the grave								
			1	No. 6	Adult	Grave C	P.	L.	N.							1				
108	1	Hole			Adult	Grave	P.					Pot sherds						Clay		
109	1	Heap			Adult & Child	Mound	S.				Part of 3 burnt daggers	Burnt human & animal bones.						Clay	Worked flints and pot sherds.	
	1	Hole			Adult	Hole	P.						1				Bone pin	1 U		A cavity left by something gone to decay.
88			1	A	Adult	Base	P.	B.	E.	3 poor flints		Animal bones	1					Clay		
			1	B	Adult	Base	P.	L.	E.	Pig's tooth								Clay		
			1	C	Youth	Base	P.	L.	W.									Clay		
			1	D	Adult	Base	P.	?	W.	Arrow head										
	1	Hole		a	Adult	Mound	?												Many human & animal bones.	
	1	Hole		b	Adult	Mound	?													
			1	E	Child	Base	P.		E.	5 worked flints									Animal bones & worked flints.	
			1	F	Child	Base	P.		E.											

GROUP III., DIVISION A—continued.

	BURNT.		UNBURNT.						ARTICLES DEPOSITED WITH INTERMENTS.										
No. of Barrow	No. of Body	Urn, Dish-shaped Hole, or Circular Heap.	No. of Body.	Description.	In Grave or Body of Mound, or at Base.	Primary or Secondary Burial.	On Back, Right, or Left Side.	Direction of Head.	Bone or Stone Tools with Bodies.	Bronze Implements.	Worked Flints; Pot Sherds; Detached, Unburnt, Human and Animal Bones scattered in the Grave.	Food Vase.	Ossuary Urn.	Incense Cup.	Drinking Cup.	Bodkins, Pins, Buttons, or Ornaments.	Clay from a Distance, and Dish-shaped Cavities without Burnt Bones	Detached Bones, Relics, &c., from the Body of the Mound, not with Interments.	Item.
256	1	Urn	?	?	?	?	...	...	...	...	...		1					{ Animal bones, pot sherds and flint flakes. }	
52	1	Heap	1	A	Grave	P.	...	...	Flint spear	...	...					{ Bone pin & whistle }	...	...	
	...		1	No. 1	Grave	P.	B.	W.	...	...	...					...	...	...	
	...		1	No. 2	Grave	P.	B.	W.	...	...	Human tibia	1				...	...	...	
	...		1	No. 4 Dismembered	Grave	P.	In a heap	In a heap	...	...	Human arm bone					...	Clay	...	
	...		1	No. 3 Dismembered	Grave	P.	B.	W.N.W.	Flint knife	...	...					...	...	...	
53	...		1	No. 1	Grave	P.	In a heap	In a heap	...	...	Pot sherds					...	...	...	
	...		1	No. 2	Grave	P.	? L.	S. E.S.E.	...	...	Many snail shells				1?	...	...	...	
	...		1	No. 3	Grave	P.	B.	W.	{ Bone pick, points of broken picks. }	...	{ Human and animal bones. }					...	...	...	
54	...		1	No. 4	Grave	P.	B.	W.	{ 2 more picks, and many animal bones. }	...	...					...	...	...	
	...		1	No. 5 dismembered 2	Grave	P.	In a heap	N.E.	...	...	Tooth of pig					...	...	...	
	...		1	No. 6 Child	Grave	P.	?		...	...	...					...	...	...	
	...		1	No. 7 Several	Grave	P.	Large heap	Large heap	...	...	...					...	...	...	
87	...		1	No. 8 Several	Mound	S.	Long heap	Long heap	...	...	...				1	...	...	...	{ An u num disme bodies sec
	1	Urn	1	... Adult	Grave	P.	R.	S.S.E.	Flint spear.	...	...	2	1			...	Clay. 1 U	{ 40 worked flints and pot sherds. }	}
	8		27							3		5	2	...	7		2	2	

			No.				P.?			Flint disc. Flint flake	Pot sherd	jet bead. bone pin.			
30	1	Hole		1	...	Base	P.?	...	L.	...	...	...	1	...	1 Flint flake.
119	1	Heap		1	Adult	Base	P.	...	B.	...	...	...	...	...	...
	1	Heap		1	Adult	Be	P.	...	L.	...	...	...	...	...	...
C30	1	Urn		1	Adult	Base	P.	...	R.	...	...	...	1		My flakes, and this, part of a polished stone axe, the lower jaw of a dog, and other animal bones.
			No. 1	1	Child	Mound	S.	E.		Flint flake				{ much clay	
C59			No. 2	1	Yg. M.	Base	P.?	S.					1		
			No. 3	1	Child	Mound	P.?	N.					1		
			No. 4	1	Child	Mound	P.?	S.					1		
			No. 5	1	Male	Grave	P.	S.S.W.	R.						
			No. 6	1	Adult	Mound	P.?	N.W.	R.						
	1	Heap	No. 7	1	Child										Several flints.
C28	1	...		...		Base	P.	...	...	...	...	jet bead.	1	Clay	
C29	1	Hole		...		Ba s	?	...	...	...	...	bone pin.	...	...	...
6	7			6									5 1 0 0		

(This Cluster was remarkable for the absence of clay from a distance.)

					S.?		Animal bone	Hammer-head of red deer horn			
C76	{ 1	Heap	...	Mound	S.?	...	...	{ Hammer-head of red deer horn }	...	...	{ Human and animal bones.
C81	...	...	Youth	Grave	P.	R.	...	...	1	...	...
C77	1	Hole	Adult	Hole	P.	...	Animal bones	...	...	...	...
C80	...	...	2 disturbed bodies	Base	P.	...	{ Barbed arrow & flint knife }	{ Jet link }	...	...
C78	...	...	1 broken up body 1 disturbed youth	Grave	P.	...	...	...	...	...	animal bones.

No. of Barrow	No. of Body (Burnt)	Urn, Dish-shaped Hole, or Circular Heap	No. of Body	Description	In Grave or Body of Mound, or at Base	Primary or Secondary Burial	On Back, Right, or Left Side	Direction of Head	Bone or Stone Tools with Bodies	Bronze Implements	Worked Flints; Pot Sherds; Detached, Unburnt, Human and Animal Bones scattered in the Grave	Food Vase	Cinerary Urn	Incense Cup	Drinking Cup	Bodkins, Pins, Buttons, or Ornaments	Clay from a Distance, and Dish-shaped Cavities without Burnt Bones	Detached Bones, Relics, &c., from the Body of the Mound, not with Interments	Remarks
C 75	… …		1	No. 1	Adult	Base	P.	L.	W.	42 Flint flakes / A beautiful flint knife	…	…	…	…	…	…	…	…	…	
			1	No. 2	Adult	Base	P.	R.	N.	…	…	…	…	…	…	…	…	…	…	
	1	Heap	…	A	?	Base	?	…	…	…	…	…	…	…	…	…	…	…	{ Flint flakes and animal bones.
C 74	1	Hole	1	…	Adult	Base	P.	…	…	…	…	…	…	…	1	…	2 bone pins	…	…	
C 79	1	Hole	1	…	…	Base	P.	…	…	3 Flint flakes	…	…	1	…	1	…	…	…	…	
	1	Hole	1	…	Child	Grave	P.	…	…	…	…	…	1	…	2	…	…	…	…	
8	6		7									2		2					

DIVISION D.

No. of Barrow	No. of Body (Burnt)	Urn, Dish-shaped Hole, or Circular Heap	No. of Body	Description	In Grave or Body of Mound, or at Base	Primary or Secondary Burial	On Back, Right, or Left Side	Direction of Head	Bone or Stone Tools with Bodies	Bronze Implements	Worked Flints; Pot Sherds; Detached, Unburnt, Human and Animal Bones scattered in the Grave	Food Vase	Cinerary Urn	Incense Cup	Drinking Cup	Bodkins, Pins, Buttons, or Ornaments	Clay	Detached Bones, &c.	Remarks
113	1	Heap	…	…	Mound	?	…	…	Flint knife	…	…	…	…	…	…	…			
	1	Heap	…	Adult	Mound	?	…	…	…	…	…	…	…	…	…	…			
	1	Heap	…	Adult	Grave	P.	B.	S.	…	Pricker	Human bones	…	…	1	…	6 bone pins			
	1	Heap	1	Adult	Grave 1	P.	…	…	…	…	…	…	…	…	…	…			
	…	…	1	Aged F.	Grave 2	P.	L.	E.	3 Flints	…	Human bones	…	…	…	…	…			13 Worked flints.

No.					Type		Dir.	Finds					Material	Remarks
97	{ 1 / 1	Heap / Hole	...	Adult / Child	Base / ate	P. / P.	... / ...	1 Flint knife	...	...	...	...	Clay	4 Flint flakes.
50	... / ...	...	1 / 1	{ Two or more dismembered bodies.	Grave / Grave	P. / P.	In a heap / In a heap	...	{ Human and animal bones and pot sherds. }	...	1	...	...	Worked flints, 3 pot sherds, human and animal bones.
51	...	...	2	Children	Grave	P.	W.	2 Worked flints	...	...	...	...	Clay	3 Horn picks, worked flints.
C 47	{ 1 / ...	Heap / Hole	... / 1	...	ate / ate	? / ?	... / R.	...	...	...	...	...	Clay	Portions of a food vase, 20 worked flints,
49	1	...	1	...	Grave / ate	P. / P.	S. / B.	Pot sherds / 3 Flint knives	...	...	1 / 1	...	Clay	5 pot sds.
6	8		8											

DIVISION E.

No.					Type		Dir.	Finds					Material	Remarks
125	...	...	...	...	Grave	...	...	...	...	...	...	...	Clay	{ Crossed by a V-shaped trench
126	2	Urn	...	...	Base	P.	...	...	...	...	...	...	...	{ Crossed by a V-shaped trench leading to a spring of water.
117	...	...	...	...	...	...	...	...	...	1	...	Clay	Pot sherd, and 9 worked flints.
C 48	{ 1 / 1	Urn / Heap	... / 1	Adult / Adult	Mound / Grave	S. / P.	... / R.	...	{ Animal bones {	1 / ...	Clay / Clay	2 Worked flints.
94	... / ...	...	...	Adult	Grave	P.	R. / S.	1 Flint knife	...	1	...	...	6 Worked flints.
5	4		2							1 1 1 1			

GROUP IV.

Table of Barrows, Interments, and Articles deposited with Interments.

INTERMENTS. ARTICLES DEPOSITED WITH INTERMENTS.

No. of Barrow	BURNT No. of Bodies	Urn, Dish-shaped Hole, or Circular Heap.	UNBURNT No. of Bodies	Description.	In Grave, or Body of Mound, or at Base.	Primary or Secondary Burial.	On Back, Right, or Left Side.	Direction of Head.	Bone or Stone Tools with Bodies.	Bronze Implements.	Worked Flints; Pot Sherds; Detached, Unburnt, Human and Animal Bones scattered in the Grave.	Food Vase	Cinerary Urn	Incense Cup	Drinking Cup	Bodkins, Pins, Buttons, or Ornaments.	Clay from a Distance, and Dish-shaped Cavities without Burnt Bones	Detached Bones, &c., from the Mound, not with Interments.	REM.
92	1	Urn	…	Adult	Base	P.	…	…	…	…	…		1					{ Pot sherds and 25 worked flints. }	
123	…	…	1	Mle	Grave	P.	L.	N.N.E.	Barbed arrow	…	…	1				4 jet buttons	little clay	…	
202	1	Hole	…	Adult	Mund	?	…	…	…	…	…						…	…	
203	…	…	Body probably destroyed by interring cattle during the cattle plague.	…	…	?	R.	N.	…	…	…			1			little cl'y	…	
204	(1)	Heap	1	Child	Base	?	R.	N.E.	…	…	Pot sherds						…	…	
			1	Adlt	Grave	?	B.	S.E.	Flint knife	…		1			1		Clay	…	A previ‑ ing h‑ troyed hunner
			1	Infant	Grave	P.	B.	N.E.	…	…							…	…	
			1	Youth	Grave	…	L.	W.	…	…							…	…	
			1	Old Mle	Nève	S.	R.	N.E.	Flint knife	…							…	…	
205	…	…	1	dlt F.	Grave	P.	L.	N.W.	Flint knife	…		1					Clay	…	Very ta femur tibia hume
			1	Male	Grave	P.	L.	N.E.	…	Dagger							Much	…	
			1	dlt	Grave	P.	L.	…	…	…							Clay	…	
			1	Adult	Gve	P.	L.	E.	{ Flint instrument & battered pebble. }	…								…	

No.				Age/Sex	Site			Direction	Flints, &c.		Other objects				
206	...	...	...	Adult	Grave	P.	R.	N.N.E.	...	...	...	...	...	...	...
207	{1} Hole	1	...	Adult	Grave	P.?	...	...	...	...	...	1	...	...	...
208	...	...	...	Adult	Grave	S.	R.	W. E. of S.	Flint knife	...	Urinal calculus. 1	1	...	Clay	} Several Flints.
...	...	...	...	Adult	Grave	P.	B.	...	...	...	...	...	...	...	
209	1 Hole	1	...	Adult	Grave	?	...	S.S.W.	Portion of antler	...	(Animal bones and tooth of Urus.	...	...	Clay	
210	1 Hole	1	...	No. 1	Hole	?	...	...	...	...	...	...	...	...	
				No. 2	Grave	P.	...	...	...	...	...	...	...	...	
				No. 3	Grave	P.	B.	S.E.	Flint knife	...	...	...	...	...	
124				No. 4 Male	Grave	P.	B.	N.N.E.	(Flint dagger, flint knife & 2 other flints.)	...	A lump of pyrites. 1	1	Pin of bone. Jet ring & stud; also amber D stud.	...	
124a	...	...	Disturbed b dy		...	...	...	...	...	...	...	...	...	...	
211	...	...	...	Adult	Grave	P.	L.	E.	(Bone tool and 6 worked flints)	...	(Animal bones and pot sherds. 1	1	...	1 U	
212	...	...	No. 1	Adult	Grave	P.	R.	...	...	...	(Pieces of animal bones.	...	...	Clay	
			No. 2	Adult	Grave	P.	R.	...	...	...	...	...	...	...	
			No. 3	Adult	Grave	P.	...	...	...	...	...	...	...	...	
	6	24										6 2 1			

GROUP V.

Table of Barrows, Interments, and Articles deposited with Interments.

INTERMENTS.

ARTICLES DEPOSITED WITH INTERMENTS.

No. of Barrow	BURNT — No. of Bodies	BURNT — Urn, Dish, shaped Hole, or Circular Heap.	UNBURNT — No. of Bodies.	UNBURNT — Description.	UNBURNT — In Grave, or Body of Mound, or at Base.	UNBURNT — Primary or Secondary Burial.	UNBURNT — On Back, Right, or Left Side.	UNBURNT — Direction of Head.	Bone or Stone Tools with Bodies.	Bronze Implements.	Worked Flints; Pot Sherds; Detached, Unburnt, Human and Animal Bones scattered in the Grave.	Food Vase.	Cinerary Urn.	Incense Cup.	Drinking Cup.	Bodkins, Pins, Buttons, or Ornaments	Clay from a Distance, and Dish-shaped Cavities without Burnt Bones	Detached Bones, Relics, &c., from the Body of the Mound, not with Interments.	REMARKS.
61	...	...	1	...	...	Cist	P.	...	...	...	...	...	...	...	...	...	...	...	...
	...	...	1	?	Adult	Grave	?	R.	...	...	...	...	...	...	...	...	...	...	Detached hmn bones.
	...	...	1	Child	Grave	P.	...	...	...	...	...	...	...	...	...	...	...	...	...
89	1	Heap	...	...	Grave	P.	...	...	...	...	...	...	...	...	...	...	...	(Pot sherds, animal bits, and 19 worked flints.
90	1	wooden receptacle	...	...	Adult	Base	P.	...	...	Stone hammer	...	...	...	...	...	...	...	Much clay	(Pot sherds, animal bones, and 7 worked flints.
56	1	Heap	...	No. 1	...	Hole	S.?	...	...	...	...	Adult & child's bones.	...	...	...	...	...	...	...
	1	Urn	...	No. 2	...	Hole	S.?	...	...	...	...	...	...	1	...	...	...	...	...
	1	Heap	...	No. 3	...	Hole	S.?	...	Flint knife	...	...	...	...	...	...	Clay	...
	...	...	1	No. 1	Adult	Base	P.	R.	W.	Flint knife	...	...	...	...	...	...	Much clay	Human and animal bones.
	...	...	1	No. 2	Adult	Base	P.	R.	W.	...	...	...	...	...	...	...	6 forked flints.
	...	...	1	No. 3	Adult F.	Grave	P.	R.	S.W.	...	...	...	...	...	1	...	...	...
	...	...	1	No. 4	Adult	(Western grave.)	P.	L.	E.	...	...	...	...	...	1	...	...	...
	...	...	...	No. 5	Adult	...	P.	L.	E.	...	...	...	...	...	...	...	...	...
57	1	Heap	...	...	...	Grave	P.	...	...	...	...	...	...	...	...	jet button	...	...

			No.	Age					Flint implement	Dagger	Bones, &c.			Metal object	Clay	Relics	Remarks
55		1		No. 1	Adult	Base	S.?	L.	S.E.	Flint knife	...	...	...	...	...	...	...	Animal bones, worked flints, & pot sherds.
		1		No. 2	Adult	Base	S.?	L.	E.	...	...	...	...	...	...	...	...
		1		No. 3	Female	Base	S.?	B.	W.	...	...	...	...	1	...	...	...
		1		No. 4	Child	Base	S.?	B.	W.	...	...	...	...	...	...	...	...
	1 to 4	1		No. 5	On edge of grave.	P.	L.	E.	...	...	...	...	...	...	...	...
		1		No. 6	Dismembered. Gr.	P.	B.	W.	...	...	Numerous small pieces of human bone in the grave.	...	...	...	...	...
		1		No. 7	Adult	Grave	P.	...	N.	Flint knife	...	4 large pieces of human leg.	...	...	...	...	...
		1		No. 8	Adult	Grave	P.	L.	...	Flint knife	...	...	...	...	...	...	...
				No. 9	Adult	Grave	P.	...	N.	...	...	...	...	...	...	...	...
		1		No. 10	Adult	Grave	P.	?	?	Flint knife	...	25 hand-struck flint chips.	...	1	jet button	...	...
		1		No. 10a	Infant	Grave	P.	L.	N.	...	...	...	...	1	...	...	...
		1		No. 11	Youth	Grave	P.	L.	N.	...	...	...	...	...	...	...	...
58	1		Hole	...	?	Hole	P.	...	...	...	...	...	...	...	...	...	7 flint chips and 1 pot sherd.
59				...	Adult	Grave	P.	R.	S.S.E.	...	...	Pot sherds.	...	...	...	...	...
91	1	1	Hole	...	Adult	Hole	P.	...	...	...	...	...	...	...	...	No clay	...
110	1 to 4		Hole	...	?	Graves	P.	L.	...	...	...	Human & many animal bones, in fragments.	...	...	...	...	Animal bones.
12		1		A	Adult	Grave	P.	R.	N.W.	Flint knife	...	...	...	...	...	...	...
		1		B	Adult	Grave	P.?	R.	S.	...	...	...	...	...	...	...	...
				C	?	Grave	P.?	L.	S.	...	...	...	...	...	...	...	...
		1		D	?	Grave	P.	R.	S.W.	...	...	...	...	...	...	...	...
		1		...	Child	Grave	P.	L.	N.E.	Flint knife, 2 flint discs	...	...	...	...	...	Clay	60 old flints.
8	1		Hole	...	Adult	Hole	S.	R.	W.	...	...	...	...	1	Bone pin	...	30 old flints.
		1		...	Child	Mound	...	...	...	Flint knife	...	...	...	1	...	Blue clay	20 old flints and animal bones.
9		1		...	(trace of body.)	Base	P.	...	...	Barbed arrow & minute flints.	...	...	...	1	...	...	...
		1		...	Adult	Base	S.	B.	...	...	...	...	...	...	...	Clay	Pot sherds, 2 flint axes, and ...
10	1		Hole	...	...	Hole	P.	...	...	...	1 Dagger	...	...	...	...	Clay	A pit dwelling.

GROUP V.—continued.

	BURNT			UNBURNT					ARTICLES DEPOSITED WITH INTERMENTS.			Vessels of Pottery.							
No. of Barrow	No. of Bodies.	Urn, Dish-shaped Hole, or Circular Heap.	No. of Bodies.	Description.	In Grave or Body of Mound, or at Base.	Primary or Secondary Burial.	On Back, Right, or Left Side.	Direction of Head.	Bone or Stone Tools with Bodies.	Bronze Implements.	Worked Flints; Pot Sherds; Detached, Unburnt, Human and Animal Bones scattered in the Grave.	Food Vase	Cinerary Urn	Incense Cup	Drinking Cup	Bodkins, Pins, Buttons, or Ornaments.	Clay from a Distance, and Dish-shaped Cavities without Burnt Bones.	Detached Bones, Relics, &c., from the Body of the Mound, not with Interments.	Remarks.
11	1	Hole {3 deposits in a hole}	...	... ?	Hole / Hole	P. / S.?	...	...	...	...	Piece of knife.	...	...	...	...	...	...	Flint chips.	
26	1 / 1 / 1	Urn / Hole / Urn / Hole	...	C / B / A / a	Mound / Hole / Hole	S.? / P. / P.	...	...	{Flakes of flint & bone tool.}	...	{Skull of a child & ox bones.}	...	1 / 1	...	...	...	Blue clay	...	...
27	...	...	1	Adult	Grave	P.	L.	N.	3 grains of wheat	...	...	1	...	...	...	...	Clay	Pot sherds.	
131	...	...	0 / 0	1 / 2	Grave / Grave	Empty / Empty	...	...	Flint scraper / Flint knife	...	...	...	...	...	...	...	...	Pot sherds.	{A curiou[s] location hip join[t]}
132	3 in holes.	...	0	... ? ...	Hole / Grave	P. / Empty	...	...	Animal bone.	...	...	...	...	...	...	...	...	...	
19	28	28										9	3	0	5				

Table of Barrows, Interments, and Articles deposited with Interments.

No. of Barrow	INTERMENTS — BURNT: No. of Bodies	Urn, Dish-shaped Hole, or Circular Heap.	UNBURNT: No. of Bodies	No.	Description.	In Grave, or Body of Mound or at Base.	Primary or Secondary Burial.	On Back, Right, or Left Side.	Direction of Head.	Bone or Stone Tools with Bodies.	Bronze Implements.	Worked Flints; Pot Sherds, Detached, Unburnt, Human and Animal Bones scattered in the Grave.	Food Vase.	Cinerary Urn.	Incense Cup.	Drinking Cup.	Bodkins, Pins, Buttons, or Ornaments.	Clay from a Distance, and Dish-shaped Cavities without Burnt Bones U	Detached Bones, Relics, &c., from the Body of the Mound, not with Interments.	Remarks.
4	1	Heap (centre grave)	…	No. 2	Child	Mound	S.	…	S.E.	3 Flint flakes	…	Animal bones	1	…	…	…	…	…	Over 20 A.S. bodies, animal	…
	…		1	No. 3	Old M.	Base	P.	L.	N.	Bone tool	…	Human bones	…	…	…	…	…	Clay	bones, pot	…
	…		1	No. 4	Youth	Grave	P.	L.	W.	1 Flint knife	…	Pot sherds	…	…	…	1	…	…	sherds, a wet-	…
	…		1	No. 5	Aged F.	Grave	P.	L.	W.	…	…	Many detached unburnt human bones.	…	…	…	1	…	…	stone, and a	…
	…		1	No. 6	Adult	Grave	P.	R.	S.	2 Flint knifes	…	…	…	…	…	…	…	…	large jet bead.	…
	…		1	No. 7	Adult	Grave	P.	L.	S.E.	1 Flint knife	…	…	…	…	…	…	…	Clay	…	…
	…		1	No. 2a	Adult	Mound	S.	R.	W.S.W.	…	…	…	…	…	…	…	…	…	…	…
	…		1	No. 3a	Adult	Grave A	P.?	R.	W.	…	…	…	…	…	…	…	…	…	…	…
	…		1	No. 4a	Adult	Grave B	P.?	…	…	…	…	…	…	…	…	…	…	…	…	…
	…		1	No. 8	Child	Grave A	P.?	R.	S.	1 Flint knife	…	Pot sherds	…	…	…	1	…	…	Flint knife	…
	…		1	No. 5a	Adult	Grave C	P.?	L.	S.E.	…	…	…	…	…	…	…	…	…	…	…
	…		1	No. 7a	Child	Grave D	P.?	…	W.	…	…	…	…	…	…	…	…	…	…	…
	…		1	No. 9	Child	Edge of grave C	P.?	R.	…	…	…	…	…	…	…	…	…	Clay	…	…
83	…		1		Youth	Mound	S.	R.	N.E.	…	…	Pot sherds	…	…	…	1	…	Clay	A circle of stones.	Skull minus under-jaw.
	…		1		Adult	Grave	P.	L.	E.N.E.	Flint saw	…	…	…	…	…	…	…	2 U		
	1	Heap			Youth	Grave	P.	L.	E.N.E.	Flint knife	…	…	…	…	…	…	…	1 U	7 flint chips	
	1	Heap																		
84	1	Heap			…	Base of mound	P.?	…	…	…	…	…	1	…	…	…	…	…	19 flint flakes	
					Youth															
85	1	Heap			…	…	P.?	…	…	…	…	…	…	…	…	…	…	…	99 flints	
	1	Heap			…	…	P.?	…	…	…	…	…	…	…	…	…	…	…		
115	…				…	…	…	…	…	…	…	…	…	…	…	…	jet button; 3 jet buttons	…	…	
200	…		1		Male	Grave	P.	L.	E.	…	…	Animal bones	1	…	…	…	…	Clay	A.S. remains	
201	1	Heap		No. 1	Adult	Mound	P.?	…	…	…	…	Animal bones	…	…	…	…	…	…	…	
	1	Heap		No. 2	Adult	Base	S.	…	…	…	…	…	…	…	…	…	…	…	…	
	1	Heap		No. 3	Adult	Base	S.	…	…	…	…	…	…	…	…	…	…	…	…	
	1	Heap		No. 4	Adult	Mound	S.	…	…	…	…	…	…	…	…	…	…	…	…	
	1	Heap		No. 5	Adult	Base	P.?	…	…	…	…	…	…	…	…	…	Bone button	…	…	
	…		1	No. 6	Adult	Grave	P.	R.	N.	Flint knife	…	Animal bones	…	…	…	…	…	…	…	

No. of Barrow	BURNT – No. of Bodies	BURNT – Urn, Dish-shaped, Hole, or Circular Heap.	UNBURNT – No. of Bodies.	Description.	In Grave or Body of Mound, or at Base.	Primary or Secondary Burial.	On Back, Right, Left Side.	Direction of Head.	Bone or Stone Tools with Bodies.	Bronze Implements.	Worked Flints; Pot Sherds, Detached, Unburnt, Human and Animal Bones scattered in the Grave.	Food Vase.	Cinerary Urn.	Incense Cup.	Drinking Cup.	Bodkins, Pins, Buttons, or Ornaments.	Clay from a Distance, and Dish-shaped Cavities without Burnt Bones.	Detached Bones, Relics, &c., from the Body of the Mound, not with Interments.	REMARK
99	1	Heap	…	A	Adult	Grave	P.?	…	…	Flint burnt	…	Human bones						Clay	…	
	1	Heap	…	C	…	Base	P.?	…	…	…	…	…							…	
		…	1	B	Adult	Base	P.?	…	…	…	…	…					2 jet buttons	…	…	
		…	2	D	Adult	asB	P.?	…	W.	24 Flint flakes, arrow & spear heads / 4 Flint flakes	…	Bones of a dismembered body.	2					…	20 flakes, 1 arrow of flint	A.S. ren
102		…	1	E	Old F.	Base	P.	L.	…	…	…	Animal bones						…	Human bones Flint knife	
		…	1		Youth	Grave	P.	L.	…	…	…	Human bones						…		
95		…	1		Adult	Hole	P.	Undefinable	…	5 Flint flakes	…	…						…	5 flakes	
60	1	Hole			Adult	Base	S.?	L.	N.	…	…	Human bones						Clay	…	
		…	1		Adult	Grave	S.			…	…	…		1				…		
	1	Urn			Child	Mound	S.	B.	N.	…	…	…	1					…		
		…	1	A	Child	Grave	S.?	L.		Flint knife	…	Animal bones	1				jet pendant	…	…	
	1	Urn		B	Adult	Base	P.	L.		Bone pick	…	…	1		1			…		
		…	1	C	Youth	Mnd	P.			…	…	…	1					…		
	1	Hole		D	Child	Mnd	S.			…	…	…	1 1					…		
		…	1	α E	Child	Mnd	S.			…	…	…	1					…		
		…	1	F	Infant	Mnd	S.		N.	…	…	Animal bones	1				Jet link	…	…	
		…	1	G	Infant	Grave	P.	L.	W.	…	…	Antler of deer, human head, K						…	Pot sherds, hips of ... ox, ... than bones.	
118		…	1	J	Male	Grave G	P.	R.	S.E.	…	…	Pot sherds						…		
		…	1	K	Adult	Grave G	P.?	L.	W.	…	…	Human and animal bones.					Jet link	…	…	
		…	1	L	Adult	Base	P.	R.	N.	…	…	Animal bones	1		1			…		
		…	1	M	Adult	Grave D	S.	B.	N.E.	…	…	…						…		
	1	Urn		N	Child	Mound	S.	L.	N.	Flint knife	…	…					jet pendant	…	…	

			No.	Age												
121	...	...	No. 1	Adult	P.	...	Grave	Flint spear	...	Burnt wood	...	...	Bone pin	...	U	...
		Hole	No. 2	Child	S?	...	Grave	Flint knife	...			1			little clay	Pieces of animal bone and 16 worked flints.
111	1	Hole	A	...	S?	N.	Mound	...	...			1	...		U	...
			B	...	S?	W.	Mound	...	...	Human bones	...	...	...		little clay	...
	1	...	...	Child	P.?	E.	Mound	...	...			...	...		...	B t sherds
	1	...	...	Female	P.?	N.W.	Grave	...	...			1	...			B t sherds
	1		...	Infant			Grave	...	...			...	...			Pot sherds
	1		...	Child			Hole	Flint knife	...			1	Bone pin		little clay	20 flint flakes
93a	1	Hole	...	?	P.		Hole	...	...			...	...		clay	
93	1	Hole	...	Youth	S.?		Hole	...	...			1	...		...	5 other flints
	1	Urn	No. 1	Adult	P.		Grave	...	...			...	...			B t sherds
	1	Urn	No. 2	Adult	S.		Mound	2 Flint knives	...			1	...		little clay	Animal and any human b ne s
	1	Heap	No. 3	Adult & Child	S.		Mound	...	...	Pot sherds	...	1			clay	
98	1	Hole	No. 5	Adult & Child	S.		Mound	Flint knife	...			1	...			B t sherds
	1		A	Youth	P.	L.	Grave A	Horn pick	...			1	...		little clay	
	1		B	Child	P.	R.	Grave B	3 Flint tools	...	Fossil shell, beaver's tooth, snail shells.	...	2	bone bodkin		clay	
	1		B	Adult	P.	R.	Grave B									
		...	C	Female	P.	R.	Grave C	...	...			...	...		...	...
78	1	Hole	...	...	P.		Base	...	...			...	...		...	...
217	1	Hole	...	...	P.		Base	...	...			...	...		...	...
19	29	50									18 6 0 4					

Table of Barrows, Inte[rments, &c., dep]osited with Interments.

BURNT			UNBURNT						ARTICLES DEPOSITED WITH INTERMENTS.										
No. of Barrow	No. of Bodies	Urn, Dish-shaped Hole, or Circular Heap.	No. of Bodies.	Description.	In Grave, or Body of Mound, or at Base.	Primary or Secondary Burial.	On Back, Right, or Left Side.	Direction of Head.	Bone or Stone Tools with Bodies.	Bronze Implements.	Worked Flints; Pot Sherds; Detached, Unburnt, Human and Animal Bones scattered in the Grave.	Food Vase.	Cinerary Urn.	Incense Cup.	Drinking Cup.	Bodkins, Pins, Buttons, or Ornaments.	Clay from a Distance, and Dish-shaped Cavities without Burnt Bones.	Detached Bones, Relics, &c., from the Body of the Mound, not with Interments.	REMARKS
104	…	…	1	No. 1	Grave A	P.	B.	S.	Flint knife	…	Many human bones.	…	…	…	…	…	Much clay	Flint scraper 3 in. long	
	…	…	1	No. 2	Grave A	P.	R.	S.	Flint knife	…	Teeth and bones of an ox	…	…	…	3	…	clay	…	
	…	…	1	No. 3	Grave B	S.	L.	W.	…	…	…	…	…	…	…	…	…	…	Vase with
	…	…	1	No. 4	Base	P. ?	R.	S.W.	Flint knife + flakes	…	…	…	1	…	…	…	…	…	
101	…	…	1	A	Grave A	P.	R.	E.	…	Pricker	Bones of pig	1	…	…	…	…	Clay	Flint knife and 8 other worked flints	Vase had l
	…	…	1	…	Grave B	P.	B.	S.	…	…	Bone pick, boar's tusk, &c	1	…	…	…	…	…	…	
	…	…	1	…	Grave C	P.	R.	E.	Flint knife	…	Animal bone	1	…	…	…	…	Clay	…	
64	…	…	1	No. 2	Grave	P.	R.	E.	…	Pricker	Animal bones	…	…	…	…	…	Clay	…	
C 68	1	Heap	…		Grave	S.	…	W.	…	…	…	…	…	…	…	…	…	…	
	1	Heap	1	Adult	Mound	S.	R.	W.	…	…	…	…	1	…	…	…	Little	Pot sherds	
	1	Urn	1	a	Mound	S.	…	…	…	…	…	…	1	…	…	…	…	…	
	1	Urn	1	A	Mound	S.	…	…	…	…	…	…	…	…	…	…	…	…	
	1	Heap	1	E	Mound	P.	R.	E.	…	…	…	1	…	…	…	206 jet beads	…	Several flint flakes	
C 69	…	…	1	C	a B	P. ?	R.	W.	…	…	…	…	…	…	…	…	…	…	
	…	…	1	No. 1	a B	P.	R.	W.	…	…	…	…	…	…	…	…	…	…	
	…	…	1	No. 2	a B	P.	R.	W.	…	…	…	…	…	…	…	…	…	…	
	…	…	1	No. 3	a s B	P.	L.	W.	…	…	…	…	…	…	…	…	…	…	
	…	…	1	No. 4	Base	P.	L.	E.	…	…	…	…	…	…	…	…	…	A barbed arrow-head	
	…	…	1	No. 5	Base	P.	L.	E.	…	…	…	…	…	…	…	…	…	…	
	…	…	1	No. 6	a B	P.	L.	W.	…	…	…	…	…	…	…	…	…	…	
	…	…	1	No. 7	Base	P.	R.	W.	…	…	…	…	…	…	…	…	…	A stone ...head	
	…	…	1	No. 8	Base	P.	B.	W.	…	…	…	…	…	…	…	…	…	…	
	…	…	1	No. 10	Base	P.	R.	E.	…	…	…	…	…	…	…	…	…	Animal bones	
	…	…	1	No. 11	Base	P.	L.	W.	…	…	…	…	…	…	…	…	…	…	
	…	…	1	No. 12	Base	P.	B.	E.	…	…	…	…	…	…	…	…	…	…	
	…	…	1	No. 13	Base	P.	R.	W.	…	…	…	…	…	…	…	…	…	…	
	…	…	1	No. 15	Base	P.	L.	E.	…	…	…	…	…	…	…	…	…	…	
	…	…	1	No. 9	M...	P. ?	L.	E.	…	…	…	…	…	…	…	…	…	…	

					Age	Position	P./S.	R./L./B.	Direction	Implements				Bone pin	Clay	Contents	Remarks
39			1	...	Adult	Base	P.		Uncertain	...	...	...	1	...	...	Pot sherds, animal bones, worked flints	
62			1	No. 1	disturb'd	Base	P.		...	...	...	...	...	...	Clay	...	
			1	No. 2	disturb'd	Base	P.		...	...	...	...	1	...		...	
			1	No. 3	disturb'd	Grave	P.		...	...	...	...	1	...		...	
			1	No. 4	Adult	Grave	P.	R.	E.	Flint knife 13 flakes	Knife	...		...	Clay	Worked flints and pot sherds	
63			1	No. 1	Adult	Grave	P.		S.		...	...	1	...		...	
			1	No. 2	Adult	Grave	P.	R.	...	Flint knife	...	...		...	Clay	Flints & pot sherds	
68	1	Heap	1		Youth	Grave	P.	R.	S.S.W.		...	...	1	...			
C 97			1		Adult	Grave	P.	B.	N.		...	...	1	...		8 worked flints, animal bones	
C 98			1		Youth	Grave	P.	R.	E.	Spear-head and flint knife	...	...	1	...	Clay	Human bones and 4 worked flints	A.S. body also.
42	1	Hole			Adult	Hole	P.			...	...	...		Bone pin	...		
69			1		Adult	Graves	P.	B.	S.		...	...	1	...		Animal bones, 14 worked flints	Hand severed.
31			1	No. 1	head only	Mound	S.?	L.	N.		...	Lower jaw of dog	1	...	Clay		
		Heap	1	No. 2	Youth	Base	S.?	B.	...		...	...		...		Many pot sherds, bones and teeth of animals, many worked flints, the end of a stone axe	
32			1	A No. 3	Adult	Base	P.	L.	S.		...	...	1	...	Clay in grave		
			1	No. 4	Adult	Grave	P.		S.	End of bone	...	Pot sherds	1	...	...	Portions of 8 distinct vessels.	
120			1	No. 1	Adult	Grave	P.	L.	S.E.	Flint knife	Bronze Dagger	...	1	...			
			1	No. 2	Adult	Grave	P.	B.	N.		...	...	1	...			
			1	No. 3	Child	Mound	P.	R.	S.E.		...	Animal bones	1	...	Little clay	2 flint knives	
			1	No. 4	Adult	Mound	S.?	R.	N.W.		...	...	1	Bone pin			
		Heap	1	No. 1		Edge of Gr.	S.?				...	...		...			
	1	Heap	1	No. 2	more than 1 body	Grave	P.		...		...	A pot sherd and 2 pieces of animal bone		...	clay		
C 43	1	Heap	1	No. 3	Adult	Grave	P.	R.	W.		...	...		...	Clay	Barbed arrow-head, 9 worked flints, 110 pt sherds of many vessels and animal bones	
			1	No. 1	Adult	Grave	P.	R.	E.		...	...	1	...	...		
		Hole	1	No. 2		Hole	P.		...		...	...		...			
104a	1	Hole				Mound	S.?		...		...	...		...			
C 99	1	Heap	1	No. 1	Adult	Grave	P.	R.	E.S.E.		...	...	1	Bone pin	...	Iron umbo of a shield and ... of other A.S. articles	
			1	No. 2	Child	Grave	P.		...		...	Pot sherds	1	...			
		Hole				Hole	S.?		...		...	...		...			
19	15		48										18 2 0 3				

3 G

GROUP VIII.

Table of Barrows, Interments, and Articles deposited with Interments.

No. of Barrow	BURNT: No. of Bodies	Urn, Dish-shaped Hole, or Circular Heap.	UNBURNT: No. of Bodies	Description.	In Grave or Body of Mound, or at Base.	Primary or Secondary Burial.	On Back, Right, or Left Side.	Direction of Head.	Bone or Stone Tools with Bodies.	Bronze Implements.	Worked Flints; Pot Sherds; Detached, Unburnt, Human and Animal Bones scattered in the Grave.	Food Vase.	Cinerary Urn.	Incense Cup.	Drinking Cup.	Bodkins, Pins, Buttons, or Ornaments.	Clay from a Distance, and Dish-shaped Cavities without Burnt Bones.	Detached Bones, Relics, &c., from the Body of the Mound, not with Interments.	Remarks.
23	...	...	1	Male	Grave	P.	B.	S.	Perforated hammer-head	...	...	1	...	...	...	...	Clay	Chips of flint	bones of left hu... anchylosed, r... mains of dwelli...
24	1	Urn	...	?	Hole	P.	...	...	...	...	Rare carbonized seds or this...	...	1	...	...	...	...	6 Flint flakes	
25	1	Hole	...	...	Hole	P. ?	...	...	...	...	...	...	...	...	...	...	Clay	3 Flint flakes	
14	1	Heap	...	No. 1	Grave	P.	...	...	...	...	Portions of a drinking-cup	...	...	...	...	...	Clay (Much clay)	Worked flints & animal bones	
	1	Heap	1	No. 2 Adult male	Grave	P.	?	?	Flint knife	...	...	...	...	...	...	...	Clay	Also 107 flints,	
	...		...	...	Grave	P.	?	?	2 Flint scrapers	...	...	1	...	...	...	...			
	1	Heap		C	Base	P. ?				...	Unburnt ... calvarum	...	...	...	...	...			
100	...	...	1	(Large female) No. 1	Grave	P.	B.	S.	Bone tool	...	Pieces of 3 drinking ups, 14 flint flakes, 44 bits of animal bone	...	...	...	...	...	3 parts clay	any pot sherds, 1 tooth of horse (?), 8 teeth of ox, and ... nes of small animals	Body at full length.
	...	...	1	No. 2 male	Grave	P.	B.	N.E.	...	...	...	...	...	...	...	...		...ny flints and ...nl obes	
38	...	...	...	...	...	...	...	...	...	...	Pot sherds & flints	...	...	...	...	...	Clay		

	1	Heap	...	No. 1	Adult	Mound	S.	...	...	...	...	...	...	...	...	...	...	...	...	
	1	Urn	...	No. 0	?	Mound	S.	..	...	...	...	...	...	1	...	...	...	..	Barbed arrow-head	
	1	Heap	...	No. 2	Youth	Mound	S.	...	...	...	...	...	...	...	...	...	...	..	...	
	...	...	1	No. 3	Adult	Base	P.	R.	S.E.	...	...	...	...	...	...	...	...	...	...	
	...	...	1	No. 4	Part of Adult	Mound	P.?	?	?	...	...	...	...	...	...	...	...	...	...	
	1	Heap	...	No. 5	Adult	Grave	P.P.	...	...	...	...	8 pot sherds, many human bones, 8 pieces animal bone	...	...	...	...	...	...	...	
275	...	...	1	No. 6	Child	Mound	P.?	?	S.	...	...	...	...	...	...	...	...	Much clay	...	
	...	...	1	No. 7	Adult	Base	P.	R.	E.	...	...	Pieces of burnt human bone scattered among the 10 bodies	...	...	...	...	...	...	We picked from near the base several pieces of bone, 3 pot sherds, 5 flint chips, 1 saw, 2 sling-stones, and 80 flakes and chips of flint	
	...	...	1	No. 8	Adult	Base	P.	R.	E.	...	...		...	...	...	...	...	Clay		
	...	...	1	No. 9	Adult ?	Base	P.	R.	E.	...	...		...	...	...	...	...	...		
	...	...	1	No. 10	Adult	Base	P.	L.	E.	...	...		...	...	...	...	...	...		
	...	...	1	No. 11	Adult	Base	P.	L.	E.	Skull of a child, leaf-arrow of flint	...		...	...	...	...	...	...		
	...	...	1	No. 12	Adult ?	Base	P.	L.	W.		...		...	...	...	...	...	...		
	...	...	1	No. 13	Adult ?	Base	P.	R.	W.		...		...	...	...	...	...	...		
	...	...	1	No. 14	Adult	Base	P.	L.	W.	...	...		...	...	...	...	...	...		
	...	...	1	No. 15	Adult	Base	P.	R.	E.	2 Leaf-arrows	...		...	...	...	...	...	...		
	...	...	1	No. 16	Adult	Base	P.	R.	W.	...	...		...	...	...	...	...	...		
C 72	...	...	1	...	Adult	Grave	P.	L.	N.	...	...	Bodies of a pig and 2 goats	...	...	...	...	...	...	Sherds of 4 kinds of pottery	
	1	Invert'd urn	...	No. 1	Adult	Mound	S.	...	...	...	...	3 flint arrow-heads	...	1	...	...	jet button	Clay	1 Flint knife	
	1	Urn	...	No. 2	Adult	Mound	S.	...	...	...	...	2 flint spear-heads	...	1	...	...	...	...	1 large hand-stone [illegible]	
13	1	Hole	...	No. 1	?	Grave	S.	...	...	Heat-splintered flints	Piece of bronze	2 bits of green glass*	...	...	...	...	...	...	98 flint flakes, 4 sling-stones	* A unique find under the circumstances.
	1	Hole	...	No. 2	?	Grave	S.	...	...	...	...	...	...	...	...	...	Jet necklace of 623 beads or pieces	...		
	...	...	1	Decayed	?	Base	P.	?	?	...	...	...	...	...	...	...		...		
103	1	...	...	No. 1	Young Person	Base	P.	...	...	...	...	...	1	...	...	...	...	1 U	...	
	1	...	...	No. 2	...	Base	P.	...	...	...	...	...	1	...	...	...	...	...	...	
105	1	Urn	...	...	...	Base	P.?	...	...	...	...	...	...	1	...	...	...	1 U	10 flint flakes and 2 pot sherds	

INTERMENTS.

ARTICLES DEPOSITED WITH INTERMENTS.

No. of row	BURNT		UNBURNT						Bone or Stone Tools with Bodies.	Bronze Implements.	Worked Flints; Pot Sherds; Detached, Unburnt, Human and Animal Bones scattered in the Grave.	Food Vase	Cinerary Urn	Incense Cup	Drinking Cup	Bodkins, Pins, Buttons, or Ornaments	Clay from a Distance, and Dish-shaped Cavities without Burnt Bones	Detached Bones, Relics, &c., from the Body of the Mound, not with Interments.	REMARKS.
	No. of Bodies.	Urn, Dish-shaped Hole, or Circular Heap.	No. of Bodies.	Description.	In Grave, or Body of Mound, or at Base.	Primary or Secondary Burial.	On Back, Right, or Left Side.	Direction of Head.											
15	1	Hole	…	No. 1 ?	Base	P.	…	…	…	…	{Burnt woven cloth}	…	…	1	…	…	Clay	{11 flint flakes, &c., and a leaf arrow-head, and a barbed one}	
	1	{Urn in hole}	…	No. 2 ?	Base	P.	…	…	Flint disc	…		…	…	1	…	…	abundn't		
86	…	…	…	…	…	…	…	…	…	…	…	…	…	…	…	…	Clay	{30 odd flints, a piece of a stone axe, and my pt sherd}	
96	1	Hole	…	…	Base	P.	…	…	Pointed flint	…	…	1	…	…	…	…	…	…	
	…	…	1	Child	Grave	P.?	…	…	…	…	…		…	…	…	…	…	…	
14	1	Urn	…	No. 1	Base	P.	…	…	…	…	…	…	1	…	…	…	…	…	
	1	Urn	…	No. 2 Adult	Base	P.	…	…	…	…	…	…	1	…	…	{9 jet beads, 2 of vitrious paste}	…	…	
	…	…	1	No. 3 Adult	Mound	S.	…	…	…	…	…		…	…	…		…	…	
	…	…	1	No. 4 Adult	Mound	S.	…	…	…	…	…		…	…	…	…	…	…	
70	1	Urn	…	No. 1 Adult	Base	P.	?	W.	…	Knife	…	1	1	…	…	…	…	Splinters and flakes of flint	{The two inhumed bodies may have been Anglo-Saxons.}
	…	…	1	No. 2 Adult?	Base	P.	R.	E.	…	…	…	1	…	…	…	…	…	1 Food vase	
	…	…	1	No. 3 Adult	Grave	P.	B.	E.	Lump of flint	…	…		…	…	…	…	…	…	
25	22											7	10	2	0				

GROUP IX.

Table of Barrows, Interments, and Articles deposited with Interments.

No. of Barrow	BURNT — No. of Body	BURNT — Urn, Dish-shaped Hole, or Circular Heap	UNBURNT — No. of Body	Description	In Grave or Body of Mound, or at Base	Primary or Secondary Burial	On Back, Right, or Left Side	Direction of Head	Bone or Stone Tools with Bodies	Worked Flints; Pot Sherds; Detached, Unburnt, Human and Animal Bones scattered in the Grave	Bronze Implements	Food Vase	Cinerary Urn	Incense Cup	Drinking Cup	Bodkins, Pins, Buttons, or Ornaments	Clay from a Distance, and Dish-shaped Cavities without Burnt Bones	Detached Bones, Relics, &c., from the Body of the Mound, not with Interments	Remarks
C 49	1	...	1	No. 1 — Youth	Grave 1	P.	R.	E.	...	Flint flakes	...	1				...	Clay	30 worked flints and the bottom half of a cinerary urn.	
	1	...	1	A — Adult	,, 2	P.	L.	S.E.	...	do.	...					...	Clay		
	1	...	1	B — ?	,, 2	P.	L.	N.N.W.	...	do.	...	1				...	...		
		...	1	No. 4 — Adult	,, 3	P.	R.	E.	...		...	1				...	...		
36	1	Heap		... — Adult	Grave	?	R.	W.	...	Flint flakes	...	1				...	...	Pot sherds, many human bones, flint flakes, at the base, over the mound, the grave in the centre.	Urn inverted.
			1	C — Child	Over Grave	P.	R?	E.	...	{ Many human and some animal bones; a tine from the antler of a red deer.	...	1				...	Clay		A skull, minus under jaw.
	1	...	1	D — Yng. Ad.	Grave 2	P.	R.	E.	...		...	1				...	...		
	1	...	1	E — Adult	,, 2	P.	L.	E.	Flint flake	}	...					...	...		
C 42a	1	Urn		No. 1 — Youth	Base	...	L.	N.N.W.	...	...	...		1			...	...	Flint knife.	
		...	1	No. 2 — Female?	Grave	P.	B.	S.	...	...	...	1				...	...		
	1	Urn	1	No. 1 — Male	Mound	S.?			...	...	...	1				...	...		
33	1	Heap		No. 2 — ?	Base	P.?			...	...	...		1			...	...	24 worked flints.	
	1	Hole		No. 3 — ?	Hole	P.?			...	...	...	1				...	...		
	1	Hole		No. 4 — ?	Hole	P.			...	...	...	1				...	...		
20	...	...	1	... — Male	Grave	P.	R.	S.	...	{ Flints, tools, pot sherds }	...	1				...	Clay	Many worked flints, pot sherds.	
16	...	...	1	... — Child	Base	P.	R.	E.	...	...	...					Jet link	...	... pot sherds.	

GROUP IX.—continued.

		INTERMENTS							ARTICLES DEPOSITED WITH INTERMENTS										REMARKS.
	BURNT			UNBURNT								Vessels of Pottery.							
No. of Barrow	No. of Bodies	Urn, Dish-shaped Hole, or Circular Heap.	No. of Bodies.	Description.	In Grave, or Body of Mound, or at Base.	Primary or Secondary Burial.	On Back, Right, or Left Side.	Direction of Head.	Bone or Stone Tools with Bodies.	Bronze Implements.	Worked Flints; Pot Sherds; Detached, Unburnt, Human and Animal Bones scattered in the Grave.	Food Vase.	Cinerary Urn.	Incense Cup.	Drinking Cup.	Bodkins, Pins, Buttons, or Ornaments.	Clay from a Distance, and Dish-shaped Cavities without Burnt Bones.	Detached Bones, Relics, &c., from the Body of the Mound, not with Interments.	
17	1	Heap	...	C. No. 1	?	Mound	S.	...	...	...	...	1	...	...	...	...	...	Worked flints, 2 food-vases, 1 with a cover.	
	1	Heap	...	C. No. 2	?	Base	P.	...	...	...	...					...	Much Clay		
19	...	Heap	Youth	C. No. 3	Grave	P.	R.	E.	...	...	...	...	...	...	...	...	...	Worked flints.	
	1	Hole	...	...	Hole	P.	...	...	...	...	...								
34	...	...	1?	...	Base	?	...	...	...	...	...	1	...	...	...	...	Clay	Worked flints and pot sherds.	Remains of dwelling.
35	1	Urn	...	...	Hole	P.	...	...	...	...	...	...	1	...	...	...	Clay		
41	(1	Heap)	1	Youth	Grave	P.	B.	S.	Flint knife	...	(Antler of red deer.)	1	...	...	...	...	Much Clay	Many worked flints and a food vase	Used as a r...
C 83			...	No. 1 Adult	Grave A	P.	...	...	...	...	...	...	...	...	...	Bone pin	Much clay	Portions of the antlers of a stag.	
	(1		1	No. 5 Female	Grave A	P.	R.	S.	Burnt flint flakes (Top part of the antler of red deer)	...	...								
C 84	1	Heap	1	No. 2 Adult	Grave B	P.	R.	N.	Flint knife	...	...	...	...	...	...	...	1 U		
	...	...	1	No. 4 Male?	Grave B	S.?	R.	W.	...	...	...								
	...	...	1	No. 3 Child	Grave				...	...	...						1 U		
				No interment could be found.	Hole	P.	...	...	...	...	...	...	...	...	...	...	1 U	Worked flints and pot sherds.	
29	1	Hole	...	?	Hole	P.	...	...	Flint disc Carbonised (button of wood)	...	...	1	...	...	...	...	1 U		
	1	Hole	...	?					...	...	...								
14	15		18									14	3	0	0				

GROUP X.

Table of Barrows, Interments, and Articles deposited with Interments.

INTERMENTS									ARTICLES DEPOSITED WITH INTERMENTS.										
BURNT.			UNBURNT.									Vessels of Pottery.							
No. of Barrow	No. of Bodies.	Urn, Dish-shaped Hole, or Circular Heap.	No. of Bodies.	Description.	In Grave or Body of Mound, or at Base.	Primary or Secondary Burial.	On Back, Right, or Left Side.	Direction of Head.	Bone or Stone Tools with Bodies.	Bronze Implements.	Worked Flints; Pot Sherds; Detached, Unburnt and Animal Bones scattered in the Grave.	Food Vase.	Cinerary Urn.	Incense Cup.	Drinking Cup.	Bodkins, Pins, Buttons, or Ornaments.	Clay from a Distance, and Dish-shaped Cavities without Burnt Bones U	Detached Bones, Relics, &c., from the Mound, not with Interments.	Remarks.
5	...	...	1			...	...					...	...	...	...	...	...	Bits of iron, a piece of British food-vase, animal bones, and mediæval pottery and some bronze.	A deep + cut into the ground under this mound.
C 33	... / 1	Heap	1	No. 1 ?	Grave	P.	...	(Only a trace remaining.)	Flint axe and flint flakes.	...		...	...	...	...	...	...	...	
			1	No. 2 Adult	Base	S.?	?	?	...	...		...	...	...	...	...	...	...	
			...	No. 3 ?	Base	?	B.	...	...	...	Animal bones and portions of 3 vases, tusk of a boar.	...	...	...	...	Bone pin shell (Pecten)	...	...	
			1	No. 4 Adult	Grave	P.	R.	N.W.	(3 small flakes and half a spear head.)	...		...	...	...	...	...	...	...	
C 82	...	...	1	... Adult	Grave	P.?	...	W.	...	...		1	...	...	...	...	Clay.	A.S. & Romano-British pottery, and A.S. interments.? Flint flakes.	
3	1		4									1	0	0	0		3 U		

GROUP X A.

Table of Barrows, Interments, and Articles deposited with Interments.

INTERMENTS. ARTICLES DEPOSITED WITH INTERMENTS.

No. of Barrow	BURNT — No. of Bodies	BURNT — Urn, Dish-shaped Hole, or Circular Heap	UNBURNT — No. of Bodies	Description	In Grave or Body of Mound, or at Base	Primary or Secondary Burial	On Back, Right, or Left Side	Direction of Head	Bone or Stone Tools with Bodies	Bronze Implements	Worked Flints; Pot Sherds; Detached, Unburnt, Human and Animal Bones scattered in the Grave	Food Vase	Cinerary Urn	Incense Cup	Drinking Cup	Bodkins, Pins, Buttons, or Ornaments	Clay from a Distance, and Dish-shaped Cavities without Burnt Bones	Detached Bones, Relics, &c., from the Body of the Mound, not with Interments	Remarks
28	...	...	1	No. 1 Youth	Base	S.?	?	N.	.	...	...	1	...	...	...	...	...	Many animal bones, pot-sherds, and flint flakes.	
	...	...	1	No. 2 Adult	Grave	P.	{ Dismembered body. }	N.	...	...	...	...	...	...	...	...	...		
	1	Heap	...	No. 3 ?	Grave	P.	...	?	...	...	...	...	...	...	...	...	...		
268	...	...	1	{ Young adult male }	Grave	P.	L.	?	Disc of flint and large flint knife.	...	{ Human and animal bones and *Helix nemoralis.* }	...	...	...	...	...	...		
	...	...	...	Adult	Grave	P.	B. ?	N.	Antler of a roebuck — a tool.	...	...	1	...	...	...	...	...		
270	...	Heap	1	Small	Grave	P.	...	...	...	...	...	1	...	...	...	...	...		
271	...	...	1 ?	?	Grave	P.?	{ Only a trace remaining. }	...	...	...	...	1	...	...	...	...	...		
294	...	Heap	1	No. 1 A { Adult M / Adult }	Grave 1	P.	B.	E.	Knife & splinters. Knife.	Knife Pricker	...	...	...	...	...	...	...	Head of an ox.	
	...	...	1	No. 2 Female	,, 2	P.	R.	W.	Knife.	...	...	...	...	...	...	tusk-tool	...	Head of badger.	
	...	...	1	B Child	Base	...	R.	N.	{ Knife, scraper, and pebble. }	...	...	...	...	...	...	...	...		
	...	...	1	No. 3 Male	Grave 3	P.	R.	E.	...	...	{ Many bones of a young adult. }	1	...	...	...	...	...		
295	...	...	...															{ Worked flints & animal bones. }	
122	...	...	...																
7	**3**		**9**									**5**	**0**	**0**	**0**				

This barrow had been removed, and no interment was found.

Is called Mill Hill, and its original contents have been destroyed by having a large cross excavated in its centre.

GROUP XI.

Table of Barrows, Interments, and Articles deposited with Interments.

No. of Barrow	No. of Bodies (BURNT)	Urn, Dish-shaped Hole, or Circular Heap.	No. of Bodies (UNBURNT)	Description	In Grave, or Body of Mound, or at Base.	Primary or Secondary Burial.	On Back, Right, or Left Side.	Direction of Head.	Bone or Stone Tools with Bodies.	Bronze Implements.	Worked Flints; Pot Sherds; Detached, Unburnt, Human and Animal Bones scattered in the Grave.	Food Vase	Cinerary Urn	Incense Cup	Drinking Cup	Bodkins, Pins, Buttons, or Ornaments	Clay from a Distance, and Dish-shaped Cavities without Burnt Bones	Detached Bones, Relics, &c., from the Mound, not with Interments.	Remarks.
37	...	...	1	No. 1	?	Mound	S.	R?	S.W.	...	...	...	...	...	...	1	...	...	...	
	...	...	1	No. 2	?	Mound	...	R.	S.W.	...	...	...	...	...	...	...	...	...	...	
	...	...	1	No. 3	Adult	Mound over Grave	P.?	R.	N.E.	...	...	...	...	...	...	...	Bone pin	...	...	
	...	...	1	No. 4	Adult	Grave	P.	L.	N.E.	...	...	...	...	...	...	...	...	...	...	
	...	...	1	No. 5	Only the cranium	Base	?	?	?	...	...	Animal & human	...	...	...	...	...	...	...	Calvarium, no mandible.
	...	...	1	No. 6	Male	Grave	P.	B.	N.E.	Flint dagger, hammer head, worked flint, and lump of pyrites	...	...	...	...	...	...	...	...	...	
	...	...	1	No. 7	Adult	Base	P.?	R.	N.E.	...	...	...	...	...	...	1	jet button	...	...	
	1	Heap	...	A	?	Base	?	...	...	...	...	Rib of small animal	1	...	...	...	...	...	...	
	...	...	1	No. 8	Youth	Shallow Grave	P.?	R.	N.W.	...	...	...	...	...	...	...	Bone pin	...	...	
	...	...	1	No. 9	?	Grave	?	B.	E.	...	...	Snail shells	...	...	...	...	...	...	Animal bones	
	...	...	1	No. 10	Small Adults	Shallow	?	B.	W.	...	...	...	...	...	...	...	...	...	...	
	...	...	1	No. 11	Small Adults	Trench	?	L.	W.	...	...	Bones of human foot and lower end of fibula	...	...	...	...	...	...	...	
	...	...	1	No. 12	Adult	Trench	S.?	B.	E.	Stone pounder and flint flake	...	Animal bone	...	...	...	...	...	...	Pick made of the antler of the red deer	
	...	...	1	No. 13	?	Mound	S.?	R.	E.	...	...	...	...	...	...	...	...	...	...	
	...	...	1	No. 14	Youth	Grave	S.?	R.	N.E.	...	...	...	...	...	...	...	...	...	...	
	...	...	1	No. 15	Adult	Grave	S.?	R.	S.W.	Bone instrument	...	...	...	...	...	...	...	...	...	

GROUP XI.—continued.

BURNT			UNBURNT (INTERMENTS)						ARTICLES DEPOSITED WITH INTERMENTS			Vessels of Pottery							
No. of Barrow Bodies	Urn, Dish-shaped Hole, or Circular Heap	No. of Bodies	No. of Bodies	Description	Primary or Secondary Burial	In Grave or Body of Mound, or at Base	On Back, Right, or Left Side	Direction of Head	Bone or Stone Tools with Bodies	Bronze Implements	Worked Flints; Pot Sherds; Detached, Unburnt, Human and Animal Bones scattered in the Grave	Food Vase	Cinerary Urn	Incense Cup	Drinking Cup	Bodkins, Pins, Buttons, or Ornaments	Clay from a Distance, and Dish-shaped Cavities without Burnt Bones U	Detached Bones, Relics, &c., from the Body of the Mound, not with Interments	Remarks
C 61																			
1	…	…	1	… Male	P.	Grave	B.	N.N.E.	Flake of flint	…	…	…	…	…	1	Jet button	6 U	…	
1	Hole	1	…	A Adult	S.	Hole	…	…	Flint flake	…	Bones of a child	…	…	…	…	…	…	…	
1	Hole	…	…	B Adult	S.?	Hole	…	…	…	…	…	…	…	…	…	…	…	…	
1	dp	…	…	C ?	S.?	Mound	…	…	…	…	…	…	…	…	…	…	…	…	
1	dp	1	…	a ?	P.?	Edge of Gr.	…	…	…	…	Human bone	1	…	1	…	…	1 U	…	
C 62																			
…	…	…	1	No. 1 Child	P.	Grave I	L.	N.E.	2 Bone articles	…	…	…	…	…	…	…	…	…	
…	…	…	1	No. 2 Adult	P.	Grave	R.	N.	(Bone tool made of a human femur)	…	…	…	…	…	…	…	…	…	
…	…	…	1	No. 3 Female ?	P.	Grave	Face	S.S.W.	…	…	…	…	…	1	…	…	…	…	
…	…	…	1	No. 4 Adult	P.	Grave	B.	S.S.W.	Flint knife	…	…	…	…	…	…	…	…	…	
…	…	…	1	No. 5 Adult	P.	Grave	B.	N.E.	…	…	…	…	…	…	…	…	…	…	
…	…	…	1	No. 6 …	S.	Shallow Grave J	R.	S.S.W.	…	…	…	…	…	…	…	…	…	…	
…	…	…	1	No. 7 Adult	S.	Shallow Grave K	R.	S.S.W.	…	…	…	…	…	…	…	…	…	…	
C 63																			
…	…	…	0 / 1	No. 1 ? / Adult	P. / P.	Grave A / Grave B	L.	S.E.	Worked stone / Flint knife	…	Animal bones	…	…	1	…	…	…	…	
…	…	…	1	No. 2 Male	P.	Grave C	Chest	E.	Flint axe, flint knife, flint flakes	…	Very many human bones	…	…	…	1	Bone pin	…	…	
…	…	…	1	No. 3 Female ?	P.?	Grave C	R.	N.W.	7 Flint flakes, 1 Stone tool	Pricker	{ human bones }	…	…	…	1	…	…	…	The u… had b… left si… locate… time… de…
…	…	…	1	No. 4 Adult	P.?	Grave D	R.	S.W.	…	…	…	…	…	…	1	…	…	…	

Barrow	Heap	No.	No.	Age/Sex	Position	P./S.	R./B./L.	Direction	Flint implements	Pricker / Rings	Bones		Jet / Ochre	U	Other	Remarks
1	...	1	No. 1	?	Grave	P.	R.	N.E.	...	...	Human bones	1	...	...	...	The head, neck vertebre, and right scapula had been removed.
	...	1	No. 2	Youth	Grave	P.	?	?	...	...	...	...	...	...	...	
2	1 (Heap)	...	No. 1	?	In Trench	S.	B.	S.	2 Flint flakes, Flint knife	Pricker	...	...	...	...	...	
	...	1	No. 2	Female	Grave A	P.	B.	N.		...	...	...	...	...	...	
	...	1		Old	Grave B	P.	R.	S.		...	...	...	...	...	...	
3	...	1	No. 3	Adult	Grave B	P.	L.	N.	2 Flint knives, 1 Lump of flint	...	...	...	...	...	...	
	...	1	No. 4	Adult	Grave B	P.	R.	S.		...	...	...	Jet button	...	...	
	...	1	No. 5	Adult M	Grave B	P.	L.	N.	Flint dagger, flint knife	...	...	...		1 U	...	
	...	1	...	Adult	Grave C	P.?	L.	N.	...	...	...	...	Jet spindle, lump of yellow ochre	2 U	...	
	...	1	...	Adult	Grave	P.	R.	W.	...	...	...	...			...	
	...	1	...	Youth	Grave E	P.	L.	E.	Flint flake, and a portion of an ammonite	2 Rings	Animal bones	1	...	...	Flint knife and a kidney-shaped stone	
4	...	1	...	Adult	Base	P.	L.	N.W.	...	...	Animal bones	1	...	1 U	...	
	...	1	No. 1	Male	Grave	P.	R.	N.N.E.	2 Flints	...	Animal bone	...	...	...	...	Near this mound was a pit dwelling containing the lower ends of 2 humeri of 2 urus, and other animal bones.
	...	1	No. 2	Adult	Grave	P.?	L.	N.N.E.		...	Pot sherd	...	...	...	...	
5	...	1	No. 1	Female	Grave	P.	B.	N.E.	2 Flint flakes	Pricker	...	...	...	2 U	...	
	...	1	No. 2	Adult M	Grave	P.?	L.	N.E.	...	...	...	...	...	...	...	
6	...	1	No. 1	Adult	Base	S.?	R.	E.	...	...	...	...	...	...	...	
	...	1	No. 2	Youth	Grave	P.	R.	E.	Flint knife, 5 small flakes	...	Animal bones	1	...	...	...	2 bits of small animal ribs were found in the vase.
	...	1	No. 3	Child	Base	...	R.	E.	10 Worked flints	...	...	...	...	...	...	

GROUP XI.—continued.

	BURNT.		INTERMENTS. — UNBURNT.							ARTICLES DEPOSITED WITH INTERMENTS.		Vessels of Pottery.							
	No. of Bodies.	Urn, Dish-shaped Hole, or Circular Heap.	No. of Bodies.	Description.	In Grave or Body of Mound, or at Base.	Primary or Secondary Burial.	On Back, Right, or Left Side.	Direction of Head.	Bone or Stone Tools with Bodies.	Bronze Implements.	Worked Flints; Pot Sherds; Detached, Unburnt, Human and Animal Bones scattered in the Grave.	Food Vase.	Cinerary Urn.	Incense Cup.	Drinking Cup.	Bodkins, Pins, Buttons, or Ornaments.	Clay from a Distance, and Dish-shaped Cavities without Burnt Bones	Detached Bones, Relics, &c., from the Body of the Mound, not with Interments.	Remarks.
5	1	Heap		A No. 1	?	Base	P. ?	..	W. ?	Flint knife	Pricker	Stag's horn	1						Human and animal bones, worked flints.	
	1	Heap		B	Female	Ba s	P.	R.	W.	Flint knife	..	Flint flakes	1							
			1	No. 2	Female	Grave 1	P.	L.	W.	..	Pricker	Animal bones	1				Jet necklace			
6	1	Heap		C	Adult	Grave	P.	R.	W. ?	..	..	..			1				Animal bones, 175 flint flakes and splinters, and 30 other worked flints.	
			1	No. 3	Adult M.	Grave	P.	..	W.	..	..	2 stag's horn picks								
			1	No. 4	Male Ad.	9 in. Below the base	S.	R.	S.	..	..	..	1							
	1	Heap		E	?	Base	S.	?	?	..	..	Head of a dog		1						
	1	Urn	1	No. 5	Child	Grave 2	S.	?	..	..	..	..								
				..	Adult	Base	P.	..	..	..	..	..								
7			1	Broken up	..	Base	P. ?	?	?	..	..	Animal and human bones							125 flint flakes, 7 worked pieces, and 13 pot sherds.	
71			1	No. 1	dult	Grave A	P. ?	R.	E.	..	..	Human bones							Many human and a few animal bones.	
			1	No. 2	Adult	Grave A	P.	B.	E.	..	..	..	1							
			1	No. 3	Portion	Grave A	P.	?	?	..	..	..								
			1	No. 4	Child	Grave A	P.	L.	E.	..	..	..								
			1	No. 5	Child	Grave A	P.	L.	E.	..	..	..								
			1	B	Adult	Grave B	S.	R.	W.	..	..	Burnt human bones								
			1	No. 1	Adult	Grave C	?	L.	W.	..	..	..								
			1	No. 2	Adult	Grave C	?	R.	W.	..	..	..								
64	1	Holes		Several	?	Holes	Post-British	Post-British	..	Small bits of a British vase	Ring	Bones					Bone pin		Bones & Roman pot sherds.	

			No.	Age/Sex	Site	Pos.		Orient.	Relics		Animal and human bones		Button of oak'd clay	Flint scraper & animal bones	Remarks
0	...	1	No. 1	Adult	Base	?	B.	S.	1 flint knife, 2 lumps of yellow ochre	...	Various animal bones	1	...	...	Teeth of the pig.
7	...	1	No. 2	Adult	Grave	P.	L.	N.	...	...	Many human and many animal bones	...	...	...	
	...	1	Dismembered / In fragments		Grave B	P.	?	...	...	...	Human and animal bones	...	...	...	
	...	1	No. 2	Male	Grave A	P.	R.	E.	...	...	...	...	...	...	
	...	1	No. 3	Female	Grave F	P.	B.	E.	...	...	...	...	...	...	
	...	1	No. 4	Child	Grave C	P.?	L.	E.	...	...	...	...	1 ⊃	...	
	...	1	No. 5	Adult M.	Grave E	S.	B.	E.	Bone handle	Dagger and other articles	4 teeth of an ox	1	...	...	
2	Hole	1	No. A	Child	Mound	S.?	R.	E.	...	...	...	...	...	...	
	Hole	1	B	Adult	Base	S.?	...	...	...	...	...	...	...	...	
	Heap	1	B	Adult	Base	S.?	...	...	...	...	Portion of the antler of a red deer	...	...	A few worked flints	This grave originally was probably a pit dwelling.
	...	1	E	Adult	Grave C	P.	...	E.	4 flint chips	...	Many human bones 2 splinters of burnt animal bones	1	...		
	Heap	1	D	Adult	Grave C	P.	L.	E.	...	...	...	...	...	...	
	...	1	C	Adult	Grave C	P.	...	...	...	...	Animal bones	...	...	...	(A fibula showed abnormal growth at the upper end.
	...	1	F	Adult	Grave F	S.	L.	W.	2 worked flints	...	Portions of twisted string, also pieces of woven and knitted texture	...	...	...	
	...	1	H	Adult	Grave H	S.	Chest	N.N.E.	...	...	...	...	...	...	
	...	1	I	Old F.	Grave I	S.	L.	N.N.E.	...	...	Human bones	...	...	...	
16	Heap	1	K	Adult	Grave I	S.	R.	N.	...	...	...	...	...	...	
	...	1	J	Male?	Grave J	S.	B. extended	...	...	...	...	...	...	...	Probably of Post-British date.
	...	1	...	Male	Grave	S.		S.	Piece of iron	...	...	...	...	...	

INTERMENTS.   ARTICLES DEPOSITED WITH INTERMENTS.

	BURNT		UNBURNT									Vessels of Pottery							
No. of Barrow	No. of Bodies	Urn, Dish-shaped Hole, or Circular Heap	No. of Bodies	Description	In Grave, or Body of Mound, or at Base	Primary or Secondary Burial	On Back, Right, or Left Side	Direction of Head	Bone or Stone Tools with Bodies	Bronze Implements	Worked Flints; Pot Sherds; Detached, Unburnt, Human and Animal Bones scattered in the Grave	Food Vase	Cinerary Urn	Incense Cup	Drinking Cup	Bodkins, Pins, Buttons, or Ornaments	Clay from a Distance, and Dish-shaped Cavities without Burnt Bones	Detached Bones, Relics, &c. from the Body of the Mound, not with Interments	REMARKS
80	…	…	1	No. 1 Adult	Mound	P.	R.	W.	…	…	…	…	…	…	…	…	…	…	
	6	{Trough-formed structure}	dispers'd	Adult	Base	P.	…	…	…	…	Unburnt human and animal bones	…	…	…	…	…	…	Human and animal bones
	…	Hole	1	No. 2 E Adult	Grave	P.	L.	E.	…	…	…	…	…	…	1	…	1 U	…	A cremator… Animal bo… unburnt
	1	Heap	1	F Youth ?	In trough Mound	P.	…	…	…	…	…	…	…	…	…	…	1 U	…	
	…	…	…	No. 3 Adult	Mound	S.	R.	W.	…	…	…	…	…	…	…	…	…	…	
	…	…	1	No. 1 Female	Base	P.?	R.	W.	{A flint knife, A flint scraper}	…	…	…	…	…	…	Bone pin	…	All the bones of a human foot in position	
	1	…	…	A Child	Mound	?	Dismembered		Flint knife	…	…	…	…	…	…	…	…	…	
81	1	crem'torium	…	{Portions of several bodies}	…	…	…		…	…	…	…	…	…	…	…	…	…	
	…	…	…	…	Base	P.	…	…	…	{Trace of bronze}	…	…	…	…	…	…	…	…	
	…	…	1	No. C Youth	Grave	P.	Dismembered, with urinal calculi		…	…	…	1	…	…	…	…	…	…	
	…	…	…	No. 2 Young F.	Grave C	S.	R.	W.	…	…	{Many human bones and pot sherds}	…	…	…	…	{Jet button}	…	Animal bones	A cremator… containing… burnt hu… bones, also charcoal, large pie…
	…	…	1	No. 3 Adult	Grave C	S.	R.	W.	…	…	{Many human bones}	…	…	1	…	…	…	…	{Mandible, … had more … 14 teeth.}
C 42	1	Heap	…	…	Base	?	…	…	…	…	…	…	…	…	…	…	…	…	

No.	Sex/Age	Mound/Grave	Position	Aspect	Implements/Finds	Human bones	Count	Other	Notes
No. 2	Child		L.	E.N.E.	...	Human bones	1	...	Pieces of a stone axe
No. 3	Aged F.	Grave	L.	N.E.	...	...	...	...	{ The sk missin the un was fo the }
No. 4	Male	Grave	R.	?	{ Flint flake, Stone weapon }	Snail shells	...	...	
No. 5	Dism. C.	Grave	?.	?.	...	...	...	...	
No. 6	Aged F.	Md	R.	S.W.	...	Bones of dog or fox	...	...	Animal bones
No. 7	Adult	Base	...	...	...	...	...	...	
No. 8	Adult	Base	...	...	...	...	...	...	
No. 1	Adult	{ Md or Grave 1 }	?	Disturbed	...	...	...	...	
No. 2	Child	Grave 1	?.	E.	...	...	...	...	
No. 3	Ad. F.?	Grave 1	R.	N.N.W.	3 Flint knifes	...	2	...	Animal bones
No. 4	Adult	Grave 2	P.	E.	...	...	...	...	
No. 5	Ad. F.?	Grave 3	Chest.	E.N.E.	...	...	1	...	
No. 6	Child	Grave 4	R.	S.S.E.	...	...	...	...	
No. 7	Child	Grave 4	R.	S.S.E.	...	...	...	...	
No. 8	Child	Grave 5	R.	N.	{ Several minute flint chips }	...	1	...	
No. 1	{ Large Male }	Grave A	B.	S.	...	...	...	...	
No. 2	?	Grave A	B.	W.	...	Many human bones	1	...	
No. 3	Child	Grave B	B.	W.	...	...	1	...	
No. 4	Adult	Grave B	R?	E.	...	...	...	Bone pin	
No. 5	Child	Base	L.	W.	...	...	...	Bone pin	
No. 6	Child	Base	L.	W.	...	...	...	Bone pir	
...	Large M.	Base	P.	?	...	...	...	...	
No. 1	Child	Grave 1	?	?	...	...	...	...	
No. 2	Child	Grave 2	?	?	...	...	...	...	
No. 3	Child	Grave 3	?	?	...	...	...	...	
No. 6	Adult	{ Shallow grave 6 }	R.	S.	{ Worked flints and pot sherds }	{ 2 destroyed adult bodies }	1	Bone pin	
No. 6a	Infant	Grave 6	?	?	Few burnt bones	...	...	...	
a	Child	Grave 4	R.	E.	Bones of infant	...	1	...	
No. 5	Adult		?	S.E.	Iron knife?	...	...	...	{ Some o probab Di Anglo- ? }
No. 7	Adult	Trench	?.	W.	...	Bones of a pig	...	...	
No. 8	Adult	Trench	R.	N.	...	...	...	...	
No. 9	Child	Grave 9	R.	S.	...	...	...	...	

79   C 67   C 40   C 45   112

GROUP XI.—continued.

	INTERMENTS.								ARTICLES DEPOSITED WITH INTERMENTS.									
	BURNT.			UNBURNT.									Vessels of Pottery.						
No. of Barrow	No. of Bodies	Urn, Dish-shaped Hole, or Circular Heap	No. of Bodies	Description.	In Grave or Body of Mound, or at Base.	Primary or Secondary Burial.	On Back, Right, or Left Side.	Direction of Head.	Bone or Stone Tools with Bodies.	Bronze Implements.	Worked Flints; Pot Sherds; Detached, Unburnt, Human and Animal Bones scattered in the Grave.	Food Vase	Cinerary Urn	Incense Cup	Drinking Cup	Bodkins, Pins, Buttons, or Ornaments	Clay from a Distance, and Dish-shaped Cavities without Burnt Bones	Detached Bones, Relics, &c., from the Body of the Mound, not with Interments	Remark
C 34	1	{Trough-shaped structure}	1	…dispers'd	Base	P.	…	…	…	…	…	1	…	…	…	…	…	Animal bones	Roman
C 41	…	…	1	No. 1 Female	Grave	P.	L.	E.	…	…	{ Human and animal bones }	…	…	1	…	…	…	…	Vase with
	…	…	1	No. 2 Male	Grave	P.	L.	E.	…	…		…	…	…	…	…	…	…	
C 57	…	Heap	1	No. 1 S mall F.	Grave 1	P.	L.	W.	…	…	…	…	…	…	…	…	…	Animal bones	
	1		1	No. 2 ?	Grave 1	P.?	R.	N.	…	…	…	…	…	…	…	…	…		
	…		1	No. 3 Child	Grave 2 Md	S.	Broken up	…	Worked flint	…	Pot sherds	…	…	…	…	…	…		
	…		1	No. 4 Inft	Grave 2	S.	L.	S.	…	…	…	…	…	…	…	…	…		
	…		…	No. 5 Infant	Grave 3	P.	…	…	…	…	…	…	…	…	…	…	…		
C 58	1	Hole	1	Adlt?	Hole		…	…	…	…	…	…	…	…	…	…	…	{ Part of a flint knife	
C 35	…	…	0	…	…	…	…	…	…	…	…	…	…	…	…	…	…	Flint flakes	
C 36	…	…	1?	No. 1 Adult	Grave	P.?	{ Fragments only }	…	Bone tool	Pricker	{ Human and animal bones }	1?	…	…	…	…	…	…	
	…		1	Adult Yg. Per.	Hole	P.?	?	S.	Worked flints		Teeth of an ox	…	…	…	…	…	…	…	
C 37	1	Urn	1	?	Grave	S.	?	…	…	…	…	1	1	…	…	…	…	Pot sherds (Roman or Saxon)	
	1	Urn	…	…	Hole		R.	…	…	…	…	1	…	…	…	…	…		
274	…	…	1	Adult	Grave	P.	R.	S.	…	…	Dark matter	1	…	…	…	…	…		
36	**37**		**120**									**25**	**3**	**2**	**9**				

GROUP XII.

Table of Barrows, Interments, and Articles deposited with Interments.

No. of Barrow	BURNT — No. of Bodies	BURNT — Urn, Dish-shaped Hole, or Circular Heap	UNBURNT — No. of Bodies	Description	In Grave or Body of Mound, or at Base	Primary or Secondary Burial	On Back, Right, or Left Side	Direction of Head	Bone or Stone Tools with Bodies	Bronze Implements	Worked Flints; Pot Sherds; Detached, Unburnt, Human and Animal Bones scattered in the Grave	Food Vase	Cinerary Urn	Incense Cup	Drinking Cup	Bodkins, Pins, Buttons, or Ornaments	Clay from a Distance, and Dish-shaped Cavities without Burnt Bones	Detached Bones, Relics, &c., from the Body of the Mound, not with Interments	Remarks
C 38	...	...	1	No. 1, Male	Cist	P.	L.	E.	Stone armlet	Dagger	Hawk's head, linen cloth	...	...	...	1	3 amber beads, linen cloth	1 U	Worked flints, animal bones, British and A.S. pot sherds	Bits of linen cloth
	...	...	1	No. 3, ?	Base	P.?	R.	N.W.	...	...	...	...	...	...	...	...	None	Many A.S. interments with iron weapons	
	...	...	1	No. 5, ?	Base	P.?	?	S.W.	Flint spear-head	...	...	1	...	...	...	Bone dress fast'ner	...	Pot sherds, animal bones, a barbed arrow-head, and 5 worked flints	
C 50	...	...	1	?	Grave	P.	...	E.	Flint spear-head	...	...	...	...	...	...	...	...	...	
C 86	...	...	1	Adult	Grave	P.	...	W.	Flint flakes	...	Human calvarium 1	...	...	...	...	...	...	...	
212a	...	...	1	No. 1 Adult	Grave 1	P.?	R.	E.	...	...	...	...	...	...	...	...	...	...	
	...	...	1	No. 2 Adult	Grave 2	P.?	R.	E.	...	...	...	...	...	...	...	...	...	...	} Probably Romano-British
	...	...	1	No. 3 Adult	Grave 3	P.?	R.	N.	...	...	...	...	...	...	...	...	...	...	
212b	...	...	1	No. 1 Adult	Grave 1	P.?	R.	N.E.	...	...	...	...	...	...	...	...	...	...	
	...	...	1	No. 1 Adult	Grave 1	P.	B.&L.	N.E.	Flint arrow-head	...	...	...	...	...	...	...	...	...	
C 44	1	Hole	...	Probably a British grave ?	Hole	...	...	...	...	...	...	...	...	...	...	...	...	Many A.S. bodies	
	1	Hole	...	?	Hole	...	...	...	...	...	...	...	...	...	...	...	...	...	
	1	Hole	...	?	Hole	...	...	...	...	...	...	...	...	...	...	...	...	...	
278	...	...	1 ?	?	Mld	S.?	...	...	...	...	...	...	...	...	...	...	Clay	3 scrapers, 3 knives, 100 flint flakes, and pot sherds	
279	...	...	1	No. 1 Adult	Grave	P.	L.	E.	...	...	...	1	...	...	...	...	...	...	
279a	...	...	1	No. 2 Adult	Oak tree coffin	P.	?	E.	...	...	...	...	...	...	...	...	...	...	
	...	...	1	No. 3 Adult	...	P.	?	W.	...	...	...	...	...	...	...	...	...	...	
9	**3**		**15**									**3**	**0**	**0**	**1**				

GROUP XIII.

Table of Barrows, Interments, and Articles deposited with Interments.

No. of Barrow	BURNT — No. of Bodies	BURNT — Urn, Dish-shaped Hole, or Circular Heap	UNBURNT — No. of Bodies	UNBURNT — Description	In Grave or Body of Mound, or at Base	Primary or Secondary Burial	On Back, Right, or Left Side	Direction of Head	Bone or Stone Tools with Bodies	Bronze Implements	Worked Flints; Pot Sherds; Detached, Unburnt, Human and Animal Bones scattered in the Grave	Food Vase	Cinerary Urn	Incense Cup	Drinking Cup	Bodkins, Pins, Buttons, or Ornaments	Clay from a Distance, and Dish-shaped Cavities without Burnt Bones	Detached Bones, Relics, &c. from the Body of the Mound, not with Interments	Remarks
221	...	...	1	Adult	Grave	P.	(Destroyed by a former opening)	(Destroyed by a former opening)	Flint flake	...	A tablet of lead, on which is stamped, Jas. Silburn	...	...	...	...	...	...	...	
222	1	{ Wooden recept'cle }		?	Base	P.?	...	S.	3 Worked flints	...	...	...	...	...	...	...	...	...	
				B — Adult	Grave	P.?	L.												
224	{ 1 or more heap, 1, also heap A }		1	A — Adult?	Base	P.	B.	N.	Flint knife and a flake	...	...	...	...	...	...	...	...	} Human and animal bones	
			1	No. 1 — Infant	Grave B	P.	R.	E.				1					1 U		
225	1	{ Urn inverted }	...	No. 3 — Adult	Grave A	P.	...	...	Worked antler	...	} Animal and many human bones	...	1	...	...	...	Clay	...	
			1	No. 2 — Adult	Base	P.?	L.	S.E.				1					Clay		
			1	No. 4 — dult	Grave B	P.	R.	W.									Clay		
			1	No. 3 — Young	Grave A	P.	B.	N.											
226	...	...	1	No. 1 — Decayed	over Grave A	?	Decayed	Decayed	Flint knife	...	...	1	...	...	...	...	Loamy Clay	...	
			1	No. 2 — dult	Grave A	P.?	R.	S.									Clay		
			1	No. 4 A — Adult	Grave A	P.	L.	S.E.											
			1	No. 3 A — Adult	Grave A	P.	R.	S.E.											
			1	No. 5 — Adult	Grave B	S.?	L.	E.											
			1	No. 6 — Adult M.	Grave B	S.?	B.	E.	{ Flint tool, Circular knife }	...	...	...	...	...	...	...	...	...	

No.		Mound		Sub	Age	Position			Direction	Relics	Deposits		Jet	Clay	Other relics
223			1	disturb'd	Adult			?	?	Lead tablet					
			1		Infant										
227	1	Hole	1		?	Hole	P.	L.	S.E.		Animal and human bones	1			
228			1	No. 1	d..lt	Base	P.	L.	W.		Antler of red deer				Animal bones
			1	No. 2	Adult	Grave	P.	B.	S.W.		Human bones				
			1	No. 3	Ad. F.?		P.	B.	W.		Pot sherds	1			
			1	No. 4	..th	Grave	P.	L.	N.E.						
			1	No. 5	AgedM.?	Grave	P.	L.	N.E.						
			1	No. 6	Child		P.	L.	S.W.						
			1	No. 7	Female	Base	S.								
245	1	Heap	1	A	?	?	S.	R.	S.	Flint disc				Clay	Several work'd flints
229	1	Heap	1	No. 1	d..lt	Base	P.	R.	E.	Many human & animal bones				Clay	Chipped flints, human bones, animal bones, pot sherds, portion of a bone knife
			1	No. 2	Young	Grave	P.	R.	N.	A beautiful flint spear					
230			1	No. 1	Adult	Grave	P.	R.	S.	Another spear				Clay	
			1	No. 2	?	Grave									
231	1	Disturbed	1	Disturbed	?	?									
220	1	Disturbed	0	Disturbed	?							1 ?			
235						Grave				3 Worked flints					Half a flint spear; 19 Flint flakes and 8 worked flints
218	1	Hole			?	Base	P.							Clay	
215	1	Heap			Adult	Base	P.			Jaw bones of a small animal	Bottom part of urn	1			
216	1	Urn	1	No. 1	Yg. Per.	Grave	P.	L.	N.N.W.	Flint knife			Jet bead		
			1	No. 2	Child	Grave	P.?	R.	N.N.W.	Flint knife		1			
219			1	No. 3	Adult	Grave	P.	B.	W.			1 ?			
18	12		28									7 3 0 0			

GROUP XIV.

Table of Barrows, Interments, and Articles deposited with Interments.

| | INTERMENTS | | | | | | | ARTICLES DEPOSITED WITH INTERMENTS | | | | | | | | | | |
| | BURNT | | UNBURNT | | | | | | | | Vessels of Pottery. | | | | | | | |
No. of Barrow	No. of Bodies.	Urn, Dish-shaped Hole, or Circular Heap.	No. of Bodies.	Description.	In Grave, or Body of Mound, or at Base.	Primary or Secondary Burial.	On Back, Right, or Left Side.	Direction of Head.	Bone or Stone Tools with Bodies.	Bronze Implements.	Worked Flints; Pot Sherds; Detached, Unburnt, Human and Animal Bones scattered in the Grave.	Food Vase.	Cinerary Urn.	Incense Cup.	Drinking Cup.	Bodkins, Pins, Buttons, or Ornaments	Clay from a Distance, and Dish-shaped Cavities without Burnt Bones	Detached Bones, Relics, &c. from the Body of the Mound, not with Interments.	Remarks.
242	…	…	1	disturb'd Male	Grave	P.	?	?	Stone axe	…	Animal	1						Many flakes, worked flints, and pot sherds	
263	1	Heap	…	disturb'd ? Male	Base	P.	?	?	…	…	…					Slip of lead, 'Jas. Silburn,' st'mp'd on it	Clay		
243	…	…	1	adlt No. 1	Grave	P.	R.	S.	…	…	…								
244	…	…	1	adlt Kild No. 2	Grave	P.	R.	S. N.W.	…	…	…							3 Worked flints	
246	…	…	1	Adult	Grave	P.	L.	E.	Worked flints	…	Human & animal bones and pot sherds					Bone pin			
247	1	…	0	?	Grave	P.	…	…	…	…	…	1							
248	1	Urn inverted	…	Adult	Base	P.?	…	…	…	…	…		1					17 Flint flakes and a pot sherd	

No.					Age	Location	P.	B.	Dir.	Implements	Pricker	Remains	Bone pin					Clay	Pot sherds
249	1	Heap		AA	-	Base	P.?		N.	Bone spatula and flint flakes	Pricker	Many human bones, unburnt (& a few burnt)							29 Flint flakes, and the sharp end of a stone axe
	1	Heap		a	Ad. M.?	Grave B	P.	B.											
					Adult	Grave C	P.		S.E.				Bone pin						
250	1	Urn			Female	Grave	?		S.					1					Animal bone, pot sherds, and 14 flint flakes
	1				Adult	Base	P.	B.	?						1				Flint flakes
251			disturb'd		?	Grave	?	?	N.N.E.									Clay	Flint flakes, barbed arrow-head, and bones, and pot sherds
	1	Heap	No. 2		Male kild	Base	P.	B.	W.			My human & and ds, also 17 pot sherds, the head of an ox, and a human cranium		1					Many animal and human bones, and flints, and pot sherds
					Adult	Grave	P.	?	?					1					
264			A		Infant	Grave	P.?	?	?							1			
			B		Child	Mound	P.?							1					
	1	Heap			Yg. Per.	Grave	P.			Flint knife									
252					Male	Grave	P.	In a heap				Lead tablet							Two discs of chalk, pot and many flints (87)
	1				Adult	Grave	P.	?	?			Lead tablet							Pot sherds and many flints
253			disturb'd		disturb'd bodies	Grave	P.	?	?										
255	2		disturb'd body		disturb'd body	Base	P.	?	?	Flint scraper		Human foot				1			Flint flakes
254	1		No. 1		Adult	Base	P.	R.	W.			Human bones				1			Trace of much burning
	1		No. 2		Adult	Base	P.	R.	W.		Pricker	Pot sherds				1			
	1		No. 3		Adult	Trench	P.	R.	N.										
15	**8**				**22**									**7**	**2**	**1**	**3**		

GROUP XV.

Table of Barrows, Interments, and Articles deposited with Interments.

No. of Barrow	BURNT: No. of Bodies	BURNT: Urn, Dish-shaped Hole, or Circular Heap	UNBURNT: No. of Bodies	UNBURNT: Description	UNBURNT: Urn, Dish-shaped Hole, or Circular Heap	Primary or Secondary Burial	On Back, Right, or Left Side	Direction of Head	Bone or Stone Tools with Bodies	Bronze Implements	Worked Flints; Pot Sherds; Detached, Unburnt, Human and Animal Bones scattered in the Grave	Food Vase	(Cinerary) Urn	Incense Cup	Drinking Cup	Bodkins, Pins, Buttons, or Ornaments	Clay from a Distance, and Dish-shaped Cavities without Burnt Bones	Detached Bones, Relics, &c., from the Mound, not with Interments	REMARKS
2	... / 1	... Hole	1 ...	Male ?		P. / P.?	? ...	W. ...	Green stone pin	Knife	Many snail shells	...	...	...	...	...		Animal bones / Pot sherds	
89	1	Heap	...	...		P.	...	...	Hammer-head / 3 flint flakes	...	...	1				Bone pin			All burnt
90	1	Hole / Heap	...	No. 1 Sm. Per. / No. 2 Adult		P. / P.	... / ...	... / ...	3 Flint flakes / Flint knife and splinters of burnt flint	...	...					...		...	
91	1	Heap	...	?		P.	...	...	...	...	...		1			...		...	
92	1 / 1	Urn / Hole	...	No. 1 Child / No. 2 Adult		P. / P.	... / ...	... / ...	... / ...	...	...		1			...		...	
93	1	Heap	...	Female and child		P.	...	...	...	...	...	1				...		...	
94	1	Urn	...	...		P.	...	...	Flint drill	...	...	1	1	1		...		...	
95	0	Probably destroyed	...	...		...	...	...	...	...	...					...		...	
96	1	Heap	...	Adult		...	...	...	...	...	...					...		2 Flint knives / Several work'd flints	
97	0	Probably destroyed	...	...		...	...	...	...	...	...					...		77 Chipped flints and a flint axe	
36	1	Hole	...	...		P.	...	...	Flint flake	...	...					ne		Flint flips, hammer stone, animal bones	
237	... / ... / ... / ...	...		No. 1 Boy / No. 2 Adult / No. 3 Child / No. 4 Child / No. 5 Adult	Grave / Grave / Mound / Grave	S. / P. / P. / ? / P.	R. / R. / L. / R. / B.	W. / E. / W.	... / ... / Flint flake / ... / Flint scraper	...	Animal bones					...	1 / 1	Found axe and a deposit of animal bones	

No.			No.	Age		P.				Human and animal bones	1	2	3	0			Remarks
238	...	...	No. 1	Adult	Grave	P.	B.	E.	...	Human and animal bones	...			1	...	...	Animal bones, pieces of burnt wood in the supposed pit dwelling / Teeth of ox and worked flints
240	...	...	No. 2	Adult	Grave	P.	Broken up	W.	...	...	...			...	Jet button	...	...
	1	1	No. 3	Adult	Grave	P.	R.B.	S.S.W.	...	...	...			...			
241	1		...	Adult	In pit dwelling	P.	...	...	Flint knife / Flint knife	Animal bones, flint flakes, and barbed arrow-head	...			1	Bone pin	...	Flint chips
257	...	Hole	...	...	Grave	P. ?	Previously emptied	...	Flint flakes	...	...			...	...	...	Flint chips
	1		...	?	Hole	P. ?	...	...	...	...	...			...			
258	...	0	...	Adult	the	P.	Disturbed	...	Slip of lead, with 'Jas. Silburn' on it	...	...			...	...	...	Portion of antler of a red deer, and burnt wood
259	...	1	...	...	Grave	P.	Disturbed	...	...	...	...			...	...	...	Teeth of an ox, worked flints
260	...	1	...	?	Grave	P. ?	Disturbed	...	...	...	...			...	...	...	1 Knife and 2 scrapers, both of flint
261	...	1	...	Adult	Grave	P. ?	Previously emptied	...	Flint flake	...	...			...	...	...	Worked flints, animal bones } Probably pit dwelling
265	1	Heap	...	Adult	Over grave	P. ?	R.	W.	...	...	...			1	...	...	Flint chips, animal bones, and pt sherds / 7 Flint flakes
	...		No. 1	Adult	Grave	P.	(Broken up or dismemb'r'd)	...	...	...	...			1	...	...	
	1		No. 2	Youth	Grave	P.	...	...	...	...	...			1	...	...	
	1		No. 3	Adult	Grave	P.	...	...	...	Pot sherds	...			1	...	...	
266	1	Heap	...	Yg. Per.	Base	P.	...	...	The centre of this mound had been cut away	...	...			...	...	...	2 Pieces of iron, few pot sherds, & animal bones
269	0		...	Adult F.	Grave	P.	R.	E.	...	...	...			1	...	...	
262	1	Heap	...	Child	the	P. ?	R.	S.	2 Flint flakes	...	...			...	...	...	
232	...		...			P.	L.										Few pieces cremated human bone
C. 88	0		...						Believed to have been previously opened by the late Jas. Silburn in 1851.								
26	16										12	3	1	0			19

MISCELLANEOUS BARROWS.

Table of Barrows, Interments, and Articles deposited with Interments.

No. of barrow	BURNT — No. of Bodies	BURNT — Urn, Dish-shaped Hole, or Circular Heap	UNBURNT — No. of Bodies	Description	In Grave or Body of Mound, or at Base	Primary or Secondary Burial	On Back, Right, or Left Side	Direction of Head	Bone or Stone Tools with Bodies	Bronze Implements	Worked Flints; Pot Sherds; Detached, Unburnt, Human and Animal Bones scattered in the Grave	Food Vase	Cinerary Urn	Incense Cup	Drinking Cup	Bodkins, Pins, Buttons, or Ornaments	Clay from a Distance, and Dish-shaped Cavities without Burnt Bones	Detached Bones, Relics, &c., from the Body of the Mound, not with Interments	REMARKS.
A	1	Hole	...	No. 4	Grave	P. ?	...	...	Unburnt human bone	...	...	...	...	...	...	...	...	...	This is a lo... barrow
	1	Hole	...	No. 5	Grave	P. ?	...	...	Flint flake	...	...	...	...	...	...	...	...	...	
209a	...	...	...	Three	graves	P.	...	...	...	...	Animal bones	1	...	...	...	1 Jet button	...	A pit dwelling	6 Anglo-Sax interments
210	...	...	Remains of broken up bodies						...	...	...	...	...	...	...	1 Jet ring	...	Pot sherds, animal bone, and corroded iron	+ Shaped ex... vation
277	...	...	1	No. 1	Mound	S.?	L.	S.S.W.	Flint knife	...	Animal bones	...	...	...	...	...	...	Stone & flint tools	
	...	...	1	No. 2	Mound	S.?	R.	N.N.E.	...	...	...	...	...	...	...	...	...		
	...	...	...	...	Grave	P.	...	...	...	...	...	...	...	...	...	...	...		
272	1	Heap	...	...	Base	P.	...	N.	...	...	...	...	...	...	...	...	...	Several flint flakes	
280	...	...	1	Adult	Base	?	...	...	...	...	...	...	...	...	...	...	...	...	
	...	...	1	Adult	Position not ascertain'd	...	...	...	...	...	...	...	...	...	...	...	...	...	
	...	...	...	Child	Grave	P.	B.	...	Flint knife	...	4 Flint knives	3	...	...	...	Bone pin	...	100 Worked flints	
	1	Heap	1	Male	Grave	P.	B.	E.	...	...	Animal bones		...	...	...	...	...	...	

		Page	No.	Age	Position		Direction	Arrow-head		Animal bones				Animal and human bones
1	...	281	No. 1	Adult	Cist 1	P.?	...	...	...	Animal bones	...	...	...	...
1	...		No. 2	Adult	Cist 2	P.?	...	...	...	...	...	...	...	Animal and human bones
...	Heap		A	Adult	In Mound	S.?	R.	...	...	...	1	...	...	1
1	...		B	Adult	Cist 3	P.	W. Bled	...	...	Animal bones	...	...	...	...
1	...		one Cist 2	Child	Cist 3	S.?	Much decayed	...	...	Human bones	...	...	1	...
1	...		Adult	Cist 5	P.?	L. W.	...	...	..	...	...	...	...
1	Heap	284	No. 1	Kild	Mound	S.?	...	...	...	Animal bones and pot sherds	...	...	3 pipes of an urn, several lips of the bones of frgs & tds, my animal bones, sandstone per, large sling-stone & 63 flint flakes, and a large ther of a red ther
6	...		2 to 6	Adult	Base	P.	Various positions	...	...					
1	...		No. 7	Adult	Mound	S.?	R.	Arrow-head	...	..	...	...	...	...
1	...		No. 8	Adult	Mound	S.?	E.S.E.	...	...	...	...	...	...	...
19	7	8									5 0 0 1			

3 K

UNBURNT BODIES.

Total	Category
41	Bodies with Flint Tools.
3	With Stone Hammer.
43	With Food-Vase.
45	With Cinerary Urn.
8	With Incense Cup.
0	With Drinking Cup.
15	With Bone Article.
7	With Jet Article.
10	With Bronze.
4	Stag's Horn Tool.
351	No. of Adult Bodies.
148	No. of Children and Youths.
66	No Age not Known.
565	Total No. of Bodies.
197	No. on Right Side.
117	On Left Side.
82	On Back.
5	On Chest.
164	Position not Known.
47	S.
9	S.S.W.
20	S.W.
4	W.S.W.
94	W.
1	W.N.W.
14	N.W.
6	N.N.W.
42	N.
12	N.N.E.
30	N.E.
4	E.N.E.
96	E.
4	E.S.E
33	S.E.
4	S.S.E.
155	No. not known.
11	Bone.
13	Pounders and Stone Hammers.
147	Flint Tools and Flakes.
25	Bronze.
10	Hammers and Picks of Stag's Horn.
119	Food Vases.
1	Cinerary Urns.
4	Incense Cups.
38	Drinking Cups.
20	

Group headings (right margin): HEADS POINTING TO THE VARIOUS POINTS OF THE COMPASS; BODIES WITH INSTRUMENTS; BODIES WITH POTTERY.

INDEX.

3 L

A SELECTED LIST OF BOOKS

RELATING TO

EAST YORKSHIRE.

———————

Further particulars respecting these, and other similar Works, will be gladly
Mailed Free to any Address on application to the Publishers.

THE EARLY HISTORY OF
THE TOWN AND PORT OF HEDON

IN THE COUNTY OF YORK.

By J. R. BOYLE, F.S.A.

495 pages, uncut edges, Demy 8vo, half-bound and gilt top, 21s. net.

A few hand-made paper copies, Demy 4to, bound in buckram and gilt top,
42s. net.

CONTENTS :—The Origin of Hedon—The Borough of Hedon—The Port of Hedon—
The Churches of Hedon—The Institutions of Hedon—The Topography of Hedon—Tenure
of Hedon—An Appendix of 34 Notes, occupying 207 pages—Glossary—Index.

BYGONE YORKSHIRE :

Its History, Romance, Folk-lore, &c., &c.

EDITED BY WILLIAM ANDREWS, F.R.H.S.

Elegantly bound in stout cloth boards, demy 8vo, price 7s. 6d.

CONTENTS.—Lake-Dwellings of Yorkshire—An Ancient Monolith—Relics and
Remnants—Yorkshire Castles : some of their Historic Associations—York Castle—Castles
and Castle Builders : Bolton Castle and the Scropes—Ramparts, Walls, and Bars of York—
The Ivanhoe Country—Knights Templars—St. Mary's Abbey, York—Byland Abbey : Its
Historical Associations—Robin Hood in Yorkshire—The Pilgrimage of Grace—Traditions
and Curious Customs of York Minster—A Story of the Gunpowder Plot—The Spinning-
Wheel—Ripon Minster—Ripon Spurs—Captain Cook—Farnley Hall.

HOLY TRINITY CHURCH, HULL,

A GUIDE AND DESCRIPTION.

By J. R. BOYLE, F.S.A.

99 pages and 3 illustrations, 16mo, paper cover, 1s. net ; also a large paper
edition, 4to, in ornamental cloth, 2s. 6d.

CONTENTS.—The Chapel of Myton—Present Church—Early Brickwork—Plan—
Exterior—Tower—Interior—Transepts—Choir—Chantry Chapels—Nave—Ancient Woodwork—Monuments—Font—Stained Glass Windows.

CHURCH BELLS OF HOLDERNESS.

By G. R. PARK.

A very interesting Volume.   Crown 8vo, bound in cloth, gilt top, price 1/6 net.

In this volume the Author has attempted to give a brief account of the bells formerly
used in the various services of the Church, including those which have been since the
Reformation dispensed with in Protestant Churches, as well as those used at the periodical
ecclesiastical seasons and in commemoration of national events.

LONDON : A. BROWN & SONS, LTD., 5, FARRINGDON AVENUE, E.C.
AND AT HULL AND YORK.

GEOLOGICAL RAMBLES IN EAST YORKSHIRE,

By THOMAS SHEPPARD, F.G.S.

247 pages, Demy 8vo, suitably bound in cloth, 7s. 6d.

With over 50 Illustrations from Photographs, &c., by GODFREY BINGLEY and others, and a Geological Map of the District.

CONTENTS.—Introduction—Spurn and Kilnsea—Kilnsea to Withernsea—Withernsea to Hornsea—Hornsea to Bridlington—Bridlington to Danes' Dyke—The Drifts of Flamborough Head—South Sea Landing to Speeton—Speeton to Bempton—The Speeton Clay and Filey Bay—Filey Brig — Filey Brig to Gristhorpe—Gristhorpe to Scarborough— Scarborough—Scarborough to Robin Hood's Bay—Robin Hood's Bay—Robin Hood's Bay to Whitby (The Yorkshire Lias)—Whitby to Redcar—The Humber—Hull to Hessle— Hessle—Hessle to Brough—The Oolites of Brough and South Cave—The Yorkshire Wolds—Holderness—Index.

Nature.—"The work of a sturdy local Geologist, who shows himself to be master of his subject, and of the literature past and present. The book is admirably illustrated with photographic views, and from its clear and accurate descriptions, it is well calculated to rouse up and foster an interest in Geology."

THE FLORA OF THE EAST RIDING OF YORKSHIRE,

Including a Physiographical Sketch,

By JAMES FRASER ROBINSON.

With a List of the Mosses, by J. J. MARSHALL, and a specially prepared Coloured Geological Map, showing the Botanical Divisions of the District.

253 pages, Demy 8vo, bound in cloth boards, 7s. 6d.

A special Interleaved Edition has also been prepared for Notes, 10s. 6d. net.

This work supplies a want long felt, not only by field naturalists and scientific men in general, but by all who are interested in the country's flora. The author has for twenty years been carefully studying the plants of the East Riding, and, besides having made a very large collection of its plants, he has also compiled from all possible sources anything pertaining to the plant inhabitants of the vice-county.

The district is a particularly interesting one, embracing chalk wolds, sandy plains, glacial mounds of clay and gravel, alluvial and marshy flats, an estuary and a sea board. Around the docks at Hull are certain "waste" grounds, upon which large numbers of interesting "aliens" flourish. Full particulars of these are given in the Flora.

The book is one which can be recommended alike to field botanists and to those taking an ordinary interest in wild flowers.

Yorkshire Post.—"We welcome 'The Flora of the East Riding of Yorkshire,' for the book not only covers a hitherto neglected district, but contains a large amount of information in little space, the plan of the whole being well arranged and clear."

LONDON: A. BROWN & SONS, LTD., 5, FARRINGDON AVENUE, E.C.

AND AT HULL AND YORK.

NOTES RELATIVE TO THE MANOR OF MYTON.

By J. TRAVIS-COOK, F.R.H.S.

One volume, cloth bound, uncut, Demy 8vo, 4s. 11d. net.

Large paper, Demy 4to, 9s. 9d. net.

Also a limited edition of the latter on hand-made paper, 15s. 6d. net.

Illustrated with a facsimile from the Doomsday, and three Maps.

CONTENTS.—Of Manors Generally—Etymology of the Name "Myton"—History of Manor of Myton—Manor of Tupcoates, with Myton—The Change in the Course of the River Hull.

THE LOST TOWNS OF THE HUMBER.

With an Introductory Chapter on the Roman Geography of South-East Yorkshire.

By J. R. BOYLE, F.S.A.

One volume, cloth bound, uncut, Demy 8vo, 3s. 6d. net.

Large paper, Royal 4to, 7s. net.

CONTENTS.—In Roman Times—In Saxon Times—Ravenser Spurn—Sites of Ravenser—Tharlesthorpe—Frismerk—Sunthorpe—Pemthorpe - Orwythfleet, &c.

EVIDENCES RELATING TO THE EASTERN PART OF THE CITY OF KINGSTON-UPON-HULL.

By THOMAS BLASHILL, F.R.I.B.A.

(Author of " Sutton-in-Holderness," &c.).

One volume, containing many Full-page Plans and Illustrations, bevelled cloth boards and gilt top, Demy 8vo, 3s. 6d. net.

SUTTON-IN-HOLDERNESS.

THE MANOR, THE BEREWIC, AND THE VILLAGE COMMUNITY.

By THOMAS BLASHILL, F.R.I.B.A.

(The Superintending Architect of Metropolitan Buildings)

336 pages, Demy 8vo, numerous Illustrations, bevelled cloth boards and gilt top, 7s. 6d. Large paper edition, Demy 4to, morocco back, cloth sides, gilt top, and uncut edges, 21s.

LONDON: A. BROWN & SONS, LTD., 5, FARRINGDON AVENUE, E.C.

AND AT HULL AND YORK.